10.00

GARRIE L. TUFFORD

DEPARTMENT OF GEOLOGY & MINERALOGY

UNIVERSITY OF MINNESOTA

DEC 2 3 1960

Principles of Stratigraphy

Principles

NEW YORK · JOHN WILEY & SONS, INC.   London · Chapman & Halt, Limited

PUBLICATION NUMBER: _____

of Stratigraphy

CARL O. DUNBAR

Professor of Paleontology and Stratigraphy
Yale University

JOHN RODGERS

Associate Professor of Geology
Yale University

To Charles Schuchert

whose life and work are an abiding inspiration to the authors of this work and to a host of other stratigraphers.

"He mapped the ancient seas and fathomed the geologic past."

Preface

:::

UPON THE RETIREMENT OF CHARLES SCHUCHERT at Yale in 1924 the senior author of this book inherited a graduate course in the stratigraphy of North America. The first few weeks of the course were then devoted to principles and the remainder to a systematic account of the stratigraphic record in this continent. In following years the discussion of principles was gradually expanded at the expense of the rest of the course, and after the junior author joined the Yale staff in 1946 *Principles of Stratigraphy* became a full year course, shared equally by Dunbar and Rodgers.

The urgent need of a textbook for a course of this scope had long been felt, but its preparation first became feasible when we could share the labor. During the first year we divided the subject matter so that one of us would lead in the discussion of certain topics and the other would lead in other topics, but both of us met every class and took part in the discussions. In the second year we reversed the assignments, each leading in the presentation of the subject matter taught by the other during the first year, and again we both attended all class meetings. In the third year we reverted to the original distribution of subject matter and each began preparing a complete manuscript on the topics discussed, each instructor meeting the class in turn. As the book shaped up, each criticized the parts written by the other, and both subject matter and methods of treatment were modified in the light of experience. To an unusual degree, therefore, the present work represents collaboration of two authors with different backgrounds of experience and, in some instances, of different points of view and even of conviction.

Stratigraphy is a rapidly growing science in which there is still much to learn. Where wide differences of opinion still exist among stratigraphers we have tried to present conflicting views, feeling sure that future discoveries rather than any fiat on our part will determine which views are correct.

The literature on stratigraphy is vast, complex, in part conflicting, and rapidly expanding. We are acutely aware that we have not fully covered the field. To do so would require several volumes of text. We have felt it best, therefore, to present such matters as would give the student a grasp of general principles and would introduce him to the special literature in which he can pursue the subject further.

ACKNOWLEDGMENTS

In the preparation of this work we have received help from many sources. We are especially indebted to John E. Sanders who read the entire manuscript and made many helpful suggestions. Richard F. Flint likewise read five of the chapters, and Preston E. Cloud a sixth. Maurice Ewing generously placed at our disposal important data regarding the work of turbidity currents, and numerous other friends helped with specific problems. Our greatest debt is to the many students with whom the ideas here set forth have been debated and discussed over the years; the pool of their knowledge has broadened our understanding even as their thoughtful questions have sharpened our thinking on many problems.

Illustrations supplied by several institutions and numerous friends are identified in the figure legends; we wish to express to each of these our grateful thanks for this indispensable aid, as also to Werner F. Gossels and Shirley P. Glaser for assistance in drafting certain of the figures.

Our thanks go also to Mrs. Lorna Hodgson for her careful preparation of the typescript, and to Clara Mae LeVene for making the index.

New Haven, Connecticut   CARL O. DUNBAR
April 15, 1957   JOHN RODGERS

Contents

Introduction:
the scope of stratigraphy

STRATIGRAPHY—literally writing about strata—is the study of stratified rocks. The term stratum (L. *sternere,* to spread) refers to planar units of rock that were originally spread as sheets over a surface of accumulation. The principles of stratigraphy were worked out primarily in sedimentary rocks, but they may be useful also in the study of such layered igneous rocks as ash falls and lava flows, and of metamorphic rocks insofar as they reflect an original sedimentary character.

The study of sedimentary rocks has three main aspects. The first is *sedimentary petrography,* the study of the rock material as such, its composition, texture, and structure. The second is *sedimentation,* the study of the processes by which sediments are formed, transported, and deposited. The third is *stratigraphy* proper, which deals with the overall relations of the stratified rocks, areal and temporal, and with the history they record.

Stratigraphy is necessarily based upon knowledge of sedimentary petrology and the principles of sedimentation. Here as elsewhere in geology, the present is the key to the past, and we can only infer the conditions under which ancient sedimentary rocks were formed when we understand how their modern counterparts are being produced. But stratigraphy goes beyond these basic disciplines in dealing with the broader relations of the layered rocks in the Earth's crust. In attempting to summarize the general principles used in stratigraphy we have necessarily introduced into this book much material belonging to sedimentary petrology and sedimentation, but no pretense has been made of covering those fields fully; each has its own vast literature and special devotees. Fortunately the literature in both sedimentary petrology and sedimentation has been summarized in recent standard works, and to these reference is frequently made in this book.

Stratigraphy in its restricted sense may be further subdivided into three phases.*

---

* Speaking humorously, we might in imitation of the trio petrography, petrology, and petrogeny, christen these subdivisions stratigraphy, stratilogy, and stratigeny; but in seriousness, the wholesale coining of such new compound terms from the classical languages is not a trend we wish to encourage.

First is the description of the strata as they occur in sequence in local areas—a necessary if somewhat tedious procedure that provides the basic data for all further interpretation.   Second is the correlation of these local sections—the determination of their mutual time relations and their place in the standard scale that forms the framework of historical geology.   To many geologists these two parts make up the whole of stratigraphy, which is considered profoundly boring by all but those immediately concerned with the specific descriptions and correlations.   But we believe that these, important and indispensable as they are, are but the means to a further end that constitutes the real core and interest of stratigraphy—namely, the interpretation of the stratigraphic record, both the rocks and their contained fossils, in terms of the past history of the Earth. Thus, though we have endeavored in this work to cover fully the subjects of description and correlation, we have devoted more than half the book to the discussion of principles and methods by which the stratigrapher interprets the data of description and correlation and builds up out of them a living picture of the geologic past.

The subject of stratigraphy has both an immense practical value and a broad philosophical interest.   The stratified rocks contain the vast fuel deposits of the Earth's crust—all the coal and petroleum and much of the fissionable atomic fuel; they provide the reservoirs for ground water; and they include economic resources of many other kinds—stratified iron ore and numerous metalliferous deposits in sedimentary rocks, phosphate deposits, potash, sodium and other salts, gypsum, and limestone.   Even where metalliferous deposits occur in intrusive igneous rocks or at their contacts in metamorphic aureoles the study of the surrounding framework of sedimentary rocks is commonly useful, even necessary, in working out the regional history that will permit an understanding of ore genesis and localization.   From the broader philosophical point of view, stratigraphy provides the basis for understanding the past history of local regions and of the whole Earth—the changing patterns of land and seas, fluctuations of climate, even the history of the evolution of life on the Earth.

PART I

ENVIRONMENTS OF DEPOSITION

Figure 1. Relief model of part of the northeastern United States showing the continental shelf in its relation to the land and the continental slope. Vertical scale exaggerated 5 times.

1. *Sedimentary processes*

A SEDIMENTARY ROCK is composed of material eroded from some pre-existing terrane, transported to its place of accumulation, and deposited there. Such material is the grist of the sedimentary mill, and its ultimate nature is determined by what goes into the mill at the source, by what happens to it in transit and while exposed at the site of deposition, and by modifications during and after burial.

INFLUENCE OF THE SOURCE

The source area determines what goes into the mill. The Little Colorado River, for example, flows out of the Painted Desert in Arizona choked with mud as red as the Triassic redbeds from which it is derived. Ausable River, on the contrary, leaves the Adirondacks carrying clean white sand derived from the Potsdam formation (Cambrian), and the Wabash River, flowing through the fertile plains of Indiana, is roily with fine dark mud rich in organic matter.

Climate and relief also play an important role in determining the nature of the sediment at its source. A granite mass in a subarctic region will crumble into gravel and sand largely made of fresh feldspar, but in a warm humid climate, where deep weathering prevails, it will yield chiefly clay minerals and quartz. Even in the humid tropics, however, the same granite will produce feldspathic sediment if the slopes are steep and the rainfall is torrential so that physical erosion out-

strips chemical decay (Krynine, 1935a). And if a deeply weathered surface be exposed to rapid erosion, as along the margins of a rising fault block, a mixture of much-decayed material and of fresh feldspar may be produced, like that of the Newark group (Triassic) of the Connecticut Trough (Krynine, 1950).

A mass of sediment deposited near its source will necessarily bear a strong impress both of the source rock and of the environment of the source area. Correct interpretation of a sedimentary deposit may be complicated, however, if the source rock itself bears the distinctive impress of an earlier sedimentary cycle. The till in the Central Lowland of Connecticut, for example, is locally as red as the underlying Newark beds (Triassic) from which it was largely derived, but over the crystalline uplands, both east and west, the till is entirely gray. In this instance, of course, the red color was not formed under glacial conditions but was inherited from a Triassic environment. In similar fashion, if the red mud of the Little Colorado River were spread over a nearby arid basin it would remain red even though the present environment in Arizona does not produce red color. Unless the source area were known and considered, the geologist of some future age would completely misinterpret the environment under which such a deposit was formed. Concentrations of clean sand, such as the St. Peter sandstone (Ordovician) of the Mississippi Valley and

3

the Ridgeley sandstone (Devonian) of the Appalachian region, can hardly be the product of a single erosion cycle; their immediate sources must have been in vast sandy deposits concentrated during previous cycles.

TRANSPORTATION

Sedimentary material is normally transported in one of three ways—in solution, in suspension, or by bottom traction. The chief agents are flowing water, wind, and ice.

Transportation by Streams

Solution

The more soluble products of weathering go into solution and are carried away by ground water or by surface runoff to the streams and lakes and ultimately to the sea. At any stage in this journey, however, chemical reaction with other materials in solution may take place, precipitation may occur because of evaporation or of other changes in the physical-chemical equilibrium, or certain materials may be extracted by organisms and built into skeletons or living tissue. If none of these changes occur, the dissolved substances remain in solution. Scarcely any minerals are completely insoluble, and colossal amounts of all the common ions of which minerals and rocks are formed are present in streams, in lakes, and especially in sea water.

Suspension

Particles that do not settle readily to the bottom in a fluid are said to be held in suspension. The roily water of streams in flood owes its turbidity to mud carried in this way.

Influence of size and shape of particles. Particles of clay size settle very slowly and will remain in suspension for many hours, even in standing water. Large grains settle faster than small ones and those of high specific gravity more rapidly than light ones. Spherical particles likewise settle faster than irregular ones of equal mass because they offer less frictional resistance.

Rubey (1931, p. 28) made critical experiments

TABLE 1. SETTLING VELOCITIES OF SEDIMENT IN STILL FRESH WATER. FROM RUBEY (1931).

	mm/sec
Very fine sand	>3.84
Coarse silt	0.96–3.84
Medium silt	0.24–0.96
Fine silt	0.06–0.24
Very fine silt	0.015–0.06
Coarse clay	0.00375–0.015
Medium clay	0.0009375–0.00375
Fine clay	<0.0009375

to determine the rate of settling of sediment in pure, still water, with the results shown in Table 1.

At these rates it would require about 2 hours for very fine sand to settle 100 feet, whereas fine clay would require about a year; to reach the ocean floor at a depth of 12,000 feet, very fine sand would need about 10 days and very fine clay would require more than 100 years. Neeb (1943, p. 94–95) reported that fine volcanic ash from the great eruption of Tamboro in 1815 is still settling out in some of the deep basins of the East Indies.

The settling velocity in still water is determined by the ratio of two forces, a downward force equal to gm (where g is the acceleration of gravity and m is the mass of a given particle), and an opposing or upward force, f (the frictional resistance), caused by the viscosity of the fluid. For particles smaller than fine sand the mass is small as compared with the viscous resistance of water and for such particles Rubey (1931, p. 17–31; 1933) showed that the settling velocity varies with the square of the diameter (Fig. 2, steeper curve), but for particles larger than coarse sand the mass is so great that viscous resistance is negligible and the settling velocity varies with the square root of the diameter (Fig. 2, flatter curve). For particles of intermediate size—fine to coarse sand—both mass and viscosity are important, and the settling velocity is intermediate between that for finer and coarser grades. The heavy curve in Figure 2 represents a general formula for all sizes.

The role of turbulence. In moving water, turbulence is an additional factor tending to keep sediment in suspension. In this connection two kinds of flow must be distinguished. At low velocities a fluid moves by a smooth gliding of fila-

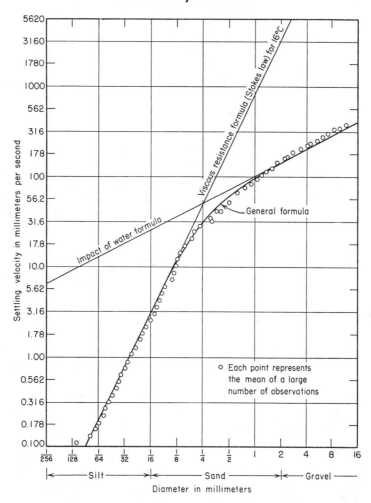

Figure 2. Settling velocity of quartz particles in still water, plotted on double logarithmic scale. From Rubey (1933). Experimentally determined velocities are represented by small circles.

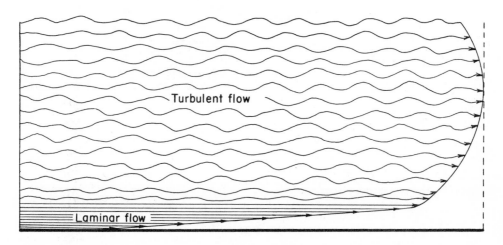

Figure 3. Laminar and turbulent flow in a stream. Velocity is indicated by the relative length of the flow-lines. Adapted from Rubey (1938).

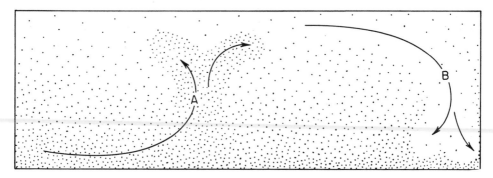

Figure 4. Role of turbulence in keeping sediment in suspension. The concentration of sediment is greater near the bottom and progressively less upward. The ascending eddy (A) therefore carries more sediment per unit volume than the descending eddy (B).

ments of current past one another, but at higher velocities the motion becomes irregular and distinctly eddying (Fig. 3). The first is *laminar,* the second *turbulent* flow. In laminar flow, particles of sediment settle as readily as in still water, but in turbulent flow, they are given repeated upward boosts that retard their settling. Of course, the upward eddies are on the whole balanced by downward eddies, and if the sediment were uniformly distributed throughout the current their effects would cancel out, the one carrying sediment downward as fast as the other carries it upward. But since solid particles constantly sink through the surrounding fluid, regardless of its motion, there is always a greater concentration of sediment near the bottom (Fig. 4). Thus ascending currents carry more sediment per unit volume than descending currents.

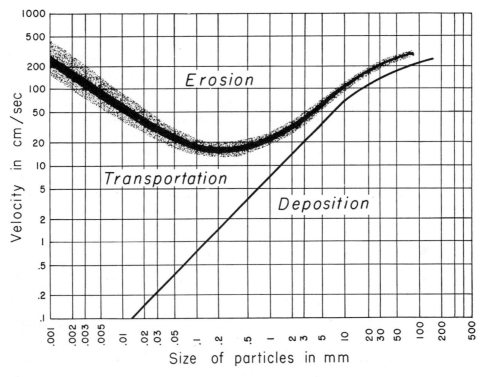

Figure 5. Graph showing velocities at which different size grades of sediment will be eroded, transported, or deposited; plotted on double logarithmic scale. After Hjulström (1935, p. 298).

Friction between a current and the surface of its confining channel causes a steep drop in the velocity gradient near the contact, where laminar flow is maintained. If the average velocity is considerable, the laminar flow may be limited to a mere film covering the surface of the materials on the bottom (whether they be solid bedrock or loose sediment), but in the movement of fine particles this layer plays an important role.

Resistance to movement after deposition. Hjulström (1935, 1939) showed that, after loose sediment of uniform size has come to rest, the velocity required to erode it is relatively high for the finest size grades, falls to a minimum for particles about 0.5 mm in diameter, and then increases again for coarser size grades (Fig. 5). There are two reasons for this apparent anomaly. First, a surface of uniform fine sediment has only microscopic relief, and individual particles project but little above the general level. Their exposed summits therefore lie within the bottom film of laminar flow or project but slightly above it and offer little surface for the turbulent current to work on. Second, the force of cohesion exerted by the clay minerals that are concentrated in the finest size grades inhibits the movement of individual particles. This explains the anomaly that silt and clay are more easily transported than sand but, once deposited, may be more difficult to move again.

Bottom traction

Coarse sediment is largely moved on the bottom where individual particles go leaping and tumbling along. Unhappily, the precise manner in which those at rest are picked up and set in motion, and the laws governing their movement, are not clearly understood. Gilbert's classic experiments on the transportation of debris by running water (Gilbert, 1914) were based on size-graded sediment in troughs having a flat bed of uniform cross section. While they provide a great mass of valuable data, the conditions represented in these experiments scarcely approach the complexity that exists in nature. Rubey's critical analysis of the force required to move particles on a stream bed (Rubey, 1938) shows the difficulty of the problem and gives references to the extensive and highly technical literature on the subject. Only the more general considerations need be presented here.

The analysis is simplified in the following discussion by assuming that the particles are spherical, but it should be remembered that in nature most of them are more or less irregular and that this adds complexity to their behavior.

Rolling. The simplest form of bottom traction occurs where spherical particles rest on a smooth surface. Here the force of the water is applied directly against the upstream side of the particles. Because of friction on the bottom and because the current striking its summit flows faster than that below, a particle tends to roll.

The influence of size is illustrated if we consider two particles, one having twice the diameter of the other (Fig. 6). The force exerted against such particles is mvk, in which m is the mass of water intercepted in a unit of time, v is its velocity, and k is a constant. The constant is needed because toward the margins of the sphere the water is deflected and only a small component of its force is exerted in the direction of movement. The mass of water intercepted is proportional to the cross section of the sphere, πr^2, but the mass of the particle to be moved by this force varies with

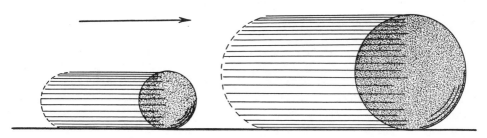

Figure 6. Influence of size of particles on velocity required for rolling on bottom. Horizontal lines represent direction of flow.

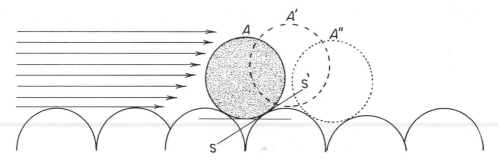

Figure 7. Beginning of saltation of a sand grain (A) resting on a surface of comparable grains.

the volume of the sphere, $\frac{4}{3}\pi r^3$. Accordingly, the larger of the two particles intercepts 4 times as much of the current but weighs 8 times as much as the smaller (assuming, of course, that they are made of the same material and that the velocity of the current is equal for both). This accords well with the common experience that sand is moved more readily than gravel and that as the velocity of a stream declines the coarsest particles of sediment come to rest first.

Saltation. In a stream the relations are rarely, if ever, so simple. Figure 7 illustrates a more normal condition in which particles of sediment are rolled over others. Here a particle, A, cannot be moved directly forward but must be pushed up an incline, s————s′, to a position A′ in order to get over the particle in front of it. Moreover, it is partly shielded from the current by the particles behind it. Both these circumstances tend to inhibit movement. Other forces are brought into play, however, for on such an irregular surface the flow is inevitably turbulent, and the eddy formed in the lee of an exposed particle produces suction. Moreover, the velocity of flow is not the same at all depths in a stream (Fig. 3, p. 5). Because of friction, it is least near the bed and the sides and rises to a maximum near the center of the channel and some distance above the median depth. The change per unit depth is rather gradual until the bed is approached and then the velocity gradient becomes very steep. Because the pressure diminishes with increase of velocity, a pressure difference is set up in the zone of steep velocity gradient and this produces a "hydraulic lift" (Hjulström, 1935, p. 267–270).

It is impossible to measure these competing forces experimentally, because any sort of gauge introduced will of itself create further disturbances. Rubey (1938) has given a theoretical analysis of the problem.

The force required to roll the particle A up the slope s————s′ to position A′ (Fig. 7) greatly exceeds that needed to roll it forward and down to position A″. Moreover, at position A′ it is elevated into current flowing more rapidly than at its original position or at A″. As a result, from position A′ it tends to leap forward into suspension until it has time to settle to the bottom again where the process is repeated. Consequently, the particle does not roll steadily along the bottom but proceeds in a series of leaps. Gilbert (1914, p. 26–30) termed this *saltation* and concluded that it is the chief mode of bottom traction in streams.

Isolated larger particles resting on finer, as a pebble or boulder lying on sand, tend to roll, and their movement is aided by excavation of sand in front of them by turbulent eddies.

Competence versus capacity

Gilbert (1914, p. 35) made an important distinction between the *competence* of a stream, which is a measure of the size of particles it can move, and the *capacity,* which is a measure of the total load it can transport. Competence depends largely on velocity, and capacity more on volume. For example, a small mountain torrent may be competent to move large boulders while lacking the capacity to transport a large quantity of sediment. The Mississippi River, on the contrary, lacks competence, in its lower reaches, to move boulders, but it has the capacity to carry the colossal load of some 500,000,000 tons of fine sediment that it delivers yearly to the Gulf of Mexico (Fisk and others, 1954, p. 80).

Load

The quantity of sediment actually being transported by a stream is its *load*. It is usually expressed in terms of weight (or of volume) of the material transported through a given cross section in a given unit of time, and normally refers to the solid material in suspension plus that moved along the bottom (some authors include material in solution as well). The material carried by rolling and saltation may be distinguished as the *traction load*.

The load of a stream of given velocity is influenced by the size of the loose particles available. A mountain brook, for example, may babble along crystal clear over boulders it is incompetent to move. Its load is zero. A second stream of identical size and velocity flowing over uniformly sorted gravel just within its capacity will carry a certain amount, but a third stream flowing over uniform sand will carry a larger load, and a fourth flowing over very fine sediment will carry a still larger load. Ideally, there is a capacity load for each size grade of sediment, the maximum being attained where all the available particles are of very fine size. In nature the sediment is normally heterogeneous, and a considerable range of size grades appears in the load.

Once fully loaded, a stream is unable to pick up additional sediment, however much may be available, and it may then flow along over a valley floor composed entirely of loose material.

As the velocity of a loaded stream decreases, both its competence and its capacity are reduced and it becomes *overloaded*. As competence declines, the coarsest particles are dropped first. The stream may then expend more of its energy on the remaining particles and may even pick up additional sediment, exchanging coarse for fine. The proportion of coarse material will vary from stream to stream and from place to place in a single stream. Rubey (1938, p. 139) concluded that, in a stream free to pick up much sand and gravel as its velocity is increased, the capacity load per unit of width will vary roughly as the cube of the velocity.

By-passing and total-passing

Since fine particles in motion are carried more readily than coarse ones of similar composition, and light ones more readily and more rapidly than comparable heavier ones, it is clear that even in a steady current a mass of heterogeneous sediment will not move as a unit. Even within the size range for which the current is competent, the finer particles will, in general, move faster and farther than the larger and heavier ones and, as the velocity eventually declines, the latter will come to rest while the former continue to move. Thus there is a constant passing of some particles by others during transportation. This phenomenon, termed *by-passing* by Eaton (1929, p. 714), is the means whereby a body of sediment becomes size-graded and the different components are winnowed out and segregated into deposits of gravel, sand, and silt. It is also probably the chief factor involved in the wear and rounding of gravel in transit.

Total-passing occurs where the current is able to transport all its load and none comes to rest.

Effects of stream transport on sediment

During transportation particles of sediment are modified by many factors. Kuenen (1956) recognizes seven distinct processes that operate to shape particles and reduce them in size. (1) Splitting is involved when a particle breaks into two or three subequal pieces. (2) Crushing occurs when a weak or small particle, caught between large ones, is pulverized. (3) Chipping involves the breaking of small flakes from the sharp edges of angular pebbles. It is important in the early stages of rounding but becomes negligible when the edges lose their sharpness. (4) Cracking produces tiny surface fractures by concussion when pebbles collide. Minute wedges may then be loosened between adjacent cracks and drop out. (5) Grinding is a form of abrasion produced when one pebble, pressed against another or against a rocky stream bed, is pushed bodily along. The result is similar to that involved in grinding thin sections. (6) Chemical attack, involving both rock decay and solution, is especially important where sediment lies exposed on the floodplain. Its effect varies, of course, with the mineral composition of the particles and with the climate, the rate of movement of the ground water, and the amount and kinds of organic acids in the soil. (7) Sandblasting is the normal effect of the by-passing of sand grains past each other or past gravel. Gregory (1915) experimented by drilling holes one inch deep in opposite faces of a number of large boulders in streams; 5 years later those on the downstream faces were not perceptibly modified whereas, due to sandblasting, those on the upstream faces were mostly obliterated and the plainest one was only 0.4 inch deep.

In general the boulders and gravel decrease in coarseness downstream from their source. This is in part due to breakage and to abrasion, but it is also in part due to selection, the coarsest particles coming to rest first as the velocity declines and thus lagging behind the finer so that they may never be carried as far.

Although rounding is the result of abrasion in transit and should increase with distance from the source, it is possible for the more angular particles to be concentrated farther downstream than the well-rounded ones, because they offer more resistance to the current and are therefore moved more readily than the well-rounded. Flakes of mica, for example, are commonly transported far beyond sand grains of equal mass.

In wear during transportation, weak materials are the first to be reduced to fine dimensions and carried away as silt or clay. Particles that are subject to chemical decay likewise tend to break down. Thus during long travel the coarser particles (boulders, gravel, and sand) are more and more reduced to a residue of such durable materials as quartz, quartzite, and chert.

Perhaps the most important effect on the sediment during transportation is sorting and size-grading. During flood a stream may carry a wide range of size grades, but even then sorting is taking place. The finer material goes into suspension and travels rapidly, while the coarser moves more slowly along the bottom. Sand and gravel can be carried only in the channel where the current is strongest, but mud and silt may be spread over the floodplain settling from the backwater. As the flood declines and the current loses momentum, coarse material comes to rest first and finer grades are carried progressively farther. Thus a mass of heterogeneous sediment becomes separated into deposits of gravel, sand, silt, and clay. In streams, however, the sorting is generally less perfect than in the sea, because most of the work is done during flood when the currents vary greatly from place to place and from hour to hour.

Transportation in the Sea

Marine currents

Currents in the sea are generated by winds, by tides, and by differences in specific gravity.

Friction of the wind blowing over the surface creates *drift currents,* including such great ocean currents as the Gulf Stream in the Atlantic and the Japan Current in the Pacific. Here the surface water is driven westward in the equatorial region under the influence of the trade winds until it impinges against the land and is deflected. Since the frictional force is applied only at the surface, its effect dies out rapidly with depth and is negligible below 600 feet. In the open oceans such currents move slowly and are shallow, but where constricted by the contour of the continental margins they gain both depth and velocity. Where the Gulf Stream passes through the Florida Strait, for example, it attains a surface velocity of 3 to 4 knots and sweeps the continental margin with sufficient velocity to remove fine sediment from the surface of Blake Plateau, even where the depth exceeds 2,500 feet (Stetson, 1939, p. 236). Northward toward Cape Hatteras it spreads out again and streams much more slowly to the northeast under the influence of the prevailing westerlies; its velocity is about 1 knot off Cape Hatteras.

Storm winds create local drift currents but these are highly variable in direction and velocity. Heavy storms rarely cover an area more than 300 miles in diameter at one time and seldom persist for more than a few days. Moreover, the wind normally changes velocity and direction as the storm passes. The net result of a passing storm, therefore, is to generate a temporary drift current that reaches maximum velocity after 2 or 3 days and then rapidly subsides, meanwhile changing or even reversing its direction; thus the general effect of a series of passing storms on a shallow sea floor is to stir up the bottom sediment and move it relatively short distances, first in one direction and then in another. In case the prevailing storms come from one direction, as in the belt of the westerlies, the net effect may be a progressive shift of the bottom sediment, but this is accomplished by many short journeys interrupted by long pauses and even reversals of direction. Near the land, however, where configuration of the shore influences the movement of the water, storm-generated drift currents may be more constant in direction.

The depth to which such currents affect the bottom is difficult to determine directly because gauges would have to be operated during the height of the storm, but study of the bottom sediment affords some indirect evidence. According to Shepard (1948, p. 53–54), such currents are negligible below 25 to 50 fathoms (150 to 300 feet).

Tidal currents arise because the earth rotates between two tidal bulges like a locomotive wheel between its brake shoes. As a result, the tidal bulges race each other around the earth from east to west. In the open ocean the bulges are very low and the movement unimportant, but as they impinge against the continental shelf a current flows and ebbs with each passing tide. Unlike the drift currents, these are not limited to the surface. As the tides enter shallow water, the currents are affected by the bottom contour and by the coastal profile. Here they are highly variable in direction and velocity, and locally they attain greater velocity than any other kinds of current in the sea with the exception of the turbidity currents discussed below (p. 13). Maximum velocity is attained in tidal inlets and in such embayments as the Bay of Fundy, San Francisco Bay, the Strait of Belle Isle, and Seymour Narrows between Vancouver Island and the mainland. In such places currents up to 5 or 6 knots are common. In Seymour Narrows a maximum velocity of 14.1 knots (16.5 miles per hour) has been measured; at the entrance to the Bay of Fundy the tidal currents run as high as 3.5 knots and in the upper reaches of the Bay they flow much faster. As the tide ebbs and flows in rhythm, the

velocity normally rises to a maximum, then declines to zero, and is reversed with each passing tide. Where influenced by suitable configuration of the coast line, however, the flow may be stronger than the ebb so that the predominant movement is in one direction.

Density currents arise wherever masses of water differ in specific gravity, the heavier mass flowing under the lighter which it displaces. Such inequalities may arise from differences in temperature (the specific gravity varying inversely as the temperature), in salinity (the specific gravity increasing with salinity), or in suspended sediment (which tends to add weight to a water mass). Water also tends to flow from areas of high barometric pressure to those of low. Cold surface water from the polar regions settles to the bottom and spreads over the ocean floor all the way to the equator. In favored places, especially in the tropics, rapid evaporation increases the salinity so as to give rise to descending currents. Streams of fresh water entering the ocean may ride far out to sea as a surface current resting on the salt water. It is even possible for a mass of water of intermediate density to flow out in a sheet between a lighter mass above and a denser one below.

Excepting only the turbidity currents discussed below, all such density currents have low velocity.

The role of waves

Waves play a very important role in the movement of sediment on the shallow sea floor since each exerts a lift as it passes.

The simplest movement is seen in the symmetrical waves that continue after the wind has died down. As shown in Figure 8, a water particle at the surface then moves in a circle whose diameter equals the height of the wave, rising and moving forward as the crest of the wave passes and then sliding down and back in the trough to its original position. Each particle below the surface also moves in a circle but the diameters of the circles decrease exponentially with depth. The rate of decrease is a function of the wave *length, L,* rather than its height. Theoretically the diameter of the orbit of movement will be reduced to one-half at a depth $\frac{1}{9}L$, to one-fourth at

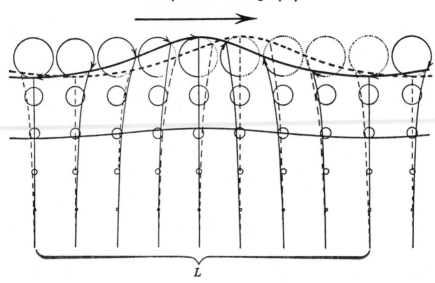

Figure 8. Movement of water particles during the passing of a low symmetrical deep-water wave. "The size of the orbits below the surface is shown to scale, and the lower wave profile shows the amount of vertical movement at that level. The dashed lines show corresponding positions one-eighth of a period later than the equivalent solid lines." From Kuenen (1950b, Fig. 42).

$\frac{2}{9}L$, to one-eighth at $\frac{3}{9}L$, and so on. At this rate, a wave having a height of 10 feet and a length of 300 feet will produce an orbit of about 15 inches at a depth of 100 feet, but of only 2 inches at 200 feet and less than $\frac{1}{4}$ inch at 300 feet. A shorter wave will reach to lesser depth. If, for example, it were 10 feet high and had a length of only 100 feet, the movement at a depth of 100 feet would be less than $\frac{1}{4}$ inch. Obviously, therefore, even large storm waves cannot affect the bottom below a depth of a few hundred feet. Some of the great swells that persist after a storm and travel far beyond the storm area have a height of 5 or 6 feet and a length of 1,000 to 2,000 feet. In spite of small height, such swells must affect the bottom to depths exceeding that of storm waves.

Thus far we have considered only waves in which the particles of water move in closed orbits. But when the wind is driving the waves, friction with the water surface carries each particle forward somewhat, so that it does not return quite to its previous position. Drift currents are thus produced, and if the water is shallow enough they may move bottom sediment.

Where waves reach the sea floor, the lowest water particles cannot rise in a circular orbit, lifting the water free and leaving a vacuum under each wave. Accordingly the orbits change to flattened ellipses very near the bottom, and the movement is largely to and fro. Where waves agitate the bottom in the absence of currents, this to-and-fro movement tends to form oscillation ripples in the sediment but produces no real transportation. In the presence of even a gentle bottom current, however, the lift given by each passing wave permits the current to shift particles it would otherwise be incompetent to move. Thus the waves strongly abet the bottom currents.

Sublevation

On the land, flowing water is confined to channels, where it tends to carve valleys and so to exaggerate the relief. Locally marine currents also flow in channels as in the tidal inlets of the shore zone and in the enigmatic submarine canyons. In narrow straits or along some coast lines, also, tidal currents are confined so as to cut into bedrock. With these exceptions the sea floor is generally mantled with loose sediment, and the currents are broad and ill-defined sheets of moving water that gently sweep the bottom. The erosion that takes place under such conditions differs in important respects from that on the land, both in the processes involved and in the results achieved. To distinguish this special type of submarine erosion we suggest the term *sublevation* [L. *sublevare,* to lift up]. It is to be used for the degradation of a sea floor composed of loose sediment.*

Agitation by waves plays an important role in lifting the particles so that bottom currents can move them. Such particles are free to move individually, the finer ones going into suspension and the coarser being swept along the bottom. Tidal currents and drift currents tend to move as a sheet, riding above local depressions in which sediment can come to rest. The net effect of sublevation is, therefore, to keep the surface of the shallow sea floor graded by filling up local depressions while planing down the higher areas. The topographic effect is the antithesis of that produced by streams on the land, and the net result is to keep a shallow sea floor remarkably flat and its slopes gentle wherever tectonic disturbances do not interfere.

Turbidity currents

It has long been observed that both where the Rhone River enters Lake Geneva and where the Rhine enters Lake Constance, the turbid river water pours steeply down under the clear lake water and spreads over the bottom toward the deepest parts of the lakes. Obviously the river water has higher specific gravity than the lake water. This was attributed to the lower temperature of the river water until Forel (1887) emphasized that the turbid water is heavier because of the suspended sediment. That sediment in suspension increases the specific gravity of a mass of water and will cause it to flow down a bottom slope is now well known both from observations in nature and from laboratory experiments, as explained below.

Daly (1936) was the first to arouse the interest of geologists in this phenomenon when he advanced the hypothesis that the submarine canyons have been carved by currents of muddy water flowing down over the continental margins. He referred to them as density currents, but Johnson (1939, p. 27) introduced the name *turbidity cur-*

* The verb *sublevate* is also useful. For example, storms generate waves and currents that sublevate the sea floor even in areas of general aggradation.

rents to distinguish them from other kinds of density currents caused by variations in temperature or salinity.

Kuenen (1937) first showed experimentally that sediment-laden water will flow down a bottom slope and (1950a) that it can attain relatively high velocity. In a series of brilliant studies he has since applied this idea to the interpretation of sedimentary deposits, both modern and ancient (Kuenen, 1950b, p. 238–248, and subsequent papers).

Since construction of the Hoover Dam, Lake Mead has provided a natural laboratory for study of this phenomenon. When the Colorado River is in flood its turbid water plunges beneath the clear water at the head of Lake Mead and streams along the bottom, following the old river channel the full distance of 120 miles to the dam, its flow being compensated by a surface current moving in the opposite direction (Gould, 1951).

The velocity of a turbidity current depends on the mass and the concentration of suspended sediment, and on the steepness of the bottom slope. Where a muddy stream debouches into a lake a persistent but rather gentle current is produced, capable of transporting and depositing sediment essentially as a normal stream does. According to Gould (1951, p. 45), for example, when the Colorado River is in flood, the flow of turbid water at the bottom of Lake Mead commonly attains a velocity of 1 foot per second (about 0.7 miles per hour) near the river mouth, but it is slowed to less than 3 inches per second (about 0.17 miles per hour) by the time it reaches the dam. In contrast, a submarine landslide on a steep slope (as at the continental margin) may suddenly set in motion a great mass of loose sediment that will incorporate water as it moves until it becomes a heavily weighted fluid mass pouring down the slope with great speed and carrying an enormous volume of sediment in suspension. A catastrophic movement of this kind is necessarily of short duration—an episode of a few hours or a day or two at the most. When it reaches the base of the declivity and the bottom slope flattens out, the moving mass of sediment-laden water rapidly loses velocity as it fans out over the ocean floor. As it does so the coarsest particles settle out first and progressively finer

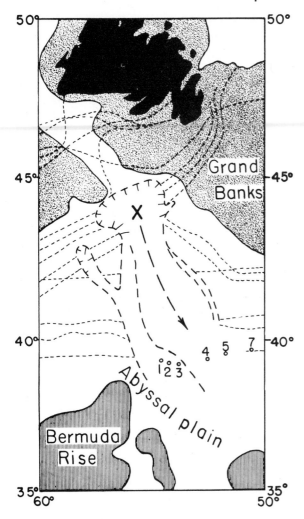

Figure 9. Area of Grand Banks earthquake of November 18, 1929. Black, Newfoundland; light shading, continental shelf; darker shading, Bermuda rise and related mid-Atlantic highs; dotted lines, transatlantic cables. The scar of the landslide is at X; arrow indicates direction of turbidity current. Numbers 1 to 7 indicate deep-sea coring stations. After Heezen, Ericson, and Ewing (1954, Fig. 4).

introduced if a number of submarine landslides occur in close succession (Kuenen and Menard, 1952, p. 92).

As Kuenen and Menard pointed out, the deposit laid down by a cataclysmic movement of this sort differs greatly from one formed by a persistent and gentler stream of muddy water. The difference is so important that these contrasting types of turbidity currents should bear distinct names. We propose to distinguish them as *steady* and *spasmodic*.

Steady turbidity currents arise when a continuing supply of turbid water flows over a sloping bottom, as where a muddy stream debouches into a lake or where sediment is lifted into suspension along a slope by storm waves. Daly (1936) postulated that such currents were generated on a vast scale along the continental margins during the glacial epochs when the low stand of sealevel permitted the waves vigorously to stir up the sediment on the outer part of the continental shelves. Where streams enter the sea they are less likely to generate turbidity currents than in lakes because the higher specific gravity of the salt water tends to counterbalance the weight of the sediment in the fresh water. Perhaps a turbidity current could be produced, nevertheless, if the river water is very heavily loaded with sediment; or perhaps sediment could settle from silt-laden river water into underlying sea water, which would then be heavier than the surrounding sea water and would flow down the slope. The idea needs confirmation.

Spasmodic turbidity currents develop only where a large volume of loose sediment is suddenly thrown into suspension, as by a landslide, on a steep submarine slope. Such slides may be triggered by earthquakes along the continental margin, as in the case of the Grand Banks earthquake described below, but they may form also without such a stimulus where a sedimentary deposit builds the sea floor up locally to an unstable gradient, as off the mouths of large rivers. Of course, not all submarine landslides develop into turbidity currents; it depends on the steepness and the extent of the slope, and probably on other factors such as the nature of the bottom sediment. Where the bottom slope is gentle, simple slumps or landslides may occur; but if the

ones follow so that the resulting deposit is a single layer graded from coarse at the bottom to fine at the top (Kuenen and Migliorini, 1950). Such a layer is said to show *graded bedding* (Figs. 50, 51, p. 107 and 109). Deposits of this nature have long been known, but their origin remained an enigma until turbidity currents were recognized and studied.

Although a spasmodic flow normally produces a single graded layer, more complexity may be

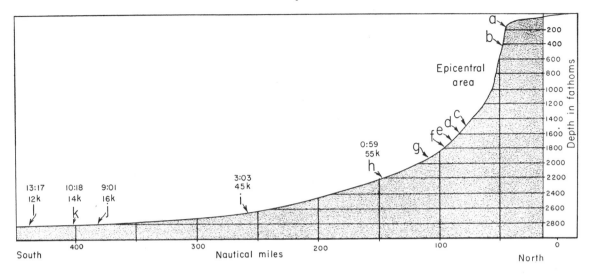

Figure 10. Profile showing progress of the turbidity current south of the Grand Banks induced by the earthquake of November 18, 1929. Adapted from Heezen and Ewing (1952). The positions of twelve submarine cables (a to l) are indicated. For each of the last five (h to l) the upper figure indicates the time interval between the earthquake and the arrival of the current that broke the cable, and the lower figure indicates the calculated velocity of the current in knots as it passed.

slope is steep and the initial movement is sufficiently rapid, the moving mass of sediment may incorporate enough of the surrounding sea water to become a fluid mass in which nearly all the solid particles are in suspension; it will then flow rapidly and may gain momentum and continue to grow by picking up additional sediment as it races down the slope.

Since a spasmodic turbidity current is of short duration and occurs far below the surface of the sea there is little chance of direct observation. Ewing and his colleagues have nevertheless been able to document several such flows. The first and most spectacular case was discovered from the records of the Grand Banks earthquake of November 18, 1929 (Heezen and Ewing, 1952). The epicenter of this quake was on the continental slope south of the Grand Banks (Fig. 9). More than a score of transatlantic cables cross this area, spread out so that a number lie upon the continental shelf, seven lie along the upper part of the continental slope, and five more are spread out farther down the slope and out on the Atlantic floor.

Following the earthquake many of these cables were broken and the precise time of each break is known. Study of these data showed that the cables lying upon the continental shelf were unbroken, the seven lying along the upper margin of the continental slope were broken simultaneously (a to g, Fig. 10), and the five lying farther down the slope were broken in sequence during a period of 13 hours and 17 minutes. Heezen and Ewing inferred that the earthquake jarred the continental slope, setting slumps and landslides in motion along its upper part over an area of 150 by 80 miles. These incorporated more water and were transformed into a vast turbidity current that raced down the slope and out onto the ocean floor to a distance of more than 400 miles from the source. The time of its arrival at successive cables gives evidence of the velocity of the current (Fig. 10). Heezen and Ewing found that a velocity of 55 knots was attained near the base of the steepest slope and at a distance of about 100 miles from the initial landslides. The velocity decreased gradually as the slope flattened but was still 45 knots at a distance of 200 miles, where the depth was 15,600 feet and the bottom slope was only 25 feet per mile, and 12 knots at a distance of 400 miles where the bottom slope was less than 4 feet per mile. Obviously, the current must have continued far beyond the last cable, fanning out over the ocean floor.

Kuenen (1952) analyzed these data, checked the velocities, and, by extrapolating experimentally determined constants to this large-scale occurrence, estimated that the transported sediment was spread over 100,000 square miles of the ocean floor as a graded layer averaging between 40 and 100 cm thick. His estimate has since received striking confirmation through a string of deep sea cores taken just south of the last broken cable (Ericson, 1953; Heezen, Ericson, and Ewing, 1954). The two western cores (1 and 2 of Fig. 9), lying near the western margin of the path swept by the current, revealed a graded bed of gray sandy sediment lying at the surface and resting with sharp basal contact on brownish abyssal clay rich in pelagic foraminifera. Core 7, taken about 160 nautical miles farther east, showed brownish abyssal clay at the surface; it was just east of the area of deposition by the Grand Banks flow. Three attempts to take cores in the intermediate area were unsuccessful, the coring tube coming up bent and empty. It is inferred that at these locations the sandy layer was too compact for the coring tube to pass through it and that, in the absence of a plug of the underlying clay, the sand trickled out of the tube as it was raised. In cores 1 and 2 the thickness of the graded bed produced by the turbidity current of 1929 measured 70 cm and 130 cm respectively.

Striking evidence of another such current was discovered about 30 miles southeast of the Bermuda Islands (Ericson, Ewing, and Heezen, 1952, p. 498) where, at a depth of nearly 3 miles (2,325 fathoms), a deep sea core revealed a graded surface layer of calcareous sand about 5.5 feet thick. The lower part of this layer includes abundant shell fragments of mollusks that live only in shallow lagoonal water, and pieces of the calcareous alga, *Halimeda,* which grows only in the presence of sunlight. Ericson, Ewing, and Heezen inferred that the material comprised in this graded layer had its source in the upper slope of the Bermuda pedestal and was transported by a turbidity current down a 30-mile slope into the deep sea. Since the deposit is not covered by abyssal clay or globigerina ooze, they conclude that it is of very recent origin.

Spasmodic turbidity currents at the mouth of Magdalena River, Colombia, were recently described by Heezen (1955). A submarine cable lies along the continental slope about 15 miles north of the river mouth and at a depth of some 4,200 feet. This cable has been broken 14 times within the last 25 years under circumstances that clearly indicate spasmodic turbidity currents. Here massive landslides from the steep slope just beyond the river mouth have been triggered, not by earthquakes but by harbor construction. Once, for example, a large section of a jetty being constructed at the terminus of the channel disappeared during the night of a cable break.

Spasmodic turbidity currents clearly provide a means, previously unsuspected, whereby terrigenous sand and mud can be transported into deep water and spread over the ocean floor at great distance from shore. The importance of this process is suggested by the recent work of Ewing and his colleagues in the North Atlantic (Heezen, Ewing, and Ericson, 1955; Ericson, Ewing, Heezen, and Wollin, 1955; and other papers). Surveys with a newly developed precision depth recorder have revealed vast abyssal plains in which the surface slopes are less than 1 foot per 1,000. One such plain lies south of Newfoundland and another borders the continental slope of eastern North America; together they cover half a million square miles (Ewing, personal communication). Some 230 cores taken by Ewing and his colleagues on these plains show evidence of turbidity-current deposition. Here graded sandy layers are separated by normal abyssal clay and globigerina ooze. The sandy beds have certainly come from the continent, and they are inferred to be the product of turbidity currents because they are graded, because they commonly contain benthonic species of foraminifera that live only in shallow water, and because no other agent is known that could transport such material far out into deep water and deposit it in this way. These appear to be aggraded plains in which turbidity-current deposits have covered the normal irregularities of the ocean floor.

The foraminifera contained both in the sandy layers and in the associated abyssal clay and ooze indicate Pleistocene age, even in the deepest parts of the cores. This suggests surprisingly rapid deposition for the deep ocean floor. If such deposition had been normal throughout geologic time, the ocean basins should be filled, or should at least be floored by a very thick sedimentary deposit, yet seismic evidence shows clearly that there is no such deposit. For this reason Ewing (personal communication) is inclined to believe that the turbidity-current deposits in the Atlantic are somehow associated with the glaciation of the Pleistocene epoch. Nevertheless the graded deposits now known in many parts of the geologic column clearly indicate that under favorable conditions spasmodic turbidity currents have been an important agent of transportation and deposition.

The well-documented spasmodic turbidity currents discussed above all reached abyssal depths, but it is not necessary to infer that such currents cannot operate in much shallower water. A steep slope of considerable length is presumably necessary for the flow to pick up enough speed to spread its sediment far from the source but perhaps several hundred feet of depth would suffice. Further research is needed to determine the minimum depth at which turbidity-current deposits can be formed.

Transportation by Wind

Wind is a powerful agent of transportation, especially in arid regions, but its effect on loose sediment differs in important respects from that of flowing water. In part this difference stems from the great difference in density and viscosity between air and water. A grain of quartz, for example, weighs only about 2.65 times as much as an equal volume of water but approximately 2,000 times as much as an equal volume of air. As a result the largest particles that can be moved by wind are far smaller than by water, and particles of sediment settle much more rapidly in air than in water. On the other hand the velocity of winds may greatly exceed that of currents in water and it commonly changes more abruptly. Whereas a current of water, losing velocity, drops progressively finer and finer particles so that the resultant sedimentary deposit grades laterally from coarse to fine, ordinarily without abrupt change, the wind tends to select sand grains of a limited size range and to concentrate them into ridges or dunes, meanwhile lifting the finer particles into suspension and scattering them far and wide as dust. We are indebted to Bagnold (1941) for a magnificent study of the movement of sediment, especially sand, by the wind.

Distinction between sand and dust

Sand is moved by traction and thus travels close to the ground; but dust, being carried in suspension, may be borne aloft by ascending currents and transported to great distance. During a dust storm, vision is obscured by the clouds of fine particles that rise to great height. Under such conditions it is impossible to see what is happening to the sand. But in deserts where the wind blows across large areas of clean sand, the sky remains clear and distant vision is unimpaired as the sand skims along the surface "like a moving carpet" below waist level of a walking man.

Wind-blown sand is normally fine-grained and exceptionally well size-sorted. According to Bagnold (1941, p. 6), desert sand is generally between 0.15 and 0.30 mm in diameter and never less than 0.08 mm, the finer material being blown away as dust. Udden (1898; 1914) and Wentworth (1931, p. 12–17) found similar sizes to predominate in some of the American dunes. Wentworth published histograms of 42 sands from dunes scattered across the United States, and these show that a large percentage of the sand falls within the range of 0.125 to 0.50 mm in diameter. Under exceptional wind conditions and near its source, wind-blown sand may be much coarser. For example, Newell and Boyd (1955) observed ridges of wind-blown "sand" along the Peruvian coast in which the bulk of the grains exceed 3 mm in diameter.

Movement of sand

By ingenious experiments, Bagnold (1941, p. 33 ff.) discovered that sand is transported by the wind in two distinct ways—by saltation and by surface creep.

Saltation. Saltation starts in air, as it does under water, when the pressure of the moving fluid becomes great enough to push the most exposed grains up over those before them (Fig. 7, p. 8). A grain of quartz, however, moves more

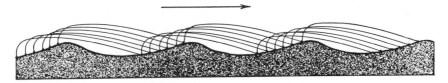

Figure 11. Relation of ripple length to average distance of saltation in wind-blown sand. Adapted from Bagnold (1941).

freely in air than under water and behaves quite differently. When a flying quartz grain strikes a rigid surface of bare rock, for example, or a pebble too large to move, it bounces off like a ping-pong ball with little loss of momentum, behaving as an almost perfectly elastic solid. The direction of its rebound depends on the angle of incidence, but in a strong wind some of the grains may bounce to a height of many feet, and to the casual observer will appear to be traveling in suspension.

If, on the other hand, the flying grain descends upon a surface of loose dry sand, it disperses most of its energy among the several grains that it strikes, ejecting them into the air and forming a small crater in the sand. Since the energy of the fast-moving grain is thus shared by several other grains, none of these rises more than a few centimeters and the original leaping grain rebounds but slightly.

The important role of this spattering action in lifting sand into saltation was demonstrated by Bagnold by means of an ingenious experiment. He floored a long wind tunnel with well-sorted dry sand, leveled to a smooth surface. A current of air was then drawn through the tunnel and its velocity gradually increased to just below the threshold at which saltation would begin. A small quantity of sand was then introduced through the roof of the tunnel near its intake. These falling grains were caught by the air stream and driven forward so that they hit the surface of the sand with considerable velocity. As each grain struck, it could be seen to form a small crater by spattering away several grains where it hit. Each of the grains thus ejected into the air stream was in turn driven forward in an arching trajectory and, upon landing, formed another crater and ejected several more grains. Thus was set in motion a veritable chain reaction that spread rapidly along the tunnel. When the velocity of the air flow was re-

duced, the movement quickly died out. The current was then gradually accelerated again until saltation began naturally (without the introduction of grains from above) and when the first grains began to leap they immediately started a chain reaction as before. Obviously the spattering greatly increases the quantity of sand lifted into the air stream.

Observations in the wind tunnel, later confirmed during sand storms in the desert, proved that in saltation over a surface of loose sand few of the grains reach a height of 3 feet in their flight and most of them travel within less than 2 feet of the surface.

Surface creep. Regardless of the height and direction of the rebound, all the grains are driven forward by the wind, those that bound highest being carried farthest, and Bagnold found that after making an arching trajectory they all strike the surface again at a surprisingly uniform angle slightly less than 15° from the horizontal (Fig. 11). As each grain hits, part of its momentum is transmitted to the grains it spatters away, but a part is dissipated in moving other grains that are not lifted but merely pressed forward. In a strong wind the net result of the bombardment of the grains in saltation is thus a slow creep of all the grains at the surface. Bagnold (1941, p. 34) found that between 20 and 25 percent of the total weight of sand passing a given line during active saltation was thus transported. He also found that in heterogeneous sand the finer grains move by saltation and the coarser ones chiefly by creep, because the impact of a high-speed grain in saltation can move grains too large to lift.

Dune building

Sources of sand. The chief requisite for dune formation is an adequate supply of loose sand. This is available in arid regions where the mantle is not held by moisture and vegetation. On large parts of the great deserts, such as the Sahara and the Arabian Desert, the mantle is removed by the wind as fast as it forms, the finer material being blown away as dust to settle outside the desert, the sand being concentrated into dunes. This leaves a large part of the desert floor exposed as bare rock or covered with a veneer of gravel which the wind cannot move.

In regions of higher relief where streams descend into the desert from more humid uplands, they bring an endless supply of loose sediment that is spread out on piedmont slopes or broad floodplains. In the absence of a cover of vegetation this sediment is at the mercy of the winds, and sand may be winnowed out to form dunes.

In semiarid regions the mantle is effectively held by a sod cover, but the sand-choked channels of through-flowing streams provide a continuous supply of loose sand. Even in humid regions sandy beaches afford a perpetual supply of loose sand and, where prevailing winds blow landward, the shore is commonly bordered by a belt of dunes. Impressive examples may be seen along the east side of Lake Michigan, and along parts of the coast of Europe, notably in the Bay of Biscay and in Holland. Cape Cod, likewise, is largely covered by dunes.

It should be emphasized that, although most dunes are made of quartz sand, calcareous dunes are formed of foraminiferal shells and of shell-sand along the shores of many coral islands. The Bermuda Islands, for example, rising to peaks as much as 265 feet above present sealevel, are formed entirely of wind-blown calcareous sand heaped into dunes during a lower stand of sealevel in Pleistocene time when the fringing coral reefs were killed and exposed.

Causes of accumulation. Wind-driven sand, like snow, tends to settle in drifts in the wind-shadow of topographic obstructions. In the "Dust Bowl" of West Texas and eastern Colorado we have seen recent examples of sand drifts along fence rows and in the lee of farm buildings. In arid or semiarid regions wherever the winds are prevailingly from one quarter, sand likewise tends to accumulate in the lee of hills, behind ledges, or even behind clumps of vegetation; if the obstructions are large, the sand drifts may grow to the size of dunes. Such deposits are stationary, because they depend on the protection given by a fixed obstruction that checks the wind.

Vegetation may also cause sand to accumulate even on a low and exposed surface. Along a sandy beach, for example, where the climate is humid so that the adjacent land is covered by grass or shrubs, the sand blown inland is checked in its flight in two ways. In the first place, the leaves break the fall of the flying grains so that they do not bounce as they would on a bare surface, and they lack the force to spatter other grains into the air current; thus saltation is inhibited. In the second place, the vegetation exerts a strong drag on the wind, slowing the layers near the surface. Once a grain has fallen, it therefore escapes the fast-flowing wind that started it in motion. Thus the sand blown inland from the beach accumulates to form drifts that grow into dunes. Where moisture is adequate, vegetation may continue to grow up through and over the dunes until they reach great size. Once a line of such dunes is formed near the shore, the vegetation may be unable to hold all the sand either because it is smothered or because the water table is too low, and dunes then migrate inland, broadening the belt of sand accumulation.

In the great flat deserts where most of the dunes of the world exist, neither topographic obstructions nor vegetation can account for the concentration of moving sand, yet isolated dunes will maintain their distinctive form, and even grow in size while migrating across the desert floor. Here, it can be shown, the dune itself serves as a trap to catch and hold sand. Consider, for example, the effect of a patch of loose sand isolated on a stretch of rocky desert floor across which storm winds are moving sand in saltation. The sand may have come from an outside source (e.g., a stream bed) or it may have been gleaned from the loose material freed by the weathering of the desert floor. In either case there is a limit to the quantity of sand a wind of given velocity can keep in motion. Since a grain of quartz sand weighs some 2,000 times as much as an equal volume of air, the energy absorbed from the wind in accelerating a sand grain to a given velocity is equivalent to that required to stop completely 2,000 times as great a volume of air moving at the

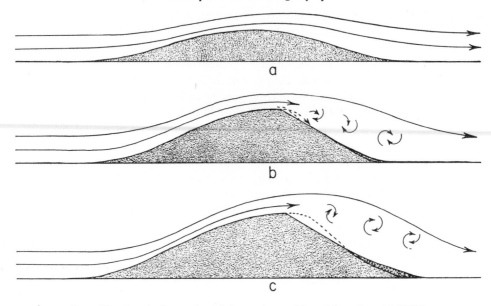

Figure 12. Growth of a sand patch into a dune. Adapted from Bagnold (1941).

same speed. The sand in saltation therefore acts as a brake, tending to slow down wind near the ground. In traveling across a gravel-covered or rocky floor, the wind gathers as many sand grains as it can keep in saltation, but upon reaching a patch of loose sand, each of these grains spatters several others into the air and suddenly a powerful brake is applied by the large quantity of sand in the air. The wind near the surface is thus checked, and it cannot carry away as much sand as it brought. The overload is dropped, and the sand patch grows even though some sand is carried away.

The evolution of a sand patch into a dune is shown in Figure 12. As the sand patch grows deeper, it assumes the form of a low mound. Now the windward slope adds a further obstacle to check the air flow. At the same time it is inclined so as to receive the maximum concentration of impacts from the arriving grains in saltation, and surface creep becomes active here, pushing sand up to the crest and over onto the leeward slope which, because of its inclination, receives few impacts from the fast-moving grains. Turbulence here may keep some of the sand in motion, but back eddies tend to retard its progress. As the mound grows higher, the wind tends to shoot ahead at the summit leaving a dead-air pocket behind the mound. Now the sand that leaps over or is forced over by creep rolls down the leeward slope to accumulate at the angle of repose (which may be as high as 34°). But since this sand is constantly added at or near the summit, the slope becomes oversteepened and is restored to equilibrium when a thin face shears off and rolls down to the bottom of the slope. This initiates the steep slip-face that is maintained on the leeward side of the dune by repeated shearing or slipping. After the dune has attained a height of several feet, the air pocket in its lee is so large that grains in saltation cannot cross it in a single leap. Thereafter it is an almost perfect trap for moving sand.

If the supply of oncoming sand is sufficient, part of it will come to rest on the stoss slope while a part is being shifted to the leeward slope, and thus the dune may grow larger by expanding upwind as well as downwind and by steadily increasing in height. If the supply of new sand is less than that moved over the crest, however, the windward slope will be degraded as the leeward grows, and thus the dune will migrate with the wind by transfer of sand from one slope to the other.

Types of dunes. Various attempts have been made to classify dunes according to their manner of growth and their shape. Recent schemes have been advanced by Melton (1940), H. T. U. Smith (1940), Hack (1941), and Bagnold (1941). For our purpose a very simple scheme will suffice.

The simplest and most distinctive type is the *barchan* dune (Fig. 13), which has the form of a crescent lying transverse to the wind with a gentle convex slope to windward and a steeper concave face to leeward. The tips of the crescent are formed of the sand that is diverted along the flanks of the dune, and they grow forward in the direction of wind flow. This appears to be the stable form where the winds blow only from a single direction. The steep leeward slope is a slip-face. If the dune is growing, sand layers may be added simultaneously over the convex windward slope and over the concave leeward slope. In this event, layers on the two sides have a steep original dip in opposite directions. They also differ in compactness. The windward slope is constantly hammered by the impact of grains in saltation, and here the sand is crowded into the most com-

pact arrangement, but on the slip-face the sand shears off from time to time and rolls loosely down the steep slope to accumulate without further agitation.

The predominant dunes in the great deserts are longitudinal ridges running parallel to the wind and separated by broad troughs so that from the air they resemble windrows of hay on a meadow. These are the longitudinal or *seif* dunes. Some of them attain great size, running as continuous ridges for as much as 50 or 60 miles and rising to a height of 200 to 300 feet. Some in southern Iran even attain a height of 700 feet. The distance apart, from crest to crest, of such parallel dunes is commonly 5 to 6 times their height, according to Bagnold.

Longitudinal dunes are stable in areas where the strong winds come alternately from two directions in the same quadrant, blowing obliquely along first one flank and then the opposite. While the wind is blowing from the right flank, sand is

Spence Air Photos

Figure 13.   Barchan sand dunes west of Yuma, Arizona.

Carl O. Dunbar

Figure 14. Cross-bedded Navajo sandstone (Jurassic) in Zion National Park, Utah.

moved obliquely to leeward and over the crest which becomes unsymmetrical, with a slip-face along the leeward side; when the wind is from the left flank the symmetry is reversed.

Great *transverse* dunes form where the wind blows across a copious supply of loose sand. In the deserts such supply may be found along the shores of a lake, along sand-choked stream courses, or where the desert floor is made of friable sandstone. Transverse ridges become unstable as they migrate away from the source and tend to break up into barchan or longitudinal dunes, depending upon the prevailing wind conditions.

In more humid areas where moisture and vegetation play a leading part in checking the movement of sand near its source, the dunes assume a more irregular form and may grow to great height as irregular mounds with intervening hollows, resembling the surface of a choppy sea.

Internal structure. Because of the manner of their deposition, wind-blown sands are almost invariably marked by conspicuous cross-stratification of a distinctive type (Fig. 14). Each added layer conforms to the surface of some part of a dune. It is invariably inclined to the horizontal plane, but the dip may vary widely in steepness and direction. Where the surfaces are curved, as in barchan and most irregular dunes, the inclined layers are also curved; but on the outer flanks of longitudinal dunes the dips may be low and gentle and fairly uniform. Because of the normal size of dunes, cross-stratification appears on a large scale. Frequent reversals of the direction of dip may be due to shifts in the wind causing growth first in one direction and then in another; they may also be due to simultaneous growth on opposite flanks of the dune or to alternations of growth and denudation on the windward side during progressive growth on the leeward slope.

There is nothing in the dune regimen to produce horizontal bedding of wind-blown sand, but the water table may protect the sand from removal at approximately one level while the upper part of a mass of dunes migrates away; if dunes reappear in the area at a later date they may rest upon a truncated surface of earlier dune sands.

Of course, offshore winds may carry sand into the sea or into a lake where it settles in water. Probably the well-rounded quartz grains in the sandy dolomites of Precambrian and Cambrian age (e.g., the Mallett formation of northwestern Vermont) are wind-blown. However, since sand travels chiefly by saltation it could not normally be carried far from shore by the wind.

Loess

The fine sediment transported as dust is widely dispersed. During a three-day windstorm in a relatively small area of the "Dust Bowl" of western Texas in 1953, the air was so densely clouded that street lights were turned on in cities as far away as Kansas City and Chicago, and the sky was conspicuously tinted all the way across the continent to New England. From time to time storms in northern Africa have likewise spread a pall of dust widely across Europe. It is normal for the dust carried aloft by storms in arid regions to be widely dispersed. If it settles in the desert its sojourn is transient, for the next storm will lift it aloft and spread it farther. If it settles outside the desert where there is moderate or heavy rainfall, it is transported into the streams by surface runoff and is carried away. If it settles on flat uplands where rainfall is only moderate and erosion is negligible, it may accumulate to form loess. Such accumulation is favored by a sod cover where the dust, settling among the grass blades, is protected from further movement by the wind and from surface runoff.

The bodies of outwash that formed about the waning ice sheets provided an important source for the loess that is so widespread about the glaciated regions of the Pleistocene. This is the *cold loess* of Obruchev (1945, p. 258). Such deposits are widespread in the Central Lowland of the United States, in European Russia and in Siberia, and about the glaciated mountains of Central and Eastern Asia.

In addition there are vast deposits of loess formed to the leeward of the great deserts of Central Asia, not dependent on glaciation but formed of dust blown out of the deserts. This is the *warm loess* of Obruchev. Such is the red loess of North China and western Manchuria.

Dust blown to sea may settle to mingle with pelagic sediments far from shore and at great depth. In the Cape Verde Islands region west of the Sahara, for example, such wind-blown dust collected aboard vessels has been analyzed by Radczewski (1939, p. 499), and Correns (1934) found the bottom sediments of this region to include notable increments of such material. Reddish-coated quartz grains were recognized by Correns as "desert quartz" (*wüstenquartz*). Such grains range in size mostly from 1 to 50 microns and thus fall in clay and silt sizes.

Transportation by Ice

Sediment is transported by glaciers and by floating ice. In either case it is carried and dropped without sorting or size-grading, and the resulting deposit is unstratified. The characteristics of till are too well known to need description here. Since rock fragments frozen in the ice are not free to move, those in the sole of the glacier are commonly faceted and striated as a result of abrasion on the floor over which the ice moves. Even those well above the base may be rubbed one against another, because of differential movement in the glacier. There is almost no limit to the size of blocks or masses of stone that can be moved by ice, and for this reason glaciation has been invoked to account for almost every very coarse rudite in the stratigraphic record. Other agents that may form such deposits are suggested in Chapter 9.

During continental glaciation, a spreading ice sheet scrapes off the mantle and scours the bedrock over a wide region, thus transporting a colossal amount of sediment. Only part of this sediment accumulates as till, the rest being reworked and carried farther by the meltwater and deposited as outwash. Though its composition may reveal its glacial origin, the outwash is really water-laid and has all the characteristics of a stream deposit.

Since ice sheets spread across country, overriding hills and valleys, they may carry "foreign rocks" into an area such stones could not otherwise reach. During the Pleistocene glaciations, for example, distinctive types of rock were transported into the British Isles from Scandinavia, having crossed the North Sea floor. Likewise, many types of rock were carried into the Mississippi Valley from sources in the Canadian Shield north of the Great Lakes.

Where glaciers reach the sea and break off into icebergs, the rocky debris in the latter is rafted away to be dropped gradually as the bergs melt. Very extensive glacio-marine deposits are now forming in this way about Antarctica (Stetson and Upson, 1937). This entire continent is being degraded by glacier ice, which spreads to a floating margin where it eventually breaks off in very large tabular bergs. The shallow sea floor is largely protected from wave action by the bergs and by floe ice. As a result the debris released from the melting bergs settles to the bottom and accumulates without further movement. It therefore has all the characteristics of till, except that it may contain the remains of marine animals. Since depth of water has no effect on such transportation, these glacio-marine deposits now extend into deep water with no appreciable change. If present conditions persist, the thickness of material thus accumulated will eventually be very great. The glacio-marine beds of the Permian System in Australia (David and Browne, 1950, p. 337–371) appear to have formed under comparable circumstances.

Carsola (1954) has shown that deposits closely resembling glacio-marine beds are now forming over the continental shelf north of Alaska, as a result of transportation by floe ice (see also p. 52).

Finally, ice rafts in streams may be responsible for the transportation of boulders into environments where flowing water could not move them. Wentworth (1928) advanced this explanation for what appeared to be glacial erratics in the terrace gravels of eight of the Southeastern States (p. 175). Boulders normally melt free before river ice begins to move, since they absorb warmth from the sun more rapidly than ice does, but in exceptional cases, where floods occur in the headwaters of a stream, the rising water may lift and break ice in the channel farther along and start it moving before thawing has occurred there. More observations on this problem are needed.

DEPOSITION

Above all else, the character of a sedimentary deposit is influenced by the precise manner in which it is laid down and the environment under which it comes finally to rest.

This subject is the center of interest in much of this book. Some aspects of it are developed in the preceding discussion of transportation, and it is the theme of the next three chapters.

CHANGES AFTER DEPOSITION: DIAGENESIS

Even after sediment reaches its final resting place it may still undergo important changes during its transformation into rock. Walther (1894, p. 693 ff.) introduced the term *diagenesis* * to embrace all such changes that result from sedimentary processes—but excluding metamorphism.

Compaction

Perhaps the simplest of these changes is *compaction*. The weight of accumulating sediment presses the mineral particles together, reducing the pore space and squeezing out part of the contained water. The change is generally negligible in sand since the grains already rest in solid contact when deposited, but fine, recently deposited mud may include much water (up to 90 percent or more) in which the clay particles are loosely suspended. In the transformation of such soupy mud into shale, most of the water is squeezed out and the original thickness greatly reduced. Furthermore, when the clay particles are pressed tightly together they cohere, thus giving real, if rather slight, strength to the sediment and transforming it into rock.

Where mud has been deposited over ridges or

* This term was first used by Guembel in 1888 and applied to metamorphic changes, but Walther specifically excluded these, and his usage has since been generally accepted.

hills of already compact rock, the compaction results in less thinning over a buried hill than over its flanks where the mud is thicker. Such differential compaction has produced many important oil-bearing structures (p. 105).

Fossils preserved in shale are commonly compressed during compaction of the enclosing sediment, and the amount of flattening gives some evidence of the amount of thinning thus produced. Graptolites preserved in black shale, for example, are generally compressed to a thin film whereas in their rare occurrences in limestone they are generally not deformed and are roughly as thick as they are wide.

Cementation

Another method by which loose, discrete particles are indurated into stone is by the precipitation of cementing materials that partially fill the voids and bond the particles together. Probably calcium carbonate is the commonest cement, with silica a close second and iron oxide, gypsum, and other less common minerals falling far behind.

Where clay minerals are present, as in mudstones, many siltstones, and some impure sandstones, they form a matrix between coarse particles and, after compaction, may form an effective bonding material; but pure sand remains loose and friable unless some cementing material is added to fill up part of the voids and bond the grains together. Some sandy deposits, indeed, have remained loose and friable for long geologic ages. In the Baku oil fields west of the Caspian Sea, for example, the Miocene beds are still so unconsolidated that vast quantities of free sand are carried up by gushing wells. The St. Peter sandstone (Ordovician) likewise is still generally so poorly cemented that it can be easily cut by a spade or pickax at its outcrops, and Dake (1921, p. 136–150) showed that it is commonly more than 99 percent SiO_2 underground.

The common cement, $CaCO_3$, may be deposited from solution in the water occluded at the time the sediment was laid down or it may be derived from the solution of shell fragments after burial. In the weathered zone, calcareous cement is commonly dissolved away leaving the sand loose and friable again. The Ridgeley sandstone (Lower Devonian), for example, crumbles readily into loose sand in many places on the summits and slopes of the sugar-loaf ridges that it forms in Pennsylvania, but below the water table, or in deep quarries, it is an extremely tough, hard rock with rather low porosity and a high content of $CaCO_3$.

Siliceous cement may be in small measure supplied by the original connate water, but since the concentration of SiO_2 in solution is normally very low, other sources are probably important. Organic structures made of opaline silica (e.g., sponge spicules and radiolarian shells) are more readily soluble than quartz and may be dissolved after burial and redeposited as cement. Under heavy load or dynamic stresses some solution may take place at the points of contact between grains. In some instances the silica is deposited in optical continuity with the sand grains, building them out into an interlocking mass of angular units, but in others it fills the voids between grains with a matrix of minute crystals. Siliceous sandstones are hard and tough and appear harsh to the touch. A good example is the Tuscarora sandstone (Lower Silurian), the great ridge maker in the central Appalachians.

According to Correns (1950), cementation is favored by changes in the pH of the water contained in accumulating sediment, the solubility of SiO_2 increasing with the alkalinity (pH) whereas that of $CaCO_3$ decreases. If the contained water is just saturated with respect to these minerals, changes in the equilibrium may cause the solution of shells or shell fragments or of minute mineral crystals (e.g., aragonite needles), or it may cause the precipitation of SiO_2 or of $CaCO_3$ in the voids. Bacterial action on contained organic matter, for example, may generate NH_3, increasing the alkalinity so that microscopic siliceous shells (diatoms, radiolaria, sponge, etc.) are dissolved. On the contrary, the precipitation of $CaCO_3$ will increase the concentration of CO_2 in the water and this will tend to cause reprecipitation of some of the SiO_2. Increased concentration of CO_2 may also result from the decay of organic matter, or from other chemical changes in the accumulating sediment, causing solution of the minute calcareous shells or shell fragments and especially of aragonite needles for which the solubility is 6 to 8 percent higher than for calcite. Repreprecipitation of this material elsewhere in the mass of sediment, or at a later date when the chemical equilibrium has changed, will partially or completely fill the voids and form a bond cementing the particles of sediment together. Correns believes that the more finely divided particles may be undergoing solution even while the coarser ones are growing.

Chemical Alterations

Reduction. In the presence of free oxygen, organic tissue is readily oxidized to CO_2 and H_2O, leaving a small residue of ash that represents the mineral constituents of the organic materials. The results are identical whether the organic matter is consumed by burning or is slowly oxidized in contact with the air; thus on land, fallen trees and forest litter, like the organic matter in the soil, disappear about as fast as they are formed. But where organic matter is protected from the air by standing water, the only oxygen available is the small trace of free oxygen held in solution. If the water is stirred by the waves and kept aerated the supply of oxygen is renewed, but if it is stagnant the free oxygen is soon exhausted and, in the presence of decaying organic matter, an oxygen-hungry or *reducing* environment is created—one in which the oxygen content of compounds tends to be reduced. Even where the water above the bottom is well aerated, reducing conditions commonly develop within the sediment below.

The ferric iron compounds are especially vulnerable to reduction, the iron readily changing valence from the ferric to the ferrous condition. This has a striking effect on the sediments since hematite (Fe_2O_3) is the chief red pigment and nearly all brown and yellow colors are due to the ferric hydroxides, goethite ($HFeO_2$) and lepidocrocite [$FeO(OH)$]. Ferrous compounds, on the contrary, are largely colorless. In a reducing environment, therefore, red, brownish, or yellowish sediment turns gray.

Destructive distillation of organic matter. In a reducing environment the organic matter in the sediment does not decay by oxidation but by slow destructive distillation, freeing molecules of CO_2 and H_2O. The common plant tissue cellulose ($C_6H_{10}O_5)_n$ may be used to illustrate the change. As each molecule of water or carbon dioxide is lost, the residue contains a higher proportion of carbon, until finally, if the process is carried to completion, only uncombined carbon is left. This is essentially what happens when wood is artificially transformed into charcoal, or when plant tissue is naturally transformed, first into peat or brown coal, then into bituminous and anthracite coal, and finally into graphite. The end product in each case, providing that the destructive distillation is carried to completion, is uncombined or "fixed" carbon which, of course, is black. The comparable alteration of organic oils and fats into bituminous hydrocarbons may be more complex, but the general principle is the same—the large complex organic molecules are simplified as the liberation of molecules of CO_2 and of H_2O reduces the hydrogen and oxygen content, leaving the residue richer in carbon (generally as hydrocarbons). Thus, after burial in the sediment, much of the organic matter turns black, and where abundant and finely divided it strongly colors the sediment.

The work of anaerobic bacteria. On stagnant parts of the sea floor where decaying organic matter has exhausted the dissolved oxygen, animal life is impossible and only the anaerobic bacteria can thrive. These bacteria secure the oxygen they need by stealing it from some of the oxygen-rich compounds that are present. One group of these bacteria attacks organic matter (e.g., $C_6H_{10}O_5$) and, in extracting the oxygen, releases free hydrogen. This hydrogen immediately unites with sulphur, derived from the ever-present sulphates, to form H_2S, a toxic gas readily soluble in sea water that makes the bottom doubly inhospitable to all forms of animal life. Furthermore, H_2S attacks soluble iron compounds to form FeS_2 which is highly insoluble and is precipitated in the form of marcasite or pyrite.

A second group of anaerobic bacteria attacks the sulphates to secure the oxygen needed in metabolism and thus frees sulphur, facilitating the formation of H_2S.

The iron sulphide formed by the anaerobic bacteria may be precipitated as a finely divided dark pigment scattered through the bottom sediment; it may replace the shells of organisms that fall or drift into the area, producing pyritized fossils; or it may be concentrated in the form of marcasite or pyrite concretions.

Where bottom water is stirred by waves or refreshed by descending currents, sufficient oxygen is present to support a bottom fauna, and then scavengers tend to devour much of the organic matter and transform it into new living tissue, so that very little accumulates. In general, however, enough organic matter is present in the sediment on the sea floor to produce at least mildly reducing conditions.

The work of mud-eaters. On the more normal sea floor lives a varied assemblage of animals that feed on mud, passing it through their alimentary tracts in order to digest from it the contained bits of organic matter. Among such animals are the holothurians, many of the echinoids, and a great variety of marine worms. Where deposition is not rapid, much or all of the bottom sediment may thus pass through the digestive mill of the several mud-eating animals where much of the organic matter is removed and the mineral particles are subjected to the chemical attack of the digestive juices. This is still another way in which sediment may be chemically altered after burial. Furthermore, the original lamination may be obscured or completely obliterated as the sediment is worked and reworked, not only by the mud-eaters but by groveling and burrowing forms as well.

Recrystallization

After burial the less stable mineral particles tend to change to a more stable form. Shells originally made of the more soluble aragonite may thus be changed to calcite or may simply be slowly dissolved, leaving only molds in the sediment. The dissolved material may then be reprecipitated on fragments of calcite to build out their crystal form, or it may be deposited as cement between the grains of sediment, reducing the pore space and solidifying the deposit into rock. Minute needles of aragonite are especially susceptible to such alteration. Furthermore, calcite may itself be dissolved in one part of a rock (where finely divided or where under pressure) and reprecipitated in another. Such recrystallization is especially common in porous limestone like reef rock, reef talus, and coquina, and explains their rapid solidification. Similar changes may redistribute the silica in a sandstone, producing a partially recrystallized rock.

Two additional diagenetic changes of great importance are *dolomitization* and *silicification;* the first is discussed in Chapter 13 and the second in Chapter 14.

2. Non-marine environments

ENVIRONMENTS OF DEPOSITION

An important part of the task of the geologist reconstructing geologic history is to determine the former distribution of land and sea, mountain and plain, desert and glacier and jungle—in short, paleogeography. As stratigraphy deals with stratified rocks, it can provide direct evidence only for those areas on the land surface and the sea bottom where deposition was going on, though the deposits of a given time may furnish much indirect evidence also about adjacent areas of non-deposition, erosion, volcanic activity, and so forth. The deposits in any given area will be greatly conditioned, if not entirely controlled, by the geography of the area, whether it is marine or non-marine, part of a wide lowland or continental shelf or close to high mountains, humid or arid, warm or cold. The sum total of these various factors is the geographic environment. The task of reconstructing the geographic features of past environments of deposition is best approached by a careful study of deposits in present environments of which the geography is known. In the following chapters, we attempt to describe some of the principal environments of today in which deposition is going on, and to show how this information may be used to interpret deposits in the geologic record.

It is convenient to group the environments studied as non-marine environments, marine environments, and mixed or shore environments, those in which both marine and non-marine processes play a part. Not all possible environments need be considered, however; the environments with which stratigraphy is primarily concerned, whether marine or non-marine, are those in which deposits are not only forming but are being preserved in considerable thickness. Hence in general these environments have this much in common: they lie low with respect to at least some surrounding areas, and they subside as (or in some cases before) deposition takes place. For present purposes, other kinds of environments may be ignored.

FLUVIAL ENVIRONMENTS

The Piedmont

Thick sedimentary deposits are now forming in belts miles wide at the foot of many of the mountain ranges in the western United States (Fig. 15). The west side of Owens Valley at the foot of the Sierra Nevada in California affords an excellent example, which has been described in detail by Trowbridge (1911). In such localities, a line of coalescing alluvial fans slopes down from the dissected face of the mountains, usually a fault-line scarp, the individual fans being reasonably distinct near the mouths of the mountain canyons but merging farther down into an undulating slope that flattens steadily toward its lower edge. In

Figure 15. Alluvial fans in southern part of Death Valley, California. View looking southeast, the Confidence Hills in the center foreground.

many places the deposits are hundreds and perhaps thousands of feet thick, and generally they consist of nearly unconsolidated and unweathered fragments of whatever rocks form the mountain range. In front of the Sierra Nevada, for example, these fragments are largely granitic, still almost fresh, produced by frost and glacier action in the high part of the range and brought down rapidly by the steep streams. More susceptible materials may show somewhat greater weathering, and where limestone is present, $CaCO_3$ in the ground water commonly cements the fan materials firmly; in general, however, unstable minerals and rocks are still common in the deposit if they were common in the source area.

The size of the fragments varies tremendously, even at a single locality or in a single layer, but normally the maximum size (and probably the average size also) decreases steadily away from the mountains (probably exponentially, like the degree of slope of the fan surface and hence the original dip of the bedding; see Krumbein, 1937, p. 586–589; Blissenbach, 1954, p. 182). Sorting is never very good; in the average desert fan, layers of medium-sorted to poorly sorted sand and gravel (deposited by ordinary streams) alternate with completely unsorted layers (deposited by mudflows, p. 171), which may consist of all sizes from very large boulders to clay if the materials are available in the source area. Blissenbach's work (1954, p. 179) indicates that the proportion of mudflow deposits increases with decreasing rainfall and may reach 40 percent of the total. The fragments are in general only slightly rounded and retain their original shapes, though Blissenbach reports sub-rounded particles at the lower end of a fan in Arizona. Organic matter is virtually absent in fans in arid regions, except locally where it is preserved in clayey mudflow layers, for the porosity of the other layers and the generally low water table permit oxidation throughout. Organic remains that might become fossils are likewise

W. H. Bradley, U. S. Geological Survey

Figure 16. Bishop conglomerate, a mid-Cenozoic piedmont deposit. Large boulders are about a foot across. South end of Little Mountain, Sweetwater County, Wyoming.

rare, though battered tree trunks and vertebrate bones may be preserved here and there.

The bedding of such fan deposits (McKee, 1953, p. 29–31) is in general very crude (Fig. 16). Over all it is parallel to the fan surface, dipping a few degrees basinward, but in detail it is very irregular. By the nature of the fan-building process, the stream on each fan tends to shift continually back and forth from one position to another; in each position it tends to form natural levees and build the channel between them higher until it becomes unstable there. Each unit of stream deposition is therefore stringlike, radiating from the fan head and exhibiting cross-stratification dipping roughly downfan with imbricated pebbles dipping upfan, and the sum total is heterogeneous cut-and-fill cross-bedding. Mud-flows may spread wide sheets of material over the upper part of the fan, or they may follow previous channels far down the slope; their deposits ordi-narily show no internal bedding whatever. Despite this great heterogeneity in detail, however, the deposits on any one part of the fan are likely to be about the same as those on any other part, except for the decrease in grain size and slope outwards, so that the piedmont deposit, taken as a whole, tends to be homogeneous if it follows the front of a mountain range of uniform height, lithology, and structure.

In the United States, piedmont deposits are forming today almost exclusively in arid or semi-arid regions, but in other parts of the world, such as the Alps and Himalayas, they are forming in humid climates; they result from the sudden decrease in velocity where rugged relief is adjacent to basins of deposition and, although favored by aridity, can occur in any climate. Large fans are forming today in Japan under 60 inches of rainfall, especially around partly enclosed down-faulted basins like that of Lake Biwa. The deposits of such humid fans differ from those of arid areas in that the materials may be considerably more weathered—in Japan feldspars are no longer fresh and rather more clay is present—and organic matter may be much more abundant because the water table is high. Deposition is apparently at least as rapid as in arid basins, and the sizing, sorting, and rounding are little different, though the unsorted layered deposits of mudflows and the very large boulders associated with them are absent (except in volcanic regions).

Deposits with these characteristics are known in several parts of the geologic record. Much of the upper Cenozoic of the Basin and Range province of the Western States consists of piedmont deposits, showing that deposition has been about the same since the beginning of block-faulting in Miocene or early Pliocene time (e.g., Longwell, 1936, p. 1414–1440). A particularly carefully studied example in California is the San Onofre breccia (Miocene) (Woodford, 1925), though apparently here the sea washed the base of the fans so that the piedmont deposits grade directly into marine deposits. In the Newark group (Triassic) of eastern North America, piedmont deposits lie next to those basin margins where faulting contemporaneous with deposition produced mountains beside the subsiding basins (east margin of the Connecticut Valley and Deep River belts, northwest margin of the other large belts; Barrell, 1915, p. 29; Longwell, 1922, p. 234–235). Krynine (1950) showed that the climate here was probably humid with strongly seasonal rainfall (p. 213), and he explained the small amount of weathering of the feldspar and other unstable minerals as the result of very rapid erosion and deposition next to the active faults. Similarly, conglomeratic deposits in the Pennsylvanian rocks of Oklahoma and Colorado were derived from nearby granitic mountains on the sites of the present Arbuckle, Wichita, Sangre de Cristo, and Uncompaghre Mountains and others.

The Floodplain

At the other extreme from short mountain torrents that debouch onto piedmont alluvial fans are the great rivers of the world that wind across vast alluvial plains. Several of these rivers and their floodplains have been studied in detail, none perhaps more intensively than the lower Mississippi, whose habit of flooding productive areas led to the establishment of the Mississippi River Commission of the U. S. Army Engineers, who have given it a great amount of scientific and engineering study. The geological results of this study have been ably set forth by Fisk in a series of publications (1944, 1947, 1952), which provide much detailed information on floodplain deposits in the making. To be sure, the deposits now forming are not representative of the whole mass of the alluvial fill but form a mere veneer, mostly less than 100 feet thick, over the deposits of a different regimen of the river; at present, the Mississippi is adding little alluvium permanently to its floodplain except on the marine delta proper, which is treated in Chapter 4. Nevertheless, the lower Mississippi floodplain, above the marine delta, can serve as a type for the floodplain environment.

The first important fact about these deposits is that they are sharply differentiated into several kinds. The primary contrast is between the deposits close to the river channel and those on the floodplain farther away, but the deposits near the river can also be subdivided. The different kinds of deposits are briefly described below, then their interrelations.

The channel of the river is 80 to 150 feet deep during bankfull floods; sediment tends to accumulate in the bottom of the channel when the floods subside. These channel deposits are, of course, only temporary, unless the channel shifts before the next major flood. But the channel shifts perpetually, especially at meanders, and as a result deposits are built up on the inside of the meander from channel bottom to flood level. Commonly they are built up piecemeal, as after individual floods, and each piece tends to be expressed at the surface as a *point bar* (or *meander scroll*) on the inside of the bend.

These deposits consist of the coarsest materials available in the stream; in general the coarsest of all are at the bottom of the old channel, and somewhat less coarse materials follow. The lower Mississippi carries all sizes of sand and a little fine gravel past Cairo, Illinois, at the head of its alluvial plain, but virtually nothing coarser than fine sand reaches the marine delta; hence the channel and point bar deposits are of these sizes. The deposits made just after floods are not very well sorted and include considerable silt, but the deposits on the point bars tend to be winnowed clean of silt at ordinary river stages. After the point bars are formed, fine material accumulates in the swales between them, forming surficial stringlike bodies of clayey silt. Little or no organic matter accumulates in these deposits, except in the clayey silt patches, and only a few potential fossils are present, such as worn bones and logs. The channel-bar deposits can be expected to show strong cross-stratification, partly of the tabular variety (p. 105) but partly more irregular. The dip of the cross-stratification swings with the meandering stream but should show statistical orientation downvalley.

R. D. Russell (Russell and Taylor, 1937; Russell, 1937) has studied the sand of the lower Mississippi in some detail. This sand, of course, comes from the whole vast drainage basin of the river; 60 to 70 percent of it is quartz, but it also includes much feldspar and a rich suite of heavy minerals, many of them supposedly non-resistant to long-distance transportation. Rounding is low and, contrary to expectation, decreases slightly downstream.

On either side of the channel the natural levees form, produced by the rapid deposition of material during overbank floods as water is checked in passing from the rapid current in the hydraulically efficient channel to the sluggish and shallow sheet of water over the floodplain. Once formed they tend to accentuate this difference in current and hence to perpetuate themselves, developing a definite crest next to the channel and an outward slope toward the floodplain. They consist chiefly of silt —very fine sand and coarse silt at the levee crest and finer silt down the slope. Sorting is only fair, poorer than in the channel deposits. Bedding is mostly very even, dipping gently away from the river. The inner face of the deposit is marked by a scoured surface against some other type of near-river deposit; the outer edge grades into the floodplain deposit.

Meanders and natural levees are at perpetual war with each other, the one tending to shift, the other to resist shifting. In some streams, meanders shift so rapidly that natural levees have no time to form; on others the natural levees constrain the river so that true meanders are absent. On its delta the Mississippi is of the latter type, largely because the channel there is cut into fine-grained deltaic silt, relatively resistant to river scour; above the delta, however, it is largely in easily moved sand and coarse silt, and meanders and levees are evenly matched. Though they are particularly open to erosion on the outer side of the meanders, the natural levees are nevertheless thickest and widest there, for during floods more water and silt leave the stream there than elsewhere.

The natural levees are occasionally broken at times of exceptional flood by crevasses, out of which water and silt pour onto the floodplain. When the flood subsides, however, the very inefficient crevasse channel is almost always quickly clogged by deposits, commonly nearly to the height of the original levee. The crevasse fillings consist of coarser material than the rest of the levee and are more irregularly bedded, resembling rather the channel deposits though not as well sorted.

When the river shifts, not by gradual migration of meanders but by cutting one off, or more drastically by diversion to an entirely new course, deposition in the abandoned channel changes abruptly. Just below the point of diversion it fills with a plug of material like a crevasse filling, which may extend some distance down the channel if the diversion was not rapid, but the rest becomes a lake or swamp and then gradually fills in with finer silt and clay, with a few layers of coarser material brought in by floods. (The stringlike bodies of clayey silt that accumulate in the swales between point bars are miniature examples of the same kind of deposit.) This material is very poorly sorted and tends to be well-bedded and high in organic matter. At some stages of filling, indeed, almost pure organic muck may form. The resulting deposits, called clay plugs on the Mississippi, are irregularly distributed through the mostly much coarser channel–bar–levee complex.

Away from the channel, except close to tributary streams, whose deposits are similar to those along the Mississippi but on a smaller scale, the rest of the floodplain receives sediment principally or only during floods when (under natural condi-

Figure 17. Silt deposited in two and a half days in a first-floor room in Dayton, Ohio, during flood of March 1913 (the specimen is approximately three inches across). Collected by August F. Foerste in his own house.

tions) it is covered with a vast sheet of slowly moving water from which silt and clay settle out. Near crevasses much coarse silt and even fine sand is laid down in a thin layer. Considerable amounts of such material may be deposited in a single flood—for example, half an inch in 3 days in a ground-floor room in the Dayton, Ohio, flood of March, 1913 (Fig. 17). The resulting interchannel floodplain deposit is normally very poorly sorted, thinly and evenly laminated (unless disturbed by vegetation, etc.), and high in organic matter. If the area remains swampy between floods, the clay and silt layers may alternate with organic muck.

The fairly high rainfall in the valley of the lower Mississippi is, of course, reflected in the deposits there; in a less humid climate, some features would be different. Thus the amount of organic matter in the finer deposits is much less in such a climate; on the other hand, large areas of the floodplain dry out periodically and may be covered with mudcracks. Calcium carbonate may be an important cement or, in sufficiently arid climates, may accumulate at the surface as caliche. Lakes in abandoned channels or on the floodplain may fill not with organic silt and muck but with fresh-water limestone. The wind may play a part, heaping up sand in dunes on the lee side of the channel and mixing loess with the fine-grained deposits of the floodplain.

At any one time, probably the largest part of a floodplain like that of the Mississippi lies far from a river channel and receives the fine-grained interchannel deposits last described. The other kinds

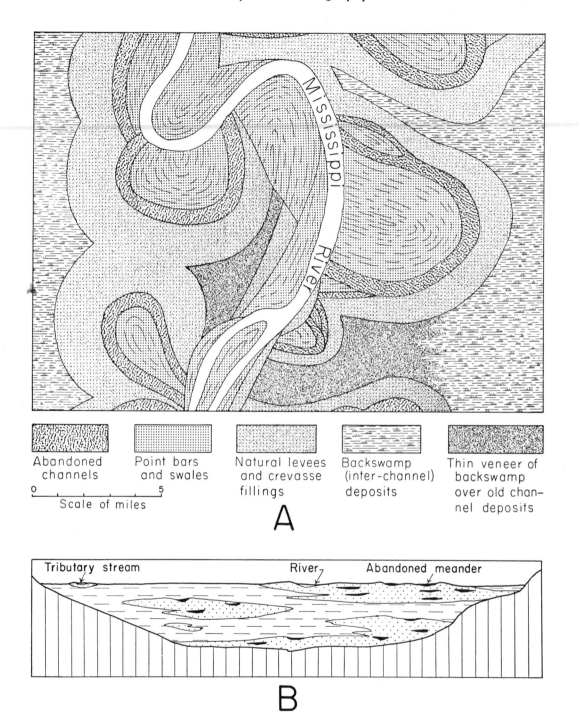

Figure 18. Floodplain deposits. A. Schematic plan of deposits along Mississippi River near Lake Providence, Louisiana. Based on Meyerdale quadrangle, Miss. River Comm., and on Fisk (1944, 1947). B. Schematic cross section of floodplain deposits of a meandering river, showing lenses of channel deposits (dotted, clay plugs in solid black) in matrix of interchannel deposits. Length of area shown, several tens of miles; large vertical exaggeration.

H. R. Wanless

A

Carl O. Dunbar

B

Figure 19. A. Channel conglomerate in the Pass Peak formation (Eocene), Hoback Basin Divide, about 30 miles northwest of Pine-dale, Wyoming. B. Upper Benwood sandstone near the middle of the Monongahela Series (Upper Pennsylvanian) in highway cut in McMechen, about 6 miles south of Wheeling, West Virginia. The sandstone here fills a channel cut through the underlying fresh-water limestone bed.

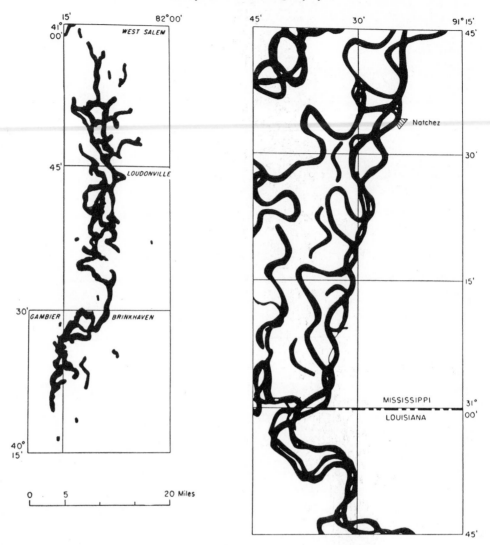

Figure 20. Diagram showing similarity of configuration of the channel deposits in the Red Bedford Delta (Lower Mississippian) of Ohio (left) and the meandering channels of the lower Mississippi River (right), both on the same scale. From Pepper, de Witt, and Demarest (1954, Fig. 28).

of deposits, intricately interwoven, form a sinuous strip of mostly coarser deposits following the actual river channel; similarly, generally narrower strips follow the tributaries (Fig. 18A). With time, of course, the river will shift its position and probably, sooner or later, will cross every part of its floodplain. When it abandons a channel, the strip of sandier deposits will gradually be buried by fine-grained interchannel deposits building up around and over it, or by channel deposits formed along a new alignment. Along the Mississippi (above the marine delta) the total floodplain deposit is so thin that newly formed channels cut entirely through it, but if subsidence were to keep pace with floodplain deposition so that a considerable thickness could accumulate, the new channels would normally be superposed on interchannel deposits. In three dimensions, then, the deposit as a whole would consist of a matrix of the fine-grained interchannel deposits surrounding many striplike sand bodies, sinuous in plan and mostly lenticular in cross section (Figs. 18B, 19), threaded through it along past alignments of the river channel. Thus, though in detail each kind of deposit on such a floodplain is much more homogeneous than the average piedmont fan deposit, in general the whole body of deposits is not homogeneous but is sharply differentiated into several contrasting types.

Deposits of just this sort are well known in the geologic record. Wanless (1923; also 1922) has carefully described such a deposit, the White River group (Oligocene) of South Dakota, formed in a rather less humid climate than that of the lower Mississippi. Rubey and Bass (1925, p. 57–62) have traced an ancient river channel in the "Dakota" formation (Cretaceous) of western Kansas. Much of the Morrison formation (Jurassic) of the eastern Rocky Mountains probably represents similar deposition. One of the best-documented examples of ancient channel sands (Fig. 20) is that of the channels in the Red Bedford Delta (p. 88 and Fig. 36, p. 87), worked out by Pepper, de Witt, and Demarest (1954, p. 46–53) on the basis of many well records. The pattern of these deposits strikingly resembles that of the well-known channel sands of the Mississippi River (Fisk, 1944).

Intermediate Fluvial Environments

Though the deposits on alluvial fans in desert basins and those on the floodplain of the lower Mississippi are in strong contrast, they are merely end-members of a gradational series of stream deposits. At the sharp break in slope at the foot of a steep mountain range, load dominates over energy available to move that load, especially if water is lost in the basin by evaporation or by sinking into permeable deposits. As a result, individual stream channels are barely established before they are clogged, and the stream shifts rapidly back and forth, almost year by year, spreading its load fairly homogeneously over the growing fan. At the other extreme, the relatively efficient channel of the lower Mississippi today is fully competent to handle its load; thus, the channel stays put or meanders within a fixed meander belt, and major shifts occur only at intervals of several centuries or so, while elsewhere on the floodplain what we have called interchannel deposits are formed.

Rivers of intermediate character produce intermediate kinds of deposits. Allied to piedmont deposits are those of braided streams, like parts of the Platte River in Nebraska and Colorado; the broad shallow channel is inefficient and the main threads of current anastomose and shift back and forth within it, piling up the load in ever-shifting sand bars that show cut-and-fill cross-stratification. More like the lower Mississippi are parts of the Missouri River, where a fairly definite channel meanders across the whole (rather narrow) floodplain, little hampered by natural levees and reworking any fine-grained interchannel deposits before they can be preserved.

River deposits of the past can be expected to show the same gradational spectrum of deposits. According to Fisk (1944), the lower Mississippi itself, having cut a trench in its valley floor during the low stand of the sea in Wisconsin time, was forced to aggrade again as sealevel rose and the waning glacier contributed its heavy load. Unlike the present river, it appears to have been a rapidly shifting braided stream, and it formed a thick body of roughly homogeneous gravel and sand that underlies the present floodplain deposit. Moreover, in each preceding glacial age during the Pleistocene, the river apparently produced a similar fill, consisting of undifferentiated braided-stream deposits below and well-differentiated floodplain deposits above.

Other ancient fluvial deposits that exhibit not just typical piedmont or typical floodplain characteristics but parts of the spectrum between include: the Pliocene deposits of the High Plains, so carefully described by W. D. Johnson (1901) half a century ago; much of the Eocene fill of the intermont basins of the Rocky Mountains; the Newark group (Triassic) of eastern North America; much of the Old Red sandstone of England and Scotland. All these deposits (and many others) used to be attributed to vast lakes, coextensive with their basins of deposition, but the work of W. D. Johnson, Davis (1900), and Hatcher (1902), among others, showed at the turn of the century that this view is untenable for most of the Cenozoic deposits of the Western States, and the same is true for many other supposed lacustrine deposits.

DESERT ENVIRONMENTS

By etymology a desert is simply a place without people, but geographically the word has come
to mean an area that is barren because it is dry.
A number of different attempts have been made
to define the term more precisely. The simplest
is based on annual rainfall, but it fails to exclude
arctic areas that, despite very low precipitation,
are sodden with water when not frozen. A much
better climatic definition depends on the ratio of
precipitation to evaporation: an area in which
evaporation exceeds precipitation is semiarid; an
area in which (potential) evaporation is more than
twice precipitation is truly arid or a desert. Another definition points to the barrenness itself: deserts are areas with a discontinuous cover of vegetation (the barrenness is assumed to depend on
dryness, so that beaches in humid climates would
be excluded). The most strictly geographic definition perhaps is that a desert is an area with interior drainage; obviously this is simply a corollary
of the climatic definition but ignores through-going
streams like the Nile and the Colorado. Nevertheless, from the point of view of depositional environments, it is perhaps the best, for it empha-
sizes that, in contrast to humid areas where streams
continue to the sea, all the products of erosion
remain in a desert region and are deposited in its
lowest portions, except for what dust the wind
blows entirely away. By this definition, desert
areas cover about 13 million square miles, one-
quarter of the land surface of the Earth.

Two rather distinct desert environments are
here discussed: vast and barren desert plains like
the horse-latitude deserts of Africa and Australia,
and rain-shadow deserts with basin and range topography like those of southwestern North America. As rather more data are available on the
deposits in desert basins enclosed by mountains,
they are considered first.

Deposits in Enclosed Desert Basins (Bolsons)

A terminology for enclosed desert basins was
established by Tolman (1909); among descriptions of the deposits in such basins may be mentioned his paper and those by Thompson (1929)
and Blackwelder (1931b). The whole enclosed
basin Tolman called a *bolson* [Spanish for large
pouch], and he divided it into three main parts.
The rock surface of the surrounding mountains is
largely the site of erosion and can hence be ignored here. Next within is the *bajada* [Spanish
for descent, slope; pronounced ba-ha'da], the belt
of alluvial fans extending out from the foot of the
mountains. In the center of the basin is the *playa*
[Spanish for shore, beach, but used locally for the
"dry lakes"], an almost perfectly flat floor, covered
with a few inches of water for a short time after
heavy floods but otherwise bare and dry. Tolman
further distinguished as *semibolsons* those basins
whose drainage lines are tributary to others; in
these a playa is seldom well exhibited. Another
unit of such basins, the *pediment,* was added by
Bryan (1922, p. 52 ff.; the term was first used
by McGee, 1897, p. 92, 110); it is a piedmont
slope superficially like the bajada but mainly erosional, being underlain by bedrock· under at the
most a few feet of alluvium. The pediment is not
a site of permanent deposition and hence need not
be further considered here; as a geomorphic form
it is the subject of a voluminous literature.

The sediments of the bajada of a typical desert
basin are simply piedmont deposits in an arid
climate, exactly as discussed above (p. 28);
normally a large part is laid down by mudflows.
The sediments of the playa, on the other hand,
are the materials carried across the bajada and
deposited in the lowest part of the basin as the
water finally evaporates. The detrital material is
mainly fine silt and clay, though coarser material,
locally up to pebbles, may be strewn over the
playa surface near the foot of the fan down which
each flood came. Mixed with the detrital material, either disseminated through the clay or as
separate layers, are the salts originally dissolved
in the flood waters; these differ greatly from playa
to playa. Ordinarily $CaCO_3$ and $CaSO_4$ are important, but in many playas sodium salts—
Na_2CO_3, Na_2SO_4, or $NaCl$—or combined salts
are common, and in a few, there are unusual salts
such as borates and potash salts. Searles Lake
in California, one of a series of playas that were
probably part of a single drainage system during
the somewhat less arid Wisconsin age, is particularly rich in borates, yet the other members of the
series are dominated by more ordinary salts—the

less soluble carbonates in the higher ones and the more soluble chlorides and sulphates in the lower ones.

The deposits of the playa are normally well-bedded, in thin continuous layers. At the margins, they intertongue with the less well-bedded bajada or piedmont deposits, and tongues of sand or even gravel extend well into the playa locally, where floods debouched onto the flat. Mudcracks tend to open or reopen on each desiccation; unless the next flood washes silt or sand into them, they will not be clearly preserved in the deposit. Locally the new flood may rip off pieces of the older layers and incorporate them as mudgalls in the new sediment. The playa clays normally have little organic matter and are pale gray or green, but locally, where conditions are right, they may be nearly black and high in sulphides. Red colors are absent, unless the source area contains red rocks. Potential fossils, except tracks, are normally rare, though on a few playas with favorable ground-water seepage more nearly permanent salt pools may resist evaporation, and in these certain peculiar forms of life may swarm.

In a typical desert basin, wind adds its work to that of water. After a flood, the sand and gravel carried out onto the playa are particularly open to wind attack until the slow growth of the playa sediment covers them. Much of the sand is picked up by the wind, along with whatever can be blown from the lower bajada slope, and carried across the playa and a little way up the bajada on the leeward side. Here the wind, forced to rise to leave the basin, loses its carrying power, and the sand accumulates in patches of dunes (Fig. 13, p. 21). The sand bodies become incorporated in the growing bajada deposit, or locally in the edge of the playa deposit; theoretically they should show the usual features of wind-blown sand—wedge cross-bedding, well-sorted, well-rounded sand showing ground-glass surface texture and made almost entirely of resistant minerals like quartz—but in the small dunes of such desert basins these features are less likely to be obvious than in larger dune areas. The pebbles left behind on the playa as a lag gravel may be shaped by the wind into ventifacts, which remain with the last of the sand, interbedded in the playa silt and clay.

The fine-grained playa sediments may also be attacked by the wind; the efficiency of such erosion depends on the degree to which the clay is bound, either because cemented by the soluble salts or because kept moist by their deliquescence or by seeping ground water, and also on the relative rate of wind erosion and water deposition. Blackwelder (1931a) has discussed a playa in southeastern California where the evidence of considerable recent wind erosion is clear, but few other North American examples have been described. The dust removed by the wind is normally blown entirely out of the desert basin.

Deposits in Wide Low-Lying Deserts

Rather less is known of the deposits of great deserts like the Sahara and the desert of Western Australia. Indeed, some maintain that deposition in such deserts is negligible; it is true that erosion predominates generally over much of their area, but basins of deposition are present also, in which the products of the erosion accumulate. Wind plays a much larger part than in the small enclosed basins, but even so the present land forms were shaped by water in much of the Sahara, which exhibits integrated water courses hundreds of miles long, though at any one time, even in floods, water flows along only a small portion of their total length.

The Sahara is the subject of an outstanding book by Gautier (English edition, 1935). In general the main deposits there resemble those of the smaller deserts, though the proportions are notably different. Stream deposits of relatively coarse material follow the lower parts of the stream courses and accumulate in broad basins near their lower ends. Deposits of playa type are forming in many local basins, notably the great *chotts* of southern Tunisia and vicinity, which are tens of miles across. And sand dunes cover areas hundreds of miles across in the vast *ergs;* several of these are situated close to the wider areas of stream deposits, from which they probably derive much of their sand, but much is also derived from the weakly cemented "Nubian sandstone," a partly marine, partly continental formation of Cretaceous and older age that forms the bedrock of much of the Saharan platform.

Stream deposits seem to be scantier in the desert portion of Western Australia, and even playas, though widespread, have mostly very thin deposits, the wind removing material probably about as fast as it reaches the playas. There are large areas of sand dunes. In general the low relief of the area, much of which preserves old peneplanes, makes stream erosion (and hence deposition) even less effective than in the Sahara.

Ancient Desert Deposits

The late Cenozoic deposits in the present desert areas of North America are likewise in large part the deposits of enclosed desert basins— for example, the bajada and playa deposits described by Longwell (1928, p. 68–96) in southern Nevada. On the other hand, the Navajo sandstone (Jurassic) of the Colorado Plateau, with its spectacular wedge cross-bedding (Fig. 14, p. 22), appears to have been formed in a vast *erg* like those of the Sahara, though perhaps less arid, for thin carbonate deposits, locally interbedded near the top of the cross-bedded sandstone unit, suggest temporary lakes between the dunes, perhaps like the lakes in the present Nebraska sand hills.

The Navajo sandstone may be merely the last of several desert deposits in the same area, for the Triassic Chinle and Moenkopi formations include many thick beds and lenses of gypsum which suggest strong evaporation and aridity. These formations are, however, bright red, whereas apparently no present desert deposits are red unless derived from a red source rock; this matter is discussed in more detail in Chapter 12. The New Red sandstone of England, and the contemporaneous red formations in the Permian and Triassic of northern and eastern Europe (Rotliegendes, Buntsandstein, and Keuper of the German section; Ufimian or continental Kazanian, Tatarian, and Vetlugian of the Russian section) present the same problem; they are associated with thick beds of gypsum and less directly with great deposits of halite and potash salts, which prove great aridity, and they

are also reported to contain ventifacts and bodies of dune sandstone.

LAKE ENVIRONMENTS

The study of lakes is a science in itself (limnology) with a profuse literature, much of it not readily accessible to geologists; fortunately Bradley (1948) has provided a simplified summary of its geological implications. Lakes occur in basins of many different origins, but thick lake sediments are likely to accumulate only in relatively large and permanent lake basins, especially those produced by tectonic subsidence. Modern examples are the lakes in the East African Rift Valley and Lake Baikal. Even more instructive for the student of lake deposits are the extinct Pleistocene lakes of the western United States, such as Lakes Bonneville and Lahontan, the subjects of the classic monographs of Gilbert (1890) and Russell (1885).

Consider first the shore deposits of a large fairly deep lake whose level remains stable. Wherever the shore of the lake is open to the waves, the finer debris is swept out into deeper water, but the sand and gravel tend to remain and to be formed into beaches along shore or into bars and spits across the mouths of bays. The reworking given these materials should remove some at least of the less resistant materials, but in fact some will probably remain if any are present to begin with. Sorting will be fairly good to very good, at least in detail, though sand and gravel layers may alternate. Cross-stratification will be on a rather small scale and will generally dip lakeward, except on the back sides of the spits and bars where it will be on a large scale and will dip into the bay. Little or no organic matter will be present, and few if any potential fossils.

In protected coves, or elsewhere where the waves have no fetch, such sandy deposits will be poorly developed or lacking, and deposits like those of the lake bottom may reach almost or quite to the shore. On exposed headlands, of course, permanent deposits may not be formed at all.

Where streams transporting debris enter the lake, they build deltas of the classical type described by Gilbert (1890, p. 65–70) from Lake Bonneville (Fig. 21A). Such a delta consists

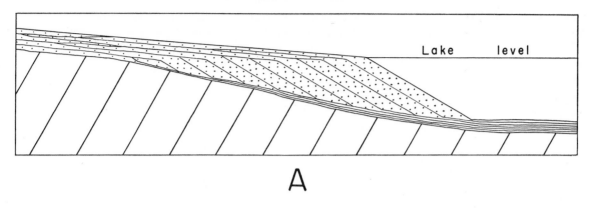

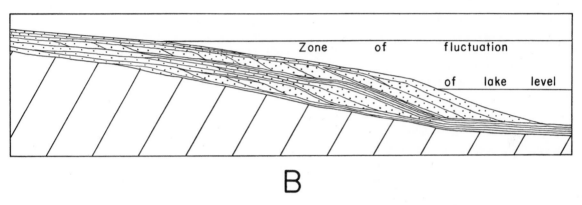

Figure 21. Lake deltas (schematic cross sections). A. Stable level. B. Fluctuating level.

of nearly horizontal *topsets,* strongly dipping *foresets,* and *bottomsets* parallel to the lake floor. Of these, the topsets are simply an extension of the normal river deposits out over the growing delta, and the bottomsets are thickened lake-bottom deposits underneath and in front of it; thus foresets are the characteristic feature of the delta. In a delta built into a lake with stable level and and not too powerful waves, the foreset beds with their high original dip are sharply set off from the others, and consist of all the coarser materials carried by the stream, dumped suddenly as the stream current is checked by the standing water of the lake. Organic matter may be trapped here, but in general will probably not be preserved.

If, however, the lake level is not stable but fluctuates considerably, the shore deposits will be somewhat different. They will begin to form, of course, at each level, only to be destroyed again as the level shifts up or down, and in gen-

eral they will appear to be smeared out over the zone of fluctuation, particularly its lower part. Beaches, bars, and spits will become quite unrecognizable or will be represented only by sandy lenses interbedded in the marginal bottom deposits. Deltas likewise will lose their classical perfection. If the lake level shifts by abrupt steps, a series of steplike deltas may be formed, but if it shifts more irregularly, the three kinds of beds in the delta will interfinger very complexly. In particular the foreset beds, the special mark of the Gilbert delta, will be reduced in importance, and in extreme cases the resulting deposit will be simply a zone of extra thickness in which the coarser stream deposits to landward interfinger with the finer lake bottom deposits to lakeward, with only scattered beds of cross-stratified sand to represent the foresets (Fig. 21B).

The bottom deposits of a large lake consist largely of the finer material—fine sand, silt, and clay—that is winnowed from the shore deposits by the waves or carried past the deltas by the stream currents, mixed with organic matter and any chemical precipitates that may form; much the most common precipitate is $CaCO_3$. Commonly the deposits show some sorting and lamination; the perfection of both depends on the yearly regimen of the lake. In lakes with regular overturn, the lamination is especially uniform; in lakes that in addition freeze over, the separation of the clay from the silt and sand is almost complete. The normal result is varves (p. 108), pairs of contrasting laminae that represent one year. Where non-detrital material is important, the alternate laminae may be dominated by $CaCO_3$ and organic matter (Bradley, 1929b). In semi-arid climates, $CaCO_3$ may become an important fraction of the total lake deposit, forming not only laminae but thicker layers, some of them oölite, and also algal reefs (see p. 229) and tufa deposits (Russell, 1885, p. 189–222). In still more arid climates, other salts may be precipitated in the bottom deposits, and the lake deposits will grade over into those of the playa.

Deposits in smaller lakes normally consist of the same kinds of sediments as those in larger lakes, but the proportions vary greatly, depending on the climate and the source of fill. Beach deposits are apt to be much less important, as the waves have less fetch and hence less power. One lake may have little but chemical or algal $CaCO_3$ ("lake marl"); another may be quickly filled in by a stream delta; a third may fill slowly with organic muck and be transformed into a swamp.

Among ancient lakes, we have mentioned above the Pleistocene lakes of the western United States. One of the most carefully studied lake deposits in the geologic record is the Green River formation (Eocene) of Wyoming, Utah, and Colorado (Bradley, 1926, 1929b, 1931a, 1948, and papers there cited). This formation was laid down in three contemporaneous lakes in a climate with only moderate rainfall; the lakes were reasonably permanent, though occasionally they may have dried up altogether, yet they were without outlets for much of their history, so that the salts brought into the basin (largely carbonates) remained there. Another famous ancient deposit is that of Lake Florissant, an Oligocene lake in

west-central Colorado. As mentioned above (p. 37), however, many deposits that have been called lacustrine are much more probably fluvial.

GLACIAL ENVIRONMENTS

Like lakes, glaciers are a study in themselves, and they and their deposits are the subject of a major branch of geology with its own literature, where the student can find descriptions not only of modern glaciers and their deposits but also of the deposits of the great Pleistocene ice sheets. As a thorough summary of the subject is provided in Flint's *Glacial Geology and the Pleistocene Epoch* (1957), only brief remarks need be made here. In general, glacial deposits (drift) fall into several classes. First is till, the direct deposit of the glacier itself. Characteristically it consists of completely unsorted, virtually unweathered material of all size grades (Fig. 22), but the largest-sized boulders occur only where massive rock like granite occurs in the source area, and the silt and clay-size material (it is normally rock flour and not true clay) may be washed out of some kinds of till deposits, such as ablation moraine. Typically the fragments of all sizes are angular or subangular, unless they were round in the source rock, but many of the pebbles and larger blocks show snubbed corners and smoothed faces with crisscross striations. Bedding of any kind is exceptional, but the deposit is typically blanketlike; it may rest on a polished and striated floor if the underlying rock is fairly resistant.

In addition to the direct deposits of the glacier, much material is deposited by the streams of meltwater that issue from it. These streams are typically overloaded, and hence their outwash deposits resemble those of ordinary braided streams or even alluvial fans, but the material in the deposits may betray its glacial origin. Certain special very coarse and siltless deposits, such as those of kames and eskers, should be readily recognizable, but they are small in amount.

In many glacial areas the wind is also an effective agent for transporting and depositing material from areas bare of vegetation, such as the

R. F. Flint

Figure 22. Coarse Pleistocene till. End moraine near Dinwoody, Wyoming.

outwash plains of the meltwater streams. Sand may be heaped into dunes beside the streams, but more important quantitatively is the dust that settles as a loess blanket downwind from each wide outwash plain. Loess consists almost entirely of silt-size particles—the sand is too heavy for the wind to lift, the clay is too fine to lift readily or it is carried entirely away—of relatively unweathered minerals, including much $CaCO_3$ if the original glacial debris was calcareous. Land snails are commonly found in the Pleistocene loess deposits. The loess shows little or no bedding, being reworked on deposition by rainwash or plant roots, but generally it displays pronounced vertical jointing. The loess blanket is thickest on the lee side of the source streams, and the thickness (and perhaps also, but less obvi-

ously, the grain size) decreases exponentially to leeward.

Glaciers are also normally accompanied by lakes, whose deposits reflect the glacial association. Shore deposits are like those of any large lake; because the lake level is apt to remain fixed for some time and then to shift abruptly as new outlets are uncovered, beaches and especially deltas are generally well developed, commonly at several levels. For example, such deposits mark the limits of the Pleistocene Great Lakes and Glacial Lake Agassiz. The bottom deposits are normally well varved clay, rather low in organic matter in the larger lakes, though some of the smaller lakes may fill with organic muck.

Glacial deposits have been reported in many parts of the geologic record behind the Pleisto-

C. R. Longwell

Figure 23. View of Dwyka tillite and glaciated pavement, Nooitgedacht near Riverton on the Vaal River, Union of South Africa.

cene. Coleman (1926) brought together all these reports, but his compilation is entirely uncritical, and many of the examples he cites are certainly not glacial at all. (A shorter more recent summary of climatic fluctuations is that by Schwarzbach [1950].) By no means all poorly sorted bouldery deposits are till or tillite, and to distinguish glacial deposits from alluvial fan deposits made partly by mudflows is not always easy (p. 172). Probably the best criteria are faceted and striated pebbles or a striated floor (though mudflows can probably striate a few pebbles and, if the deposit has been deformed, slickensides can resemble striations). Areal relations, association with other probably glacial deposits such as varved clay, and the presence of truly exotic boulders may be decisive.

There can be no question about the glacial origin of the basal Karroo or Gondwana tillites of the southern hemisphere and India. In South Africa (Fig. 23) these deposits extend over a distance of nearly 1,000 miles and reach thick-

nesses of hundreds of feet; moreover, in the south they contain boulders whose only source seems to be 800 miles to the northeast (du Toit and Haughton, 1954, p. 271–277). Similar deposits are known in the Paraná Basin of South America, in Australia, both southeastern and southwestern, and in peninsular India; in all three regions the ice evidently reached the sea, producing glaciomarine deposits.

A supposedly contemporaneous deposit in North America is the Squantum tillite of eastern Massachusetts, but even if it is a tillite it is hardly more than the deposit of a valley glacier, and its geologic age is far from established.

No other universally accepted glacial deposits are known in post-Cambrian rocks, though many have been announced. Precambrian tillites of several ages are known, however. Especially noteworthy are the tillites that occur in several continents a few hundred to a thousand feet below and in conformable or nearly conformable sequence with the lowest beds with Lower Cambrian fossils; tillites in this position are known in the Wasatch Range in Utah; in northern and probably central Norway; in Sinkiang and in central China proper; and above all in South Australia. A widespread upper Precambrian tillite in Central and South Africa has been assigned to this age also but, in the absence of unequivocal Cambrian rocks, its exact age is not known; it may well be older. Older Precambrian tillites are reported in South Africa, in the Huronian rocks of Ontario, Canada, and in the Medicine Bow Mountains of Wyoming.

3. Marine environments

MARINE WATERS now cover about 70 percent of the Earth's surface, and during much of the past they probably were even more extensive. Conditions of marine deposition vary widely but are less well known than those of the land because of the difficulty of direct observation. For the most part, expensive equipment and ocean-going vessels are required for such study and, until recently, little more than widely spaced sampling had been attempted. The last two decades, however, have witnessed enormous advances in the study of the sea floor, and the geologic results have been effectively summarized by Shepard (1948) and by Kuenen (1950b). Several well-equipped oceanographic laboratories are now engaged in such research, using revolutionary new devices. Among the latter may be mentioned the Piggot gun (Piggot, 1937) and its outgrowth, the Kullenberg piston corer (Kullenberg, 1947, 1955), which yield core samples of the bottom sediments to a depth of many feet, regardless of the depth of the water; the adaptation of cameras to photograph the bottom at any depth (Ewing, Vine, and Worzel, 1946; Shepard and Emery, 1946); a device for measuring current velocities at or near the bottom regardless of depth (Stetson, 1937); and the sonic depth finder, which gives a quick and accurate measure of the depth of water in continuous record from a moving ship.

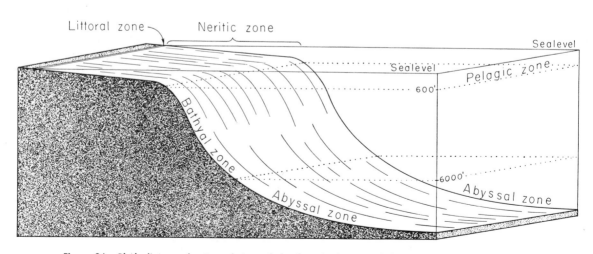

Figure 24. Block diagram showing relations of the four depth zones of the sea and of the pelagic zone.

For purposes of analysis and description various criteria might be used to subdivide the marine realm, but the most widely used and perhaps the most fundamental is depth. Four major depth zones are commonly recognized as indicated in Figure 24. The *littoral zone,* embracing the area between extreme high and low tide limits, is alternately a part of the land and of the sea, and it is treated in the next chapter.

NERITIC ZONE

General

The *neritic zone* extends from lowest tide limit to the "break in slope" at the edge of the continental shelf. This break is generally a real and natural boundary.

On the assumption that the continental shelf is a constructional terrace made of sedimentary deposits built into the sea, the break in slope has commonly been supposed to mark the depth to which waves are effective and currents are able to move sediment on the bottom; thus it would coincide with the baselevel toward which the shelf is graded. Oceanographers of the last century believed this depth to lie at about 600 feet below sealevel, and for this reason most hydrographic charts show the 100-fathom contour as a conspicuous datum line.

The edge of the continental shelf does not follow the 100-fathom line very closely, however, being somewhat deeper in some areas and appreciably shallower in many others. The variation in depth may be the result of local conditions that influence the depth at which waves and bottom currents are effective, or it may be due to warping since the break in slope was established; some students challenge the basic assumption that the break marks the edge of a graded terrace. At present the matter is controversial (Stetson, 1949; Dietz and Menard, 1951; Shepard, 1948, p. 190 ff.) but, whatever the explanation may be, the break in slope at the edge of the continental shelf is a more significant lower limit to the neritic zone than the arbitrary depth of 600 feet so commonly cited.

The neritic zone is an area of active bottom currents, affected by storm waves and by storm-

drift and tidal currents. It borders all the lands, and its width varies from less than 10 miles to more than 200 miles, averaging about 50 miles. At present it includes about 10,000,000 square miles, an area equal to more than one-sixth that of the land surface.

The neritic zone is subject to agitation by waves and to appreciable variation in temperature, and is generally swept by bottom currents capable of moving and sorting sediment. It is reached by sunlight so that algae and other forms of plant life can exist at the bottom, and it is the home of the most varied and prolific bottom faunas. All the terrigenous sediment reaching the sea (excepting only wind-blown dust) must cross this belt or come to rest within it. It is the region in which a large part of the *recoverable* stratigraphic record has been formed and its importance in stratigraphy is, therefore, out of all proportion to its area.

Flatness of the Neritic Zone

Table 2 gives the normal depth at stated distances from shore in four different types of neritic seas. The data for wide lagoons are from Pamlico Sound, North Carolina, for a quiet landlocked sea from the Baltic Sea, for a stormy landlocked sea from the North Sea, and for a stormy shelf sea from the Atlantic continental shelf between Long Island and Cape Hatteras. In all cases, a profile from the shore seaward is concave near the land, dropping down more rapidly within the first mile or two and then flattening out to a gentle seaward slope.

Since the published diagrams of submarine profiles invariably exaggerate the vertical scale enormously, we unconsciously visualize bottom

TABLE 2. NORMAL DEPTH OF NERITIC SEAS AS A FUNCTION OF DISTANCE FROM SHORE. FROM BARRELL (1917, P. 780).

Distance from shore	5 mi	10	20	80	100
Stormy shelf sea	95 ft	110	140	300	300
Stormy landlocked sea	55	70	90	110	110
Quiet landlocked sea	35	50	70	90	90
Wide lagoons	15	15	—	—	—

slopes as much steeper than they are.* Actually, off our mid-Atlantic coast the *average* slope outside the 5-mile limit is only 2 feet per mile for 100 miles from shore. If the sea were withdrawn from this shelf and an observer were parachuted down in the midst of it, he could see neither the old shore line nor the sea, and he would be unable to judge from the slope which direction to take in returning landward. In regions of recent tectonic activity, where the continental shelf is much narrower, the slopes are, of course, steeper, but even where a depth of 300 feet is reached within 10 miles of shore, the bottom slope averages only 30 feet per mile.

Sharp relief occurs locally within the neritic zone, as along faulted coast lines, or in areas of submarine volcanoes, coral reefs, or submarine canyons. In other places, such as the Gulf of Maine, considerable relief has been inherited from a drowned land surface. But, by and large, the neritic zone is a region of very gentle slopes and vast areas of nearly flat sea floor (Fig. 1, p. 2). Here bottom sediment is transported chiefly by tidal currents and by storm-generated drift currents aided by storm waves, all of which are variable in force and direction and operate discontinuously. Such sediment must travel far over a nearly horizontal surface before attaining depths below the reach of waves and currents. The net result is that bottom sediment in the neritic zone is shifted about many times before eventually coming to rest, under circumstances that favor sorting and size-grading.

Present Non-Graded Condition of the Neritic Zone

Deductive reasoning would suggest that sediments should be well graded across the continental shelf with the coarsest material near shore and the finer farther out. This distribution was widely assumed until about 1930, and oceanographers commonly recognized a sandy zone

* To draw a profile across the floor of the stormy shelf sea to true scale, draw a thin horizontal chalk line on the blackboard, using a scale of $\frac{1}{24}$ inch per 100 feet. The first 100 miles from shore will be represented by a base line 18.3 feet long and the depth at this distance (300 feet) will be $\frac{1}{8}$ inch.

extending out to a depth of 200 or 300 feet and a muddy zone beyond this. Shepard (1932) challenged this assumption, pointing out that the bottom samples recorded on hydrographic charts of various continental shelves indicate large areas of sand and even of gravel on the outer part of the shelf and of silt and mud nearer shore. This condition he attributed to the lowered sealevel during Pleistocene glaciation, which laid bare a large part of the continental shelf. During this low stand of sealevel, till was spread across the shelf in high latitudes while elsewhere sand and gravel were carried far out by major streams.

Shepard drew the further conclusion that since the waning of the glaciers and the corresponding rise in sealevel, the mud has been trapped in estuaries and other embayments near shore and not enough has spread seaward to blanket the coarse material. Kuenen (1939b) challenged this interpretation on two grounds. First, the Piggot cores from the North Atlantic basin between Newfoundland and Ireland (Fig. 25) had revealed a layer of postglacial mud that ranges from less than 6 inches to nearly 2 feet thick over the ocean floor but thickens to over 9 feet near the continental margin (core 3) east of Newfoundland (Bramlette and Bradley, 1940). Obviously most of this terrigenous mud must have come off the continental shelf. Second, no globigerina ooze is found on the shelf, as it is on the ocean floor wherever terrigenous mud is sparse. Kuenen concluded, therefore, that the entire shelf is swept by some sort of currents that are winnowing out the fine mud and carrying it over the continental margin, leaving the coarse material exposed. Certainly the non-graded condition is in part a result of the recent low stand of sealevel due to glaciation, but recent work by Stetson (1938; 1939) and by Ewing and his associates (e.g., Northrop, 1951) has shown that processes of gradation are actively at work and have already been effective over the inner half of the shelf off the coast of southern New England.

Modern Neritic Environments

Stetson's critical study of our Atlantic continental shelf (1938; 1939) showed clearly that

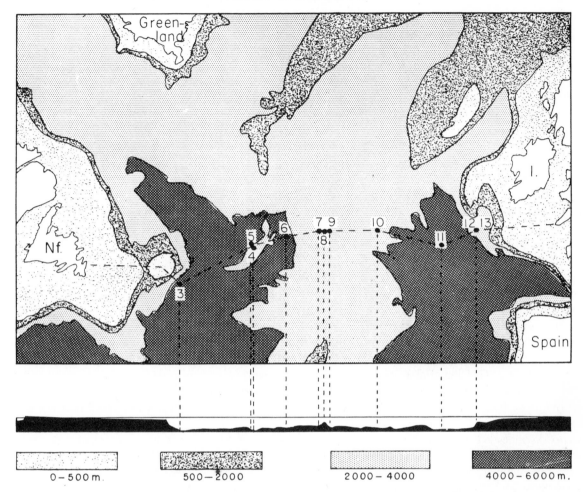

Figure 25. Bathymetric chart of a part of the North Atlantic Ocean, showing distribution of the deep-sea cores between New-foundland and Ireland. The submarine profile in solid black follows the line of core stations. Adapted from Bradley (1940, Pl. 1).

the bottom is being brought into equilibrium with the forces at work, and that factors other than depth are important, and he suggested that different areas should be treated separately, each in its proper geographic setting. The nine regions described in the following paragraphs illustrate the wide range of environments that obtain in the existing neritic zone; they are only samples, however, from an enormously varied complex of environments. One of the urgent needs of stratigraphy is a critical and more detailed study of the conditions of deposition in a wide range of settings in the modern shallow seas.

Glaciated shelf off the New England coast. Stetson recognized that Pleistocene glaciation spread a mantle of highly heterogeneous drift over the entire continental shelf from Cape Cod northward, completely upsetting the normal graded condition. But off Cape Cod he found a broad belt of well-graded sand extending out to a depth of some 70 meters (230 feet) and, beyond this, a wide zone of silt and clay. Obviously the mud has been winnowed out from the sandy zone and spread seaward so that here a well-graded condition obtains over the inner half of the shelf. But beyond the mud zone wide areas near the edge of the shelf are floored with very sandy deposits in which the grains are notably rounded and frosted, as though they have been extensively wind-blown. Obviously, this sand has not been transported from the present shore zone across the intervening mud. Stetson interprets this anomalous sandy deposit as a vestige of extensive sand dunes that formed over the outer part of the shelf during the low stand of sealevel. As the glaciers waned and the sea returned rather rapidly to its present position, waves and currents had time to destroy the form of the dunes by spreading the sand, but not to remove all sand from the area.

Northrop (1951) extended these observations by study of two profiles running south from Buzzards Bay and Martha's Vineyard to the continental margin. He gathered bottom samples at closely spaced stations, and with an ingenious apparatus he simultaneously photographed the bottom. His observations clearly showed four zones of sediment on the shelf. The first, extending to about 30 miles from shore, consists of gravel from which the fine sediment has been winnowed. The gravel is poorly sorted and but slightly rounded and is the coarser residue of reworked glacial till. The second zone, some 10 miles wide, is floored by compact and well-sorted sand and silt. This material is obviously being moved by present currents since overturned shells are more or less filled with it. The third zone consists of soft mud, largely silt, extending from 45 to 75 miles off shore and out to a depth of about 300 feet. Beyond this to the edge of the shelf the sediment is sandy, and Northrop confirms Stetson's conclusion that it was originally a wind-blown deposit laid down during Wisconsin time when the shoreline was near the continental margin. It is still exposed because such fine mud as now reaches the area is swept on over the edge of the shelf.

All this suggests an early stage in the development of a normal submarine profile with size-graded bottom sediment, but one that is already far enough advanced for equilibrium to be approached over at least the inner half of the shelf out to a depth of some 300 feet.

Neritic zone off the mid-Atlantic States. Conditions over the continental shelf between Cape Cod and Cape Hatteras differ greatly from those farther north. Shepard and Cohee (1936) studied some 700 bottom samples from the northern part of this area and showed that it is almost entirely covered with sand, lacking the mud zone that is prominent off the New England coast.

According to Stetson (1939), sand persists as far south as Cape Hatteras, making this the largest known area of sandy sea floor. The reason is not far to seek. During the low stand of Pleistocene sealevel a wide coastal plain developed here on the underlying sedimentary formations which consist largely of clean sands. The extensive sandy mantle then formed is now being worked over by the sea while the major streams on the land are deeply drowned and drop most of their mud in estuaries and bays near shore. Stetson thinks the whole shelf in this region is now subject to winnowing action whereby the small amount of mud originally present in the sandy mantle has been carried on out to deep sea.

Probably such widespread formations of clean sandstone as the St. Peter (Ordovician) of the upper Mississippi Valley, the Tuscarora (Silurian) of the Appalachians, and the Oriskany (Devonian) of New York and Pennsylvania formed under somewhat comparable conditions from a vast sandy mantle already largely devoid of mud.

Florida region. South of Cape Hatteras conditions change rapidly. The shelf narrows progressively from about 90 miles at Savannah to 10 miles off Miami, but it is over 100 miles wide along the west side of Florida (Fig. 41, p. 94).

Fine sand is carried southward by longshore currents from the coast of South Carolina and Georgia, covering the inner part of the shelf to about the middle of east Florida. It is represented by fine and remarkably well sorted beach sand at Jacksonville and Daytona. Farther south the sediments are almost entirely calcareous, since the underlying sea floor and the adjacent land are made exclusively of limestone and no streams bring in detrital material.

The southern half of the east coast of Florida is swept by the Gulf Stream, which continues northeastward over the outer part of the shelf toward Cape Hatteras. Bottom sediment on this part of the shelf, and likewise on the adjacent Blake Plateau down to 2,500 feet or more, consists of lime mud and lime sand, the latter formed of shell fragments and oöids. Here the lime sand is coarser on the outer margin of the shelf, and even on the much deeper Blake Plateau, than it is near shore. Stetson (1939) is convinced, however, that this is not due to lack of adjustment to the marine forces. On the contrary, he thinks the Gulf Current is strong enough to winnow out and carry away the finer increments of lime mud where it impinges against the continental margin, leaving a sandy residue of the larger particles it cannot move. This suggests that Blake Plateau is reduced below what would otherwise have been its normal profile because of sublevation and non-deposition resulting from the impact of the Gulf Current.

The neritic zone is 75 to 120 miles wide along the west side of Florida with an average slope of 2.6 feet per mile out to the break in slope, which here lies at a depth of only about 35 fathoms. Gould and Stewart (1955) found the shelf to be covered generally by very fine white sand that varies in composition from the shore seaward. Out to a depth of about 30 feet the sand is more than 50 percent quartz with shell sand playing a minor role. This inner sandy zone is between 10 and 30 miles wide. Beyond it is a second zone in which shell sand predominates over quartz. A third zone, several miles wide, is covered by shell sand without quartz, and a fourth zone extending to and beyond the break in slope is largely covered by algal sand. This algal zone lies mostly between the depths of 25 and 40 fathoms.

Extensive coral patches are scattered over the shelf, but actual reefs are limited to the keys near the southern tip of Florida. A very large fauna of shell-bearing mollusks thrives on the shelf, and foraminifera make an important contribution to the deposits. This is an area of very low tides, and it is shielded from the great storm waves of the Atlantic and by-passed by the Gulf Current. Wave action is important in agitating the sediment, but bottom currents are relatively gentle.

The deposition of limestone is discussed in Chapter 13, but it may be noted in passing that the shelf about Florida and the Bahama Islands constitutes one of the chief areas of calcareous sediment in the modern world, and that the thick Cenozoic limestones underlying this area probably were formed in a similar environment.

Neritic zone off the western Gulf Coast. The shelf between the Mississippi River Delta and the Rio Grande is an area of great interest and of present active research. The Mississippi delta is treated in Chapter 4, but it should be noted that much sediment from the Mississippi drifts westward into the area under discussion and little, if any, goes directly southward over the edge of the shelf. The neritic zone along the coast of Texas, and of Louisiana west of the delta, has been discussed by Storm (1945), by Lowman (1949), by Stetson (1953), and by Shepard and Moore (1955a, b).

The neritic zone in this region has a maximum width of about 130 miles east of Galveston, but narrows to 50 or 60 miles along the western side of the Gulf. It is almost entirely covered with detrital sediment. In general a zone of well sorted sand is present near shore, grading seaward into finer sandy and silty mud. Barrier islands of sand are developed here on an exceptional scale separating the open sea from wide lagoons and estuaries. Shepard (1953) has shown that the embayments are being rapidly silted up, not so much by delta building as by deposition on the flat bay floors. Outside the barriers the grain size decreases generally toward the continental margin, though the sorting is less perfect in the finer sediment on the outer part of the shelf. Storm (1945, p. 1313–1314) described interesting variations in the bottom sediment near Corpus Christi where, within a zone 40 miles wide, the shore is paralleled by alternating belts of sandy and of muddy bottom. The innermost sandy belt is the barrier island about 1 mile wide separating the lagoon from a 12-mile belt of finer silty mud. The next sandy belt is narrow and is separated by an 8-mile belt of finer mud from an outer sandy zone 10 miles or more in width. Storm found that the outer sand belt follows the path of a bottom current that parallels the shore, flowing northeastward, and the middle sandy belt marks the path of a counter current, flowing southwestward. The barrier island, of course, is due to onshore waves. Thus, in spite of the segregation of the sediment into distinct bands, there is close adjustment to existing waves and currents. This banding parallel to the shore is probably a local phenomenon.

South of Galveston considerable patches of coral and algae are found over the middle part of the shelf at distances of 20 to 40 miles from shore. These appear on "plateau-like hills" that rise somewhat above the general level of the muddy plain of the continental shelf, but it has not been determined whether they are entirely due to construction by lime-secreting organisms or merely form a veneer over some kind of structural feature (Stetson, 1953, p. 20–23).

Continental borderland off southern California. Off southern California is a region of recent and continuing tectonic disturbance in which the shelf is narrow and by no means flat. Large-scale maps by Shepard and Emery (1941) show that the continental margin is from 25 to 50 miles from shore off middle California, increasing to more than 150 miles off San Diego, but that the submerged area is not really a shelf, but a "continental borderland"—a region of basin and range topography comparable to that of southern California. The summits of some of the ranges stand exposed as islands (Santa Catalina, San Clemente, Santa Cruz, Santa Rosa), others form shallow banks (Tanner Bank, Thirtymile Bank, Cortes Bank), and others are deeply submerged (Northeast Bank, Santa Lucia Bank, Rodriguez Seamount). The intervening basins reach bathyal and even abyssal depths. Only a small part of this area falls within the neritic zone, which borders the coastline and surrounds each island in a narrow belt varying from less than 3 miles to 10 or 12 miles in width. The complex distribution of sediments in this area has been described by Revelle and Shepard (1939).

There are several sources of sediment in this area. Streams from the mainland supply mud, sand, and gravel to the coastal belt; submarine erosion locally yields detrital sediment about the shores of the islands; benthonic organisms form shelly deposits near the islands and on the shoals; and both pelagic and benthonic foraminifera are abundant. Finally, in places on the outer ridges Shepard found coarse sand and gravel; these he thinks were inherited from a previous low stand of sealevel.

Distribution of these sediments shows marked topographic control. Scattered areas of rock floor about the islands and on some of the shoals are evidently being swept clean, but in general the banks and shoals are covered with sand or sandy mud. The basins, on the contrary, are floored by fine clay rich in organic matter. Evidently the fine material is being winnowed out and carried from the banks and shoals even at considerable depth.

For some distance out from the mainland, the sand is largely terrigenous, but on the outer shoals and banks it is almost entirely made of foraminiferal shells. The "sands and sandy muds" of this region are therefore highly calcareous. Locally the bottom is covered with sand and gravel made of molluskan shells, and Cortes Bank shows a considerable area of calcareous sand made almost entirely of bryozoan fragments, in part "old and worn."

Arctic shelf off Alaska and northwest Canada. A wide shelf sea borders the Arctic Ocean from Novaya Zemlya eastward along the Siberian coast and across Bering Strait to the Arctic Archipelago of North America. Carsola's study (1954) of a representative area of some 35,000 square miles along the north coast of Alaska, and extending as far east as Banks Island, shows the shelf to be rather shallow, the break in slope occurring on the average at a depth of about 200 feet.

East of the Alaskan-Canadian boundary, glacier ice pushed out to sea during Pleistocene time, but the northern border of Alaska was not glaciated. However, most of the region under study is covered by floe ice from 9 to 11 months in the year. In the summer a belt of open water develops along the shore, but during periods of onshore wind ice is driven against the land and at times piles up so that it extends from the surface to the bottom in depths as great as 120 feet. The tide is very low and waves are generally weak because the floe ice leaves the wind relatively short fetch across open water. As a result bottom currents are gentle, and the shelf is covered with mud.

Mechanical analysis of many of the sediment samples gives bimodal frequency curves, indicating two independent sources of the material. Carsola finds that the fine mud and much of the silt has been carried in suspension, whereas the coarser material (cobbles, pebbles, and sand) has been rafted out by floe ice. In support of this interpretation he reports that "dirty" floe ice carrying much sediment may be seen early in the season but disappears (by melting) before late summer. Just how the sediment gets into the ice has not been determined. Some of it is undoubtedly frozen in when the ice is driven against the land by onshore winds, and some of it may be washed onto the ice by streams during spring thaws. Wind-blown dust and sand are probably not important since the coastal plain is low and swampy.

It may be noted that the sediment on this shelf would normally be interpreted as glacio-marine, but that glacier ice is actually not involved. A good illustration of true glacio-marine deposits now forming has been described by Stetson and Upson (1937) and by Hough (1956) around Antarctica (see also pp. 24, 174).

Shelf off the west coast of South Africa. From Walvis Bay southward for a distance of some 200 miles to near Cape Town the neritic zone presents an unusual environment that has been described by Brongersma-Sanders (1948). The coast line is nearly straight here and the adjacent land is arid and without important streams, so that but little terrigenous sediment is brought into the sea. The continental shelf is only 25 to 30 miles wide but is essentially flat, sloping gently seaward. The climate of the area is subtropical.

At intervals of 4 or 5 years an upwelling of deeper water brings abundant nutrients to the surface. When this coincides with a few days of still weather, the surface water is suitably warmed and certain microscopic pelagic organisms (such as the dinoflagellate, *Noctiluca*) increase to epidemic proportions. These tiny creatures become so abundant as to stain the water red (producing the "red tide"), and they liberate some sort of toxic substances causing mass destruction of all the animals living in the area. The dead animals then accumulate on the bottom where, in the absence of scavengers, the organic matter is attacked by anaerobic bacteria that generate large amounts of H_2S. This also is toxic and keeps the water poisoned for a considerable time. Although fish and other pelagic organisms return after a time, and diatoms and foraminifera quickly thrive, the shell-bearing benthonic animals migrate so slowly that they make little progress at repeopling the bottom before another "red tide" repeats the cycle.

Here, then, is a stretch of the neritic zone with an area of more than 5,000 square miles in which the bottom is almost void of animal life. Brongersma-Sanders calls it an *azoic zone*.

In the absence of terrigenous mud, the bottom sediment consists largely of the shells of diatoms that rain down from the surface. Following one of the "red tides" the "remains of dead fish may be brought up by the bucketful," but invertebrate shells are virtually absent. In the deposit now forming, fish remains will, of course, appear in great numbers in certain layers, corresponding to episodes of mass mortality. Brongersma-Sanders suggests that the diatomite in the Monterey formation (Miocene) of California may have formed under such an environment. Bramlette's monographic study (1946) of· the Monterey formation indicated, however, that conditions of deposition differed in important respects from those off the present coast of South Africa. The diatomites and related siliceous rocks of the Monterey (p. 252) clearly formed in a region comparable to the modern continental borderland off the coast of southern California, in which structural basins reaching depths below the neritic zone were separated by thresholds shallow enough to cause the bottom waters to be largely stagnant. The notable sparseness of benthonic mollusks and the great abundance of fossil fish confined to certain bedding planes strongly suggest, however, that red tides may have played an important role in creating an environment in which only pelagic organisms could thrive.

North Sea. Fully 90 percent of the floor of the North Sea lies within the neritic zone, and because it is largely landlocked, this sea may present an environment much like that in many epeiric seas of the past. However, it was rather thickly blanketed during the Pleistocene epoch by heterogeneous and irregularly distributed glacial deposits on which the waves and currents are still at work. Lüders (1939) gives an excellent summary of the environment and of the distribution of bottom sediments, as far as now known.

In general the North Sea is shallowest at the south; at the Strait of Dover the maximum depth is only about 100 feet. Its floor slopes irregularly to the north, and it goes below the neritic zone in the Norwegian Trough along its northeast margin. During the low stands of sealevel in the glacial ages, the North Sea floor was emergent, and according to Lüders an area of large sand dunes formed in the central southern part; these now form the great shoal known as Dogger Bank. As sealevel rose, the northern part of the region was flooded first while extensive swamp deposits formed at the south before the Strait of Dover was opened.

The North Sea is an area of heavy storms and of rather strong, but very complex, tidal currents. Impressive evidence of marine erosion is seen along the British and the Norwegian coasts, but along the low coasts of Denmark, Holland, and Belgium, the sea is working upon the vast sandy deposits of the great Rhine–Ems–Scheldt delta complex (Fig. 33, p. 82).

According to Lüders, coarse sand and gravel covers nearly 20 percent of the floor of the North Sea, medium and fine sand about 60 percent, and mud and sandy mud a little less than 20 percent. The mud is almost entirely in the deeper water below the neritic zone. Coarse sand and gravel are widely distributed in irregular patches and appear to represent largely the coarser residue of Pleistocene deposits from which the finer material has been removed. Probably much of the floor is subject to sublevation and the finer sand is still being moved during storms, but gradation of the bottom sediments in adjustment to the waves and currents is far from complete except very near the shore.

Baltic Sea. The Baltic Sea floor lies entirely within the neritic zone and, as one of the few examples of an epeiric sea now extant, challenges the interest of stratigraphers. Unfortunately, from this point of view, it lay wholly within the glaciated region and thus displays features probably quite different from those normal to most epeiric seas of the past. Gripenberg (1939) gives an excellent account of the sediments and the bottom conditions in the Baltic.

Unlike the North Sea region, which was covered by glacial drift during the Pleistocene ice ages, the Baltic area was scoured clean by the ice sheet that pushed across it to the plains of Germany, and during the waning phases of glaci-

ation it became a lake in which varved silt and clay accumulated.

The adjacent highlands on the west had been stripped clean of mantle so that they have yielded but limited postglacial sediment. To the northeast, Finland is low and its streams so extensively ponded that they carry practically no terrigenous sediment. Moreover the great rivers from the south flow so far across the low plains of Germany and Poland that they carry only fine mud. As a result the Baltic Sea has received a surprisingly small amount of sediment during Recent time, and fully 50 percent of its floor is composed of late glacial varved clay or of similar but non-laminated clay. Other parts are covered with a thin veneer of fine sand. Dark muds rich in organic matter occur in the deepest parts of the basin and in sheltered bays along the Polish and German coast. The chief source of this mud is apparently the rivers that flow through the low fertile plains of Germany and Poland.

In sheltered places along this coast, as about the Esthonian islands of Ösel and Moon, such soft black mud accumulates in very shallow water, right up to the shore line (Twenhofel, 1915). Grabau (1917, p. 953) reports that some 615 square miles of the floor of Danzig Bay is covered by such mud, locally called pitch because of its black color, in which Bischof found over 20 percent by weight to be organic. This mud has been brought in largely by the Vistula River. The more exposed parts of the Baltic Sea floor are apparently subject to gentle action by bottom currents that have shifted fine sand about and have moved some of the fine mud into the deepest depressions.

A notable feature of the environment in this nearly landlocked sea is the low salinity which drops progressively from the normal 33 permille at the Skagerrak to a low of about 3 permille near the head of the Gulf of Bothnia. It is probable that the salinity was similarly reduced in many of the epeiric seas of the past.

Summary on the Neritic Zone

In summary it may be emphasized that there is no single *typical* neritic environment. The character of the bottom sediment and of the environment under which deposition is taking place differs from region to region, as clearly shown by the examples described above. Other areas would certainly display additional local peculiarities. The distribution of sediments on the east Asiatic shelf, plotted by Shepard, Emery, and Gould (1949), for example, shows many interesting relations.

These differences are due in part to local climatic conditions, but the geographic setting plays an all-important role, determining whether the shallow sea will be landlocked or exposed to the full force of storm waves from the open ocean, and whether tidal currents will be strong or weak. The local source of the bottom sediment may be a dominating factor largely responsible for such great differences as the gravel bottom off the New England coast, the lime mud of the Florida shelf, and the vast sandy flats off the mid-Atlantic States. Even within a single province many distinct local environments may be recognized, each characterized by distinctive sediments and faunas. Along the Gulf Coast, for example, Shepard and Moore (1954, 1955a, b) recognize as many as 16 such local environments.

In spite of such impressive local differences, however, the neritic zone as a whole has certain characteristics that stand in strong contrast to those of other parts of the sea floor. First of these is variability itself, which results from the shallowness and the nearness to land. A second is that it lies generally within the reach of waves and bottom currents capable of repeatedly lifting and moving the bottom sediments. A third is the richness and variety of its bottom life, resulting from the penetration of sunlight and the growth of plant life—especially the microscopic plants that form "the ultimate pastures of the sea."

BATHYAL AND ABYSSAL ZONES

The break in slope provides a natural basis for separating the neritic from the bathyal zone, but the boundary between bathyal and abyssal is entirely arbitrary, being placed by widely accepted definition at 6,000 feet.

As thus defined, the bathyal zone occupies the upper part of the continental slopes (Fig. 1, p.

2), varying in width from about 10 miles to more than 100 miles, with a total area of approximately 12,000,000 square miles or a little more than that of the present neritic zone. The rest of the deep ocean floor constitutes the abyss. It has an area of about 120,000,000 square miles, of which some 90,000,000 exceeds 12,000 feet of depth.

The continental slope is normally steepest in its upper part, and with increasing depth it gradually flattens out to merge imperceptibly with the broad ocean floor. Locally, along faulted coasts such as that of California, the break in slope at the top is abrupt and the upper part of the continental slope is steep, but in general the break is broadly rounded and the slope below is gentle. For example, where the bathyal zone is only 10 miles wide, the average slope is about 1 foot in 10, and where it is 25 miles wide the slope is about 1 foot in 25.

The boundary between the bathyal and abyssal zones lies in the midst of this slope and is not marked by any appreciable change in environment or in the character of the bottom sediments. We have therefore no criteria for separating the sedimentary rocks formed above this limit from those formed a considerable distance below, and it will be convenient to discuss the bathyal and abyssal zones together.

The surface layers down to a depth of 600 feet constitute the *pelagic zone* of the sea (Fig. 24, p. 46). It is important as the source of the organic oozes discussed below.

Bathyal and abyssal conditions are found in two quite distinct situations, first in the broad ocean basins and, second, in the mediterraneans —the deep basins enclosed within and between the continental platforms. The first, being the more normal and widespread, will be considered first.

Bottom Environments in the Open Ocean

General environmental conditions

Below a depth of 600 feet the ocean floor is a region of total darkness, of quiet, and of cold. Even the great storm waves do not disturb the bottom, and with local exceptions discussed below, it is touched only by currents so gentle as to have little effect on the bottom sediment. Spasmodic turbidity currents (p. 14) are, of course, an important exception but they operate only very briefly and locally and at long intervals. With these exceptions material brought in suspension, as well as that derived from the surface, settles directly and permanently to rest.

The most general circulation is that of cold water from the polar regions, which settles to the bottom and spreads over the entire ocean floor. Although its movement is extremely slow, it reaches to the tropics and has produced a general density stratification in the oceans, based upon temperature. This arrangement is locally disturbed by other types of ocean currents as, for example, the density currents due to water masses of unequal salinity, so that the decrease in temperature with increasing depth is not uniform even though it is general, but at depths below 6,000 feet the water is everywhere within a few degrees of freezing.

Table 3 shows the temperature (centigrade) recorded at various depths in the Atlantic, between the latitudes of Spitzbergen and the South Orkney Islands.

TABLE 3. TEMPERATURES AT DIFFERENT DEPTHS AND LATITUDES IN THE ATLANTIC OCEAN. AFTER SCHOTT.

Depth in Meters	Latitude							
	80°N	60°N	40°N	20°N	0°	20°S	40°S	60°S
0	2°	9°	16°	20°	27°	17°	15°	<0°
200	2°	6°	12°	15°	15°	11°	10°	<1°
400	1°	9°	12°	12°	9°	9°	10°	<1°
800	0°	8°	11°	8°	5°	5°	4°	<1°
1000	<0°	7°	9°	6°	5°	4°	3°	<1°
2000	−1°	3°	4°	4°	3.3°	3°	2°	<0°

Locally, where ocean currents are confined to narrow passages, they gain sufficient velocity to sublevate and remove fine sediment or to prevent deposition even at great depth. Thus in Florida Strait the fine sediment is being winnowed out and carried away from the continental slope and

from the surface of Blake Plateau down to depths as great as 2,500 feet (Stetson, 1939, p. 236). A part of the steep continental slope west of California is likewise bare of modern sediment down to abyssal depths (Hanna, 1952).

Some unknown agent seems also to be winnowing out part of the finest sediment from the summit of the mid-Atlantic Ridge in more than 8,000 feet of water. Thus in the North Atlantic cores taken between Newfoundland and Ireland (Fig. 25, p. 49), the several distinct layers of sediment individually thin on the mid-Atlantic Ridge (core 8) while the average grain size increases because of scarcity of the finest sizes (Bramlette and Bradley, 1940, p. 14). Whether this winnowing is due to tidal currents, to occasional tsunamis, or to something else, is not yet known, but in any event the current must be very gentle.

Likewise, some of the seamounts that stand far above the ocean floor, but have flat summits half a mile or more below the surface, show ripple-marks (Dietz and Menard, 1951, p. 2004, Fig. 6), or are swept clean of sediment (Carsola and Dietz, 1952), indicating some form of current action at intermediate depths that is not yet understood.

Sources and character of sediments

In their classic study of the deposits in the deep sea Murray and Renard (1891) proposed a classification of deep sea sediments that has since been generally adopted and is used in the following paragraphs.

Terrigenous muds. The bathyal zone is generally floored by fine lead-colored or bluish-gray terrigenous mud that also extends out to a variable distance into the abyss. It commonly has a surface film of reddish or brownish color due to oxidized iron, but reducing conditions obtain below the surface, and as fast as the mud is covered the iron is reduced to a ferrous state and the reddish tint is lost.

Where the neritic zone is covered with calcareous sediment, however, limy mud spreads down over the continental slope and may extend into deep water, as off both east and west coasts of Florida, the Bahama Banks, the Yucatan Peninsula, the northeast coast of Australia where it is fringed by the Great Barrier Reef (p. 92), and about tropical islands that are capped or fringed by coral reefs.

The terrigenous mud is obviously derived from the land whence it has been carried to the sea in suspension. As noted in Chapter 1 (p. 4), clay and fine silt settle so slowly that they may require many years to reach the ocean floor. Thus very gentle ocean currents are able to spread fine mud far from the land. That accumulation of such mud is more rapid near the continental margin than far at sea was strikingly shown by the string of cores taken across the North Atlantic between Newfoundland and Ireland (Bramlette and Bradley, 1940, Pl. 3). In these cores a layer of postglacial sediment could be clearly identified all the way from the continental margin to the mid-Atlantic Ridge. In cores 4 to 8, far out in the ocean floor, this layer consists largely of globigerina ooze and ranges in thickness from less than 2 feet in core 4 to less than 6 inches in core 8. In core 3, however, near the foot of the continental slope east of Newfoundland at a depth of 15,500 feet, this layer consists of fine, calcareous blue mud more than 9 feet thick (the calcareous material consisting of included globigerines).

Abyssal red clay. In the abyssal region the most widespread sediment is the so-called red clay. It covers about a quarter of the floor of the Atlantic and Indian oceans and nearly half that of the Pacific (Sverdrup, Johnson, and Fleming, 1942, p. 977), lying chiefly in the deeper regions far from shore, almost entirely below 12,000 feet. Its color varies from brick-red to chocolate-brown and nearest shore grades locally into blue. It is extremely fine-grained, and chemically it approaches the composition of the average igneous rock from which it differs in a somewhat higher content of aluminum, iron, manganese, and magnesium, and a lower content of calcium, potassium, and sodium. Manganese oxide occurs in the form of concretions, as scattered grains, as coatings over shells, or as matrix, and is one of the most distinctive features of the abyssal red clay.

The source of the red clay is less obvious than that of any other oceanic sediment, and it probably is not simple. It may be derived from wind-blown dust, from meteoric dust, from volcanic ash, and possibly from terrigenous sediment of colloidal dimensions. The red color is due to oxidation of the iron to the ferric condition. Since the cold deep water carries free oxygen in solution and the very minute particles of sediment that make up the red clay settle so slowly, they have ample opportunity to be oxidized before reaching the bottom; and the extreme sparseness of organic matter at great depth permits them to remain so after deposition.

Calcium carbonate is dissolved in cold water rich in carbon dioxide below about 15,000 feet; hence shell-bearing animals are very rare or absent. Even such large shells as that of the nautilus (or of ammonites) that might settle from above would be dissolved on the bottom, leaving at most a "ghost" of the shell as a faint impression in the clay. Such insoluble objects as the earbones of whales remain, however, and siliceous shells, notably radiolaria, are common.

Organic oozes. The surface waters of the ocean support vast numbers of a few kinds of organisms, mostly microscopic, that are adapted to pelagic life and make shells of $CaCO_3$ or of SiO_2, which they extract from the great store carried in solution. These shells eventually settle to the bottom and, where accumulation of mud is very slow, they form the so-called organic oozes.

Globigerina ooze. The most widespread of these is globigerina ooze, which covers nearly 50,000,000 square miles of the ocean floor. It is made by some 30 species of foraminifera belonging to the families Globigerinidae and Globorotaliidae. Only these 2 of more than 50 families of the foraminifera are adapted to a floating habit (the rest living at the bottom), but having made the adaptation to pelagic life they thrive in incredible numbers throughout the surface waters of the ocean.

Like other single-celled organisms these creatures reproduce by subdividing. At spawning time the protoplasm of each subdivides into zoospores that swarm out and scatter, leaving the empty shells to sink to the bottom. Normally these are not shells of the dead, as so commonly stated, but are those abandoned by the living, and the ooze includes very little organic matter.

Where mud is accumulating, foraminiferal shells commonly are included, and thus all gradations occur between terrigenous mud and globigerina ooze. The sediment is commonly considered to be ooze if more than 30 percent shells. Since the globigerines live at the surface, their shells may settle to the bottom in water of any depth, but areas of globigerina ooze actually lie almost exclusively at depths between 6,000 and 15,000 feet, because at shallower depths, mostly near shore, mud accumulates much more rapidly than the shells, and at greater depths the shells are dissolved and disappear.

Pteropod ooze. The pteropods are a minor group of gastropods adapted to pelagic life. Their small and delicate calcareous shells appear commonly in globigerina ooze and locally they form a calcareous "ooze" that covers small areas at intermediate depths.

Radiolarian ooze. Radiolarians are truly microscopic, single-celled animals, the majority of which make their shells of SiO_2. Although many of them live at great depth, others thrive in vast numbers in the pelagic zone. Like the foraminifera, they reproduce by subdivision, leaving their empty shells to settle to the ocean floor. Being siliceous, these shells are insoluble even at great depth, and they may accumulate wherever there is a dearth of other bottom sediment. At present, radiolarian ooze covers some 5,000,000 square miles of the deep ocean floor. Normally it is by no means a pure concentrate of shells but rather a variety of red clay rich in radiolarians. Some of the radiolarian cherts may represent deposits of this sort.

Diatom ooze. Diatoms are microscopic, single-celled plants that thrive in the sunlit surface waters where certain nutrients are plentiful. They form delicate siliceous shells which are shed at the time of reproduction. They live in greatest abundance in cold water and at present have formed belts of diatom ooze in high latitudes, one in the southern hemisphere roughly girdling the continent of Antarctica and another in the northern hemisphere confined largely to the northern part of the Pacific Ocean basin.

It must be emphasized that diatoms accumulate also in shallow water. An extensive deposit now flooring the neritic zone off the west coast of South Africa is discussed above (p. 53). According to Brown (1924) living diatoms drift ashore in the Marquesas Islands to form foamy green masses several millimeters in thickness and extending for hundreds of feet along the shore. A similar phenomenon occurs along the coast of Oregon. The diatomite beds in the Miocene deposits of the Chesapeake Bay area are associated with very shallow-water deposits. Finally, diatom oozes also form in fresh-water lakes.

Summary on organic oozes. Pelagic organisms, such as the diatoms, the radiolarians, the pteropods, and the globigerines, each have a preferred distribution in the pelagic zone, depending on the temperature and on the distribution of the dissolved nutrients on which they feed and from which they make their shells. They are not sharply limited, however, and commonly are associated, both as living creatures and in the bottom sediment.

Although diatoms and pteropods live only in the pelagic zone, different groups of the radiolarians inhabit preferred depth zones and some kinds live only at great depths. When their distribution is better known, radiolarians may be useful, at least in the Cenozoic formations, as a criterion of the actual depth of deposition. Inferences about depth are increasingly hazardous, however, when applied to the older rocks and are especially to be decried where the preservation is poor so that even generic identification is open to question. Furthermore, although radiolarian ooze is now forming only at abyssal depths, the mere presence of abundant radiolarians in a shale is not of itself valid evidence of deposition at great depth. Such radiolarians as live near the surface may drift into shallow water and be killed by changes of temperature or salinity and may accumulate in abundance. This appears to have been true, for example, of the radiolarians in the Stanley shale (Mississippian) of Oklahoma.

The overwhelming majority of foraminifera live at the bottom, creeping over its surface or over seaweeds or other organisms. Where the environment is suitable, as in parts of the neritic zone where terrigenous sediment is lacking, foraminiferal shells make up the bulk of the bottom sediment. Such accumulations are not to be confused with globigerina ooze. Shallow-water foraminifera, for example, are particularly abundant about coral reefs and locally make up most of the so-called coral sand. The chalk of the Cretaceous system in Europe likewise includes vast numbers of foraminifera, the majority of which are benthonic forms, and its associations clearly indicate that it is not a deep sea deposit.

Benthonic foraminifera do show a distinct zonation in depth (actually controlled by temperature which in turn is related to depth) as first emphasized by Natland (1933). Further investigation along this line has already provided convincing evidence of the depth of deposition of Cenozoic deposits and, among other things, has demonstrated that the thick Pliocene deposits of the Ventura and Los Angeles basins in California were mostly, if not entirely, formed in the bathyal zone (Natland and Kuenen, 1951; Crouch, 1952). This use of benthonic foraminifera is more fully discussed below (p. 148).

Deposits of turbidity currents in deep water. Until recently it was generally believed that no coarse sediment could be transported into the bathyal or abyssal zones because of the lack of strong bottom currents. It was recognized, of course, that landslides and taluses might form immediately adjacent to active submarine faults, and that icebergs could raft coarse debris to sea and drop it far from land, but with these exceptions it has been commonly assumed that conglomerates and breccias are prima-facie evidence of deposition on the land or in the neritic zone.

Intensive interest in the submarine canyons, beginning about 1935, led to researches by Kuenen (1937; Kuenen and Migliorini, 1950) and others that show the previously unsuspected power of turbidity currents to transport coarse sediment far out into the ocean basins. Whether such currents have actually eroded the canyons is still a moot question, but it now seems certain that from time to time the sediment that has accumulated in them is flushed out, starting as landslides that generate turbidity currents of high velocity capable of carrying sand and gravel down to the base of the continental slope and far beyond. The colossal current that developed on the slope south of the Grand Banks following the earthquake of November 18, 1929 (Heezen and Ewing, 1952), reached a velocity of more than 60 miles per hour (55 knots) on the lower part of the continental slope at a distance of more than 100 miles from the edge of the continental shelf and at a depth of more than 12,000 feet (p. 15). A velocity of 60 miles per hour exceeds that of any currents known to operate on the land and would be competent to transport enormous quantities of sediment. The vast submarine plains of the western Atlantic Basin described in Chapter 1 (p. 16) are believed to be formed of deposits carried into the abyss in this way. A segment of the plain flanking the continental margin east of New York has been considered by Ewing and his colleagues to be a "delta" built by turbidity currents originating in the submarine canyon of the Hudson. It lies at a depth of 14,000 to 16,000 feet, has an area of some 6,000 square miles, and extends some 400 miles beyond the present shore. Cores from this area, studied by Ericson, Ewing, and Heezen (1951, 1952), revealed a sequence of graded layers of fine clean sand alternating with layers of abyssal clay, the sand layers making up about 30 percent of the deposit. Each graded sand layer is interpreted as the deposit formed by a single spasmodic turbidity flow.

The deposit produced by a recent spasmodic turbidity current southeast of Bermuda is described on page 16. Northrop (1954) has reported an even more extreme example from the Puerto Rican Trough which has a flat floor about 10 miles wide lying at a depth of 26,000 feet. Cores from this depth show red clay (which is normal) alternating with layers of calcareous sand that show graded bedding and include shells of shallow-water benthonic organisms.

It now seems certain that if coarse material is available in the source area from which turbidity currents arise it may be carried into abyssal depths and even to many tens of miles from shore. Sandstones and conglomerates in the very thick Pliocene deposits of the Ventura and Los Angeles basins have recently been attributed to such currents (Natland and Kuenen, 1951; Crouch, 1952).

Rate of deposition in the deep sea

Deposition on the deep ocean floor is undoubtedly slow and must vary from region to region, but until recently there was little real evidence as to its rate. Study of radioactive materials in long cores of the abyssal clays now appears to have opened up new possibilities, and on this basis Pettersson (speaking before the National Academy of Sciences on April 26, 1954) estimated that the average rate of deposition of abyssal red clay is 1 to 2 mm per 1,000 years. Subsequently, Kröll (1955) has published results from several widely spaced deep sea cores that confirm this figure, but 2 cores of calcareous sediment, 1 in the equatorial mid-Atlantic and 1 in the western Pacific, suggest a rate of some 20 mm per 1,000 years.

Globigerina ooze probably accumulates more rapidly. The most convincing data on this rate come from a study of the North Atlantic cores between Newfoundland and Ireland (Fig. 25, p. 49). Here a late glacial layer is clearly recognizable (p. 48) above which there is a postglacial layer of globigerina ooze. Bramlette and Bradley (1940, p. 13) found that over the western Atlantic basin (cores 4 to 7) the postglacial layer averages 34 cm thick, and they estimated that it represents the last 9,000 years. They concluded that the average rate of deposition has been 1 cm in about 500 years. From his study in the South Atlantic, where the deposits are also foraminiferal, Schott (1935, p. 129) had previously concluded that the average rate is 1 cm in about 800 years.

The pelagic foraminifera did not evolve until Cretaceous time but probably have been as common as now throughout the Cenozoic Era. If so, at the rate of 1 cm in 500 years they should have made a deposit some 5,000 feet thick during the last 60,000,000 years. If only 60 percent of the sediment is $CaCO_3$, as Schott found in the South Atlantic, it would still represent more than 3,400 feet of $CaCO_3$. All this calcium has been extracted from the lands, taken to sea in solution, and permanently locked up on the deep ocean floor. It represents a cumulative loss of calcium from the continental areas, and has probably made the most profound change in the geochemistry of the earth since early geologic time. It might be interesting to speculate what the effect would have been if pelagic foraminifera had evolved at the beginning of the Paleozoic Era, for even at half the current rate they should have accumu-

lated to a thickness of 20,000 feet (disregarding compaction) in the 500,000,000 years since the Cambrian Period began.

Spasmodic turbidity currents probably occur at long and irregular intervals, but the extensive deposits recently brought to light on the floor of the western Atlantic by Ewing and his colleagues stand as a graded plain forming a slope down toward the adjacent areas that are covered only by globigerina ooze (like a bajada slope around a playa, p. 38). This suggests that sediment brought in by turbidity currents has on the average accumulated more rapidly than that formed by pelagic organisms. Such a rate can hardly be normal for all geologic time, however; else the ocean basins would have been completely filled. On the contrary, seismic studies of the Atlantic floor by Ewing and his colleagues indicate that the sedimentary layer over the western Atlantic basin averages only about 1.2 km thick and that it rests on the basaltic layer of the crust (Ewing, Sutton, and Officer, 1954). Probably the abnormal activity of turbidity currents in this region resulted from Pleistocene glaciation.

Bathyal and Abyssal Environments in Closed Basins

Deep basins that are separated from the open oceans by shallow thresholds present a variety of special conditions. Some such basins are nearly landlocked (e.g., the Mediterranean, the Black Sea, the Red Sea) while others are deeps within the continental platforms joined to the oceans by wide stretches of shallow sea (e.g., the Japan Sea, and the Banda, Halmahera, and other basins in the East Indies). The most important effect of the shallow threshold is that it tends to cause stagnation of the deeper water within the basins. The effects of this stagnation are further influenced by the local climate and the nature of the surrounding lands.

Black Sea. The Black Sea is a classic example of the enclosed basin in a rather extreme form. It has been described by Androussow (1897), Arkhangelsky (1927), Wolansky (1933), and many others. It has an area of about 170,000 square miles and an extreme depth of 7,360 feet, yet its only outlet is through the Bosporus, which at one place is only half a mile wide and forms a threshold only about 130 feet deep. Fresh water brought in by the Danube, the Dnieper, and other large streams dilutes the surface layer in the Black Sea, creating a density stratification that prevents vertical circulation. Near the surface the water teems with swimming and floating organisms, both plants and animals, but the oxygen has long since been exhausted from the stagnant water below, and the bottom is almost lifeless. When an organism dies and settles down from the surface there are no scavengers to devour it, but anaerobic bacteria attack it and extract the oxygen they require by breaking down the organic compounds. In doing so they liberate H_2S which is toxic to other organisms and creates a strongly reducing environment. Under these conditions finely divided marcasite (FeS_2) is precipitated and this, with a carbonaceous residue of the disintegrated organic matter, colors the bottom mud dark gray. Around the shore in the neritic zone, the bottom is sandy and light gray to a depth of about 120 feet, but from there to 600 feet it is muddy and dark gray, while below this the entire floor is covered with fine gray clay and calcareous marl, having an organic content of 3 to 10 percent by weight (Trask, 1939, p. 449).

Mediterranean Sea. The Mediterranean Sea, in turn, is largely landlocked, but the Strait of Gilbraltar is 8 miles wide at the narrowest point and the threshold is 1,050 feet deep. A surface current from the Atlantic streams in at a velocity of some 2.5 miles per hour and is counterbalanced by an outward flow at greater depth. This provides circulation capable of replacing all the water in the Mediterranean within a period of 75 years (Kuenen, 1950b, p. 43). As a result, the bottom is not stagnant like that of the Black Sea. But, because the water in the Atlantic is stratified according to temperature, the cold water from the polar regions cannot get over the threshold, and the minimum temperature in the Mediterranean is about 13°C. even in its greatest depth. Since few large streams enter the Mediterranean, organically formed calcium carbonate (largely foraminiferal) accumulates about as fast as terrigenous material, and the bottom sediment is a remarkably uniform pale-brownish calcareous mud (Bøggild, 1912).

Red Sea. The Red Sea has a maximum depth of about 7,200 feet with a threshold at the south only 240 feet deep. The region is arid, so that evaporation greatly exceeds precipitation and there is no runoff from the surrounding lands. To make up for the excess evaporation, a strong current flows in from the Gulf of Aden. Owing to the rapid evaporation the salinity rises to between 40 and 41 permille in the northern part of the basin during the hot summer months; during the cold winter months this highly saline water is chilled and settles to the bottom. As a result the entire Red Sea basin below its threshold has become filled with dense water having a salinity of 40 to 41 permille (Sverdrup, Johnson, and Fleming, 1942, p. 687). The oxygen content is also very low, and in general the bottom is remarkably barren of animal life. The high temperature of the water facilitates chemical decay and this, together with the sparseness of organic matter, probably explains why the bottom mud is not black but greenish (Strøm, 1939, p. 365).

Basins off southern California. The basins off southern California (p. 52) present quite different conditions. The area off the coast from Santa Barbara to San Diego includes 11 roughly oval basins, ranging from 10 to 20 miles wide and 50 to 100 miles long. These have broad bottoms and range in depth from about 3,000 to more than 6,000 feet. Thresholds range in depth from less than 3,000 feet for one nearshore basin to more than 5,000 feet for the outer ones. Tidal currents sweep the ridges and saddles to considerable depth, but the water in each basin is relatively stagnant below the threshold level.

The basins are floored with gray calcareous mud rich in organic matter. The mud is mostly clay that has been carried in suspension from the shallow areas. The organic matter, having approximately the specific gravity of water, is easily swept into the basins where it accumulates with the clay. Its destruction is there inhibited by the low oxygen content of the stagnant bottom water. Trask (1932, p. 240) showed that these muds contain as much as 7 percent by weight of organic matter, the maximum in any open sea deposit examined (p. 206).

The relatively high content of $CaCO_3$ is attributed largely to the pelagic foraminifera that thrive in the surface waters of this area, settling equally over the basins and the shoals. Their shells are sparse, however, in the bottom mud of the basins, the CaCO$_3$ appearing rather in the form of minute particles. According to Revelle and Shepard (1939, p. 260–261), the shells are largely dissolved under the conditions that obtain on the stagnant bottoms, and the CaCO$_3$ is reprecipitated in the form of lime mud.

East Indian Archipelago. In the highly mobile area of the East Indian Archipelago large islands alternate with shallow sea and with marine basins of great depth, active volcanoes are abundant, and coral reefs abound along some of the shores and shoals. The marine environments are therefore uncommonly complex. The submarine geology has been described by Molengraaff and by Kuenen (1939a, 1942, 1950b), and extensive bottom samples collected by the Snellius Expedition of 1929–1930 have been described by Neeb (1943).

The movement of water through the deep straits and into the closed basins is extremely complex, varying with the submarine topography and with the depths of the thresholds. Only the warm shallow layers can spill over the shallower thresholds, so that the bottom water in the basins is moderately warm even at great depth.

The chief types of bottom sediment in this region are (1) terrigenous blue mud, (2) globigerina ooze, (3) mixed volcanic and terrigenous mud, (4) volcanic mud, and (5) "coral" mud. These occur in highly irregular patches and their distribution is determined rather more by source than by depth of water. Downwind from active volcanoes the bottom sediment is largely volcanic mud, grading laterally into mixed volcanic and terrigenous mud regardless of depth. Blue terrigenous mud surrounds the non-volcanic islands, spreading from near shore with decreasing coarseness into the depths and away from land; in this regard distance may be more important than depth. Coral mud is limited to small patches in the vicinity of reefs and occupies a very small percentage of the area. Globigerina ooze predominates where terrigenous and volcanic sediments are inadequate, regardless of depth. Pelagic foraminifera are abundant throughout the region and form an important component of the terrig-

enous and volcanic muds so that the bottom sediments are moderately calcareous.

In general there is circulation of the water within the deep basins, but a small deep in Kaoe Bay, embraced by two arms of the island Halmahera, is so stratified that the bottom presents strongly reducing conditions. Here the bottom mud is greenish (not black) and is rich in H$_2$S and FeS$_2$ (Kuenen, 1942, p. 28–29).

An excellent example of an ancient deposit formed in density-stratified water behind a shallow threshold is the Bone Spring "black limestone" in the Leonard Series (Permian) of the Delaware Basin, West Texas (King, 1948, p. 26–27). It is a monotonous succession of thin-bedded, nearly black limestone, in part laminated and platy. Its dark color is due to a large concentration of organic matter, yet fossils are extremely rare. The normal benthonic faunas of the contemporaneous shelf deposits are entirely lacking and the chief fossils found are ammonites, which presumably could swim at the surface and whose shells could certainly float and drift after death. Where they are found, their thin-walled living chamber is generally preserved, suggesting that they settled onto quiet bottom where they were never disturbed.

The deposits of the overlying Guadelupian Series in the Delaware Basin show evidence of similar though less extreme restriction of circulation and are in sharp contrast to the reef deposits that nearly surround them (p. 93).

CRITERIA FOR DISTINGUISHING MARINE FROM NON-MARINE DEPOSITS

Most fossiliferous strata can be assigned with some assurance to the marine or to the terrestrial environment, but even for these, caution may be needed. Where diagnostic fossils are absent several criteria may be invoked, one or more of which may be convincing, but it must be confessed that in a surprising number of instances marine or non-marine origin is difficult to prove.

Fossils. Land plants and terrestrial vertebrates are distinctive, and certain large groups of shelled invertebrates live only in the sea while other groups are confined to fresh water. Where any of these are present in abundance there is usually no uncertainty.

It may be noted, however, that logs drift to sea and may be buried in marine sediments. Leaves are not likely to survive such transportation. Even land animals may bloat after drowning and drift to sea, as witness an articulated skeleton of the dinosaur, *Claosaurus agilis* Marsh, found in the Niobrara chalk (Cretaceous) of Kansas. The land snail, *Cerion,* which is common in the vegetation on the Bahama Islands, is blown to sea in great numbers during hurricanes and settles in lime-mud where other shells are lacking (p. 232). The well-known lithographic limestone (Upper Jurassic) at Solenhofen, Bavaria, has yielded a great abundance of marine fossils, but beside these have been found a small dinosaur, the bird *Archeopteryx,* and many insects. The lithographic stone represents the mud laid down within the lagoon of an atoll, and these creatures from the land were blown or drifted out to mingle with the remains of marine organisms.

Conversely, marine shells appear locally in non-marine deposits. Gulls commonly fly inland a short distance carrying clams, which they drop from considerable height in order to break the shells and get at the soft parts. Crows, likewise, carry echinoids inland. Small shells may be rolled with the sand grains and appear in dunes near shore. Indeed, dunes on some of the Pacific islands are largely composed of foraminifera tossed up by the waves and then drifted inland by the wind. Likewise, fossil sea shells are in places weathered out of older formations and redeposited in fluvial sediments far from the sea.

Probably such abnormal occurrences seldom cause confusion because the exotic fossils are associated with more abundant ones normal to the environment of deposition, but they indicate the need for caution when fossils are rare.

The presence of diagnostic fossils in certain layers does not prove, however, that intervening, even closely associated beds, were formed in the same environment. The cyclothems of the Pennsylvanian system in Illinois (Fig. 52, p. 110) illustrate this point. Here a typical cyclothem includes 10 very distinct lithologic units, several of which consist of a single bed or a group of beds only a few feet thick; the whole is some tens of feet thick or may reach a hundred. The basal sandstone (unit 1) of each cyclothem commonly rests on an erosion surface, varies much in thickness, and is cross-bedded; even in the absence of fossils it appears to be a fluvial deposit. Units 2, 6, and 10, consisting of rather thinly laminated gray shale or siltstone and yielding no fossils, offer no obvious criteria of either marine or non-marine origin. The underclay (unit 4), on the contrary, which commonly includes fossil tree roots in place of growth was clearly formed on a land surface, and the coal (unit 5) is a swamp deposit with abundant evidence of land plants. The lower one of the three limestones (unit 3) is commonly interpreted as a "fresh-water limestone" since it yields no fossils, is lenticular and discontinuous, as though deposited in a series of lakes and ponds rather than in the sea, and it lies between beds thought to be non-marine. The higher limestones (units 7 and 9), on the other hand, and also the intervening shale (unit 8), bear abundant and distinctive marine fossils. Such cyclothems succeed one another through a thickness of hundreds of feet of the Illinois Coal Measures, marine and non-marine beds alternating in cyclical fashion.

Shell-bearing animals are so generally present on the sea floor and their chances for preservation are so good that the absence of fossils in a sedimentary rock suggests that it is non-marine. Nevertheless, the thick, widespread, and mostly unfossiliferous Cambrian and Lower Ordovician dolostones of the Appalachian region (e.g., the Copper Ridge dolomite) are certainly marine, and the lack of fossils in these is probably due to diagenesis. Furthermore, most marine organisms cannot survive in either brackish or hypersaline water. For this reason salt-bearing and gypsiferous shales are generally unfossiliferous. The Salina shale (Upper Silurian) of New York and the thick Ochoan Series (uppermost Permian) of West Texas and New Mexico are good examples.

Red color. Redbeds are treated separately in Chapter 12, but it may be noted here that they are generally unfossiliferous or include lenses of sandstone bearing terrestrial vertebrates or plant fossils. The red color is due to thorough oxidation and suggests an environment in which sediments are exposed to the atmosphere during deposition. Under such conditions organic remains of any kind are likely to decay and dissolve and so disappear. Such an oxidizing environment is widespread over well-drained floodplains but hardly exists in the sea, except at great depths and far from shore where deposition is extremely slow.

In the Bedford sandstone of Ohio (Lower Mississippian) Pepper, de Witt, and Demarest (1954, p. 45–58) recognized the structure of a great delta which they named the Red Bedford Delta. Its subaerial portion is marked by red color, channel sands, and abundant mudcracks; the contemporaneous shallow marine beds are gray and lack both channel sands and mudcracks.

Nevertheless, some highly fossiliferous marine formations are partly red, notably those that grade laterally into non-marine redbeds as the Sequatchie limestone (Upper Ordovician) grades eastward in East Tennessee into the Juniata redbeds. Such red marine deposits must have accumulated where red muds from the land were being carried into shallow sea in such volume that they could not be reduced before burial. While red color is much more common in non-marine than in marine deposits, therefore, it is not an absolute criterion.

Mud blebs (clay galls). Where balls of clay accumulate with gravel or coarse sand, they are squashed during settling and compaction and appear as mud blebs, or clay galls, in the resulting conglomerate. Such clay balls commonly form where meandering streams undercut floodplain deposits. As the banks cave, the sandy and silty layers quickly fall apart, but clay layers crumble into chunks with sufficient cohesion to roll along as pebbles. In a flooded stream these are likely to come to rest in the next gravel bar where they may be buried and preserved. If carried to the sea, however, such clay balls would be destroyed at the beach by the ceaseless agitation of the waves. On the sea floor itself, waves and currents erode by sublevation, picking up detrital particles individually; hence clay balls could hardly form there. Thus clay galls should be an excellent criterion of fluvial deposition. They might easily form, however, where submarine landslides give rise to turbidity currents; clay galls are common in the coarser parts of graded

beds and appear to be made of chips of the fine-grained part of the underlying layer.

Mudcracks. Mudcracks form in soft sediments containing clay minerals that shrink on desiccation. Normal mudcracks cannot form under standing water. They are widely distributed over floodplains and the subaerial parts of deltas and on the floors of pools or ponds or lakes that have dried up. They form less commonly on tidal mud flats, because periods of exposure are not ordinarily long enough to let the mud dry. In general, therefore, mudcracks are highly characteristic of non-marine environments (see Chapter 11, p. 199). They are common and widely distributed in redbeds such as the Mauch Chunk formation (Mississippian) and the Catskill facies of the Devonian in Pennsylvania, both of which show additional evidence of fluvial deposition.

Channel sands. Floodplain deposits normally include silt and clay spread widely beyond the channel during flood, and relatively linear bodies of sand or gravel representing the channel fill and natural levees (Figs. 18, 19, pp. 34 and 35). The channel sands normally show evidence of cut-and-fill and of irregular cross-lamination. In the sea, on the contrary, sand is normally spread in sheets, since there are no confining channels. Barrier beaches, however, as well as spits and bars are also linear and, where incompletely exposed, may resemble channel sands. The "shoestring sands" of the oil fields of Kansas, for example, have been interpreted by some as channel sands and by others as barrier beaches (p. 70).

Two criteria may distinguish channel sands from submarine bars. In the first place channel deposits normally rest unconformably upon and cut into the underlying finer-grained beds, whereas bars and barriers are built up by the waves above the adjacent sea floor. In the second place, channel deposits commonly include fossil driftwood or land animals, whereas bars and sand barriers commonly include the shells of marine animals.

Fisk and others (1954) have shown that, in the Birdfoot subdelta of the Mississippi, linear bodies of sand radiate like the veins of a leaf through the finer sediments of the delta (Fig. 31, p. 79). These are capped by the natural levees which are, of course, non-marine, but these are only a surface veneer; the bulk of each linear body of sand was formed by forward growth of the submarine lunate bar at the end of the distributary. Although formed below sealevel, the lunate bar is constantly bathed by the escaping fresh water so that few, if any, marine organisms can live on it. Such linear sand bodies may therefore retain little evidence of a marine environment.

Cross-stratification. Cross-stratification is one of the most obvious structural features of the coarser detrital rocks and has received the attention of many stratigraphers (p. 105). The many forms in which it appears should afford useful criteria for environments of deposition, but unfortunately we need many more critical observations on the production of cross-stratification in modern environments before it can be fully used in interpreting sedimentary rocks. Studies by Hack (1941), Bagnold (1941) and McKee (1938a, 1939, 1953) have made notable advances but, as McKee observes, there is still much to be done.

Perhaps the wedge type of cross-stratification seen in dunes is most distinctive (Fig. 14, p. 22). It normally occurs on a large scale with sets of cross-strata intersecting one another in several directions and without any normal horizontal layers. Such wind-blown deposits are, of course, non-marine, but they may form in several distinct environments. Dunes are characteristic of desert areas far from sea, but they also form along sandy shores (as on Cape Cod and in the Netherlands) where rainfall is plentiful. A large area of dunes forms the Sand Hills of central Nebraska and another lies along the east side of Lake Michigan. Calcareous dune sands are common along many shores in the tropics. Fine examples of ancient dune sands may be seen in the Navajo sandstone (Jurassic) and the Coconino sandstone (Permian) of the Colorado Plateau (McKee, 1945b) and in the Lower Bunter sandstones (Triassic) of the Birmingham region, England (Shotton, 1937). The exposed bedrock of the Bermuda Islands consists entirely of calcareous dune sands blown together during a low stand of sealevel during Pleistocene time.

Size-sorting. In general marine sediments are better sorted than fluvial deposits. With local exceptions near the shore, marine currents sweep the bottom gently and are aided by the lift of passing waves. This gives time and maximum opportunity for size-sorting. On the contrary much of the transportation by streams is accomplished in brief periods of flood. Here current velocity varies rapidly and irregularly depending on the configuration of the channel, and it fluctuates from hour to hour with the flood stage. Sand and gravel are commonly rushed along rapidly for a brief period and then allowed to settle quickly until the next flood, escaping the ceaseless agitation that the waves produce on the sea floor.

Nevertheless, the clay and silt that settles from suspension over the floodplain may be well size-sorted and evenly laminated. Probably no stream-deposited sand is as cleanly sorted and even-grained as a normal marine sand, and no ordinary marine sediment as poorly sorted as an alluvial fan or a stream-channel deposit, but between these extremes there are many deposits in which the degree of sorting would not be a definitive criterion—at least not in the present state of our knowledge.

Clay mineral composition. Recent studies by Millot (1949), Grim, Dietz, and Bradley (1949), Van Houten (1953), and others, suggest that the composition of the clay minerals will give valuable clues to the environment of deposition of sediments. The literature on the clay minerals, especially those in soils, is vast, and in recent years considerable attention has been directed to both recent and ancient sedimentary deposits. The problem is complex, however, and little more than a beginning has been made in the application of the technique. Present knowledge has been effectively summarized by Grim (1953).

The chief types of clay minerals found in sediments are illite, montmorillonite, and kaolinite, each of which may result from the weathering of many kinds of rock. Whether at a given place one or another will form depends in part on the source rock but even more on the chemical environment. Furthermore, after its formation, one may be altered to another if the chemical environment changes in certain respects.

From the point of view of criteria of environments, the significant fact is that in the marine en-

vironment kaolinite tends to disappear by alteration into montmorillonite or illite, so that in a
general way kaolinite-rich clay is characteristic
of non-marine and illite-rich clay of marine deposits.   This generalization is altogether too
sweeping to be applied to specific cases, however.
Thus Millot (1949) found that kaolinite was
lacking in some marine sediments but present in
others and in one sample constituted 50 percent
of the clay.   Grim, Dietz, and Bradley (1949)
found that marine bottom cores off the California
coast all contained mixtures of illite, montmorillonite, and kaolinite but that illite was generally
most abundant and kaolinite least abundant, and
they concluded that kaolinite "is slowly lost during diagenesis under marine conditions."   Clearly
the percentage of kaolinite remaining in a marine
clay may vary widely, depending on the rapidity
with which it is introduced and the local environment.   No definite ratio of kaolinite to montmoril-

lonite and illite can be used, therefore, as a criterion of marine or non-marine deposition, but
where a given stream, as in a delta, is dropping
part of its load on the subaerial surface and
carrying the rest to the sea, there should be an
appreciable drop in the proportion of kaolinite in
the clay fraction at the shore line.   K. M. Waagé
(personal communication) has found this an extremely useful criterion in locating the boundary
between contemporaneous marine and non-marine
parts of the Dakota sandstone group (Cretaceous).

Still further caution is needed, however, since
even slightly saline lakes may act like sea water
in altering kaolinite to montmorillonite and illite.
Thus Keller (1953) has found that certain zones
in the Morrison formation (Jurassic) are rich in
kaolinite and others in illite and montmorillonite,
although the whole of the Morrison is regarded as
non-marine.

4. Mixed environments

THE ZONE where land and sea meet is an area of maximum geographic complexity, where many different kinds of processes operate. Deposits in this zone show the imprint of these different processes, commonly as a confusing mixture of the criteria ordinarily supposed to indicate marine or non-marine deposition. But if they are rightly interpreted, such deposits can provide a maximum of paleogeographic information.

The shore, or the littoral zone, is normally defined as the area between the extreme low and high (storm) tide lines, the area that is alternately land and sea. Sometimes the term beach is defined in the same way, but more usually it means a deposit on the shore or (taken still more narrowly to exclude tidal flats) a sandy or gravelly deposit on a shore open to the waves. For the student of sediments, however, not all "shore" deposition takes place between the tidal limits; that is, shore processes strongly condition some deposition above the high tide line, as on sand dunes behind a beach, and especially below the low tide line, as in lagoons behind barrier beaches or in river estuaries, where tidal currents directed by the shape of the shore play an important part. Above all, in the marine delta the actually littoral sediments are an insignificant part of the total deposit, yet it is the presence of the shore, checking the current of the incoming river, that is ultimately responsible for the entire edifice. In discussing the environments transitional between the marine and the non-marine, therefore, we can by no means confine ourselves to the area between high and low tide.

The genetic classification of shorelines has been carried far by the geomorphologists, but in the study of the mixed environments of deposition what is significant, as for marine and non-marine environments, is the general geographic setting and the processes that are dominant, not the origin of the shoreline. The main agents and some of the depositional environments they dominate are: waves and the longshore currents they induce (cliffed shores, beaches), tides and tidal currents (tidal flats and lagoons, estuaries), silt-laden rivers (marine deltas), and organisms (organic reefs).

ENVIRONMENTS DOMINATED BY WAVES

Cliffed Shore Environment

A cliffed shore in hard rock is hardly likely to be the site of much deposition. Nevertheless, a talus or a narrow boulder beach may form, and the material worn from the cliffs accumulates especially as pocket beaches between the headlands (though even here a large part of the material may be derived rather from the alluvium of the valleys between the headlands). Despite the intrinsic unlikelihood of preservation in such localities, a few deposits of just this nature are

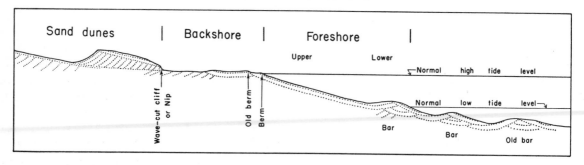

Figure 26. Diagram of a beach and its parts. Length of area shown, several hundred feet; vertical exaggeration about twice.

known in the geologic record; for example, the talus or boulder beach material at the base of the Cambrian Tapeats sandstone in the Grand Canyon of Arizona (Sharp, 1940, p. 1253, 1263), where the Cambrian sea, advancing over the nearly peneplaned continent, encountered monadnocks of resistant rock. Similar deposits are known on the same unconformity in Missouri (Bridge, 1930, p. 64–66), Wisconsin (Weidman, 1904, p. 91–92), and Minnesota (Fig. 85, p. 171).

Where waves attack a high shore made of weak rock, such as friable sandstone or till, much more material is supplied in a unit of time and deposits are more likely. The coarser material, gravel (if it is present) and sand, accumulates to form a beach, narrow around the headlands but wider in the re-entrants or across alluvial patches between the higher parts of the shore. If longshore currents are consistent in direction, the sand may migrate considerable distances along shore, perhaps entirely out of the source area into a low shore environment.

On the beach near the source cliffs, the sorting, rounding, and mineral content of the sand and gravel are rather heterogeneous, if the source was heterogeneous, but downcurrent the sorting and rounding improve and non-resistant materials decrease (probably exponentially) as the materials are reworked and transported by the waves. Some shape-sorting of pebbles and sand also goes on, but it appears to differ from locality to locality, for on some beaches spherical particles become dominant, on others relatively flat ones; moreover the lithology of the pebbles, especially planes of weakness, strongly influences the re-

sult. If the material is transported out of the source area, it may then come to resemble beach deposits produced entirely in the low shore environment, though it may remain somewhat more heterogeneous.

Low Open Shore (Beach) Environment

If strong waves beat on a low shore, unless very large quantities of material are constantly supplied by a great river, they produce a continuous line of wide beaches; if the shore had a gentle enough slope to begin with, these will be barrier beaches. Such beaches line almost the entire Atlantic Coast of the United States from the tip of Cape Cod to the tip of Florida. Similar beaches follow the south shore of the Baltic and North Seas along the lowland of Poland, north Germany, and the Netherlands, and also the coast of southwestern France and elsewhere where alluvial plains front open water, except close to the mouths of the greater rivers.

Beaches have been much studied, in America notably by the Beach Erosion Board of the U. S. Army Engineers, in whose technical reports and memoranda has been published much of the best scientific work done on beach and shore processes. The typical beach (Fig. 26) is divided into the relatively smooth sloping *foreshore,* which extends from lowest low water to a normally well-marked break in slope, called the *berm,* at about normal high water, and the rougher but relatively flat *backshore,* extending from the berm back to the farthest point reached by waves, which in natural conditions is commonly the base of a sea cliff or nip or the edge of a beach ridge or a line of sand dunes. Berms are mainly built during storms, and the bigger the storm the higher and more marked the berm; indeed, if a beach has experienced a series of storms of diminishing intensity, it may exhibit several berms, though the lower ones will be destroyed in the next great storm. The foreshore can commonly be further divided into the upper foreshore, which has a smooth profile, and the lower foreshore, which is broken by bars formed by the breakers at high stands of tide; similar bars may be present beyond low tide level, and the outer limit of the foreshore is not a line of major discontinuity. As with berms, the heaviest storms build the biggest bars and the farthest to sea, destroying all older bars; later weaker storms, or simply steady breakers of relatively constant size, can build smaller bars farther in, so that a given beach may have one bar one month and three or four another.

Except for the bars, the slope of the foreshore is a very shallow curve, slightly concave upward and flattening outward into the shelf profile (p. 128). Its slope is governed by a number of factors; in general it is steeper if the material is coarse, if the shore is fully open to ocean waves, if the regimen of the sea includes heavy storms (and it is steeper right after heavy storms than after periods of ordinary weather), and perhaps also if the tidal range is high, provided tidal flats do not form. It does not appear to depend at all on the original slope of the terrain, and it is considerably steeper than the slope of most plains or continental shelves; hence if a shift in sealevel brings the shore onto such a plain or shelf, the waves gouge and build where they break until they have fashioned the proper beach profile, thus producing a barrier beach with an eroded zone in front and a lagoon or salt marsh behind. Relative to the rest of the over-all profile, this somewhat steeper part at the shore is called the *shore face*.

The material on such a beach is mostly or entirely sand. Finer materials are winnowed out by the waves and carried either into deep water or into protected bays and lagoons; gravel-size material, except for broken shells which are quickly worn down, is rarely available on low shores. At any one state of the waves, the size-sorting is apt to be excellent, each size having its appropriate station on the beach; but with alternating storm and calm, adjacent laminae commonly have rather different sizes, and the over-all sorting is only moderately good. Ordinarily the more resistant minerals, above all quartz, are concentrated on the beach, but there are many exceptions where non-resistant minerals are common or even dominant, as for instance where waves are relatively weak or have been at work only a short time or where quartz is uncommon or even lacking in the source area. Many Pacific islands have no quartz, and their beaches consist of calcite and aragonite grains, commonly fragments of shells and tests of foraminifera, of fragments of basalt, or of augite or olivine grains. Heavy resistant minerals, like ilmenite, magnetite, and zircon, are commonly sorted out from the quartz or other light minerals and concentrated in separated layers; on the Atlantic beaches of the southeastern United States, especially on older beaches now well above sealevel, commercial deposits of zircon and monazite have thus been formed. The coarser sand grains may be well rounded, but there seem to be as many exceptions as examples for this generalization. Shells may be present in abundance, and, of course, some beaches are made entirely of shell fragments, but on the whole potential fossils are relatively rare in the final deposits of normal quartz-sand beaches.

The stratification of beach deposits has been studied particularly by Thompson (1937) and by McKee (1953, p. 4–16). It differs markedly from one part of the beach to another. The upper foreshore has the most regular bedding, with long even laminae and cross-laminae exhibiting ordinarily only rather low-angle cross-stratification, commonly with a herringbone arrangement. The general dip is seaward at varying angles; the laminae may appear especially even and parallel in sections parallel to the shoreline, unless the beach is cusped. The lower foreshore with its bars is much more strongly cross-stratified, with cut-and-fill cross-bedding dipping both landward and seaward. The backshore is the most irregular; some beds show gentle even cross-stratification like that of the upper foreshore, but obvious cut-and-fill cross-bedding is also common, and patches of much disturbed sand and even lenses of silt or clay may be present. The dips of the cross-strata are irregular but most commonly are landward.

If material is being added to a beach by long-shore currents or otherwise, the foreshore slope tends to remain nearly constant but the backshore widens as the beach advances seaward. As the landward parts of the backshore cease to be reached even by storm waves, beach ridges form parallel to the shore, marking the stages in the advance. If much material is available, as where streams contribute much sediment but the waves are strong enough to prevent delta formation, a wide belt of beach ridges may be formed; small ponds or swamps may be left between them. Almost invariably the wind becomes an important agent in these ridges, unless they are of gravel, and the belt behind the beach becomes a belt of sand dunes. If the supply of sand is large, the sand dunes may migrate inland and bury old lagoons, floodplain deposits, or whatever lies in their path.

The deposits of such sand dunes do not differ greatly from those of a desert except for their restriction to a belt just inland from a beach. The sand is normally considerably better size-sorted than on the beach and notably rounder, perhaps as much because round grains are selectively transported from the backshore by the wind as because of increased wear. Strong wedge-shaped cross-bedding is the rule. Lenses of silt and clay or even peat record lagoons or inter-ridge lakes and swamps buried by the dunes.

Unequivocal beach deposits do not appear to be common in the geologic record. Late Cenozoic beaches are known in several areas where beaches are forming today; Thompson (1937) describes some in California, and the ancient zirconiferous beaches of the southern Atlantic States are well known, though not well described in the literature. Bass (1934) has described the shoestring oil and gas sands of Greenwood and Butler Counties, Kansas, as being beach deposits of the Pennsylvanian sea, because they are fairly straight in plan and lens-shaped in cross-section, with the upper surface convex and the lower plane. Their rather high silt content (roughly 25 percent) is surprising, however. Rich (1923, 1926, and discussion in Bass, 1934) has discussed other shoestring sands in Kansas, of which some may

be old beach deposits but others may be the deposits of delta distributaries or tidal channels. The Second Berea sand (Lower Mississippian) of southeastern Ohio has been identified by Pepper, de Witt, and Demarest (1954, p. 54–56) as a large barrier beach formed along the east side of the Red Bedford Delta (p. 88, and Fig. 36, p. 87).

Certain sheets of clean sand in the Paleozoic section of the eastern United States may be partly beach deposits. The Whirlpool sandstone (basal Silurian) at Niagara Falls shows rill marks and other beach structures; it lies at the base of the thin northwestern edge of a vast sheet of clean quartz sandstone and conglomerate (Clinch, Tuscarora, Shawangunk) that extends along the Appalachians from eastern Tennessee to eastern New York, representing the return of the sea over the continental Upper Ordovician Queenston-Juniata redbeds and, farther east, over the eroded edges of Middle Ordovician rocks folded in the Taconian orogeny. How much of this sheet of sandstone was finally deposited in a beach environment is unknown, but its purity suggests long winnowing by competent agents like waves, whether at the shore or in shallow water offshore. A similar case might be made out for the Oriskany sandstone (Devonian) of New York and Pennsylvania and the St. Peter sandstone (Ordovician) of the Mississippi Valley, both of which represent marine transgression after a period of emergence and some erosion (Dapples, 1955, discusses the St. Peter). Parts of the St. Peter have been claimed as sand dune deposits, because of the fine size-sorting, rounding, and ground-glass surface texture, and quite possibly much of the rest of it accumulated first in dunes and was then reworked by the advancing sea. Except for the Whirlpool sandstone, however, probably most of each of these sheets of sandstone was finally laid in place under a shallow sea rather than between the tides (p. 50).

ENVIRONMENTS DOMINATED BY TIDES

Tidal Flat Environment

Large tidal flats occur on coasts where much silt and clay is brought into the sea by rivers and where the tidal range is high, and along those parts of such coasts where the waves are unable to beat in full strength against the shore. For example, along the China coast near the mouth of the Yangtze River (Fig. 34, p. 83), the tidal range is 10 feet or more and the sea is turbid with mud from the river. Here tidal flats cover hundreds of square miles; they are found in virtually every bay and strait in the rugged Chusan Archipelago and along the adjacent mainland coast south of the mouth of the river, except that in those bays that face east into the open waters of the East China Sea there are normal sand beaches. In the more indented and protected bays, the flats are 3 or 4 miles wide and slope evenly and very gently from the sea wall that protects the cultivated alluvial flats at the bayheads to the low water mark, and indeed the slope continues seaward into the bays. In the less indented bays or on the sides of straits, wherever major tidal currents sweep by, the tidal flat has the same low slope near the seawall, but at its outer end it is truncated by tidal scour, the bottom dropping off rapidly from mid-tide level or above into several fathoms of water. On the otherwise smooth surface of the tidal flat, meandering tidal channels that bring tide water in and out are normally incised.

The tidal flat sediments that partially fill the Waddenzee, a large shore lagoon behind barrier beaches along the northwest coast of Germany and in the northern part of the Netherlands (Fig. 33, p. 82), have been described by Häntzschel (1939) and by van Straaten (1954). Van Straaten found two principal types of deposits between mean high and mean low tide, one along the main tidal channels and one on the high unbroken flats between. The sides of the main tidal channels are scored with many gullies that help to bring the water onto and drain it off the main flats with each tide. Channels and gullies tend to shift laterally, and sediment is deposited relatively rapidly in the abandoned portions or along banks from which the channel or gully is receding. This sediment is generally fine grained and none too well sorted, but distinctly laminated, with alternating commonly thinly lenticular laminae of silty clay and silty sand (Fig. 27A); because of the rapid deposition, the lamination is not de-stroyed by burrowing worms. Mussels form large beds on the flats between the gullies, and their shells accumulate in the bottoms of the gullies where they are covered up as the gully shifts. Thus deposits near the channels come to consist of relatively fine-grained sediment with good though somewhat lenticular lamination and a few shell layers.

On the higher flats deposition is much slower and hardly exceeds the rate of relative rise of sealevel in the area. As a result, the finer mud tends to be winnowed out by the repeated flood and ebb, and only coarse silt and fine sand remains. This material is well laminated when deposited, but because deposition is slow the laminae are soon disturbed or destroyed by the innumerable burrowing organisms and replaced by a contorted streaking (Fig. 27B).

Near the landward edge of the flats, especially close to mean high tide and between that and extreme high tide, salt grasses are able to take hold; they trap sediment and quickly build the flat up into a salt marsh, commonly barely awash at high tide but seamed with little tidal creeks kept stable by the vegetation and bordered by natural levees. The sediment here accumulates more rapidly than on the high flats until extreme high tide is reached, and it shows fairly even laminae, alternately of sand and silty clay (Fig. 27B, top). In areas where sediment is less abundant, considerable bodies of salt-water peat may form. As in the high flats, the ultimate thickness of the deposit (and indeed of the whole complex of tidal-flat deposits) is determined by the rate of subsidence of the area or the rise of sealevel.

The main tidal channels of the Wadden Zee and similar tidal flats extend below low tide level, and hence they are not strictly part of the tidal flat. Their sediments are deposited in strong currents and show coarser bedding than the tidal-flat deposits, and also prominent ripple marks and cross-bedding. They lace through the tidal-flat deposit just as the channel deposits in a large floodplain wind through the fine-grained interchannel deposits.

Van Straaten compares the tidal-flat sediments of the Wadden Zee with the Psammites du Condroz (Devonian) of the Belgian Ardennes, which show many of the same sedimentary details (Fig.

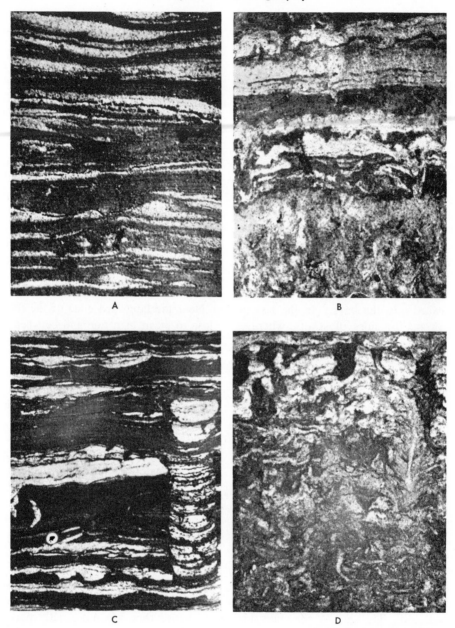

Figure 27. Mudflat sediments, recent and ancient. From van Straaten (1954); A originally from Häntzschel (1939). A. Recent deposit from low mud flat, north of Wilhelmshafen, Germany. B. Recent deposit from high mud flat, overlain by salt marsh deposit, north of Groningen, the Netherlands. C. Devonian sandy shale, Yvoir, Belgium. D. Devonian argillaceous sandstone, Yvoir, Belgium.

27C, D). He suggests, however, that, though some of the Psammites du Condroz may be tidal-flat sediments, a larger part was more probably deposited in a shallow shore lagoon like those parts of the Wadden Zee now below the low tide mark. Few other ancient tidal-flat sediments have been reported. Richter (1931) has suggested a very shallow-water or tidal-flat origin for the black well-laminated Hunsrückschiefer (Devonian) of the Rhineland (p. 205). Possible tidal-flat sediments in the United States are the thinly laminated, strongly mudcracked, very clayey limestones of the upper Silurian of the central Appalachians and New York (parts of the Tonoloway and Manlius limestones, etc.), but proof is lacking.

Shore Lagoon Environment

Where barrier beaches form, lagoons form behind them, as on virtually all the coasts listed above as showing beaches (p. 68). If there is any tide at all, considerable bodies of water must sweep in and out of these lagoons every day, through whatever channels remain in the barrier beach. Within the lagoon, with its negligible waves, any fine sediment suspended in the water brought in by the tidal currents has a chance to settle out, and hence these lagoons become the resting place for much of the fine material that the waves have winnowed from the sand they have shaped into beaches.

An excellent example of such a lagoon, Barataria Bay on the Mississippi Delta (Fig. 29, p. 77) has been studied by Krumbein and his associates (summarized by Krumbein, 1939). In the larger shallower part of the bay, rather ill-sorted silt or very fine sand is being deposited, but in the deeper channels, through which the tidal waters move in and out, somewhat coarser better-sorted sand is present; these channels are very similar, of course, to the main tidal channels of a tidal flat. There is less than half a percent of organic matter in the coarser sand, more (up to $7\frac{1}{2}$ percent, but mostly 1 or 2 percent) in the silt. Except in the most protected areas, not much clay is present. The close correlation between depth, grain size, sorting, and (inversely) organic content is notable. Krumbein does not discuss the bedding of the deposits; in rather finer and more organic lagoonal deposits McKee (1953, p. 39) found, surprisingly, no visible stratification, except where lenses of sand and broken shells may represent former channels. Fairly regular lamination might be present, however, in the more silty deposits, and the sandy channel deposits would show coarser bedding and cross-stratification.

The depositional pattern in such a lagoon resembles that on a tidal flat, and in a broad way that on a floodplain also; of course, a marginal lagoon may in time fill up and become a tidal flat. Criteria to show that the fine-grained deposits were marine, tidal, or non-marine (p. 62) would help to distinguish these environments. A further criterion of the lagoon might be close association with the relatively coarse deposits of a barrier beach (and its dunes), which would abut against and might interfinger with the fine silt of the protected bay, provided the beach deposits were preserved at all. Pamlico Sound in North Carolina, however, is 20 miles wide behind its barrier beach (ignoring the embayed rivers that penetrate still farther inland); deposition in such a "lagoon" approaches that in any marine bay.

Shepard and Moore (1955a) have described in detail the sediments of part of the almost continuous shore lagoon along the Texas coast of the Gulf of Mexico. The part they studied lies between major passes and shows only a few distinct sandy channels; the sediments are chiefly silty clay in the central parts of the lagoon (depths from 5 to 12 feet) and become sandier toward the shore in most directions. In addition, the sediment pattern is diversified by many large oyster reefs and areas of reef debris. Shepard and Moore recognize eight different subenvironments within the lagoon, each characterized by such sediment properties as size, composition (reef or terrigenous), and fossils (especially forams and ostracodes). Moreover, drilling showed that about the first 50 feet of sediment beneath the floor of the lagoon was deposited under very similar conditions, behind a barrier beach.

As noted above, van Straaten (1954) interprets the larger part of the Psammites du Condroz of Belgium as the deposit of a shore lagoon. Similar deposits ought to be preserved also in the Cenozoic around the Gulf of Mexico, especially in ancient Mississippi deltas (p. 86). Bass (1934, p. 1345) was unable to recognize any lagoon deposits behind his Pennsylvanian barrier beaches (p. 70).

Estuary Environment

The term estuary, as here used, refers to a river mouth, commonly wide and funnel-shaped, in which the tide causes daily reversals of the river current. The river may have been drowned, but not all drowned rivers need have estuaries. The word has also been used much more broadly for any river mouth or river-mouth district (or even for large enclosed bodies of shallow sea such as Chesapeake Bay); such a usage appears to be preserved in the name of the Estuarine Series (Jurassic) of England, which is evidently a deltaic deposit.

Though the world's largest rivers have generally formed typical marine deltas, many fairly large ones have estuaries, or mouths with some features of both. North American estuaries include the Columbia and the Delaware, and perhaps also the Hudson, though the extreme length of the tidal Hudson (150 miles) and the bottleneck of the Highlands make it very unusual. The Río de la Plata in South America is the estuary of the Uruguay River; the Paraná appears to maintain a delta on the side of the estuary. In Europe, the Gironde, the Loire, the Weser, and the Elbe may be mentioned, and also the Thames and the Severn. The estuary of the Severn was described long ago by Sollas (1883); no better description of a modern estuary and its deposits has come to our attention.

The essential feature of an estuary, as here defined, is that tidal currents are more effective than the river current in distributing sediment at the river mouth. As a result, incoming sediment is swept back and forth repeatedly, presumably inching its way slowly downchannel. On the way it accumulates in streamlined silt and sand bars or islands between the main threads of the tidal currents; bars and channels shift their position from time to time. The material in the estuary depends, of course, on the material contributed by the river; in most cases it appears to be largely silt and fine sand. (That some sediment comes from the seaward side was proved by Sollas for the Severn, but it need not be very much.) Presumably coarser materials would be concentrated in the channels and finer on the bars, but a sharp distinction between channels and intermediate flats, as in the tidal flat and lagoon, would be unlikely. If those environments resemble floodplains in pattern, the estuarine environment resembles the braided river.

By the nature of the estuary, permanent deposits would be minor as compared with a marine delta, unless they were trapped by special local subsidence. The tidal currents would tend to keep the material in transport until it could finally escape from the estuary altogether and be deposited under entirely marine conditions beyond their sphere of influence. In fact, no authenticated deposits of an estuary, as the term is used here, are known in the geologic record.

MARINE DELTA ENVIRONMENT

In the great marine deltas the littoral zone reaches its maximum breadth. Here shallow shore lagoons and salt-water marshes alternate with land areas over a belt that may be 25 to 30 miles wide. In plan, marine and non-marine deposits are intimately interlocked, and in vertical section they normally are deeply intertongued because the shoreline has shifted in and out during deposition. Although a very large part of the delta is made of entirely marine or entirely non-marine beds, these are so intimately associated with each other and with littoral deposits that all must be considered parts of a genetic whole.

Great rivers naturally flow toward subsiding areas; hence their deltas may grow to great thickness and will have the maximum chance of permanent preservation. They therefore form an important part of the stratigraphic record.

Parts of the Marine Delta

In his classic study of marine delta deposits, Barrell (1912) recognized the same elements that were defined by Gilbert (1890) for the small lake delta (p. 40, and Fig. 21. p. 41), but he showed that the relative importance of topset, foreset, and bottomset beds may be very different in the two kinds of deltas. In particular, the topsets are much more important and complex in a marine delta. In a small lake, where waves are weak and currents negligible, the bottom load of the stream is dropped at once on reaching standing water, and it accumulates at the angle of repose to form a steep foreset slope. As long as lake level remains constant, the delta builds out instead of up and the topset beds remain a thin veneer, liable to be completely eroded. In the sea, on the other hand, waves and currents work to slice off the exposed part of the delta and to spread the resulting sediment under water, building out the neritic zone as a shallow *subaqueous topset plain*. Thus the topset area of a marine delta consists of two parts, one subaerial and the other subaqueous, both sloping very gently seaward. They are separated by the shore face or foreshore slope carved by the waves (Fig. 35, p. 85, and p. 68). The subaqueous topset plain is built out to the depth at which the waves and currents lose the power to transport sediment on the bottom. Beyond this lies the foreset slope over which finer sediment settles out of suspension. Unlike the steep foreset slope of the small delta built into quiet water, the foreset slope in the marine delta is gentle, yet it may extend down into the bathyal zone.

The great streams that build marine deltas break up into several or many distributaries before reaching the sea. Each of these tends to build a fingerlike salient at the delta front. They are opposed by the waves and currents, which tend to cut back the salients, carrying the finer material seaward and shifting the sand laterally to form spits and bars across interdistributary basins, thus straightening the shoreline. The result of this struggle differs widely among deltas, depending on whether local conditions permit the river or the sea to dominate. In this regard the deltas of the Nile and the Mississippi stand at opposite extremes.

Nile Delta

The delta of the Nile is the classic example to which the name was first applied and, as befits a type, it is almost ideal in its symmetry and structure (Fig. 28). Distributaries begin near Cairo, more than 100 miles inland, and fan out seaward over a great triangle whose base extends about 150 miles along the shore. The shoreline indeed is remarkably simple. Beyond the shore face lies the shallow subaqueous topset plain, which slopes scarcely 5 feet per mile for the first 15 to 25 miles and then gradually steepens out to the break in slope, 35 to 45 miles from shore and about 300 feet deep. Beyond

this lies the foreset slope, which descends for the next 20 miles at 100 to 150 feet per mile and forms a broad bulge on the floor of the Mediterranean.

These relations are shown in the profiles beneath the map (Fig. 28). Profile A follows the 31st meridian across the middle of the delta from near Cairo (C) to the floor of the Mediterranean. Profile B follows the 29th meridian, which lies west of the delta and shows the normal contour of the continental margin. Subsidence has accompanied accumulation in this area, so that the floor under the delta has some such position as the dashed profile; it may be deeper but is probably no shallower. The shaded area on the diagram thus represents a vertical median section through the delta and shows its lenticular form. In these profiles the vertical scale is greatly exaggerated; the true proportions are shown in solid black at the bottom of the figure.

The land surface of the delta is almost flat and is largely covered for a short time each year by the floodwaters of the Nile, which spread over it a thin layer of silty mud. This annual "gift of the Nile" has kept the area fertile during the thousands of years of human occupation. Excavations at Memphis, a short distance above Cairo, have shown that about 9 feet of river-borne sediment has accumulated there during the 3,000 years since the statue of Rameses II was erected.

Mississippi Delta

Pattern of growth. The delta of the Mississippi River is roughly the same size as that of the Nile but differs in several important respects. Its structure, method of growth, and recent history are perhaps better known than those of any other great delta (Trowbridge, 1930; Russell, 1936; Russell and Russell, 1939; Fisk, 1944; Fisk, McFarlan, Kolb, and Wilbert, 1954). Fisk's monograph of 1944 sets forth the results of extensive geologic and engineering research done for the Mississippi River Commission of the U. S. Army Engineers.

Unlike the Nile, which once a year spreads widely across the whole of its subaerial delta plain, the Mississippi River is confined to its channel except in very unusual floods until it has

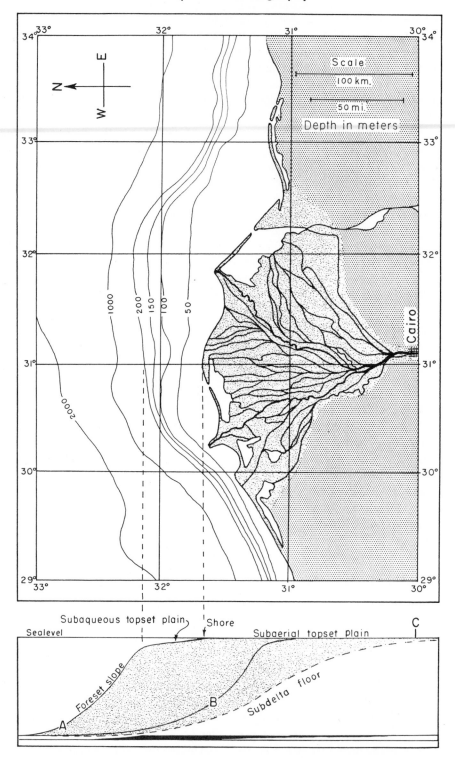

Figure 28. The Nile Delta. Map: subaerial part of delta shown by darker shading, subaqueous part by submarine contours (depths in meters). Cross sections: profile A along 31st meridian in center of delta—shading shows probable thickness of delta sediment (upper section exaggerated about 80 times; lower section nearly true scale); profile B along 29th meridian west of delta.

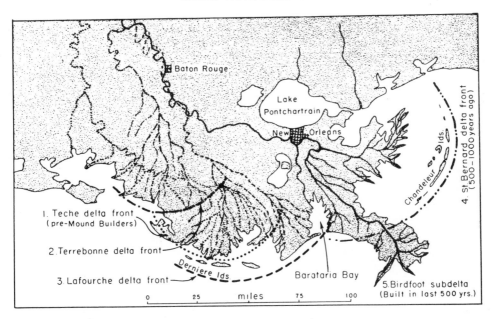

Figure 29. The Mississippi Delta and its five most recent subdeltas. Adapted from Fisk (1944).

passed New Orleans, more than 100 miles below the head of the delta. Even below New Orleans about 85 percent of the water is confined to the main channel as far as Head of Passes, far out near the front of the Birdfoot subdelta, where the river splits into three main distributaries (Fig. 30). By thus concentrating on a small sector of the delta front, the river has rapidly built out the great salient known as the Balize or Birdfoot subdelta, most of which has formed within the last 500 years.

This has long been the habit of growth of the Mississippi Delta. After one sector is built far out, the entire flow of the river is shifted to some other sector and the process is repeated there. Figure 29 shows the sequence of subdeltas that have succeeded one another in Late Pleistocene and Recent time, as worked out by Russell (1936) and by Fisk (1944) and his colleagues. Fisk and others (1952) have shown that in another couple of decades the Mississippi will shift again unless man intervenes, this time to the present course of the Atchafalaya River (between the old Teche and Terrebonne channels).

Stage of active growth. The growing Bird-foot delta (Fig. 30A) illustrates the stage of active growth of the Mississippi Delta. It forms a rather simple bulge, mainly under water and extending some 50 miles out onto the continental shelf. Its total area is 700 square miles, but the highly irregular land area occupies only about one-fifth of that. The subaqueous topset plain extends out to about the 60-foot contour; it is some 15 miles wide on the west and even wider on the east but narrow on the front where forward growth is most rapid. The foreset slope descends from 60 to 250 or 300 feet within 5 or 10 miles. The subaerial topset plain is nowhere more than 5 or 6 feet above sealevel and consists of the natural levees (solid black on Fig. 30), together with the intervening marshes, lakes, and lagoons.

Figure 30B shows the distribution of different kinds of sediment in part of the same area. The natural levees are about 1,000 feet wide and 5 to 6 feet high in the vicinity of Head of Passes; they consist of fine sand dropped as the floodwater spreads beyond the channels. Because they develop progressively as the channels lengthen, they are both lower and narrower toward the ends of the passes, beyond which they are extended by underwater bars. Beyond the jetties, where the stream meets salt water, the channels become shallower, and the coarser sand soon comes to

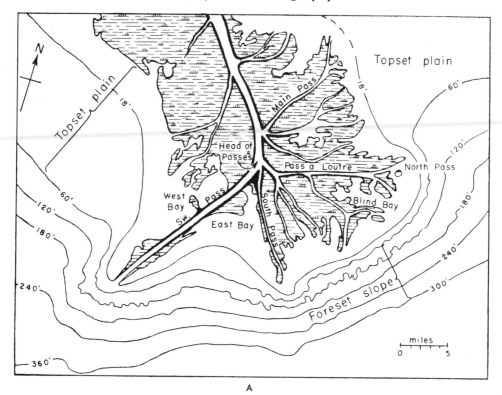

A

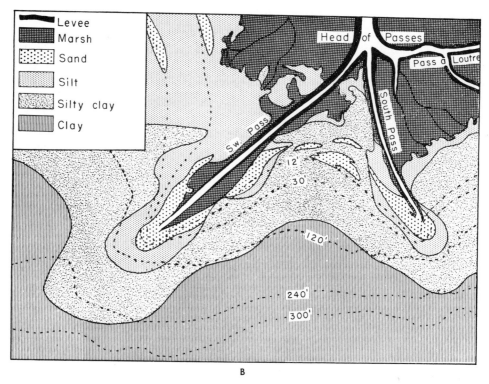

B

Figure 30.   Birdfoot subdelta of the Mississippi, after Fisk and others (1954).   A. Outer part of subdelta; submarine contours show depths in feet.   B. Distribution of different sizes of sediment on southwest side of subdelta.

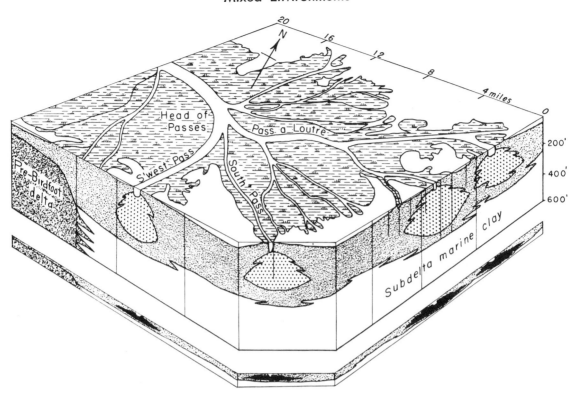

Figure 31. Block diagram of the Birdfoot subdelta, modified from Fisk and others (1954). Linear sand bodies made by main distributaries shown in open stipple on main diagram (vertical exaggeration about 30), in black on cross section below (vertical exaggeration about 5).

rest in the form of *lunate bars* about the ends of the distributaries. Finer sand is carried farther forward, grading downslope into silt. In this way long ridges are built forward under water on which the distributaries advance. Waves and currents shift some of the sand back alongside the ends of the natural levees in the form of spits, and also spread the silt and some of the clay into the interdistributary embayments while carrying the finer clay out to greater depths.

The distribution of sediment according to grain size does not correspond very closely with depth (Fig. 30B). At the end of each distributary, much of the sand is carried forward over the lunate bar to a depth of 30 feet, where it spreads over an area 2 or 3 miles wide. Silt spreads still farther out and down to a depth of more than 100 feet in front of each distributary. As the natural levees grow forward they form a thin veneer over the lunate-bar sands. The relations in cross section are shown in Figure 31. Russell and Rus-

sell (1939) have aptly compared such delta deposits to a pile of leaves, in which the slender fingers of sand built out along the distributaries are the veins of the leaves.

Later stages of development. Comparison of the Birdfoot subdelta with successively older subdeltas shows the important changes that ensue after the stream abandons a subdelta and surrenders it to the attack of the sea. Between 500 and 1,000 years ago the St. Bernard subdelta (Fig. 29) extended eastward even beyond the line of the present Chandeleur Islands. Since being abandoned by the river, it has been largely drowned, and the advancing sea has reworked the sand of the outer distributaries and thrown it up to form the curving barrier of the Chandeleur Islands. The lagoon behind has widened and deepened during subsidence to form Chandeleur Sound. In the normal course of events, if subsidence is not too rapid, the sand barrier will be prograded closer and closer to shore and eventually will be transformed into an ordinary beach along a straight shoreline.

Such an evolution can actually be traced in the older subdeltas. On the Lafourche subdelta, which is next older than the St. Bernard, the Derniere Islands represent the sand barrier formed by the sea; they are much closer to shore than the Chandeleur Islands and, to the east, they are continued in the smoothly curving beach along the shore west of Barataria Bay. The still older Terrebonne subdelta was largely buried by the Lafourche subdelta, but toward the west its long sandy beach is exposed, suggesting that its barrier had already reached the shore. The even older Teche subdelta is both largely drowned and largely covered by the Terrebonne subdelta.

It is noteworthy that all these subdeltas, save the one now rapidly growing, show evidence of drowning, presumably because of slow subsidence of the whole delta area, compaction of the recently accumulated sediments, or both. In any event the sea has advanced as much as 20 to 30 miles across what was previously land surface and has reworked and redistributed the upper parts of the great fingers of sand, the veins of the leaf, that run through the topset beds. The extensive sandy bottom about the Chandeleur Islands indicates that they have there been transformed into a sheetlike bed of marine sand.

Comparison with the Nile Delta. Although the Nile Delta has not been studied in such detail, clearly its growth has been much more symmetrical than that of the Mississippi Delta and has followed a different pattern. The reason apparently lies in the different regimens of the two great rivers, for marine conditions are somewhat comparable—the tides are so small as to be negligible on both shores, and neither is exposed to the great waves of the open ocean. The Mississippi River carries a colossal load of sediment throughout the year, nearly all confined to the river channel and its few distributaries. Where these debouch they completely dominate over the marine forces and build steadily forward, thrusting out long fingerlike salients. The Nile, on the other hand, carries relatively little sediment except during a month or so of its annual flood when the water rises some 40 feet at Cairo and spreads across nearly the whole of the subaerial delta

surface, distributing the sediment widely along the shore front. Then, after the flood subsides, the waves and shore currents have most of the year in which to work almost unhindered, straightening the shoreline by building spits and bars and by filling the interdistributary embayments. There is a close analogy here to the contrast between floodplain deposition by a normal stream and that by a braided stream, the Nile corresponding to the braided stream.

Colorado River Delta

The delta of the Colorado River (Fig. 32) offers an interesting contrast to that of the Mississippi. Its subaerial portion has been studied in great detail by Sykes (1937), and some of its features have been critically analyzed by McKee (1939). It is being built in an arid environment and into a gulf with exceptionally high tides (as much as 30 feet). Because of the aridity, the Colorado River has largely cut itself off from the sea, and during the last 50 years it has dropped almost all its load on the subaerial part of its delta, spreading fine sand and silt across the middle and upper portions and carrying only fine mud to the seaward margin. For some 20 miles below Yuma, at the head of the delta, fine sand is now being deposited in thin deltaic fans formed about distributaries. This material shows intricate cross-lamination on a small scale, resulting from shifting ripples. Farther downstream, over the middle portion of the delta, beds of crosslaminated fine sand alternate with beds of horizontally laminated mud. The seaward third of the delta is covered only during high floods, and there the water spreads in sheets from which fine mud settles to form even laminae. Mudcracks are excessively developed in such layers. Because of the great aridity, this part of the delta is impregnated with salts and is almost without vegetation; deposits formed here would be largely barren of fossils.

Rhine–Ems–Scheldt Delta

The Low Countries of western Europe occupy a broad coastal lowland where several large streams have joined in building a broad com-

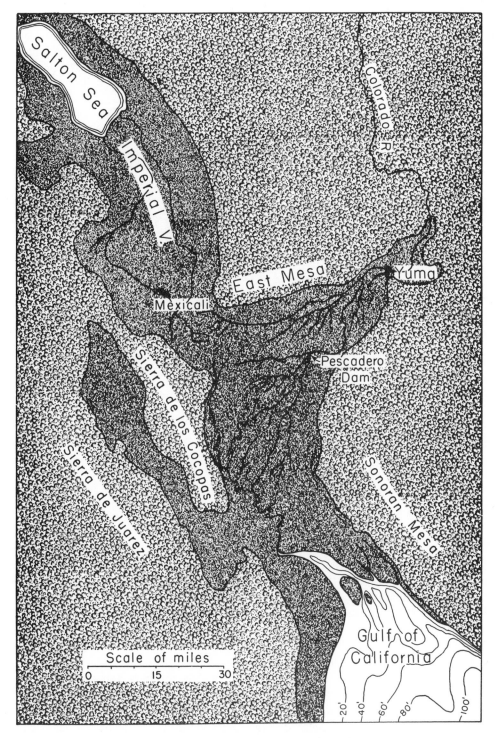

Figure 32. The delta of the Colorado River, after Sykes (1937).

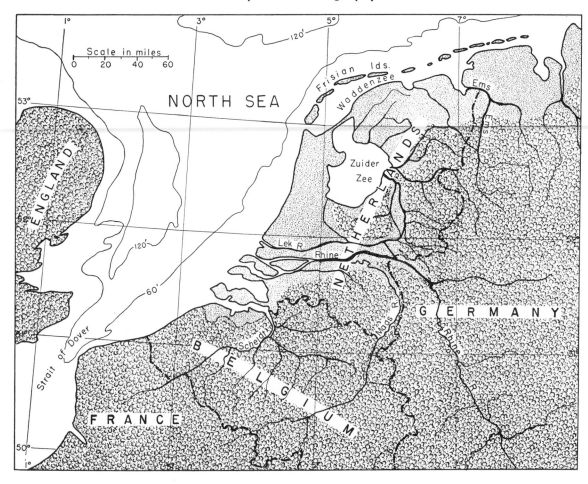

Figure 33. The compound delta of the Rhine, Ems, and Scheldt Rivers.

pound delta (Fig. 33). The subaerial part stretches for more than 200 miles from Belgium across Holland to northwestern Germany and reaches 75 to 100 miles inland; the subaqueous part floors the North Sea.

The contributing streams are less subject to great floods than the Nile and are mostly confined to channels, yet they have been unable to build out salients like the Mississippi's because the sea is dominant. Heavy northwest storms have cut a relatively steep shore face and have thrown up beaches and bars, back of which lie extensive lagoons and tidal flats (p. 71). Pronounced subsidence has taken place here, especially during the last 800 years, and only active human intervention has kept the sea back and prevented large areas of lowland from becoming salt marsh.

The Frisian Islands represent an extensive sand barrier built up by the sea off the north coast of the Netherlands and the northwest coast of Germany. Because the prevailing winds are from the sea, sand is blown inland to form extensive dunes back of the shore zone. Lateral movement of sediment along the shore has completely welded the deposits of the several streams into a single delta that forms a wide bulge in the coastline facing the North Sea.

Outside the bars and sand barriers, the shore face descends rather steeply to a depth of 30 feet or more; beyond this a broad subaqueous topset plain slopes gently away to merge with the floor of the North Sea. No foreset slope is recognizable, because the entire floor of the North Sea is subject to wave and current action.

Similarly in the past, deltas must often have been built into shallow epeiric seas. Thus the Catskill Delta (Devonian) of New York and Pennsylvania was almost certainly a compound delta built by numerous streams flowing out of Appalachia into a shallow embayment, and all its deposits appear to be topset beds.

Hwang Ho Delta

The delta of the Hwang Ho or Yellow River forms the plains of north China and floors the Gulf of Pechili and nearly the whole Yellow Sea (Fig. 34). The subaerial surface forms a great triangle with its apex at least 250 miles inland where the Hwang Ho leaves the mountains; its base, more than 350 miles long, is interrupted by the island-like upland mass of the Shantung Peninsula. The seaward slope of the delta averages only 1⅓ feet per mile, and the repeated floods over its surface have long been the scourge of China (United Nations, 1950, p. 77–81, Fig. 25). In 1887 flood waters covered some 50,000 square miles, and the loss of human life has been estimated at 1,000,000. During later historic time the river discharged into the Yellow Sea, where its delta is confluent with that of the Yangtze River, but during a great flood in 1855 it suddenly shifted to a northern course and discharged into the Gulf of Pechili. It followed this course until 1938, when, to impede the Japanese invaders, the Chinese shifted it back to a southern

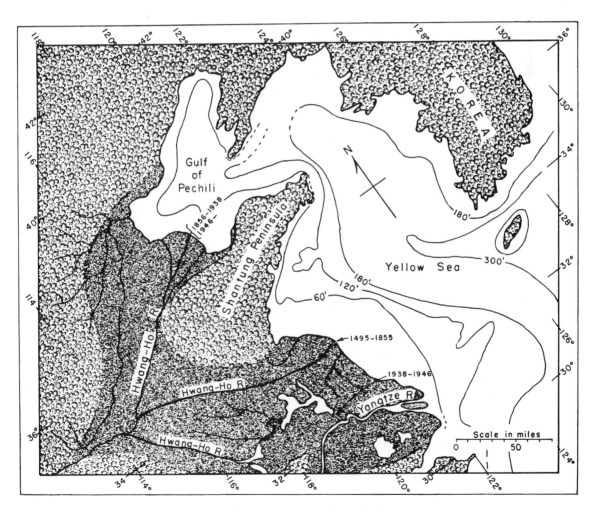

Figure 34. The delta of the Hwang Ho (Yellow River).

course, where it flowed through a maze of large shallow lakes and swamps into the Yangtze River. In 1946, with United Nations help, the Chinese restored the river to its northern course. Between the north and south courses and to the west of the Shantung Peninsula lies a vast swamp of approximately 1,000 square miles.

The subaqueous topset plain occupies the whole Gulf of Pechili (some 7,000 square miles) and most of the Yellow Sea. Between the Shantung Peninsula and the mouth of the Yangtze, the 60-foot submarine contour shows a broad bulge of shallow sea floor where the surface slope is approximately 1 foot per mile for as much as 50 miles from shore. U. S. Hydrographic Chart 3175 warns that junks frequently ground here at 20 to 30 miles from the coast. Indeed, it is almost impossible to approach the land from the sea along this coast because of the great width of extremely shallow water and the broad tidal flats. Keulegan and Krumbein (1949) think it probable that storm waves are damped out as they come in across this gently shelving sea floor and never break at the shore. Yet the rivers have not built out great salients at the mouths of their distributaries, like those of the Mississippi Delta, perhaps because of the very fine grain of the sediment which goes readily into suspension and thus is easily spread, perhaps because of the high tides and strong tidal currents which help to move material quickly away from the river mouths. The notable lack of sandy beaches and barrier islands may be due both to the fineness of the sediment and the absence of breakers.

Modern critical studies of the bottom environment and the faunas of this shallow sea floor are much to be desired. According to Grabau (1931, p. 538), the salinity is reduced to 25.54 permille in the Gulf of Pechili, and of the salts present NaCl is low (52.16 percent instead of 77.76 percent), $MgCl_2$ is high (32.59 percent instead of 10.88 percent), and $MgSO_4$ is high (9.46 percent instead of 4.74 percent). As a result, certain groups of marine animals (hydroids, brachiopods, corals, echinoderms) are rare or absent, and the fauna is dominated by dwarfed mollusks, commonly not over half as large as in the Yellow Sea.

It may be noted that a relative lowering of sealevel by 100 feet would transform the whole floor of the Gulf of Pechili into land and move the shore south of the Shantung Peninsula as much as 50 miles seaward. On the other hand, a rise of 100 feet would bring the sea far in over the present subaerial plain and transform the Shantung Peninsula into an island.

Perhaps the Pennsylvanian strata in the Mid-continent region of the United States were laid down in such an environment. There marine and non-marine conditions alternated repeatedly as streams converged into a shallow epeiric sea, bringing fine sediment from distant Appalachia. In this setting, the Oklahoma Mountains (Arbuckles, Wichitas, and Amarillos) stood as rugged uplands, surrounded at some times by the sea and at other times by a vast alluvial plain like that of the Hwang Ho Delta.

Preservation of Deltaic Deposits

Factors controlling volumetric proportions of parts of the delta. From the viewpoint of stratigraphy, the volume of the deposits laid down in the different parts of a delta is more important than their relative areal extent. The relative volume will be influenced by (1) depth of the sea, (2) rate of subsidence (or of rise of sealevel), (3) rate of supply of sediment, and (4) strength of waves and currents.

If the stream enters water that is deep close to shore, most of the sediments will come to rest on the foreset slope. As long as the region is stable and sealevel remains constant, the delta must then grow outward, and most of the sediment will accumulate as foreset beds, as in small deltas built into lakes, the topset beds remaining only a thin veneer (Fig. 35a).

On the contrary, if the sea is so shallow that its entire floor is within reach of the waves, all the deposits will be spread across it as topset beds. This is true of the Rhine Delta, now being built into the North Sea, and it must have been common in the epeiric seas of the past. Here the ratio of subaerial to subaqueous beds will depend on the relative strength of the stream and of the waves and currents. In the presence of weak marine forces a powerful stream will rapidly push forward the shoreline and extend the subaerial

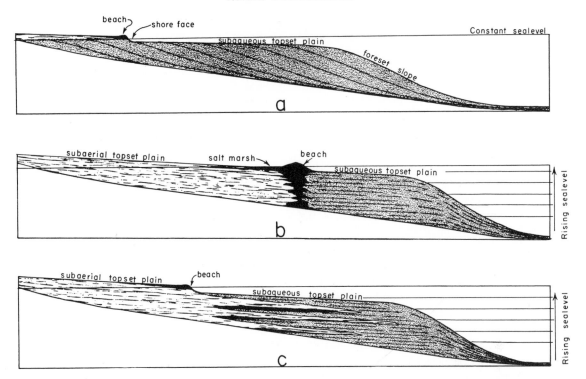

Figure 35. Diagrammatic cross sections through marine deltas built into fairly deep open water with (a) constant sealevel, (b) steadily rising sealevel, (c) intermittently rising sealevel. Length of area shown, several tens of miles; vertical scale greatly exaggerated. Uneven shading, non-marine deposits of subaerial topset plain; even shading, marine deposits of subaqueous topset plain and foreset slope; black, littoral deposits of beach and salt marsh.

part of the delta until the entire basin is transformed into land. Subsidence may interfere, however, tending to drown the subaerial surface and extend the subaqueous beds. With the proper balance between subsidence and stream load, the shoreline may remain fixed while delta deposits accumulate to great thickness, both subaerial and subaqueous portions being volumetrically important (Fig. 35b).

If the source area is rising so that the load of the stream steadily increases in volume and coarseness, the shoreline will be pushed seaward and the non-marine beds will spread progressively over the marine. This clearly happened in Devonian time in the Appalachian region, when Appalachia was rising under the influence of the Acadian disturbance and the subaerial part of the Catskill Delta spread ever farther to the west.

Intermittent subsidence will, of course, lead to deep intertonguing of marine and non-marine deposits, the shoreline retreating landward by drowning during rapid subsidence and advancing seaward during times of stability (Fig. 35c). This appears to have been the situation over the interior of the United States during the Pennsylvanian, for the Coal Measures show repeated recursions of marine beds extending from Oklahoma and Kansas as far east as Ohio and Pennsylvania. Eustatic changes of sealevel like those induced by continental glaciation would, of course, produce the same result.

The importance of marine forces may be further illustrated by comparing the deltas of the Mississippi and the Amazon. Both rivers are building deltas in subsiding regions, and both carry a colossal load of fine sediment. The Amazon, however, faces the full force of the Atlantic storm waves and the subaerial part of its delta is relatively small; the Mississippi is building in a more protected gulf where waves are smaller and tides are negligible, and its land surface is large and is being rapidly extended.

The littoral record. Although the littoral zone is most expanded in the great marine deltas, there are still relatively few examples of littoral deposits known in the stratigraphic record. Barrell (1906, p. 442–446) explained why this should be so. In a region that is emerging from the sea, the littoral deposits form only a thin veneer subject to destruction by erosion before lithification has begun. Where, on the other hand, an old land surface sloping gently seaward is slowly subsiding so that the sea transgresses landward, the depth of the littoral deposits behind the beach or the sand barrier cannot in general be as great as the depth of the sea in front of the shore face. The advancing sea will therefore cut away and destroy whatever littoral deposits were made ahead of it.

Littoral deposits have their best chance of preservation in marine deltas, but even here they will be only partly preserved. Where the subaerial part of the delta is growing during subsidence, shallow shore lagoons will be filled up and salt marshes, as well as beaches, will be covered with river-laid deposits, but the subdeltas of the Mississippi show that such burial may give the littoral deposits only transient respite from destruction. Within the 500 years or so since the river completed the St. Bernard subdelta and shifted to another sector, slow subsidence has let the sea sweep inward several miles, reworking the upper part of the subdelta, spreading marine sands over the floor of Chandeleur Sound, and building the sand barrier of the Chandeleur Islands. The previously formed beach and salt marsh deposits of this subdelta have been largely, if not entirely, destroyed. The same fate has befallen each of the older subdeltas in turn. Permanent preservation will occur only where the sea has been held back while subsidence has carried the littoral deposits at least 30 to 50 feet below sealevel. In the vertical section of a delta, therefore, the littoral deposits would appear only sporadically between marine and overlying non-marine beds (Fig. 35c).

Ancient Delta Deposits

The present delta of the Mississippi River, composed of its several successive subdeltas (Fig. 29, p. 77), appears to have been built entirely since sealevel returned to about its present height after the maximum of the Wisconsin glaciation. But a similar delta was apparently formed after each of the preceding Pleistocene glaciations also (Fisk, 1944), along with a body of floodplain deposits farther upstream (p. 37). The present delta is thus the last of a series of superposed deltas that make a mass of deposits thousands of feet thick.

The recent phase of Mississippi delta building dates only from the Pleistocene, when ice sheets created the present vast river system by diverting many north-flowing streams to form the Missouri and Ohio Rivers. Twice before during the Cenozoic, however, great rivers built a large marine delta in the central Gulf region. Climaxes of deltaic deposition in the Miocene and the Early Eocene are recorded by many thousands of feet of fluvial or nearshore marine sandstone; at other times (Late Eocene and Paleocene) marine clays spread far to the north. The Cretaceous deposits of the area may record a still older delta. Other deltas were built by other rivers along the Atlantic and Gulf Coasts at various times in the Cenozoic, especially to the west in Texas, where the Rio Grande built (and is still building) a series of deltas.

During the later Cretaceous, a vast seaway extended northward across North America from the west end of the Gulf of Mexico to the western Arctic Ocean, on the site of the present Great Plains and eastern Rocky Mountains. A series of large coalescing marine deltas was built out into this seaway in front of spasmodically rising mountains (early pulses of the Laramide orogeny) to the west. These deltas are recorded by thick bodies of coal-bearing sandstone (Mesaverde, Judith River, Belly River formations or groups, and others) that tongue eastward into marine Cretaceous shale (Stebinger, 1914; L. S. Russell, 1939; Sears, Hunt, and Hendricks, 1941; Pike, 1947; Spieker, 1949). Non-marine sediments pushed forward first here, then there, but finally toward the end of the period spread eastward over the whole area driving the sea entirely out.

The *Catskill Delta* (Middle and Upper Devonian) of New York and Pennsylvania is especially well exposed and is one of the best documented of all ancient deltas; its stratigraphy is discussed in Chapter 7 (p. 137, and Fig. 71, p. 139). Older deltas in the Appalachian geosyncline are the

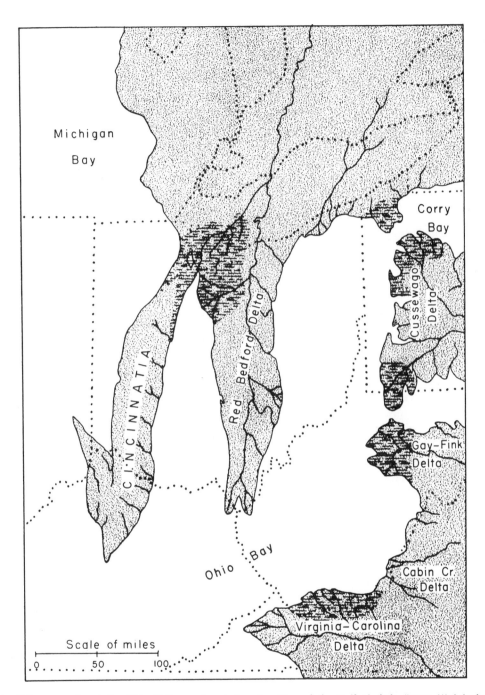

Figure 36. Paleogeography of the Ohio Valley region during deposition of the Bedford shale (Lower Mississippian). Cincinnatia was a low peninsula formed by the Cincinnati Arch and was not an important source of sediment. Unshaded areas, shallow sea. After Pepper, de Witt, and Demarest (1954, Pl. 13C).

Queenston Delta (Middle and Upper Ordovician) of New York and Pennsylvania, and the *Blount Delta* (Middle Ordovician) of East Tennessee. The Pennsylvanian rocks of eastern and central United States appear to be an intertonguing complex of deltaic and marine deposits indicating that large deltas formed repeatedly along the eastern side of a vast, shallow epeiric sea.

The Bedford shale and Berea sandstone (Lower Mississippian) of Ohio and adjacent states form a particularly interesting complex of deltaic deposits. In a monumental study of these formations, based on outcrops and some 43,000 well records, Pepper, de Witt, and Demarest (1954) have produced an analysis of the delta deposits built into a shallow epeiric sea that will become a classic. Figure 36 shows the paleogeographic relations during late Bedford deposition as worked out by these authors. At this time 4 distinct deltas were building simultaneously from different sources; the *Red Bedford Delta* was formed by a large stream flowing southward from the Canadian Shield, the others by rivers flowing west out of Appalachia. The subaerial surface of the Red Bedford Delta alone was approximately equal in area to that of the present Mississippi or Nile deltas.

In a shallow sea so completely landlocked and so far from the open ocean, tides were probably negligible. With the Cincinnati Arch forming a long peninsula, Cincinnatia, on the west, the Ohio Bay must have lacked great storm waves so that the rivers were completely dominant over marine forces. Nevertheless, the bay was so shallow that locally produced waves could reach bottom everywhere, helping to spread the fine sediment. No break in slope can be detected, and the entire complex apparently consists of topset beds. This probably was a common situation in the epeiric seas of the past.

ORGANIC REEF ENVIRONMENTS

General

Life flourishes in the shore zone, ordinarily adapting itself to the inorganic environment and the processes at work in it. In clear tropical seas, however, certain organisms such as corals can create their own shore environment and build edifices that support whole islands; these edifices are the coral reefs, or, better, organic reefs, for many kinds of organisms share in building them today and many others were important in the past. Only a small part is actually deposited between the tide lines, for the waves heap up some material into permanent islands and much more settles into place under water, but ordinarily shore processes play a vital role in producing the reef proper and hence the whole deposit.

The organic reef proper is a solid mass of $CaCO_3$ built up by organisms nearly or quite to the surface of the ocean where it intercepts the waves; * indeed the reef ordinarily grows best

* The nautical term *reef* was originally applied to edifices of this sort in present-day seas precisely because they intercept the waves and are hazards to navigation; some writers have therefore wished to restrict the term (organic) reef to such wave-resistant structures. Because it is rarely possible to determine whether a given structure built in a Paleozoic sea was or was not a hazard to navigation, the word reef if so defined could rarely be applied in stratigraphy, and hence Cumings (1932) proposed the term *bioherm* "for reeflike, moundlike, lenslike or otherwise circumscribed structures of strictly organic origin, embedded in rocks of different lithology." (For bedded rather than lenslike structures he proposed the term *biostrome*.) More and more, however, geologists have refused to restrict reef in this way; see, for example, the detailed definition of the word in its modern geologic application that was presented by Wilson (1950) at the 1949 Reef Symposium sponsored by the American Association of Petroleum Geologists and accepted in principle by the participants in the symposium, most of whom either implicitly or explicitly treated bioherm and (organic) reef as synonyms. In this book, bioherm is not used, and organic reef, as applied to ancient sediments, means a deposit composed of the remains of organisms, mainly colonial, that have accumulated approximately in the position of growth to form non-bedded or at best poorly bedded masses of solid rock, while better bedded normally fragmental sediments were accumulating on all sides (Pia, 1933, p. 11–12).

More recently, MacNeil (1954) has proposed to include in the organic reef or reef-rock the whole body of organic deposits here called the reef complex, both that in position of growth (his "bioherm" or "biohermal reef rock," our "reef proper") and that produced by erosion (his "detrital reef rock"). It is certainly true that the fragmental debris may be quickly indurated into material as solid as the "reef proper" and as much a part of the hazard to navigation, especially if slightly where the waves can beat vigorously upon it, for though they are continually breaking it up into rubble and sand, the fresh nutrients and aerated water they bring enable the organisms to build faster than erosion can proceed. Thus the reef can continue to grow, though it supplies a great amount of fragmental debris, which in turn surrounds and half buries the reef. Further, the mere presence of the reef greatly modifies the action of the waves and other shore processes and provides a new and more sheltered environment for other kinds of organisms, which then add their contributions to the growing deposit. The whole deposit—the reef proper and the sediments accumulating around it in the environment it creates—is called a *reef complex* (Henson, 1950, p. 216).

With respect to form, present-day reefs are grouped into three main classes: *fringing reefs*— reef strips that hug the shoreline; *barrier reefs*— reef strips that follow the shoreline but are separated from it by a more or less continuous lagoon generally tens of fathoms deep; and *atolls*— doughnut-shaped reef strips that surround empty lagoons. Some add a fourth class: *table, patch,* or *platform reefs,* which are isolated patches of reef smaller than atolls and lacking central lagoons. Islands are generally scattered here and there along barrier reefs and atolls or surmounting table reefs. Fringing reefs and barrier reefs accompany already existing shores and are built on continental or island shelves or slopes; atolls and table reefs dot the open tropical oceans, some on continental shelves or banks but many standing on isolated pedestals that rise from great depths. The origin of these different reef forms has been debated for a century in a voluminous literature (see Ladd and Tracey, 1949, for a short historical summary); we are concerned with the matter only as it bears on the sediments produced.

---

exposed by a fall in sealevel, and it is also true that the two rock types may be and ordinarily are intimately intermixed in any reef complex. But to stratigraphers studying the sediments in three dimensions, the original organic framework is the true reef, responsible for all the rest of the deposit, and needs to be sharply distinguished from the surrounding fragmental debris, which is derivative and secondary (cf. Newell, 1955a, p. 302).

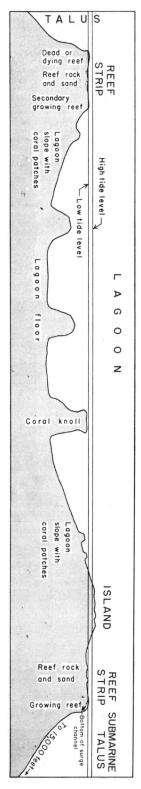

Figure 37. Diagrammatic cross section of an oceanic atoll. Total width measured in miles or tens of miles; vertical scale considerably exaggerated, tidal range greatly exaggerated.

U. S. Geological Survey, J. I. Tracey, Jr.

Figure 38. Oblique aerial view of Eninman Island and leeward reef, Bikini Atoll. From Ladd, Tracey, Wells, and Emery (1950).

Atolls

A number of atolls in Micronesia have recently been studied in detail, notably Bikini and Eniwetok; surface study has provided detailed information on the modern reefs and associated sediment (see especially Emery, Tracey, and Ladd, 1954; also Tracey, Ladd, and Hoffmeister, 1948; Ladd, Tracey, Wells, and Emery, 1950), and deep wells have provided data on the underlying deposits (Ladd, Tracey, and Lill, 1948; Ladd, Ingerson, Townsend, Russell, and Stephenson, 1953).

Figure 37 is a diagrammatic cross section of an atoll like Bikini, crossing the reef ring once through an island and once between islands, and Figures 38 and 39 show aerial photographs of parts of Bikini (see also Fig. 76, p. 150). The most actively growing part of any reef is at the seaward edge of the reef strip, especially on the windward side; here coralline algae like *Lithothamnion,* with some help from corals and other organisms, build forward on the uppermost part of the outer slope and upward to a bit above low tide level. The front of the windward reef is normally deeply notched by marginal grooves and surge channels, apparently adjusted to absorb the shock of the waves efficiently; as the algae build forward on the buttresses between the grooves and channels, the inner parts of these may be roofed over and then filled with debris. Debris is constantly being torn from the front of the reef by the waves; much of it tumbles down into the deep water below, where it builds a submarine talus of rubble and sand, along with coral and algal material produced on the slope below the main zone of building and wave action, but much of the debris is also tossed up onto the flat top of the reef strip and is carried inward across it. On flourishing reefs and parts of reefs, the erosion so produced is more than balanced by new growth, but on less flourishing reefs erosion may become dominant and cut deeply into reef rock produced under more favorable conditions. On Bikini, the windward north and east flanks are growing, the west flank is about stable, and on the south flank, leeward to the trade winds but subject to occasional violent storms, the outer edge of the reef strip is being eroded.

Back of the most actively growing zone, patches of growing coral become more important than algae, but the modern deposits on the main reef flat are largely loose material, much of it the debris from the reef front (sand, rubble, and even large blocks), but much of it simply the tests of foraminifera. On most modern reefs, however, the reef flat is actually made of consolidated limestone, deposited apparently at the slightly higher stand of sealevel that accompanied the so-called postglacial climatic optimum, over which the modern deposits (debris, coral heads, foraminiferal tests) form at most only a thin veneer. Originally this older rock consisted of precisely the same sediments as those forming today—reef rock, reef debris, coral patches, foraminiferal sand—but since the last fall in sealevel it has been indurated and then beveled, chiefly by solution, down to the present low tide level or a bit beyond.

Inward the veneer of loose sand and rubble, interspersed with coral patches, commonly becomes thicker and, where an island is present, merges with the beach, though there may be a slightly deeper boat channel between, in which large flat coral heads are growing. The island itself is made of sand and rubble heaped up by the winds and by the waves during extreme storms (in part probably at the earlier higher stand of the sea). Some islands are only temporary sand bars, others are reasonably permanent and support plant and animal life and human villages, but all are subject to continual shifting or to partial destruction by the greatest storms.

The inward side of the islands, or the sandy inner part of the reef strip where islands are absent, slopes down into the lagoon. Down this slope, the sand of the island beach or on the reef grades into finer calcareous sediment on the lagoon floor. Coral patches are also prominent here, forming mounds and miniature reefs, and on the leeward side of the lagoon, where the lagoon waves strike the inner edge of the reef strip, they may coalesce into a growing reef zone that is a smaller replica of the zone at the windward edge of the atoll. Much of the sand and silt in the

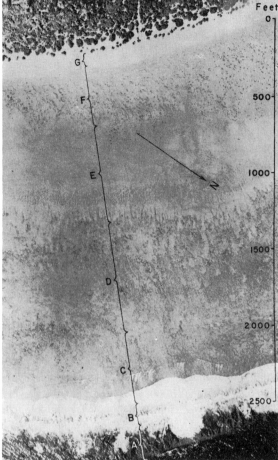

U. S. Navy

Figure 39. Vertical aerial view of windward reef in front of Bikini Island, showing reef zonation. A. Marginal grooves and spurs below low tide level. B. *Lithothamnion* ridge, interrupted by surge channels. C–F. Reef flat with coral heads and patches. Algae are prominent in C; E is mostly bare reef rock with traces of an old reef front. G. Beach. Arrow points north. From Ladd, Tracey, Wells, and Emery (1950).

lagoon, especially around the sides, is derived from the reef, but much is also produced in the lagoon itself by the organisms living in its quieter waters, notably the delicate calcareous alga *Halimeda,* which grows in profusion in the deepest parts. From the floor of the lagoon many coral knolls rise steeply; they are alive with corals, algae, and mollusks, all contributing to the growth of the structure.

Roughly speaking then, the accumulating sediments of a growing atoll are: the outer submarine talus; the actively growing reef rock proper; the lime-sand and lime-rubble, mixed with coral patches, that cover the main part of the reef strip and form the islands; and the lime-sand and lime-silt that accumulate, along with and around scattered coral knolls, in the lagoon. Of these the reef rock proper is perhaps the smallest in volume (not more than 10 percent), yet it is responsible in a sense for the whole.

The drill holes that have penetrated various Pacific atolls have encountered similar sediments thousands of feet thick. On several, the deposits reach back to the Lower Miocene, and on Eniwetok to shallow-water Eocene sediments overlying olivine basalt at a depth of more than 4,000 feet (the surrounding ocean is about 3 miles deep). Thus we now know what was long suspected, that the Pacific atolls are built on volcanic foundations rising above the ocean floor, and that the entire thickness of the overlying sediments was deposited in the atoll environment, presumably at depths hardly if at all greater than the present atoll sediments. Presumably also—and the information from the drill holes is not contradictory—the proportions of the different kinds of sediments are roughly the same in these piles of sediments as in the present-day atoll. If so, the reef rock proper is only a small part of the total reef complex, yet it is an important part, "as important as the sides of a pail that holds water" to quote Ladd's happy phrase (Ladd and Tracey, 1949, p. 299), and indeed erosion of the growing "pail" produced the "water." Whether the pattern of concentric rings shown by the various deposits today has been constant enough through geologic time to render the pail analogy geometrically correct as well, the evidence is not yet sufficient to tell us. We know at least that in many ancient reefs the reef rock proper is as small a part of the whole complex as in modern atolls (p. 95 and Fig. 40).

One would not expect to find oceanic atolls like Bikini in the geologic record of the continents; nevertheless, we have discussed them at some length because they illustrate in a simple form the interrelations of the various kinds of deposits found around organic reefs. The islands of Kita- and Minami-Daito, nearly 200 miles east of Okinawa in the Philippine Sea, appear, however, to be raised ancient atolls; on each a central depression close to sealevel is surrounded by a complete ring half a mile wide and 100 to 200 feet high. The surface rock is dolomitized "Plio-Pleistocene" limestone; drilling on Kita-Daito encountered such rock to a depth of 340 feet, beneath which are mostly poorly consolidated and undolomitized Miocene sediments.

Furthermore, atolls are not restricted to the deep open oceans but occur also in shelf seas—for example, the Marquesas Islands near Key West, Florida, and a number on the Sahul Shelf northwest of Australia (Teichert and Fairbridge, 1948). In the geologic record, the famous lithographic limestone of Solenhofen, with its extraordinarily well preserved fossil birds, reptiles, fish, and invertebrates, appears to have been deposited as fine lime-mud in the lagoon of a shelf atoll. Another such atoll in the Pennsylvanian limestone of Scurry County, Texas, is famous as an oil reservoir (Stafford, 1955; Myers, Stafford, and Burnside, 1956).

Barrier Reefs

A small but flourishing barrier reef along an open coast shows most of the same features as the windward side of an atoll—submarine talus, actively growing reef front, reef flat with scattered islands, lagoon with coral knolls—and the deposits formed ordinarily differ only in the lagoon, where much terrigenous detritus may be brought by streams from the adjacent land mass to stifle the coral colonies and interfinger with the limey deposits of the reef complex. At places along the coast, such detritus may encroach all the way across the lagoon and reach the reef proper; here reef growth itself may be inhibited and the strip of calcareous deposits come to an end, interfingering along the reef trend as well as landward with the terrigenous sediments.

The greatest reef complex in the world today is the Great Barrier Reef of Australia, which follows the coast of Queensland for 1,000 miles at distances of 20 to 150 miles from shore. It has been considerably studied, and two fairly deep holes have been drilled in it; Fairbridge (1950) has recently provided a summary of information

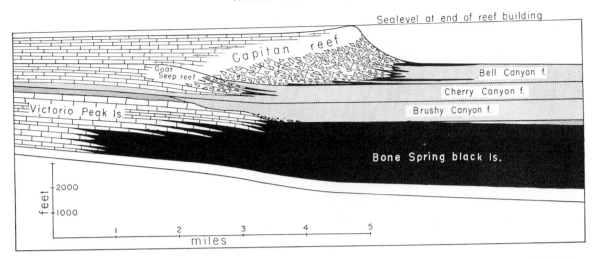

Figure 40. Diagrammatic cross section of Capitan Reef, West Texas, at end of Guadalupe epoch. From King (1948). Dots, sandstone; black, deep-water basinal limestone; blank, reef limestone; triangles in blocks, reef talus limestone; blocks, other limestone or dolostone.

on this and other Australian reefs. This is no simple barrier strip; instead, as Fairbridge points out (1950, p. 332), every kind of reef is here represented. On the outer side is a line of reefs like a string of kidney-shaped half-atolls separated by narrow but apparently permanent passes; few islands occur on these reefs. Next within these is a less regular line of platform or patch reefs, like immense coral knolls in the outer part of the vast lagoon; these commonly support islands. Fairbridge (1950, p. 357–359) believes there is an evolutionary sequence of such reef patches, which include some shelf atolls with shallow lagoons. The inner part of the lagoon is the more open Steamer Channel; terrigenous sediment floors most of it, probably helping to inhibit coral growth there, and also encroaches far into the lines of reefs, locally entirely across them. To the north, on the other hand, terrigenous matter is scant and fringing reefs skirt the shore on the landward side of the lagoon. In the resulting reef complex, all the types of calcareous deposits found on the atoll are present, but they intertongue with each other and with the terrigenous sediments in a far more complex pattern than on either atoll or simple barrier reef. The holes drilled on the Great Barrier Reef penetrated 400 to 500 feet of reef complex and then 200 feet of quartzose foraminiferal sand, of which they

did not reach the bottom. There is little doubt that the reef complex rests on a fairly gentle continental slope, but probably it is separated from the continental "basement" by non-calcareous deposits like those now forming in the inner lagoon, to which the quartzose foraminiferal sand may be a transition.

Superb examples of ancient barrier reefs are found in the Permian rocks of West Texas and adjacent New Mexico (King, 1942, 1948); here at several epochs barrier reefs surrounded deep enclosed basins (like atolls turned inside out) and had very shallow lagoons between them and the shore. The best known of them is unquestionably the Capitan Reef in the Guadalupe Series on the north side of the Delaware basin; this reef and the related deposits on both sides are described in detail in the recent memoir by Newell and others (1953).

A diagrammatic cross section of the Capitan Reef (Fig. 40) shows a sequence of facies from "open water" to lagoon and shore, some of them resembling deposits in modern barrier reefs or atolls but others differing because of peculiarities of the particular geographic setting, a nearly enclosed marine basin in an arid land. The deposits in the deeper part of the basin are quite unlike the open ocean deposits around atolls or in front of the Great Barrier Reef because circulation in

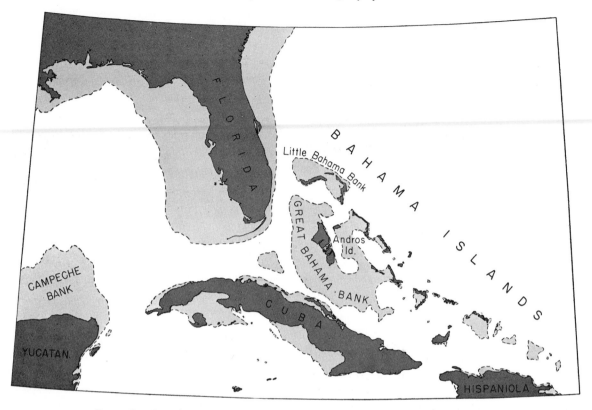

Figure 41. Map of Florida-Bahama region. Dashed line is 200-meter submarine contour.

the basin was restricted (p. 62); moreover, much sand was brought into the basin, either through passes or over the reef itself. Between basin deposits and reef proper are submarine talus deposits, composed of lime-sand and lime-rubble and showing high primary dips (p. 104); in places tongues of this material extend far out into the basin, partly as the result of submarine slides. Next comes the reef proper, now massive largely structureless rock that was formed chiefly by calcareous algae and sponges, with some help from bryozoa; brachiopods and fusulines, and to a less extent echinoderms and corals, inhabited the reef though they contributed little to the solid framework. Inward from the reef proper are deposits of lime-sand worn from it, and also cemented coquinas of fusulines and fragments of brachiopods, mollusks, and other organisms. These in turn grade and tongue landward into the deposits of the shallow lagoon—pisolitic (apparently algal) limestone and dolostone, fine-grained dolostone (believed by Newell and others

to have been originally a chemical deposit of aragonite mud), thick evaporites (chiefly anhydrite), and, interbedded with all these, terrigenous quartz sandstone and finally redbeds. Reef-talus, reef, and backreef lime-sands are like the deposits of modern reefs, except for the unfamiliar organisms, but because of the aridity the lagoon was a great evaporating pan whose high salinity inhibited organic deposition like that in modern reef lagoons, and favored chemical deposition except close to the reef where new water streamed in to replace what evaporated.

Other Kinds of Reefs

Fringing reefs, rarely large, display the outer zones of the atoll, but the lagoon is absent and terrigenous matter may encroach well into the reef strip. Likewise table reefs may show several of the atoll zones, especially a veneer of lime-sand that typically covers the central portion of the reef. Table reefs, like atolls, are not confined to the deep open ocean but grow in lagoons like that of the Great Barrier Reef and also on open continental shelves or in epeiric seas in tropical areas where terrigenous detritus is lacking; modern examples are the reefs on the Sahul Shelf off northwestern Australia (Fairbridge, 1950; 1953) and some of the Florida Keys. Table reefs of this kind appear to have been especially plentiful in Paleozoic seas in North America; they are now found as bun-shaped or more irregular reef masses surrounded by their own debris in Cambrian rocks in Texas (Fig. 94, p. 180), Ordovician rocks in Virginia and Tennessee, Silurian rocks in Indiana and Illinois, Devonian rocks in Michigan and Alberta, and Pennsylvanian rocks in Texas and New Mexico, to mention only a few localities (Twenhofel, 1950). In some ways these reefs resemble the coral knolls of the atoll lagoon, but the "lagoons" in which they formed commonly had no reef rim but were vast shallow epeiric seas floored by other carbonate deposits.

Reefs of still another kind are the Bahama Banks (Fig. 41); these are something between very large atolls with very shallow lagoons and table platform reefs. The deposits here have been described by many workers, notably Black (1933), Thorp (1935; 1939), Newell and others (1951), Illing (1954), and Newell (1955b). Around the edges of the banks, especially where winds or currents bring in new water, are growing reef strips surmounted by lines of sandy islands (cays), but most of the platform surfaces are covered with vast amounts of aragonite particles ranging in size from coarse sand to fine needles 1 to 3 microns long. These particles were apparently produced by chemical (or biochemical) precipitation (p. 231), but now they are being transported and deposited by the waves and currents like any other sand and mud in shallow water; the coarser sand accumulates in areas of moderate currents and the finest mud in relatively protected waters like those west of Andros Island. Great banks like those of the Bahamas may have been present in ancient seas; Cloud and Barnes (1948, p. 79 ff.) believe that much of the Ellenburger group (Lower Ordovician limestone and dolostone) of Central Texas was deposited on such a bank on the site of the present Llano uplift.

PART II

BASIC STRATIGRAPHIC RELATIONS

Figure 42. The great unconformity at Siccar Point, Berwickshire, Scotland, where the meaning of unconformity was first perceived by James Hutton in 1788. Old Red sandstone (Devonian) here rests on steeply dipping Silurian strata. British Crown copyright.

5. Stratification

NATURE OF STRATIFICATION

Definitions. As stratigraphy is the study of stratified rocks, it must include a study of stratification, which is not only one of the most obvious features of those rocks (Figs. 43–46) but also one of the most significant for their interpretation. A number of terms are available to describe this and related features—on the one hand the concrete terms *layer, stratum* (plural, *strata*), *bed,* and *lamina* (plural, *laminae*), and on the other the corresponding abstract terms *layering, stratification, bedding,* and *lamination.* In current usage these different terms carry different shades of meaning to many geologists, but to others some of them seem interchangeable or at least intergradational. The terminology in this book is based mainly on the practical suggestions of McKee and Weir (1953) as supplemented by Ingram (1954).

The broadest terms, layer and layering, are not restricted to stratified rocks. A layer is a planar unit limited by differences in composition, texture, or structure of the rock material, and layering therefore includes not only stratification but all other planar arrangements such as, for example, gneissic banding. Stratum and stratification [L. *sternere,* to spread out] imply that the layers were deposited separately and successively, one after and upon another, and are applied only to rocks of sedimentary origin. Thus stratification is defined as the kind of rock layering formed during deposition by changes of some kind in the materials being deposited or in the conditions of deposition, and a stratum is defined as a layer so formed. By common consent lamina and lamination refer to stratum and stratification less than 1 cm thick. Some geologists consider the terms bed and bedding direct synonyms of stratum and stratification, but McKee and Weir (1953, p. 383) propose to define bed as a unit more than 1 cm thick and to distinguish various classes of bedding and lamination quantitatively. Their scheme, modified by Ingram (1954) to insure more nearly equal classes, is given in Table 4.

TABLE 4. CLASSIFICATION OF BEDDING ACCORDING TO THICKNESS. AFTER MCKEE AND WEIR (1953) AS MODIFIED BY INGRAM (1954).

Beds	very thick-bedded
	———100 cm (about 3 ft)———
	thick-bedded
	——— 30 cm (about 1 ft)———
	medium-bedded
	——— 10 cm (about 4 in.)———
	thin-bedded
	——— 3 cm (about 1 in.)———
	very thin-bedded
	——— 1 cm (about ⅖ in.)———
Laminae	laminated
	——— 0.3 cm (about 1/10 in.)———
	thinly laminated

Carl O. Dunbar

Figure 43. Irregularly bedded, lenticular sandstone and shale. Oswego sandstone (Ordovician) at Salmon River Falls, New York.

A uniform scheme of this sort for describing bedding in quantitative terms will be as useful as the widely accepted Wentworth scheme for grain size (p. 161), and we urge its adoption.

Both McKee and Weir (1953) and Ingram (1954) define bedding without reference to any parting that may be shown by the strata, and suggest separate quantitative terminologies for units defined by their parting. To many geologists, however, the word bed (in such compounds as well-bedded, for instance) carries the additional connotation that the strata are visibly distinct units, separated by bedding planes that are actual partings or else planes along which partings tend to develop. Such partings are especially brought out by weathering, so that a given unit may appear thick-bedded where fresh but weather into very thin beds. Lamina and lamination, on the other hand, carry no connotation of partings and indeed may imply their absence in rocks that have a thicker "bedding" as well. Thus lime-stone may show very minute lamination but be called thick-bedded, if there is no tendency to part along the laminae (Fig. 47).

Certain other terms may be mentioned. *Band* and *ribbon* are properly two-dimensional and should be used only to describe the appearance of layering of various kinds on surfaces that intersect the layering. *Fissility* is the tendency of a rock to split or part into thin layers or plates (Ingram, 1953); it is ordinarily the result of the parallel arrangement of flaky mineral particles. In many sedimentary rocks the most prominent fissility is parallel to the bedding, but in others it is not; fissility akin to slaty cleavage and cutting the stratification at large angles can be found in rocks that show no other sign of metamorphism and, if mistaken for bedding, it can lead to serious errors (Fig. 48).

Basis of stratification. The changes during deposition that produce stratification may be of several kinds. Mere cessation of deposition ordinarily does not produce it, unless some additional change takes place before or with the renewal of deposition. If, for example, uniform sand is poured into a beaker a little at a time, stratification is not likely to appear unless the beaker is shaken between times to compact the sand already present before more is added. Changes in the composition of the material being deposited are the most obvious causes of stratification; even very minor changes may produce distinct stratification if they affect the constituents that give the rock its color. Changes in grain size, as from sand to gravel, may also cause pronounced layering, and changes in other textural characteristics, such as roundness, may distinguish one stratum from the next. Changes in structure are also significant—variations in degree of compaction or cementation, or other variations in the arrangement or fabric of the particles.

In shale, the stratification is commonly emphasized by the parallelism of flaky mineral particles, producing a bedding fissility, but of course such fissility must be distinguished from other kinds. Differences in composition are also present in most shale, but they may be subtle and difficult to detect. In sandstone and limestone, such changes are apt to be more obvious; indeed, the beds of many sandstone and limestone units are separated and made obvious by thin "shaly partings," perhaps representing accumulations of fine particles during a cessation in the normal influx of coarser material. Differences in texture may also be very important in these rocks.

The regularity and lateral extent of stratification and bedding vary within wide limits. In some rocks, notably some varieties of shale, lamination and grosser bedding are remarkably even (Fig. 45), but in others, especially impure limestone, the beds pinch and swell or are broken into nodules (Figs. 43 and 46). The lateral extent

Carl O. Dunbar

Figure 44. Two massive beds (a and b) in a thin-bedded and shaly Cretaceous formation. Pan-American highway south of Comitán, Mexico.

Carl O. Dunbar

Figure 45. Even bedding in siltstone. Schenectady formation (Ordovician) near Schoharie Creek, 1 mile south of Sloansville, New York.

of the layers is very roughly related to their evenness; even beds may extend for miles, but uneven irregular beds may tongue out between bedding planes in a short distance or may coalesce with beds above or below as the intervening bedding plane disappears. The lateral persistence and regularity of stratification is, of course, a reflection of the persistence and regularity of the depositional agent. Thus agents that operate in channels or over small areas (for example, stream currents, wind currents around dunes) produce irregular strata that are not persistent, whereas agents that spread evenly over wide areas (for example, spasmodic turbidity currents, many neritic currents away from the irregularities of the shore, or the atmospheric currents that distribute volcanic ash) produce very even strata that are very persistent.

Recognition of stratification. Stratification is such a fundamental property of sedimentary rocks that its recognition might seem automatic, but in fact the determination of its attitude in a given outcrop may be anything but obvious. By no means may one simply assume that the most prominent parting present is the bedding; in many rocks cleavage, or a set of joints, is far more prominent. Changes in the rock material itself—compositional, textural, or structural—are the best criteria. Commonly such changes are much more apparent on weathered than on fresh surfaces, the processes of differential weathering having "developed" latent differences that are virtually invisible in the unweathered rock. Color changes may be very helpful, though color layering or banding resulting from weathering along the weathering surface, and thus aligned parallel to it rather than to the stratification, can often mislead. Fissility or other partings alone are generally unsafe guides, because of the danger of confusion with cleavage or joints. Often, however, a prominent direction of parting furnishes a first clue to the bedding, which can then be confirmed by the discovery of actual differences in rock composition or texture.

But such differences may be difficult to find, especially in areas of slightly metamorphosed rocks, and the geologist may be forced to rely on less satisfactory criteria. Thus he may often discover other clues that are helpful or even diagnostic in the rocks of a given region. The mere shape of a large outcrop may be expressive to a geologist familiar with the outcrop habits of the local formations. For example, in parts of the central and southern Appalachians, outcrops of the Lower Cambrian quartzite units, which are

very thick-bedded and considerably deformed, may be devoid of lamination or other layering and may show three variably spaced and mutually perpendicular sets of partings, one of which is presumably the bedding. But if it is known that in the particular unit the beds are roughly 25 feet thick and that their original upper surfaces may be sprinkled with small isolated pebbles, then the geologist observing an extended outcrop can locate the stratification with reasonable accuracy. Another local clue in these rocks is furnished by the tubes called *Scolithus,* an animal boring that is extremely abundant in certain layers of these units, and that is always perpendicular to the stratification (except in cases of extreme deformation).

In summary, it should be emphasized that in many cases the very attitude of stratification as recorded by the geologist is not a fact directly

Carl O. Dunbar

Figure 46. Uneven bedding in shaly limestone. Trenton limestone (Ordovician) at Trenton Falls, New York.

Figure 47. Lamination in medium- to thick-bedded limestone. Conococheague limestone (Upper Cambrian) at Waynes Castle, 4 miles west of Waynesboro, Pennsylvania.

observed in the outcrop but only a more or less probable inference from what can be observed.

ATTITUDE OF STRATIFICATION

Original Attitude

The almost universal assumption in both stratigraphy and structural geology is that the stratification of sedimentary rocks was originally horizontal. This assumption is certainly a reasonably valid approximation in the vast majority of cases, but a discussion of limitations and exceptions is in order.

Deposition takes place by the accretion of material on a surface or floor, either by chemical growth or far more commonly by mechanical settling of particles. The fundamental controls on the attitude of the stratification are this surface or floor and, at least in the mechanical deposits,

the direction in which gravity pulls the particles. When deposition begins, the stratification will be parallel to the surface or floor or will be in a compromise position between that and the horizontal (perpendicular to gravity). As deposition proceeds, irregularities tend to be evened out and the stratification tends to approach the horizontal more and more. Where deposition has been long continued and uninterrupted by pronounced erosion or by structural deformation—as in most parts of the preserved stratigraphic record— nearly or quite horizontal stratification is the expectable result. So far the assumption is justified.

Originally non-horizontal stratification is fairly common, however, and the geologist who makes this assumption should always be ready to question it and to recognize the criteria of an original dip. The term *original dip* is here used to mean the dip of a layer at the moment it was deposited; *primary dip* is usually considered a synonym.

Initial dip, on the other hand, may best be reserved for the dip *after* consolidation, slumping (if any), or any tilting or warping resulting from further deposition in the basin, but *before* tectonic warping has taken place. It is the initial dip that chiefly interests the structural geologist, the original dip that interests the stratigrapher.

One variety of original dip is that which reflects a pre-existing steep surface, such as the slope of a hill of older rock buried or partly buried by the strata showing the original dip. An excellent example in Missouri has been described by Bridge and Dake (1929; Dake and Bridge, 1932). The surface of Precambrian rocks on which the first Cambrian strata in the central Ozark region were laid down was rough and hilly, the relief amounting to more than 1,500 feet and the slopes reaching 45°. The various Cambrian units and even the lowermost Ordovician units lap up around these hills, and the sandstone and dolostone of

which they are composed is contaminated or almost replaced, near the hills, by grit or conglomerate made of fragments of Precambrian rhyolite. The rocks that show this contamination also show unusually high dips for the Ozark region, commonly 20° and locally 30°. The pattern of dips shows no structural control but is closely related to the distribution of Precambrian rock hills. The close association of overlap and marginal conglomerate with steep dips away from the buried hills makes this example unusually clear and instructive.

Similar or even steeper dips are found in talus slopes beneath cliffs and also in the debris around organic reefs that stand boldly above their surroundings, both in modern seas and in the geologic record, for example in the Silurian rocks of Indiana (Cumings and Shrock, 1928a; 1928b, p. 142–144). Here the steep surface of deposition was not a pre-existing erosion surface, as in the

Carl O. Dunbar

Figure 48. Slaty cleavage in mudrock, easily mistaken for bedding. The inked line indicates the true bedding, which dips gently away to the right. Esopus "shale" in roadside quarry, about 5 miles north of Kingston, New York.

Missouri example, but grew up in the same sea and probably only a little ahead of the deposit showing the original dip. An original dip of 65° is recorded in Indiana.

Less spectacular but more widespread original dips partly dependent on the inclination of the depositional floor are dips in piedmont fan deposits (p. 28) and other non-marine deposits (such as till or loess deposits) and presumably also in the deposits on the continental slope. Recognition of such dips would not be at all easy, and would depend on determination of the environment of deposition and of the source of the sediments. For example, the Triassic rocks of central Connecticut now dip 15° east on an average. But they were piedmont deposits at the west foot of a faulted mountain range; therefore the original dip of any layer must have been a few degrees west. Some of the eastward tilt of the lower layers was produced, however, by tilting during further deposition, as shown by Krynine (1950, p. 117–123; Krynine calls the dip after the tilting during deposition the primary dip rather than the initial dip).

In another large group of original dips, those in which cross-stratification on all scales is produced (p. 106), a non-horizontal surface of deposition need not pre-exist but is created by the depositional processes themselves. The material, brought by currents from one side, is not dumped evenly over the floor but is swept into bars or dunes or ripples, on the lee side of which deposition proceeds along a surface tilted at or near the angle of repose of the material. The classical example is the delta formed by a stream in a lake (Fig. 21, p. 41); the stream brings more material than the lake can distribute, and the material builds up the lakeward-dipping foreset beds of the delta. The angle of repose in these cases depends on a number of variables (Van Burkalow, 1945); for angular blocks it may pass 50°, for dry sand it is of the order of 35°, but for sand under water it is considerably less. In general the angle of repose is a limit to the original angle of deposition for mechanically deposited material (there is, of course, no limit to the original dip of chemically deposited material, for travertine may form on overhanging slopes).

Original dips of this sort occur not only in lacustrine deltas but wherever ordinary currents deposit sandy material—in the deposits of streams (especially braided streams), in sand dunes, in shallow-water marine deposits, and on a small scale wherever ripple marks are formed. In the smaller examples, where the cross-stratification is obvious, such dips are readily recognizable as originally non-horizontal, but in the larger examples the original dip may extend unchanged over large outcrops or groups of outcrops and may lead to serious errors in both stratigraphy and structural geology. For example, in the Whitehorse sandstone (Permian) of Oklahoma, sets of sandstone strata tens of feet thick and hundreds of feet long show consistent dips, sharply different from one set to the next; if the cross-stratification were not recognized as such, many non-existent structural features would be mapped (Reeves, 1921, p. 52–54). The criteria for such large-scale original dips must be the regional distribution of the dips and an occasional exposure showing the true relations; apparently such large-scale dips are confined to sandstone units and mostly to certain continental wind-blown deposits, though they may occur in limestone formed of sand-size particles.

The organic equivalent of such cross-stratification is illustrated by the great Capitan Reef (Permian) of West Texas (Fig. 40, p. 93). The geologists who first discovered that the front of the Guadalupe Mountains, formed by the reef, contained rocks of the same age as those over a thousand feet lower in the basin to the south postulated a fault or a sharp flexure to explain the discrepancy. It is now known, however, that the difference was original, that the reef grew up from a gentler flexure on the sea floor until it stood high and steep over the basin, and that a reef talus (p. 95) accumulated in front of the reef along surfaces inclined perhaps 20° basinward. Stratification is very obscure in the "dipping" rocks, so that the original dip is hard to observe, but even if it were obvious the true relations could have been deciphered only after the regional picture of the reef and its environment had been worked out.

Later Changes in Attitude

A layer once produced is liable to further tilting or warping as deposition proceeds above it.

The upper surface of a bed may be truncated at a bevel by later scouring before the deposition of the next bed, though of course this would not affect the layering within the bed. If more than one kind of material is present in variable thickness, compaction or other consolidation may cause differential warping of the layers. The differential compaction of shale over buried hills of crystalline rock or over lenses of less compactible sandstone has been much studied by petroleum geologists (Hedberg, 1926, 1936; Athy, 1930), and it can produce appreciable dips in the shale on the flanks of the other rock bodies. Differential subsidence of the basin of deposition also warps the already deposited layers. Dips produced in these ways can usually be recognized as such only after detailed study of thickness data, construction of isopach maps, and so forth. The results of compaction over buried hills may be mistaken for original dips around such hills, or the reverse.

More spectacular changes in attitude are associated with submarine slumping and gliding, as where unconsolidated mud slides downslope, becoming churned up or completely destratified in the process. There are well-known examples in the Silurian rocks of Wales (Jones, 1937; Straw, 1937; Earp, 1938). The resulting structural features may be hard to distinguish from tectonic features, and, indeed, much debate has raged over specific examples (compare Jones, 1937 and 1940, with Boswell, 1937 and 1949). In the better-displayed examples, at least, the layering is clearly not in its original attitude. Such features also record an original slope to the depositional floor great enough to cause gliding, though apparently the slope need not have been more than a few degrees.

Finally the attitude of layering may be altered after deposition by tectonic deformation, producing folds and faults, but study of such attitudes lies in the province of structural geology.

SPECIAL VARIETIES OF STRATIFICATION

Cross-Stratification

Cross-stratification is also called cross-bedding, false bedding, current bedding, and so forth (for a full list of synonyms, see Shrock, 1948a, p. 242).

McKee and Weir (1953, p. 382) define a cross-stratum as "a single layer of homogeneous or gradational lithology deposited at an angle to the [overall] original dip of the formation." Sets of cross-strata, within which the layering has a consistent orientation or original dip (p. 102) range from microscopic to tens of feet thick and long; in the larger examples the individual cross-strata may be inches thick. The angle between the cross-strata of adjacent sets ranges up to 35° in exceptional cases but is rarely over 20°. Cross-stratification normally occurs in sand-size and silt-size material (including of course lime-sand and lime-silt), locally in gravel, rarely if at all in clay-size material. McKee and Weir (1953, p. 383) and Ingram (1954) have worked out a terminology for cross-stratification, based on thickness, corresponding to their terminology for ordinary bedding mentioned above (p. 97).

[margin handwritten note: However, there must be a variation of particle sizes to be observed as cross-stratification.]

As seen in cross section, cross-stratification appears to take three different forms (Fig. 49A, B, C), though all transitions between can be found. In perhaps the commonest form, the sets of cross-strata appear *tabular* (A),* bounded by ordinary "horizontal" subparallel bedding planes or by strata or sets of strata showing no cross-stratification. In some cases, where the cross-stratification has resulted from migrating ripple marks, the bounding planes themselves may have an original dip (McKee, 1938a, 1939). Commonly the cross-strata in set after set have the same inclination, but in certain deposits the inclination changes or reverses from set to set, producing a "herring-bone" effect in cross section. In this form, the cross-strata ordinarily have a nearly constant inclination, but each cross-stratum may be vaguely or distinctly concave upward at the base and concave downward at the top. The top is rarely preserved, however, ordinarily being truncated by erosion before the deposition of the overlying stratum.

In another common form (so-called compound foreset bedding), the sets of cross-strata appear

---

* This type of cross-stratification has commonly been called torrential cross-bedding, but the term is a complete misnomer; its evenness is almost certain proof that it was formed not by torrents but by steady and probably broad currents in river, lake, or sea, especially by currents building into shallow standing water.

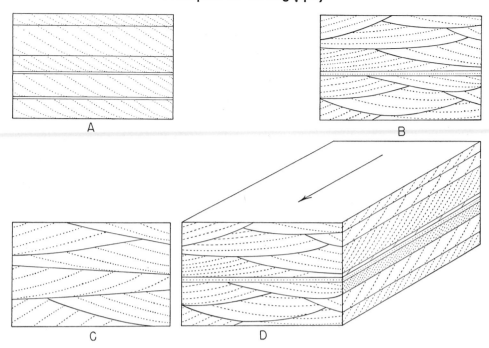

Figure 49. Cross-stratification (A to C after Shrock, 1948a, Fig. 208). A. Cross section showing tabular cross-stratification. B. Cross section showing lenticular cross-stratification. C. Cross section showing wedge-shaped cross-stratification. D. Block diagram showing common relation between tabular and lenticular cross-stratification; arrow shows direction of current.

lenticular (B), and their rounded bottoms, concave upward, rest on the truncated edges of the underlying sets and their cross-strata, and are themselves truncated beneath overlying sets. The cross-strata in these sets are commonly strongly concave upward and are parallel to at least part of the bottoms of the sets. There may or may not be truly "horizontal" strata cutting at intervals across the lenticular sets of cross-strata.

In the third form, less common perhaps, the individual sets appear *wedge-shaped* (C), the boundaries between being nearly straight or only slightly concave upward and inclined at various angles to each other, higher boundaries always truncating lower ones and the strata of underlying sets. The cross-strata in the sets may or may not be parallel to the boundaries of the sets and may or may not be concave upward; in rare cases, indeed, specially placed cross sections may show them concave downward. Truly "horizontal" bedding is rare or absent. There are, of course, bodies of cross-stratified material of which the cross sections conform to none of these neat categories.

Inclined cross-strata form primarily, as already noted (p. 104), where a current brings material from one side and dumps it in such a way as to build up a surface inclined away from the source at about the angle of repose, parallel to which deposition then takes place until some change in the current initiates a new set of cross-strata. The currents may be marine or lacustrine currents, streams, or the wind; well-known examples of cross-stratification in the making are found in deltas and sand dunes, but every braided stream deposit or ripple, and indeed almost any product of current action composed of sand or silt, should show it. The surprising thing, in fact, is to find sandy deposits formed by ordinary currents that lack it. Water currents produce chiefly the first two forms of cross-stratification described above; to some extent that produced by steadier currents (as in deltas) approaches the tabular form, that by more shifting currents (as in braided streams) the lenticular form. More generally considered, however, these two cross-sectional forms are commonly exhibited by the same deposit, depending on how the cross section is cut

(Fig. 49D), and the actual three-dimensional form of the sets of cross-strata is tonguelike, with the long dimension parallel to the direction of flow of the current and with the cross-strata inclined downstream.

Though beach deposits commonly show several varieties of cross-stratification, they are perhaps especially characterized by the "herringbone" variety of the tabular form, at least on a small scale. Moreover, the boundaries between the tabular sets, which correspond roughly to temporary positions of the surface of the beach, may themselves be inclined at low angles to the over-all bedding, making two orders of cross-stratification (in such cases the larger is commonly roughly wedge-shaped, though the angles remain low). The direction of inclination here tells little about the general direction of the currents, though under favorable conditions it may indicate the direction of the body of water.

Wind deposits tend to exhibit wedge-shaped or lenticular cross-sectional forms, commonly on a large scale (though in wind ripples the scale is small), and without any persistent "horizontal" layering or parting. If consistent, the direction of inclination indicates the direction toward which the prevailing wind blew.

Repetitive Stratification (Cyclic or Rhythmic Bedding)

Sequences of strata that show a consistent repetition of two or more kinds of rock, alternating monotonously through considerable thicknesses, are common in the geologic record, and more are being discovered every year. Several different varieties are known, some reasonably well understood, others less so. Some are known to be cyclic, the product of rhythmic changes in the environment, and of many others the same is suspected, but some, at least, may be the products of repeated but quite non-periodic alterations in the conditions of deposition.

Graded bedding. In a typical graded bed (Fig. 50), coarse detrital material below grades up into fine above, and this is succeeded along a sharp contact by the coarse base of the next graded bed. The individual beds range from a few tenths of an inch to several feet thick, and they may build

Gary M. Boone

Figure 50. Natural graded bedding in Paleozoic mudstone, 5 miles northeast of Farmington, Maine.

up great thicknesses of rock, even thousands of feet, characterized throughout by a monotonous repetition of coarse and fine materials, with the gradation always in the same sense. The coarser bottom parts of the beds may be anything from very fine sandstone to coarse conglomerate, though the largest size is apt to be about the same through hundreds of beds in any one sequence; they are typically very poorly sorted as to both size and composition, containing considerable silt and clay along with the coarser materials and having enough dark rock fragments to be classed as typical graywacke. Upwards in each bed the coarser sizes drop out, and the uppermost part normally contains only silt and clay; it may be a fairly fissile shale. In some sequences, shaly chips of the finer material are found in the coarser parts of the beds along with ordinary pebbles, but otherwise evidence of reworking is scant. The beds are generally even, commonly remarkably so, and individual beds appear to have extraordinary lateral extent, locally even miles, though in view of the normal monotony of the sequences and the considerable deformation that they have characteristically undergone, such an extent can rarely be proved.

A reasonable explanation of graded bedding in terms of the standard processes of stream or shallow-water deposition has proved difficult. The facts seem to demand that material be dumped suddenly yet fairly evenly over a large area and then allowed to settle quietly in accordance with size, coarser before finer, undisturbed by scouring currents, and that the dumping be endlessly repeated though separated by intervals of complete quiet. On the other hand, those currents in streams or in shallow seas that are capable of handling material as coarse as much of the material in the graded beds produce a totally different arrangement; they sort the material better and ordinarily separate widely the coarser and finer particles, and moreover they rarely place coarse material directly on top of fine without obvious scour. In addition they regularly produce coarse cross-stratification, which is very rare in association with graded bedding.

The problem has now been solved by Kuenen and Migliorini (1950) who have shown, by comparing field observation and laboratory experiment, that graded bedding is produced by another quite different depositional process—spasmodic turbidity currents in bodies of standing water (p. 14). Because they are heavy with suspended sediment, these currents can flow down the slopes and out onto the floors of lake or ocean basins; thus even coarse debris, brought to the shore or shelf area by ordinary currents, can be transported on into deep water, where otherwise only the finest material would be deposited. As the head of such a current sweeps by a given spot, it deposits a poorly sorted mass of material including the coarsest sizes present; as the tail passes, both the maximum and the average size of material deposited becomes finer and finer, until at the last the finest sediment suspended in the water settles out. The degree to which the next current will scour the deposits of the preceding one is not certain; on steep slopes the energy may be sufficient to cause erosion, but on gentle slopes or flat floors apparently none is accomplished. That such currents produce graded bedding has been proved by experiment (Fig. 51).

From these results further conclusions about deposits showing graded bedding may be deduced. Great thicknesses should accumulate chiefly below relatively steep underwater slopes, such as continental slopes, at the top of which material is being constantly supplied, as by streams or by bottom currents on the continental shelf. Rapidly subsiding basins beside rapidly rising highlands or islands in orogenic belts would be the ideal locations; in such basins vast amounts of material might accumulate in a geologically very short interval (a small fraction of a period). Earthquakes or volcanic explosions may commonly serve as triggers to set off the spasmodic turbidity currents, but they are probably not essential. Finally, the repetition of the graded bedding implies no strictly periodic or rhythmic process.

Varves. Another variety of repetitive stratification, and one that is reasonably well understood, is annual layering or varves. The typical case is that of deposition in a proglacial lake. During the summer, meltwater brings much material into such a lake, and some of this is spread well out into the lake by currents (probably in good part steady turbidity currents, p. 14). The coarsest fraction of this material settles quickly to the bottom, but the finer part remains suspended, because the water is cold and therefore relatively viscous and is free of electrolytes or other flocculating agents. During the winter, when the lake freezes over, no new material is added, and the fine suspended matter settles slowly to the bottom. Thus is formed a couplet of coarser and finer material like a graded bed, except that the coarse layer is rarely coarser than fine sand and both layers tend to be better sorted. Ideally each couplet represents one year, but complications such as an early spring thaw and freshet followed by weeks of freezing weather may produce double or even multiple couplets for each year.

Varves are not confined to glacial-lake deposits, though perhaps most clearly and unequivocally shown there. Bradley (1929b) has described and discussed non-glacial varves in the Green River formation (Eocene) of the Rocky Mountains, and Rubey (1931, p. 40–52) and Bradley

Figure 51. Artificial graded bedding, produced by Kuenen in his laboratory (from Kuenen and Migliorini, 1950, Pl. 3B).

(1931b; bibliography in Bradley, 1937) have discussed possible marine varves in detrital formations. Udden (1924) has considered the laminations in the Castile anhydrite (Permian) of West Texas as annual, and similarly Sander (1936, p. 198; trans., p. 145) has suggested that certain apparently rhythmic, thin laminations in the Triassic carbonate sequence of the Tyrolean Alps are also annual.

Cyclothems. A much larger scale form of repetitive stratification is the cyclothem, independently discovered in the Lower Carboniferous Yoredale Series of Yorkshire (Hind, 1902; Hudson, 1924) and the Pennsylvanian rocks of Illinois (Udden, 1912, p. 47–50; Weller, 1930; Wanless and Weller, 1932, first use of term), and now recognized in Carboniferous rocks in many parts of the world and also, though generally with somewhat different characteristics, in rocks of other ages. In Illinois, the typical cyclothem (Fig. 52) consists of the following sequence (Weller, Henbest, and Dunbar, 1942, p. 10):

10. Shale with ironstone concretions
 9. Marine limestone
 8. Black sheety shale with black limestone concretions or layers
 7. Impure, lenticular, marine limestone
 6. Shale
 5. Coal
 4. Underclay
 3. "Fresh-water" limestone
 2. Sandy shale
 1. Sandstone, locally unconformable on underlying beds

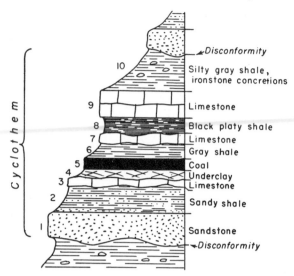

Figure 52. Typical cyclothem from Pennsylvanian of Illinois.

Typically the cyclothems are somewhat more or less than 50 feet thick; not all the units are present in each cyclothem, but enough occur to make the regular repetition clear. Such a succession is evidently the record of a cycle of deposition, first non-marine (units 1 to 5 and part of 6), then marine (units 6 to 10, though non-marine conditions recurred before the following unconformity in some cycles), preceded and followed by erosion.

East and west from Illinois, facies modifications of this sequence appear. To the east, the sequence tends to lose its marine members and to become, in descending order (Wanless and Shepard, 1936, p. 1182; Waagé, 1950, p. 46):

Shale, partly or wholly fresh-water
Coal
Underclay, locally with fresh-water limestone, gradational below through sandy shale into
Sandstone, commonly conglomeratic

Westward, on the other hand, more and more marine limestone appears, commonly in several units. Here also cycles of cycles appear, and Moore (1936, p. 29) has called the deposits of such super-cycles megacyclothems. Figure 53 illustrates a typical megacyclothem from the Pennsylvanian of Kansas. Whether the typical Illinois cycles correspond to the larger or smaller cycles in Kansas does not seem certain.

Quite different cycles of sedimentation are also known—for example, the following sequence (total thickness about 10 feet) in the Upper Cambrian Gatesburg dolomite of central Pennsylvania, described by Krynine (mimeographed guidebook for Twelfth Annual Field Conference of Pennsylvania Geologists, 1946, p. 2–4):

Buff silty dolostone with sand grains
Cryptozoon bed (dolostone, locally silicified)
Massive black dolostone, oölitic above
Thin-bedded dark dolostone
Sandstone

Such striking phenomena as the Pennsylvanian cyclothems call for explanation. There is little question that each records a cyclical advance and retreat of the sea over the land, the sea standing in Kansas through most or all of each cycle but reaching Pennsylvania only at the climax of certain cycles. But the cause of the cyclical change in the position of the sea relative to the land is in debate. Weller (1930) has maintained that the land has been diastrophically active, sinking and rising cyclically so that the shoreline swept in and out repeatedly and sand was supplied periodically from the rising land. If so, the regularity of the repetition is certainly extraordinary. Wanless and Shepard (1936) have suggested that the sea rather than the land was active, its level changing eustatically in cyclical fashion, probably as the result of waxing and waning glaciers in other parts of the world, especially the Southern Hemisphere. If so, there were more than 50 such glacial advances and retreats in the late Paleozoic, far more than the evidence at present available in the glaciated areas would indicate. The problem remains open.

STRATIFICATION AND ROCK SEQUENCE

The Law of Superposition

Stratification obviously records the position of the surface of deposition of the rocks in which it is found, but it does more, for it permits the determination of relative age. The first fundamental generalization of stratigraphy, without which virtually no history could be read from sedimentary rocks, is the law of superposition; to wit, in a sequence of layered rocks, any layer is older than the layer next above. Steno in the seventeenth century appears to have been the first

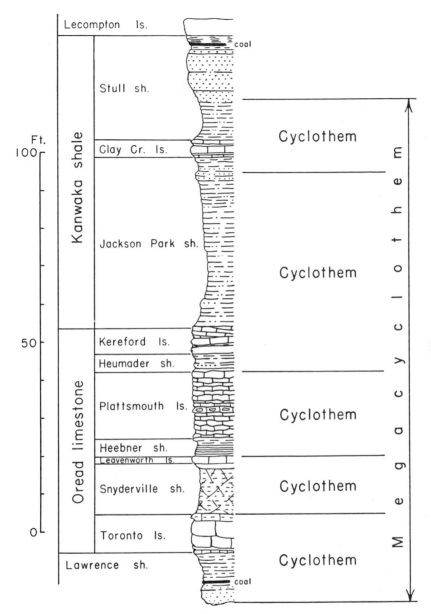

Figure 53. Megacyclothem from Pennsylvanian of Kansas (from Moore, 1936, Fig. 3).

firmly to grasp this generalization, and during the eighteenth century it became the basis for deciphering history from rocks through the work of such men as John Strachey, Johann Gottlob Lehmann, Giovanni Arduino, John Michell, and Georg Christian Fuchsel (p. 289).

It is possible to imagine exceptions to this general rule; thus if beds were deposited in a cave, they would be younger than the overlying rocks. This explanation has actually been invoked in a few cases. Ulrich (1931), studying the faunas from the Lower Ordovician section of carbonate rocks at Philipsburg, Quebec, found in the Naylor Ledge formation a fauna which he believed to be younger than that in the overlying Luke Hill formation. He therefore concluded that the Naylor Ledge was formed in a cave beneath the Luke Hill. When mapping showed, however, that the Naylor Ledge formation is a perfectly regular mappable unit traceable for miles, so that the

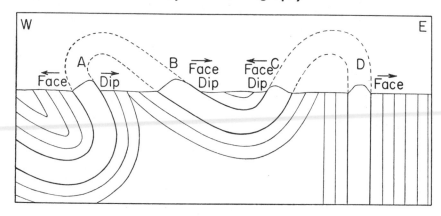

Figure 54. Dip and face of beds. After Shrock (1948a, Fig. 8).

cave would have had to be 30 feet high and 5 miles long, the cave hypothesis collapsed of its own weight.

A much more debatable case is that of the Independence shale of Iowa (argued by Cooper and Warthin and by Stainbrook in Cooper and others, 1942, p. 1765–1767). The Independence is a dark fossiliferous shale in a sequence of carbonate rocks. Its apparent stratigraphic position is between the Wapsipinicon limestone below and the Cedar Valley limestone above, both of which were referred by Cooper and others (1942) with some question to the Middle Devonian, but it contains a well-defined Upper Devonian fauna. As it was known only in local patches, Cooper and Warthin suggested that it was a cave deposit, thus removing the anomaly in the faunal succession, but Stainbrook, who has studied the formations intensively in the field, believed it to be in normal position and therefore preferred to revise the age assignment of the overlying Cedar Valley limestone. More recently Stainbrook (1945) has summarized all the available field data and concluded again that the Independence underlies the Cedar Valley in normal order and that the cave hypothesis is untenable.

Criteria of Superposition

The other important possible type of exception to the law of superposition is that of tectonically overturned beds, which are by no means uncommon in areas of strong deformation. The exist-

ence of overturned sequences has led to a search for criteria by which the original order of the strata can be determined. The literature on this subject is voluminous, but it has recently been summarized in masterly fashion by Shrock in his book *Sequence in Layered Rocks* (1948a). As Shrock's book discusses the subject in detail, only a few of the main criteria need be mentioned here; students are urged to delve into that book for further details on these and other criteria, and also for the mass of valuable information it contains on all aspects of stratification. We have made much use of it, not only in the present section but throughout this chapter.

In discussing criteria of superposition, Shrock (1948a, p. 17–18) defines *face* as the direction faced at present by the original upper surface of the strata, in contrast to *dip*, the direction they incline without respect to superposition (Fig. 54). If dip and face have the same direction, the strata are in normal sequence; if opposite directions, they are overturned. Another useful term is *geopetal* [Gr. *geos*, earth, + L. *petere*, to seek], introduced by Sander (1936, p. 31; trans., p. 2) for any features "that enable us to determine what was the relation of 'top' to 'bottom' at the time when the rock was formed."

The criteria of superposition may be classed generally into (1) stratigraphic criteria, those based on original features of the rock formed by the processes of deposition, and (2) tectonic criteria, those based on features impressed on the rock by processes of deformation.

Stratigraphic criteria. *Local sequence.* If the local sequence is known, it can, of course, be used to detect overturning. Commonly, however, criteria of superposition are needed to establish the local sequence.

Graded bedding. Most forms of repetitive stratification are geopetal, especially typical graded bedding, which commonly occurs, moreover, in sequences where other criteria are rare and wanting and where, because of the absence of fossils and the presence of considerable deformation, the local sequence is difficult to determine. The use of graded bedding depends on the gradation from coarser to finer upward within each bed (Figs. 50, 51, pp. 107 and 109). Reverse gradation is virtually unknown, for it would require very special conditions to deposit fine materials first and then, without disturbing them, to cover them with gradually coarser materials. Graded bedding is probably, therefore, the strongest of all criteria of superposition, and it is practically unimpeachable if, as is typical, a number of beds with consistent gradation can be observed.

Cross-stratification. Normally cross-strata are truncated by the upper surface of the cross-stratified set; they may either swing into parallelism with the lower surface or intersect it, commonly at an angle less than that at which they intersect the upper surface. As a result of the swing into parallelism or near-parallelism, the cross-strata are commonly concave upward, especially in the lenticular form of cross-stratification (Fig. 49, p. 106). Either one-sided truncation or concavity may therefore be used to establish sequence, but it should be noted that isolated exceptions to both rules occur. As with graded bedding, therefore, the observer should not rest content with a single example but should look at a number and assure himself that they are consistent before reaching a firm conclusion as to top and bottom.

Evidence of unconformity. If any kind of unconformity (Chap. 6) can be recognized, it can be used as a criterion of superposition. Thus basal pebble layers, weathered zones, crevice fillings, and other criteria of unconformity are also criteria of superposition.

Minor stratigraphic features. Many minor features can be used as supporting evidence for superposition, such as mudcracks and oscillation ripples (but less commonly current ripples) or, in lava flows, pillows and the distribution of vesicles. In many areas, local criteria can be worked out; for example, in the Upper Devonian rocks of New York many sandstone beds have certain characteristic markings (ripple marks, tracks) on the upper surface and other different but equally characteristic markings (so-called flow markings, and groove casts) on the lower surface. A geologist acquainted with these features could determine very readily which way the beds face. Another local criterion is furnished by the silicified layers commonly present immediately beneath thick beds of altered volcanic ash in certain sequences, such as the Middle Ordovician of the Appalachians, the Upper Cretaceous of the northern Great Plains and Rockies, and the Monterey formation (Miocene) of California (p. 250).

Fossils. The first use of fossils in establishing superposition depends on the direct evidence they give of relative age, by correlation with a standard succession whose superposition is known (Chap. 16). This evidence commonly permits the determination of the relative position of major units but rarely of individual beds, if the structure is complex. The fossils themselves may give clues, however, apart from their age significance. Fossils in position of growth (such as corals, or stromatolites like cryptozoon), worm tracks or burrows (if the local habit of occurrence is known), partial fillings of shell interiors—all these may be used as geopetal criteria.

Tectonic criteria. The principal tectonic criteria of superposition are drag folds and slaty cleavage. Slaty cleavage is ordinarily parallel to the axial planes of the major folds of the region (and slip cleavage is not far from parallel if deformation has not been intense or compound), and likewise the axial planes of the drag folds are normally about parallel to those of the major folds. Now the location of a given outcrop of steeply dipping strata with respect to the nearest major anticline and syncline can usually be worked out, if the attitude of the axial planes of the major folds is known, provided that the strike of the strata and that of the axial planes do not differ more than about 45°. Imagine the strata pro-

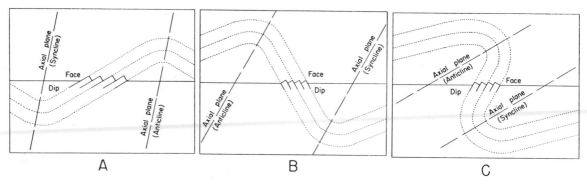

Figure 55. The use of tectonic criteria in determining superposition. The axial planes of the major folds on either side of the outcrop being studied are assumed to be parallel to slaty cleavage or the axial planes of drag folds within the outcrop. A. Beds dip in the same direction as axial planes but more gently: beds right side up. B. Beds dip in the opposite direction from axial planes: beds right side up. C. Beds dip in the same direction as axial planes but more steeply: beds overturned.

jected upwards and downwards to intersect one axial plane on each side of the outcrop; then the beds face in the direction of the axial plane that intersects the strata projected downwards, which is the axial plane of the major syncline (Fig. 55). A rule of thumb is: if the beds dip in the opposite direction from the axial planes, or if they dip more gently, they are right side up, but if they dip more steeply in the same direction they are overturned; if they are vertical they face in the opposite direction to the dip of the axial planes. (If the folds are isoclinal, the strata should be parallel to the axial planes and the rule would fail, but in that case the axial-plane attitude as deduced from cleavage or drag folds is ordinarily not the true attitude but is normally rotated a little in the direction that makes the rule work.)

As with stratigraphic criteria, a single drag fold or cleavage plane is not enough to establish the sequence with assurance; several consistent observations are needed. Furthermore, several assumptions enter into the train of reasoning; namely, that the larger folds are part of the same deformation pattern as the lesser features, that the strikes of strata and axial planes do not diverge too greatly (if they do, the axes of the folds probably plunge steeply and the distinction between anticline and syncline loses its meaning), and finally that there has been only one period of deformation. In general the tectonic criteria, having been impressed on the rock after its formation, are of a lower order of reliability than the stratigraphic criteria, which are the direct results of the depositional process.

Northeast Tennessee provides an instructive example of the failure of tectonic criteria. In a belt of near vertical Lower Cambrian quartzite and shale units striking northeast, the drag folds sketched in Figure 56A may be observed. The axial planes of the drag folds dip northwest; therefore, by the usual rule the beds lie between an anticline to the northwest and a syncline to the southeast, and they face southeast. Not far away in the same strike belt, weak slaty cleavage (the rocks are otherwise unmetamorphosed) dipping northwest less steeply than the bedding enforces the same conclusion. But the well-established local sequence shows that the beds face northwest, and this is confirmed in the exposure in question by cross-stratification. The discrepancy can be resolved by seeing the exposure in its regional setting (Fig. 56B). It is part of one of a series of thrust sheets which, after being stacked one on top of another, were then folded into a synclinorium to the northwest and an anticlinorium to the southwest. The tectonic criteria fail because of the two periods of deformation. If the later folding is removed, by tilting the exposure in question through 90° or more to the southeast, the tectonic criteria square perfectly with the stratigraphic criteria (Fig. 56C).

A much less reliable tectonic criterion of age relations, which may nevertheless be needed in reconnaissance or in complexly deformed areas, is the relative degree of deformation or metamorphism. Ordinarily one would expect crystalline schist to be older than adjacent little or not metamorphosed sedimentary rocks, and rocks intruded and metamorphosed by a large granite body to be older than rocks equally close to the granite but not affected by it. But exceptions to these rules are all too common, and such criteria are at best merely suggestive and should be used only as a last resort.

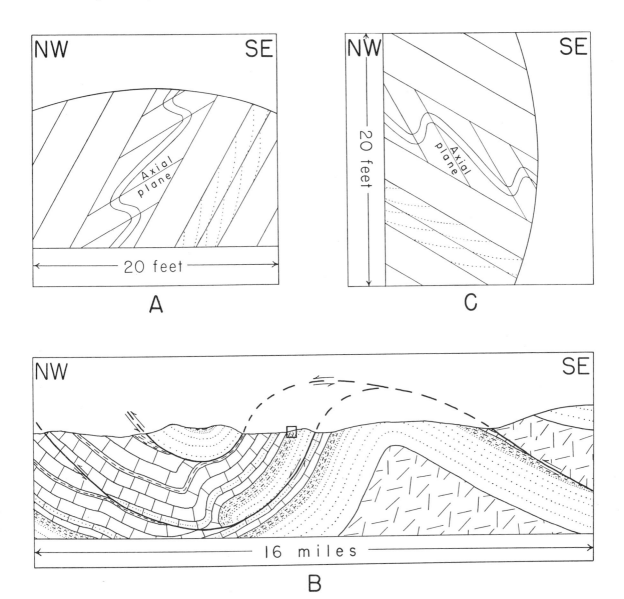

Figure 56. Failure of tectonic criteria of superposition because of double deformation, based on field example in East Tennessee. A. Diagram of actual outcrop; axial planes of drag folds indicate overturning, but cross-stratification denies it. B. Regional setting; small square shows location of A. C. Outcrop rotated through 90° to remove effect of second deformation; cross-stratification and drag folds now agree.

6. Breaks in the record

UNCONFORMITIES

The Concept of Unconformity

Growth of the concept. Deposition of sediment has been going on somewhere ever since erosion began on the Earth, and a continuous record of all geologic time may be present in parts of the ocean floor. But if such a record exists it is now beyond our reach; on the continents there are gaps, large or small, wherever sedimentary rocks have been studied. The lost intervals range in magnitude from the short span of time between storms, recorded only as obscure bedding planes, to the great breaks where Pleistocene till rests on early Precambrian rocks and virtually all of geologic time goes unrecorded.

Recognition of such temporal breaks in the stratigraphic record began with James Hutton who in the company of Sir James Hall and John Playfair visited Siccar Point, Berwickshire, Scotland, in 1788 and for the first time saw the Old Red sandstone (Devonian) resting upon the upturned edges of Silurian strata (Fig. 42, p. 96). The three visitors were emotionally stirred to realize that what they saw proved that the "Primary schistus" [Silurian] had been uplifted, deformed, and partly eroded away before deposition of the "Secondary strata" (Hutton, 1795, v. 1, p. 458). Hutton soon discovered the same relation at other localities in southern Scotland, and Playfair (1802, p. 217) described comparable relations in the north of England where, about Ingleborough, the Great Scar limestone (Lower Carboniferous) rests on the peneplained edges of strongly folded Silurian and Ordovician strata (Fig. 59, p. 119).

These pioneers had seen and correctly interpreted a great unconformity, though neither of them used that now familiar term. The word *unconformable* was apparently introduced from German into English by Bakewell (1815, p. 48), and it soon became firmly established, but in what seems to us now a restricted sense, referring only to the relations observed by Hutton and Playfair. Lyell, for example, wrote (1838, p. 74): "Strata are said to be unconformable, when one series is so placed over another, that the planes of the superior repose on the edges of the inferior." The same or a similar definition was repeated by Lyell, Dana, and other textbook writers throughout the nineteenth century.

At first, to be sure, only such obvious breaks could be recognized, but with the rapid growth of stratigraphy after 1800, as fossils came to be used to date the rocks, less conspicuous breaks were detected, even in the midst of parallel strata, and in his monumental *Origin of Species,* Charles Darwin (1859) emphasized the incompleteness of the stratigraphic record and argued that probably more of geologic time is represented by breaks than by beds. The remarkable insight shown by Darwin is now evident.

As important breaks come to be recognized

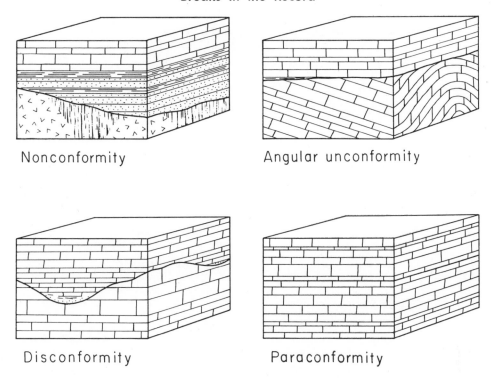

Nonconformity

Angular unconformity

Disconformity

Paraconformity

Figure 57. The four types of unconformity.

even where discordance was lacking, these too were regarded as unconformities, and thus the scope of the term broadened. After describing several such breaks in New York State, Grabau (1905, p. 534) observed: "We need a term to express the relation where two formations thus conform in their bedding but comprise between them a time break of greater or less magnitude. To speak of such strata as unconformable, without qualifying the term, is misleading, since it suggests that the older strata have suffered folding and erosion before the deposition of the latter." He then proposed to call them *disconformable,* restricting the term unconformable to cases in which discordance of bedding occurs. And in 1913 (p. 821) he wrote: "Strata separated by an unrepresented time interval are generally spoken of as unconformably related. Two types of such unconformable relation may be recognized. . . . For the first type, in which no folding of the older set of strata is involved, the term *disconformity* has been proposed, with the corresponding limitation of the term *unconformity* to the second type, or that in which folding plus erosion of the first

set of strata precedes the formation of the second set."

Pirsson (Pirsson and Schuchert, 1915, p. 291–293), on the contrary, proposed to retain the term unconformity in a generic sense to cover all types of important breaks in the stratigraphic sequence. He clearly recognized the four basic types of structural relation shown in Figure 57, but did not name them. Instead, he accepted Grabau's term disconformity for the two types in which the break is between beds that are parallel, and proposed *nonconformity* to embrace the other two.

The meaning attached to unconformity has varied also in another way. Hutton and Playfair were impressed with the significance of the *hiatus* in the record and of the events that had occurred during the lost interval. Lyell and Dana, on the contrary, focused attention on the *structural relations,* and Pirsson (Pirsson and Schuchert, 1915, p. 288–289) defined an unconformity as the *surface* separating two unconformable formations. Clearly, however, the break or hiatus in the record is the one feature that gives significance to unconformity and the only one that would justify recog-

Charles Schuchert

Figure 58.   Nonconformity at Montmorency Falls, east of Quebec City.   Here Trenton limestone (Middle Ordovician) overlaps on Precambrian granite.

nition of an invisible unconformity between parallel beds.

Definition.   An unconformity may be defined as a temporal break in a stratigraphic sequence resulting from a change in regimen that caused deposition to cease for a considerable span of time.   It normally implies uplift and erosion with the loss of some of the previously formed record. In this sense it is a hiatus representing a certain span of time.   It is located at a surface of unconformity, and the beds above and below are unconformable, that is, they do not fit together as parts of a continuous whole [L. *un,* not + *con,* together + *formare,* to shape or form].

The term unconformity is still commonly used also in the two other senses mentioned above. It refers to the *structural relations* of the beds

above and below the break rather than to the hiatus itself, as when we distinguish different types of unconformity, and it is sometimes applied also to the *surface* separating the unconformable units. The context normally shows which meaning is intended so that no ambiguity results from these varied usages.

Types of unconformity.   Structural relations between unconformable units fall into one of the four types illustrated in Figure 57.   In the first, stratified rocks rest upon non-stratified (Fig. 58), either igneous or metamorphic; in the second, an angular discordance separates two units of stratified rocks (Figs. 42, p. 96, and 59); in the third, all the strata are parallel but the contact between two units is an uneven erosion surface (Fig. 60); and in the fourth, the contact is a simple bedding plane (Fig. 61, and Fig. 115, p. 256). The evidence of a break in sequence is obvious in the first three, but in the fourth type it must be inferred from other than structural criteria.

Each structural type needs a distinct name to facilitate accurate and objective recording of observed relations, and we face the choice of restricting names currently used in a broader sense or of coining new ones. We propose to restrict the term *nonconformity* to the first type, in which stratified rocks are unconformable with non-stratified, either igneous or metamorphic. For the second type, in which two units of stratified rocks are discordant, the term *angular unconformity* is in common use. We propose to restrict the term *disconformity* to the third type, in which two units of stratified rocks are parallel but the surface of unconformity is an old erosion surface of appreciable relief, and to introduce a new term *paraconformity* for the fourth type, in which the beds are parallel and the contact is a simple bedding plane. In the last case the two units may be described as *paraconformable.**

There is special need for a term for this non-evident type of unconformity in which the contact is a simple bedding plane, since its recognition is commonly subjective, especially during recon-

* L. *para*, beside (in the figurative sense of being not quite the same or not really) + *con*, together + *formare*, to shape or form. The prefix *para* is used in this sense in many technical terms; for example, the *paragaster* of a sponge is *not really* a gaster (stomach).

Courtesy of Her Majesty's Geological Survey

Figure 59.   Unconformity between the Horton flags (Silurian) and the Great Scar limestone (Lower Carboniferous) in Comb's Quarry 1 mile west-northwest of Helwith Bridge, Yorkshire. British Crown copyright.

Edward T. Schenk, courtesy of National Park Service

Figure 60. Disconformity between the Mead and the Peasley limestones (both Cambrian) in the south wall of the Grand Canyon, 1 mile east of Grand Wash Cliffs.

naissance study or where fossils are rare or lacking. Important breaks of this sort have often been recognized by one stratigrapher only to be denied by another. Commonly the hiatus is inferred because of an abrupt faunal change, but such changes may be susceptible of more than one interpretation. They may be due to loss of part of the evolutionary record, for example, or to a mere change in the environment without loss of time. It will make for objective reporting, therefore, if such inferred breaks in the sequence are identified by a distinct name.

When traced laterally a single unconformity may appear locally in more than one guise. In southeastern Wyoming, for example, the great unconformity below the Pennsylvanian System (Fig. 62) illustrates three of the four structural types shown in Figure 57. Along the flanks of the Front Range, the Fountain arkose rests nonconformably on Precambrian granite, including

in its basal layers fossiliferous chert pebbles derived from Mississippian limestones that once covered the region but were eroded away before Pennsylvanian deposition began. The Hartville Uplift some 25 miles to the northeast brings the base of the Pennsylvanian to the surface again, and there it rests disconformably on the Guernsey limestone (Lower Mississippian), filling narrow canyons 50 feet or more in depth. Here the strong relief at the contact is made the more striking because the limestone is white and the basal beds of the Pennsylvanian are red. Where exposed again in the rim of the Black Hills a hundred miles farther northeast, the basal Pennsylvanian beds are light-gray limestone resting paraconformably on the Lower Mississippian limestones, and the contact is inconspicuous in most outcrops although more than half a geologic period is unrecorded, yet the hiatus is even greater here than in the Hartville Uplift.

Criteria for Recognition and Evaluation

Recognizing an unconformity is only the first step toward understanding it; the more important objective is to determine the magnitude of the hiatus (Blackwelder, 1909). Since most of the criteria used for recognition also throw some light on the importance of the break, we may avoid repetition by discussing recognition and evaluation together as the more important criteria are considered in turn.

Nonconformity. Where stratified rocks rest upon igneous or metamorphic rocks, a marked change in regimen is evident. If the lower rock is plutonic and the sedimentary rock shows no contact metamorphism, or if it includes in its base pebbles of the igneous rock, a major hiatus is indicated during which a thick cover was eroded from the intrusive mass.

If the lower rock is a sill, its intrusive rela-

tions should be revealed by alteration of the immediately overlying sedimentary layers and by a chilled border in the intrusive rock; if the igneous rock is volcanic, no hiatus is necessarily implied. Along the eastern border of the Columbia Plateau, for example, basalt flows intertongue with the fossiliferous Latah formation (Miocene) in a manner proving that the lava flowed into a basin in which sediment was being deposited. Similar relations may be seen about the southern margin of the Absaroka Plateau in Wyoming where several Eocene and Oligocene sedimentary formations rest upon thick masses of lava or of volcanic ash. Here no loss of time is necessarily implied between the igneous outburst and deposition of its sedimentary cover.

Where sedimentary rocks rest upon metamorphic, a major hiatus is normally indicated, and its importance may be inferred by the intensity of the

Charles Schuchert

Figure 61. Beargrass Quarry near Louisville, Kentucky, showing paraconformity between the Louisville limestone (Middle Silurian) and the Jeffersonville limestone (lower Middle Devonian). This hiatus is represented by more than 3,000 feet of strata in parts of the Appalachian trough.

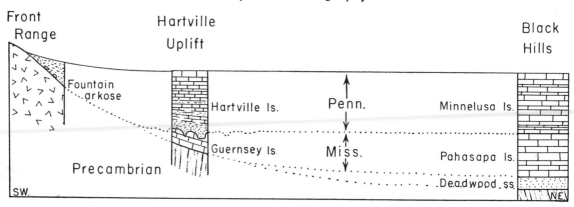

Figure 62. Variable expression of the great unconformity at the base of the Pennsylvanian System in southeastern Wyoming: nonconformity to SW (left), disconformity in center, paraconformity to NE (right).

metamorphism and the kinds of minerals present, since they will suggest the environment of temperature and depth under which the metamorphism occurred. Where, however, a resistant sedimentary formation such as quartzite or massive limestone rests upon weaker beds and both have been somewhat deformed, the weak rock may display strong slaty cleavage and appear much more strongly metamorphosed than the overlying formation. Geikie (1903, p. 687) has described a locality on the west coast of Islay, Scotland, where massive grit overlies slate with what might be mistaken for a profound unconformity (Fig. 63). The bedding in the slate has been largely obscured by slaty cleavage, but it can still be detected, and

it proves that the two formations were folded together.

On the other hand, severe deformation may wipe out the evidences of unconformity even where there has been angular discordance or nonconformity. Near certain faults in Dutchess County, New York (Balk, 1936, p. 732–736), the Poughquag quartzite (Lower Cambrian) has been sheared and recrystallized until it appears entirely conformable with the underlying Precambrian gneiss. Thus in metamorphic terranes, conformity of foliation may mask an original unconformity, or for that matter an original thrust fault.

Angular discordance. Angular discordance is one of the most obvious marks of a hiatus since it

Figure 63. Deceptive appearance of unconformity between slate (a) and overlying massive grit (b) on the west coast of Islay, Scotland. From Geikie (1903).

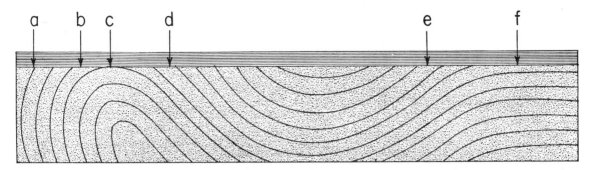

Figure 64. Diagram of an angular unconformity between folded and non-folded beds, showing variation in the angular discordance according to position on the folds.

normally implies that the older beds were deformed and then truncated by erosion before the younger ones were laid down.

It must not be inferred, however, that the angle of discordance indicates the relative importance of the hiatus. As shown in Figure 64, where the folds in an older formation have been truncated and then covered by younger beds, the angle of discordance varies widely according to position on the folds. At locality *a*, for example, it is about 80°, but at *b*, *d*, and *e* it is only about 45°, and at *c* and *f* the beds are parallel. Too often, alas, we hear the argument that because the discordance between two formations is large the hiatus must be profound, or vice versa.

Where the older beds are closely folded the discordance may reach any angle up to 90°, but as we leave the strongly disturbed area and the folds flatten out, the discordance declines even though the hiatus does not decrease. A striking illustration may be seen along the foot of the Glass Mountains in West Texas where the Wolfcamp beds (Lower Permian) overlie the Gaptank formation (Pennsylvanian) with a profound unconformity. At Dugout Mountain in the western part of the range, the Pennsylvanian beds stand vertically and the overlying Permian strata are nearly horizontal. In this part of the range the unconformity is impressive, but in the vicinity of Gaptank some 30 miles farther northeast there is no apparent discordance and the boundary was misplaced until the fossils were critically studied.

Caution is needed where detrital beds were laid down with an initial dip about "highs" such as the Ozark Dome (p. 103) and the Arbuckle Mountains, both of which were gradually buried by onlapping Upper Cambrian deposits. In places in both regions the basal sandstone beds were laid down with an initial dip of 20° or more away from granite hills. The overlapping dolostone and limestone beds were nearly horizontal when deposited. On timbered slopes where outcrops are small, the discordance in dip could be mistaken for evidence of an important hiatus during which the granite domes had moved and the sandstone had been tilted. Careful areal study has disproved this explanation.

It is also possible to mistake cross-bedding for angular unconformity, especially where large-scale foresetting has been followed by even bedding, and outcrops are limited. Such relations are common in the Pleistocene valley fills in New England where lakes formed beside stagnant ice. Tributary streams built deltas into such lakes, and in these most of the sand and gravel was laid down as long, steeply dipping foreset beds, but eventually, when the lakes filled, meltwater flowing along the valleys deposited horizontal layers of sand and silt over the cross-bedded deposits. Similarly in large marine deltas, cross-bedded sandy deposits in the form of lunate bars, built about the mouths of distributaries, may be followed by horizontally bedded sands laid down in the form of natural levees (p. 79). Similar discordances due to cross-bedding may be seen locally in the Jurassic rocks of the Colorado Plateau, as where the marine Carmel formation rests on the Navajo sandstone (Fig. 65) (Gilluly and Reeside, 1928, p. 74). In the heated controversy over the Cretaceous-Tertiary boundary early in

Carew McFall

Figure 65. Horizontally bedded Carmel formation resting on cross-bedded Navajo sandstone (both Jurassic) 1.75 miles west of Boulder, Utah.

this century, an angular unconformity was alleged to separate the Fox Hills sandstone from the Lance formation, but the supposed unconformity was later found to be only cross-bedding (Thom and Dobbin, 1924, p. 486).

Even in cases of real structural unconformity, the local angle of discordance is relatively unimportant as a measure of the time lost by uplift and erosion, but the areal extent of the disturbance and the size of the folds may be highly significant. For this reason the importance of an unconformity must be judged not so much in a single outcrop as by regional study, and by other criteria discussed below.

Erosional relief at the contact. Where the surface of unconformity cuts across beds, it is

evident that uplift and erosion have occurred during the hiatus. Large relief makes the unconformity impressive, but is a poor criterion of its temporal value. In the first place, the relief is limited by the amount of uplift rather than the time involved; in the second place, maximum relief is produced early in the erosion cycle while the streams are cutting chiefly downward, and a much longer time is required for lowering of the interfluves and eventual peneplanation. Paradoxical as it may seem, therefore, the amount of relief at a disconformity is likely to vary inversely as the time involved. The striking disconformity shown in Figure 60 (p. 120), for example, represents a relatively minor break within the Mississippian sequence, whereas a simple bedding plane

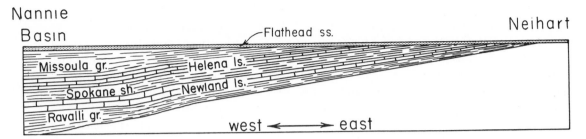

Figure 66. Stratigraphic section from Nannie Basin to Neihart, Montana, showing regional unconformity between the Belt group (Precambrian) and the Flathead sandstone (Middle Cambrian). Length of section about 125 miles. After Deiss (1935).

in Figure 61 (p. 121) conceals a hiatus representing all of Late Silurian and Early Devonian time.

Regional beveling of formations or of faunal zones. In apparently conformable rock sequences an unconformity may sometimes be recognized by the systematic appearance (or disappearance) of units at a given contact over a large region. A splendid example (Fig. 66) is furnished by the overlap of the Flathead sandstone (Middle Cambrian) on the Belt group (Precambrian) in western Montana (Deiss, 1935). In most localities the Flathead formation appears strictly conformable with the underlying Belt strata, but regional study shows that it rests on different units of the Belt group from place to place, beveling down over as much as 20,000 feet of beds from the west or northwest to the east or southeast. The disconformity thus revealed proves that the Belt group is much older than the Flathead formation,

and, indeed, it is one of the main lines of evidence that the Belt is Precambrian.

There is considerable danger, however, of confusing such a situation with one due to facies change. Assume, for example, that a stratigrapher has studied four sections and found the sequences shown in Figure 67. The thickness of shale between the limestone with fauna x and the sandstone with fauna d increases steadily toward the east, and additional faunal zones come in between, as the shale thickens; moreover, at each locality the base of the sandstone unit rests on a sharply defined surface along which the underlying shale has been scoured.

One possible interpretation is that the sandstone with fauna d is regionally paraconformable on the underlying shale, truncating the fossil zones it crosses. But another plausible interpretation is that fauna d is a facies fauna contemporaneous

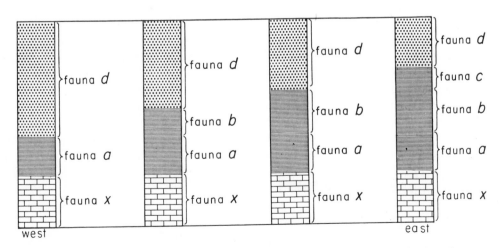

Figure 67. Four columnar sections showing progressive eastward thickening of a shale formation between an underlying limestone and an overlying sandstone.

with faunas *a*, *b*, and *c* but restricted to a sandy environment, and that the sand spread progressively eastward during the period of deposition without any major break so that the lower part of the sandstone in the western section was being deposited at the same time as the upper part of the shale in the eastern section. Evidence of scouring at the top of the shale would prove little or nothing because any current strong enough to transport sand where there was only mud before would be strong enough to scour the mud. The choice between the two interpretations would have to depend on more detailed studies between the widely spaced sections, in particular on evidence either of intertonguing of the facies or, on the other hand, of actual truncation of the shale sequence, and on more careful consideration of the faunas showing either that fauna *d* contains elements of faunas *b* and *c* or, on the contrary, that it is entirely younger.

Some of the most troublesome controversies in stratigraphy have developed out of such relations. To mention but a single example, Ulrich (1911, p. 379, 382, 576) proposed the Blount group to embrace four formations in the Middle Ordovician of eastern Tennessee, at least 3,500 feet thick, which he believed to lie between the Lenoir limestone and the Lowville limestone, younger than the one and older than the other. He believed that a great hiatus existed elsewhere in the Appalachian Trough where these formations are not present. It is now known that they merely represent different lithologic facies equivalent to other formations, and the supposed hiatus has vanished.

Abrupt lithologic change. Abrupt lithologic change implies a change in regimen and may indicate a hiatus, especially if coarse detrital sediment overlies fine; but the change in regimen does not necessarily involve a break in deposition. The walls of the Grand Canyon show several such changes, some of which are associated with major breaks and others not. At the top of the massive, light-gray Redwall limestone (Lower Mississippian) there is an abrupt change to the Supai redbeds (Lower Permian). The hiatus is a great one but the formations are paraconformable.

Some 1,800 feet higher the red Hermit shale is abruptly succeeded by massive, cliff-forming white sandstone of the Coconino formation. Again the beds are paraconformable and the change in lithology is abrupt and striking, with coarser detrital sediment resting on fine. But in this case the sand appeared as migrating dunes spreading over a lowland where mud had been forming; the formations above and below are both Middle Permian, and if there be any hiatus it is relatively unimportant. Lower down on the walls of the Canyon the lithologic change is abrupt between the Tapeats sandstone and the Bright Angel shale and again between the latter and the Muav limestone but these are all Cambrian formations, and McKee (1943, p. 103; 1945a) has proved by lateral tracing that these contacts are mere changes of facies that rise in the section from west to east and involve no hiatus whatever (Fig. 73, p. 141). On the contrary, McKee has separated the Kaibab limestone at the top of the Canyon from the similar Toroweap limestone next beneath, because there is clear evidence of a hiatus between them.

In short, a pronounced and abrupt change in lithology should be considered a warning of a possible hiatus but not proof that one exists.

Evidence of an old erosion surface. One of the most satisfactory criteria for unconformity is evidence of an erosion surface between two formations. Such evidence may be in the physical form of the surface, such as pronounced irregularities, mounds, crevices, or even caves, overlapped and filled by the materials of the overlying unit; it may be evidence of weathering of the rock below before deposition of the rock above, such as a fire clay, an old soil profile, or a rusty, silicified, or calichified zone; it may be the abrupt truncation of structural features such as joints, faults, or dikes in the lower beds; or it may be the presence of pebbles from the beds below in the basal layers above. Lag gravels and sands of any sort are suggestive of unconformity; likewise, especially in marine deposits, concentrates of phosphate, manganese, iron, or glauconite nodules or grains (though such concentrates may be evidence only of extremely slow deposition and not of a break in the record). Such evidences of unconformity, especially from well cuttings, are summarized by Krumbein (1942a).

Several of these criteria are illustrated about the flanks of the Ozark Dome where Lower

Mississippian cherty limestone is overlapped by dark Middle Pennsylvanian shale and sandstone (locally coal-bearing). Although essentially parallel, the beds above and below the contact are lithologically so dissimilar as to indicate that a major change in the environment had occurred before Pennsylvanian deposition began. Furthermore the surface of the Mississippian limestone had a karst topography with abundant sinks and a mantle that included residual chert fragments. The basal Pennsylvanian beds filled the sinks and locally include lenses of chert breccia derived from this old mantle.

Other criteria are illustrated about Syracuse, New York, where the Onondaga limestone (Middle Devonian) commonly rests paraconformably on the Manlius limestone (uppermost Silurian). But locally, as near Jamesville, the upper surface of the Manlius limestone is marked by crevices several inches deep, filled with coarse quartz sand. In the large quarry of the Solvay Company within a mile of this locality, a thin lens of fossiliferous Oriskany sandstone (Lower Devonian) is found between the Manlius and the Onondaga limestones, and the sand that fills the crevices in the Manlius limestone at Jamesville was clearly derived from the Oriskany formation.

Thin beds of ganister or of fire clay are common in the Coal Measures, and buried soil profiles or gumbotil are common in Pleistocene deposits.

Paleontological evidence. The relative importance of a hiatus is immediately evident if the beds above and below bear fossils by which they can be assigned their proper position in the geologic column. In most instances this is the final and the only criterion that gives quantitative results for the large unconformities. In the Grand Canyon walls, for example, where Redwall limestone can be dated as Lower Mississippian and the underlying Muav limestone as Middle Cambrian, we know that the paraconformity represents more than three geologic periods, yet the physical evidence for the break is less obvious than for that which separates the Toroweap and the Kaibab limestones, both of which are Middle Permian. Many large unconformities would never be suspected if it were not for such dating of the rocks above and below. Over a large area in the Ohio Valley, for example, Middle Devonian lime-

stone rests paraconformably on similar Middle Silurian limestone, as in the Beargrass quarries near Louisville, Kentucky (Fig. 61, p. 121). This hiatus may be seen also in a large quarry at Newsom, west of Nashville, Tennessee (Fig. 115, p. 256) where two paraconformities are present. Here the Chattanooga shale (Middle (?) and Upper Devonian, Hass, 1956) rests on the Pegram limestone (basal Middle Devonian), which is only 6 feet thick and in turn rests on the Lego limestone (lower Middle Silurian). The same widespread paraconformity separates Middle Silurian from overlying Lower Devonian limestones in the Western Valley of Tennessee, where the contact can be located only when fossils are found in the bounding layers.

Such large faunal breaks prove a hiatus and at the same time indicate its temporal value by placing the beds above and below in widely different divisions of the geologic column. Unless the faunas differ appreciably in age, however, an abrupt faunal break is no evidence of a hiatus, for it may be due to a change in bottom ecology without interruption of deposition. Such environmental change might be a result of difference in depth or salinity, or in the quality or quantity of sediment being introduced. For example, a cyclothem in the Pennsylvanian rocks of Illinois (Fig. 52, p. 110) normally includes 10 distinct lithologic units most of which have a fauna (or flora) largely distinct from that of any other member, yet the same fossil assemblages largely reappear in corresponding members of the next cyclothem above and below. Obviously these faunal changes are not due to loss of part of the record but to migrations in response to changing environment.

DIASTEMS

Introduction

The discovery of radioactivity, just before the turn of this century, proved an open-sesame to many wonders of this atomic age. Not the least of these was an absolute time scale for geologic history. When Boltwood (1907) first proposed to use the ratio of lead to uranium in a mineral as a measure of the time in years since it crystallized, we were still assuming that the Earth is not over one hundred million years old. Use of the lead-uranium ratio, however, soon demonstrated its age to be more than two thousand million years, and placed the beginning of Cambrian time at approximately 500,000,000 years ago.

To some thoughtful stratigraphers this amazing discovery presented a dilemma, for if the known stratified rocks have been accumulating throughout this vast span of time the average rate of deposition must have been extremely slow, yet there is very good evidence that individual beds accumulated rapidly. Thus Schuchert (1931, p. 49) found that if a geologic column were built up by superposing the thickest known part of each of the geologic systems in North America, from Cambrian to the present, the composite record would be about 259,000 feet thick. If we combine his results with the latest estimates of time based on radioactive minerals, we get the figures in Table 5, in which the last column indicates the estimated average rate of deposition.

TABLE 5. AVERAGE RATES OF DEPOSITION IN GEOLOGIC TIME, AS POSTULATED BY SCHUCHERT (1931).

	Thickness in Feet	Time in Years	Average Rate of Deposition
Cenozoic	61,400	70,000,000	1 ft in 1,400 years
Mesozoic	86,600	130,000,000	1 ft in 1,500 years
Paleozoic	111,000	300,000,000	1 ft in 2,700 years

Internal evidence in the strata, however, belies these estimates. In the Coal Measures of Nova Scotia, for example, the stumps and trunks of many trees are preserved standing upright as they grew, clearly having been buried before they had time to fall or rot away. Here sediment certainly accumulated to a depth of many feet within a few years. In other formations where articulated skeletons of large animals are preserved, the sediment must have covered them within a few days at the most. Abundant fossil shells likewise indicate rapid burial, for if shells are long exposed on the sea floor they suffer abrasion or corrosion and are overgrown by sessile organisms or perforated by boring animals. At the rate of deposition postulated by Schuchert, 1,000 years, more or less, would have been required to bury a shell 5 inches in diameter. With very local exceptions fossil shells show no evidence of such long exposure. Evidently then, either our estimates of

geologic time are grossly exaggerated, or else most of the elapsed time is not represented in any given section by sedimentary deposits.

Such considerations led Barrell (1917) to a critical analysis of the manner in which sediments are laid down. He recognized, of course, that unconformities would account for part of the time, but Schuchert's measurements were taken from the deepest parts of the geosynclines where deposition was presumably most rapid and most nearly continuous. Outside the geosynclines where unconformities are common, the stratified rocks are very much thinner. Barrell concluded that unconformities are quite inadequate to reconcile the immensity of geologic time with the evidence for rapid accumulation of sedimentary deposits, and that innumerable short breaks due to non-deposition, or to sublevation of loose sediment on the sea floor, must account for most of the elapsed time. For these small breaks he coined the term *diastems*. This concept, which he first applied to marine strata, will be clear from the following considerations (Barrell, 1917, p. 776–809; Eaton, 1929, p. 713–741).

Temporary Baselevel of Aggradation

With local exceptions due to recently drowned topography, to recent tectonic movement, or to the growth of organic reefs, the continental shelf is a remarkably flat sea floor sloping gently seaward (p. 47, and Fig. 1, p. 2). A submarine profile from the shore to the continental margin has the form represented in Figure 68, concave for a few miles from shore, then nearly flat for many miles, and finally convex where the shelf grades over into the continental slope. The concavity near shore is due to degradation by the waves and currents, and the convexity is due to aggradation.

Between the concave zone where degradation is dominant and the convex zone where deposition prevails, the profile is intersected by an imaginary horizontal plane toward which the sea floor is being graded. From one viewpoint it is the baselevel of erosion, but from the stratigrapher's point of view it is the *baselevel of aggradation*. Below this ideal plane deposition will take place whenever sediment is available, but above this level no

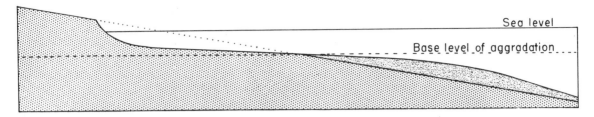

Figure 68.   The base level of aggradation in relation to the submarine profile across a continental shelf.   Vertical scale very greatly exaggerated.   If this diagram were drawn to true scale to show the relations off the mid-Atlantic States, the entire profile of the shelf would lie within the line here marking sealevel.

sediment can come permanently to rest, regardless of time.   The depth of this plane below sealevel is influenced by several factors each of which varies from place to place and from time to time.   It is not a fixed baselevel, therefore, but a *temporary baselevel of aggradation* which rises and falls with fluctuations in these controlling factors.

Factors Controlling the Depth of the Baselevel of Aggradation

Currents.   Bottom currents (p. 11) control the movement of sediment on the shallow sea floor.   They are due chiefly to tides and to storms, and are highly variable.   When bottom currents are strong they tend to sublevate and move loose sediment, but as they decrease in velocity they lose carrying power and drop their load.   In general they lose velocity with depth.

Waves.   Where waves reach the bottom they exert a lift with each passing crest (p. 11), and thus facilitate movement by bottom currents.   The effectiveness of waves reaches a peak during great storms and falls to zero during quiet weather.

Load.   Both the volume and the coarseness of the sediment influence the depth of the baselevel of aggradation.   Since bottom currents normally lose velocity with depth, coarse particles will come to rest first while finer ones are carried beyond into deeper water.   If all the sediment were coarse, the sea floor would be graded to one depth; if all fine, it would be graded to a deeper level.   In short there is a different baselevel of aggradation for each size grade of sediment.   For this reason the continental shelf would not be perfectly horizontal even if it were perfectly

graded; coarse material near shore would be in equilibrium at shallower depths than the finer sediment farther out, and the perfectly graded surface would therefore slope gently seaward.

If the volume of sediment available exceeds the capacity of the waves and currents, part of it will accumulate, and the baselevel of aggradation under these conditions will be higher than if the load were less.   Where large amounts of sediment are introduced by streams, the sea floor may thus be graded up to sealevel and the land surface extended, as it is in great deltas.

Even if a temporary baselevel were established under a given set of waves and currents and a part of the sea floor were graded to it, equilibrium would be upset by a change in the load of the streams bringing in sediment.   If the load became finer or decreased in volume, the baselevel would drop and currents would begin to sublevate sediment and degrade the floor, but if the load were increased in volume or in coarseness, the baselevel of aggradation would be raised and some of the sediment could come to rest.   Such fluctuations in load could arise from climatic changes or from uplift or subsidence in the drainage basin of the streams far inland.

Intermittency of Deposition

If waves and currents of given competence operated constantly and uniformly over a considerable area of the neritic zone, and if a constant supply of loose sediment were available, the sea floor in this area would eventually be graded to a monotonously flat surface in equilibrium with all these controlling factors.   The increment of sediment introduced from outside the area would then be transported beyond it into deeper water, thus extending the graded surface areally without changing its depth. Total-passing (p. 9) and non-deposition would then persist over the entire graded area until some change in waves, currents, or load intervened. If the sediment available were homogeneous in size and specific gravity, the graded surface would be horizontal and the sea floor would coincide with the baselevel of aggradation. If the sediment were heterogeneous, size-grading would occur during transportation with finer and finer material coming to rest progressively away from the source, and the sea floor would slope very gently in that direction. It would nevertheless be in equilibrium with the environment, and neither deposition nor sublevation could take place over the graded area.

Either downwarping or eustatic rise of sealevel would, of course, shift the sea floor below the baselevel of aggradation, and deposition could then take place. Uplift of the sea floor or lowering of sealevel would, on the contrary, subject the loose sediment to stronger wave and current action, and some of the particles would begin to move, being swept along the bottom until they reached deeper water. Thus, by sublevation, the sea floor would be lowered, yet if the changes were slow, it would be kept perfectly graded during the process. Once a shallow sea floor approaches a graded condition in equilibrium with the forces at work, subsidence (or rise of sealevel) is necessary to permit further deposition, and the rate of deposition is therefore dependent primarily on the rate of subsidence. Speculation to the effect that coarse sediment accumulates faster than fine, or that calcareous sediment accumulates more slowly than terrigenous sediment, is therefore baseless because it rests on false assumptions. On a shallow sea floor that is graded to equilibrium in a given environment, further deposition cannot take place regardless of the nature or the coarseness of the sediment so long as the controlling factors do not change.

An exception must be made, of course, for a largely landlocked epeiric sea, where the bottom may be silted up to sealevel because waves and currents have no means of removing and disposing of the excess after the floor is built up to the baselevel of aggradation.

Thus far we have considered the situation that would obtain over a large area of the neritic zone if waves and currents were uniform and constant in their force and were operating on a uniform load of sediment until equilibrium was achieved and the sea floor had been graded to the baselevel of aggradation.

Of course, no such condition exists in nature. The depth of wave action falls almost to zero in calm weather and may rise to 300 feet or more during heavy storms. It varies from day to day with the passing storms, and from season to season as the prevailing weather changes. Currents generated by the winds likewise vary, and they commonly change direction with the shifting winds. Thus the baselevel of aggradation constantly fluctuates, so that perfect equilibrium is never attained over any considerable area or maintained for any considerable length of time. During storms it is depressed and the surface of the sea floor is subject to sublevation. A surface film of loose sediment begins to move as the currents and waves increase in force, but, as the storm passes, this sediment soon comes to rest again. Fine material lifted into suspension will travel at the velocity of the currents but the traction load, carried by saltation or by rolling along the bottom, will move much more slowly. With local exceptions near shore, bottom currents are very gentle, moving a few tens of miles per day at the most. An ordinary storm would probably shift sediment by bottom traction a distance of rods rather than miles.

A storm sweeping across the neritic zone stirs a surface layer of sediment and sets it moving for a few days, only to come to rest in a new place, but since the neritic zone is so broad and so flat, little of the material will be carried directly out to the continental margin. Although the net result over a long period of time is to shift the sediment seaward, it may be moved in one direction by one storm and in a different direction by the next. Thus it is shifted about many, many times on the shallow sea floor before reaching its final resting place, lying at rest for the most part during fair weather and moving chiefly during storms.

Over most of the neritic zone, therefore, little or no deposition takes place most of the time. Fine sediment carried in suspension may settle widely during fair weather, but it will be lifted and moved from time to time during stormy weather. For short periods, even the coarser material at the surface will be shifted by bottom traction, but both coarse and fine will come to rest again in a new location forming a fresh layer deposited in a brief span of time. The breaks in the sedimentary record caused by these periods of non-deposition, or of sublevation, are diastems. They are responsible for the bedding planes in shallow-water marine strata.

Fluvial deposits, likewise, form intermittently. A stream does most of its work when in flood, and only then does it spread beyond its channel to deposit mud and sand over the bordering lowlands. Even large floods seldom persist for more than a few days or at most a few weeks, and the intervals between are long and irregular. In the exceptional case of the Nile, the floods come annually and last for a couple of months, spreading a film of silt over the delta, but for the remainder of the year nothing is added. Along more normal streams, like the Colorado River and the Mississippi, large floods occur at intervals of a few years, and in arid regions cloudbursts may result in sudden floods lasting but a few hours, interspersed with periods of several years' duration in which the streams are dry.

Temporal Value of Diastems

The diastems, the relatively short breaks in the record, are not ordinarily susceptible of individual measurement, even qualitatively. The lost interval is too short to be reflected in the evolutionary changes of the associated fossils, and there are no relevant structural criteria. Radiocarbon dating may give quantitative results, however, in Pleistocene deposits where suitable fossil material is present in beds immediately above and below a break, and pollen analysis may permit qualitative estimates of the lost time during which adjustments of the vegetation to climatic changes were taking place.

Brinkmann (1929, p. 79–83) used an ingenious technique to measure the relative amount of time represented by beds and by breaks in the Oxford clay (Upper Jurassic) about Peterborough, England. This locality is famous for its ceramic industry, and extensive quarries in the Jurassic clay afforded an unusual opportunity for detailed study. The clay is thinly bedded and very richly fossiliferous, abounding in small ammonites of the genus *Zugokosmoceras*. Brinkmann collected zonally from each centimeter of the clay through a thickness of some 1,300 cm. He then made a biostatistical study of the suite from each zone. This study revealed a gradual increase in the number of ribs as well as progressive bundling of the ribs at the umbilical nodes during the time represented by the 42 feet of clay (Fig. 69). The rate of evolution of these and other characters could then be plotted as a curve. In the curve A in Figure 69, for example, the abscissa is scaled in centimeters of thickness of the section and the ordinate in terms of the number of ribs. Thus each specimen can be plotted by a dot recording its position in the section and the number of its ribs. In spite of scattering, it is clear that the number is increasing upward in the section, and a curve can be drawn to represent the mean value. At a shelly layer at the level 864.5 cm, however, there is a break and sudden rise in the curve after which it proceeds to climb gradually as before. This marks a diastem, and the break in the curve is due to a loss of part of the record. Now by spreading the curve at this place, as in curve A', until the two segments of the curve are in line, we have a measure of the size of the break in terms of the rate of sedimentation. B is a comparable curve based on the coefficient of bundling of the ribs near another diastem at horizon 1093.5 cm. If we assume that the normal rate of deposition was uniform, then this diastem represents a time loss equivalent to that normally required to form 80 cm of deposit (curve B'). Obviously, small diastems equivalent to the time commensurate with that involved in the deposition of a centimeter of clay would not be revealed.

The validity of Brinkmann's method of measuring the temporal value of a diastem could be checked by comparing the breaks at the same level in curves based on other characters. Unfortunately Brinkmann did not go so far and did

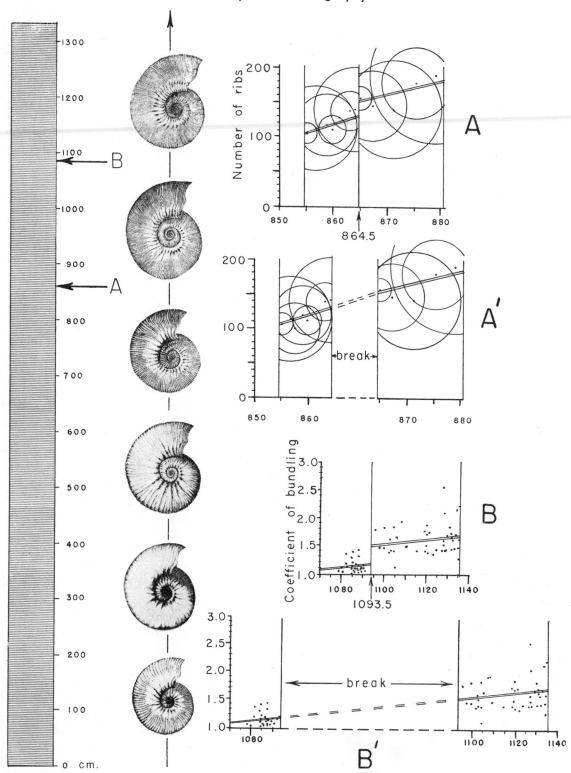

Figure 69. Measurement of temporal value of diastems in the Oxford clay (Jurassic) about Peterborough, England. Adapted from Brinkmann (1929).

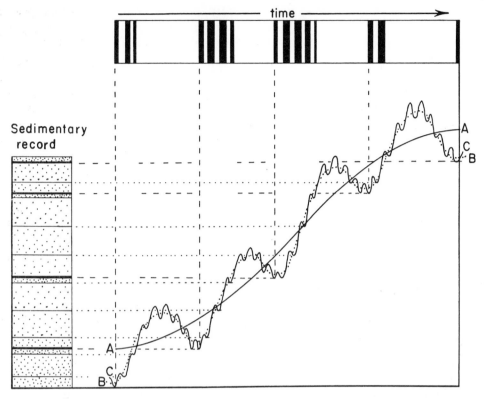

Figure 70. Diagram showing (left) the sedimentary record resulting from hormonic oscillations in the base level of aggradation and (top) the relative time value of deposition and breaks. After Barrell (1917).

little more than demonstrate how the technique could be applied. Of course, it would be applicable only in exceptional places where rapid evolution was recorded by very abundant fossils that could be collected zonally in great detail.

Figure 70 is an ingenious device of Barrell's (1917, p. 796) that illustrates hypothetically the temporal values of the diastems and unconformities as compared with the beds in a stratigraphic deposit. It is based on the premise that deposition of sediment is a rhythmic process controlled by cyclic changes, both diastrophic and climatic. Time is measured from left to right, and the rise in baselevel is measured vertically. The resultant stratigraphic record is shown as a columnar section at the left.

Curve A———A represents the rise of baselevel (with respect to the sea floor) during the negative phase of a diastrophic cycle such as those indicated by the coming and going of epeiric seas during the geologic past. During the subsiding phase a sedimentary record could accumulate. Curve B———B represents the rise and fall of baselevel when oscillations of smaller amplitude and shorter period are superposed on the first, oscillations such as the eustatic changes in sealevel during the Pleistocene epoch resulting from the alternate growth and disappearance of the continental ice caps. Curve C———C represents the final pattern of movement of the baselevel when rhythms of a still smaller order are superposed. Such minor oscillations might represent the smaller climatic cycles to which diastems are largely due.

As the baselevel rises the sedimentary deposit is built up to the corresponding level, but as it falls, part of the sediment is removed. If the drop is slight, the sea floor will be lowered by sublevation producing a diastem; if it be great enough, subaerial erosion will create an unconformity. The black bars in the time band at the top of the diagram show the time represented by the beds in the column at the left, and the blanks indicate the hiatuses. Barrell emphasized that these curves are hypothetical and the scale indeterminate. If a more rapid rate of subsidence were assumed, the curve would be steeper; if a slower rate, it would be flatter. If more than three independent variables were introduced the curve would be more complex, and if the diastrophic or climatic changes were not cyclic but irregular, the curve would be more uneven. In most of these cases the percentage of the time represented by deposits would be even less than on Barrell's diagram. Finally, wherever the sea floor is entirely below the baselevel of aggradation, the analysis would not be applicable. Over the shallow sea floor or on the land, however, it gives a significant picture of the intermittent nature of the deposition of sediment and explains how, even in a simple sequence of strata, rapid deposition of individual layers may be reconciled with great total elapsed time.

DISTINCTION BETWEEN DIASTEMS AND UNCONFORMITIES

As clearly seen by James Hutton, an unconformity records a change in the overall conditions of deposition, commonly involving, at the least, regional uplift and erosion if not tectonic disturbance or metamorphism of the rocks that were formed before the break. Diastems, on the contrary, are smaller breaks resulting from the normal changes that occur without any basic change in the general regimen. The distinction is parallel to that between the regimen and the stage of a stream (or of a glacier), or to that between climate and weather. The stage of a stream fluctuates from day to day, from season to season, and from year to year, but if no changes take place in the average rainfall or its seasonal distribution, or in the topography or other features of the drainage basin, these stages are only the normal fluctuations about an average stage. The whole complex of such fluctuations—highs, lows, and means—constitutes the regimen of the stream, and that regimen changes only if some basic factor influencing the river or its basin changes so that the whole complex of stages is altered. Diastems, then, are breaks resulting from fluctuations of stage, as in a stream or a body of standing water; unconformities are breaks resulting from changes in regimen, as a result of which new conditions of deposition (or of non-deposition) prevail. The distinction can thus be generalized from the sediments of shallow marine waters to sediments of all environments. Of course, there are many borderline cases where the distinction cannot be unequivocal and where judgments by competent observers will differ, but the two main groups of breaks are different enough in character and origin to warrant separation.

7. Facies and facies change

::

GENERAL CONSIDERATIONS

The concept of facies. During the early study of stratified rocks, the most impressive fact discovered about them was the extraordinary persistence in rock type displayed by each stratum or group of strata when traced laterally. So striking was this fact that it was quickly generalized into the doctrine that all strata are persistent in rock type as far as they go and that each was deposited as a separate act in a "Universal Ocean." This doctrine was especially promulgated and championed by Abraham Gottlob Werner toward the end of the eighteenth century and is called from him "Wernerian." With the discovery of the "Law of Faunal Succession" by William Smith in England and by Cuvier and Brongniart in France, the same principle was carried over to the fossils, and was generalized by d'Orbigny and others into the doctrine of catastrophes, according to which each fauna was created, distributed throughout the world, and then destroyed, giving place to another newly created and more complex fauna.

The gradual growth of uniformitarianism, stemming in the first place from James Hutton and spread especially by his British followers from Playfair to Lyell and Darwin, checked the most pernicious effects of these doctrines and led geologists to anticipate that, just as sediments and animal assemblages vary today over the globe, so they must have varied in the past, and that the deposits and faunas of any given age should include a wide range of types, though the faunas at least would be characterized by certain broad uniformities resulting from the stage of development or evolution then reached. Nevertheless, theoretically sound and acceptable as this view was and is, the obvious persistences of both rock types and faunal assemblages displayed in the stratified rocks have commonly overshadowed it in practice, and many a stratigrapher and paleontologist has proceeded in fact on almost classically Wernerian lines in his interpretation of the observed data.

One of the very first well-documented and clearly formulated applications of uniformitarian ideas to the interpretation of sedimentary rocks and their faunas was that by Gressly (1838), who studied the Triassic and Jurassic rocks of the eastern Jura Mountains in Switzerland. In the Triassic and Lower Jurassic rocks he found that rock types and faunas were persistent throughout the area and, indeed, far beyond into the standard sections of southwest Germany, but the higher in the Jurassic he worked, the more diverse each unit became from area to area, until in the highest Jurassic unit he could distinguish five separate lithologic varieties (in addition to subvarieties), each dominant over parts of the region he studied and each characterized by its own fauna. To these different but contemporaneous rock types and faunas he gave the name *facies,* the Latin (and also the French) word for aspect, especially facial aspect. (A comparable usage in non-technical English occurs in the idiom "That puts a different face on the matter.") In his own words (Gressly, 1838, p. 10–12, trans. by JR; italics in original):

I have succeeded, in this manner, in recognizing, in the horizontal dimension of each formation,* diverse well characterized modifications, which present constant peculiarities in their petrographic constitution as well as in the paleontologic characters of the assemblage of their fossils, and which are governed by appropriate and hardly variable laws.

And at once there are two principal facts which characterize everywhere the assemblages of modifications that I call *facies* or *aspects of formations:* one is that *a given petrographic aspect of any formation necessarily implies, wherever it occurs, the same paleontologic assemblage; the other* is that *a given paleontologic assemblage rigorously excludes fossil genera and species frequent in other facies.*

I think that the modifications, whether petrographic or paleontologic, shown by a formation in its horizontal extent, are produced by the different locations and other circumstances that so powerfully influence, nowadays too, the different genera and species of organized beings which people the Ocean and the seas of the present.

Gressly's concept of facies is still valid after more than a century; indeed, his application of it to the Jurassic rocks of the Jura is more up-to-date than many studies made within the past few decades. Geologically, then, the term facies means the general aspect of the rocks, lithologic and biologic (and by extension, structural or tectonic and even metamorphic), as that aspect reflects the environmental conditions under which the rocks were formed. Almost implicit in the definition, as shown by Gressly's remarks, is the idea that the rocks of a given stratigraphic unit show more than one aspect, each aspect being a facies; and the term has its characteristic use in the combination *facies change,* which indicates variation in aspect, reflecting variation in the

---

* The French word *terrain,* here translated "formation," might equally well be rendered "stratigraphic unit." Gressly used the word formation for units like Triassic and Jurassic which modern American usage calls systems; thus he divided the Jurassic "formation" into four "groupes" and nine "terrains."

original environment, within the rocks of the stratigraphic unit.

As mentioned above, the concept of facies, though theoretically entirely acceptable, has had in practice to make its way against the dead weight of the Wernerian assumption of perfect lateral persistence of rock type and fauna. In North America, particularly, the idea of facies was adopted rather slowly, and during the first part of the present century its progress was indeed checked for some time. At that time the outstanding protagonist of facies in North America was A. W. Grabau, who was greatly influenced by Johannes Walther and others in Germany, where the idea was commonplace. The outstanding proponent of views minimizing facies and stressing lateral persistence, both of rock type and fauna, was E. O. Ulrich. This controversy is dealt with more fully in Chapter 16 (p. 284); suffice it to say that when Grabau left America for China in 1920, Ulrich's views were entirely dominant, and only since about 1930 has the facies idea again come into its own here. The present state of the matter is well displayed in the symposium of 1948 on "Sedimentary Facies in Geologic History" (Longwell, Chairman, 1949), though even yet the old Wernerian assumptions are by no means powerless.

Definitions. Before we proceed to discuss the different kinds of facies and facies changes, we must define certain terms. A *fauna* is a natural assemblage of animals living together, a *flora* is a corresponding assemblage of plants, and a *biota* is a natural assemblage of both plants and animals. Thus we speak of the bottom fauna of Long Island Sound, the flora of New England, or the biota of the Arctic tundra. These terms may also be applied to fossil assemblages—for example, the fauna of the Oriskany sandstone or the flora of the Coal Measures. In discussing the accumulated remains of organisms, however, whether recent or fossil, we must commonly distinguish between assemblages of forms that actually were associated in life and assemblages of forms merely brought together after death. An assemblage of the first sort is a *biocoenosis* [Gr. *bios,* life + *koinos,* common, shared in common], of the second a *thanatocoenosis* [Gr. *thanatos,* death + *koinos*]. A good example of a thanatocoenosis is a collection of foramini-fera dredged from the ocean floor, made in part of pelagic forms from the sunlit surface waters and in part of benthonic forms from the cold dark bottom. The two groups live in totally different regions and environments, but they are generally found together after death.

According to Gressly's definition of facies quoted above, the term clearly refers to a facies or aspect of some definite stratigraphic unit, and the unit has both its lithologic and biologic aspects, its *lithofacies* and *biofacies*. By exten-sion, the term biofacies also refers to a local aspect of some larger life assemblage or biota, especially a modern biota, more or less limited by some environmental control (and faunal facies and floral facies refer to such aspects of a fauna or flora). In the timbered upland of New Eng-land, for example, the plants living in an open meadow are almost entirely different from those in a deeply shaded part of the timber, and those on a well-drained southern slope are largely dif-ferent from those in a nearby bog. These are all local aspects or facies of the New England flora. In the sea, likewise, the bottom fauna varies with the local environment. The assem-blage living on a rocky bottom is largely different from that on a sandy or muddy bottom; where the waves and currents are strong, special as-semblages of plants and animals tend to thrive (as on the face of coral reefs), whereas a very different assemblage occupies protected nooks or deeper water.

Thus each local assemblage of animals and plants constitutes a *facies* of the larger fauna, flora, or biota of the region; the environment itself, under which the assemblage lives or lived, is called a *biotope* [Gr. *bios,* life + *topos,* place]. For example, a warm, clear, well-aer-ated, normally saline sea floored with sand is one biotope; a stagnant, foul mud bottom another. The record of such an environment (and of its biota) in the rocks is called a *lithotope* [Gr. *lithos,* rock + *topos*]; * black shale is a litho-tope, for example—any or all black shale.

* This terminology follows Wells (1947), Moore (1948, p. 310), and current usage in ecology, but differs from that of Krumbein and Sloss (1951, p. 194, 227), who have redefined both lithotope and biotope as *areas*

We may use black shale to illustrate the appli-cation of these terms to stratigraphy. The black shale *biotope* is a soft muddy sea floor below active wave base over which the water is defi-cient in oxygen and foul with dissolved H_2S. It is inhabited by the black shale *biocoenosis,* which includes anaerobic bacteria and possibly *Lingula* and burrowing worms, but few if any bottom-dwelling mollusks. In this specialized environ-ment many different black shale deposits have formed. These deposits are the black shale *lithotope,* consisting of brownish to black, fissile, pyritiferous, bituminous shale, in whatever area or part of the stratigraphic column it may occur. In it is found the black shale *thanatocoenosis,* in-cluding driftwood, spores of land plants, fish re-mains, and seaweed, in addition to the forms that lived in the original bottom mud. A particular black shale deposit may thus be at once a facies of some stratigraphic unit, an example of the black shale lithotope, and the surviving record of a biotope.

In the rest of this chapter, the discussions of physical and biological facies and facies changes are largely separated, but it must never be for-gotten that the two kinds are intimately related and strongly condition each other. Thus faunal facies dependent on bottom conditions are the result of and faithfully reflect physical facies, and on the other hand the physical facies changes around an organic reef are the direct result of ecologic differences in fauna. The Permian Sys-tem in various parts of the world displays several outstanding examples of such interrelations (Dun-bar, 1941).

PHYSICAL FACIES CHANGE

Examples

The Catskill Delta. One of the most carefully studied examples of facies changes in the North

characterized by uniform lithology or biology. It should also be noted that when Moore presented the opening paper of the 1948 symposium on sedimentary facies (p. 136), on the meaning of the term facies, he used facies and lithotope as recommended here, but that in the paper as published (Moore, 1949) he substituted lithofacies for lithotope, a confusing mixture of meanings for the word facies.

American record is that in the Middle and Upper Devonian rocks of New York State and adjacent Pennsylvania. Now that these changes are understood, we know that they record the gradual growth of a great delta, called the Catskill Delta (p. 86), fed by a stream or more likely several streams from rising mountains to the east and southeast. But early geologists did not have this hindsight, and the difficulties that facies changes presented to them (and in other cases still present to us) need emphasis, as well as the conclusions that can be drawn from them when they are properly understood.

The Devonian rocks of New York State are laid out in perfect order, occupying most of the western part of the state and extending eastward almost to the Hudson River. Moreover, the regional strike is east-west, almost transverse to the trend of the Appalachian geosyncline, so that the gently dipping strata exhibit an excellent cross section of the Devonian deposits of the geosyncline (Fig. 71). The perfection of this record was early recognized, and it became, largely through the work of James Hall, the standard for Devonian correlation throughout North America. The lower part of the Middle Devonian all across the state is the Onondaga limestone, a distinctive cherty coralliferous limestone that can be recognized physically and biologically and that served as a firm base for all studies of the overlying rocks. Above the Onondaga, Hall and his colleagues (especially Timothy Conrad and Lardner Vanuxem) found everywhere a black shale with relatively sparse, unusual, and delicate fossils, which they called the Marcellus shale, and above that a thousand feet or so of gray, partly calcareous, partly sandy, highly fossiliferous shale, which they divided in places into several units but called collectively the Hamilton group. Above this, from near the middle of the state westward, follow a rather thin limestone (Tully) and another black shale (Genesee), but these units cannot be recognized farther east. Following either the second black shale or the calcareous or sandy shale is a thick mass of gray to brown interbedded shale, flagstone, and sandstone, sparingly fossiliferous, which these men divided variously but generally into the Portage group or Sherburne flagstones

below and the Ithaca and Chemung groups above. Finally, above these in all sections, though to the west it lies mainly south of the state line in Pennsylvania, they found a great thickness of red, silty, and sandy shale with red, brown, and gray sandstone, which they called the Catskill group or division, from the Catskill Mountains at the east end of the Devonian area, which are largely composed of these rocks. Thus in all sections from east to west they had encountered the same succession of rocks (leaving out of account the Tully and Genesee), from black shale at the base to redbeds at the top.

To this sequence, established in 1842, later work added many refinements and subdivisions, and in particular application of the facies concept by H. S. Williams, C. S. Prosser, and J. M. Clarke in the last twenty years of the nineteenth century resulted in some changes—for example, that the Ithaca is not part of the Chemung group but a facies of the underlying beds (as indeed Vanuxem had originally suspected), and that both Chemung and Ithaca grade eastward into redbeds of Catskill type. But no changes were made in the overall sequence (Fig. 71A).

In the 1920's George H. Chadwick began to restudy the Chemung group and G. Arthur Cooper the Hamilton group, and their work (Chadwick, 1924, 1933; Cooper, 1930, 1933) precipitated a major revision in our understanding of these rocks, showing that the facies concept had hitherto been applied far too cautiously. It is now known (see Cooper and others, 1942, p. 1734–1736 and columns for New York State) that the change from each lithology to the next was not roughly contemporaneous across the state but started in the east and advanced slowly westward, and that redbeds of the Catskill unit were already being deposited in the Catskill Mountain area well before the end of the Middle Devonian, while black shales of Marcellus type were still being deposited in western New York. Thus planes of time equivalence, instead of roughly paralleling the boundaries between the rock types, as tacitly assumed by Hall and his colleagues, cut diagonally across them. They rise steadily to the east (Fig. 71B), so that even the highest of the Catskill redbeds in the Catskill Mountains, hitherto supposed to be the

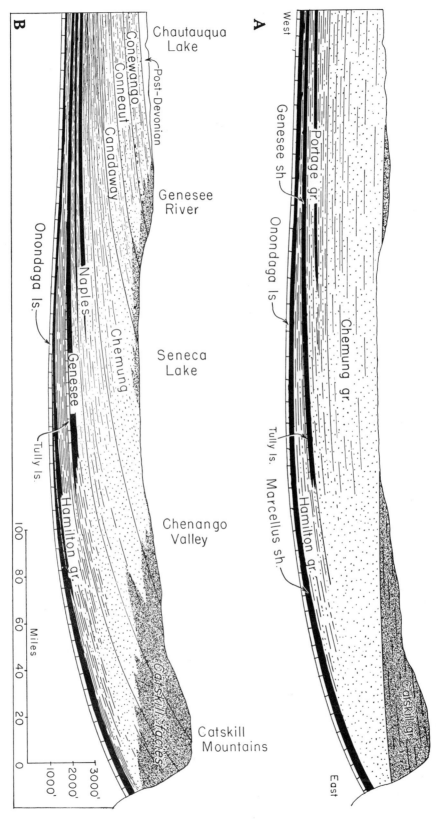

Figure 71. East–west sections across the Catskill Delta (Devonian) in southern New York. A, interpretation of Middle and Upper Devonian stratigraphy current before about 1930. B, present interpretation following the work of Chadwick and Cooper. Stratification lines indicate supposedly isochronous deposits.

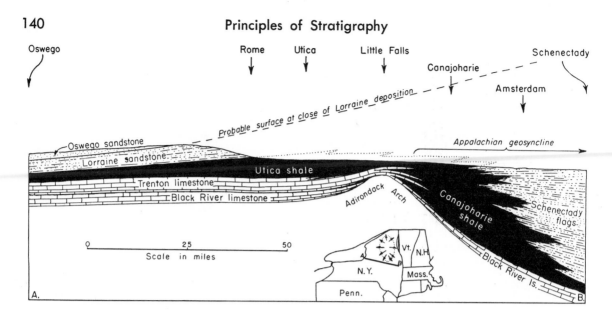

Figure 72.   East–west section of the Middle and Upper Ordovician formations from central New York to Albany.

youngest Devonian rocks in the state, are as old as the lower part of the Upper Devonian in the western part of the state, which is in turn overlain by many hundreds of feet of younger Devonian rocks, divided into three great groups.

It must not be supposed that facies relations of this sort, simple as they appear in generalized diagrams like Figure 71, p. 139, are obvious in the field.   On the contrary, their elucidation required detailed and painstaking tracing of key units and collecting and carefully identifying many fossils, but, even more, it required the vision to break away from the accepted interpretation and apply the facies concept boldly wherever it led.

Other examples.   A somewhat similar reorientation of our understanding had been accomplished earlier by Ruedemann in the Ordovician rocks cropping out in a belt across the eastern half of New York north of the Devonian rocks (see Ruedemann, 1925a, and historical review therein).   Here a highly fossiliferous body of limestone (Trenton) is succeeded through most of the area by black shale carrying graptolites (Utica), gray shale and sandstone with some fossils (Hudson River), and gray sandstone (Oswego)—the names given are those applied by the pioneer geologists in 1842.   (Redbeds called Queenston come in above the gray sandstone in western New York to complete the parallel with the Devonian, but they need not enter the present

discussion.)   This sequence was recognized both in north-central New York east of Oswego on Lake Ontario and in the lower Mohawk Valley west of Schenectady.   But Ruedemann, by zoning the graptolites in detail, was able to show that here also lithologic changes were not contemporaneous everywhere but shifted westward through a large part of Ordovician time, and that gray sandstone was already being deposited in the lower Mohawk Valley well before limestone deposition had ended in the central part of the state (Fig. 72).

Another magnificent example of shifting facies has been beautifully worked out by McKee (1945a) in the Cambrian rocks of the Grand Canyon region, again by painstaking tracing of units and attention to the fossils.   Here (Fig. 73) three lithologic units—in ascending order, the Tapeats sandstone, Bright Angel shale, and Muav limestone—were shown to transgress eastward with time, so that again, though in any one section the three rock types are successive, deposition of the highest facies had already begun at the west before deposition of the lowest had stopped to the east.

In the Mesozoic of North America, splendid examples of facies change are offered especially by the Upper Cretaceous rocks of the Rocky Mountain region, for example (Fig. 78, p. 155) in central and eastern Utah as described by

Spieker (1949). Outside North America, many similar examples are known. One of the most instructive, and also one of considerable significance for geological nomenclature, is provided by the Permian rocks of Russia. Here typical Lower Permian shale, sandstone, and conglomerate (Artinskian and Sakmarian Series) in the Urals grade westward into the so-called Uralian limestones, long held to be Carboniferous (Dunbar, 1940, 1942). The confusion created by failure to recognize this facies change is still reflected in some geological literature, where "Uralian" fossils are cited as evidence of pre-Permian age.

A rather different sort of facies change, involving organic reef deposits is displayed by the Permian of West Texas, discussed in Chapter 4 (p. 93 and Fig. 40, p. 93). Now that the relations of the various facies around the ancient reef are known, the pattern they present is exceptionally clear and instructive, but it should not be forgotten that this pattern had to be built up piece by piece from scattered and puzzling data, that each facies change and each original dip formed at first a glaring exception to the expected relations instead of, as now, an integral part of the whole regional pattern.

General Analysis

The vast number of complexities in most actual cases of facies change obscure somewhat the fairly

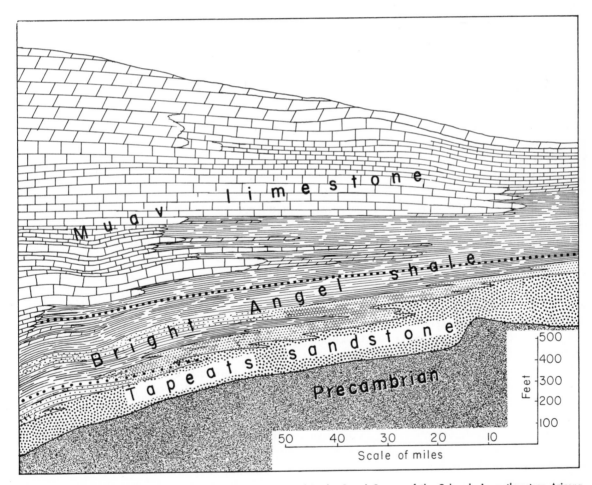

Figure 73. East–west section of the Cambrian formations exposed in the Grand Canyon of the Colorado in northwestern Arizona. After McKee (1945a). Stratification lines indicate isochronous deposits. The row of heavy round dots shows the position of a high lower Cambrian (*Olenellus*) faunal zone; the row of heavy square dots shows the position of a low Middle Cambrian (*Glossopleura*) zone.

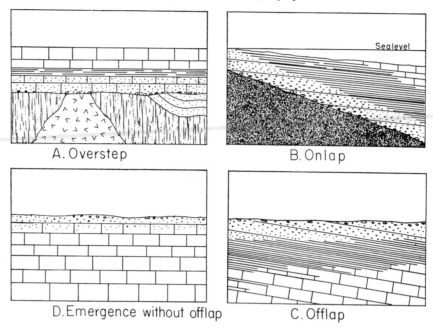

A. Overstep

B. Onlap

D. Emergence without offlap

C. Offlap

Figure 74. Idealized types of marine facies relations.

simple relations that are the essence of the idea. Some of these relations can be readily analyzed in simplified theoretical cases, as they would appear in cross section perpendicular to an advancing or retreating shoreline; such an analysis has been carried out especially by Grabau (1906; 1913, p. 723–745). Of course, such theoretical cases do not correspond to any actual occurrences, in which the facies fluctuate and shift irregularly, both perpendicular and parallel to the shoreline, or are interrupted or interpolated as they progress and regress. Some facies relations, moreover, notably those involving different kinds of limestone, do not fit this kind of analysis at all. But in fact the facies changes in the Cambrian rocks of the Grand Canyon (Fig. 73) approach remarkably close to the theoretical case of marine onlap, with instructive variations produced by the brief interpolated regressive phases.

Facies changes in strictly marine terrigenous deposits. The distribution of facies changes in terrigenous sediments is controlled by the balance between the relative subsidence—or emergence—of the basin of deposition (or relative rise or fall of sealevel for marine deposits) and the supply of the terrigenous material. Several cases can

be distinguished; the first group of such cases includes those in which there is only marine deposition, so that emergence from the sea results in non-deposition or erosion.

A. If subsidence very greatly exceeds supply, ordinarily because of very limited supply rather than very rapid subsidence, the deposits of the spreading sea will be little affected by the land-derived material. What material is supplied will be spread discontinuously at the base of the marine deposit, probably as local patches of basal sandstone or conglomerate, and these basal layers will be followed directly by open sea deposits (commonly limestone) virtually free of terrigenous matter (Fig. 74A). The relation of the deposit to the underlying rocks will be that of *overstep,* and lateral facies changes (at least as conditioned by the overstep) will be negligible. An example is the overstep of Ordovician limestone over Precambrian rocks on the south margin of the Canadian Shield from the north shore of the St. Lawrence River to Lake Timiskaming and the Hudson Bay lowland. Locally there is a basal sandstone or conglomerate, but elsewhere clean limestone rests directly on the Precambrian basement, and corals are found where they grew in clefts in or attached to the surface of the crystalline rocks (Fig. 58, p. 118).

B. If subsidence exceeds supply but supply is not negligible, the material supplied, sorted by the waves and currents, should ideally be distributed in belts parallel to the shoreline, coarsest in and finest out. As the sea encroaches, the result will be a steady landward shift of several different lithotopes, beginning with a transgressive basal sandstone or conglomerate, whose relation to the floor beneath will be that of *marine onlap* (Fig. 74B). The Cambrian rocks of the Grand Canyon (Fig. 73) furnish an almost ideal example.

C. If supply becomes greater than subsidence, though not so much greater that the waves and currents are incompetent to distribute the material, the results will be similar except that the lithotopes will shift seaward as the shoreline retreats (Fig. 74C). The individual facies in a unit deposited during retreat may be different from those deposited during advance, however, as well shown by McKee (1945a) for the minor regressions in the Cambrian rocks of the Grand Canyon region. Theoretically the last lithotope will be a regressive sandstone or conglomerate, above which will follow an unconformity, and the relation of the beds beneath to this unconformity will be that of *marine offlap*. Actually in most examples, either the subsequent erosion destroys the continuity of the regressive deposit or non-marine deposition succeeds marine; hence the case is seldom clearly displayed. Perhaps, however, the Middle and Upper Ordovician rocks of eastern New York (Fig. 72) illustrate it.

D. If in the presence of considerable supply subsidence is negligible, or if there is actual emergence, the seaward shift of lithotopes may be disrupted, resulting in a discontinuous regressive deposit over largely open sea sediments (Fig. 74D). In the nature of the case, the evidence for such regressions is likely to be destroyed by immediately following erosion, but they may have occurred several times during the early and middle Paleozoic in the central United States, as after the deposition of the Lower Ordovician or the Middle Silurian rocks.

Facies changes in marine and non-marine terrigenous deposits. Ordinarily deposits will form and be preserved on the land as well as in the sea only if both supply and subsidence are considerable; therefore, cases corresponding to the two extreme cases just discussed (A and D) can be neglected. If supply exceeds subsidence, the lithotopes will shift seaward, and one or several non-marine lithotopes will follow and cover the last marine or a littoral lithotope. The result is a *continental replacement* (marine regression). An unconformity may and commonly does terminate the sequence, or at least its landward part, and the relation of the beds to the unconformity is that of continental offlap, but if the regression is followed at once by another transgression, this unconformity will not normally extend out into the marine deposits. Clear examples of continental replacement are numerous, for instance the Catskill Delta (Fig. 71, p. 139) and the Upper Cretaceous of the Rockies, cited above (Fig. 78, p. 155).

The reverse case, where subsidence exceeds supply, is theoretically entirely similar and will result in *marine replacement* or transgression and, at least in the landward area, in a continental onlap over an unconformity. The lithotopes may be different, however, and in particular a littoral lithotope is commonly absent; indeed, if supply is not very great, the advancing waves may rework most or all of the material so that no continental rocks are preserved; this case then merges with the second strictly marine case (B) discussed above. Good examples of this case involving continental deposits are rare; perhaps the Pennsylvanian of the eastern United States may be cited though the facies shifts are enormously complicated by the many cyclothems. An example of marine transgression over continental deposits is the transgression of the Silurian over the Upper Ordovician in western New York and central Pennsylvania.

Theoretical cases involving only non-marine deposits could be constructed, but they have little application, for the distribution of facies in non-marine sediments is largely controlled by the specific environment (Chap. 2).

The commonest among these various cases are those of continental replacement and marine onlap. Of course, each of these in practice is complicated by numerous minor fluctuations which are in essence minor interpolations of their opposites, marine replacement and marine offlap, but these are much more rarely the dominant patterns. Moreover, the two main patterns not uncommonly occur in combination, forming detrital wedges, regional tongues of coarser terrigenous material, commonly with a continental core, that project into finer marine deposits. Examples are common among the cases already cited—the Catskill Delta (including the overlying Lower Mississippian rocks of New York and Pennsylvania) and such tongues as the Judith River sandstone in the Upper Cretaceous shale of Montana or the Mesaverde group in the corresponding rocks in Utah and Colorado (Fig. 78, p. 155). Such wedges are almost invariably the reflection of some significant tectonic episode, ordinarily a pulse of orogeny, and thus they have meaning over and above the depositional history they record.

Because tectonic uplift proceeds slowly to its climax, deposition of detrital sediment begins during the uplift and continues until the highlands are worn down again. A great detrital wedge, such as those just mentioned, therefore records both growing and declining phases of the disturbance, and if traced toward its source generally includes an unconformity that grows in magnitude toward the area of uplift, where it may even show angular discordance (Spieker, 1946). Toward the basin of deposition, on the other hand, it may die out completely. Such a break ordinarily lies within the detrital wedge, not at its base (Fig. 78, p. 155).

Both the Acadian and the Taconian disturbances produced relations of this sort in the Appalachian region. During the latter half of the Ordovician Period, for example, detrital sediment spread ever farther west as the Queenston Delta grew across New York and Pennsylvania, and by the close of the period the shoreline was west of the longitude of Niagara Falls and the eastern part of a broad piedmont coastal plain was being degraded. As a result of this regional offlap, the late Ordovician formations are missing in the eastern half of New York and Pennsylvania; when deposition was resumed during early Silurian time, the Tuscarora-Medina sandstone spread eastward across progressively older Ordovician

formations. In central Pennsylvania (as from Lewiston to Bellefonte), where the Upper Ordovician is fully represented and the Juniata sandstone (Richmondian) is succeeded by the Tuscarora sandstone (Early Silurian), the two systems appear accordant and transitional, but along the eastern folds in Pennsylvania (as at Harrisburg and eastward) the Tuscarora sandstone rests on Middle and lowest Upper Ordovician shale, and along the Hudson Valley in New York (as at Rondout and at Becraft Mountain) only the very youngest Silurian beds (Manlius limestone) are present, resting with striking unconformity on folded Middle Ordovician and older shales. In this case, indeed, the unconformity lies at the top of the detrital wedge and the first deposits above it were marine through most of its extent.

Comparable relations exist in the Devonian and Mississippian Systems in the same region as a result of the Acadian disturbance. In the westernmost part of the Appalachian geosyncline (e.g., northwestern Pennsylvania) deposition continued under the same regimen from Late Devonian into Mississippian time, and it has been difficult to determine which of several minor breaks represents the climax of the orogeny, but toward the east more and more of the upper part of the Devonian is missing (Fig. 71, p. 139) and the front of the Catskills includes nothing higher than Middle Devonian. No Mississippian deposits are preserved this far east, but if present they would surely overlie the Middle Devonian with a great hiatus.

Facies changes involving limestone. In his classical analysis, Grabau assumed that limestone is simply the facies farthest from shore, beyond the last terrigenous mud, and that only so does it participate in facies shifts. Possible examples are the Muav limestone in the Cambrian of the Grand Canyon, the Trenton limestone in the Ordovician of New York, and presumably the Onondaga and Tully limestones in the Devonian of New York and the Greenhorn and Niobrara chalks of the Upper Cretaceous of the Great Plains. But more commonly the analysis breaks down, for limestone is deposited wherever terrigenous material fails to arrive in quantity in relatively warm shallow seas, and distance from shore is only one of several possible reasons for this failure. Thus limestone may form on a shallow bank near shore onto which the mud cannot spread and may grade seaward or parallel to the shore into mud deposited in deeper water; complex longshore currents may mix calcareous and non-calcareous deposits in intricate patterns, especially if terrigenous material is supplied only along part of a coastline; and limestone made of sand particles may accumulate near shore or even on the beach while mud is by-passed beyond it. In such cases, sandstone along shore may grade directly into limestone, as in the Upper Cambrian rocks on the continental platform of the Central United States, for example, in the Upper Mississippi Valley and the Ozarks. Early in the Late Cambrian Epoch, indeed, some of the contemporaneous mud appears to have by-passed entirely off the platform into deeper water in the Appalachian geosyncline to form the Nolichucky shale.

Furthermore, several facies may be present within the limestone. In some examples, these facies progress and regress fairly regularly, like the terrigenous facies already discussed, as shown by McKee (1945a) for the Muav limestone (though the regressive facies are not the same as the progressive) and by Moore (1936; 1948, p. 310) for the limestone involved in the Pennsylvanian cyclothems, which may be considered miniature specialized repetitions of marine and continental replacement. In others, however, more complex patterns are found, especially where organic reefs are present. The analyses of these cases are progressing vigorously at present, because of the importance of organic reefs as oil reservoirs; among such analyses may be cited the pioneer work of Cumings and Shrock (1928a, b), and recent studies by Ladd (1950), Henson (1950), and Link (1950). The Guadalupian reefs of West Texas, cited above, provide a wellnigh ideal example of a regressive shift of reef facies (Fig. 40, p. 93).

BIOLOGICAL FACIES CHANGE

The discovery and interpretation of biological facies changes in the geologic record presents more difficulties even than physical facies changes, for the very existence of the different facies hampers the use of fossils to prove that the facies are indeed contemporaneous aspects of a larger unit. We must therefore study first the "facies changes" of the present, for which problems of correlation do not arise, and then apply the principles so learned to the facies of the past. Fortunately these matters have been intensively studied by biologists interested in the distribution of plants and animals (biogeography) and in their mutual interrelation in communities or life assemblages (ecology). Moreover, some biologists, and especially paleontologists of a biological bent, have already begun the application of these studies to the past (paleobiogeography and paleoecology). The literature on these subjects is vast, uneven, and rather chaotic; as possible introductions we may cite the books on biogeography by Ekman (1953), by Hesse, Allee, and Schmidt (1951), and by Cain (1944), and the forthcoming *Treatise on Marine Ecology and Paleoecology* being prepared under the direction of H. S. Ladd (Hedgpeth and Ladd, Editors, 1957).

Distribution of Organisms in Space

Means of dispersal

Every species of animal or plant is capable of producing far more young than can possibly survive. As a result each species tends to spread beyond its existing range and to invade new areas until it has occupied all available living space to which it is adapted. To this end many devices, some highly specialized, have been developed to aid in dispersal.

Direct locomotion. Animals that are free to move about display the simplest means of dispersal, for whether they crawl, run, swim, or fly, each could ultimately spread over the whole surface of the earth, if not inhibited by some sort of barrier.

Attachment to moving objects. Many creatures that lack powers of locomotion manage to "thumb a ride" on some moving object. Barnacles, for example, attach themselves to the hulls of ships or to driftwood, and certain species grow on whales or other living animals. Bryozoans and hydroids grow on drifting seaweed, and corals, bryozoans, and many kinds of worms grow on pilings or driftwood that may raft them to far places. The boring clam, *Teredo,* has spread around the world because it infests the hulls of wooden ships, pilings, and driftwood. A common tree-dwelling land snail, *Cerion,* has been carried from South America throughout the West Indian Islands on rafts of driftwood, because it has the ability to seal its shell so tightly that it can survive immersion in salt water for 3 or 4 days at a time (Bartsch, 1920, p. 53–54).

Floating. Creatures that float constitute the *plankton* of the seas and lakes [Gr. *planktos,* wandering]. They drift with the currents and commonly are widely distributed. Thus the common brown seaweed, *Fucus,* which lives generally in the tidal zone on rocky coasts the world around, can be kept afloat by the air pods in its branching thallus; when pieces are torn loose during storms, they can float indefinitely and continue to live and grow. Related forms that are never attached make up the sargasso that accumulates in abundance in the central portions of the open oceans. Some of the graptolites of Paleozoic seas had similar air bladders that enabled them to float. Jellyfish are also dispersed by floating and drifting with the currents. A host of microscopic organisms, both animals and plants, live perpetually floating in the surface waters of the sea; among these globigerines, radiolarians, and diatoms are geologically the most important, but there are many others.

Meroplanktonic stage. Perhaps the commonest way that sessile or slow-moving organisms are dispersed is by means of a free larva or seed. Nearly all aquatic animals pass through a larval stage, in which they are free to float and swim, even though later they settle to the bottom and become attached (like corals and barnacles) or crawl slowly (like snails and clams). Such larvae constitute the *meroplankton* [Gr. *meros,* part + *planktos,* wandering]. This free stage lasts only a few hours in some groups of animals but as long as 30 days in others. In the meantime, currents may carry the young animals far from their point of birth. Many shallow-water species have been widely distributed among the islands of the Pacific by drifting from island to island across deep open water during this free-living stage.

One of the most remarkable specializations for dispersal is the larval stage (glochidium) of the common river clams. An ordinary meroplanktonic stage would be useless for dispersal in a river with its one-way current, but the clam larvae possess strong hooks by which they attach themselves to passing fish, and thus they can be carried upstream against the current.

Dispersal by the wind. What may be considered the terrestrial equivalent of a meroplanktonic stage is exhibited by many land plants whose seeds are scattered by the wind. The tumbleweed and the milkweed have particularly remarkable specializations for this purpose. Likewise spores of many of the lower plants, and of some lowly animals, are blown about as dust and appear almost everywhere, awaiting favorable conditions under which to germinate and grow. Other plants have developed seeds that cling to the hair of passing animals. "Beggar's lice," the Spanish needle, the cocklebur, and the sandbur are familiar examples. Many kinds of plants are widely distributed by birds, which may carry a fruit or seed some distance before dropping it, or may swallow the fruit and pass the seeds unharmed hours later. Finally, some land plants produce seeds capable of floating in the ocean for a considerable period before germinating; the coconut and some other tropical plants have been distributed among the far-flung Pacific islands in this way.

Rates of migration

If fossils are to be used in correlation, it is pertinent to ask whether the means of dispersal will permit a new species to spread over the world so rapidly that its appearance in different areas will be geologically contemporaneous. The answer is unequivocally affirmative; unless inhibited by barriers that it cannot cross, almost any kind of animal or plant could spread over the earth so quickly that from the geological point of view the migration would appear instantaneous. Grazing cattle, for example, would need to travel less than a mile a day to cross the North American continent in 10 years. A postman who walks 10 miles each day travels the distance to the most remote point on the planet in about 3½ years. Even the proverbial snail's pace is rapid, geologically speaking, as shown by well-documented observations on two species. The common shore snail, *Littorina littorea* (Linn.), was a European species until shortly after 1850, when specimens were dropped by some unknown ship near Halifax, Nova Scotia. By 1868 it had reached the coast of Maine, whence it spread gradually southward to Cape Cod and then westward into Long Island Sound. By 1880 it had reached New Haven, and the record of its migration was documented by Verrill (1880). It had required 12 years to travel the 360 miles from Maine to New Haven. At this rate, the snail could have migrated half way round the world since Columbus discovered America or 12 times around the world since the Mankato glacial advance.

The migration of *Littorina* is facilitated by its meroplanktonic larva, but a more remarkable case is that of *Crepidula convexa* Say, which has no meroplanktonic stage (Vokes, 1935). This small snail, a native of our Atlantic coast, was accidentally introduced into San Francisco Bay with oysters transplanted from the East. It was first observed there in 1899. By 1918 it had reached a point 12 miles away, and by 1933 it had got through the Golden Gate and down the coast to Moro Beach, a distance of 46 miles from the original planting. At this rate (about 1⅓ miles per year) it could have migrated to the most distant place on Earth since the climax of the last Pleistocene glaciation.

Barriers to dispersal

In spite of the strong tendency to spread, the many devices that facilitate migration, and the rapid rates that are possible under favorable circumstances, none of the higher animals or plants is world-wide, and most of them are restricted within well-defined limits by one or more barriers to dispersal.

Major geographic barriers. Land bridges, such as the Isthmus of Panama, are at once an avenue of dispersal for land animals and plants and a barrier to marine organisms, especially effective where the connected lands cross climatic belts. Dall found, for example, that 517 species of shell-bearing mollusks live on the Caribbean side of the Isthmus of Panama and 805 on the Pacific side, but that only 24 species are common to both.

Open water is an equally obvious barrier to the migration of most land animals and plants. The unique fauna of Australia, for example, came into existence because Australia was completely isolated from the Asiatic land mass by open water during most of the Cenozoic. The Cenozoic faunas of South America likewise developed in almost complete isolation from those of North America while the present Isthmus of Panama was submerged.

Large bodies of deep open water may in addition prove almost insuperable barriers to the migration of the benthonic organisms of the shallow sea floor. Such creatures are adapted to moderate temperatures, to sunlight, and to definite types of food, and the whole environment on the deep ocean floor is so different that few if any of the shallow-water species can survive there. If the distance across is not great, they may cross deep water during a meroplanktonic stage, provided the currents are favorable, and some forms, such as corals and bryozoans, may be rafted across while attached to driftwood or seaweed, but a shelf fauna as a whole could hardly cross a large body of deep water, such as the present Atlantic Ocean. In the past, migration routes from Europe to America or vice versa were probably the long way around along the continental shelves.

Currents. Currents may be both an aid and a hindrance to migration. Floating or drifting creatures, including meroplanktonic young, may be carried in the direction of flow while unable to migrate in the opposite direction. Clams, for example, were unable to invade the land waters until Devonian time because they had no means of migrating against the river currents. They now depend on their highly specialized larva, the glochidium, which can attach itself to fish in order to "hitch a ride" upstream (p. 146).

Temperature. Most animals and plants are limited in their distribution to a restricted range of temperature. Few species of plants, for example, could live both in the Everglades of Florida and the uplands of New England, or in either of those places and the barrens of Labrador. Marine faunas likewise change greatly with

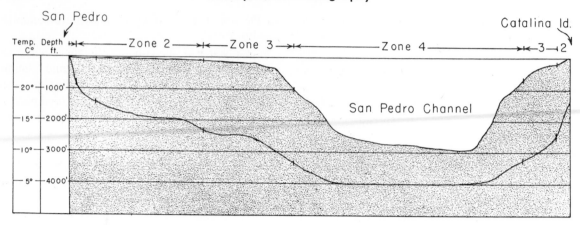

Figure 75. Profile across the San Pedro Channel between San Pedro and Santa Catalina Island showing relations of 4 foraminiferal depth zones. The lower profile is a corresponding curve showing mean temperature at the bottom. After Natland (1933).

latitude. Dall and Harris (1892, p. 26–27) compiled the following census of the shell-bearing mollusks that live on the continental shelf of eastern North America:

Fauna off the Greenland coast .... 180 species
Fauna of the Gulf of Maine .... 277 species
Fauna off the Carolina coast .... 305 species
Fauna on the shelf west of Florida .... 681 species
Fauna off the coast of Panama .... 517 species

If it be assumed that each of these provincial faunas is entirely distinct from the rest, the total number of species should be 1,960. Actually there are 1,772 different species; hence only about 200 range from one of these areas into the next, even though unbroken shallow sea stretches from Greenland to Panama. Temperature is clearly the limiting factor.

On the shelf off the mid-Atlantic States, the cool Labrador current hugs the shore as far south as Cape Hatteras, inside the warm Gulf Stream, and according to Dall and Harris (1892, p. 24) the boundary between these currents is an invisible but effective barrier separating entirely different bottom faunas.

The temperature in the sea decreases with depth as well as with higher latitude. Thus Natland (1933) showed that the benthonic foraminifera (not, of course, the planktonic ones) off the coast of California are segregated into 5 depth zones related to the bottom temperature (Fig. 75). Zone 1 is in brackish lagoonal water less than 10 feet deep. Here the temperature fluc-

tuates with the seasons. Zone 2 ranges from 14 to 125 feet deep and the bottom temperature ranges between 13.2°C. and 21.5°C. Zone 3 ranges from 125 to 900 feet deep and the bottom temperature ranges between 8.5°C. and 13.2°C. Zone 4 ranges from 900 to 6,500 feet deep and the bottom temperature ranges between 4.0°C. and 8.5°C. A fifth zone appears in the deeper part of the channel between depths of 6,500 and 8,340 feet where the bottom temperature is between 2.4°C. and 4.0°C.

Furthermore, a fauna adapted to a certain temperature range may spread into lower latitudes by shifting to deeper water. According to Pratje (1924), for example, a small coral fauna thrives along the west coast of Europe following a preferred temperature zone. Its depth range off the coast of Norway is from 600 to 1,800 feet, but the depth increases to the south, and west of Gibraltar it is found as much as a mile below the surface.

On land a precisely similar zonation takes place with height above sealevel. Thus the flora of the high upland in the Great Smoky Mountains has many "Canadian" forms otherwise unknown in the southeastern United States, and the Rockies and the Sierra Nevada have a timber line similar in some respects to the tundra timber line in northern Canada.

Moisture. The amount of rainfall and its distribution through the year plays as important a role as temperature in controlling the distribution of land plants and hence of land animals, which are bound to the plants in biologic communities. The total difference in the biotas of the forested Appalachians, the grassy Plains, and the desert basins of the Cordillera, even within the same range of annual temperatures, is too well known to need comment. Even some apparent exceptions prove the rule; thus a small prickly pear cactus is fairly common in limestone areas in the Appalachian Valley of Virginia and Tennessee and is even found locally in very sandy areas in New England, but only where excessive underground drainage removes water from the surface soil so fast that the normal undergrowth adapted to the humid climate cannot survive.

Salinity. Salinity plays a role in the ocean comparable to that of moisture on land. Most aquatic organisms are as sensitive to changes in salinity as land plants and animals are to differences in rainfall; only a very few can pass from fresh water to sea water or vice versa. The salinity is nearly uniform in the open ocean, both in the concentration of salts (33 to 37 permille) and in the proportions of different salts, but in more or less landlocked embayments it may vary in both regards. In the Baltic Sea, for example (p. 54), the salinity falls from 33 permille at the Skagerrak to only 3 permille at the upper end of the Gulf of Bothnia. Tolerance to such a change is very different in different groups of organisms; thus the corals, crinoids, and echinoids are very sensitive, whereas the starfish and some of the pelecypods and gastropods can live in a wide range of salinity. Accordingly, decreasing salinity exerts a screening effect on the faunas, which are reduced to fewer and fewer species of the more hardy groups, and even those species fail to reach normal size and generally have abnormally thin, fragile shells (Goldring, 1922). Many kinds of marine organisms likewise avoid the mouths of large streams, and the fresh water of a great river like the Mississippi may serve as a barrier to coastwise migration.

If the water becomes very hypersaline, on the other hand, as in the Dead Sea or the Gulf of Kara-Boghaz on the east side of the Caspian Sea, few if any organisms can survive. Likewise, where the proportion of different salts departs appreciably from that in normal sea water, the effect on the faunas may be marked, as in the Gulf of Pechili (p. 84).

Edaphic and ecologic barriers. Besides being limited by the temperature and by the aridity or the salinity of their environment, sessile organisms are strongly controlled by the nature of the substratum on which they live—by the soil on land and the sea bottom in the oceans—and all organisms are affected by the relative abundance of other organisms, such as predators, food organisms, parasites, or hosts, in the biologic communities in which they live. The controls exercised by the substratum are called *edaphic* [Gr. *edaphos,* bottom or soil], those by other organisms or by the community as a whole *ecologic* [Gr. *oikos,* dwelling or habitat + *logos,* study]. Spectacular examples of edaphic controls are the black belts of the Southern States; these are underlain by Cretaceous chalk and possess fertile black calcareous soils, whereas the adjacent sandy and clayey strata produce red soils from which all the lime has been leached. The black belts were originally grassy prairies and now they are intensively cultivated for cotton, but the adjacent areas of red sandy soils supported forest and are still largely covered with pine barrens. Here the original edaphic control has resulted in an ecologic control that has even influenced the distribution of man; such examples could be multiplied.

Similarly the local environment on the sea floor exerts a profound influence over the distribution of the bottom life and hence to a considerable degree over the life in the waters above. Many animals require or prefer a hard rocky surface; others, such as oysters, live on muddy bottoms but must find solid supports to avoid suffocation; still others, like the "long-necked" clams and many worms, burrow in muddy bottoms and find their food there.

In the sea the amount of disturbance of the water by waves and currents is also important (just as windiness might be on land). Corals thrive best in shallow water where the breaking waves provide both microscopic food and abundant oxygen, but they can grow only on solid bases that lift them above the bottom sediment that would otherwise smother them. In the Bahama region, for example, coral reefs form a

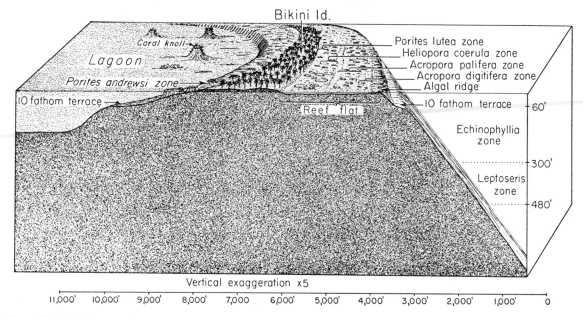

Figure 76. Block diagram showing edaphic faunal zones about Bikini Island, on the windward side of Bikini Atoll. Adapted from Ladd, Tracey, Wells, and Emery (1950). Compare Figure 39, p. 91.

narrow fringe along the windward eastern side of Andros Island (Fig. 41, p. 94), but the broad shallow bank west of the island is almost barren of bottom life because during stormy weather a vast quantity of fine lime-mud is lifted into suspension and then settles out again as a smothering blanket. In this area, thousands of square miles of shallow subtropical sea floor that one might expect to be teeming with shell-bearing organisms is actually almost barren. Neither corals nor mollusks can survive, and the only common animal on the bottom is a small crustacean that burrows in during stormy weather and digs out afterwards.

Wide sand flats were called "the deserts of the sea" by Walther because they are commonly so sparsely settled. Here the sand that shifts during storms tends to bury and kill off the bottom-dwelling organisms, and only those that burrow find it a favorable environment. Yet a few specially adapted forms like the sand-worm, *Sabellaria,* prefer this environment and thrive locally in great abundance (Richter, 1927).

The differentiation of bottom faunas into local facies reaches its greatest complexity in and about coral reefs; Figure 76 shows typical relations on

the atoll of Bikini (Ladd, Tracey, Wells, and Emery, 1950). Thus, though corals and calcareous algae grow on all parts of the reef, preferring, indeed, shallow and turbulent water, only the more massive kinds can survive the pounding of heavy surf on the growing reef face, and the more delicate species are restricted to somewhat deeper water or to protected places. The same differentiation is illustrated by two large species of echinoids. The "slate-pencil urchin," *Heterocentrotus mammillatus* (Linn.), thrives in a narrow zone where the surf breaks on the reef front, using its stout blunt spines to brace itself in crotches among the algae and corals. Another form, *Echinothrix calamaris* (Pallas), lives on and about the coral knolls in the quiet shallow water inside the lagoon. Its long needlelike spines protect it against predators, but they would quickly be broken to bits by the pounding surf on the reef front. Although these genera live but a short distance apart, neither can survive where the other thrives.

Over the more normal sea floor, different facies are less narrowly restricted geographically and commonly less sharply defined, but they are none the less real and important. Good examples have been described (Walther, 1910; 1919–1927, p. 60) from the Bay of Naples (Fig. 77). Here a limy shoal, Pigeon Bank, provides an area of rocky bottom about 125 feet below sealevel. Upon it live 310 species of shell-bearing invertebrates. The adjacent mud bottom, about 100 feet deeper, has only 45 species of shell-bearers, and only 14 species are common to the two environments.

The limiting conditions for faunal facies may be much less obvious than in these cases. Swan (1953) has recorded the distribution of three related species of the echinoid, *Strongylocentrotus,* in the Puget Sound area, all living in the lower part of the intertidal zone. On exposed coasts in water of normal salinity, the three species live together, but in the quieter slightly less saline water of San Juan Channel, *S. purpuratus* (Stimpson) becomes rare, and in Puget Sound *S. franciscanus* (A. Agassiz) also becomes rare and only *S. droebachiensis* (O. F. Müller) is com-

mon. Where it is common, *S. franciscanus* is generally found clinging to vertical faces of rocky ledges, whereas *S. droebachiensis* is common on horizontal surfaces, and *S. purpuratus* lives in crevices. Here then we have salinity controls and edaphic controls, and perhaps purely ecologic controls as well.

Realms, provinces, and facies

The large geographic barriers of land and water subdivide the Earth's surface into a series of faunal and floral realms. Thus each large continental land mass is a distinct faunal realm; South America, Africa, and Australia are well defined, but the northern continents, Eurasia and North America, have been so recently connected by a Bering land bridge that they are commonly included in a single Holarctic realm (sometimes divided into Palearctic and Nearctic portions). Each such faunal realm is further subdivided by

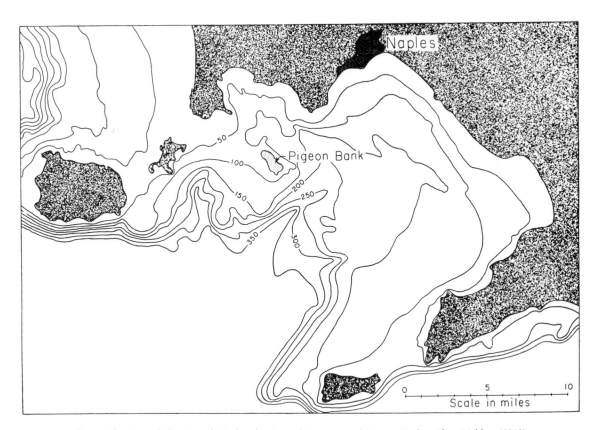

Figure 77. Map of the Bay of Naples showing relations around Pigeon Bank. After Walther (1910).

climatic and topographic barriers into a series of faunal provinces. The individual oceans likewise form faunal realms for marine animals. Although the Atlantic and Pacific Oceans are broadly connected by open water in the far south, their faunas are largely distinct because the climate of the high latitude connection prevents migration around the American land mass. And within each realm, temperature has produced several distinct faunal provinces, as shown by Dall and Harris' figures quoted above (p. 148). Finally, within each province, local and particular differences in soil and bottom or in the biologic community itself produce faunal and floral facies.

Changes in the Distribution of Organisms through Time

From the beginning, life has slowly evolved, new species and genera appearing as older ones disappeared either by evolving into something else or by extinction. This ceaseless change has made possible the use of fossils in dating rock strata. If each new fauna as it evolved had spread over the whole Earth, replacing its predecessor, such dating would be an easy matter, but in fact some organisms and groups have been "conservative," evolving little if at all over long stretches of time, while others have proliferated rapidly into many branches with different and complicated histories, and still others have evolved at a meteoric rate (comparatively speaking) and as quickly died out. Moreover, as we have just seen, the Earth at any time such as the present has supported many diverse faunas and floras in different regions. Finally, our knowledge of the life span in geologic time of any biologic unit is based only on experience—on what we have been able to discover about its stratigraphic range in the rocks that have been studied—and we must realize that the rocks in any one region will rarely record the full range.

Effects of changing barriers. A species or genus, or a whole fauna, may be confined for a time to a single facies or province or realm by any of the barriers discussed above. But if the environments shift or the restraining barriers are broken, the organisms will quickly spread into other areas, appearing there later than in the area where they evolved. The formation of a land bridge may permit the sudden migration of land animals and plants from one continent to another; such an interchange took place between North and South America when the Isthmus of Panama was formed late in Pliocene time. The breaking of such a land bridge would in turn allow the rapid mingling of marine faunas hitherto separated.

Climatic changes may also permit, or indeed enforce, mass migrations such as those that occurred in Europe and North America during the Pleistocene glaciations. Thus for a time the reindeer spread southward over much of Europe and the musk ox ranged into Arkansas. These animals still persist in the high Arctic, but they vanished from the lower latitudes with the waning of the ice sheets. Conversely a flora adapted to a warm humid climate spread almost uniformly from the Gulf Coast to Alaska during Paleocene and Eocene time; then as the climate gradually became more arid and cooler, it retreated southward, but it still persists almost unchanged on the Gulf Coastal Plain.

On a smaller scale, the gradual shift of edaphic or ecologic environments may permit or require faunas to shift their geographic range and even to persist in new areas after they have disappeared from where they were first found. Thus during the growth of the Catskill Delta in Devonian time (Fig. 71, p. 139), several different edaphic environments shifted steadily westward, and the faunas migrated with them, evolving but slowly as they went, so that genera and perhaps even species appeared and flourished in the western part of the region a considerable time after they had been driven out of the eastern part.

To summarize, the appearance of an organism or a fauna in a given region may represent its evolution in place, or it may merely record the breaking of a barrier somewhere else or the shifting of a favorable environment.

Extinction, extermination, and asylums. Similarly the disappearance of a fauna in a given region may record its extinction or only its extermination. The dinosaurs, the woolly mammoth, the dodo, and a host of other creatures are *extinct* [L. *extinguere,* to destroy completely] —they are no longer living anywhere. But a species, or a whole fauna, may disappear locally or even regionally while surviving elsewhere. It may be driven away by changing environments or by competing rivals, or it may be killed off by disease. If it persists elsewhere, it is not extinct but merely *exterminated* [L. *ex,* out of + *terminus,* boundary or limit]—an important distinction (Tolmachoff, 1928). The rats exterminated in one village may return again. The horse and the camel and the elephant died out in North America late in Pleistocene time, but they survived in the Old World, and the horse especially has returned to flourish here in historic time. These great mammals were merely exterminated here, but their contemporaries, the ground sloths and the saber-toothed cats, are extinct.

Areas that are sufficiently isolated and undergo little environmental change may permit a fauna to persist locally long after it has been exterminated everywhere else. Such places form *asylums* for the contained faunas. Australia with its rich marsupial fauna is a striking example.

Large islands commonly serve as asylums. J. P. Smith (1895, p. 487) reported 5 species of mollusks that live on Santa Catalina Island but are known only as fossils on the mainland. Dall (1916) stated that on the shore of Socorro Island, some 800 miles south of Catalina and 300 miles west of Mexico, there are several species of northern origin, at least four of which now live on the mainland shore only in cooler water 200 to 800 miles farther north than Socorro Island. These boreal species migrated south during the Pleistocene and later retreated up the coast, except those that were trapped about Socorro Island.

China has been an asylum for two striking plants, *Ginkgo* and *Metasequoia,* both of which were widely distributed and common in the Mesozoic floras of the world. *Ginkgo* was discovered by early European visitors to China growing about certain of the temples where it had been husbanded since time immemorial; apparently it no longer lived wild. It is now a common urban shade tree in North America. *Metasequoia* was believed to have been extinct since Miocene time until living trees were found in an isolated valley in central China in 1941 (Chaney, 1948a, b).

Seedlings have since been introduced into the United States, and the genus will probably become widespread again. Equally noteworthy is the discovery within recent years of *Latimeria,* a relative of the Devonian lungfish and a member of a subclass listed in the textbooks as extinct since the Cretaceous, which is still living along the coast of East Africa. Eleven specimens have thus far been taken.

The most remarkable asylum yet recorded from the geologic past was on the site of the present Indonesian island of Timor, whose Permian rocks have yielded a rich fauna of crinoids and blastoids including many genera otherwise known only from Mississippian or older rocks (Wanner, 1916, 1924). Indeed, the whole class Blastoidea was believed to have become extinct near the beginning of Pennsylvanian time, until the Permian faunas of Timor were discovered. Some of the most bizarre of these have since been found, however, in the Permian of Australia.

Heterochroneity and recurrence. Should conditions change so that an organism or a fauna, preserved in some asylum, could spread again, it might reappear in a region from which it had previously been driven. The organism or fauna would be found in the strata of that region at two different levels, though absent between, and would be said to be *recurrent* (Williams, 1913). On the other hand, it might enter a new region where the time of its appearance would be quite different from that of the region it had previously inhabited. In this new region, not only its first appearance but its whole stratigraphic range might be quite different from that in the original region, and it would be said to be *heterochronous*. In North America, for example, the blastoid genus *Schizoblastus* is a guide to Mississippian rocks, but in Timor it is known only from the Permian, the Mississippian being unrecorded. A good many such heterochronous appearances of fossils are known, though few are so extreme. Large stellate discocyclinid foraminifera, for example, are confined to the Upper Eocene (Ocala limestone) in Florida and to the Upper and Middle Eocene of the Caribbean region, but along the California coast (as in the Santa Ynez Range) they occur in the Lower Eocene (Woodring, 1931). On the contrary the foraminifer, *Nonion* *pizarrenze* (Berry), is a very useful guide to Miocene rocks in the Atlantic Coastal Plain, yet it is still living off the coast of Peru and Chile, and a variety has been described off California.

It is commonly possible to recognize strongly heterochronous species in a fauna by study of the whole fauna. Among the Permian blastoids of Timor, for example, the conservative Mississippian genus *Schizoblastus* is associated with the highly specialized and exclusively Permian genera *Pterotoblastus* and *Timoroblastus,* more advanced than any known Mississippian blastoids, and with a variety of ammonites and other fossils of undoubted Permian age. But where a fauna spread slowly as a favorable environment gradually shifted, its first appearance might be considerably higher in one section than in another, yet concrete evidence to prove the difference might be hard to come by.

His study of the restriction of the living benthonic foraminifera to distinct depth zones along the coast of California (Fig. 75, p. 148) led Natland (1933) to a discovery at once disturbing and significant. Nearly all these species have been living in the region since Miocene or early Pliocene time, and presumably they have been zoned into distinct faunas adapted to different bottom temperatures throughout their existence. In Hall Canyon 1 mile north of Ventura, California (and about 75 miles north of where he had studied the living forams), Natland studied a thick section of Pliocene and Pleistocene strata that have been upturned and transected by Hall Creek. Here he found essentially the same 5 faunas that he had recognized as living in successive depth zones today, but they occur in vertical succession in the rocks, with zone 5 at the base of the section and zones 4 to 1 in regular sequence up to the youngest deposits. As all the species are still living in the region, this sequence in the rocks has no time significance and cannot be used for detailed correlation; instead each fauna records the depth (or at least the bottom temperature) at the time of deposition. Natland concluded that in early Pliocene time the sea was more than 6,000 feet deep in the vicinity of the present Hall Canyon; as it was gradually filled and the water became shallow, the appropriate faunas migrated in and established themselves in their turn. This method of estimating the depth of deposition of late Cenozoic deposits has since been applied in the Los Angeles basin also (Crouch, 1952).

RECOGNITION OF FACIES CHANGE

Difficulties. If the geologic history of a region is to be correctly understood, it is obviously necessary to recognize changes of facies wherever they occur. In the case of the Mesaverde group (Fig. 78), for example, it would be easy to assume, in the field, that the coal-bearing deposits are of one age, since in almost every section they are overlain by fluvial sandstones and shales and are underlain by marine sandstone that in turn rests on the Mancos shales. With this assumption the history would be inferred as follows: (1) the region was covered by open sea while a great thickness of mud accumulated to form the Mancos shale; (2) as the sea finally shoaled, sand was spread widely across the area; (3) the whole region was soon transformed into a vast swampy lowland in which vegetation accumulated to form the coal; and finally (4) it was aggraded into a broad well-drained alluvial plain.

But the relations indicated in Figure 78 tell a very different story. During Star Point deposition a rising land mass lay a short distance west of the Wasatch region while an interior sea covered the area represented by the diagram, its floor being shallow and sandy along the western margin and deeper and mud-covered elsewhere. As uplift progressed in the land to the west, an ever-increasing volume of detrital sediment was delivered to the sea, gradually building an alluvial coastal plain and pushing the shore eastward until, before the end of Price River deposition, a vast delta had formed over eastern Utah and west central Colorado—a delta as large as that of the modern Hwang Ho. But because of unequal uplift to the west, and possibly unequal subsidence of the sea floor, the shore line fluctuated back and forth in its advance, and from time to time sand was spread far out over the shallow sea floor. As the delta grew, its swampy seaward margin shifted eastward, following the shore line while a broad fluvial plain sloped

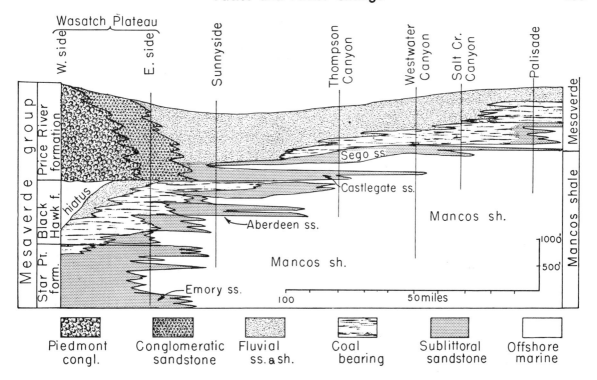

Figure 78. Facies changes in the Mesaverde group (Upper Cretaceous) in east-central Utah and west-central Colorado resulting from early episodes of the Laramide orogeny just to the west of the present Wasatch Plateau. Isochronous lines are horizontal. Adapted from Spieker (1949).

gently up to a piedmont belt over which coarse gravel was accumulating.

Several criteria may be used to demonstrate lateral change of facies, as explained below, but it cannot be too strongly emphasized that such complex relations as those shown in Figures 71–73 and 78 are not readily evident in the field, where only a tiny facet can be seen at one time, and can only be worked out bit by bit by careful mapping and the comparison of local details.

Intertonguing. Where two distinct facies intertongue, it is evident that they are at least partially contemporaneous. Such widespread thin tongues of sublittoral sand as the Castlegate and Aberdeen sandstones in Figure 78, for example, prove clearly that part of the Mancos shale is equivalent to non-marine beds farther west. Likewise it was the intertonguing of redbeds into the marine part of the Catskill Delta (Fig. 71, p. 139) that gave the first clue to the real age of the Catskill facies. The thin but extensive tongues of limestone that extend far east into the Bright

Angel shale (Fig. 73, p. 141) demonstrate in the same manner that most of the shales of the east end of the Grand Canyon are equivalent to the lower part of the Muav limestone farther west in the canyon.

Key beds or faunal zones that cross facies boundaries. In the Cambrian section of the Grand Canyon (Fig. 73), McKee (1945a) discovered two thin but persistent faunal zones that do not parallel the facies boundaries. The lower, bearing the Lower Cambrian trilobite *Olenellus,* is about 150 feet above the top of the Tapeats sandstone at the west end of the Canyon, declining gradually eastward until it is lost at the top of the sandstone within about 40 miles. A second faunal zone, bearing the Middle Cambrian trilobites *Alokistocare* and *Glossopleura,* lies near the top of the Bright Angel shale at the west end of the Canyon, but at the east end it is only a short distance above the Tapeats sandstone. Clearly then, part of the Bright Angel shale is of Early Cambrian age at the west end of the Canyon, and all or nearly all of it is of Middle Cambrian age at the east end of the Canyon.

In his study of the Hamilton group in New York (Fig. 71), Cooper (1933; Cooper and Williams, 1935) was able to carry the *Hypothyridina venustula* fauna far to the east of its normal lithotope (the Tully limestone) and thus to locate the top of the Hamilton group in the sandstone facies high up in the Catskills. Within the Hamilton group itself, he could use three thin but persistent limestones that extend far across the center of the state forming key beds tonguing into the shale facies on the west and the sandstone facies on the east.

Such key beds or faunal zones are commonly less extensive and generally do not extend completely through a facies complex, but if they extend far enough to tie one section to the next, other key beds or faunal horizons may then be found to tie in a further section. Thus bit by bit, like pieces of a jig-saw puzzle, the evidence may be built up.

Lateral gradation within a known stratigraphic interval. In some instances the lateral change of facies is gradual rather than abrupt. If overlying and underlying units do not change facies, or at least do not change at the same place, the equivalence of two facies may be evident. In the lower part of the Hamilton group in western New York, for example, the Stafford limestone, a few feet thick, is a fine key bed at the top of the Marcellus stage, but in the Finger Lakes region it gradually becomes sandy and passes over into the Mottville sandstone tongue, which is used as a key bed much farther east. The change of several of the Muav tongues from limestone in the west to dolomite farther east is also evident from the field relations (Fig. 73).

Faunal zones independent of facies. In spite of the faunal facies emphasized earlier in this chapter, the faunas entombed in the rocks are,

for a variety of reasons, commonly not limited strictly to a single lithotope. For one reason, many organisms have wide tolerance and will live simultaneously, though not in equal abundance, in a wide range of ecologic and edaphic situations. For another, the groups that float or swim are relatively independent of local bottom conditions; such creatures provide some of the best guide fossils for correlation regardless of lithology. And finally, shells may be transported after death and appear in thanatocoenoses outside their actual biotope. In this case it is not necessary that they be widely distributed across several facies, but only that they "spill over" some distance from one lithofacies into another.

In summary it may be emphasized again that the working out of a facies complex is not easy. It is much like solving a jig-saw puzzle, for at first the relations are not visible and we must begin by fitting together such bits and pieces as match up. In the puzzle we may be guided by shape or size or color of the pieces until parts of a general picture begin to appear. At first the puzzle may seem confusing—even hopeless—but once the pieces are fitted together and the picture emerges as a consistent whole, we can be reasonably sure of our solution.

In stratigraphy we start with such local details as we can observe and map; while mapping and matching such bits and pieces, we begin to watch for the larger picture that will tie them all together into a consistent whole. It took almost 100 years to discover the real relations of the varied facies in the Catskill Delta (Fig. 71, p. 139), but now that the picture is completed no one doubts the modern interpretation. Likewise, the complex facies relations in the Permian rocks of West Texas were utterly confusing until after 1925, and now they are so clear that one is inclined to forget how much careful and tedious work went into the solution of the problem.

PART III

INTERPRETATION OF
SPECIFIC LITHOTOPES

Charles Schuchert

Fig. 79. Exposure of the Cow Head breccia in the shore zone on the southwest coast of Cow Head Island, western Newfoundland. A large block of thin-bedded limestone, weaker than the surrounding material, has been largely ripped out by the waves to form the tide pool in the foreground.

8. Sedimentary rock nomenclature

GENERAL REMARKS

In order to discuss individual rock types and their origins, we must have names for them. And the subject of rock names leads directly into the vigorously debated subject of rock classification. Many writers bemoan the haphazard and patchwork nature of sedimentary rock terminology, envying the logical (if mutually contradictory) systems of classification that abound for the igneous rocks. But whether or not such classifications are satisfactory for igneous rocks (a point that can be debated), sedimentary rocks are many and very diverse, and it is doubtful whether their diversity can be properly expressed by any simple classification based on two or three variables only.

Most sedimentary rock terminology derives directly from field usage. Field names are rarely precise, but as laboratory study of sedimentary rocks has progressed, it has suggested many valuable precisions of the field terms. In the thirties, the Committee on Sedimentation of the National Research Council made an effort to standardize sedimentary rock nomenclature by general agreement among interested workers; the results were published in a series of five papers (Wentworth and Williams, 1932; Wentworth, 1935; Allen, 1936; Twenhofel, 1937; Tarr, 1938), each discussing one important group of sedimentary rocks. No systematic over-all classification was proposed, for none would have met with general approval; instead, the Committee tried to define existing terms more precisely and in such a way as to gain maximum acceptance. The series of papers is not complete, and no one is likely to agree with all the recommendations, but it provides a very useful basis for discussion.

If the Committee just mentioned failed to obtain unanimous agreement on nomenclature, it is hardly to be expected that the terminology chosen for this book can command it. Accordingly our discussion is directed more toward explaining existing conflicts in the use of terms and the ambiguities to which they may lead than toward attempting to establish once and for all a "correct" usage, though we have not hesitated to express our opinions on controversial terms. Although uniform usage is a desirable goal, it is not likely to be achieved now by the fiat of any textbook, and in the meantime it is less important for young geologists to be inculcated with any particular teacher's "correct" usage than for them to realize what differences exist, to be on the watch for them in the papers they read, and to be careful to explain their own usage without ambiguity in the papers they write. What can be dangerous to scientific understanding and progress is not so much that a term is being used in two senses, annoying as that may be, as that the men so using it are unaware of their difference.

Most of those who classify sedimentary rocks

TABLE 6. GROSS CLASSIFICATION OF SEDIMENTARY
ROCKS.

Class	Chief Rock Type
Silica and silicates dominant	
Fragmental	
Coarse	Conglomerate
Medium	Sandstone
Fine	Shale
Not obviously fragmental	Chert
Carbonates dominant	Limestone
Soluble salts dominant	Gypsum and rock salt
Phosphate dominant	Phosphate rock
Carbonaceous matter	
dominant	Coal
Miscellaneous	Other unusual rock types (e.g., iron-formation)

begin with a division into two groups, generally called mechanical and chemical (including organic), a genetic distinction. In fact, however, they then proceed to assign only the conglomerate–sandstone–shale sequence to the mechanical group and all the others, including the limestones, to the chemical, though many limestones and a few phosphates, etc., are mechanical in origin; in other words, the classification is really descriptive though masquerading as genetic. Grabau's classification (1904, 1913) is, to be sure, uncompromisingly genetic—limestone is parceled out into four or five separate categories and the term does not even appear in the index of his book, *Principles of Stratigraphy*—but precisely for this reason it has proved of little value for that description of rock types that must precede any discussion of genesis.

The subject of terminology may best be introduced, then, with a simple descriptive classification that breaks the multiplicity of sedimentary rocks down into manageable and generally recognizable classes containing rocks that, at least superficially, seem to be alike; the diverse genesis of the rocks in these groups can then be considered. A first breakdown can be compositional, into rocks composed mainly of silica and silicates, of carbonates, of soluble salts (especially sulphates and chlorides), of phosphates, of carbonaceous matter, etc. All but the first of these is a reasonably compact group, but the silica-silicate rocks comprise two-thirds to three-quarters of all sedimentary rocks and require to be further sub-

divided. They may be divided first into those that are clearly composed of fragments (of older rocks) and those that are not; the latter include the cherts and their allies. The fragmental rocks in turn are normally divided, according to the dominant fragment size, into three main categories: coarse, medium, and fine. The preliminary classification comes out, then, as in Table 6.

The rest of the present chapter is concerned only with the fragmental silica-silicate rocks; the detailed terminology of limestone and chert is considered in chapters devoted to those rock types, and space limitations prevent us from considering at length the other kinds of sedimentary rocks which, though very interesting and instructive, are relatively minor in amount.

GRADE SCALES

As the main subdivision of the fragmental siliceous rocks is by fragment size, some sort of scale of sizes must be adopted. Very early in the history of geology a general three-fold division into coarse, medium, and fine was accepted, but not till the end of the last century was precision introduced, principally by specifying exact numerical limits to named size grades. A system of such limits is called a grade scale. Some early grade scales simply chose convenient if arbitrary limits such as 1 inch, 0.5 inch, 0.2 inch, etc., but with the advent of statistical methods for treating sedimentary rock properties such as fragment size, it became necessary to construct grade scales with equal class intervals, and by common consent all such scales have been based on the metric system. Class intervals can be made equal in either arithmetical or geometrical progression but, despite the greater simplicity of arithmetical progression, it is manifestly absurd to use a grade scale that would lump, for example, all fragments smaller than 0.1 mm in one grade and then attempt to distinguish the grades 1.1–1.2 mm and 1.2–1.3 mm. Hence only geometrical scales have been seriously considered.

The scale most commonly used in America by geologists, hydrologists, sediment engineers, and students of ceramics, etc. (but not soil scientists), is the Udden-Wentworth scale, which begins at 1 mm and proceeds by powers of 2. This scale was proposed by Udden (1898, p. 5 n; 1914), revised and strongly championed by Wentworth (1922, 1933), and recently codified by a Subcommittee of the American Geophysical Union, representing students of geology, fluid mechanics, and sediment engineering (Lane and others, 1947); it is shown in Table 7.

In Table 7 we have substituted pebbles where the Lane Subcommittee wrote gravel and have retained Wentworth's more expanded use of the term gravel for all sediment made of (rounded) fragments larger than 2 mm. On the other hand, we approve the deletion of Wentworth's term granules (for particles between 2 and 4 mm), and also the use of clay size rather than clay for the finest sizes, as the term clay should be restricted to materials that are plastic when wet.

On the above scale, the boundaries of the three major classes of fragmental sediments are 2 mm and $\frac{1}{16}$ mm; these boundaries are not merely arbitrary but correspond in a rough way to important distinctions in the type of particle making up the sediment. Thus fragments in gravel are usually rock fragments, and in water they are transported almost entirely by bottom traction; sand grains are generally individual mineral grains (though they may be fragments of very fine-grained rocks like slate or phyllite), and they are the principal saltation load; the particles of mud are either very small detrital mineral grains (as in most silt) or particles of clay minerals produced during weathering, and they generally move in suspension. Moreover, mud shows a greater resistance to erosion by pure water than sand precisely because of the small particle size (p. 7 and Fig. 5, p. 6).

Of course, most fragmental sediments have grains belonging to several of these classes, and the over-all distribution of grains by size is best described in terms of statistical measures. Figure 80 shows the derivation of some of the simpler measures from size data determined by sieving a beach sand. From these data a *frequency histogram* was first constructed (shaded blocks bounded by solid lines); it shows the percentage of particles in each size grade. From it a *cumulative histogram* was made (blocks bounded by dashed lines) by adding on top of

TABLE 7.   MODIFIED WENTWORTH GRADE SCALE.

	Grade Limits (mm)	Grade Name	ϕ Units (See p. 163)
Gravel	4096		−12
		Very large boulders	
	2048		−11
		Large boulders	
	1024		−10
		Medium boulders	
	512		−9
		Small boulders	
	256		−8
		Large cobbles	
	128		−7
		Small cobbles	
	64		−6
		Very coarse pebbles	
	32		−5
		Coarse pebbles	
	16		−4
		Medium pebbles	
	8		−3
		Fine pebbles	
	4		−2
		Very fine pebbles	
	2		−1
Sand		Very coarse sand	
	1		0
		Coarse sand	
	$\frac{1}{2}$		+1
		Medium sand	
	$\frac{1}{4}$		+2
		Fine sand	
	$\frac{1}{8}$		+3
		Very fine sand	
	$\frac{1}{16}$		+4
Mud		Coarse silt	
	$\frac{1}{32}$		+5
		Medium silt	
	$\frac{1}{64}$ (approx. 16 microns)		+6
		Fine silt	
	$\frac{1}{128}$ (approx. 8 microns)		+7
		Very fine silt	
	$\frac{1}{256}$ (approx. 4 microns)		+8
		Coarse clay size	
	$\frac{1}{512}$ (approx. 2 microns)		+9
		Medium clay size	
	$\frac{1}{1024}$ (approx. 1 micron)		+10
		Fine clay size	
	$\frac{1}{2048}$ (approx. $\frac{1}{2}$ micron)		+11
		Very fine clay size	
	$\frac{1}{4096}$ (approx. $\frac{1}{4}$ micron)		+12

each block the sum of the blocks to the left; it shows the percentages in each size grade added to the percentages in all larger size grades. The smooth curve passing through the mutual corners of the cumulative histogram blocks is the *cumulative curve* (solid curve); it shows the cumulative distribution at all sizes, not just the sizes that bound the classes (the sieve sizes). The first derivative (or graph of the slope) of the cumu-

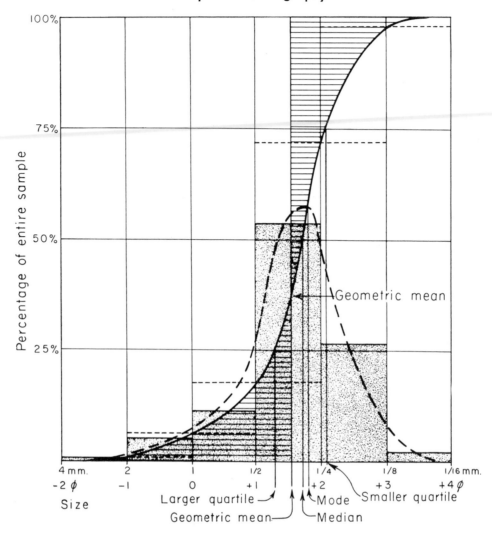

Figure 80. Methods of portraying size distribution of particles in a sediment, and measures of the average size. The data are for a beach sand from Lake Erie (Pettijohn and Ridge, 1932, sample 22), and the statistical measures were calculated by Krumbein (Krumbein and Pettijohn, 1938, p. 240–250).

lative curve is the *frequency curve* (dashed curve); it shows the frequency distribution at all sizes. (The ordinate for the frequency curve is not percentage, as for the others, but the slope of the cumulative curve; it was arbitrarily drawn to pass through the modal point on the cumulative curve.)

The *mode* of the distribution is the most frequent size; it is therefore the high point of the frequency curve and the steepest point (point of inflection) of the cumulative curve. The *median* of the distribution is the size of the middle par-

ticle; it is the 50 percent point on the cumulative curve, and the line passing through it should divide the area under the frequency curve into two equal parts. Similarly the larger and smaller quartiles are the 25 and 75 percent points on the cumulative curve and divide the area under the frequency curve into quarters. The *geometric* (or *logarithmic*) *mean* is the center of gravity of the area under the frequency curve, or the size that makes the two ruled areas (enclosed between it and the cumulative curve) equal. It is geometric because the abscissa shows millimeters in geometric progression, i.e., on a logarithmic scale (it is the *arithmetic mean* of the ϕ distribution).

The sediment as a whole is ordinarily assigned to that class containing either the mode, the median, or the geometric mean of the size distribution; these seldom differ much, but when they do the last is the most accurate expression of the size, though the others may be easier to determine (one should indicate which is being used). A neat method of indicating by adjectives the spread of grain sizes outside the mean or median class was proposed by Niggli (1935) and adapted to the Wentworth scheme by Pettijohn (1957, p. 26); the scheme is shown in Figure 81.

If finer subdivisions are needed, the Wentworth grade classes can be split geometrically into halves by multiplying the grade limits by the square root of 2, or into quarters by the fourth root of 2. Sieves are available that automatically separate Wentworth classes, half-classes, and quarter-classes.

Krumbein (1934, p. 76) has proposed an elegant mathematical transformation that eliminates the necessity for using the fractional limits of the Wentworth classes, which are very awkward in statistical calculations. He defines a size measure ϕ, equal to the negative logarithm to the base 2 of the size in millimeters; thus 1 mm = 0 ϕ, ½

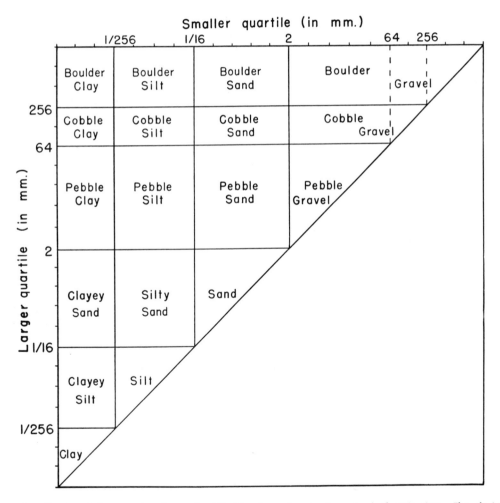

Figure 81. Classification of fragmental sediments by Niggli's scheme for showing spread of grain sizes. The abscissa is the smaller quartile, that size exceeded by 75 percent of the grains of the sediment; the ordinate is the larger quartile, that size exceeded by only 25 percent of the grains. Modified from Pettijohn (1957).

TABLE 8. ATTERBERG GRADE SCALE. AFTER
ATTERBERG (1904, P. 402–403).

Grade Limits (mm)	Atterberg's Terms	Approximate English Equivalent
(No specified upper limit)		
	Block	Boulders
———200———		
	Sten	Stones
———20———		
	Grus	Gravel
———2———		
	Sand	Sand
———0.2———		
	Mo	? (fine sand or coarse silt)
———0.02———		
	Lättler	Silt
———0.002———		
	Ler	Clay
(No specified lower limit)		

mm = +1 ϕ, ¼ mm = +2 ϕ, etc. (see the last
column in the table on page 161). The Wentworth scale, which is geometric when expressed
in millimeters, is thus transformed into a simple
arithmetic scale in ϕ units, each class being 1 ϕ
unit wide, each half class ½ ϕ unit, etc. The
principle is identical to that of pH as a measure
of alkalinity. After the initial strangeness of the
system has worn off, its great simplicity and usefulness become apparent, and geologists should
make more use of it.

Though the Udden-Wentworth scale is now
standard with American geologists, European geologists and soil scientists, and also, increasingly,
American soil scientists, use the Atterberg scale,
which begins at 2 mm and proceeds by powers
of 10, as shown in Table 8. The Atterberg
grade classes are much larger than those of the
Wentworth scale; they can be subdivided by the
second and fourth roots of 10. Krumbein has
suggested a transformation of this scale into ζ
units exactly like the transformation of the Wentworth scale into ϕ units, except that 2 mm = 0 ζ.

A similar grade scale, based on powers of 10
but beginning at 1 mm, has been suggested by

Alling (1943) after Hopkins (1899) for the description of size measurements in thin or polished
section as opposed to measurements of separated
fragments by sieves, pipettes, etc.

We strongly recommend the use of the Wentworth scale.

TERMINOLOGY OF THE COARSE-GRAINED FRAGMENTAL SEDIMENTS AND ROCKS

Coarse-grained fragmental rocks and sediments
may be subdivided either by size, according to the
Wentworth grade scale, or by shape, as in Table 9.

Shrock (1948b, p. 120–121) objects to this
use of breccia; he prefers to use conglomerate as
the general term for coarse-fragmental consolidated rocks and to divide them into roundstone
and sharpstone conglomerates. It is true, of
course, that the term breccia is also used for non-
sedimentary rocks that consist of angular fragments in a solid matrix, but this seems no bar
to its use here. Commonly enough the origin of
a specific rock of this sort cannot be determined
at once but only after painstaking field and laboratory study, and it seems best to retain the descriptive word breccia for all such rocks, whether
sedimentary or not, qualifying it with genetic adjectives when the origin has been ascertained.

The Latin-root words *rudite* and *rudaceous*
come from Grabau (1904; 1913, p. 285); the
corresponding Greek-root word *psephite* is rare
in America but more common in Europe.

TABLE 9.   CLASSIFICATION OF COARSE-GRAINED
FRAGMENTAL ROCKS AND SEDIMENTS.

	Individual Fragment	Uncon- solidated Aggregate	Consoli- dated Rock
General term	———	Ruda- ceous sedi- ment	Rudite, pse- phite
Fragments rounded	Roundstone (di- vided by size into boulders, cobbles, peb- bles)	Gravel	Conglom- erate
Fragments angular	Sharpstone	Rubble	Breccia

Rudites lend themselves to subdivision according to their composition, along the same lines as the sandstones or arenites, as discussed in the following paragraphs.

Genetic subdivision of the rudites is discussed in the next chapter.

TERMINOLOGY OF THE MEDIUM-GRAINED FRAGMENTAL SEDIMENTS AND ROCKS

The medium-grained sediments are the sands, and the corresponding rocks are the sandstones. To many geologists, however, the unqualified words sand and sandstone carry the connotation of high quartz content; the common use of the phrases pure sandstone and impure sandstone illustrate this point. In our opinion this compositional connotation should be rejected and sand should be solely a size term, but the possibility of ambiguity must be recognized. Many therefore use instead the Latin-root words *arenaceous* sediment and *arenite* (and in Europe the Greek-root word *psammite*).

The sands are subdivided by size according to the Wentworth grade scale. Rounding is much less used than with the coarse sediments; it has been suggested that the word *grit* be defined as coarse sandstone with angular grains and subdivided as follows: 2 to 1 mm, coarse grit; 1 to ½ mm, medium grit; ½ to ¼ mm, fine grit. As rounded grains smaller than ¼ mm are rare, no distinction is necessary for finer sizes. The word grit has been commonly used, however, in other quite different senses, as for a sandy fine-pebble or very-fine-pebble conglomerate (like the Carboniferous Millstone Grit of England), or for a silty or fine sandy mudrock (like the Devonian Esopus "grit" of New York). The word is therefore so ambiguous as to have lost much of its value, and those using it are urged to specify very clearly just what they mean by it.

A far more fruitful subdivision is by composition. The following main types are now generally recognized:

1. *Quartzose sandstone* (or quartz sandstone or quartz arenite or "normal" sandstone): grains are dominantly quartz (the limit variously taken as 80, 90, 95, and 99 percent quartz; 90 is recommended). Two varieties are *quartzite* * (strongly enough cemented with silica to break across the grains) and *"greensand"* or *glauconitic sandstone* (containing "considerable" glauconite, the rest normally quartz).

2. *Arkose:* contains 25 percent or more feldspar, the rest normally quartz and kaolin-clay matrix. (For a history of usage, see Oriel, 1949.)

3. *Graywacke:* contains 33 percent or more dark decomposable material, whether rock or mineral fragments or matrix; the rest normally quartz with or without feldspar, light-colored rock fragments, and dirty well-lithified silt and clay matrix.

4. *Calcarenite* or *lime-sandstone:* grains are dominantly calcite (we recommend 90 percent) (p. 227).

Intermediate varieties can be described by qualifying adjectives, such as arkosic sandstone, quartzose calcarenite.

A precisely similar subdivision of rudites can be made:

1. *Quartzose conglomerate* (breccias are rare)
2. *Arkose conglomerate* and *arkose breccia*
3. *Graywacke conglomerate* and *graywacke breccia*
4. *Calcirudite* or *lime-conglomerate* and *lime-breccia*

Of these terms graywacke is the most likely to be ambiguous. Troost in 1841 wrote "Geologists will rejoice that henceforth the name of graywacke will be doomed to oblivion," but the name has refused to die, precisely because it describes an important class of rocks, the "dirty" sandstones with much silt and clay matrix. Definitions vary widely but most include about the same rocks; † the one used here comes from the Re-

---

* If the silica cement was introduced during diagenesis or normal sedimentary burial, the quartzite is an *orthoquartzite,* but if the rock is the product of metamorphism, it is a *metaquartzite.* Krynine (1948, p. 149–152) has further extended the term orthoquartzite to include all "clean" or quartzose sandstones with little or no fine-grained matrix, whether the rock breaks across or around the grains and whether the cement is silica or calcite, but this extended usage does not seem desirable.

† On the other hand, graywacke is occasionally defined as "the basic equivalent of an arkose," though there are extremely few rocks made only of gabbroic debris and

TABLE 10.　CLASSIFICATION OF FINE-GRAINED FRAGMENTAL ROCKS AND SEDIMENTS.

	Unconsolidated Aggregate	Consolidated Rock		
		General term	Non-fissile	Fissile
General term	Mud if wet, dust if dry	Mudrock or lutite	Mudstone	Shale or mud shale
Particles mainly larger than 4 microns	Silt	Siltrock	Siltstone	Silt shale
Particles mainly smaller than 4 microns, normally composed of clay minerals	Clay	Clayrock	Claystone	Clay shale
Very weakly metamorphosed (after Flawn, 1953)	—	—	Argillite	Clay slate

port of the Committee on Sedimentation (Allen, 1936, p. 46). To many the term carries the additional connotation of strong lithification, approaching incipient metamorphism. The rocks are commonly subdivided further by the presence or absence of feldspar (which is normally but by no means exclusively plagioclase, commonly contributed from volcanic rocks). Krynine (1948) calls these classes high-rank and low-rank graywacke; Pettijohn (1957, Chap. 7) and Krumbein and Sloss (1951, p. 132–134) call them graywacke and subgraywacke. Krynine's terms, though they imply genesis, are preferable as they do not exclude from graywacke the original Saxon rocks; perhaps simply feldspathic graywacke and non-feldspathic or lithic graywacke (Krynine, 1948, p. 153; Pettijohn, 1954) would serve. In any case, it is evident that one should exercise caution in reading about these rocks and frame explicit and precise definitions in writing about them.

Recently proposals have been made for dividing the sandstones into two main groups. Fischer (1934, p. 326–327) divided them by the character of their size sorting into sandstone proper, whose grains fall into relatively few size grades, and wacke, whose grains are distributed fairly evenly over many size grades. In the same way, Gilbert (Williams, Turner, and Gilbert, 1954, p. 289 ff.) divided them at 10 percent fine silt and

the rocks first called graywacke in Saxony were not such rocks; the term is too useful to be squandered on these rare rocks.

clay (coarse silt is classed with the sand); those with less he called arenite, those with more, wacke. This restriction of arenite by composition contradicts, however, Grabau's specific statements of his purpose (1904, p. 242; 1913, p. 285) in proposing the term originally, to avoid the ambiguity inherent in the compositional connotation of sandstone; it would thus compound confusion and should be rejected. Whether Fischer's restricted use of sandstone is desirable can also be debated. Wacke may be useful, though apparently it was originally used for weathered basalt (Allen, 1936, p. 32). Packham (1954) has made a somewhat similar division into an arkose-quartzose sandstone suite and a graywacke suite, but on largely genetic grounds, using the sedimentary structures exhibited by the sandstones. Whether these proposals will gain acceptance remains to be seen.

TERMINOLOGY OF THE FINE-GRAINED FRAGMENTAL SEDIMENTS AND ROCKS

The principal bases for dividing the fine-grained sediments and rocks are particle size and fissility. The scheme shown in Table 10, largely after Ingram (1953), is recommended. Finer subdivisions by size are rarely useful as size sorting in these materials is ordinarily poor.

The most controversial term here is *mudstone*. The following four definitions have been advocated in recent years:

1. Fine-grained sedimentary rocks that slake readily to mud when wetted repeatedly (Shrock, 1948b, p. 124; cf. early use by Murchison, 1839, p. 204 n)

2. Fine-grained sedimentary rocks that show no fissility (Ingram, 1953, and many others)

3. Fine-grained sedimentary rocks, whether fissile or not (Knopf, in Longwell, Knopf, and Flint, 1939, p. 514)

4. Fine-grained sedimentary rocks and unconsolidated sediments (Twenhofel, 1937, p. 98)

Of these, the last is improper for a term ending in -stone, and the first seems too restricted to be of much use. The second is the most usual and fills the greatest need, especially as the third usage can now be replaced by Ingram's happy suggestion of *mudrock*. Nevertheless, all using the term are urged to make their definition explicit and unambiguous.

Argillite has recently been used by some for all argillaceous rocks, whether weakly metamorphosed or not; this is roughly equivalent to mudrock or clayrock of the present scheme. Though logical, this usage flies in the face of well-established practice and merely introduces a new ambiguity into an already ambiguous terminology, and it should be rejected. For those who prefer classical words, the Latin-root *lutite* and the Greek-root *pelite* are available in common use and are reasonably unambiguous.

One other term may be discussed. The name *bentonite* was given by Knight (1897, 1898) to a light yellow-green to yellow soft clay, greasy and soapy to the touch; it possesses extraordinary powers of swelling when wet, absorbing several times its own weight of water. Such clay is widespread as thin layers in the Upper Cretaceous of the Great Plains and Rocky Mountains. Later Hewett (1917) demonstrated that the bentonite of the West is altered volcanic ash. Since then, a volcanic origin has been made part of the definition, so that altered volcanic ash layers like those in the Middle Ordovician of eastern North America (p. 250) have commonly been called bentonite even if they do not swell, whereas clays that do swell have been rejected as bentonite because volcanic shards had not been seen in them. This seems like an unwarranted perversion of a sound descriptive name into a genetic one. The Ordovician ash beds are neither bentonite, since they do not swell, nor "metabentonite," since they are not metamorphosed bentonite; they are simply soft weakly fissile clayrock.

9. Rudites

THE PRECEDING CHAPTER presented terminology for the description of sedimentary deposits. We now turn to the genetic interpretation of different lithotopes.

The coarse clastic rocks have special interest because they commonly involve unusual agents and conditions of deposition.

RUDITES FORMED WITHOUT TRANSPORTATION

Residual breccia. In the weathering of cherty or siliceous limestone, the $CaCO_3$ is normally carried away in solution leaving a mantle filled with chunks and fragments of chert. Modern examples may be seen in the Flint Hills of Kansas, in outcrops of the Boone chert about the flanks of the Ozarks, and in exposures of the Knox dolomite in the southern Appalachians. Locally a chert rubble of this sort accumulates to a thickness of several feet. Soil creep and surface wash may aid in its concentration in low places, but transportation is not an important factor.

Such deposits of cherty mantle were common on the surface of the Knox dolomite when the Middle Ordovician seas spread over the region of Tennessee and Virginia, and are incorporated as a basal breccia (Bridge, 1955) in the Blackford and Lenoir limestones (basal Middle Ordovician). At the base of the Pennsylvanian shale around the flanks of the Ozark Dome there are similar residual breccias derived from the underlying Boone chert (Mississippian).

Less frequently quartzites and other types of resistant rocks weather to a residue of gravel or loose blocks. In desert areas where the fine debris is removed by the wind, a "desert pavement" of residual gravel and cobbles commonly forms. Lag gravel appears as a comparable residue on pediments where the finer material is removed by sheet wash. Any such accumulations of residual gravel or boulders may be incorporated as a breccia in the base of the succeeding sedimentary deposit. Such rudites are normally not more than a few feet thick, and they are discontinuous and irregularly distributed. Where they rest directly on their source rock they can be readily identified by the field relations as well as by their lithology.

Karst breccia. In regions of active underground drainage the collapse of the roofs of caverns produces local masses of rubble that may later be cemented into breccia. The great masses of fallen rock in Carlsbad Caverns, now largely covered by stalagmites, illustrate the process. In areas of pure limestone like that about Mammoth Cave in Kentucky or Luray Caverns in Virginia, the breccia will be a jumble of angular blocks of limestone; but in formations of interbedded chert and limestone the latter may be dissolved, leaving the chert to collapse. Such breccias occur in the Boone chert (Mississippian) on

Carl O. Dunbar

Figure 82. Reef talus on the flank of the Shikhan Tra-Tau, an early Permian reef near Ufa, west of the southern Urals, U.S.S.R.

the flanks of the Ozarks as a result of pre-Pennsylvanian karst development.

Where salt beds are present they normally disappear by solution near the outcrop, permitting the overlying strata to settle. If the rock is weak it may slump and crumple, but if resistant it may collapse into a jumble of angular blocks. The Mackinac breccia (Devonian) of northern Michigan is a spectacular example. It occurs in local patches over an area of 50 to 60 square miles along the north side of Mackinac Strait where most of the surface is formed of nearly flat-lying Middle Devonian limestone. The breccia is more resistant than the bedded rock and tends to weather out into stacks and hoodoo rocks. These masses of breccia, of limited areal extent, reach to depths of several hundred feet below the surface. They consist wholly of angular pieces of the Devonian limestone, ranging in size from gravel to blocks several feet in diameter. Deep below lies the Salina shale (Upper Silurian), which contains thick beds of salt. According ·to Landes (1945), the solution of part of this salt during Middle Devonian time caused the local collapse of all the overlying beds, and the fallen rubble was later cemented to form the Mackinac breccia.

RUDITES INVOLVING TRANSPORTATION

Rudites Resulting from Mass-Wasting

Coarse debris brought downslope by mass-wasting commonly reaches the margins of basins of deposition where it may accumulate to form talus breccia or cenuglomerate. Sharpe (1938) has given a fine analysis of the ways in which such material is transported.

Talus breccia. The talus formed at the foot of a cliff owes its position chiefly to gravity. In part the debris falls and rolls down the slope, but creep and frost-heaving aid in its movement and may carry large blocks a mile or two from their source into the edge of a subsiding basin where the surface slope is gentle.

If the small pieces of rock are slabby, they

Figure 83. Profile of the north slope of Lookout Mountain in the Cascade Range, Washington. The mountain is made of weak
John Day beds (Miocene) capped by 200 to 300 feet of basalt. After I. C. Russell (1900).

tend to slide down the slope and may give the appearance of crude bedding with a steep initial dip (Fig. 82). Russell (1900, p. 193–200) found, however, that large tabular masses tend to ride up over the finer debris and thus to be gradually rotated back toward their source as they slowly creep down the slope (Fig. 83). Carew McFall (unpublished thesis) observed the same phenomenon along the south face of the Aquarius Plateau in Utah where great tabular masses of the capping lava, as much as a mile in length, have crept down the slope rotating so that they dip back toward their source at angles up to 60°.

Figure 84 shows a large block of massive Capitan dolostone that has crept down the slope along the face of the Glass Mountains in West Texas. Similar blocks, several feet in diameter, have

reached the floor of the Marathon basin and are largely buried in finer debris.

Submarine talus is formed where sea cliffs descend below water level. If the water is shallow, the fallen pieces may be somewhat rounded by the passing of finer particles moved by storm waves, but if it is deep, or if the shore is protected from large waves, the fallen debris will remain angular.

A fine example of submarine talus breccia, described by Berkey (1897–1898, p. 375–377), is exposed along a cliff of Keweenawan lava within the edge of the city of Taylors Falls, Minnesota (Fig. 85). It consists of angular fragments of amygdaloidal basalt, obviously derived from the cliffs above. The blocks are coarse near the cliff but become finer away from it, and within a hundred feet or so give way to silty shale filled with the late Cambrian brachiopod *Obolus matinalis* (Hall). In the sandy matrix among the blocks of basalt near the base of the cliff the peculiar shore-dwelling Cambrian snail, *Hypseloconus,* may be collected. Clearly this talus was formed while the late Cambrian sea was beating against this very cliff, which was later buried and is being exhumed by modern erosion. A very similar deposit of the same age occurs at Ableman in the Baraboo region of Wisconsin (Weidman, 1904, p. 91–92).

Submarine talus likewise forms about organic reefs which tend to grow up and out toward the open sea. The growing organisms, such as corals and algae, are frequently broken loose during storms and roll down to form a long talus slope. Modern deposits about the islands and coral atolls in the mid-Pacific have recently been described by Emery (in Emery, Tracey, and Ladd, 1954, p. 70–72), and Newell and others (1953,

Carl O. Dunbar

Figure 84. Large block of Capitan dolostone (Permian) on the front slope of the Glass Mountains, West Texas. This block has crept down the slope from the distant cliff at the left during the present cycle of erosion.

p. 67–69) have described comparable deposits in the Permian reef complex of the Guadalupe Mountains of West Texas (p. 93). Figure 82 shows a similar talus breccia on the flanks of Shikhan Tra-Tau, a great reef in the lower Permian limestone of the Ufa Plateau west of the Urals.

A crude stratification may be seen in many talus breccias, due either to the preferred orientation of slabby fragments parallel to the original slope, or to variations in the coarseness of the debris from time to time, and showing a steep initial dip away from the source. On the basinward side talus breccia grades into finer grained and distinctly bedded sediments. Such a deposit should be readily identified by its linear form and its position against the cliff from which the coarse debris was derived.

A spectacular talus deposit of late Miocene and Pliocene age is the Violin breccia that lies along the north side of the San Gabriel fault south of Bakersfield, California (Crowell, 1955). It consists of granitic and gneissic debris in angular and subangular blocks up to 6 feet in diameter. Near the fault, bedding is indistinct, but less than 500 feet from the fault, the breccia grades rather abruptly into finer material and intertongues with the well-bedded sandstone and graywacke of the

Ridge Basin formation which is partly marine and partly non-marine. This breccia reaches the phenomenal thickness of some 27,000 feet and indicates that repeated uplift maintained a steep San Gabriel fault scarp in this area from late Miocene to late Pliocene time.

Cenuglomerate. Rockfalls, landslides, and mudflows are important in regions of high relief and are one of the chief sources of coarse breccias. For rudites so formed, Harrington (1946) has proposed the apt term *cenuglomerate* [L. *coenum,* mud + *glomerare,* to roll together].

A typical rockfall occurred near Frank, Alberta, in 1903 (Daly, Miller, and Rice, 1912). Here the face of Turtle Mountain, a great cliff of Carboniferous limestone, towers some 3,000 feet above the valley of Old Man Creek. After heavy rains in 1903, a mass of stone about half a mile long and 150 feet thick fell from the upper part of the cliff, crashing down and spreading into a bed of rubble that covered about 1 square mile of the valley floor. As is common in such falls, the rock was so completely shattered that the largest fragments remaining were scarcely 6 feet in diameter.

Rockfalls occur chiefly in regions of high relief where they are removed as erosion proceeds, but along moving faults they may at times have

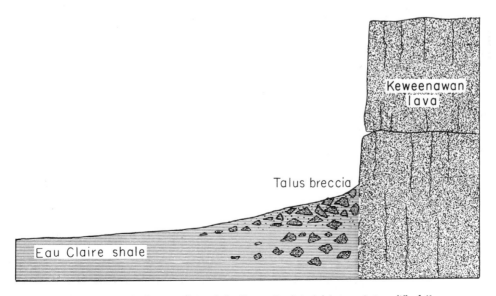

Figure 85. Talus breccia in the Eau Claire shale (Upper Cambrian) lying against a cliff of Keweenawan lava in the city of Taylors Falls, Minnesota.

played an important role in transporting rock debris down a scarp into a subsiding structural basin.

In mudflows there is sufficient water to permit the debris to move as a fluid, like cement coming from a mixer. Troxell and Peterson (1937) have described a mudflow, of the type characteristic of arid regions, that occurred in La Canada Valley, a structural basin lying south of the San Gabriel Range in southern California. It originated in a part of the mountain slope that had been laid bare by forest fires in November, 1933. Then on New Year's Day, 1934, after a few days of very heavy rain, the mantle began to slide off into the headwaters of several small, subparallel streams. In these it flowed like soupy cement, with a front wall 8 to 10 feet high as it raced down the valleys. An observer at the mouth of one of the streams was pinned against the side of his automobile as the flood swept over him and quickly passed, leaving him upright but buried to his shoulders in debris. Within 20 minutes some 600,000 cubic yards of sediment were thus transported onto the floor of La Canada Valley. Two boulders, estimated to weigh 60 tons each, were brought down Dunsmore Creek and left in a city street at the north edge of Glendale.

A similar mudflow occurred near Wrightwood, California, in 1941 (Sharp and Nobles, 1953). This one traveled some 15 miles before coming to rest in the edge of the Mojave Desert where the gradient was only 75 feet per mile. Observers described it as like slimy, gray cement that went splashing and slithering along at a velocity of 10 to 15 feet per second. A similar flow occurred in the same area in 1943, and others have occurred there in the past. From a fluid sample taken at the time, Sharp and Nobles estimated that the water content in the flow was 25 to 30 percent by weight.

The Volcán mudflow of July, 1943, in Argentina has been vividly described by Harrington (1946). It started with a great rockfall, similar to that of Turtle Mountain in Alberta, but, immediately following the fall, the rainsoaked debris began to move down the canyon El Volcán. It traveled some 3 miles from its source, emerged from the mouth of the canyon, and streamed out across a great alluvial fan as a flow some 200 meters wide and 2 miles long. Here it left a deposit of coarse rock debris 25 to 30 meters thick at the center of the stream, thinning to about 1 meter at the margins. Observers reported that the flow moved with a velocity of 6 to 9 miles per hour and that it appeared as a turbulent stream of rock debris in which large blocks bobbed about like corks, frequently disappearing and then reappearing at the surface.

After settling, the matrix of this flow was a rather fine and superficially homogeneous, cream-colored mud. The bulk of the deposit, however, consisted of blocks of stone ranging up to 5 meters in diameter with a weight of 10 to 20 tons. Their shapes were highly varied and irregular, and some of them showed marks of abrasion.

According to Harrington, this is only the latest of a series of mudflows that have contributed to the building of the alluvial fan in front of El Volcán. He estimated that sediments of the fan, partly fluvial and partly mudflow, have a present thickness of at least 1,000 feet.

Blackwelder (1928) has emphasized the importance of mudflows as a geologic agent in arid regions and has illustrated numerous examples. Mudflows occur also in the tropical rain forests. Here the lush vegetation normally protects the soil and mantle from wash and gullying, but at times of exceptionally heavy rainfall small landslides on steep slopes may gather momentum and go crashing down a long slope, carrying away the timber and the mantle. Figure 86 shows a steep slope in the rain forest northeast of Caracas, Venezuela, that is scarred by many such landslides. In 1950 a comparable mudflow from the opposite side of the mountain reached and partly destroyed the town of La Guaira which lies on the coastal lowland. In the province of Tabasco, southern Mexico, rapid erosion of this sort brings down quantities of feldspathic debris onto the edge of the coastal plain where it is accumulating under conditions of heavy tropical rainfall yet will form an arkosic rudite (Krynine, 1935a).

Solifluction is a special type of mudflow seen in high altitudes and high latitudes where alternate freezing and thawing of a surface layer over permanently frozen ground facilitate creep.

In summary it may be noted that cenuglomerates closely resemble tillite. They are heterogeneous, unsorted, and unstratified, and may include very large blocks of stone. Furthermore, the boulders may be striated as a result of friction against each other during movement.

Skid boulders. In the Death Valley region of California, isolated boulders are scattered over the floors of some of the playas, resting on fine mud. They are mostly angular blocks of stone clearly derived from outcrops near the margins of the playas, and they are associated with trails or skidmarks indicating that they have recently slid across the surface of the mud, in some instances as much as 1,000 feet (Fig. 87). In size they range up to blocks estimated to weigh a quarter of a ton.

If such angular blocks had been found embedded in an ancient mudstone, they would almost certainly have been attributed to ice rafting. These modern boulders obviously have not been rafted into place, but the agent of transportation is a puzzle. Several students (McAllister and Agnew, 1948; Kirk, 1952; Clements, 1952) have concluded that the boulders have been skidded about by strong winds after rain had softened a surface film of the mud, which then served as a lubricant while the underlying layers were still firm. Shelton (1953) suggested that thawing after a freeze may have produced the slick surface on which the boulders were moved and that a gelatinous film produced by blue-green algae may have played a part. Stanley (1955), on the contrary, has presented convincing evidence that ice, driven by the wind, has played a part. According to him the boulders have been moved only during the winter when the playas are covered with a few inches of water that is frozen over. Then as the ice begins to melt it can be broken up and moved about by strong winds, the ice bringing much more force to bear against the protruding boulders than the wind could exert directly on them.

Piedmont Conglomerates

As explained in Chapter 2, gravel is spread over the piedmont slopes in front of many mountain ranges. Where the mountain front is abrupt, boulders of considerable size may be swept out

John T. Miller

Figure 86. Naiguatá Peak a few miles northeast of Caracas, Venezuela, showing scars where landslides have ripped through the heavy rain forest.

By LIFE photographer, Loomis Dean, © TIME, Inc.

Figure 87. Skid boulder and trail on the floor of a playa near Death Valley, southern California.

2 or 3 miles from the canyon mouths by heavy floods or by mudflow. Smaller gravel up to a few inches in diameter will be carried much farther out from the mountains to be left in irregular and lenticular deposits within finer material. Johnson (1901, p. 633 and Pl. 118) found gravel as coarse as cobbles, widely distributed more than 250 miles from the front of the Rockies, along the eastern escarpment of the High Plains all the way from Kansas to Texas. Grabau (1913, p. 594) has reported that the pebbles in the western exposures of the Pottsville conglomerate of Pennsylvania (early Pennsylvanian) have made a journey of more than 400 miles from their source. In general the piedmont gravels of the more humid environments are more rounded and better sorted than those of arid basins.

The term *fanglomerate* was introduced by Lawson (1912, 1913) for the lithified counterpart of the coarse, poorly rounded and poorly sorted deposits that form the upper part of the alluvial cones about the ranges in arid regions.* Instead of fanglomerate, Norton (1917, p. 167) used the term *bajada breccia* (p. 38).

Rudites Formed by Glaciation

The characteristics of glacial till are too well known to need a long description here. It shows a complete lack of sorting and of stratification; blocks or boulders of large size may be isolated in much finer material; and some or many of the boulders may be striated and soled.

It is important to note that mudflows also show all these features, though a typically soled and

---

* Unfortunately the name was first applied to a formation of quite different origin, "a detrital rock at Battle Mountain, Nevada." In an abstract (1912) of a paper given before the Geological Society of America, Lawson interpreted this deposit as probably a Mesozoic counterpart of the deposits now forming about the Basin Ranges. In the paper published later (1913), he began with a description of the modern deposits and then described the one at Battle Mountain as an example of a fanglomerate. Roberts (1951) later studied this deposit, named it the Battle formation, and showed that it is of Pennsylvanian age and is at least largely marine. Although Lawson completely misinterpreted this deposit, it is clear what he intended fanglomerate to mean, and the term has since been widely used in that sense. We

striated glacial boulder could hardly be duplicated in a mudflow. A heavily scored and polished rock floor under such a deposit would afford the most convincing evidence of glaciation (Fig. 23, p. 44).

In modern valley glaciers the fine increment of the sediment is chiefly "rock flour" made of fresh rock ground up or scraped off the boulders or the floor, with a minimum of clay or other products of chemical decay. This criterion would be less applicable to the deposits left by continental ice sheets that move far out over the plains, incorporating in their load the soil and weathered mantle of the region.

Ancient tillites are well known from the Permian of South Africa and of Australia and India, and from the late Precambrian in several parts of the world. There are undoubtedly other tillites, but many of the alleged glacial deposits were probably formed by some of the other means discussed in this chapter.

Rudites Formed by Rafting

Glacio-marine deposits. The capacity of floating ice to transport rock debris has long been recognized. A vast belt of the sea floor surrounding Antarctica is now covered by sediment dropped from floating bergs (Stetson and Upson, 1937). It has all the characters of till except that it is being deposited on the sea floor and includes the remains of marine animals (p. 24). The glacial beds in the Lower Marine Series of the Permian of Australia almost certainly were formed in similar fashion. In the cores from the floor of the North Atlantic (Bramlette and Bradley, 1940), four "glacial layers" have been recognized on the basis of gravel and coarse sand presumably dropped from bergs and floe ice during four late glacial advances. Such debris must have virtually covered the Atlantic ocean floor above 50°N, for the glacial layers could be recognized in each of the widely spaced cores.

Coarse material may thus be carried to sea and dropped into quiet deep water beyond the

---

therefore recommend its continued use even though the original "type fanglomerate" is a deposit of entirely different nature.

reach of waves or strong currents, and scattered boulders may thus be embedded in fine sediment. The capacity of bergs to transport masses of rock of almost unlimited size is so well known that, in the past, glaciation has been invoked to explain almost every rudite that contains blocks more than a few feet in diameter, or in which scattered boulders are embedded in a fine matrix.

It is important to understand that this is only one of several ways in which coarse rudites may be formed.

Ice-rafted stream boulders. Wentworth (1928) recorded well-striated cobbles in Pleistocene terrace gravels in eight of the eleven Southeastern States. They were found at 20 localities in the Tennessee River system and at numerous localities in the Chesapeake Bay region. All these places are far south of the known limits of glaciation, and Wentworth concluded, therefore, that the cobbles must have been transported by floating ice in the rivers and must have been striated by dragging bottom during such transportation.

Boulders rafted by drift logs. Price (1932) described a remarkable occurrence of erratic boulders within the Sewell coal bed at Leslie, West Virginia. From this coal he records 40 boulders, ranging in size up to 160 lbs, with 13 exceeding 10 lbs each. They are of varied lithology—sandstone, quartzite, vein quartz, and granite—and are mostly well rounded. Their source must have been in the Blue Ridge country at least 60 miles to the east. They could hardly have been ice-rafted into the midst of a Pennsylvanian coal swamp, and presumably they were carried by floating trees. They probably had been entwined by the roots of trees that were eventually undercut during floods and set adrift with boulders held among their roots (Fig. 88).

Boulders rafted by kelp. In the sea certain of the seaweeds develop rootlike holdfasts by which they attach themselves to the sea floor, or to solid objects lying upon it. *Laminaria*, the "devil's apron string," is a conspicuous example. It normally grows offshore in water more than 20 feet deep. During heavy storms a large clump of such algae attached to loose gravel or boulders may "drag anchor" and thus transport even large cobbles considerable distances. After a heavy

Carl O. Dunbar

Figure 88. Boulder held in the roots of an uprooted tree. Although the roots were partly broken away, the boulder was still so firmly held that it could not be dislodged when the picture was taken.

storm in July, 1927, one of the writers found on the sandy beach at Lighthouse Point near New Haven a large number of such clumps of *Laminaria*, each attached to a cobble. The largest of these was a cluster of 12 straplike thalli, the longest exceeding 10 feet, attached to a granite cobble weighing 4 lbs. It had been transported into an area of fine sand.

Emery and Tschudy (1941) have emphasized this role of kelp in the transportation of rock.

Rudites Related to Faulting

Talus and turbidity flows from submarine fault scarps. Probably the coarsest of all rudites have been formed in connection with submarine faulting. Here the masses of rock dislodged from a scarp may accumulate as talus, but in the sea, especially if soft mud is present below the scarp, conditions are favorable for landslides that may develop into spasmodic turbidity currents capable of transporting very large blocks.

One of the most spectacular of all known rudites is the Cow Head breccia of western Newfoundland, described by Schuchert and Dunbar (1934, p. 73–86). It is a limestone breccia consisting of fragments of Upper Cambrian, Lower Ordovician, and Middle Ordovician formations that are widely exposed in the region (Figs. 79,

Charles Schuchert

Figure 89. A block of massive Upper Cambrian limestone about 45 feet thick in the Cow Head breccia near the village of Cow Head, Newfoundland.

p. 158, and 89, 90). The breccia occurs discontinuously for a distance of more than 200 miles along the coastal belt in front of the Long Range Mountains, and it is probably a series of lenses not strictly contemporaneous. It is therefore not a geologic formation but a facies of the Humber Arm group (Middle Ordovician).

The size of the blocks—average as well as extreme—varies greatly from place to place, but many blocks exceed 100 feet in diameter and the largest observed is of massive white limestone

Charles Schuchert

Figure 90. Close view of Cow Head breccia on Cow Head Island, Newfoundland, showing a thin-bedded slab that was brought into place without separation of its layers but has been bent by the weight of the load above.

approximately 400 feet by 600 feet by 20 feet. In most places the lower contact of the breccia is not exposed, but along the coast some 3 miles northeast of Port au Port the breccia rests on black graptoliferous shale that clearly was soft when the great boulders descended upon it, settling partly into it and squashing the mud aside.

At Cormorant Head on the west side of Port au Port Peninsula, a large mass of the breccia is exposed in the sea cliff in relations that clearly indicate its association with a submarine thrust fault and at the same time give the geologic date of formation (Fig. 91). For about 3 miles southwest of Cormorant Head (inset) a 300-foot sea cliff is formed of nearly horizontal St. George dolomite (Lower Ordovician) and Table Head limestone (basal Middle Ordovician). About a mile south of Cormorant Head, a thrust fault, A, is clearly exposed where the St. George dolomite has been thrust up over the Table Head limestone. A similar fault, B, is inferred to lie beneath Cormorant Head, because of large-scale drag in the Table Head limestone and the relations in front of it. Against the front of this thrust mass lies very coarse limestone breccia in which the blocks are of Table Head limestone, all angular and for the most part large. This deposit shows no trace of bedding and is clearly a submarine talus. The front of the thrust mass is so shattered that the exact boundary between it and the breccia is in part not clearly defined.

In the lower sea cliff to the north of the Head a long sequence of the succeeding Humber Arm beds is exposed. These begin with dark silty shale but include numerous beds of limestone-breccia and of calcarenite. Four of the coarsest beds of breccia are indicated in Figure 91. These include boulders of both Table Head limestone and St. George dolomite and were in part derived from the posterior thrust sheet (above fault A). These thick beds of breccia show no internal evidence of stratification, but the finer ones, farther out and higher in the section, show every gradation into well-bedded calcarenite in which the grains are fine angular fragments of the same source rock. The interbedded shales bear graptolites and inarticulate brachiopods at the positions shown in Figure 91, proving that the breccia was formed on the sea floor. They repre-

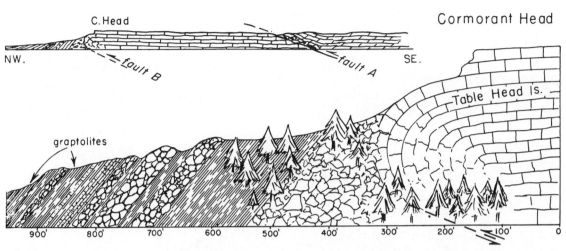

C.Head   Cormorant Head

NW.   fault B   fault A   SE.

Table Head ls.

graptolites

900'   800'   700'   600'   500'   400'   300'   200'   100'   0

Figure 91. Sea-cliff section at Cormorant Head on the west coast of Port au Port Peninsula, western Newfoundland.

sent a fauna that occurs normally at the summit of the Table Head group, indicating that the faulting occurred at the close of Table Head deposition. In this connection it is significant that a profound change in regimen of regional extent occurred at this time, the overlying Humber Arm group being detrital whereas the underlying Table Head and St. George formations, with a combined thickness of more than 3,000 feet, are largely calcareous. Although the contact relations of the Cow Head breccia have not been observed elsewhere, it can hardly be doubted that all the coarse masses are connected with submarine faulting of this time. The largest and coarsest mass at Cormorant Head appears to be a simple talus deposit, but the higher beds are probably lenses formed by landslides, and in other places spasmodic turbidity currents may have played a part.

Bailey and Weir (1933) described another very coarse breccia, associated with submarine faulting of Late Jurassic age, along the coast of Dornoch Firth in northeastern Scotland. There dark shales of Kimmeridgian age alternate with boulder beds in which exceptional blocks exceed 100 feet in length. The boulder beds are closely associated with a great fault on which aggregate movement is estimated to have exceeded 2,000 feet, and the boulder beds are considered to represent repeated landslides into the sea.

The remarkable boulder beds of the Johns Valley shale in the Ouachita Mountains of Arkansas have been interpreted (Miser, 1934, p. 992–1004; Moore, 1934) as the product of submarine landslides from an unknown fault scarp on the sea floor in early Pennsylvanian time.

Chaos and megabreccia. The name *chaos* was proposed by Noble (1941, p. 961 ff.) for a phenomenal type of breccia associated with thrusting. The type example is the Amargosa chaos, a widespread deposit in the Death Valley region of California. This deposit, some 2,000 feet thick, lies upon the surface of the Amargosa thrust and is in turn overlain in part by the Funeral fanglomerate (Pliocene?). It consists of enormous blocks and masses of the formations that crop out in the region, ranging in age from Precambrian to Tertiary. These blocks are in a confused, chaotic arrangement, tightly packed together with very little finer grained material. "Most of them are more than 200 feet in length, some are as much as a quarter of a mile, and a few are more than half a mile in length. . . . Each block is minutely fractured throughout, yet the original bedding in each block of sedimentary rock is clearly discernible. . . . Commonly the bedding, even of incompetent beds, is not greatly distorted" (Noble, 1941, p. 964).

Noble believed the Amargosa chaos to be entirely of tectonic origin, even though it appears as a somewhat extensive sheetlike deposit. Jahns and Engel (1950) note that related breccias are

Carl O. Dunbar

Figure 92. Rockledge breccia south of St. Albans, Vermont. The white block in the near foreground is about 8 feet across.

widespread both in the desert and in the coastal region of Southern California, but in most places they are not as coarse as the type chaos. Admitting that locally this type of deposit represents "the crackled soles, tongues, or other parts of low-angle thrust faults," they suggest that much of it is of sedimentary origin. More recently, Noble (Noble and Wright, 1954, p. 152) has accepted one part of the chaos as sedimentary in origin rather than tectonic.

Under the term *megabreccia* Longwell (1951) described similar coarse deposits, including individual blocks as much as a quarter of a mile long, flanking some of the basins in the Lake Mead area of southern Nevada and western Arizona. These he showed have formed downslope from large thrusts in the ranges, and the field relations prove that they are at least largely sedi-

mentary rather than tectonic. Of the mass in the valley west of Black Mountains he writes:

Evidence bearing on the exact cause and the detailed mechanics of sliding is meager. Logically we may suppose that uplift of the Black Mountains fault block played an important part in setting the stage, if not in the continuing performance. Active rise of the hanging wall would produce an oversteepened front, from which masses of bedrock might shear off under their own weight and build up an unstable slope of coarse debris. Material under such a slope might move slowly in a chronic slide, or at a time of unusual saturation by ground water it might slide catastrophically. Moreover the upthrust hanging wall may have developed conditions for instantaneous release of immense bedrock masses, to hurtle down the slope in the manner of the Frank, Alberta slide in 1903. Such a mechanism may be urged to explain the large thickness of megabreccia in its present outcrop, three or four miles from the mountain front, and its absence or much reduced thickness nearer the mountain source. Less favorable to this hypothesis, perhaps, is the interfingering of megabreccia with ordinary fan material in the northern and western part of the outcrop area; this evidence of extensive reworking in transit seems to accord best with the concept of leisurely progress down the slope. [He adds that in places a low-angle thrust fault may have helped to push such debris down slope before it.] Clear evidence of such action connected with the Glendale thrust, near the Muddy Valley, Nevada, is provided by the Overton fanglomerate, which includes blocks up to half a mile long, some of them samples of the thrust plate itself, others torn from the underlying bedrock and pushed by the plate onto the fan slope. A thrust plate of this kind, moving forward on a low-angle incline, might override an extensive sheet of its own debris. Megabreccia developed under such conditions would be of mixed origin —partly sedimentary, partly tectonic (Longwell, 1951, p. 349–350).

Shoal Breccias

On a flat sea floor, organic knolls and banks will cause heavy storm waves to break if the water is sufficiently shallow, setting up strong hydraulic forces that may rip up both the knolls and the surrounding bottom. But in this situation the broken material is not transported away and may be recemented to form a thin lens of limestone-breccia.

The Cambrian-Ordovician sequence in northwestern Vermont (Schuchert, 1937) includes four zones of breccia believed to have formed in this way. Of these the Rockledge breccia is best known and will serve for illustration. It lies between the Hungerford slate below and the Georgia slate above, both Upper Cambrian and accordant in dip and strike. The lower of these formations is a "banded" slaty shale some 700 feet thick that includes numerous thick lenses of compact, light-gray limestone interpreted as algal banks.

The Rockledge breccia crops out along the strike of these beds for a distance of 4 or 5 miles south of St. Albans, but it is a thin lens having a maximum thickness of about 40 feet. It consists of limestone fragments and blocks set in a calcareous and somewhat muddy and sandy matrix. The fragments are of two sorts (Fig. 92): (1) scattered blocks of light-gray limestone and (2) much more numerous pieces of thin-bedded

Carl O. Dunbar

Figure 93. Boulder in the Rockledge breccia formed of a slightly worn algal reef mass. South of St. Albans, Vermont.

darker gray limestone. Many of the white blocks exceed 10 feet in diameter and one, called Rockledge, exceeds 100 feet in length. A few of these white blocks are angular but most of them appear more or less rounded (Fig. 93); the fragments of darker thin-bedded limestone are relatively small and generally are acutely angular. The white blocks are like the algal banks that occur scattered in the Hungerford slate below the breccia, and their subrounded shape is believed to be inherited from the shape of the original banks. The thin-bedded dark limestone is similar to the limestone in various beds in the enclosing slates.

No deep vertical sections through the breccia and associated beds are available in Vermont, but beds of about the same age and facies exposed in the bluffs of Llano River, central Texas, may be instructive. Here the Wilberns formation of thin-bedded impure limestone includes numerous bun-shaped masses of lighter, fine-grained limestone. The largest of these, shown in Figure 94, is about 100 feet across and 50 feet thick. It is believed to be a reef knoll of algal origin that during its growth stood several feet above the surrounding sea floor. None of these beds are brecciated, possibly because the water was too deep or the waves too small to break about the knolls. In Vermont, however, during a short time when such algal knolls grew extensively, occasional storm waves broke about the knolls, ripping up the thin-bedded layers

Philip B. King

Figure 94. Wilberns formation (Upper Cambrian) in the bluffs on the Great Bend of Llano River, central Texas. The enclosed algal reef is about 100 feet across and 50 feet thick.

about them and even breaking up some of the smaller knolls. Raymond (1937, p. 1135–1137) found that the same trilobites occur in the matrix and in the boulders of the breccia, proving that brecciation took place during accumulation of the deposit.

Other shoal breccias are noted by Norton (1917, p. 177–179), and a good example occurs in the Upper Devonian Davenport limestone about Davenport, Iowa (Stainbrook, 1935, p. 252). It may be noted that shoal breccias have been recognized only in limestones.

Desiccation Breccias

Where laminated or very thin-bedded sediments are exposed long enough to dry out, mudcracks commonly form and the polygons may break loose as waferlike slabs. Mudcracks form only where some component of the sediment, usually clay, produces cohesion between the particles and shrinks appreciably upon drying. A surface film of clay may curl into rolls that can be moved by the wind, but such films will soften with the return of water and be transformed into small mudballs. Lime-mud, however, will crack to form polygons that become indurated after a few days exposure and do not readily soften when wetted. They are readily moved by waves and currents when water returns, and tend to form layers of "flat-pebble" conglomerate or breccia. If they are moved chiefly by bottom currents, they tend to accumulate in windrows or lenses where they become imbricated to form the so-called "edgewise conglomerates." Such deposits are common in the Conococheague and Beekmantown limestones (Upper Cambrian and Lower Ordovician) of the Appalachian region (Stose, 1909, p. 6 and Fig. 17; Bassler, 1919, p. 86–88).

Normal Marine Conglomerates

Where gravel is transported seaward by bottom currents or is reworked by the waves and currents of a sea advancing over a land surface, marine conglomerate tends to form. In such deposits the rock fragments are relatively more rounded and worn than in any of the types of rudite discussed above.

Barrell (1925, p. 306 ff.) has emphasized that marine conglomerates will be relatively thin, commonly under 50 feet thick and rarely if ever as much as 100 feet thick, except where they form locally along a bold coast where deep water comes immediately up to shore. The reasons for this are obvious. Waves and bottom currents decrease so rapidly with depth that the gravel line is usually less than 100 feet deep. With rising sealevel the sea advances landward and the waves cut away the upper part of such a gravel deposit, tossing the coarse particles shoreward and keeping them "in the mill." Of course, where the sea is beating against a cliff, the gravel may accumulate to any thickness permitted by the depth of water at the shore. In this instance the marine conglomerate may be thick in a narrow linear belt; it cannot be both widespread and thick. Indeed, it is difficult to cite examples from the stratigraphic record of widespread marine conglomerates; river gravels are normally dropped before the streams reach the sea and those produced by wave action on headlands and sea cliffs are kept near shore.

10. *Terrigenous arenites*

THIS CHAPTER is devoted to the terrigenous arenites, the calcarenites (lime-sandstones) being reserved for Chapter 13 where they are discussed along with the other kinds of limestone, but it should be emphasized here that lime sands are transported and deposited by the same agents, and in the same manner, as the sands discussed below.

SOURCES AND MINERAL COMPOSITION

Terrigenous sand is produced by the disintegration of pre-existing rocks, but it comprises only particles of sand size that have survived chemical weathering at the source and weathering and attrition during transportation. The grains may be highly varied in mineral composition at the source, depending on the parent rock and the climatic environment. A granite will yield quartz grains in excess of feldspar if the climate and topography permit thorough chemical weathering, but feldspar may predominate over quartz if erosion is rapid and mechanical weathering prevails. Basic plutonic rocks, lacking quartz, will produce sands made of feldspar, ferromagnesian minerals, and magnetite. The sand derived from metamorphic rocks commonly includes a wide range of minerals at the source in which quartz and feldspar predominate, and garnet, magnetite, and many other minerals are locally conspicuous.

If the sediment accumulates rapidly near its source, all such minerals may survive, as they commonly do in arkose and graywacke; but if exposed to long or repeated transportation the less stable minerals gradually disappear, leaving a higher and higher concentration of quartz grains.

In the erosion of sedimentary rocks the quartz particles readily survive, to be concentrated and redeposited. Thus they may pass through a series of sedimentary cycles. Meanwhile all the less durable minerals are gradually eliminated and almost pure quartz sand remains. Such remarkably pure concentrates as the St. Peter sandstone (Middle Ordovician) of the Upper Mississippi Valley, the Tuscarora sandstone (Lower Silurian), and the Ridgeley sandstone (Lower Devonian) of the Appalachian region have probably been produced in this way. Such deposits can be distinguished from first generation sandstones by the presence of grains of chert or of quartzite, or of quartz grains having a worn rim of secondary quartz within which is a nucleus made of a smaller, worn quartz grain.

Accessory minerals. Even when a sand has been reduced largely to quartz grains, there are several durable minerals that commonly persist in small quantity and may throw light especially on the source area. The majority of these are of higher specific gravity than quartz and are readily separated by pouring the sand into a heavy fluid, such as bromoform, in which the quartz and feldspar float while the accessory minerals sink. The latter are thus easily segregated and constitute the *heavy mineral suite* of the deposit.

Heavy minerals derived from granite are chiefly zircon, monazite, sphene, rutile, and apatite; those derived from metamorphic terranes include garnet, staurolite, kyanite, tourmaline, and topaz; and those from more basic sources may include spinel, pyroxenes, amphiboles, magnetite, and olivine. Gold and platinum, likewise, appear in some sands and are important in placer deposits. Thus the heavy mineral suite may indicate the probable source area of a sandstone or, on the contrary, may rule out a suspected source area.

Heavy mineral suites may vary geographically within a sandstone formation, indicating diverse sources as different streams were simultaneously feeding sand into a basin of deposition from different directions. The heavy mineral suites may differ likewise in successive formations within a given region, indicating that the source of one formation lay in one direction and that of another in a different direction. Such differences may, however, be due to the uncovering of new types of rock in the source area as erosion proceeded.

Finally, a persistent zone of heavy minerals may be useful in local subsurface correlation, especially in cuttings from deep wells.

Beach concentrates. During transportation, some of the less common minerals that survive with quartz but differ from it in specific gravity tend to be winnowed out and concentrated locally. Placers of gold, platinum, and diamonds have been formed in this way. Beach concentrates of certain heavy minerals are even more common and widespread and some of them are of great economic importance. The beaches of Florida, for example, include local concentrates of monazite, zircon, ilmenite, and rutile that are an important source of zirconium, thorium, and titanium (p. 69); and the monazite sands of southern India and Brazil are an important source of rare earths. Many other beach concentrates are of no present economic value. Along the west side of Lake Champlain, for example, the sandy beaches locally include layers of red sand consisting almost entirely of garnet and magnetite

brought, along with much quartz, by streams flowing out of the adjacent Adirondack Mountains. Similar concentrates of black sands are common along the beaches of southern New England where they have been segregated out of the Pleistocene drift. Beaches composed almost entirely of olivine occur locally in the Hawaiian Islands and other Pacific islands that are made of basic lavas and ash, and Bennett and Martin-Kaye (1951) described beaches in Grenada made almost entirely of augite sand.

Glauconite. Glauconite is included with the terrigenous sands even though it does not come "from the lands" but is formed on the sea floor. It occurs throughout the geologic column and is an important constituent of the sedimentary rocks in many parts of the world. Relatively pure concentrates of glauconite are commonly known as "greensand." Such deposits are conspicuous in the Franconia formation (Upper Cambrian) of Wisconsin and Minnesota, in the Lower Cretaceous of western Europe, and in the Upper Cretaceous of New Jersey, to mention only a few examples. In other places grains of glauconite are abundantly scattered through a calcareous or argillaceous matrix to form glauconitic marl. Extensive deposits of this sort occur in the Lower Cretaceous of Texas and the Eocene of Alabama and Mississippi, and in other parts of the world.

Although glauconite is locally plentiful in modern sediments and has been the subject of much research, widely divergent views have been held as to its origin. Many students have attributed it to the diagenetic alteration of fragments of ferromagnesian minerals exposed on the sea floor (Glinka, 1896; Cayeux, 1897; Hummel, 1922; Galliher, 1935). Galliher, for example, showed conclusively that it is forming from the alteration of flakes of biotite in the sediments now accumulating off the coast of California.

On the other hand there are extensive deposits in which the grains of glauconite are internal molds of small shells, especially the chambered shells of foraminifera. Here it is evident that the glauconite formed within, and neatly filled, the shells, and that the shells did not take part in the chemical reactions that produced the glauconite.

Students of such deposits have concluded that clay minerals, originally filling the shells, have been transformed into glauconite (Murray and Renard, 1891, p. 378–391; Takahashi, 1939; Grim, 1951). A few (e.g., Hadding, 1932) have argued that glauconite may be precipitated directly from sea water. Takahashi concluded that glauconite may originate from a variety of materials such as clay filling of shells, fecal pellets, silicate minerals, volcanic glass, feldspar, mica, or pyroxene, and that the presence of organic matter seems to facilitate glauconitization. According to him the diagenetic change of such substances into glauconite involves the loss of alumina, silica, and alkalies (except potash), and gain in ferric iron and potash. A number of workers (Hadding, 1932; Galliher, 1935; Hendricks and Ross, 1941) have emphasized that glauconite forms only where accumulation of sediment is very slow. This accords well with Goldman's observation (1921) that in the Bend Series (Lower Pennsylvanian) of Texas, minor breaks in the sequence are marked by concentrations of glauconite. Takahashi (1939) and Hendricks and Ross (1941) suggest that a reducing environment is necessary and that bacterial action plays a part. Where now forming, glauconite grains commonly are scattered in muddy sediment, but Takahashi records some areas of modern glauconite sand about Japan. He thinks these sands have been winnowed out of the mud and concentrated by waves and currents. It is probable that glauconite marl represents the normal primary occurrence, and that greensand is a concentrate brought together like any other kind of sand during transportation on the sea floor. Sublevation and removal of the finer sediment may aid in the concentration.

Under certain conditions glauconite is stable enough to survive erosion of an older deposit and redeposition. Its presence in a particular deposit is therefore not certain proof of marine deposition, though its normal occurrence is in marine strata.

In an excellent review of the literature on glauconite formation, Cloud (1955) concludes that it is more useful in paleoecological studies than other accessory minerals.

SHAPE: ROUNDNESS AND SPHERICITY

The shape of sand grains and pebbles is one of their most obvious characteristics and one of the most significant in sedimentation; it is also one of the most difficult to describe and measure in quantitative terms. Indeed, the problem still defies satisfactory solution.

At their source, rock fragments are normally angular and almost infinitely varied in shape. Those made of minerals that are brittle or have good cleavage tend to remain angular, as they are reduced in size mainly by fracture; but those made of tough minerals, like quartz, are reduced by attrition during transportation. The wear on such particles is concentrated chiefly on the edges and angles, and as these are worn blunt the fragments are progressively rounded. *Roundness,* then, is a function of the sharpness of the edges and angles.

Wadell (1932, 1933) devised a scheme, now widely used, for measuring the degree of roundness of sand grains and gravel. It involves measurements on a projection of the particle on a plane surface. The particle to be studied is placed on a glass slide and jostled gently until it comes to rest on its broadest surface. This normally places its least diameter in the vertical position and its maximum and intermediate diameters in the plane of the slide. It may then be photographed at any desired enlargement, or its image may be projected onto a horizontal surface, for measurement (Fig. 95).

According to Wadell's scheme (1932, p. 448), the roundness of a particular corner of a particle is r/R, in which r is the radius of curvature at the corner in question and R is the radius of the maximum inscribed circle. The roundness of the particle as a whole is the average of the roundness of all its corners. In Figure 95B, for example, the roundness of the lower corner is about 0.22, that of the blunt corner at the right is 0.50, and that of the other corners, reading counterclockwise, is 0.30, 0.36, and 0.40. The roundness of the particle is, therefore, the sum of these figures, 1.78, divided by 5, or approximately 0.36. Inspection of the figure shows that the radius of curvature increases as a corner becomes more

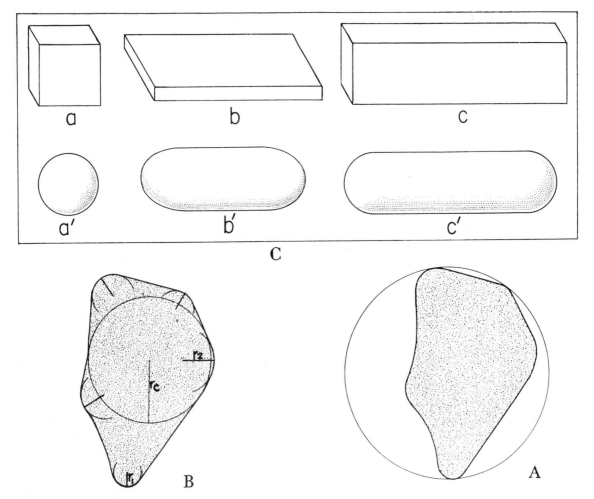

Figure 95. Shape of sediment particles. A. Projection of a particle lying on its broadest surface, showing the minimum circumscribed circle (for calculating sphericity). B. Same projection, showing the radius of curvature at each corner and the maximum inscribed circle (for calculating roundness). C. Distinction between shape and roundness. Particles in upper row have a roundness of 0, those in lower row a roundness of 1, but shapes differ greatly from left to right.

broadly rounded until it equals the radius of the maximum inscribed circle; the corner then disappears completely—it has become perfectly rounded. The particle as a whole is completely rounded when all its corners and angles have been so reduced. Perfect roundness therefore has a value of 1, and the roundness of an irregular particle, being less, is expressed as a decimal fraction.

Krumbein (1941) has prepared diagrams showing particles of varying degrees of roundness, to which actual particles can be visually compared; use of these diagrams avoids the rather tedious procedure outlined above and still gives reasonably accurate and reproducible results.

Wadell (1932, 1933, 1935) made another very important advance in the study of shape when he recognized that roundness is only one aspect of shape and that *sphericity* is an equally significant and quite distinct aspect. Sphericity is a measure of the degree of approach of a particle to the spherical shape.

The distinction between roundness and sphericity is illustrated by Figure 95C. The geometric forms in the upper row—a cube, a tablet, and a prism—differ conspicuously in shape, but they agree in having a roundness of exactly zero; every

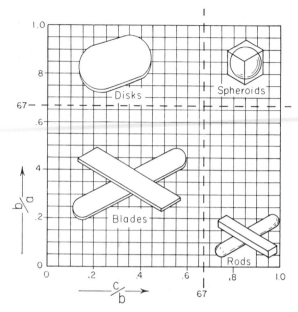

Figure 96. Diagram to illustrate the Zingg method of shape measurement and classification. Adapted from Krumbein and Sloss (1951, Fig. 4–7).

edge and corner is perfectly angular. The counterparts of these objects in the lower row likewise differ greatly in shape yet all are perfectly rounded. At the same time, it is obvious that the cube is more nearly spherical than either the tablet or the prism. A dodecahedron is even more nearly spherical.

The distinction is important because roundness and sphericity play different roles in sedimentation. Roundness gives a measure of the attrition the particle has experienced, but its influence on the movement of the particle is secondary; sphericity, on the other hand, strongly influences the dynamic behavior of a particle. A sphere not only rolls more readily than other shapes but, having the least possible surface area per unit volume, it has a higher settling velocity than any other shape.*

Wadell (1932, p. 445) defined *true sphericity* as s/S, in which s is the surface area of a sphere of the same volume as the particle and S is the actual surface area of the particle. The precise measurement of the actual surface area of an irregular particle is so difficult, however, as

---

* A tear-shaped particle may be an exception but is unlikely to appear in sediment.

to be impractical. Wadell (1933, p. 324–325; 1935, p. 264–265) therefore proposed a simpler method for measuring what he called the *practical sphericity* of sand grains, based on measurements on the image of the particle projected onto a plane surface (as in the measurement of roundness). The method is illustrated by Figure 95A. The area of the image of the particle is first measured with a planimeter. Then the radius of a circle of equal area (r_p) is calculated. Next the radius of the minimum circumscribed circle (r_c) is determined. The sphericity is then r_p/r_c. The sphericity of a sphere is 1 and that of any irregular particle is less than 1 and is expressed as a decimal fraction.

For particles that are roughly equidimensional (as quartz sand grains commonly are), such measurement gives a reasonable approximation to the *true* sphericity (see Wadell, 1935, p. 258–263); but for flattish particles it falls wide of the mark. A circular disc, for example, would register perfect sphericity. Flakes of mica and other flattish mineral grains would thus give entirely fictitious values.

A scheme proposed by Zingg (1935, p. 52–56) avoids this difficulty by measuring all three of the principal diameters, a, b, and c. It was designed to classify pebbles according to *shape*. Zingg did not recognize the distinction between roundness and sphericity, but it is obvious that he was not concerned with roundness.

By inspection, Zingg identified the longest diameter (a) of the pebble to be studied. The smallest diameter at right angles to a is the c diameter, and the diameter at right angles to both a and c is the intermediate diameter, b. These lines need not meet in a common center. The shape is defined in terms of the two ratios, b/a and c/b.

Figure 96 shows the basis for Zingg's classification of pebbles according to shape. In the graph the b/a ratio (which varies from 0 to 1) is plotted along the ordinate and the c/b ratio along the abscissa. Obviously particles of every proportion can be located on such a grid. Near the lower left corner where b is much smaller than a and c than b, the particles are slender and bladelike; toward the lower right corner where b and c are subequal but a is much longer, the particles are prismatic or, if rounded, they are subcylindrical "rollers." In the upper right corner *a*, *b*, and *c* are subequal and the particles have a high degree of sphericity. In the upper left corner, on the contrary, where *c* is very small and *a* and *b* are subequal, the particles are discoidal. Zingg recognized these four major classes of shape, as shown in Figure 96, separated by the lines $b/a = \frac{2}{3}$ and $c/b = \frac{2}{3}$. The figure shows both angular and rounded examples, to emphasize that Zingg's classification is not concerned with roundness.

Although designed primarily for the study of pebbles large enough to be easily oriented for measurement, Zingg's method can be adapted to the study of sand. If the grains are placed on a microscope stage and jostled gently until they come to rest on their largest surface, the *c* diameter will normally be vertical and the *a* and *b* diameters will lie in the plane of the stage where they can be identified by inspection and measured. The *c* diameter can be measured by the distance the microscope moves when it is focused first on top of the grain and then on the surface of the stage beneath.

Krumbein (1942b) has worked out the relation of Wadell's sphericity to Zingg's shape classification and has shown that particles of the same sphericity may have quite different shapes (for example, rods and discs) and hence different settling velocities, rolling velocities, etc. Thus Zingg's shape classification, though perhaps more difficult to apply, can give more information about the dynamic behavior of particles.

SIZE SORTING

Description of size sorting and size distribution of the particles in a sediment are discussed in Chapter 8. They are more readily determined in terrigenous arenites than in any other type of sedimentary deposit and are more commonly studied in such rocks. Except in quartzites, the matrix is generally weaker than the grains of sand which can be freed by crushing; calcareous matrix is readily removed by hydrochloric acid. Once the grains are freed they can be separated into standard size grades by sieving.

By blending a suite of samples before sieving, the average size and size distribution in a deposit can be determined, or by carefully selecting samples for individual study these characteristics can be determined for individual layers or for distinct parts of a sedimentary structure such as the crest or the trough of a ripple.

During recent years much research has been devoted to the shape-sorting and size-sorting in modern sands and gravels with a view to finding criteria that will throw light on the environment of deposition of the older sedimentary deposits (see Russell and Taylor, 1937; Goldstein, 1942; Cailleux, 1945; Keller, 1945; Hilmy, 1951; Shepard and Moore, 1954, 1955a; Mattox, 1955). Some significant conclusions have been reached but much still remains to be done.

Wind-blown sand in the deserts falls within a rather small size range (p. 17). Dune sands tend also to show higher sphericity than any other type of sand and the grains commonly have a frosted surface resulting from the endless buffeting during saltation. Once the sands have been sorted and shaped by the wind, they may retain these characteristics, however, despite reworking by the sea. The modern sands lying near the edge of the continental shelf southeast of New England, for example, are interpreted as reworked dune sands that accumulated along shore during a low stand of the sea in Pleistocene time (Stetson, 1938, p. 34–36; 1939, p. 241–242; Northrop, 1951). The remarkably rounded, frosted, and well-sorted grains of the St. Peter sandstone (Middle Ordovician) strongly suggest long transportation by the wind, but if so it was during previous sedimentary cycles for the St. Peter formation has been shown by Dake (1921) and by Dapples (1955) to be largely, if not wholly, marine.

In general, fluvial sands are less well sorted than marine sands, but where sediment is delivered to the shore in large volume faster than the waves and marine currents can rework it, as in the great deltas, sorting is poor. Here barrier beaches may, however, form local masses of well-sorted sand. In the Red Bedford Delta (Lower Mississippian) of Ohio, for example, Pepper, de Witt, and Demarest (1954, p. 51) used this criterion in recognizing the Second Berea sand and the Euclid siltstone as offshore bars.

Among the marine formations, beach deposits normally show the highest degree of sorting because here the sand is long subjected to oscillation and reworking by the waves. The beaches along the east coast of Florida, from Jacksonville to Daytona, are remarkable in this respect. This sand has been carried southward by longshore currents from the coast of the Carolinas and has thus been exposed to continued wave action during long transportation. More precise discrimination of other environments of deposition will undoubtedly be possible when modern sands have been more extensively studied.

Shepard and Moore (1954) recently opened a very promising new line of attack on the recognition of local environments of deposition in their "coarse fraction" studies of the modern sediments along the Gulf Coast. In such study, which is adapted only to loose or partly consolidated deposits, a sample of the sediment is sieved and sorted into standard size grades. The clay and silt are then weighed so that their percentage can be determined, but further study is concentrated on the sand-size fraction which is studied under a binocular and separated into different mineral and fossil components such as terrigenous sand, foraminifera, ostracoda, and other biologic units. The percentages of such diverse constituents of the "coarse fraction" of the bottom mud or sand was found to be highly diagnostic of several facets of the local environments near shore.

CROSS-STRATIFICATION

Of all the types of sedimentary rocks the arenites show cross-stratification best (p. 105). Many studies have been made of this structure—for example, Spurr (1894); Gilbert (1899); Grabau (1907; 1913, p. 701–706); Sorby (1908, p. 176–189); Andrée (1915, p. 382–395); Cressey (1928); Knight (1929, p. 56–74; 1930); McKee (1938a, 1939, 1953); McKee and Weir (1953); but much more research is needed. Basically, cross-stratification is produced when granular sediment is transported to a position where it rolls down a slope that has an appreciable angle to the surface of aggradation, as on the foreset slope of small deltas built into standing water, at the front of sand bars or "giant ripples" in stream courses, on the surfaces of shifting ripples, and on sand dunes. It is commonly produced during deposition of sand either by wind or flowing water. It is especially common in the terrigenous arenites and in calcarenites. In all cases the angle of cross-stratification at the time of deposition represents the angle of repose of the loose sand *under the local conditions that obtained at the time*. It may later be reduced somewhat by compaction of the mass of sediment.

Obviously, cross-stratification may be produced in stream-laid deposits, in wind-blown sands, and in marine deposits, all under a wide range of environments. Indeed, it seems easier to account for cross-stratification than for the even bedding of sheet sands that lack it.

Of all the varied types of cross-stratification, that of dunes is perhaps most distinctive (Figs. 14, p. 22 and 49C, p. 106). The large scale of such cross-bedding, the curvature of the laminae conforming to the dune slopes (Fig. 13, p. 21), and the varying directions of the wedges of cross-beds form a combination that can hardly be mistaken. Since, however, dunes form along the shores of large lakes (e.g., Lake Michigan) or of the sea (e.g., Cape Cod, Holland) in humid environments and along sand-choked streams in semi-arid regions, as well as in the desert, supporting criteria are needed to determine the climatic environment under which any particular deposit of ancient dune sand accumulated.

Beach sands, like dunes, show large-scale cross-stratification with wedges of cross-strata dipping in different, commonly opposite, directions (p. 69), but in these the dips are generally gentler than in dunes and the cross-strata tend to be straighter. For reasons explained above (p. 86), however, beach deposits have little chance of permanent preservation, and few have been recognized in the ancient rocks.

Cross-bedding produced by small deltas building into standing water may be on a large or small scale depending on the depth of water. In some of the Pleistocene fills built into ice-margin lakes along the Connecticut Valley, individual cross-beds reach lengths of some tens of feet. In such delta deposits built into standing water, the sand comes to rest at an angle of repose exceeding 20 degrees, and the cross-strata are almost straight rather than curved. Furthermore, unlike dune or beach deposits, the foresets tend to dip in a constant direction.

In stream deposits built into relatively quiet backwater during flood (as in the middle section of the Colorado River Delta), cross-bedded layers of sand a few feet thick may come to alternate with horizontal mud layers formed during another flood (Fig. 49A, p. 106). Far from being *torrential cross-bedding,* as this type has sometimes been called, it indicates that stream deposits were built periodically into standing water.

Cross-stratification may give clear evidence of the direction of movement of the currents during deposition, since the foresetting is in general downstream. This criterion has been used to determine the direction of the source area of many cross-bedded sandstones (Potter and Olson, 1954; Brett, 1955). It is successful only, however, when based upon a large number of well-spaced observations that can be treated statistically. This condition is necessary for at least two reasons. In the first place a meandering stream flows in many different directions, and only the statistical mean would clearly indicate its general course. In the second place the cross-bedding is produced largely at the front of migrating sand bars in the stream channels. Such bars are irregular in shape and size and perhaps never maintain an even front at right angles to the current. On the contrary they present an irregular, lobate front, and much of the sand spills off the sides as well as the front of a lobe. Thus dips are formed simultaneously in almost every direction except upstream. For this reason also the appearance of a cross-bedded sandstone may vary greatly, depending on the orientation of an exposed section (Fig. 49D, p. 106).

A further word of caution may be needed with respect to channel sands that show strong cut and fill. Much of the sand along a meandering stream may have accumulated as point bars about the concave sides of the meanders, dipping laterally into the channel and at right angles to the local flow of the current. If a stream migrates laterally, it will leave wide lenses of cross-stratified channel sand in which the foresetting is generally at a high angle to the general stream course. Prominent bodies of gray sandstone and conglomerate of this kind may be seen in the Catawissa redbeds (Upper Devonian) in the region of the Neversink Reservoir south of the Catskill Mountains of New York.

RIPPLE MARKS

The ripple marks preserved on the bedding surfaces of sandstones may throw light on the direction of the moving currents and on the environment of deposition, but here again there is need of much more research. Kindle and Bucher (1926) have given an excellent summary of the extensive literature on the subject, and van Straaten (1953a, b) has described many different kinds of ripple marks that occur along the Dutch coast.

Oscillation ripples (Fig. 97d) are formed where waves agitate the bottom in the absence of currents. They can be recognized by their symmetrical form, and in general by their broadly rounded crests. Of course, they indicate standing water at the time the ripples were formed. Sand cannot be spread over a surface in the absence of bottom currents, however, and in a sequence of layers bearing only oscillation ripples, the mass of sand that forms each layer was probably introduced and spread by bottom currents during a storm or flood and may at that time have borne current ripples, but after being deposited it remained under standing water shallow enough for oscillation waves to reach bottom.

Interference ripples (Figs. 97b and 98, b) present a distinctive dimpled surface. They are believed to form when there is a sharp and abrupt change in the direction of the wind so that after one set of ripples is formed a second set begins to form at a high angle to the first set. They may also form where ordinary waves break up into two sets of oscillations crossing each other (Kindle and Bucher, 1926, p. 473). Van Straaten (personal communication) believes that they are formed only where a gentle bottom current is flowing nearly at right angles to the

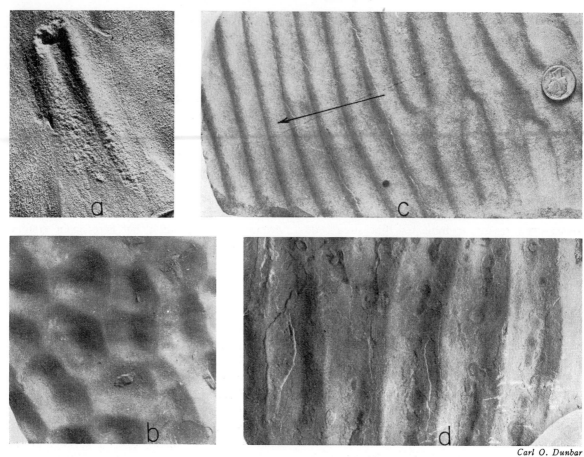

Carl O. Dunbar

Figure 97. Rill and ripple marks: (a) rill mark formed by a *Lingula* shell on a Silurian beach (Whirlpool sandstone in Niagara Gorge); (b) interference ripples in Clam Bank formation (Lower Devonian), Newfoundland; (c) current ripples (locality unknown); (d) oscillation ripples in St. Louis limestone (Mississippian), St. Louis, Missouri.

troughs of the waves; it is difficult to see, however, how bottom currents could play a part without introducing asymmetry in the ripples. The matter needs further study.

Current ripples, whether formed by wind or water, have their axes approximately at right angles to the current and are unsymmetrical (Fig. 97c), with the lee slope steeper than the stoss slope.

Bagnold (1941, p. 62–64) found that in wind-blown sand the wave length of the ripples varies with the wind velocity. For fine and well-sorted sand he found that ripples with a length of 2.4 cm are formed at the initial velocity at which saltation begins and that the length increases to a maximum of about 12 cm at a critical velocity above which the sand begins to drift as a sheet, and ripples disappear. The length, however, depends in part on the size of the grains and on the degree of sorting. With more observational data, criteria could probably be developed that would indicate the wind velocity under which the ripples in any wind-blown sand were formed. Gilbert (1914) found that underwater ripples also increase in length up to a critical velocity at which they disappear. As emphasized by Bagnold, however, the mechanism is somewhat different under water where the spattering effect (p. 18) is unimportant. The length of ripples formed under water varies greatly and is, of course, controlled by definite factors among which current velocity and coarseness of the sand are undoubtedly important, but no general law has yet been discovered covering the matter.

Attempts have been made to distinguish between current ripples made by wind and water on the basis of the ratio of their height to their length. According to Kindle and Bucher (1926, p. 481), this ratio ranges between 1:20 and 1:50 for current ripples formed by wind and between 1:4 and 1:10 for those formed by flowing water. Furthermore, Bagnold (1941, p. 152) found that, in somewhat heterogeneous sand, the wind tends to concentrate the coarser grains at the crest of the ripples because they are pushed up the back slope by the impact of the saltating grains. The smaller grains leap over the crests and tend to come to rest in the troughs, whereas no force is available to propel the coarser particles down the lee slope. On the contrary, experience shows that under water the coarser particles tend to accumulate in the troughs where they are partially shielded from the current.

Ripple marks have commonly been considered evidence of deposition at shallow depth. Undoubtedly they are most commonly so formed, but this criterion must be used with great caution. Symmetrical ripples can form only where waves are able to oscillate the bottom sediment, but current ripples have no such limits. Whenever bottom currents are able to transport sand they are likely also to be able to form ripples. Fairly coarse ripples in globigerina sand have been photographed, for example, on Sylvania Seamount at a depth of 4,500 feet (Dietz and Menard, 1951, p. 2004). The nature of the

Carl O. Dunbar

Figure 98. Oscillation ripples (a) and interference ripples (b) on the surfaces of sandstone beds in the Clam Bank formation (Devonian) near Clam Bank Cove, Port au Port Peninsula, western Newfoundland. The view is up a cliff, showing the under surfaces of the beds.

current sweeping the summit of this seamount is not understood. Possibly the ripples are due to internal waves produced at the interface between ocean currents moving at depth but with different velocities or in different directions.

GRADED BEDDING

Graded bedding is discussed in Chapter 5 (p. 107). In its most typical form it seems clearly to be the product of spasmodic turbidity currents (p. 14), the material for each layer having been carried in suspension and allowed to settle beyond the reach of waves and normal bottom currents (Kuenen and Migliorini, 1950). Thus sequences of graded beds are conspicuously free of oscillation ripples and large-scale cross-bedding, which are evidences of normal bottom traction, and where these are common, graded beds are as conspicuously lacking. Of course, current ripples may occur in graded beds.

It is now well known that sand can be transported by spasmodic turbidity currents to great depths and far out from shore, but such deposits can also form in moderate depths where deposition is rapid. Wherever the bottom slope near shore is oversteepened to instability, submarine landslides may form and may develop into spasmodic turbidity currents that will transmit masses of sediment into deeper water. More observation is needed to determine the minimum depth in which graded bedding may be formed. Thus, although graded bedding probably rules out deposition in shallow water above local wave base, it does not necessarily imply great depth. Classic examples of graded bedding occur in the Macigno sandstone of Italy, in the Flysch of the Alps, in the Silurian of Wales, and in the Franciscan group of California. Graded bedding is also conspicuous in the Coutchiching group (early Precambrian) of the Rainy Lake region of the Canadian Shield, in the Hudson River shale along the Hudson Valley, and in many other geosynclinal deposits.

FLOW ROLLS

In certain sandstones an occasional layer, or even a considerable thickness of layers, appears contorted and broken as though tectonically de-

formed, whereas the beds below and above are undisturbed (Fig. 99). Generally such deformed beds originally rested upon a layer of mud, now shale, that provided a gliding surface. The deformed layers typically show unsymmetrical folds and small thrust faults. Individual sections of such a folded bed commonly appear to be rolled or curled and have been appropriately termed *flow rolls* (Pepper, de Witt, and Demarest, 1954, p. 88). Generally some of the underlying mud has been squeezed up into the folds and faults in the deformed sandy layer. When traced laterally in outcrop the deformation is found to extend only a short distance, a few yards or a few rods, and to end abruptly though the layer continues undeformed. Commonly, however, where one such deformed lens is found, others appear higher and lower in the sequence, irregularly overlapping one another in space. In short, the slumps indicate that during deposition small local movements occurred from time to time. Examination of the upper contact of the deformed layers makes it clear that they were at the surface when deformed.

Early in this century stratigraphers commonly interpreted such phenomena as the result of violent storms that churned up the bottom and rolled up masses of the surface sandy layers. The deformed masses were therefore termed "storm rollers," a misnomer based on a complete misconception. Storm waves sublevate the sand on a sandy sea floor, moving the grains individually; the sand would not have sufficient cohesion to permit rolling in masses. Such disturbed masses simply represent small landslides formed where the bottom had been aggraded to an instable slope. In such an environment, soft mud layers formed a lubricant over which thick sand layers could slide. If the surface were steep, as at the continental margin or on the foreset slope of a rapidly growing delta, such landslides might have gained sufficient momentum to pick up water and develop into spasmodic turbidity currents. In that case the moving material would have been deposited as a graded bed much farther down the slope, and the only evidence of the loss in the area of original accumulation would probably be an obscure local diastem. The slumped

Carl O. Dunbar

Figure 99. Flow rolls in a bed of sandstone due to slumping at time of deposition. Type section of the Chemung sandstone in Chemung Narrows, 10 miles west of Waverly, New York.

masses, on the contrary, appear in areas where the bottom slope was more gentle and the overloaded mass moved only a short distance before coming to rest. Rettger (1935) made significant laboratory experiments on such movement and indicated criteria for the recognition of "soft-rock deformation."

Kaye and Power (1954) observed somewhat similar deformation in layers of sand alternating with soft mud that had been deposited in the reservoir behind Grand Coulee Dam in eastern Washington. Here, however, the sand slumped vertically into the mud without lateral movement and the mud was squeezed upward between and about the curved masses of sand, the deformation being due solely to overload on the same fluid layer of mud. Slumping due to gliding should be distinguishable from slumping due to static load by the presence of overturned folds and small-scale thrusts. Combination of the two mechanisms is also possible, however.

Flow rolls are common in the Wellsburg sandstone (Upper Devonian) in the type region of the Chemung Stage in south central New York. They are characteristic of this facies in the Catskill Delta but are not seen in the non-marine facies farther east or in the finer-grained and deeper-water facies farther west. They also occur commonly in the Artinsk facies of the Russian Permian. They are believed to be characteristic of deposits formed on the gentle slopes of the sublittoral zone where layers of sand alternate with layers of soft mud and where deposition is rapid. They are less likely to form in terrestrial environments where less water is retained in the mud layers. A fine example may be observed, however, in the upper part of the Conemaugh Series (Pennsylvanian) west of St. Marys, West Virginia. The "pockets" at the base of coarse graded beds, described by Natland and Kuenen (1951, p. 96 and Figs. 16–18), present a superficial resemblance to flow rolls but should be readily distinguishable. They apparently were formed at the base of a deposit suddenly dumped upon a surface of loose sand by a spasmodic turbidity current, and they show size-grading from the base upward but no lamination and no evidence of movement after deposition.

GROOVE CASTS

In certain types of sandstone some of the layers are embossed on the under surface by subparallel ridges. The ridges may occur singly but commonly they are in parallel sets, some larger and others smaller, and not uncommonly two or more sets are superposed with slightly divergent orientation (a, b, and c of Fig. 100). Such ridges normally occur on the under surface of sandstone beds resting on more argillaceous layers that were originally mud. It is evident that such ridges are casts of grooves made by some object or objects dragged across a muddy bottom before the sand was deposited. Shrock (1948a, p. 162) has therefore termed them *groove casts*.

The ridges are generally straight and extend for a few or even many feet. Rarely some of the ridges are ornamented for part of their length by chevron-shaped ridges and grooves somewhat resembling chatter marks on a glacial groove (X in Fig. 100).

Groove casts have been observed and illustrated by numerous geologists who generally agree that the grooves were made by objects dragged across a muddy surface, but the nature of the objects and the manner of their transportation are obscure. Shrock (1948a, p. 162–166) reviewed speculations on the subject. The grooves are in some instances an inch or more in depth and two or more inches in width. It is obvious that the objects responsible for the grooves were dragged, not rolled and, whatever their nature, they were normally carried away since none have been observed in place.

Lyell (v. 2, 1845, p. 144) thought such grooves might have been made by jagged pieces of pack ice that touched bottom, and he cited grooves on mud banks in Minas Bay, at the head of the Bay of Fundy, alleged to have formed in this way during the winter season. If they were formed by drifting ice, the disappearance of the objects that cut them is easily explained. Shrock suggests that gravel frozen in a film of ice on very shallow water might be dragged about as postulated in the explanation of skid boulders (p. 173), or that they may have been dragged by algal rafts, but in such cases some of the gravel should have remained on the bedding surface along with the grooves.

Figure 100. Groove casts on the under surface of a sandstone layer. Sherburne formation, Taughannock Falls, north of Ithaca, New York.

Another likely agent is driftwood or trees that, after dragging bottom locally, were floated away to be preserved elsewhere. Chevron marks like those in Figure 100 probably were produced by branches or roots of floating trees dragged over fairly firm mud. Preliminary experiments indicate that such marks can be produced, that they result from tension tears, and that the chevrons point upstream. On the surface shown in Figure 100 the sharpest and presumably latest-formed chevrons point toward the lower left, but partly obliterated ones in the upper right corner point in exactly the opposite direction, from which we may infer that a drifting tree was dragged first in one direction and then in the opposite, possibly recording the ebb and flow of a Devonian tide.

Groove casts occur in rocks at least as old as the Ordovician but, so far as the writers are aware, those bearing chevron marks are not found below the Devonian. It may be noted that if groove casts are due to floating ice or to drifting wood, they are evidence of extremely shallow water. However, in the Normanskill shale in the bluffs of the Hudson River at the west end of the mid-Hudson bridge at Highlands, New York, rather coarse groove casts are conspicuous on the under surface of sandstone layers that show well-developed graded bedding and may be the product of spasmodic turbidity currents in water of considerable depth.

In summary, it appears probable that groove casts have been produced by objects of several different sorts. The problem needs further study.

ARKOSE AND GRAYWACKE

The presence of abundant feldspar in a sand has been considered by many to imply an arid environment, since in the presence of warmth and humidity the feldspars tend to break down into clay minerals. Krynine (1935a) observed, nevertheless, that arkosic sediment is now accumulating over the coastal lowlands of Tabasco, Mexico, within the tropical rain belt, and he has emphasized that the presence of feldspar indicates merely that mechanical weathering and rapid deposition have outstripped chemical decay. Where relief is low and the climate is warm and humid, mechanical erosion is slow and the feldspars tend to disappear. The decay is facilitated if the sediment undergoes long transportation before final deposition. In regions of high relief, on the contrary, especially if the rainfall is torrential, rapid erosion (Fig. 86, p. 173) may rip out fresh debris and dump it into basins of deposition where it is covered before chemical decay has destroyed the feldspars. Arkose, therefore, implies a granitic or gneissic source area and rapid deposition but is not, of itself, a safe criterion of climate. The arkosic redbeds of the Newark group clearly accumulated in a warm, humid environment. On the other hand, granite ranges in arid regions also supply arkosic sediment because here the aridity inhibits chemical decay.

Graywacke is made of debris from a non-granitic source that has not been reduced by chemical weathering to stable end products. Like arkose, it indicates predominance of mechanical over chemical weathering. Pettijohn (1943) has emphasized that graywackes predominate where highlands are undergoing rapid erosion and the derived sediment is deposited rapidly and without long transportation. Blackwelder (1918) has shown that sediments produced in subarctic climate, as in Alaska, tend to be graywacke because frostwork is active and chemical decay is inhibited by the low temperature. Like arkose, however, graywacke is not of itself a safe criterion of climate.

FOSSILS

Contained fossils, of course, throw light on the environment of deposition of sandstones in many ways. First of all, they may give the surest indication whether the deposit is marine or nonmarine. Unfortunately, many sandstones are sparingly fossiliferous. In the terrestrial environment organic matter is commonly destroyed by oxidation, and shells are leached out by moving ground water. Sands laid down in the shallow sea are also commonly poor in fossils because the rapid shift of loose sand during storms smothers many kinds of benthonic animals. Here, however, worm borings are likely to be significant, especially the U-shaped tubes made by tubicolous polychaetes.

The distribution of shells within the deposit may also be significant. In the "Chemung facies" of the Catskill Delta, for example, shells of brachiopods and crinoidal debris are generally not scattered at random but are concentrated in certain layers, commonly lenticular, where the shells are literally heaped together. Many of these shelly beds are filled with the shells of *Cyrtospirifer* of the *"Spirifer disjunctus"* type. In these the valves are invariably separated and generally show wear. Commonly the thin anterior margins are lacking and only the thick umbonal parts of the shell remain. These beds were clearly deposited on shallow sublittoral sand flats on which the sand was shifted back and forth and the shells were washed about, worn, and concentrated in pockets or windrows on the sea floor. In deeper water, or where deposition is more rapid, bivalved shells are commonly buried with the valves together and are distributed more or less at random through the beds.

SUMMARY

It should be evident from the preceding discussion that whereas many different criteria may throw light on the source of sands and especially on the environment of their deposition, few of them are sufficiently diagnostic to be used alone, but when they are considered together and balanced one against another they may permit safe inferences to be drawn. It is only too evident, however, that much more research is needed.

11. Lutites

GENERAL FEATURES

Introduction. The shales and mudstones out-bulk all other types of sedimentary rock and have accumulated in a wide range of environments (Chaps. 2–4). On the land, fine sediment is deposited in lakes, on the floodplains of rivers, in the swamps and swales of humid regions, and in the playas of arid basins; and in the sea, it accumulates in shallow lagoons, in the interdistributary bays of large deltas, in protected bays along normal coastlines, in the deeper parts of the more protected epeiric seas or shelves, and over most of the bathyal zone and vast areas in the abyss. When adequate criteria are developed to distinguish deposits formed in these varied environments, the lutites will therefore aid greatly in interpreting the stratigraphic record. Even now they contribute much information, but in some respects they are more difficult to study and to interpret than any of the other lithotopes discussed in Chapters 9 to 14.

In the extensive literature dealing with such rocks, three studies are especially noteworthy—that of Marr (1925) on the Stockdale shale (Silurian) of the Lake District in England, that of Rubey (1931) on the marine Cretaceous shales of the Black Hills region, and that of Bradley (1931a) on the Eocene lake deposits of the Green River formation. Each of these is a case study involving analysis of all the evidence that can be brought to bear on the interpretation of a distinct type of shaly deposit.

Mechanical analyses. The lutites include the finest of the detrital sediments and cannot be separated and size-graded by sieving as the coarser sediments commonly are. Rubey's study of the Cretaceous shales of the Black Hills region (1931, p. 14–22) includes an excellent critique of the several methods used in the mechanical analysis of such fine-grained sediments, and of the very considerable difficulties involved, and a thorough review of these techniques may be found in Chapters 5 and 6 of Krumbein and Pettijohn's *Manual of Sedimentary Petrology* (1938). All the known methods are time-consuming and most of them are subject to large error.

Mineral composition. The lutites consist mostly of the end products of chemical decay—the clay minerals and sesquioxides—but they may also include finely divided particles of a wide variety of other minerals, particularly quartz and calcite. The rock flour produced by glaciers, for example, is largely made of fine particles of unweathered rocks or minerals of all kinds, depending on the nature of the bedrock under the ice.

In clays and clay shales the clay minerals greatly predominate over other minerals. Within recent decades notable advances have been made in the differentiation and identification of the clay minerals, and we are indebted to Grim (1953) for a fine summary of present knowledge. The clay minerals, which are all complex hydrous aluminum silicates, fall largely into three groups of closely allied species—the kaolinite, illite, and montmorillonite groups, each with a distinct type of crystal structure and certain distinctive physical characteristics but with a considerable range of chemical composition. The kaolinite minerals are almost pure hydrous aluminum silicates; they can contain only very small amounts of the other cations and do not form in the presence of large concentrations of those cations, especially calcium. Minerals of the montmorillonite group, on the other hand, contain essential cations, chiefly magnesium or iron, and in addition may hold large amounts of exchangeable cations—calcium, sodium, or hydrogen, and more rarely magnesium or potassium. Most of the illites contain small amounts of essential potassium, and also variable amounts of calcium, magnesium, and iron (up to 18 percent Fe_2O_3); structurally illites are closer to the micas than are the other clay minerals.

Grim (1953, p. 356–357) points out, however, that montmorillonite is generally absent in shales older than the Mesozoic and that kaolinite also is less abundant in the older shales than in modern muds and is rare in pre-Devonian rocks. He thinks both montmorillonite and kaolinite have been transformed in the older rocks into illite or some other form of mica. In any event the dominant clay mineral in the Paleozoic shales is illite.

Each of the three chief clay mineral groups can be produced in the weathering of almost any kind of rock, depending on the local chemical environment. In large streams, moreover, all three are generally present, since the mud brought by different tributaries from a wide variety of sources and environments is thoroughly mixed in transit.

Since, under appropriate chemical environments, any of these clay minerals may be transformed into one of the others, the proportions commonly change during transportation and especially after deposition (p. 65).

Organic matter is an important constituent of some lutites, especially the gray oil shales and the black shales (p. 202).

Bedding and lamination. By definition (p. 166), shales are fissile and they are generally thinly laminated as well; mudstones are the thicker bedded or non-bedded equivalents. The nature of the lamination in shales may throw interesting light on conditions of deposition.

The varved clays of proglacial Pleistocene lakes, for example, are characterized by couplets of layers, one produced in summer and the other in winter (p. 108). Like the growth rings in trees, they record the years and permit measurement not only of the time involved in the accumulation of a given deposit but also of the annual rate of deposition. Although marine clays are not generally varved in this way, Rubey (1931, p. 40–52) showed that pairs of very thin laminae in the Cretaceous shales of the Black Hills region are probably annual layers. Bradley (1929b) also found evidence for annual layering in parts of the lacustrine Green River shale (Eocene) of Wyoming. Without critical analysis and supporting evidence, however, it is unsafe to assume that the laminae in a shale represent annual deposition rather than deposition by a single storm or stormy spell. Several laminae may even have formed during a single flood (Fig. 17, p. 33).

At shallow depths where the sea floor is well aerated, bottom-dwelling animals may rework the mud and effectively remove evidences of lamination; but in stagnant basins where decaying organic matter produces toxic conditions in which benthonic organisms cannot survive (p. 60), fine layers of mud remain undisturbed and here the most perfectly laminated, fissile shales are produced.

The terrigenous muds now accumulating in bathyal and abyssal depths show almost no layering. This is probably because the generally fine sediment settles so slowly that the coarser particles introduced in suspension during one storm or flood overtake the finer particles of one or more preceding storms before reaching the bottom. Thus the sediment introduced by successive storms is mingled during its descent and does not accumulate in distinct layers.

When a spasmodic turbidity current carries mud into deep water, however, or even into a moderately shallow basin, it settles out to form a graded bed (p. 107). Successive flows of this kind will produce a well-bedded deposit in which the layers may be thick or thin and may persist with great uniformity over a large area. The "banded slates" (Ordovician) described by Barrell (1917, p. 803, Pl. 43) in the Slate Belt of Pennsylvania are almost certainly of this sort. The lighter layers are silty and the blacker layers are very fine grained and rich in carbonaceous matter. Each silty layer rests with sharp contact on the underlying dark layer but grades into the one above. Individual units range from mere films to layers several inches thick. Similar banding occurs in the Georgia slate of northwestern Vermont and indeed in many other lutite deposits.

Mudcracks. Mudcracks are found chiefly in the lutites. Clay shrinks notably on drying but has sufficient cohesion to hold together until cracks form to relieve the tension (Fig. 101). When wetted again the clay softens and swells, and in fairly homogeneous mud the cracks may close and disappear; but if a mudcracked surface is covered by a layer of different composition (e.g., sand or silt) before the mud has time to swell, the cracks will be filled with this new material and cannot close. Alternate deposition of clay and sand or of clay and silt therefore affords the best conditions for the preservation of mudcracks; casts of the mudcracks then appear on the under surfaces of the sandstone beds. If the mud is more or less calcareous, the $CaCO_3$ tends to "set" upon exposure to the air and mudcracks may thus be well preserved in fairly homogeneous muds, as for example, in the Moccasin formation (Middle Ordovician) of eastern Tennessee or the Manlius formation (Upper Silurian) of New York.

Mudcracks normally form only when clay is exposed to the air and dried until it has lost much of its moisture. They are commonly observed on the floodplains of aggrading streams and over the subaerial surfaces of large deltas, which are widely submerged by muddy water during great floods but are exposed for long intervals between. They are not normally produced in the tidal zone because the interval between tides is too short to permit thorough desiccation, and if they ever form under standing water it is under very local and exceptional conditions that are not understood. The few instances of mudcracks alleged to have been formed under water

Charles Schuchert

Figure 101. Mudcracks on a recent fill near New Haven, Connecticut.

are not well substantiated and may have some other explanation.*

A puzzling case is presented, however, by an 8-inch layer of limestone in the Uniontown formation (Upper Pennsylvanian) in the vicinity of McMechen, West Virginia, which over an area of several square miles bears conspicuous shrinkage cracks (Fig. 102) on its *under* surface. This layer is a rather pure, fine-grained limestone except near its base where it becomes increasingly darker and impure. The cracks are widest at the basal surface and die out upward as the rock becomes purer. Although the pattern is somewhat rectangular rather than hexagonal, these are undoubtedly shrinkage cracks. Occurring as it does in a non-marine, coal-bearing formation, this layer probably records a shallow marl lake, and the first lime deposited must have included a considerable percentage of clay or organic impurity that shrank markedly after deposition. It is quite

* Twenhofel (1923, p. 64) reported the experimental production of mudcracks under water in bentonite, but in 1925 he stated that this occurred only when lumps or layers of dry bentonite were wetted. This would be an improbable situation in marine deposits in nature, and since no mudcracks have been reported in the very abundant layers of bentonite in the Pierre shale (Upper Cretaceous) of the northern Great Plains, it appears that subaqueous mudcracks of this sort in nature are highly improbable. Moore (1914) observed mudcracks in a pond and supposed that they had formed under standing water, but this conclusion seems unnecessary.

Figure 102. Lower surface of the upper layer of the Uniontown limestone in the Monongahela Series (Upper Pennsylvanian) showing shrinkage cracks. Highway cut in McMechen, West Virginia.

possible, however, that the shrinkage was produced by desiccation after the lake had dried up.

Krynine (1935b) observed a set of dog tracks on a fresh bed of clay in a quarry near New Haven, Connecticut, that persisted with little loss of detail for more than a month during which rain fell 17 different times for a total of 5.7 inches and the surface was repeatedly flooded and laid bare. He concluded: "It seems from these observations that desiccation features which are usually considered to be associated with semiaridity can form, survive, and be incorporated in the fossil record under the climatic record of a rather wet New England spring in a locality whose annual rainfall averages 46 inches."

In general, mudcracks may be considered one of the best evidences of non-marine deposition. Pepper, de Witt, and Demarest (1954, p. 89–90) have shown, for example, that in the deposits that formed the Red Bedford Delta (Lower Mississippian) in Ohio mudcracks are abundant in the red shales and siltstones that formed the subaerial part of the delta, whereas the contemporaneous gray submarine beds lack them completely. In the Catskill Delta (Devonian) of New York and Pennsylvania, likewise, mudcracks

are confined to the red subaerial beds of the Catskill facies.

In some formations, however, mudcracked layers are interbedded with others bearing marine fossils. In the Wills Creek shale (Upper Silurian) near Cumberland, Maryland, for example, conspicuously mudcracked layers (Fig. 103) are interbedded with others bearing abundant ostracods and a few other types of marine invertebrates that suggest brackish or probably hypersaline water. These deposits were forming along the southeast margin of a great relict sea while extensive salt deposits were being precipitated in western New York and central Michigan, and probably the shore line fluctuated back and forth over a wide belt in the Cumberland region as the water level rose and fell with seasonal or longer-term variations in evaporation or in the inflow of fresh water. Thus muds deposited on the shallow sea floor may have been laid bare for relatively long periods. In general, however, the mudcracked layers are remarkably barren of fossils, and they may actually have been deposited during the retreat of the sea.

Conspicuously mudcracked layers are likewise interbedded with marine layers in the Manlius formation (uppermost Silurian) of New York. The prisms of the so-called "prismatic layer" exposed in the Vlightberg at Rondout, New York (Van Ingen and Clark, p. 1185 and Pl. 6), for example, were formed by large mudcracks that extend through the layer to a depth of 8 to 10 inches. Such deep cracks imply exposure for a period of many months, at least. A similar "prismatic layer" occurs at the top of the Decker Ferry formation on the Nearpass farm south of Port Jervis, New York.

Typical mudcracks occur rather commonly also in some of the impure layers in the Lower Ordovician limestones of the Appalachian trough. There is no evidence here of non-marine deposition, and the mudcracks seem to have formed on a very shallow sea floor that was subject to intermittent exposure over considerable areas for at least months at a time. The nearest approach to a comparable environment in the modern world may be the Rann of Cutch east of the Indus Delta, an area of some 8,000 square miles lying within the belt of monsoon winds. During half of each year, while the winds are blowing onshore, it is a very shallow lagoon, but during the dry season the strong offshore winds drive the sea water out leaving its floor exposed to be extensively mudcracked. The parallel with the Lower Ordovician seaway is not close, to be sure, for in the Rann of Cutch the sediment is detrital and includes much salt, but it does suggest the possibility that persistent winds may at times have driven the water out of very shallow parts of some epeiric seas so as to expose considerable areas of the bottom long enough to permit mudcracks to form.

Charles Schuchert

Figure 103. Mudcracked surface in the Wills Creek shale (Upper Silurian) at Roundtop, Maryland.

Fossils. The fossils preserved in shales afford some of the best evidence for the environment of deposition. They may give proof of a marine or a non-marine environment and may even indicate a particular biotope. Of course, full use of the paleontological evidence requires a profound knowledge of biology and especially of the ecology of living organisms. The forthcoming *Treatise on Marine Ecology and Paleoecology* (Hedgpeth and Ladd, Editors, 1957) will summarize existing knowledge of the criteria that can be used in interpreting ancient sedimentary deposits. The subject is also discussed in Chapter 7.

Color. One of the most obvious features of a shale or mudstone is its color. No satisfactory criteria have been developed for interpreting the gray, greenish, bluish, dun, and buff colors in shales, but the red and black colors deserve special treatment. Accordingly the redbeds are treated in Chapter 12, red shales and sandstones being considered together, and the remainder of the present chapter is devoted to the black shales.

BLACK SHALES

Nature of the Coloring Matter

A typical black shale is fine grained, thinly laminated, rich in carbonaceous matter, and very dark gray to black in color. The Dictyonema-schiefer (basal Ordovician) of western Europe, the Genesee shale (Upper Devonian) of New York, and the widespread Chattanooga shale (basal Mississippian and Upper Devonian) are good examples. These are but the norm, however, in a wide spectrum of deposits that range from dark-gray shale on the one hand to pure carbonaceous deposits (sapropel or coal) on the other hand. Most of the shales thus included are dark gray rather than black and some are brownish-black.

The pigment of most black shales is carbonaceous matter derived from organic tissues (either animal or plant) that have been buried with the sediment. It occurs both as fixed carbon and as bituminous hydrocarbons. A constant struggle is waged on the sea floor between the forces supplying organic matter and those that destroy it (p. 26), and the amount that remains at any

place to be buried in the mud, and hence to color the sediment, depends on the *ratio* of supply to loss rather than on the total amount of organic matter introduced.

In some black muds and black shales, however, finely divided iron sulphide (FeS_2) is the chief pigment. Boswell (in Marr, 1925, p. 135) reported, for example, that black mud dredged from the Irish Sea owes its color almost exclusively to FeS_2, organic matter being virtually absent, and Fearnsides (1905, p. 613) indicated that the blackness of certain of the Dolgelly beds (Upper Cambrian) of North Wales is likewise due to FeS_2 and that these beds contain but little carbonaceous matter.

Types of Black Shale as Distinguished by Field Relations

In the extensive literature on the subject, black shale has been assigned to a number of different depositional environments. The extremes range from the view of Grabau (Grabau and O'Connell, 1917) that the black shales of Scotland and elsewhere were mostly spread over the subaerial surface of great deltas and in shallow lagoons near shore, to that of John M. Clarke (1904, p. 199–201) who thought they had settled into deep stagnant basins like the Black Sea, and of Ruedemann (1934, p. 15–23) who thought they had accumulated in abyssal depths in the geosynclines that were swept by through-flowing ocean currents. While such extreme theories may or may not be tenable in specific cases, they are not necessarily mutually exclusive. Since the accumulation of organic matter in mud depends simply on the relative rates of supply and of destruction rather than on the total amount supplied, black shales have surely accumulated under a wide range of conditions. The preservation of abundant carbonaceous material sets certain limits to the possible environments of deposition, but we must depend on other features to narrow down the possibilities for each particular black shale. In this connection the larger relations and the associated deposits may be particularly significant.

Non-marine black shales. Black shales are conspicuous in the Coal Measures where they are commonly interbedded with gray sandstones and greenish-gray or even red shales that bear clear evidence of fluvial deposition. Such black shales are commonly filled with the remains of terrestrial vegetation and include beautifully preserved fern leaves that could not have been transported appreciably before burial. Coal beds are commonly succeeded by fissile black shale of this sort, known to the coal miners as "roofing slate." All such black shales are clearly the product of deposition in swamps and bogs, or in shallow lakes, where standing water and lush vegetation conspired to incorporate an excess of organic matter in the accumulating muds. In the anthracite fields of Pennsylvania no marine fossils are known throughout the entire coal-bearing sequence, and deposition was probably far from the sea. In the coal fields of Illinois and Indiana, on the contrary, the coal beds are commonly succeeded by black "roofing slates" that in turn are overlain by a "caprock" of marine limestone (Fig. 52, p. 110). Here the coal and the overlying black shale clearly accumulated in vast paralic swamps barely above sealevel, like those of the broad swampy coastal lowlands of eastern Sumatra.

Black shales of barred basins. Black muds are now accumulating in many of the fjords along the Scandinavian coast (Strøm, 1939). Although comparable deposits must be rare, if present, in the stratigraphic record, and none are now known, they nevertheless illustrate well some of the principles that govern deposition in barred basins, i.e., basins with a shallow threshold (p. 60).

In many of the Norwegian fjords, a shallow threshold left by the glaciers prevents free circulation of water from the sea into the deeper inner part of the fjord. The fresh water flowing from the land into the head of the fjord is less dense than the salt water in the depths of the fjord, and it therefore floats at the surface (Fig. 104A). The resulting density stratification keeps the bottom water stagnant, and decaying organic matter on the bottom quickly exhausts the free oxygen so that few benthonic animals can survive even though fish and other pelagic and floating organisms (mostly microscopic) are abundant near the surface. When such animals die, their carcasses settle to the bottom and, in the absence of scav-

engers, are attacked only by anaerobic bacteria. The H_2S which these bacteria generate makes the bottom still more inhospitable.

At intervals of a few years, however, the water in the fjord is overturned, normally in late winter or early spring when but little fresh water is flowing in from the still-frozen land and a sharp cold snap chills the surface water until it is denser than that at the bottom. The fresh cold water then settles, displacing the stagnant but warmer bottom water and forcing it to the surface (Fig. 104B). An overturn may also be produced at this time of year when strong offshore winds persist for a few days, generating an outflowing surface current that must be balanced by inward flow of sea water over the threshold (Fig. 104C). The sea water thus siphoned into the basin may be even denser than that at the bottom (which is constantly diluted by diffusion of fresh water from above), and it flows to the bottom of the fjord displacing the stagnant water. These overturns are completed within a few days, and they "sweeten" the bottom and permit the temporary incursion of a new bottom fauna. Meanwhile the H_2S brought to the surface during the overturn kills most of the floating and swimming animals in the surface waters and their carcasses then sink to the bottom and decay, restoring the reducing conditions (p. 26). The concentration of fossils on occasional bedding planes, so common in black shales, may in many cases be the result of such mass mortality.

Larger barred basins like the Black Sea also show density stratification and are floored with mud rich in organic matter and H_2S (p. 61), but in such basins the water is not overturned. Even in the margins of the open oceans, deep basins with shallow thresholds, like those in the continental borderland off southern California, are density stratified, stagnant in depth, and generally floored with mud richer in organic matter than the surrounding shallow areas (Trask, 1939). The importance of stagnation as a factor in the accumulation of organic matter is shown by comparison of one of these deep basins with the flat shelf sea along the west coast of South Africa where the "red tide" causes mass mortality at intervals of 3 or 4 years, covering the bottom

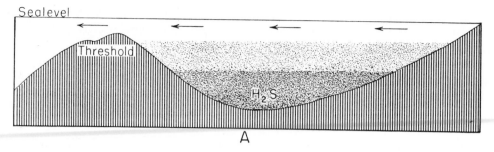

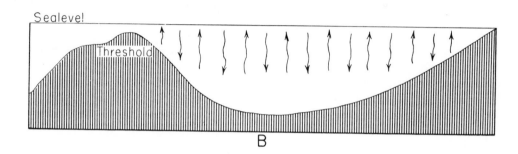

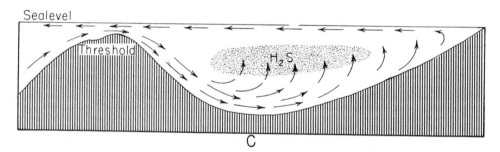

Figure 104. Circulation of water in a Norwegian fjord separated from the ocean by a shallow threshold. Adapted from Strøm (1939, Fig. 1).

with dead fish that can be dredged up by the bucketful (Brongersma-Sanders, 1948). In spite of this rich supply the shallow sea floor along the African coast, well aerated by the waves and bottom currents, retains only a small percentage of organic matter, and its bottom mud is pale-greenish gray (p. 53).

One of the best-documented examples of an ancient deposit formed in a large density-stratified marine basin is the Bone Spring formation (Permian) in the Delaware Basin of West Texas (Fig. 40, p. 93). It consists of thin-bedded, generally finely laminated, platy black limestone and interbedded black shale. It was deposited in the deeper part of the Delaware Basin while massive

light-gray limestone was forming on the surrounding shelf (King, 1942). It rests on the Hueco limestone which bears a normal benthonic fauna, and the base of the Bone Spring formation (well exposed along the face of the Sierra Diablo) also consists of normal light-gray limestone with a rich benthonic fauna of brachiopods, bryozoans, corals, and fusulines (Dunbar, 1953). Within 50 feet of the base, however, scattered dark platy and silty barren layers appear, and they increase in frequency and thickness upward as the fossiliferous gray layers become thinner and farther apart and finally drop out. The black limestone and black shale, which continue upward for hundreds of feet, are remarkably barren of fossils and have yielded no evidence of a bottom fauna. Here the transition beds at the base certainly record a change in the environment from normal open shallow water to a somewhat deeper, density-stratified basin. The even lamination of the black limestone and shale indicates deposition on a quiet sea floor below wave base and devoid of groveling and mud-eating organisms, and the absence of fossils strongly suggests a stagnant, lifeless bottom.

Black muds and shales of open bays. Goldman (1924) has described extensive areas of black mud now forming in Chesapeake Bay, (1) in deep spots off the mouths of entering streams and (2) in shallower areas midway between the sandy shore and the current-swept channels. Grabau (1917, p. 953) and others have likewise described the black muds that cover some 600 square miles of the floor of Danzig Bay on the south side of the Baltic Sea, and Twenhofel (1915) has vividly described "black shales in the making" in the bays about the Esthonian islands of Ösel and Moon (p. 54). In each of these regions there is an abundant bottom fauna, limited, of course, to types of organisms that can survive on a soft muddy bottom; all are protected from large storm waves of the open sea, but in none is the bottom water confined or stagnant. The concentration of organic matter in the mud is due merely to a copious supply which overbalances the loss by decay (p. 202).

Apparently the Hunsrückschiefer (Lower Devonian) about the Hunsrück, in the German Rhineland, was deposited in somewhat comparable shallow water. It has long excited interest because of its remarkably preserved fossils. It has been extensively quarried for roofing slate and has yielded an unparalleled variety of starfish and ophiuroids, as well as many crinoids and remarkably preserved arthropods with appendages attached. Since all these types of organisms easily fall apart after death, it is notable that so many in the Hunsrückschiefer are whole. Because of these undisturbed fossils, the fine lamination, and the black color, this formation was generally considered to be a product of deposition in a deep stagnant basin until about 1930. Then Richter (1931, 1935, 1936, 1941) and Kutscher (1931) showed that this assump-

tion was untenable. They both pointed out, independently, that these black shales are interbedded with thin silty laminae that bear clear evidence of bottom currents. Distinctive borings also prove that marine worms were living in abundance on the muddy bottoms.

Previous workers, impressed with the perfectly preserved starfish and crinoids, had overlooked many other kinds of fossils that are obscurely preserved, and had assumed that all the fossils represent creatures that had settled from above or had drifted into the basin, but Richter and Kutscher both identified a large and varied benthonic fauna including various sessile forms. Richter believes that the structure of the echinoderm skeletons favored early and rapid replacement by pyrite so that they were uncommonly well preserved, whereas most of the other shells were largely dissolved away, leaving only "ghosts" or obscure impressions in the shale. Because of the composition of the fauna, Richter and Kutscher agree that it could not have drifted into the area after death but was living on the bottom while the mud was accumulating. They visualize the environment as that of a shallow and muddy, but not stagnant, sea floor near shore. Richter thinks that rapid burial of the rich organic deposit left much of the diagenesis (reduction and pyritization) to take place in the mud below a surface on which organisms could thrive.

Thick geosynclinal deposits of black shale. In the Appalachian trough the Middle and Upper Ordovician deposits include a black shale belt along the western side of the geosyncline that grades westward into limestone and eastward into a coarser detrital facies, all the way from New York to Alabama (Fig. 72, p. 140). In this belt the shale ranges from several hundred to some thousands of feet thick and, while it was being deposited, richly fossiliferous and obviously shallow-water limestones were forming on the platform to the west. On the opposite side of the geosyncline gray sandstone, siltstone, and gray shale were forming, locally rich in fossils but in many places displaying graded bedding and other evidences of turbidity current deposition. Toward the margins of the black shale belt, where shale intertongues with limestone on the west or

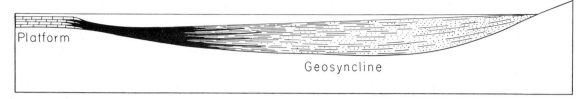

Figure 105. Hypothetical section across a geosyncline bordered on the left by a stable platform and on the right by highlands.

with coarser detritals on the east, benthonic fossils are not uncommon; but with these exceptions the faunas of the black shales consist almost exclusively of pelagic forms, chiefly graptolites (Ruedemann, 1934).

Since the various species of graptolites range all the way from north to south, Ulrich (1911, p. 517, 675) argued that ocean currents must have streamed through the geosyncline and hence the bottom on which the black mud accumulated could not have been stagnant. Ruedemann (1934) likewise invoked through-flowing currents to bring in the graptolites from a source in the Sargasso Sea in the open ocean. The sparseness of benthonic fossils, nevertheless, indicates a bottom environment largely devoid of life and strongly suggests stagnation, quite different from the environment of the Hunsrückschiefer (Ruedemann, 1935, p. 83).

Perhaps the evidence can be reconciled as follows. If the geosyncline was slowly and symmetrically downwarped (Fig. 105), the water should have been deeper along the western part than elsewhere. It would have been shallower over the adjacent platform on the west because of lesser subsidence there, and over the eastern part of the trough because of rapid filling by detrital sediment from Appalachia. The only sediment available along the western part of the trough, however, was the fine mud carried in suspension across some 200 miles or more of shallow sea floor. If filling did not keep pace with subsidence here, the water would gradually deepen as downwarping proceeded. A gentle bottom slope of 30 feet per mile on the flanks of the trough would permit a depth of 300 feet within 10 miles of the platform but would not be detectable in the modern deposits. Subsidence was likewise uneven along the 2,000-mile axis of

the geosyncline, and the shallower places must have been thresholds preventing free circulation at the bottom in the deeper basins even though surface currents flowed through the trough. Since pyrite is generally not abundant in these graptoliferous shales, however, complete stagnation seems improbable.

The organic matter concentrated in this zone of deeper water may have been largely winnowed out of the sediment that was accumulating over the broad shallow sea floor farther to the east. Trask (1932, p. 113) found that in general the organic content of the mud in basins is greater than that on ridges and slopes. This, he explains, is because the organic matter, having almost the specific gravity of sea water, is very buoyant and can be transported by very gentle currents even to considerable distances before coming to rest on the sea bottom along with the finest clays. In the Channel Island region off the coast of southern California, for example, Revelle and Shepard (1939, p. 261–266 and Fig. 8) reported that the organic content of the bottom muds exceeds 7 percent in the deepest parts of the basins but falls to less than 1.5 percent over the shoals. In the Baltic Sea, likewise, Gripenberg (1939) has shown that, although most of the open sea floor is covered with fine sand or glacial clay of light color, the slightly deeper places, far out from shore, are black mudholes.

If, then, the sand and silt accumulating during Ordovician time along the eastern part of the Appalachian geosyncline were subject to such selective sorting, much of the finely divided organic matter would have been winnowed out and transported into the deepest water along the western side of the trough, there to accumulate faster than it was destroyed even in the presence of gentle circulation of the bottom water.

Thin but widespread black shale on the platform. The Chattanooga shale (Middle (?) and Upper Devonian, Hass, 1956) seems to represent an environment unlike any of the types discussed above and possibly one without a close parallel in the modern world. It is the initial deposit of a marine inundation that spread far to the west of the Appalachian geosyncline across the peneplaned surface of the stable interior of the continent. Here it unconformably overlaps older formations ranging in age from Ordovician to Devonian. Over considerable areas it has a thin basal sandstone member (Hardin sandstone of western Tennessee; Sylamore sandstone of the Ozark region) but in many places the black shale rests directly on the old erosion surface. The great lateral extent and the thinness of the formation are noteworthy. It stretches from Oklahoma and Kansas on the west to the deformed belt in eastern Tennessee and Kentucky and probably was originally a continuous sheet of black mud covering an area of more than 200,000 square miles. Nevertheless, it generally is less than 20 feet thick, increasing to about 100 feet along its eastern margin in Tennessee and southwestern Virginia and locally exceeding 400 feet in the basin of southern Illinois. Along its eastern margin it is divided by a wedge of gray silty and sandy shale (Olinger shale) that separates a lower from an upper black shale member. Along its western margin, however, it thins to a feather edge without change of facies and is paraconformably overlapped by succeeding Mississippian formations, commonly limestones.

Lithologically the Chattanooga shale is notable for its black or brownish-black color, its fine and even lamination, and its fissility. As seen in thin section, according to Bates (1953), it consists "of grains of quartz and feldspar in a matrix of yellow to red-brown organic material which incorporates shreds of mica and probably clay particles and is dotted by small clusters of pyrite. . . . Several types of clay minerals [are] present."

The black shale is generally barren of fossils except for conodonts, spores of land plants, fragments of driftwood, and scattered fish plates or fragments thereof. Almost the only evidence of bottom life is the local occurrence in some abundance of a very small species of *Lingula*. In contrast, the gray Olinger shale member along its eastern margin carries a limited fauna of calcareous brachiopods (Swartz, 1929).

The abundance of organic matter, the fine and even lamination, the finely divided pyrite, and the general lack of benthonic fossils suggest deposition in quiet stagnant depths below wave base, and this interpretation has been advocated by Rich (1951).

On the contrary, Conant (1953), who is heading a comprehensive study of the Chattanooga shale for the U. S. Geological Survey, thinks that the postulated deep-water environment would require highly improbable conditions, and he suggests seven lines of argument in favor of extremely shallow water, for example, the larger field relations. Thus the black shale lies directly on the peneplaned land surface from which it is only locally separated by a thin and discontinuous basal sandstone member, it covers a region that was not deeply inundated at any other time during the Paleozoic Era, and it is directly succeeded by limestones admittedly of shallow water deposition.

Twenhofel (1939) has postulated that such widespread black muds could accumulate in very shallow epeiric seas surrounded by low lands and lacking appreciable tides. Here he thinks waves might be effectively damped out by the shallowness of the water and by the luxurious growth of seaweeds that would at once protect the muddy bottom and supply a large amount of the organic matter. He postulates that under these conditions low salinity might make the bottom inhospitable for most marine animals and a wide marginal zone of fresh water would prevent them from inhabiting the shore zone.

We may hope for a more definitive solution of the problem when the current project of the U. S. Geological Survey is completed.

Some of the Devonian black shales of the Ohio Valley (New Albany shale of Indiana; Olentangy and Cleveland shale of Ohio) closely resemble the Chattanooga shale in field relations and are, indeed, its northward continuation; they present similar problems.

Black shales associated with organic reefs.
Finally, small deposits of black mud may actually
accumulate in the midst of coral reefs. Yonge
(1930, p. 47–48) has observed areas of black
mud on the shelf of the Great Barrier Reef of
Australia. Ruedemann (1925b, p. 7–8) has described a small deposit of dark-brown shale rich
in graptolites (the Gasport Channel deposit), enclosed within the coralliferous Lockport limestone
(Middle Silurian) near Gasport, New York.
Troedsson and Roswall (1926) also recorded
small bodies of black graptoliferous shale in the
reefy limestone of the Leptaenakalk (Middle Silurian) at Dalarna, Sweden; and Cumings and
Shrock (1928b, p. 56–62) described the drab to
dark-gray Mississinewa shale of northern Indiana,
which flanks the large coral reefs of the Silurian
in that region and occupies the basins between
them.

In such instances relatively shallow but protected places in a region of copious organic matter
have provided the conditions for the accumulation of dark to black muds, but since corals thrive
only in well-aerated water, this is rare.

12. Redbeds

REDBEDS WERE among the first sedimentary rocks to attract the attention of geologists. They occur in many parts of the world and are of all ages from Early Precambrian to Recent (the Athabaska redbeds of Saskatchewan are not less than 1,600,000,000 years old, according to Collins, Farquhar, and Russell, 1954, p. 13). Widely divergent views have been held as to their origin, and an extensive and controversial literature has grown up about them. Probably much of the confusion has stemmed from a tendency to assume that they were all formed in the same environment.

GENERAL CHARACTERISTICS

With minor exceptions the redbeds consist of non-marine terrigenous, fragmental sediments. They range in coarseness from rudite to lutite and commonly consist of alternations of sandstone, siltstone, and shale.*

In typical redbeds the size-sorting is normally poor and the distinction between sandstone, siltstone, and silty shale is generally obscure; pure clay shale is rare. In some redbed sequences the sandstones are arkosic, but in others they are highly quartzose and in a few they contain enough

---

* Red limestones and the sedimentary red iron ores occur in other associations and present special problems; they are not considered "redbeds" and are not treated in this chapter.

---

rock fragments to approach a graywacke in composition. Some are associated with evaporites of impressive proportions and must have accumulated in a strongly arid environment, but others are intimately associated with swamp deposits and coal beds. With rare and local exceptions the redbeds are sparsely fossiliferous, but this is at least partially due to their thorough oxidation which destroyed organic tissues; in some redbeds (e.g., the Newark group of Massachusetts, Connecticut, and New Jersey) footprints indicate deposition in an environment teeming with life. It is evident, therefore, that redbeds differ greatly in their associations and must have formed in a wide range of environments; their chief common characteristic is the red color.

COLOR OF REDBEDS

Nature of the coloring matter. The pigment of redbeds is finely divided hematite (Fe_2O_3). Other types of sedimentary rock contain iron in other forms, such as goethite ($HFeO_2$) and lepidocrocite [$FeO(OH)$], which color the rock brown or, in more diluted form, yellow; marcasite and pyrite (FeS_2), which if abundant and finely divided color the rock dark gray; or various ferrous or ferro-ferric silicates (e.g., chamosite and other chlorites), which color the rock green or, more commonly, hardly contribute to its color at all. Thus it is the presence of hematite rather than some other iron mineral that distinguishes redbeds.

The hematite is normally concentrated in the finer fraction of the fragmental sediment, as indicated by Tomlinson (1916, p. 177–179). Thus in a typical redbed sequence the shales are the reddest, the siltstones somewhat paler, and the sandstones much paler or not red at all. Evidently the hematite was carried mechanically as finely divided sediment and was thus distributed with the other clay-size constituents.* In some redbeds, however, the hematite appears as a stain on the surface of grains, and in these the sands may not appear paler than the shales. In some cases, also, it can be shown that the sandstones are not red because the contained iron has been reduced to a ferrous condition.

Sources of the red pigment. The iron now present in the hematite that colors redbeds must come ultimately from the chemical weathering of ferrous silicates in igneous and metamorphic rocks. Ferrous iron is relatively more soluble than ferric iron, which is soluble only in fairly acid solutions; thus a little iron can be carried in neutral or even weakly alkaline solutions as long as they are reducing, but is precipitated at once when they are oxidized. In ordinary laboratory experiments at surface temperatures and pressures, however, ferric iron is precipitated not as hematite but as goethite. In the presence of pure water goethite is stable at all temperatures below 130°C. and generally will not dehydrate to hematite unless the temperature is considerably higher (Posnjak and Merwin, 1919; Tunell and Posnjak, 1931), but in slightly acid solutions the temperature of dehydration is somewhat lower (Tunell and Posnjak, 1931, p. 338, reported that in $\frac{1}{10}$ normal HCl, goethite changes to hematite at a temperature of about 100°C. within a few weeks). One would expect, therefore, that all ferric iron in soils, which are obviously formed at surface temperatures and pressures, would be goethite. In the brown and yellow soils of arid and temperate climates, weathering has evidently produced goethite (or its polymorph, lepidocrocite), but the red soil and mantle of the humid tropics contains much hematite. How hematite forms here is not known; Raymond (1927, p. 240–241; 1942, p. 666–667) suggested that nitrates produced by bacteria in tropical soils favored the formation of a red instead of a yellow ferric compound, but his suggestion remains unproved.

At present then, hematite is forming in red residual soils (under conditions whose physical chemistry is not yet understood) over enormous areas in Africa, Asia, and South America, in large areas in the southeastern United States and Central America, and in smaller areas in Europe (Blanck, 1929–1932; Robinson, 1932; Marbut, 1935). Apparently it forms in soils only where the rainfall exceeds 40 inches, and generally where the mean temperature is over 60°F., though the lower temperature limit is different for soils formed over different rock types; thus in the southeastern United States red soils on shale, mica schist, or granite extend northward only to North Carolina, or locally into southern Virginia, whereas on limestone and basic igneous rocks they extend to Maryland. Even within the humid tropics, of course, dark soils form where drainage is impeded, but wherever drainage is good and the soil can dry out between rains or rainy seasons, the active bacteria of the tropics quickly destroy organic matter and thus prevent the accumulation of humus and the establishment of permanently reducing conditions; if iron is present the resulting soils are red. Red soil can form even under a tropical rain forest with hundreds of inches of rainfall, but the most favorable climate is that of the warm savanna with its strongly seasonal rains and widely fluctuating water table. Here oxidation of the iron is completed in the dry season, and the hematite once formed is not reduced in the next rainy season.

Once red soils are formed, the red pigment colors all sediments washed from the areas where the soils were produced, provided the pigment is not reduced during deposition. Most marine sediments, of course, are deposited under reducing conditions, as are many non-marine sediments. But where the basin of deposition, like the area where the red soils formed, is well drained, at

---

* Iron transported in, and deposited from, solution commonly appears as one of the brown or yellow hydrous oxides, and if deposited as hematite generally is concentrated in ore bodies instead of being disseminated as pigment through the fragmental sediment.

least seasonally, there the red color will be preserved.

Several other possible sources of red pigment have been suggested (see Tomlinson, 1916, p. 238 ff.), but none of them can be significant for typical redbed sequences. Some modern marine sediments are red; the red clay of the open ocean is the most widespread, but from its position in the deepest ocean basins it can hardly be a possible source for the continental redbeds. Red terrigenous mud occurs near shore in a large area off the mouth of the Amazon River, but the red here appears to come in its turn from red soil on the continent, brought down by the river and deposited before it can be reduced; almost everywhere else along the continental shelves and slopes the terrigenous muds are grayish, bluish, or greenish. Pink and red granites contribute color to some arkose, but the red of the associated siltstones and shales is typically much stronger, so that the granites can scarcely have been the principal source of pigment. Finally, the erosion of pre-existing redbeds, as in parts of the arid southwestern United States, in the red desert of Arabia, and elsewhere, produces red sediment (p. 217), but the origin of the red pigment is not thereby explained, though the color of some particular red formations, formed in environments that do not produce red pigment, can be thus accounted for (e.g., the red Pleistocene till in the Connecticut Valley; p. 3).

Some students (e.g., Crosby, 1891; Barrell, 1908, p. 285–293) have thought that some, at least, of the ancient redbeds were brown or yellow when deposited and became red by dehydration after accumulation, either because of higher temperature resulting from deep burial or because of automatic dehydration too slow to be detected in the laboratory. The evidence opposed to this idea is so impressive, however, that it no longer seems tenable. If, for example, dehydration occurs slowly after burial, then the more ancient formations should all be red rather than brown or at least there should be a systematic variation according to age; on the contrary, the early Paleozoic sandstones and siltstones are commonly brown—for example, the Croixian Series (Cambrian) of the upper Mississippi Valley and the Black Hills. Likewise, if deep burial were responsible for dehydration there should be a systematic difference in color according to position within a thick sequence. There is no such relation. On the contrary, in the Connecticut Trough where the Newark group is perhaps 15,000 feet thick, the uppermost part, which has never been deeply covered, is fully as red as the basal part. In this sequence, furthermore, certain Triassic intrusives have baked the adjacent sediments and produced a gray contact zone; evidently the sediments were already red in Triassic time.

Miller and Folk (1955) have recently reported that in samples of 22 formations, ranging in age from Cambrian to Cenozoic and representing practically all the well-known redbeds in the United States, magnetite and ilmenite are present as detrital grains and are generally the dominant heavy minerals. In closely associated gray layers, or even in gray or greenish spots in the midst of red layers, on the contrary, they found almost no magnetite or ilmenite. From these observations they draw two conclusions: (1) under reducing conditions both magnetite and ilmenite readily disappear and cannot be reconstituted, and (2) all redbeds have been derived from sources in igneous or metamorphic rocks where magnetite and ilmenite are present. If so, the sediments of which all existing redbeds are formed must have originated in oxidizing environments, and at no time, either during transportation or after burial, could they have passed through reducing conditions. But deep red soils commonly develop in warm humid climates over limestone and shale units in which the iron is certainly in a ferrous state, and one would expect that this red soil might easily supply material for redbeds.

Miller and Folk further argue that, in the redbeds which they observed, the oxidation that produced the red pigment took place chiefly after deposition since the pigment is thin or lacking at the points of contact between sand grains. This conclusion appears to contradict the evidence in many redbeds that the red pigment is concentrated in the finest size grades where it was deposited mechanically. More study is needed to determine if the relations discovered by Miller and Folk hold for all redbeds or if some have formed as they infer and others in other ways.

Effects of a reducing environment. Although hematite is remarkably stable and highly insoluble in the presence of free oxygen, it readily yields part of its oxygen in a strongly reducing environment, the iron passing from a ferric to a ferrous condition. According to MacCarthy (1926), purely ferrous compounds of iron (ferrous hydroxide, carbonate, sulphate, phosphate, or silicate) are practically colorless; ferro-ferric compounds are blue; and mixtures of ferric and ferro-ferric compounds are greenish. Thus, in a strongly reducing environment, red sediment loses its color which is replaced by gray, greenish, or bluish tints. Some of these ferrous compounds (e.g., $FeCO_3$) are readily soluble, and in this form much of the iron may be leached out and carried away, but others are stable. Thus a gray or greenish deposit is commonly found to include as high a percentage of iron as a red one (Dorsey, 1926).

Reducing conditions are created within a sedimentary deposit wherever sufficient organic matter has accumulated with the sediment. The decaying organic matter tends to exhaust the free oxygen and to rob some from the ferric compounds, reducing them to a ferrous condition. In the soil and mantle this reduction may be counterbalanced by a continuing supply of oxygen from the air and rain water (above the water table) and from descending ground water. Thus in the humid tropics where the growth of vegetation is rapid, decay and destruction of the organic matter is also rapid, and wherever there is sufficient relief to permit ready circulation of the ground water a strongly oxidizing environment is maintained and the soil and mantle are red. But wherever the sediment accumulates under standing water, or where the water table is near the surface and the ground water is stagnant, reducing conditions are readily produced. Thus the shallow sea floor is generally a reducing environment. The net effect on the iron in the sediment will then depend on the balance of supply and depletion. If red pigment is supplied in sufficient quantity and deposition is sufficiently rapid, part of the hematite may survive; but if deposition is slower, or the amount of organic matter is sufficiently great, reduction will be complete and initially red sediment will be transformed into gray or greenish or bluish sediment or, with sufficient organic matter, it will become dark gray or black.

A study of the Middle and Upper Devonian deposits of the Catskill Delta indicates that reduction of initially red sediment occurred there on a colossal scale. The chief source of sediment for this vast deposit lay to the east and southeast in Appalachia, and the Catskill redbed facies represents the piedmont alluvial slope and the higher subaerial surface of the delta sloping westward toward the sea that then occupied the Appalachian trough. Toward the shore these redbeds grade laterally into non-red sandstones and siltstones that locally (as at Gilboa) bear unmistakable evidence of a swampy coastal lowland, but for the most part are the shallow marine equivalents of the subaerial redbeds. Clearly, the sediments that form the marine part of the delta must have been transported from the east across the area in which the Catskill redbeds were accumulating. In part the red color may have been produced there during accumulation, but since the red pigment is notably concentrated in the maroon shales, it must have been introduced originally as a fine sediment and deposited with the clay minerals; in short, the sediment was predominantly red when it reached the delta surface. If this be true, the sediment that by-passed and reached the sea must also have been red. Since the marine part of the delta is now almost if not entirely non-red, reduction on a grand scale must have taken place in the Devonian sea. The Sespe formation (Oligocene) of California bears the same implications. This thick, non-marine red formation grades westward into a non-red marine sequence, yet all the sediment had a common landward source and must originally have been red.

In the Red Bedford Delta (Fig. 36, p. 87) the muds laid down over the subaerial surface for the most part remained red, whereas contemporaneous muds carried into the sea are gray. The channel sands of the subaerial part of the delta likewise are gray.

DIVERS TYPES OF REDBEDS

As indicated above, redbeds are not all alike and they may have formed under a wide variety of environments. No attempt will be made here to discuss the varied conditions of deposition exhaustively, but a few types will be used to illustrate the problem.

Arkosic redbeds of the Newark type. The Newark group (Triassic) occupies a series of fault troughs along the axis of the Appalachians where it reaches a thickness of many thousands of feet (some 15,000 feet in the Connecticut Trough and up to 25,000 feet in New Jersey and Pennsylvania). It has been studied by numerous workers (Russell, 1892; Davis, 1898; Barrell, 1915; and others), and the deposits of the Connecticut Trough have recently been studied in a comprehensive and critical manner by Krynine (1950).

Typically these deposits are irregularly bedded, poorly sorted, and heterogeneous. Conglomerates are common along the faulted borders of the troughs where they accumulated as scree and piedmont boulder beds along the border faults, which were active during deposition. Fresh and partly weathered feldspar is abundant both in the conglomerates and in the finer sediments. At many places, and in many different beds, footprints of dinosaurs and of small sprawling reptiles and amphibians occur in amazing abundance, indicating that vast numbers of such animals were present in the basin during deposition. Mudcracks are equally abundant and to many of the earlier workers were considered evidence of aridity, but Krynine (1935b) has shown that shallow mudcracks such as these can form, and can be preserved, in regions of heavy rainfall, especially where the rainfall is seasonal (p. 200). Dune sands and salines are conspicuously absent from all the Newark troughs, and the isolated salt crystals of which casts have been found could easily have formed during the dry season of a seasonal climate. Local lenses of black shale, rich in plant remains and fossil fish, record swamps in Connecticut, New Jersey, and Pennsylvania; farther south in the Richmond Basin of Virginia and the Deep River Basin of North Carolina, layers of coal occur within the redbed sequence. Although the Newark group is predominantly red in the Connecticut Trough, Krynine has shown that a considerable thickness of beds lying between sheets of basaltic lava is not red, presumably because the lava flows disorganized the drainage and produced swampy conditions. After the last flow, drainage was reestablished and the slopes became graded again so that circulation of ground water was adequate near the surface, and then the accumulation of red sediment was resumed. Barrell (1908, p. 285–293) and others had argued that, even if the red pigment was formed under warm and humid conditions in the adjoining uplands, the basin of deposition was arid. Raymond (1927, 1942) was the first strongly to challenge this view and to argue that the basin of deposition also was humid. Krynine (1950) has since made a very strong case for this interpretation, postulating a savanna climate with warmth and heavy rainfall over both the source area and the basin of deposition, the rainfall being largely concentrated in wet seasons alternating with dry seasons. Under such conditions the dry seasons tend to inhibit forest growth and to facilitate oxidation of the soil and mantle.

Other deposits probably formed under similar conditions are the Fountain formation (Pennsylvanian) of Colorado (Tieje, 1923), the Torridonian (Precambrian) and the Old Red sandstone (Devonian) of Great Britain, and the Keweenawan and other redbeds of the Canadian Shield.

Redbeds in the Coal Measures. In the Monongahela Series (uppermost Pennsylvanian) of the Appalachian coal fields of Pennsylvania, Ohio, and West Virginia, widespread formations (or members) of red shale alternate with gray sandstones and gray or dark shales and coal beds. In the immediately overlying Dunkard Series (early Permian?) there is an equally striking association of redbeds with non-red deposits of swampy lowlands.

The Dunkard Series occupies an oval area of about 30,000 square miles in extreme southwestern Pennsylvania and adjacent parts of Ohio and West Virginia (Fig. 106). These sediments, like those of the underlying Monongahela Series, clearly had their source in the highlands of Appalachia to the southeast. Clapp (1907) described these beds in the corner of Pennsylvania, Stauffer and Schroyer (1920) made a more general study of the series in Ohio, and Cross, Smith,

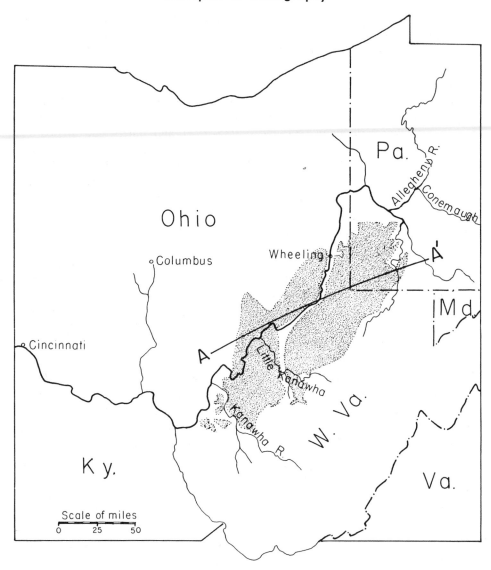

Figure 106.   Sketch map of area underlain by the Dunkard Series.

and Arkle (1950) presented a very detailed account with many sections. To the northwest of line A—A in Figure 106, this series, more than 1,000 feet thick, includes a complex alternation of gray, buff-weathering sandstones, olive-green to dark-gray to black shales, fresh-water limestones, and thin coal seams. To the southeast of line A—A red shales appear, and they increase in number and thickness toward the southern border of the basin as limestones and coals drop out. In Lewis and Gilmer Counties, West Virginia, for example "the series consists mainly of

alternating beds of brown, micaceous sandstones, sometimes massive and sometimes flaggy, and red and sandy shales" (Reger, 1916, p. 103). And according to I. C. White: "As we pass south-westward, however [from line A—A], the coal beds all disappear except one (the Washington) before we reach the Little Kanawha river, and the Limestones with one or two exceptions thin away into great masses of marly red shales" (White, 1903, p. 101). In short, the Dunkard Series is wholly non-red in the northwestern part of the basin where it includes much dark shale, many thin coal seams, and much fresh-water limestone; but along the southern border it consists mostly of gray, brown-weathering sandstone and red shale. Along the axis of the basin between these extremes, red shales alternate with darker shales and sandstones and deeply intertongue into the non-red facies. In a section west of Stanleyville in Washington County, Ohio, for example, Stauffer and Schroyer (1920, p. 121–122) record 17 units of red shale scattered through the section with an aggregate thickness of 200 feet.

Here, then, non-marine deposits were spread over a basin the northern half of which was repeatedly occupied by fresh-water lakes and by large swamps in which vegetation accumulated to form coal, while the southern part was a well-drained alluvial plain on which red mud accumulated on the interfluves while gray channel sands (now weathering brown) spread widely along the stream courses. Moreover, the source for all this sediment lay to the southeast. No difference in climate, either in the source area or in the basin of deposition can be invoked to account for the contrast in color. The sediment must have been largely red when it reached the Dunkard Basin; where it came to rest on well-drained slopes it remained red, while in the swampy lowlands the iron was reduced to a ferrous state. Likewise, Van Houten (1948) has shown how a shifting balance between oxidizing and reducing conditions in a basin of deposition has produced alternating red and drab layers and lenses in the lower Cenozoic rocks of the Rocky Mountain region.

Red shales occur also both in the Monongahela and the Conemaugh Series in the Appalachian coal fields. Similarly, in the Upper Coal Measures of the Potteries coal field in the Midlands of England, the Etruria "marl," about 1,000 feet thick, consists largely of red shale and red siltstone (Kendall, 1929, p. 276).

Redbeds of the Catskill type. The Catskill Delta (Devonian) has been described above (p. 138). Here redbeds several thousands of feet thick form a landward facies laid down over the higher part of the subaerial surface of the delta. In the eastern sections, as in the face of the Catskill Mountains, the redbeds consist of monotonous bright red silty shale in units tens to hundreds of feet thick alternating with units of gray sandstone and conglomerate up to 50 feet or so in thickness. These sandstones appear massive from a distance but are generally cross-stratified with abundant evidence of cut-and-fill. The conglomerates include a variety of resistant rock types derived from Appalachia, all much worn by long transportation. The pebbles commonly are less than 2 inches in diameter. The silty maroon shales bear obscure traces of rootlets as well as impressions of upright stems of small shrublike vegetation, but the organic tissue is generally completely missing. Occasional small lenses of green shale are included and these are locally filled with fern leaves. The conglomerates and massive, cross-stratified sandstones are clearly ancient channel deposits.

Toward the west the redbeds intertongue with, and grade into, gray sandstones and greenish-gray shales that locally (as at Gilboa) include abundant stumps of trees standing where they grew. These record forested lowlands near the shore. Still farther west these beds grade over into gray marine sandstone, siltstone, and shale.

In redbed sequences of this type, as in those associated with coal measures, the shales and silty shales are red but the interbedded sandstones are generally gray or greenish-gray and weather brownish in outcrop. Since both sandstones and shales had a common source area, this striking difference in color must be attributed to factors that operated in the basin of deposition. In part, the fine particles of hematite may have been winnowed out of the sands and concentrated with other particles of clay size, so that most of the pigment was mechanically separated from the sands before burial. In that case, of course, the percentage of iron should be decidedly lower in the sandstone than in the shales. A more important reason for the difference in color may have been the local ground water conditions at time of deposition. The sandstones and conglomerates were, of course, deposited within or near stream channels. Under a savanna climate the stream courses are bordered by timber and the interfluves are grasslands. During the rainy season both stream courses and interfluves may be extensively flooded. Then sand is swept along the channels and over the natural levees while

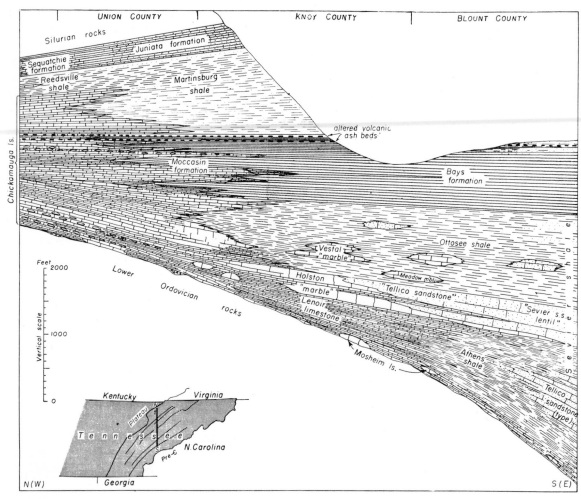

Figure 107. Facies changes in the Middle and Upper Ordovician rocks of East Tennessee. Note position of redbeds (shaded) at the climaxes of the facies shifts.

clay and silt settle out of the slowly moving water over the grasslands. In the dry season, on the contrary, the grassy interfluves may become parched, while through-flowing streams maintain a high level of the water table and support a continuous growth of vegetation along their courses. Thus reducing conditions may predominate along the permanent stream courses where the sands are chiefly concentrated, while oxidizing conditions are dominant over slightly higher ground where the fine muds are laid down. Chemical analyses commonly show little difference in the percentage of iron in the red shales and the gray sandstones but show that the iron is ferrous in the sandstones. Thus the local en-

vironment of deposition must have been the controlling factor in determining whether the iron remained ferric or was reduced to the ferrous state.

Somewhat similar to the Catskill redbeds are the Bays formation (Middle Ordovician) and the Juniata formation (Upper Ordovician) of the Appalachian region (Fig. 107). Each of these forms one facies in a great marine delta fed from rising mountains to the east, the redbeds being essentially the non-marine portion of the deltas. Most of the material carried farther out into the marine part of the delta was reduced to gray or green, but the two red formations mentioned grade laterally into red limy mudstone (Moccasin and Sequatchie formations, respectively) with marine fossils. Perhaps conditions there were locally comparable to those off the mouth of the present-day Amazon, where red mud is introduced faster than it can be reduced. These Ordovician redbeds are mainly siltstones and silty shale and are associated with layers and lenses of white or gray sandstone, chiefly quartzose but including some rock fragments. Both sandstones and mudstones show graywacke features, though they are by no means rich enough in dark fragments to be classed as graywackes.

The red Medina sandstone (Lower Silurian) also intertongues with gray marine beds from Niagara Falls westward, and near their extremities some of the red tongues are filled with marine fossils.

Redbeds associated with evaporites.

Quite different from those described above are the widespread redbeds associated with large deposits of evaporites. Such, for example, are the Chugwater formation of Wyoming, the Spearfish formation of the Black Hills, and the Pease River group of the Panhandle of Texas. Each of these Permian and Triassic formations includes vast quantities of gypsum and anhydrite as lenses or beds, either thick or thin, or disseminated in gypsiferous shales.

Halite and potash salts are regionally associated with some such redbeds, but they are generally enclosed in shales of pale gray color. Examples are the Salina salt beds (Upper Silurian) of New York, underlain by the Vernon red shale, and the potash salt deposits in the Salado formation (Upper Permian) of Texas and New Mexico, overlain by the Rustler and Dewey Lake redbeds. The vast Kungurian salt deposits of the Permian Basin in the U.S.S.R. are likewise succeeded by the Ufimian redbeds of Kazanian age. Dune sands are not uncommonly associated with evaporite-bearing redbeds (e.g., in the Whitehorse group of southern Kansas and Oklahoma, and the New Red sandstone of central England).

In such redbeds arkose is rare and the sandstone is largely quartz-sandstone. Conglomerate is uncommon and the average grain size of the sandstone is much less than in the arkosic types of redbeds. Sorting is better, though still generally only fair (except in the dune sands), and

bedding is commonly even—so even, in fact, that Branson (1915, 1927) argued that such beds could not be non-marine. In these deposits, also, the sandstones as well as the shales are generally red.

That these deposits were laid down in an arid climate, in some instances in truly desert basins, seems proved by the associated evaporites. In England dune sands and ventifacts provide supporting evidence. The relatively fine grain, even bedding, and wide extent argue for long transportation before burial and suggest that the sediment came into the desert basins from distant sources with a different climate, presumably one humid enough to produce red soils. The significant point is that, if red sediment be transported into an arid or semiarid environment, the hematite is stable and the deposit remains red when spread over a subaerial surface. Large deposits of halite or of potash salts indicate permanent bodies of water, either dead seas or large salt lakes, and under such conditions the air is excluded and reducing conditions obtain. Hence the shales enclosing such salt deposits are gray even though flanking deposits laid down beyond the shoreline, and succeeding deposits formed after the bodies of water had disappeared, are largely red.

Other redbeds, including such formations as the Chinle (Triassic) of the Colorado Plateau, are not associated with extensive evaporites but have many characteristics of redbeds that are. They may have been deposited under a less rigorous, semiarid climate.

Redbeds derived from older redbeds.

As emphasized above, pre-existing redbeds commonly weather down into red sediment that may then be deposited as second-generation redbeds in an environment that has no relation to the conditions under which the red pigment was formed. The red till in the Connecticut Valley was thus derived from the underlying Newark redbeds. Even the varved clays laid down in the proglacial lakes of this area are commonly reddish.

Quite possibly the Wingate sandstone (Upper Triassic?) of the Colorado Plateau was likewise merely derived from the underlying redbeds. It is a widespread, massive, commonly cross-stratified dune sand, formed in the midst of a vast lowland that was almost completely mantled by redbeds of Permian and Triassic age. Under these conditions, in an arid climate in which a vast field of dunes could form, hematite would not be produced—but neither would it be destroyed, and the red sands winnowed out by the wind from the surrounding landscape and concentrated into dunes would remain red. A parallel may be seen in the modern red desert of Arabia where the red sand of the dunes is being derived from a red sandstone that floors the desert.

Summary. The association of some redbeds with large deposits of evaporites, and locally of dunes, influenced many of the earlier workers in geology to consider redbeds as the product of an arid or at least semiarid environment. On the contrary, with the exception of areas where the soil and mantle are derived from underlying redbeds, the deserts are notable for their dun and buff colors; they are not red. Furthermore, world-wide soil studies have made it clear that red soil is formed only under warm, humid conditions. It now seems clear that the source area determines whether or not the sediment will be initially red and that conditions in the basins of deposition determine whether it will or will not remain red. Furthermore, just as red sediment is formed in a warm, humid environment, so also it may accumulate and remain red in a moist, humid environment if laid down on sufficiently well-drained slopes, and especially if the rainfall is seasonal. Redbeds still present many unsolved problems—for example, the conditions under which the petrified logs were deposited in the Chinle formation of the Painted Desert, and the conditions under which the gravel of the Shinarump conglomerate was so widely spread over the Colorado Plateau—but it is now evident that red color alone is not a criterion of the environment of deposition.

13. Carbonate rocks

NEXT IN ABUNDANCE among sediments to the siliceous fragmental rocks are the carbonate rocks, and among these the rocks composed of the minerals calcite and dolomite are overwhelmingly dominant. Magnesite and siderite rocks are known but mostly as local deposits; although of some economic interest, their origin is ordinarily so unusual that they provide little evidence on the genesis of carbonate rocks generally. Accordingly this chapter is concerned only with calcite rocks and dolomite rocks, i.e., with limestone and dolostone.*

* The rock made of dolomite was first recognized as a different rock type by Dolomieu (1791), and it was named *dolomie* in his honor by de Saussure, *fils* (1792). The name, in the form *dolomite,* was introduced into English by Kirwan (1794, p. 111–112). In those days the distinction between minerals and rocks was still vague and fluid, and the name dolomite was naturally applied to both, though it is clear that both Dolomieu and de Saussure were thinking principally of the rock (*pierre*). But even after that distinction became clear and sharp, the name dolomite continued, and indeed still continues, to be used for both rock and mineral, a potent source of ambiguity. Attempts to name the rock magnesian limestone, dolomite limestone, or dolomitic limestone have failed, because phrases can seldom oust single words as names and because the term limestone has been increasingly restricted to rocks in which the mineral calcite predominates. Shrock's proposal, *dolostone* (1948b, p. 126), a coined word like the original dolomite, seems to have more promise for removing the ambiguity, and we have therefore adopted it for this book.

PETROGRAPHY

Mineral Composition

Although both limestone and dolostone may contain small quantities of a great number of minerals, their chief constituents are the carbonate minerals aragonite, calcite, dolomite, and ferroan dolomite or ankerite. Of these the first is orthorhombic, the others hexagonal-rhombohedral and practically isostructural. The mutual relations of these minerals and some of their properties become more comprehensible when one understands their crystal structure.

The simple crystal structure of halite (NaCl) is well known (Fig. 108, left); it consists of effectively spherical Na^+ and Cl^- ions alternating along each of three mutually perpendicular directions, so that each Na^+ ion is placed between six Cl^- ions and vice versa. The cubic regularity of this arrangement is reflected in the excellent cubic cleavage of halite. The structure of calcite (Fig. 108, right) is similar, the Ca^{++} and the $CO_3^=$ ions alternating in three directions. The Ca^{++} ion is about the same size and shape as the Na^+ ion, but the $CO_3^=$ ion is larger and has the effective shape of three spheres fused into a triangular, somewhat planar mass. These triangular ions take more space than the spherical Cl^- ions and, in order for them to pack neatly into the structure, they must be cocked at an

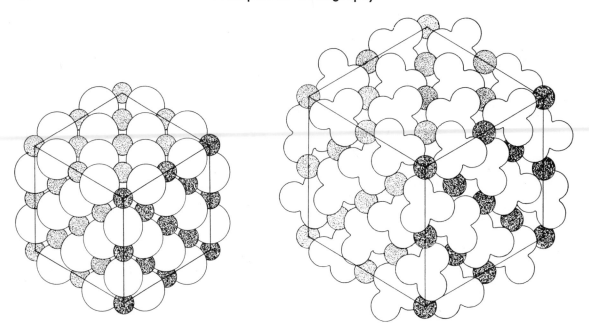

Figure 108. The crystal structures of halite (NaCl), left, and calcite (CaCO₃), right, compared. The c-axis of calcite and a diagonal to the cube of halite are perpendicular to the page. Sodium and calcium ions are shaded.

angle to fit between the six nearest Ca^{++} ions, and the whole cubic array must be squashed, as it were, along one of the cube diagonals until the three lines of alternating ions meet not at 90° but at 101°55′. This arrangement is expressed in the excellent rhombohedral (1011) cleavage of calcite, which can be thought of as cubic cleavage distorted by the presence of the non-spherical carbonate ion. As shown by Bragg (1924b; 1937, p. 120–126), the asymmetry of the carbonate ion also produces the high birefringence and negative optical sign of calcite and other carbonates. The other simple rhombohedral carbonates, such as magnesite ($MgCO_3$) and siderite ($FeCO_3$), have the same structure as calcite.

In the mineral dolomite, about half of the Ca^{++} ions are replaced by Mg^{++} ions. If the Ca^{++} ions and the Mg^{++} ions had the same effective ionic size, there could be unlimited substitution of one for the other and hence complete isomorphism between calcite and magnesite. But in fact the effective radius of the Ca^{++} ion is 36 percent larger than that of the Mg^{++} ion. Therefore, the presence of more than a small percentage of Mg^{++} ions scattered through the calcite structure would cause so great a distortion that the structure would be unstable; in other words, no such crystals ever form. Where Ca^{++} and Mg^{++} ions are present in equal numbers, however, they alternate regularly between the $CO_3^=$ ions along each of the three directions (Ca^{++}, $CO_3^=$, Mg^{++}, $CO_3^=$, repeated endlessly), producing the stable structure of the mineral dolomite with, relative to calcite, slightly different angles and a lowered symmetry.

The effective ionic radii of the Mg^{++} and Fe^{++} ions, on the other hand, are almost the same (the Fe^{++} ion is the larger by about 6 percent), and hence these ions can and do substitute for each other in any proportion. Thus there is complete isomorphism from magnesite to siderite, and also from dolomite [$CaMg(CO_3)_2$] to a ferroan analogue [$CaFe(CO_3)_2$], which has been called ferrodolomite. Material with a composition intermediate between dolomite and ferrodolomite is called ferroan dolomite or ankerite.

The degree to which one cation can substitute for another in the rhombohedral carbonates may be determined by an examination of the actual distribution of analyses of pure mineral samples. According to Figure 109, based on data from a careful study by Ford (1917), calcite can accept as much as 4 percent Mg^{++} * and 6 percent Fe^{++} ions in place of Ca^{++} ions, and dolomite can accept 15 to 20 percent excess Ca^{++} and as much as 7 percent excess Mg^{++} (these conclusions appear to hold for surface temperatures; at high temperatures much more substitution is possible).

In addition to showing the limits of substitution, Figure 109 shows which are the most commonly found mineral compositions. Thus the diagram shows a marked concentration of analyses corresponding to nearly pure calcite, with only 1 or 2 percent Mg^{++} or Fe^{++}. Another concentration corresponds to fairly pure dolomite con-

* This conclusion seems to hold only for inorganically deposited calcite; some organisms appear able to deposit much larger amounts of Mg^{++} in calcite crystals (p. 228).

taining up to 5 percent Fe^{++} and a small excess of Ca^{++} over the theoretical composition. Dolomite with greater amounts of Fe^{++} is also common, in particular dolomite in which the numerical (not weight) ratio of the cations approaches $2Ca^{++}:1Mg^{++}:1Fe^{++}$, but with slightly more Mg^{++} than Fe^{++} and slightly more Ca^{++} than the sum of the others. This suggests that carbonate with the composition $Ca_2MgFe(CO_3)_4$ has an enhanced stability, and by some the name ankerite has been used to specify material of approximately this composition. Nevertheless, analyses are spread over the whole range from this composition to that of theoretical dolomite. Analyses showing an ionic ratio $Mg^{++}:Fe^{++}$ less than 1 are not so common.

Aragonite has the same chemical composition as calcite and therefore consists likewise of Ca^{++}

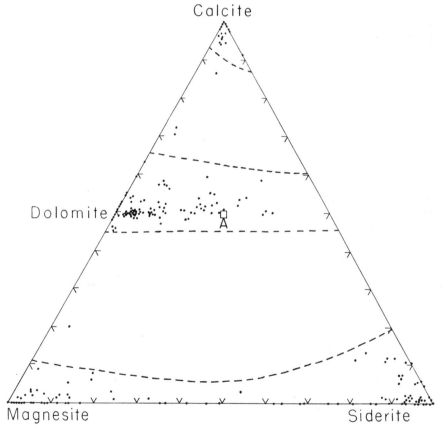

Figure 109. Chemical analysis of carbonate minerals, plotted by molar percent of $CaCO_3$ (top of triangle), $MgCO_3$ (left base), and $FeCO_3$ (right base). After Ford (1917) [includes all analyses of calcite-group minerals available to Ford]. The square, A, marks the composition $Ca_2MgFe(CO_3)_4$, theoretical ankerite.

and $CO_3^=$ ions, but the ions are packed differently * and a little more closely, producing a greater specific gravity. The aragonite structure is so built that it will not tolerate even the few percent Mg^{++} or Fe^{++} that can enter the calcite structure, though it may accept small amounts of the larger Sr^{++} and Ba^{++} ions. On the other hand, small amounts of the $SO_4^=$ ion can enter the aragonite structure.

A third form of $CaCO_3$ (μ-$CaCO_3$, sometimes called vaterite) is known (Johnston, Merwin, and Williamson, 1916; Gibson, Wyckoff, and Merwin, 1925), but it is of no importance in geology.

The stability relations of calcite and aragonite were studied with care by Johnston, Merwin, and Williamson (1916). At all temperatures and pressures likely to be encountered in sedimentary environments, calcite is the stable form. Nevertheless, aragonite commonly forms instead of calcite, and once formed it may be metastable for long periods. Conditions favoring the precipitation of aragonite rather than calcite from solutions saturated in $CaCO_3$ are: relatively warm water, supersaturation, high alkalinity (which increases the likelihood of supersaturation), seeds of aragonite or other orthorhombic carbonates or of orthorhombic sulphates, or presence of appreciable $SO_4^=$ in the solution. As $SO_4^=$ ions are present in all sea water and supersaturation is almost the normal state in the warm parts of the ocean, aragonite appears to be the form normally produced by chemical precipitation in the sea. The opposite conditions favor the deposition of calcite or the conversion of aragonite into calcite; thus meteoric water, being normally very low in salts, tends to destroy aragonite. If connate water rich in $SO_4^=$ is trapped with aragonite in sediments, however, it may preserve the aragonite for many millions of years; aragonite is known in the shells of many Triassic and Jurassic ammonites and has been reported in certain Pennsylvanian nautiloids preserved in asphalt (Fischer and Finley, 1949).

The important carbonate minerals, as they oc-

cur in rocks, can rarely be accurately distinguished by inspection, at least without carefully checked experience on the particular group of rocks being studied. Chemical analysis (though the Ca-Mg separation is tedious and subject to error), X-ray diffraction patterns, and differential thermal analysis enable one to determine them, but in a mixture one can only determine the relative amounts, not their distribution in the rock. Optical methods easily separate aragonite from the others, but distinction between the hexagonal carbonates is difficult unless there is a textural difference, as there commonly is (Fig. 114, center, p. 241). For rapid laboratory use a number of serviceable staining techniques have been developed, but as they depend mainly on the order of solubility of the carbonates in very dilute acid (the order is: aragonite, calcite, dolomite and ankerite, magnesite and the other hexagonal carbonates), they fail with very fine-grained material, the solubility of which is more affected by grain size than by mineral composition. Aragonite can be told from calcite by Meigen's reaction (Holmes, 1921, p. 262–263); it stains much more rapidly then calcite in hot $Co(NO_3)_2$, both in powdered form (if not too fine) and in polished section. Calcite can be told from dolomite because it stains more rapidly in cold $Cu(NO_3)_2$ (Rodgers, 1940). Dolomite can be told from ankerite by staining the latter with acidified $K_3Fe(CN)_6$ (Henbest, 1931, p. 362). The literature on the carbonate stains has been carefully summarized by Hügi (1945).

When relatively pure and compact, the carbonates may also be distinguished by careful measurement of their specific gravities. The specific gravities are as follows:

Aragonite	2.93–2.95
Calcite (pure)	2.715
Dolomite	2.87
[theoretical $CaMg(CO_3)_2$]	
Ankerite	2.99
[theoretical $Ca_2MgFe(CO_3)_4$]	
Magnesite	2.96 plus

In addition to the carbonates, many other minerals may be present in carbonate rocks, but rarely in large proportions. Because of the ease with which acid removes the carbonates, these impurities are readily isolated as insoluble residues,

---

* The difference is roughly that between cubic and hexagonal closest packing, but the planar $CO_3^=$ ion reduces the symmetry of calcite from cubic to rhombohedral and of aragonite from hexagonal to orthorhombic (see Bragg, 1924a; 1937, p. 117).

and they have received much study (McQueen, 1931; Ireland and others, 1947). Where the insoluble residue is fragmental, it may be treated by the same petrographic methods as any sand or clay, but commonly it consists largely or entirely of non-fragmental silica or chert. Chert in carbonate rocks is dealt with in the next chapter.

The different carbonate minerals occur in widely varying proportions in the carbonate rocks. Chemically precipitated calcium carbonate, such as travertine or the lime deposits on the Great Bahama Bank (p. 231), commonly consists of aragonite, but in deposits of any considerable geologic age aragonite is quite subordinate and is present chiefly in shells or in the oöids of oölite. Calcite and dolomite occur mixed in all proportions, but some evidence suggests that rocks consisting almost entirely of one or the other are commoner than those consisting of nearly equal amounts of the two. Steidtmann (1917, Fig. 1, p. 437) plotted the chemical analyses of 1,148 carbonate rocks from the literature and found that nearly half the analyses showed less than 10 percent $MgCO_3$ and less than 15 percent impurities. Another large group of analyses contained from 36 to 46 percent $MgCO_3$, close to the theoretical composition of the mineral dolomite, and was equally low in impurities. Analyses with intermediate amounts of $MgCO_3$ were less common and generally showed higher proportions of impurities. These analyses do not, of course, give the mineral composition directly, but in view of the known ranges of composition of the minerals, a good majority of the rocks represented by Steidtmann's analyses consist of either calcite or dolomite almost to the exclusion of the other, whereas rocks consisting of a mixture of the two minerals are distinctly less common and ordinarily more impure.

Quite possibly Steidtmann's analyses, which were taken largely from publications on commercially useful carbonate rocks, are unduly weighted in favor of the commercially valuable pure calcite and pure dolomite rocks. At least some of the same conclusions can be drawn, however, from other groups of analyses not affected by the same bias. One such group is a series of 240 chemical analyses (not used by Steidtmann) that were made for J. P. Lesley (1879) on pairs of samples taken from each bed of a 371-foot section of Lower Ordovician carbonate rocks near Harrisburg, Pennsylvania. Figure 110 is a plot of these analyses showing the relation of carbonate composition to insoluble matter (presumably chiefly silica, as sesquioxides were separately determined; a plot of carbonate composition against sesquioxide content is very similar). Like Steidtmann's analyses, these show a marked concentration below 10 percent $MgCO_3$ with low impurities, and a tendency for $MgCO_3$ and impurities to increase together. There is no concentration of analyses near the theoretical composition of the mineral dolomite, but it is known that typical pure dolostone is rare in the beds on the southeastern side of the Appalachian Valley and Ridge Province, where the specimens analyzed were taken.

A series of 252 specimens taken from the 8,000-foot Arbuckle group of carbonate rocks (Upper Cambrian and Lower Ordovician) of Oklahoma has been analyzed mineralogically by Merritt (Decker and Merritt, 1928), who distinguished calcite, dolomite, and insoluble residue. Figure 111, a triangular plot of these analyses, shows that whereas entirely pure calcite rocks and dolomite rocks are rare or absent, rocks containing a high proportion of one or the other are much commoner than rocks containing more equal proportions. A tendency for the mixed rocks to be more impure is also suggested.

How much ankerite is present in common carbonate rocks is unknown; probably much that has been reported as the mineral dolomite is actually ferroan and some may approach $Ca_2MgFe(CO_3)_4$. According to Steidtmann (1917, p. 434), staining showed that all the dolomite other than vein dolomite in the rocks he studied contained Fe^{++}, though commonly a small amount. In some of Lesley's analyses iron was determined as carbonate; generally it was a few tenths of a percent but in a few it reached 2 percent. It showed a general positive correlation with $MgCO_3$, but with many striking exceptions. A curious rock consisting of about equal amounts of calcite and ankerite (relatively high in Fe^{++}) was found by C. D. Holmes (personal communication) to be fairly common in certain bodies of glacial drift in

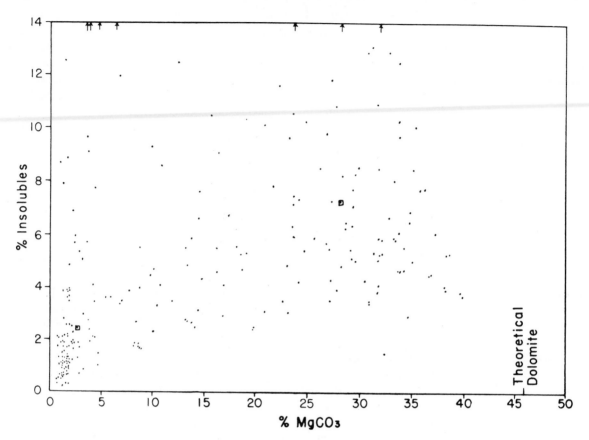

Figure 110. Chemical analyses of carbonate rocks from near Harrisburg, Pennsylvania, plotted by weight percent of MgCO3 (abscissa) and insolubles (ordinate). Analyses from Lesley (1879). Arrows at upper margin indicate analyses with more than 14 percent insolubles.

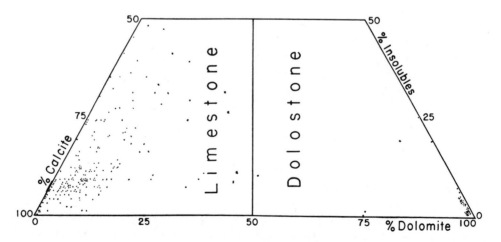

Figure 111. Mineral analyses of carbonate rocks from Arbuckle group, Oklahoma, plotted by volume percent of calcite (left base of triangle), dolomite (right base), and insolubles (top). Analyses from Decker and Merritt (1928).

central New York State, though its bedrock source has not yet been identified.

Texture

In contrast with the siliceous fragmental rocks, the grains of a carbonate rock can rarely be separated and studied individually but must be studied chiefly in the aggregate, in polished or thin section. Hence measuring the size, roundness, or three-dimensional shape of large numbers of grains in a carbonate rock is less easy and more time-consuming than in a conglomerate or sandstone or even a shale that can be disaggregated without appreciable loss. Furthermore, measurements of grain size in polished or thin section do not give quite the same results as measurements of the same grains after separation (Krumbein, 1935; Krumbein and Pettijohn, 1938, p. 129–134; Chayes, 1950). In fact, describing the texture of a carbonate rock may be more like describing that of an igneous rock than of a sandstone or shale.

Accordingly, whereas the Wentworth grade scale is now used very generally for describing the grain size of the siliceous fragmental rocks (p. 161), no such agreement has been reached for the carbonate rocks, and opinion seems fairly evenly divided between those who advocate the Wentworth scale or a modification and those who urge a clean break and a radically different

TABLE 12. ALLING GRADE SCALE FOR CARBONATE ROCKS. AFTER DEFORD (1946).

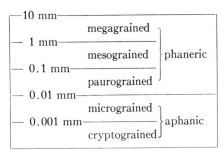

scheme. Among the former may be mentioned Payne (1942, p. 1706), who would adapt the Wentworth scheme for crystalline-textured rocks like the carbonates, as shown in Table 11. Among the latter may be mentioned DeFord (1946), who advocates using Alling's grade scale (p. 164), partly because it was deliberately proposed for use in thin section rather than on separated grains. For the size classes, DeFord proposes the terms given in Table 12. Further, each of these classes can be subdivided into four units if need be.

Faced with these divergent opinions, students must be prepared to recognize and understand scales of both types. We recommend, however, the Wentworth-type scale, because of its more practical dividing line between phaneritic and aphanitic rocks, i.e., between those in which the grains are readily visible to the naked eye and those in which they are not, and because of the advantages of having a single grade scale for all sedimentary rocks.

The range of common grain sizes in limestones runs from a micron to several millimeters. Moreover, many individual rocks exhibit a wide range of sizes; not uncommonly a few relatively large grains are set in a very finely crystalline or aphanitic matrix. Dolostones, however, are rarely either lithographic or granular crystalline, and any one rock is generally uniform in grain size. Where limestone and dolostone are associated in the same formation, the dolostone is normally the coarser.

In most carbonate rocks the grains are interlocking, even in those limestones that were evidently fragmental and still exhibit cross-stratifi-

TABLE 11. WENTWORTH GRADE SCALE FOR CARBONATE ROCKS. AFTER PAYNE (1942).

	4 mm and over	
		granular crystalline
	2 mm	
		very coarsely crystalline
	1 mm	
		coarsely crystalline
phaneritic or phanerocrystalline	½ mm	
		medium crystalline
	¼ mm	
		finely crystalline
	⅛ mm	
		very finely crystalline
	⅟₁₆ mm	
		sublithographic
aphanitic or microcrystalline	⅟₂₅₆ mm or 4 microns	
		lithographic *

* Payne distinguishes the rocks with grains less than 1 micron from the rest as cryptocrystalline, but the distinction would seldom be used.

cation; presumably the original pore spaces in these rocks have been filled with calcite deposited in optical continuity with the fragmental grains. Such a texture is, of course, well known in sedimentary quartzite (p. 25), but whereas completely interlocking texture is relatively exceptional among the siliceous fragmental rocks, it is the rule in the carbonate rocks. Hence the shape of the grains in the average limestone has little relation to their original shape at the time of deposition and is of little significance to the geologist; roundness and angularity carry none of the meaning they do for quartz sand grains. Grains of the mineral dolomite tend, however, to develop a characteristic shape, the rhombohedron $(10\bar{1}1)$. This tendency is particularly well developed in rocks containing some dolomite crystals set in a finely crystalline or aphanitic matrix of calcite (Fig. 114, center, p. 241), but commonly it is expressed in part even in rocks consisting entirely of dolomite.

Descriptive Nomenclature

The nomenclature of the common carbonate rocks is in a very unsatisfactory state (Rodgers, 1954b). Some of the commonest terms are used in several senses, and often it is difficult to determine in a given article or report which sense is intended. For example, in the nineteenth century the word limestone was generally used for all the carbonate rocks except those made entirely of magnesite or siderite, but since 1900 there has been a growing though by no means uniform tendency to restrict it to those rocks in which the dominant mineral is calcite. This narrower usage is observed in the present book; that is, limestone stands for a rock containing more than 50 percent of the common carbonate minerals, of which more than 50 percent is calcite or aragonite.

There are all intermediates between rocks composed entirely of calcite and those composed entirely of dolomite; for this series, the following terminology may be used:

Limestone: sedimentary rock containing more than 50 percent of the minerals calcite (plus aragonite) and dolomite (including ankerite), in which the calcite (plus aragonite) is more abundant than the dolomite.

Dolomitic limestone: limestone in which dolomite is more than 10 percent but less than 50 percent of the combined calcite and dolomite.

Calcitic dolostone: dolostone in which calcite is more than 10 percent but less than 50 percent of the combined dolomite and calcite.

Dolostone: sedimentary rock containing more than 50 percent of the minerals dolomite (including ankerite) and calcite (plus aragonite), in which the dolomite is more abundant than the calcite.

The term magnesian limestone is occasionally found; unfortunately it has been used in at least two quite different senses, on the one hand as a synonym of dolostone (e.g., the Magnesian limestone in the Permian of England, which is largely pure dolostone), and on the other for those calcite limestones containing an appreciable content of Mg^{++} but *not* in the mineral dolomite. The term seems to have little utility.

The term *chalk* (from the Latin *calx,* lime or limestone *) has been applied in Britain for centuries to the well-known white weakly cohesive calcite rock in the Upper Cretaceous of southern England. In America, however, it is now fairly commonly used for any weakly cohesive limestone, and even for some fairly clayey rocks (Austin chalk, Niobrara chalk). Another term more commonly applied to weakly cohesive clayey calcite rocks is *marl.* To be sure, marl has been used in some quite different senses as well—for the calcareous deposits of fresh-water lakes, whether clayey or not, and, in Britain at least, for any weakly cohesive clayey rock, whether calcareous or not, as in the name Keuper Marl, applied to red mudstones in the Upper Triassic of the Midlands. Despite these possible ambiguities, both chalk and marl are terms worth preserving with definite meanings, and we recommend the simple scheme in Table 13 for the rocks com-

* The continental languages still use derivatives of the Latin *calx* for limestone: Kalk, calcaire, calcare, caliza; they designate what the British call chalk by derivatives of the Latin *creta* (a rock from the island of Crete): Kreide, craie, creta, greda.

posed of well mixed (not merely interbedded) argillaceous and calcareous matter.

Correns (Barth, Correns, and Eskola, 1939, p. 200; also Pettijohn, 1957, Fig. 99) has proposed an elaborate scheme of intermediate subdivisions between clay, marl, and limestone or chalk (Kalk), which may be useful where detailed distinctions are needed.

Appreciable amounts of other impurities in limestone and dolostone (between 10 and 50 percent) may be indicated by such adjectives as sandy, silty, or cherty.

Size terms such as aphanitic or medium-grained may also be used as modifiers for limestone and dolostone. For limestone composed of mechanically deposited grains (such as fragments of shells, comminuted algal carbonate, chemically precipitated but mechanically transported aragonite needles or pellets, or pieces of older limestone), Grabau's terms *calcirudite, calcarenite,* and *calcilutite* (Grabau, 1903) have been widely accepted. The corresponding English terms *lime-conglomerate* (or *lime-breccia*), *lime-sandstone,* and *lime-mudstone* (and, for the unconsolidated materials, *lime-gravel* or *lime-rubble, lime-sand,* and *lime-mud*) have also been used (Cloud and Barnes, 1948, p. 17) though less widely; they are used in this chapter. The limiting diameters are taken at 2 mm and $\frac{1}{16}$ mm. (The terms drewite and vaughanite, for lime-mud and lime-mudstone respectively, are unnecessary [Thorp, 1935, p. 79–81] and should be abandoned.)

TABLE 13. CLASSIFICATION OF CALCAREOUS-ARGILLACEOUS ROCKS AND SEDIMENTS.

Weakly Cohesive Rock	Thoroughly Indurated Rock
Chalk (wider sense)	Limestone
—————75% lime carbonate, 25% clay—————	
Marl	Marlstone (Bradley, 1931a, p. 7)
—————25% lime carbonate, 75% clay—————	
Clay	Claystone (Ingram, 1953), unless fissile; in that case, shale

GENESIS OF LIMESTONE

Organic Limestone

Sources of organic CaCO₃. Calcium carbonate, deposited in the form of shells, carapaces, and other organic structures, can form thick deposits, and some at least of the limestone formations in the geologic record are composed wholly or chiefly of such material. The form or shape in which the calcium carbonate is deposited is highly specific for each organism; indeed, for most fossil invertebrate animals it is the sole record of the animal, and the infinite variety of such forms has been the principal study of the invertebrate paleontologist. For the present discussion, however, a few broad generalizations suffice.

Animals that form limy deposits take the calcium into their tissues in some soluble form and then secrete $CaCO_3$ to make compact and distinctively organized shell structures. Some aquatic plants (e.g., Characea and Dasycladacea) likewise use lime within their tissues to form distinctive structures, but many of the calcareous algae merely cause precipitation of $CaCO_3$ from the surrounding film of sea water as they extract from it the CO_2 needed in photosynthesis. This precipitate settles like frost over the surface of the larger thalli (e.g., *Halimeda*) or among the filaments of the microscopic algae, and forms a spongy deposit of loosely aggregated fine particles. Such material tends to slack down into lime-mud on the death of the plant.

The mineral composition of shells, etc., has been studied by many observers, beginning with Sorby, the father of petrography, and is fairly well known (Bøggild, 1930; Lowenstam, 1954). Among the lime-depositing algae, *Halimeda* and related green algae and certain primitive red algae precipitate aragonite; the reef-making coralline red algae, such as *Lithothamnion*, precipitate calcite. Most of the calcareous foraminifers (also those arenaceous foraminifers that use lime as a cement) deposit calcite (Bandy, 1954, has discovered some exceptions); so do most of the calcareous sponges. The hydrocorallines such as *Millepora* deposit aragonite; so do the living reef-making colonial Hexacoralla (Scleractinia), though many simple and especially cold-water corals use calcite. Most modern Octocoralla (Alcyonaria) stiffen their nitrogenous skeletons with calcite spicules, but the one important massive octocoral, *Heliopora,* deposits aragonite.

What the principal Paleozoic corals, the Tetracoralla (Rugosa) and the Tabulata, deposited cannot, of course, be directly determined, as any aragonite would by now have been converted into calcite. In view of the excellent preservation of many details of structure in the fossils of these groups, as contrasted with the invariably inferior preservation of structure in shells and deposits converted from aragonite, it seems probable that these corals deposited calcite. On the other hand, poor preservation of structure suggests that the stromatoporoids may have deposited aragonite. Living lime-depositing brachiopods and bryozoans deposit calcite (an exception among the bryozoans has been reported by Lowenstam, 1954), and there is little reason to doubt that the extinct members of these groups did likewise. The shells of some of the Paleozoic brachiopods were made of coarse crystals and have shown themselves particularly resistant to solution.

Echinoderms are characterized by dermal skeletons consisting of separate plates that grow larger during the life of the animal. Each plate is an individual, optically continuous, calcite grain; in life each is porous and the pores are filled with animal tissue, but after death and decay the pores normally fill with calcite in crystal continuity with the plate, producing a solid grain. The plates tend to fall apart after death, but each individual plate is robust and sturdy and relatively resistant to wear and solution.

Most arthropods build exoskeletons of chitin or related materials, but some stiffen the chitin with layers of calcite. Ostracodes and barnacles build their shells of calcite, and apparently the exoskeletons of trilobites were partly or wholly calcite.

The majority of mollusks build shells made entirely of aragonite, but calcite is deposited by some. An outer layer of calcite is present in the shells of many groups of streptoneuran gastropods and anisomyarian pelecypods; in some pelecypods, such as the oysters, the entire shell is calcite. Lowenstam (1954) has shown that the

ratio of aragonite to calcite may vary widely within a single genus or species among the pelecypods, gastropods, and serpulid worms; in a general way, the higher the temperature, the more aragonite. Among the shell-bearing cephalopods, calcite formed certain specific parts of the shells; thus the aptychi of ammonites, the guards (but probably not the phragmocones) of belemnites, and the siphuncular deposits of certain Paleozoic nautiloids appear to have been calcite, and in many cases these parts are found preserved where the rest of the shell, formed of aragonite, is gone.

Careful work by Clarke and Wheeler (1922) and by Chave (1954) has shown that the shells of many of the calcite-secreting organisms contain considerable quantities of Mg^{++}, whereas less than 1 percent is found in shells made of aragonite. Qualitatively this is explained by the tolerance of the calcite structure for Mg^{++} ions (p. 220), but quantitatively the amount far surpasses that known in inorganic calcite; the maximum recorded is more than 15 percent $MgCO_3$ in the Foraminifera and in four separate classes of the Echinodermata and more than 25 percent in the coralline algae. That the phase present is still calcite has been proved by X-ray analysis (Chave, 1952). Thus organisms are capable of depositing calcite with a composition that would be unstable under ordinary inorganic conditions. The Mg^{++} content of shells of a given invertebrate group is typically higher in warm-water representatives of the group than in cold-water representatives.

With some exceptions, calcite shells tend to be relatively coarse grained and to break down into lime-sand, the grains of which retain some organic structure so that the origin of the fragments can be ascertained. Aragonite shells tend, on the other hand, to be finer grained and to break down into structureless lime-mud, and even if larger fragments or whole shells are preserved, all internal structure is lost if the aragonite is converted into calcite. Aragonite also tends to dissolve more readily than calcite, and perhaps to be replaced more easily by other substances such as dolomite or silica; not uncommonly calcite shells have been preserved where aragonite shells are represented only by molds. As noted above, the calcium carbonate deposited by many of the calcareous algae, whether calcite or aragonite, tends to slack down into lime-mud.

Limestone made of organic CaCO₃. The rocks most obviously made of organic $CaCO_3$ are the deposits of *organic reefs* (p. 88). In the geologic record organic reefs are known to be composed of:

> Calcareous algae
> Sponges
> Archeocyathids
> Hydrocorallines
> Corals (hexacorals,
>   tetracorals, tabulates)
> Stromatoporoids
> Bryozoans
> Tubicolous annelids
> Rudistids
> Oysters

Similar masses may also be formed by the rapid accumulation, in place, of fragments of crinoids or of brachiopod or mollusk shells, though these should probably not be called reefs. Some reefs show excellently preserved organic structure, but in others the structure has been lost by recrystallization of one sort or another, and only the non-bedded (and commonly porous) character of the reef mass, contrasting with the bedded material around it, remains to testify of its origin. The fabric of reef rocks, recent and ancient, is described by Newell (1955a).

Smaller reef masses are commonly bun-shaped or mound-shaped (Fig. 94, p. 180), and larger ones are generally markedly linear, but all may be very irregular; the term reef is rarely applied, however, if the vertical dimension is very small relative to the least horizontal dimension. In size, reefs range up to masses like the great Capitan Reef in the Permian of Texas and New Mexico, which is not less than 60 miles long, 1 mile wide, and 1,500 feet thick. The distribution of organic reefs through the geologic column has been summarized by Twenhofel (1950) (though he forgot to mention the important rudistid reefs in the Cretaceous rocks of eastern Mexico).

Related to, and commonly part of or grading into, organic reef masses are the structures called *stromatolites* (Kalkowsky, 1908; Pia, 1928; Cloud, 1942). They appear to form on and over colonies of blue-green algae (and to some extent green algae).* The mucilaginous jelly around the cells of the blue-green algae catches whatever lime-mud drifts by, forming a thin layer of $CaCO_3$ (in addition some $CaCO_3$ may be precipitated as the algae withdraw CO_2 from the sea water in photosynthesis, stiffening the layer); the algae then grow out over the surface of the newly deposited layer, and the process is repeated. The result is a deposit of laminated but otherwise structureless $CaCO_3$, recording the position of successive growths of the algae. The laminae may be flat but more commonly they are humped up, forming bun-shaped heads of varying sizes or long parallel fingers (Fig. 112). Free ball-like masses of small size also occur. Stromatolites occur in considerable abundance in limestone formations from the Precambrian upward.†

Other types of organic limestone are those consisting of bedded accumulations of shells and shell fragments. Typical is *coquina,* lime-breccia made of shells and shell fragments with only enough cement to form a cohesive mass and hence having a high porosity. (The fully cemented equivalent has been called *coquinite.*) Coquina commonly consists of whole or partly broken shells of mollusks or brachiopods or of echinoderm plates, such as echinoid spines or crinoid stem segments. Finer-grained equivalents may consist of ostracode valves, tests of foraminifers,

---

* Some writers have maintained that stromatolites are inorganic and concretionary (Holtedahl, 1921, and references there cited). The common association of stromatolites with oölite (p. 233) may be significant, though it may only indicate conditions favorable for the precipitation of $CaCO_3$, whether inorganically or by algae.

† Generic and specific names have commonly been given to the different shapes of stromatolites. The stromatolites appear, however, to have been produced not by any single organisms but by colonies, often including species from several families or even classes of algae, and the shape of the colony is determined not by the species of organisms present but by the environmental conditions of growth. Hence names such as cryptozoon and collenia do not refer to true biological genera but merely indicate form, and they are best spelled with small initial letters. The different kinds of stromatolites are known to have great value in local correlation in many areas, like any other particularly distinctive and environmentally controlled lithology, but they cannot be used for interprovincial correlation as if they were biological genera (see Cloud, 1942).

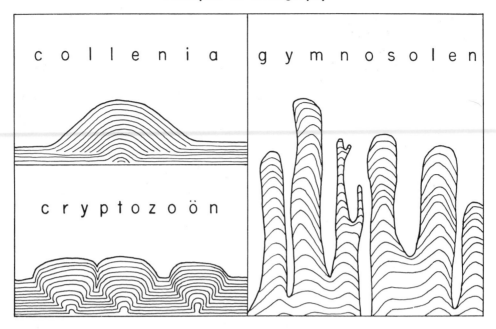

Figure 112. Shapes taken by some stromatolites. After Pia (1928).

pteropod shells, or coccoliths (minute plates and rods secreted by planktonic flagellate algae). The last three types accumulate in vast quantities in places on the floor of the deep ocean and form the widespread calcareous oozes (*Globigerina* and pteropod oozes; p. 57). Foraminifers have also accumulated in thick deposits in shallow water, as, for example, in the West European chalk and in many fusuline limestones of late Paleozoic age.

Chemical Limestone

Chemical precipitation of $CaCO_3$. Like any other soluble or slightly soluble salt, $CaCO_3$ has a definite limit of solubility in water, which varies with temperature and pressure and also with the pH and the concentration of other dissolved ions in the water. If the concentration of $CaCO_3$ in the water falls below this limit, the water is undersaturated and will tend to dissolve any solid $CaCO_3$ with which it is in contact. If the concentration rises above this limit, the water is supersaturated and, theoretically, solid $CaCO_3$ will be precipitated. Supersaturated water solutions of $CaCO_3$ are metastable, however, under

many conditions (supersaturation is apparently normal in warm sea water), so that precipitation occurs only after disturbance of the metastability, as by seeding or agitation. Nevertheless, any process producing supersaturation will tend to cause precipitation.

The solubility relations of $CaCO_3$ in sea water are complicated, and no attempt will be made to deal with them rigorously here (the student is referred to the pertinent literature: Buch, Harvey, Wattenberg, and Gripenberg, 1932; Wattenberg, 1933; Moberg, Greenberg, Revelle, and Allen, 1934; Revelle and Fleming, 1934; and to the masterly summary by Pia, 1932). The quantitatively most significant factor affecting the solubility of $CaCO_3$ in water is the CO_2 content of the water; under normal surface conditions a decrease in the CO_2 content decreases the solubility of $CaCO_3$ and tends to cause supersaturation and precipitation. The CO_2 content is itself affected by several factors, most notably the temperature; an increase in the temperature of water saturated with CO_2 and $CaCO_3$ decreases the solubility of the CO_2, driving it off and thus producing supersaturation with respect to $CaCO_3$. Plants such as algae that use CO_2 in their life processes may also deplete the water of CO_2 and cause precipitation of $CaCO_3$ if equilibrium with atmospheric CO_2 is not immediately regained, as it normally is not. A decrease in the partial pressure of CO_2 in the atmosphere may also reduce the CO_2 content of water in equilibrium with it, but the resulting decrease in the solubility of $CaCO_3$ is almost negligible. The solubility of $CaCO_3$ in sea water is also decreased by an increase in alkalinity, as, for example, when ammonia is produced by the decay of nitrogenous matter or in the life processes of certain bacteria, or by an increase in salinity, especially by an increase in the concentration of Ca^{++} ions.

Attempts to calculate the degree of undersaturation or supersaturation of $CaCO_3$ in actual sea water have led to divergent results. Early attempts led to estimates of improbably high supersaturation (14 times, for example; Gee and others, 1932, p. 147). Even after detailed investigation of the numerous factors controlling the solubility, complete agreement has not been reached. The German investigators (Wattenberg, 1933; Wattenberg and Timmermann, 1936; Wattenberg, 1936) have calculated from the best available data that warm surface sea water contains 2 to 4 times as much $CaCO_3$ as would be present at exact saturation under the same conditions; the American investigators (Gee and others, 1932, p. 151; Moberg, Greenberg, Revelle, and Allen, 1934, p. 271–272; Revelle and Fleming, 1934; Revelle, 1934) have concluded from observations and experiments that tropical sea water is at most only slightly supersaturated and that a further correction in the calculations is necessary. All agree, however, that the warm surface water of tropical seas is at least saturated and probably mildly supersaturated with $CaCO_3$, whereas the cold water of polar seas and of the deep ocean is undersaturated.

These relations are neatly demonstrated by the distribution of the calcareous oozes formed by the accumulation of the shells of pelagic foraminifers (chiefly *Globigerina*) and pteropods. The shells sink, after being abandoned by the animals, until they reach bottom or are dissolved in undersaturated water. As mentioned in Chapter 3 (p. 58), such oozes are present on the floor of the open ocean in tropical latitudes in all depths less than about 15,000 feet, unless masked by sediments from the lands, but are rare at greater depths. There is therefore a foraminiferal "snow-line" at approximately that depth, below which shells are dissolved faster than they "snow down" from above. (The elevation of this line differs from basin to basin on the ocean floor, depending on the course of the deep currents bringing cold undersaturated water from the polar seas.) Several thousand feet higher than the foraminiferal "snow-line" is a pteropod "snow-line," for the delicate aragonite shells of the pteropods dissolve somewhat more readily than the calcite shells of the foraminifers.

In view of the saturation or supersaturation of shallow tropical waters, one might expect chemical precipitation of $CaCO_3$ to be widespread, but actually it appears to occur in only a few areas, notably on a part of the Great Bahama Bank at the mouth of the Gulf of Mexico (Fig. 41, p. 94), and even here it has been denied. The bank illustrates very well the conditions necessary for large-scale chemical precipitation of $CaCO_3$ and deserves a brief summary. (The literature on the Great Bahama Bank is voluminous and contradictory; a complete bibliography to 1939 can be found in Thorp, 1939. See also Cloud and Barnes, 1948, p. 81–84. The present account follows mainly Black, 1933; C. L. Smith, 1940; and Illing, 1954.)

The Great Bahama Bank is a vast area of shoal water, not more than 25 feet deep over more than 25,000 square miles. Fairly small islands (cays) fringe its eastern edge; farther west, on the west edge of the Tongue of the Ocean, a deep embayment in the bank, lies Andros Island, composed of Pleistocene oölite and fringed by mangrove swamps on the west and organic reefs on the east. All around the bank, the bottom drops off very abruptly into deep water. The shallow water over the bank is warmed more by the sun than the surface water of the surrounding deeper seas. Evaporation, already rapid in this climate, is therefore even more rapid on the bank, and a net inflow of water onto the bank must replace that lost. Hence the salinity as well as temperature of the water on the bank is raised. Conditions are thus well nigh ideal for supersaturation with respect to $CaCO_3$, and storms, stirring up the calcareous bottom sediments, provide both agitation and seeding to induce chemical precipitation.

In the lee of Andros Island, nearly 4,000 square miles of the bank is covered by lime-mud composed of aragonite, much of it in the form of needles 1 to 10 microns long. The water is so shallow that every storm stirs up the mud and makes the water milky. Unquestionably great quantities of lime-mud are swept off the bank at every storm, probably to cascade down the slopes as turbidity currents into the surrounding deep basins, yet these losses appear to be made good by continued formation of aragonite. Virtually no macroscopic bottom organisms can survive in the mud area, and hence such organisms are found only in isolated colonies on local areas of hard rock bottom, chiefly on the margins of the mud deposit. Reportedly the only shells common in the mud itself are those of land snails blown off the island of Andros!

It would seem reasonable to believe that the aragonite mud in this area is the result of direct chemical precipitation. Some investigators have maintained, however, that bacteria are the principal agents. The original suggestion of Drew (1913) that denitrifying bacteria on the bank itself are responsible has been disproved and abandoned; a later suggestion by Bavendamm (1932) that ammonifying and perhaps sulphate-reducing bacteria in the mangrove swamps of Andros precipitate the $CaCO_3$, which is then swept out on the bank, seems quantitatively a quite insufficient explanation. Experimental work by Gee and others (1932; reviewed by Gee, 1932) has shown that, in the absence of bacteria, $CaCO_3$ is precipitated from warm supersaturated sea water as aragonite needles a few microns long, indistinguishable from the needles on the Great Bahama Bank. There can be little question, therefore, that the bulk of the mud on the bank is indeed of inorganic chemical origin.

But aragonite mud of this sort covers less than a fifth of the area of the Great Bahama Bank. In another fairly small part, mainly a strip along the islands on the eastern edge and along the east side of Andros, organic reefs are found, and also much organic debris, in part derived from and surrounding them. The major part of the bank, however, is floored by lime-sand composed mainly of micro-crystalline aragonite (the grain size of the aragonite crystals composing the sand is 1 to 4 microns) and containing few or no organic fragments. Illing (1954) has shown that this sand, too, results from chemical precipitation, the precipitated aragonite being progressively cemented, by additional fine-grained aragonite, into aggregates, at first friable and then firmly coherent, and even into aggregates of aggregates. The precipitation takes place principally where tidal currents of ocean water sweep into the bank and are warmed up; the aggregation is apparently a response to the turbulence of these currents. The currents then sort and abrade and transport the sand-sized aggregates far and wide over the bank. In some situations, the particles acquire a superficial oölitic coating, and in others, especially near the bank margins, true oöids are forming today (Newell, 1955b, p. 311–312). Bacteria and algae may be of some importance in cementing the aggregates, but probably not in the original precipitation.

Aragonite sand of this sort has not yet been reported elsewhere, although, now that Illing has called attention to it, it may well be found in other areas of shallow-water calcareous sediments. Fine needles of aragonite, like those in the mud west of Andros, have been found in bottom samples from other protected shoal areas in that region—west of Abaco Island on the Little Bahama Bank, behind the Florida Keys, and around the nearby Tortugas and Marquesas Islands, but elsewhere in the world they have been reported only at Tubuai Manu (Maiao) Island in the Society Islands (Thorp, in Williams, 1933, p. 79–80), and they appear to be absent from calcareous sediments in other tropical areas such as Samoa (Bramlette, 1926) and the Great Barrier Reef of Australia (Vaughan, 1918). Perhaps inorganic chemical deposition of $CaCO_3$, though so prominent in the Bahamas, is relatively rare in the world as a whole, even though the tropical seas tend to be supersaturated, because lime-depositing organisms thrive in those seas and normally remove the CaCO₃ from the water fast enough to prevent disturbance of the super-saturation.

Outside the sea, chemical precipitation of $CaCO_3$ is known around many springs and waterfalls in limestone country, and also in limestone caverns, wherever running or trickling water already saturated with $CaCO_3$ is warmed or evaporated or both. The deposits take the form of calcareous sinter or tufa or travertine,* and commonly exhibit fine concentric banding, though some are porous and structureless. Similar deposits, commonly structureless, may form in lakes whose water has become supersaturated with $CaCO_3$; fresh-water green or blue-green algae are thought, however, to be the principal agents of deposition in most modern lakes, whether fresh or salt. $CaCO_3$ may also be deposited chemically in the soils of semiarid or arid regions, where lime-bearing water evaporates instead of finding its way to the water table. In these areas it may form concretionary masses in the subsoil (as in the B horizon of prairie soils) or masses or layers close to the surface (as in the A horizon of more desert soils), producing the widespread calcrete deposits of many arid regions, for example, the caliche of parts of western North America.

Limestone made of chemical CaCO₃. Because of the relative instability of aragonite, ancient lithified equivalents of the lime-mud at present forming on the Great Bahama Bank would by now have been recrystallized to calcite and would have lost any direct textural evidence of their chemical origin. After recrystallization, the rock should be very finely crystalline to aphanitic lime-mudstone, having few fossils. Such rock is not uncommon in the geological record, and perhaps much of it has formed by the accumulation of chemically precipitated $CaCO_3$. Cloud and Barnes (1948, p. 79–109) have made a strong case for such an origin for the lime-mudstone of the Ellenburger group (Lower Ordovician) of Central Texas, and a similar origin has been

proposed for the high-calcium limestone of "Mosheim" facies (mainly Middle Ordovician) in the Appalachian region (Cooper, 1944, p. 282–283). Some limestones of this sort show traces of pellets and aggregates and were probably originally aragonite sands rather than muds (Fig. 114, left, p. 241), but they are still as fine-grained as the true lime-mudstones. A chemical origin is also possible for the aphanitic carbonate rock (commonly dolostone) associated with salt and gypsum deposits in many places; for example, the dolostone in the Carlsbad and Rustler formations of the Permian of West Texas and adjacent New Mexico (King, 1948, p. 65, 88, 91). Newell and others (1953, p. 121) suggest that this rock was a chemical precipitate of aragonite, like the modern Bahama mud, and was later converted to dolomite.

Oölitic texture in limestone is probably a sign of chemical precipitation. *Oölite* * is that variety of limestone largely made up of small spheroidal particles (oöids) showing concentric and commonly also radial structure. In most oöids, the structure is concentric to a core of extraneous material such as a sand grain, a chip of shell, or a piece of older limestone. Microscopic studies by Sorby (1879, p. 74–76) and others (Kalkowsky, 1908; Black, 1933, p. 462; Hatch, Rastall, and Black, 1938, p. 175–178) have shown the structure of oöids to be of three main types: very fine aragonite arranged concentrically (the *c*-axes of the grains being tangential †), fairly fine calcite arranged radially (the *c*-axes being radial), and relatively coarse calcite with little or no arrangement. Of these the first is the chief one

* Pia (1933, p. 13) suggests that travertine be used as a general term for all these materials, sinter for the solid massive chiefly inorganic variety, and tufa (German Tuff) for the weaker porous variety deposited largely by plants.

* Many recent writers have used the term *oölite* for the individual particles in such rock, but in England the word has been consistently used for the rock since the days of William Smith. Others have proposed the term oölith for the particles, but oölith is barely distinguishable from oölite, and moreover it is the German word for the rock. The term *oöid,* proposed by Kalkowsky (1908, p. 71–72), seems satisfactory. The common restriction to grains smaller than 2 mm in diameter seems reasonable; where the grains are larger the terms pisolite and pisoid are applicable.

† Eardley (1938, p. 1375) seems to doubt Sorby's statement on this point, but Sorby (1879, p. 74) indicated very clearly that he determined the optical elongation of the aragonite grains.

among modern oöids and is presumably the primary structure of most; the last is the result of ordinary recrystallization of the first. The radial calcite oöids predominate in most ancient unmetamorphosed oölite, and appear to result from a special kind of recrystallization of the aragonite oöids. As shown by Eardley (1938, p. 1384). any clay trapped with the aragonite during growth is segregated into radial spindles during such recrystallization.

The origin of oölite has been debated for over a century. Some have held it to be organic, probably algal (Wethered, 1890; Rothpletz, 1892; Kalkowsky, 1908), or else precipitated by the action of decaying organic matter (Linck, 1903); others have considered it inorganic, formed by chemical growth in colloidal suspension (Bucher, 1918), or by accretion on rolling grains, either physically (as on a snowball, Sorby, 1879, p. 74) or chemically, above water (Matthews, 1930) or below. The last view, proposed a century ago by De La Beche (1851, p. 123), has been applied to the oöids in the Bahamas by Vaughan (1910, p. 175–177), Black (1933, p. 462), and Illing (1954, p. 43–44), and virtually proved for those of Great Salt Lake by Eardley (1938, p. 1359–1387), and it may be taken as the most probable mode of origin for all. If so, oölite in the geologic record indicates chemical precipitation of $CaCO_3$ around nuclei in agitated water.

Fresh-water limestone is present in many parts of the geologic column—beds occur in the Dunkard group (Permian) of West Virginia and Ohio (Cross, Smith and Arkle, 1950); the Newark group (Triassic) of Connecticut (Krynine, 1950, p. 106–111); the Morrison formation (Jurassic) and related rocks of Colorado and Wyoming (Baker, Dane, and Reeside, 1936, p. 10, 55); the Green River shale (Eocene) of Wyoming, Colorado, and Utah (Bradley, 1929a); the White River group (Oligocene) of the Dakotas and Nebraska (Wanless, 1922, p. 194–195); and the Muddy Creek formation (Hualpai limestone) (Pliocene?) of southern Nevada (Longwell, 1936, p. 1429 ff.)—and some of it may be of chemical origin. The Newark and Green River limestone beds, however, show algal structures, and algae were at least important contributors to their deposition.

Detrital Limestone

Limestone clearly composed of fragments of older limestone is not common, but it is known in several parts of the geologic column. Examples are the "Potomac marble," lime-breccia in a fanglomerate in the Newark group (Triassic) of Maryland and Virginia; the bodies of giant lime-breccia and associated lime-sandstone in the Cow Head breccia (Ordovician) of Western Newfoundland (Schuchert and Dunbar, 1934, p. 73–86) (p. 175); and, on a smaller scale, the "edgewise conglomerate" or "intraformational conglomerate" common in the Cambrian and Lower Ordovician carbonate rocks of both the Cordilleran and Appalachian regions, and in northwest Scotland (p. 180).

Organic-Fragmental Limestone

Composition and distribution of modern shallow-water calcareous sediments. The composition of the calcareous sediments now accumulating on the floor of the shallow tropical seas has been studied by a number of observers, most of them inspired by T. Wayland Vaughan, whose interest in the problem dates from 1908 or earlier. Perhaps the most detailed such study is that by Thorp (1935; summarized in Thorp, 1939) of 74 samples of calcareous bottom sediments from the Florida-Bahama region. (Thorp's material included samples from the aragonite mud area west of Andros Island and from the organic reef belt east of it, but none from the widespread lime-sand shown by Illing [1954] to be the main deposit on more than half of the Great Bahama Bank. See p. 232.) On averaging his results, Thorp found that two-thirds of the material (66 percent) consists of fragments recognizable as certainly organic, and that another 7 percent is almost certainly organic, though the particular organism by which it was formed cannot be identified. Most abundant are fragments of the deposits of calcareous algae, which form nearly a third of the organic fragments; in order after these come mollusks (chiefly gastropods and pelecypods), foraminifers, and hexacorals. Minor constituents include sponge and octocoral spicules, fragments of worm tubes, echinoid spines and plates, ostracode valves and pieces of the tests of other crustaceans, and bryozoan fragments. Included in the almost certainly organic fragments are fairly friable pellets of lime-mud, apparently fecal pellets of mud-feeding organisms, which are concentrated in a few areas, chiefly in the littoral zone near extensive areas of lime-mud.

Also present in the samples is $CaCO_3$ of presumed inorganic origin, locally forming a large part of the sediments but averaging only about 4 percent of the whole suite of samples. This material consists of aragonite needles and oöids, the former from the chemical precipitates of the area, the latter apparently largely from erosion of Pleistocene oölite. A small portion of the samples (less than 3 percent) is non-calcareous material such as quartz grains, evidently terrigenous.

The remaining fifth of the material investigated consists of $CaCO_3$ of silt and clay size whose origin is indeterminate. Some of this is probably an inorganic chemical precipitate, but at least a good part is certainly derived from broken-down shells or algal deposits, especially from those made of aragonite. The conclusion is that well over three-quarters of the calcareous sediments now accumulating in the shallow waters of the Florida region is composed of fragments of organic origin.

Similar results have been reached in studies of other samples from the same region (Vaughan, 1910; 1918; Goldman, 1926; Gould and Stewart, 1955) and of like sediments from other parts of the world, such as Samoa (Bramlette, 1926) and the Great Barrier Reef of Australia (Goldman, in Vaughan, 1918). There are some differences in these other sediments—for example, at Samoa hexacorals are more abundant than either mollusks or foraminifers, and aragonite needles and other inorganic calcareous materials are entirely wanting—but the general conclusion that the bulk of the sediments is of organic-fragmental origin is equally applicable.

Deposits of this character are widely distributed; in fact, they appear to be the typical bottom sediments in most shallow tropical seas that are free from terrigenous material, the Bahamas offering the most conspicuous exception. Around North America they are found on both sides of the Florida peninsula, especially on the broad shoal area on the west (there passing laterally on the north into the terrigenous mud brought down by the Appalachicola River), on the Campeche Bank of Yucatán, on the banks extending northeast from Nicaragua toward Jamaica, and on many of the smaller banks and shoal areas of the West Indies region. They floor large areas in the East Indies also, especially on the Sahul shelf off the northwest coast of Australia (though not where the rivers of New Guinea supply terrigenous material) and locally elsewhere around "coral" islands like those of the eastern Java Sea and the Sulu Archipelago, and they are also found in many places around the South China Sea. Likewise around and within barrier reefs and atolls in all parts of the tropical seas, a major part of the bottom sediment is organic-fragmental (p. 90).

Although the source of much the largest part of modern shallow-water calcareous sediments is thus organic, the mode of deposition of those sediments is entirely mechanical. That is, fragments of gravel, sand, silt, and clay size, derived from shells, algal crusts, and other organic deposits, are distributed on the sea floor by waves and currents in just the same manner that detrital terrigenous gravel, sand, silt, and clay would be distributed. Hence, all the concepts and principles developed for marine deposition of siliceous fragmental sediments by Barrell and his successors (p. 128), such as profile of equilibrium, bypassing, diastems, baselevel of aggradation, are equally applicable to the calcareous fragmental sediments, which differ only in that their source is not detritus brought to the sea by rivers or eroded from the shore by waves, but shells and other deposits of organisms growing in the sea itself, and especially those that form upstanding reefs and thus invite the attack of the waves. Subject to the same waves and currents, the particles of the calcareous sediments like those of the siliceous fragmental sediments undergo on the sea floor constant working and reworking, sorting, scrambling, and resorting, so that an individual particle may travel many miles and settle down thousands of times before it reaches a permanent resting place and finally becomes part of the slowly accumulating deposit. Likewise the lime-sand and lime-mud, produced by chemical precipitation in shallow seas like the Bahama Banks, are subject to the same processes, modified only if they form so rapidly as to clog the currents or in such restricted bodies of water as to be free of disturbance by large waves. It goes without saying that the same principles apply to detrital limestone. To sum up, except for strictly non-fragmental organic limestone, like that in organic reefs, for the calcareous deposits of the deeper seas, such as the oozes, and for a few chemical sediments, such as those associated with the chemical salines perhaps, calcareous sediments are deposited in just the same way as other sediments, being governed by precisely the same laws. The significant difference is in the source of the material and in its composition, and in the resulting differences in diagenesis.

Composition of North American limestone. One of the very first detailed petrographic studies of sedimentary rocks was that of the limestone formations of England by Sorby (1879). Studying thin sections from all parts of the geologic column down to the Bala limestone of the Welsh Ordovician, Sorby recognized that limestone after limestone is made up largely of fragments of calcitic shells set in a matrix or paste of fine-grained $CaCO_3$; the matrix he believed to be chiefly the disintegration products of other shells, especially aragonitic ones. He considered the possibility of chemical deposition of the paste, but on the whole discounted it except for the Jurassic oölites, and even in them he found organic-fragmental deposits, in some of which aragonite is still preserved in the shells of ammonites. He called attention to the presence in some rocks of fragments of fragmental limestone, some at least definitely detrital from older formations, but more derived from the immediately underlying layers of the formation in which the fragments are found. In this pioneer work, therefore, Sorby recognized virtually all the different genetic varieties of limestone, established that among them organic-fragmental limestone is dominant, and

saw the evidence of the continual reworking that the materials underwent during their deposition. Many later geologists have forgotten or ignored these insights (but see Grabau, 1903), though recently they have been widely reaffirmed (for example, Hatch, Rastall, and Black, 1939, Chap. 8; Sloss, 1947; Pettijohn, 1948, p. 115; 1957, Chap. 9).

No similar petrographic survey of North American limestone formations appears to have been made, but a good deal is known about certain units. Precambrian calcareous rocks are widespread but commonly dolomitic; where unmetamorphosed they are chiefly fine grained and if organic are presumably made up mostly of algal carbonate. The common presence of stromatolites supports this suggestion, but chemical limestone may also be important. Cambrian and Lower Ordovician carbonate rocks are mainly similar, though of course fossiliferous; the shells of the animals may have contributed to the fine-grained lime-mud along with the algae. Some lime-sandstone, including rock made almost entirely of trilobite fragments, is known, but it is quite subordinate to finely crystalline or aphanitic limestone. As noted above (p. 233), Cloud and Barnes (1948, p. 79–109) have interpreted the aphanitic variety—which is rather common, especially in the Lower Ordovician—as an inorganic chemical deposit, comparable to the aragonite mud of the Great Bahama Bank. The wide distribution of "intraformational" lime-breccia in rocks of this age has already been mentioned (p. 234).

In the Middle Ordovician, several groups of animals appeared that deposited calcite shells and quickly became major contributors to the carbonate sediments: tetracorals, tabulates, bryozoans, and crinoids. At the same time the articulate brachiopods, though they had been present through the Cambrian, began their major Paleozoic expansion. As a result organic-fragmental limestone is very common from the Middle Ordovician Series up; well-known examples are the Holston "marble" of Tennessee (Ordovician), the Coeymans and Becraft limestones of New York (Devonian), the Grand Tower limestone of Missouri (Devonian) (Payne, 1942), the Burlington and Sainte Genevieve limestones of the Mississippi Valley (Mississippian), and the Pennsylvanian fusulinid limestones of the Midcontinent region. Finer-grained limestone, commonly shaly, is also widespread; the presence of abundant fossils in much of it suggests an organic-fragmental origin. A chemical origin seems more likely for thick more uniform lime-mudstone bodies, such as that in the Upper Silurian of the Central Appalachians and the Great Lakes region. Reef deposits are widely distributed from the Ordovician up, though probably they form only a small fraction of the total.

Lower Mesozoic limestone is rare in the United States and Canada, the largest body probably being the Jurassic Twin Creek-Carmel limestone of Utah and adjacent states. Much of this limestone is finely crystalline to aphanitic and sparingly fossiliferous; it is difficult, therefore, to determine whether it is mainly chemical or organic-fragmental. Jurassic limestone also occurs at the surface in eastern Mexico and underground under much of the Gulf Coastal Plain of the United States; some is fossiliferous and apparently organic-fragmental, but some is associated with anhydrite and is oölitic and probably chemical.

Cretaceous limestone is more abundant, especially around the Gulf of Mexico. Lower Cretaceous limestone covers large areas in central and western Texas and eastern Mexico; much of it is organic-fragmental (for example the typical Edwards limestone), though chalky and reef facies occur. In the Upper Cretaceous, "chalk" is widespread, including the Selma in Alabama and Mississippi, the Austin and overlying beds in Texas, and the Niobrara of the Great Plains. The rock is fine grained and full of clay, and may be in large part a chemical precipitate. Reef limestone, dominated by rudistids, is prominent in eastern Mexico.

Cenozoic limestone is common only around the Antillean region, as for example in Florida, where much of it is evidently organic-fragmental, closely resembling the calcareous deposits now forming on the shallow sea floor to the west. Oölite occurs in the Pleistocene.

Thus, although admittedly poor and scattered, the evidence suggests that, just as organic-frag-

mental deposits dominate modern calcareous sediments, so they have dominated ancient calcareous sediments since the Middle Ordovician. Strictly organic reef limestone, though prominent, has been relatively subordinate in amount, and strictly detrital limestone has probably been almost negligible. How much limestone has been of true chemical origin remains undetermined—probably a great deal before the Middle Ordovician and relatively less since. Without more detailed studies of limestones than have yet been made, such questions cannot be answered.

GENESIS OF DOLOSTONE

Although dolostone is by no means uncommon among the sedimentary rocks of the geologic record, its origin is still uncertain. Probably the chief reason for this uncertainty is that, unlike the other major types of sediments, it is nowhere known to be forming today, and therefore the present fails us as a key to the past. Hence the problem must be attacked in other ways: by detailed study of the rock as it now occurs for clues that may bear on its origin or origins, and by careful consideration of the chemistry of formation of the mineral dolomite. With this information, perhaps, the field of hypotheses can be narrowed and each can be restricted to its proper application.

Physical Chemistry of the Mineral Dolomite

The first important fact about the physical chemistry of dolomite is that critical investigations are yet to be made. A vast literature exists on the subject of the artificial synthesis of the mineral, but for practically none of the experiments were the temperature, pressure (especially partial pressure of CO_2), alkalinity, and chemical constitution of the solutions fixed exactly enough to supply quantitative results. Moreover, in many allegedly successful experiments proof that the mineral dolomite itself was formed is lacking; in most where the matter was investigated, it was found that $CaCO_3$ and $MgCO_3$ were present together as a mixture rather than as a compound. The earlier work has been reviewed by Leitmeier (1916, p. 687–696), Van Tuyl (1916), and

Clarke (1924, p. 566–569), and Leitmeier sums it up by saying (1916, p. 696): "All attempts to date . . . only show that dolomite in nature is not formed in the ways investigated." Dolomite was apparently synthesized several times, but only under high temperature and/or high pressure (especially high partial pressure of CO_2) and/or with unusual combinations of salts. Most attempts to synthesize it resulted in the precipitation of $CaCO_3$ first and a magnesium salt later (mainly $MgCO_3 \cdot 3H_2O$, but $Mg(OH)_2$ forms in sufficiently alkaline solutions).

The most detailed physical-chemical investigation yet made is that of Bär (doctoral dissertation at Frankfurt, not seen; results reported in Bär, 1924, 1932), and his principal experiments were carried out at a partial pressure of CO_2 of 1 atmosphere and hence cannot be applied directly to sedimentary dolostone. At that pressure, according to Bär, dolomite dissolves congruently, that is, the resulting solution at all times contains equal molar amounts of $CaCO_3$ and $MgCO_3$, and conversely dolomite can precipitate directly from such a solution. Bär contends, however, from a survey of the existing data on the solution of dolomite, that these relations hold over only a certain range of partial pressures of CO_2, the limits of which were not determined. Thus at higher partial pressures (probably only slightly higher) dolomite would dissolve incongruently, $CaCO_3$ being dissolved and $MgCO_3$ remaining, and conversely at the same higher pressures $MgCO_3$ would precipitate first from a solution containing equal molar amounts of the two carbonates and would only later be altered to dolomite. Finally at low partial pressures, probably including those normal at the Earth's surface, $MgCO_3$ would dissolve and $CaCO_3$ remain, and conversely $CaCO_3$ would precipitate first from an equimolar solution and would later be altered to dolomite by further reaction with the solution. This view is attractive but unfortunately cannot be taken as proved in the absence of further experimental work.*

* Halla (1935, 1936) combats this view, holding that the congruence or incongruence of dolomite cannot be affected by changes in the partial pressure of CO_2, and hence that if it is congruent at one pressure, as experimentally shown by Bär, it must be so at all, but his argument is entirely theoretical and, moreover, involves several approximations, so that his counter-conclusion likewise cannot be considered as proved.

Whether or not the mineral dolomite can be precipitated directly from solution under conditions attainable in shallow seas, there is evidence that solid $CaCO_3$ can be converted into dolomite under some conditions, especially if present in an unstable form (aragonite or μ-$CaCO_3$). Again the earlier experiments achieved results only at partial pressures of several atmospheres of CO_2, generally at high temperatures and in the presence of a considerable concentration of salts, but recently Rivière (1939a, b, 1940, 1941) has apparently succeeded in causing Mg^{++} to replace Ca^{++} in carbonate powder in ordinary sea water at ordinary temperatures and pressures. He found that the reaction was aided by high salinity and particularly by sustained high alkalinity, the pH approaching 9 (in normal sea water it is just over 8). Unfortunately it was not determined whether the mineral dolomite itself was produced, and hence Rivière's results, like Bär's, can only be suggestive. Further experimental work on the formation of dolomite by replacement of $CaCO_3$ in sea water, with special attention to pH and oxidation potentials, is badly needed.

Geologic Occurrences of the Rock Dolostone

Dolostone is almost everywhere associated with non-dolomitic limestone, but it has in general two main geologic occurrences, which reflect two main modes of origin. It may occur as widespread beds, tongues, members, or formations, normally interbedded or intertongued with limestone, or it may occur as irregular masses, normally cross-cutting the bedding of limestone formations and related instead to fracture systems, commonly the same fracture systems that seem to have guided ore deposition. In the first type of occurrence, the dolostone is clearly stratigraphically controlled; its relations with other rocks and formations are the normal stratigraphic relations of unconformity, vertical alternation, facies change, and so forth. Figure 113 shows such relations between dolostone and limestone in the Middle and Upper Cambrian and Lower Ordo-

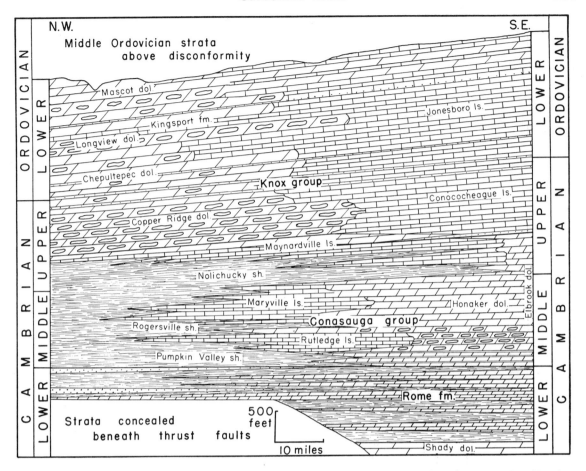

Figure 113. Facies changes in Cambrian and Lower Ordovician rocks in East Tennessee and southwest Virginia. Note intertonguing of limestone and dolostone, and evidence of a northwest source of material: sand and mud in Rome time, mud in Conasauga time, and non-fragmental silica in Knox time.

vician beds of the southern Appalachians; moreover, these relations persist along strike, and the Lower Ordovician rocks, for example, grade from dolostone on the northwest to limestone on the southeast all the way from New York to Alabama. For convenience, this type is here called S-dolostone. In the second type of occurrence, the dolostone is clearly tectonically controlled; its relations with other rocks are like those of structurally guided hydrothermal replacement deposits of ore minerals. This type is here called T-dolostone. Both types may be present in the same area, but even so they have distinguishing characteristics, and there does not appear to be a gradation between them.

Some geologists have maintained that dolostone occurs in still a third way, as blankets or bodies in limestone related neither to primary bedding nor later fractures but to the present or an ancient land surface—in other words, that it has been produced during the subaerial weathering of the limestone. Such dolostone might be called W-dolostone. Two modes of origin have been proposed: slightly magnesian limestone may be leached of its $CaCO_3$ during weathering to produce a rock of about the composition of dolomite, or magnesium-bearing surficial waters may replace the calcite (or aragonite) of the limestone by dolomite. The leaching theory is based on the observation that from a somewhat dolomitic limestone the calcite is leached first, but even assuming that the original limestone contained

15 percent $MgCO_3$, perhaps contributed by calcareous algae or other organisms, the theory demands a far greater porosity or loss of volume than has been observed. Thus it can hardly account for the production of any large bodies of dolostone from limestone, and it has not been advocated, except for very local occurrences of porous dolostone at obvious unconformities, within the present century.

The surficial replacement theory on the other hand has been more recently defended, notably by Reuling (1931) for part of the Devonian dolostone of the Eifel region of northwest Germany, supposed to have been dolomitized in pre-Triassic time, and by Landes (1946) for certain oil-bearing pockets of porous dolostone in limestone in Michigan (Devonian) and in Ohio and Indiana (Ordovician). Landes believes that the porosity of the dolostone he studied was produced during dolomitization, and that since the porosity is a surficial phenomenon beneath disconformities the dolostone is likewise. For these rocks, however, the alternative suggestion of Murray (1930), that the porosity is the result of surficial leaching of already existing pockets of slightly calcitic dolostone produced at an earlier time in some other way, seems satisfactory. The production of any sizeable quantity of W-dolostone by weathering or by circulating surficial water must be considered still unproved.

Hewett (1931, p. 57–68, 100–101) has made a detailed study of T-dolostone in the Goodsprings district, Nevada. Some S-dolostone is present in the district, but most of the dolostone there is the result of replacement of limestone by solutions working out from faults and other fractures and from or along bedding planes. This T-dolostone is generally medium to coarse grained, but some is fine grained; normally, however, it is coarser (and somewhat more porous) than the limestone from which it was formed. Much but not all is also lighter in color than the limestone. Hewett believes that the dolomitization took place during the deformation of the region and shortly after the intrusion of certain igneous rocks, which probably supplied the magnesia. The ore deposits of the area (principally zinc and lead), though not directly related to the T-dolostone, are apparently related to the same fractures and intrusions. Hewett (1928) has also summarized the facts on many other occurrences of T-dolostone, almost all in zinc and lead districts.

The East Tennessee zinc district exhibits an instructive combination of S- and T-dolostone (Newman, 1933; Oder and Miller, 1945; Brokaw, 1950; Oder and Hook, 1950; Bridge, 1956). The Knox dolomite group of Late Cambrian and Early Ordovician age, half a mile thick and the dominant rock of the district (in the northwestern part of the area covered by Fig. 113), consists mainly of gray fairly fine-grained, locally well-laminated but rather thick-bedded dolostone, at certain levels in which are beds of very fine-grained to aphanitic pale-brownish limestone. Individual beds as well as larger formations of dolostone and limestone, and also certain characteristic sandy and cherty layers, are persistent and can be recognized from outcrop to outcrop or from drill-hole to drill-hole throughout the district. In areas of deformation, however, the limestone has been replaced by medium-grained to coarse-grained light-gray dolostone, in bodies that are not persistent but are related to fractures, commonly but not invariably fractures that seem to have been channels for the zinc-bearing solutions. Indeed, stratigraphic correlation between outcrops or drill-holes is possible only if dolostone of this second type is reckoned as limestone. Thus the two kinds of dolostone are clearly differentiated, both in lithology and in distribution. Figure 114 shows unaltered, partly altered, and completely altered limestone from this district.

Although T-dolostone has thus been recorded in considerable mass in the vicinity of many zinc and lead districts, nevertheless the bulk of the earth's dolostone is S-dolostone. Whole formations of dolostone are spread over large areas; for example, the sheet of Upper(?) Ordovician dolostone of which the Bighorn of Wyoming and the Red River of Manitoba are representatives, the record of the most widespread submergence in the geologic history of North America; the Permian dolostone of northern Europe, including the Magnesian limestone of England and the Zechstein of Germany; and the Triassic dolostone of

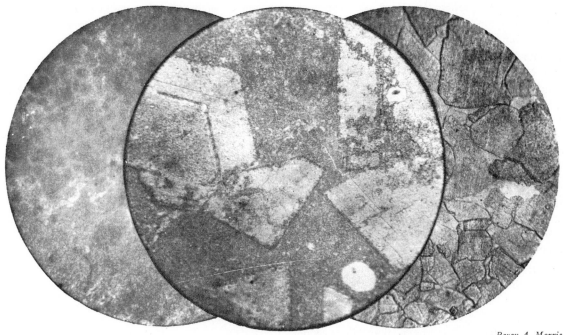

Percy A. Morris

Figure 114. Photomicrographs of limestone (left), limestone with dolomite rhombs (center), and T-dolostone (right), all from a single bed in the Kingsport limestone (Lower Ordovician) at Thorn Hill, Tennessee. Fields are about 1.6 mm across. The limestone shows pellet or aggregate structure and was probably formed from aragonite sand like that on the Great Bahama Bank (p. 232).

the eastern Alps, where the rock was first recognized. In North America, dolostone is virtually confined to Paleozoic and upper Precambrian rocks, but elsewhere Mesozoic, especially Triassic, dolostone is common, and some uplifted "coral reefs" of "Plio-Pleistocene" age in the Pacific are now dolostone, though undoubtedly they formed as calcium carbonate (for example, Kita Daito Jima or North Borodino Island in the Philippine Sea east of Okinawa; Hanzawa, 1940). Daly (1909, p. 165) has assembled analyses to show that the $CaCO_3:MgCO_3$ ratio in carbonate rocks varies from 2 or 3 to 1 for the Precambrian and lower Paleozoic to 40 to 1 for the Cretaceous and about 30 to 1 for the Cenozoic. These figures suggest that in general more S-dolostone formed in earlier periods than in later ones, but they can hardly be considered a quantitative sample of the earth's carbonate rock.

Some commonplace generalizations about S-dolostone, based on existing knowledge, may be rehearsed. Characteristically it is more uniform in texture than the associated limestone, and also slightly coarser grained. Aphanitic dolostone is fairly rare, though it is the normal carbonate rock in sequences containing saline deposits (p. 242). S-dolostone tends to be massive; massive limestone is also known, of course, but on the average, and also ordinarily where the two are interbedded, limestone is thinner bedded than dolostone. Original structures in dolostone are typically poorly preserved; thus in many dolostone formations fossils are notoriously rare and those that are present are molds, or if not molds have been replaced so that much structural detail is lost.

It is proper to point out, however, that these generalizations are indeed general, if not superficial and misleading. The most thorough and critical petrographic study of S-dolostone yet published is that by Sander (1936) of the Triassic carbonate rocks of the Tyrol, and his work offers exceptions to most of the above statements. Above all, Sander has shown that the rocks called dolostone in the field are not simple but are formed of a complex mixture of several genetically different components. Each of these components may be either calcite or dolomite, and not uncommonly, indeed, the calcite and dolomite alternate repeatedly, probably rhythmically, on a scale of meters, millimeters, or even microns (Sander, 1936, p. 182–183, 189–190; English translation, p. 128, 135–136). Thus the problem of the origin of the rock dolostone becomes the problem of the origin of the dolomite in each of these components.

Among these components, two have in the main formed the original fabric of the rocks Sander studied: an external mechanical component, consisting of carbonate-mud and carbonate-sand, including organic-fragmental material, and a "biogenic" component, consisting especially of "cheesy cavernous crusts that do not show organic structure" (Sander, 1936, p. 31; trans., p. 1). In this basic fabric, small to microscopic cavities have been formed by various diagenetic processes: mechanical washing out, chemical solution, or deformation in the form of minute crumpling. In these cavities two more components occur: an internal mechanical component, commonly distinguishable from the external mechanical component only by slightly larger grain size if by that, and an internal chemical component, consisting of sparry carbonate deposited on the walls of the cavities and commonly filling them. Finally, another chemical component consists of sparry carbonate that has "metasomatically" replaced all pre-existing components but especially the earliest ones; this component likewise may be either calcite or dolomite (if dolomite, it commonly takes the form of minute rhombs), and it may replace either calcite or dolomite.

Moreover, Sander gives evidence that the periods of formation of most of these components overlapped in time; for example, the filling of a given cavity may exhibit a small-scale rhythmic alternation of the internal mechanical and chemical components, or a layer of the external mechanical component may overlie a diastem that truncates minutely crumpled older layers of the same component partly replaced by the "metasomatic" chemical component. The evidence also shows that repeated mechanical sedimentation played a very great part in the formation of these rocks. Breccias containing fragments of breccias, mechanical deposits on the floors of cavities in mechanical deposits, numerous closely spaced sublevation surfaces—all these show that the material now forming the mechanical components has been deposited and eroded, redeposited and re-eroded, probably many times before finally becoming a permanent deposit. Thus, detailed petrographic study of older rock again confirms the conclusions drawn from the survey of existing calcareous sediments as to the great importance of continual mechanical reworking in the formation of the carbonate rocks (p. 235) and shows that the textural difference between such rocks and the similarly reworked non-calcareous fragmental rocks results not from a difference in the manner of the mechanical deposition but from the superposition on the mechanical components of diagenetic chemical components that solidify the rock by a sort of auto-cementation.

Theories of Origin of S-Dolostone

In general there have been two theories of the origin of S-dolostone (omitting those that have denied its existence and assigned it to T- or W-dolostone). One theory holds that dolomite was precipitated directly as such from sea water —this is called the primary precipitation theory —and the other that previously existing calcitic deposits were altered to dolomite on the sea floor or after but slight burial—this is called the penecontemporaneous replacement theory. (The local existence of detrital S-dolostone made of fragments of an older dolostone is, of course, acknowledged, but the question of origin is then merely transferred to the parent rock.)

Since the work of Van Tuyl (1916) and Steidtmann (1917), the replacement theory has been dominant in the American literature. The primary precipitation theory has been applied, however, to the aphanitic dolostone commonly associated with saline deposits, for the replacement theory encounters obstacles in explaining their uniformity, their very fine grain, and their association with the obviously precipitated salines but not with ordinary limestone. Yet Newell and others (1953, p. 121) have recently studied such a dolostone that formed in the highly saline lagoon behind the Capitan Reef, and they think it represents chemically precipitated aragonite mud later replaced by dolomite. For more widespread S-dolostone the primary theory in its simple form implying direct, chemical precipitation is generally rejected. Tarr (1919), indeed, suggested that all S-dolostone is deposited in restricted, somewhat hypersaline seas, but on the contrary it is found in great volume in the deposits of some of the most widespread marine invasions of the continents; for example, the sea that deposited the great sheet of Upper(?) Ordovician dolostone already mentioned (p. 240) covered western North America from Texas to the Arctic Islands and was widely inhabited by a rich and varied fauna. Moreover, positive evidence of replacement is not lacking. The granular texture of most S-dolostone and the palimpsest features it contains argue for replacement, and the case is clinched by the local occurrence of fossils or of whole organic reef masses now made of dolomite but almost certainly deposited as calcite or aragonite. A particularly striking example is the raised atoll of Kita Daito Jima mentioned above (p. 241), made of dolostone of "Plio-Pleistocene" age, but the lower part of the Funafuti reef (Ellice Islands) and many known Triassic and Paleozoic reef masses enforce the same conclusion.

Sander's study of the Tyrolean dolostones led him, on the other hand, to the conclusion that dolomite of "primary origin is especially abundant and widely distributed" (Sander, 1936, p. 177; trans., p. 123). In calling dolomite (or calcite) "primary," however, Sander means "that in the early stages of rock formation dolomite came to a place in the fabric where calcite was not earlier present" (*loc. cit.*), for he deliberately bases his definitions on observed petrographic criteria and hence classes as primary that dolomite for which there is no petrographic evidence that it was ever anything else. Thus if any particles were originally formed as calcite (organically or chemically) but were converted to dolomite on the sea floor *before* finally coming to rest in the deposit, they would be primary on Sander's definition though secondary by conventional usage, for Sander maintains that there

are no observable petrographic criteria by which this conversion could be recognized.

At least with respect to the organic-fragmental part of the "primary" mechanical component, however, petrographic criteria for the distinction in question do exist. Thus dolomitic foraminifer tests described by Sander were certainly calcite at the time of formation even if they were dolomite at the time of final burial. And if they have been converted to dolomite before final deposition, why not also the indeterminate lime-mud and lime-sand in which they are embedded? It is admitted, however, that no evidence one way or the other is likely to be found in the rocks themselves. The strictly biogenic (presumably algal) origin of the "cheesy cavernous crusts" does not seem to be demonstrated; they may have been directly, biochemically precipitated from the sea water at their present position, but they may also have been built up like ordinary stromatolites (p. 229) from passing carbonate mud particles that stuck to the mucilaginous jelly coating the algae; if the latter, this material, too, is primary in Sander's sense but not in conventional usage. The chemical sparry dolomite lining cavities must evidently be primary in every sense, but the water in these cavities, as Sander expressly mentions (1936, p. 182; trans., p. 128) need not have been normal sea water; in one case, however (p. 173; trans., p. 115–116), Sander records primary chemical dolomite formed on what appears to have been the free upper surface of the deposit in contact with normal sea water. Thus Sander's conclusion that primary dolomite "is abundant" is not proof of direct precipitation of dolomite from sea water on a vast scale, though it would, of course, be consistent with such precipitation.

As shown above, however, the replacement origin of dolostone is clearly demonstrated in some cases by the existence of dolostone reefs that were doubtless deposited as solid masses of calcite and aragonite and converted into dolomite while solid rock. Presumably, therefore, if chemical conditions are right, replacement could occur even more readily in unconsolidated lime-sand and lime-mud deposits during the constant working and reworking that such material undergoes on the sea floor, especially if Bär's suggestions as to the incongruent formation of dolomite after calcite is correct (p. 238; Bär, 1924, 1932). Many lines of evidence suggest that the control that determines whether or not dolomite shall be formed from calcite in this way (or for that matter in any other way) is in delicate balance. Thus alternating layers of limestone and S-dolostone, whether thick or thin, are commonly sharply separated by a bedding plane or shaly parting, and rocks with an intermediate composition appear to be relatively less common (p. 223). The regional extent and consistency of alternations of this sort, and of lateral gradations from dolostone to limestone (as in the Knox group of the southern Appalachians, p. 238 and Fig. 113, p. 239), point the same way; so does Sander's evidence concerning the rhythmic alternation of calcite and dolomite, and he concludes that a nonorganic chemical control is the most probable (1936, p. 183; trans., p. 128). As to what the control is, our information is insufficient and we can only guess. Sander suggests changes in temperature and especially in partial pressure of CO_2. Rivière's experiments (p. 238; Rivière, 1939a, b) suggest that salinity and especially alkalinity are important, and the oxidation potential may also be significant. Ordinarily the pH of sea water remains well below 9, the figure attained in Rivière's successful experiments, but it is well known that a rapid rate of photosynthesis in a shallow body of water not subject to mixing with deeper water may cause the pH to approach 9, the rapid rate being possible if enough nutrients are available to support a large population of planktonic algae.

We may sum up a possible theory of the origin of S-dolostone as follows. Suppose that lime-mud and lime-sand are being formed chemically and/or organically and are being distributed mechanically in clear shallow marine waters. They are constantly being worked and reworked on the sea floor and are deposited and sublevated again many times before they finally come to rest. In those parts of the sea where photosynthesis is especially rapid and where because the water is shallow the resulting alkalinity is not quickly neutralized, chemical conditions become right for the conversion of the restlessly wandering calcite particles into dolomite. Presumably the reaction is reversible, though it might show considerable lag, and a given particle might be altered several times before it is finally buried. Thus the composition, calcite or dolomite, of the mechanical components of the accumulating sediment is controlled by a delicate balance of chemical factors in the overlying water, which might be altered from time to time and from place to place, giving rise to alternating layers or intertonguing facies of limestone and dolostone. Superposed on these mechanical components would be diagenetic chemical components, either in cavities or by actual replacement, composed of either calcite or dolomite depending on the chemical balance in the diagenetic solutions. Were conditions especially favorable, layers of carbonate-sand or carbonate-mud already deposited, or even solid reef masses of calcite and aragonite, might be transformed in place into dolomite (or back again). Finally, in extremely restricted warm and hypersaline arms of the sea, dolomite might be precipitated directly as such, along with gypsum, anhydrite, or salt. It should be unnecessary to add that this theory, built on the shakiest of observational and experimental foundations is no more than a tentative working hypothesis, and that its chief value lies not in explaining the origin of dolostone but in pointing out those aspects of the subject where more work needs especially to be done.

14. *Siliceous non-fragmental rocks*

CHEMISTRY AND MINERALOGY OF SEDIMENTARY SILICA

The siliceous non-fragmental sediments are those consisting mainly of free silica that is not detritus from older rocks but has formed either organically by accumulation of siliceous tests or spicules, or chemically by direct precipitation or by replacement, at surface temperatures and pressures. The principal example is the rock chert.

Chert has been the subject of as much controversy as dolostone, and for about the same reasons: neither is known to be forming anywhere today, and the chemistry of formation of each presents difficult problems. The geological literature contains many contradictory statements about the chemical precipitation of free silica, both as to the state of the silica in the solutions from which it comes down (Roy, 1945) and as to the chemical factors (concentration of silica, catalysts, inhibitors) affecting precipitation (cf. Tarr, 1917, p. 434–437, with Lovering, 1923, p. 534–536). The chemical aspects of the matter, however, are by now fairly clear—both the facts and their theoretical interpretation. The following account depends mainly on Hurd (1938), Taliaferro (1935), and Krauskopf (1956).

In very dilute water solutions (0.01 percent by weight or less, or 1 mole of silica to 33,000 of water), silica is present as individual mole-cules of SiO_4H_4 (monosilicic acid), which are only slightly dissociated in neutral solution. In slightly more concentrated solutions, the molecules of monosilicic acid polymerize slowly into molecules of "polysilicic acid" that approach colloidal dimensions until the concentration of monosilicic acid has fallen to 0.01 percent or so, but the solution remains stable and is hardly more viscous than pure water.

In solutions containing about 0.5 percent by weight SiO_2 (molar ratio of water to silica 660 to 1), the polymerizing molecules tend to build up long molecular fibers of hydrated silica, greatly increasing the viscosity of the solution. At concentrations of 2 percent by weight SiO_2 or higher (molar ratio of water to silica 160 to 1 or less), the process goes rapidly to completion (except in strongly alkaline solutions), all the silica becomes part of the fibers, and the erstwhile solution sets to a jellylike or rubbery solid, a hydrated silica gel. Unlike many colloidal coagulations, this process is not strongly catalyzed by electrolytes; its speed depends primarily on the original concentration of silica and on the pH (within the usual range of natural waters it is most rapid at a pH of 8). Once set, the gel tends to contract (retaining its shape), expressing liquid water until the molar ratio of water to silica has decreased to 3 to 1 (53 percent by weight SiO_2) or less. In this process the specific gravity rises and the gel tends to lose its jellylike or rubbery character and starts to harden. The interpretation is that the hydrated silica fibers are pulled closer and closer together as more and more cross-bonds are established between them, the water being forced out to the surface of the gel. After this stage, water is lost more slowly and largely without contraction, the lost water being replaced by air and the specific gravity falling. Presumably the silica fibers, now nearly dehydrated, can no longer draw closer together, and the water still entangled between them is not forced out but escapes by diffusion through the "brush-heap" of fibers. When this process has reduced the water-to-silica ratio beyond 1 to 1 (77 percent by weight SiO_2), the gel approaches the geological material chert.

Opal, whether or not produced in this way by coagulation of silica solutions, is a common constituent of Cenozoic chert, being known as far back as the Eocene. It is also the only form of silica deposited by those organisms that build siliceous tests or skeletons: diatoms, silicoflagellates, radiolaria, and sponges. It is generally considered amorphous, but X-ray photographs show faintly the lines characteristic of high-temperature cristobalite, which of all the crystalline forms of silica is stable at the highest temperatures (above 1470°C.) and has the most open structure and lowest specific gravity. All the crystalline forms of silica can be described as regular three-dimensional networks of silica fibers. In opal, presumably, the still slightly hydrated fibers are for the most part not regularly arranged and their three-dimensional cross-bonding is not complete, so that the specific gravity is even lower than that of cristobalite, but small volumes of fibers may possess the simple cristobalite arrangement. (Faint X-ray lines of high-temperature cristobalite can also be obtained from freshly prepared hydrated silica gel before any contraction.)

Opal is theoretically unstable and tends either to be dissolved (especially by alkaline water), the silica being reprecipitated elsewhere, or to be converted in place into chalcedony or microcrystalline quartz. Nevertheless, veinlets of opal are known, so that it can evidently be deposited little by little from migrating solutions under certain circumstances, as well as be formed directly by coagulation.

Another form of silica found in chert is chalcedony, which is not a separate mineral species but a form of quartz containing abundant minute bubbles of water (0.1 micron) that lower the density and the refractive index (Midgley, 1951; Folk and Weaver, 1952; Pelto, 1956). Under a microscope, chalcedony appears as radiating needles a few microns thick and from tens to one or two hundred microns long, not uncommonly forming perfect spherulites. Chalcedony generally occurs filling veins or cavities, commonly in opal or other chert; more rarely it may form within bodies of opal. It is metastable and is known in Paleozoic chert.

The mass of older chert is made of ordinary microcrystalline quartz in equant anhedral grains a few microns across. Quartz is stable, of course, at surface temperatures and pressures, and microcrystalline chert is common in lower Paleozoic rocks; when chert is deformed or slightly metamorphosed, however, its grain size increases markedly, and it becomes virtually indistinguishable from metamorphic quartzite.

NOMENCLATURE AND CLASSIFICATION OF THE SILICEOUS NON-FRAGMENTAL ROCKS

The obviously organic siliceous sediments are classified, according to the organism responsible for them, into diatomaceous, radiolarian, and sponge-spicule sediments. Each group is then further subdivided, largely in accordance with the degree of consolidation. Thus the diatomaceous sediments include:

> *Diatomaceous ooze*—unconsolidated, consisting simply of separate diatom tests plus less than 50 percent impurities
> *Diatomaceous earth,* or *diatomite*—consolidated but not compact, commonly more than half pore space
> *Diatomaceous chert*—consolidated and compact, the space between the diatom tests being filled with silica that is not obviously organic in origin

A further distinction is made by some between diatomaceous earth (barely consolidated, friable) and diatomite (consolidated and cemented), the latter grading into diatomaceous chert as the proportion of not obviously organic silica increases. The term *diatomaceous shale* is used for impure diatomite with much clayey matter and with shaly partings. Similar sets of terms are used for the radiolarian and sponge-spicule sediments.

Those siliceous sediments that are non-fragmental and not obviously organic are commonly called chemical; their terminology has been discussed by Tarr (1938), and his proposals are followed here in the main. The over-all term for the compact vitreous microcrystalline silica rocks is *chert*. *Flint* is a dark variety of chert occurring as nodules in the Chalk of England and northwest Europe, and the term should probably be restricted to that material or to material very much like it. *Jasper* is a red, yellow, brown, or black variety of chert containing an appreciable percentage of iron (more than 5 percent). *Jasperoid* may be used for yellow or brown chert or coarser-grained silica stained by a smaller amount of iron, though in some districts it has been used for chert not colored at all by iron. In the United States, *tripoli* means very porous and friable chert, such as is used in the manufacture of abrasives. It is usually stated to be "weathered chert"; most of it is apparently produced by leaching of the carbonate from an intimate mixture of finely divided carbonate and chert rather than by alteration under weathering of chert itself. Abroad, however—for example, in Tripoli—tripoli means diatomaceous earth.

Other kinds of "chemical siliceous" rocks are not considered varieties of chert. *Novaculite* originally meant a rock used for honing razors. In the United States it is now used only for the mountain-forming Arkansas novaculite of Arkansas and Oklahoma and the equivalent Caballos novaculite of the Marathon region of West Texas (Devonian and Mississippian), which are very even-textured rock made of microcrystalline quartz. Though aphanitic, novaculite is generally coarser in grain than true chert, and has a dull rather than a vitreous luster. *Porcelanite* (or porcellanite) is a term used for silica rocks that are less compact than chert because of minute pores that give the rock a less vitreous and more porcelain-like texture; commonly the rock is somewhat impure and thin-bedded, and it grades into *porcelaneous shale* and mudstone ("siliceous shale"). Such rocks occur in the Mowry shale (Cretaceous) of Wyoming and adjacent states (Rubey, 1929) and in the Monterey formation (Miocene) of California (Bramlette, 1946). *Siliceous sinter* is the silica deposited around hot springs and geysers.

GEOLOGIC OCCURRENCE OF CHERT AND RELATED ROCKS

All the clearly organic siliceous sediments and also much chert occur in bedded deposits, interstratified with other sedimentary rocks. Particularly common is the association of bedded chert, locally radiolarian or diatomaceous, with thick sequences of graywacke and dark silty shale, typically showing graded bedding and including spilitic basalt flows. The chert generally occurs as relatively thin, even to nodular, beds a few inches to a foot thick, which may be separately intercalated in the graywacke sequence or may form bodies of solid chert hundreds or even thousands of feet thick, interrupted, if at all, only by thin shaly partings. American examples of such sequences containing much bedded chert are the Monterey formation (Miocene) and the Franciscan formation (Jurassic and Cretaceous) of California, and the Normanskill formation (Ordovician) of New York.

Chert also occurs very commonly in association with carbonate rocks, but here it typically takes the quite different form of nodules a few inches across, normally flattened into oblate spheroids or disclike bodies extended parallel to the bedding. Nodules may be so abundant in a given layer or layers that they coalesce to form irregular masses or an incomplete nodular bed, or even an anastomosing network in three dimensions. Many nodules show concentric color banding or alignment of impurities such as carbonate grains, and the banding shares the flattening of the nodules; normally, the nodules appear sharply set off from the enclosing carbonate rock but in some cases, at least, this appearance is deceptive, and the boundary is irregularly interlocking. If the enclosing rocks are fossiliferous,

fossils may be present in the chert, either as carbonate or silica. Excellent descriptions of nodular chert in limestone are given by Tarr (1917),
Barton (1918), and Twenhofel (1919). Chert
may also occur in these rocks, especially in dolostone, as finely divided disseminated silica interstitial to the carbonate grains.

The two kinds of occurrences so far described
differ greatly both in general form and in association, but some more or less transitional types are
known. Thus, though most of the chert in the
Monterey formation is bedded, nodules of chert
occur in the diatomite; on the other hand, the Rex
chert (Permian) of the phosphate district of
southeastern Idaho, though containing solid
bedded chert in some areas, grades laterally in
others into very cherty limestone, in which the
chert takes the form of nodular beds or nodules.
In general, however, these two kinds of chert are
distinct.

In both its bedded occurrence in graywacke
and its nodular or disseminated occurrence in the
carbonate rocks, the chert is evidently stratigraphically controlled, for it is commonly highly
specific to individual formations and the nodular
kind may be specific even to individual layers
within a formation. Thus individual cherty dolostone beds in the Kingsport formation (Lower
Ordovician) of East Tennessee (Fig. 113, p. 239)
—for example, a bed somewhat more than a foot
thick containing a double row of gray chert
nodules—can be recognized through the Mascot-
Jefferson City zinc district (Oder and Miller,
1945). All these types of chert are here grouped
as S-chert.

In contrast to these occurrences, chert is found
in a number of mining districts, especially zinc
districts, in irregular masses related to fractures
and to ore bodies. The "jasperoid" of the Jop-
lin district of Missouri and adjacent states is an
example; similar chert is known in East Tennessee (Oder and Miller, 1945, p. 2–3). In occurrence it resembles T-dolostone with which it is
commonly associated, though perhaps it is less
widely distributed in any given district, and it
may be called T-chert. In both these districts,
however, there is also much S-chert, chiefly

nodules in dolostone in Tennessee but grading
into nodular beds in Missouri.

Chert accumulates in great abundance in the
residual mantle over many formations of carbonate rocks, notably the great sheet of Upper
Cambrian and Lower Ordovician dolostone that
extends over most of the central United States
from the Appalachians to the Southern Rocky
Mountains. Although much of this chert is
merely nodular S-chert released during weathering, much more cannot be so explained. The
sheet of dolostone mentioned, where unweathered, contains considerable nodular chert—commonly most abundant in certain layers and
formations—but it also contains much very
finely divided and disseminated silica, so that the
total silica content of the rock, even excluding
the nodular chert, may pass 15 or 20 percent.
This finely divided silica appears as an insoluble
residue of chert when the rock is dissolved in
acid, and, indeed, the particular form taken by
the insoluble residue is commonly specific to individual formations and has been widely used in
recognizing and correlating them.

Now, in the residual mantle over these formations, the nodules of S-chert are joined by great
numbers of irregular chert blocks ranging in size
from small chips to masses several feet on a side
and displaying great variety in form and appearance, some massive and some friable, some compact and some porous, yet in general so distinctive of individual formations that those formations can be mapped separately by careful attention to details of the residual chert. These chert
blocks, which are not present as such in the
underlying bedrock, are apparently produced by
concentration of the finely disseminated silica
into solid blocks during weathering. This mode
of origin seems proved in certain cases, at least.
For example, a layer 10 to 15 feet thick near the
top of the Mascot dolomite (Lower Ordovician)
of East Tennessee is exposed in road cuts and
stream outcrops as a dark crystalline dolostone
lacking chert nodules but containing as much as
20 percent finely divided silica, much more than
the rest of the dolostone layers in the upper part
of this formation. On divides between streams,

however, where weathering has proceeded to considerable depths, this layer is represented by great solid masses of light-colored compact vitreous chert, some of which actually forms ledges still in the original position of the layer so that it can be mapped and its strike and dip measured. Intermediate exposures leave no doubt that the chert masses and ledges are produced by weathering of this highly siliceous layer. Chert formed, or rather concentrated and accumulated into solid masses, in this way may be called W-chert.

Similar movement of silica during weathering is demonstrated by the superficial silicification of fossils in some carbonate rocks. The conditions favoring this movement are not certainly known, but presumably they are those known to favor the leaching of silica from soils, a phenomenon chiefly important in warm humid climates with alkaline soil water and little or no humus. There is no particular reason to doubt that the formation of W-chert is going on today in favorable localities in the southeastern United States.

GENESIS OF S-CHERT AND RELATED ROCKS

Source of the Silica

Presumably the silica in S-chert, and also that in the organic siliceous sediments, had previously been in solution in the body of water in which the sediments were deposited. The ocean itself has a remarkably small silica content, on the order of 1 or 2 parts per million, actually considerably less than most of the large rivers that enter it, and this discrepancy must be accounted for. Some have maintained that the silica, being colloidal, is precipitated at once on encountering the electrolytes in the sea water, but present evidence indicates that silica in such dilute solutions is not colloidal (Roy, 1945), and that electrolytes have little effect on its precipitation (Hurd, 1938). Silica may be preferentially adsorbed, however, on some sedimentary materials, such as clay or finely divided calcium carbonate. On the other hand, those organisms that make tests of silica may be primarily responsible for the depletion of silica in the ocean; siliceous sponges are common on many muddy sea bottoms, and

diatoms and radiolaria flourish occasionally in vast "epidemics" when conditions become favorable, and little of the silica they withdraw is returned to solution.

Silica appears to find its way into solution in the ocean or other bodies of water as the result of two main processes—chemical weathering of silica-bearing rocks and igneous activity. Calculations from analyses given by Clarke (1924, p. 70–109) show that the silica content of the world's rivers ranges, with few exceptions, between 3 and 50 parts per million, being lowest for rivers in cool climates, especially those draining recently glaciated areas, moderately high and consistent for those in warm humid climates, highest but somewhat erratic for those in warm arid climates, where evaporation increases the absolute content. Studies of soil chemistry show that silica is most mobile in warm humid or seasonally humid regions, especially in areas of low relief but unimpeded drainage, such as areas approaching peneplanation. Deposition of *silcrete* (the silica equivalent of caliche) was widespread in Australia during the epoch culminating in the Miocene peneplane there, probably the best authenticated peneplane in the geologic record, and it is known also in other areas—the eastern Sudan and parts of South Africa, for example. Silica so mobilized should remain in solution until the water containing it evaporates (as in silcrete deposition) or delivers it to the ocean, unless the water should be acidified or otherwise chemically altered, or unless the silica should be removed by diatoms in a lake.

That the water discharged in igneous activity commonly contains unusual amounts of silica in solution is well known; analysis of the water of Opal Spring in Yellowstone National Park, for example, has shown 762 parts per million of silica (Clarke, 1924, p. 195 n), and siliceous sinter is deposited around many of the hot springs and geysers there as such water cools or is chemically altered after coming to the surface. Submarine hot springs could discharge such silica directly into the ocean, and emanations accompanying submarine lava flows might also add silica to the sea water. Perhaps the concentration of silica so provided might locally pass the point at which coagulation to silica gel begins.

Another igneous source of silica is the submarine alteration (halmyrolysis) of volcanic ash, especially the alteration of ash of intermediate composition to montmorillonitic material (bentonite). That this process has operated in the past is proved by the concentration of silica in layers immediately beneath ash layers in the Mowry shale (Rubey, 1929) and the Monterey formation (Bramlette, 1946), and by thin layers of chert, representing silicified limestone, beneath altered ash beds in the Middle Ordovician rocks of the eastern United States. To what degree silica so released would be taken into solution to be reprecipitated later as chert is unknown.

Origin of Nodular Chert in Carbonate Rocks

There are good grounds for believing that, in many cases at least, the silica now forming chert (other than T-chert) in carbonate rocks was brought to the ocean by rivers draining nearly peneplaned areas. W. A. Tarr (1926, p. 25–28) especially championed this view. The very existence of widespread bodies of calcareous rocks of a given age indicates that mechanical erosion was negligible on adjacent land masses. The case is particularly clear for the silica in the Knox group (Upper Cambrian and Lower Ordovician) of the Southern Appalachians (Fig. 113, p. 239). In the Cambrian rocks underlying the Knox group, beginning with the Rome formation (upper Lower Cambrian), the distribution of sandstone and shale shows that terrigenous material was entering the Appalachian geosyncline and adjacent waters principally from the west and northwest (not from the southeast, though a southeastern source supplied material both earlier, in early Early Cambrian time, and later, in Middle Ordovician time). In late Early Cambrian (Rome) time, coarse sand and even fine gravel reached into what is now the northwest part of the Appalachian Valley and Ridge province, and fine sand and silt were carried southeastward entirely across it. In Middle and early Late Cambrian (Conasauga) time, only clay and silt were washed

into the area, and the eastern limit of mud fluctuated back and forth, producing the intertonguing shale and limestone formations of the Conasauga group in East Tennessee and farther south. Finally, in later Late Cambrian and Early Ordovician (Knox) time, the sea, having spread far northwestward over the central part of the continent, cleared completely, except for occasional incursions of well-rounded sand (probably beach sand and possibly in part wind-borne) at times of temporary emergence, as at or near the end of the Cambrian. The rocks that were deposited in the Southern Appalachian area at this time, the Knox group, are chiefly dolostone to the northwest and limestone to the southeast, and the amount of silica they contain decreases with remarkable regularity from much in the northwest to little in the southeast, though in any one section certain vertical variations in silica content are superimposed. There can be little doubt that the source of the silica in the Knox group was the same as the source of the mud in the Conasauga group and the sand in the Rome formation, probably the Canadian Shield and its southern extensions to the Ozark region, which, having furnished first sand and then mud, had finally been completely worn down to a peneplane, on which there was little mechanical but intense chemical weathering, and from which the sluggish rivers brought to the sea little but dissolved matter, notably calcium and magnesium carbonate and silica.

How the silica so brought to the sea was precipitated in its present form as nodules of chert and in some cases—in the Knox group, for example—partly also as finely divided disseminated silica, is another question. Two main theories have been proposed, roughly parallel to the two main theories for the origin of S-dolostone and not infrequently advocated by the same individuals. Tarr (1917; 1926; also, Tarr and Twenhofel *in* Twenhofel and others, 1932, p. 519–546) strongly advocated a theory of primary precipitation of the silica, whereas others, such as Barton (1918) and Van Tuyl (1918), have advocated a theory of penecontemporaneous (diagenetic) replacement.

According to the primary precipitation theory

in its simplest form, the concentration of silica brought in by the rivers periodically built up to a threshold value (a very low value according to Tarr), whereupon the silica coagulated into roughly spherical blobs of gel, which contracted and hardened into chert nodules. So stated, the theory explains very simply the shape and formation of the nodules and especially the extraordinary precision with which chert nodules of one particular type occur at an exact stratigraphic horizon whereas nodules of an entirely different type occur just as precisely a few feet or inches above or below. The theory is less successful, however, in explaining the common concentric banding of impurities (usually carbonate particles) in the chert nodules, the presence in them of fossils, some unaltered and some silicified, and the merging of nodules into nodular beds or into anastomosing three-dimensional networks. To explain these facts, Tarr suggested that the blobs of gel rolled around on the sea floor, incorporating lime-mud as they grew, snowball fashion; that fossils were picked up by the rolling blobs or fell into them from above; that adjacent blobs coalesced, losing their identity; and that, at times, those parts of blobs that projected above the surrounding lime-mud continued to grow upward until the next period of general precipitation, thus attaching the nodules of a lower layer to those of an upper. But more recent evidence suggests that silica will not coagulate spontaneously in solutions of such low concentration, and that, moreover, silica gel when formed would be rubbery rather than sticky and quite incapable of picking up lime-mud particles or fossils or continuing to grow where not covered up. Thus the modifications fail to make the theory convincing and at the same time they destroy its original simplicity.

Moreover, in some highly fossiliferous limestones carrying chert nodules there is clear evidence that the chert has replaced the limestone. The Cottonwood limestone (Lower Permian) in southern Nebraska, for example, carries vast numbers of the fusuline, *Schwagerina emaciata* (Beede), lying at random but fairly evenly spaced in the matrix. Abundant nodules of light-colored chert occur in the limestone, and in these the fusulines are oriented as in the surrounding limestone, are equally abundant, and are silicified. Individual shells extending across the boundary between chert nodules and surrounding limestone are commonly only partly silicified. If the chert nodules had originated as balls of silica gel on the sea floor, the surface tension at their borders would certainly have caused a distinctive concentration and orientation of the fusulines. Twenhofel (1919) has described very similar relations in the Foraker limestone (also Lower Permian) in southern Kansas.

The penecontemporaneous replacement theory sees the chert nodules essentially as syngenetic or diagenetic concretions, like the calcareous concretions common in many sandstone, shale, and clay formations—Marcellus shale (Devonian) of New York, Dakota sandstone (Cretaceous) of Kansas, Champlain clay (Pleistocene) of the Hudson, Champlain, and Ottawa Valleys, and the Pleistocene loess of the Upper Mississippi Valley. In each case a relatively minor constituent of a sediment has concentrated around certain centers, both the location of the centers and the shape of the resulting concretions being strongly influenced by the stratification. Emery and Rittenberg (1952, p. 796) have shown how a slightly lower pH in one bed, or even one lamina, of a growing sediment might cause silica to precipitate there from the interstitial water being driven upward by the compaction of the sediment, and Newell and others (1953, p. 160–166) have explained chert nodules and desilicated sponge spicules, occurring close together in different layers of the same bed, by just such a mechanism. The chert in the growing nodules (like the calcite in at least some calcareous concretions) actually replaces the surrounding sediment, but commonly the replacement was incomplete, leaving concentric bands of carbonate particles or avoiding dolomite rhombs or fossil shells. Where centers were thick along one horizon the concretions coalesced into a nodular bed; where several horizons were closely spaced, into a three-dimensional network.

The penecontemporaneous theory, therefore, while lacking the elegant simplicity of the first form of the primary theory, is more successful in accounting for the somewhat complicated facts. But it does demand that the silica, before accumulating diagenetically to form the nodules, was present, dissolved in the interstitial water or disseminated through the lime-mud. How this disseminated silica was first trapped remains to be explained; preferential adsorption on calcium carbonate or some other catalytic reaction in the growing sediment may be suggested, but direct evidence of such a process is at present lacking. The disseminated silica does exist, however, in many calcareous formations, both those with many and those with few chert nodules; under some circumstances, at least, what silica was not concentrated into nodules of S-chert in the freshly formed deposit is now being concentrated into blocks of W-chert at the present land surface.

Origin of Bedded Chert

The origin of great thicknesses of bedded chert is even more of a problem than that of the nodular chert in carbonate rocks, and no unified theory can be presented. Several interesting studies of individual occurrences of bedded chert have been made, however, and some of the results of these studies are summarized here. From them it appears probable indeed that no one theory will explain all the various occurrences.

Certainly one of the outstanding studies of cherty rocks is Bramlette's report on the Monterey formation (1946). The Monterey is a distinctive and very siliceous facies of the marine Miocene (and locally basal Pliocene) deposits of California, occurring in the Coast Ranges from San Francisco to Los Angeles, and locally reaching a mile in thickness. The distribution of rock types and the areal variations suggest a non-uniform environment, perhaps something like that around the present Channel Islands off Los Angeles (p. 52). Thick bodies of undisturbed sediments, showing rhythmic bedding and characteristically high in non-detrital silica, mark old basins, whereas thinner bodies of reworked sediments, showing thicker less regular bedding and scour and fill features and containing much terrigenous material, were deposited on old ridges,

which appear to have been less in areal extent and more local than the basins. The total amount of terrigenous material is smaller than might be expected.

Three kinds of siliceous sediments in the Monterey are listed by Bramlette: diatomaceous, porcelaneous, and cherty; all grade into ordinary terrigenous shale, mudstone, and sandstone, though the cherty rocks show the least gradation. The very porous diatomaceous rocks consist mostly of diatoms, and their origin is clear. In the much less porous porcelaneous rocks, the pores are largely molds of diatoms; the rocks seem to represent diatomaceous rocks that have been largely cemented by silica. The compact cherty rocks appear to be the end stage of this process, and in them almost all traces of diatoms have disappeared, except where they are preserved in unchertified carbonate concretions. The three rock types grade laterally into each other, confirming the view that the cherts and porcelaneous rocks are simply diatomaceous rocks more or less altered by cementation with silica, but in any one area the diatomaceous rocks lie stratigraphically high so that the alteration appears to be in part a matter of depth of burial.

But how did the alteration take place, and, in particular, whence came the silica that converted the porous diatomaceous earth into compact chert? The diatoms in some of the diatomaceous rocks show clear evidence of much solution, suggesting that the silica was dissolved from one part of the rock to cement another. If so, however, the total body of the rock would have been compacted to a third its original volume, and though there is evidence of some compaction, it is not of this order of magnitude. Another source might be the pyroclastic material which is unevenly distributed through the formation. This consists mainly of unaltered volcanic ash in the diatomaceous rocks but of bentonite in the other rocks, and the alteration of ash to bentonite releases considerable silica, as proved by the silicification of the underlying beds as well as by chemical analysis. Here again, however, the amount of silica released is quantitatively insufficient to produce the vast amounts of cemented porcelaneous and cherty rocks. The question of the source of the cementing silica must be left in abeyance.

The source of the silica used by the diatoms themselves and the reason for the extraordinary volume of diatomaceous and altered diatomaceous material is likewise not clear. Bramlette is inclined to lay this also to marine alteration of volcanic ash freeing silica into the sea water where it was available to the diatoms. In summary, greatly increased volcanic activity in the Miocene provided silica for vast numbers of diatoms, whose tests, along with much volcanic ash, accumulated to great thickness in favorable basin environments. After deposition, probably after some burial, much of this deposit was further cemented by silica of uncertain provenance, probably in part from the diatomaceous earth itself, in part from alteration of the enclosed volcanic ash, though these sources do not appear competent to have provided the whole of it.

Bedded chert also occurs in California in the Franciscan formation; this chert was intensively studied by Davis (1918). It is now largely chalcedonic silica, much of it stained red with iron oxide. Radiolaria are found in many layers and are locally very abundant. Associated with the chert are shale (much of it siliceous and locally, at least, containing much tuffaceous material), graywacke, and basalt flows, including some pillow lava. Davis argued, largely by eliminating other probabilities, that the silica was supplied to the sea directly by emanations accompanying the basalt flows, that it formed layers of silica gel on the sea floor which solidified into the present chert, and that the radiolaria, which flourished because of the high silica content of the water, are mainly incidental. In the same study, he extended this theory of primary origin to the Monterey chert, but there, at least, it seems untenable, as Bramlette has shown. If, on the other hand, the radiolarian chert of the Franciscan were secondary after radiolarian earth, like the Monterey chert after diatomaceous earth, the evidence for the alteration has been lost in the deformation and metamorphism that the rocks have since undergone.

A different sort of siliceous sediment is the "siliceous shale" of the Mowry, in the Cretaceous sequence of Wyoming and South Dakota, described by Rubey (1929). A thick sequence of dark, dark-weathering, soft, only slightly fissile claystone or mudstone is interrupted by the Mowry, a dark, distinctly hard shale that weathers light bluish-gray and porcelaneous. The hardness of the shale is directly correlated with an abnormally high silica content. Interbedded in the Mowry (as also in the overlying and underlying less siliceous rocks) are many beds of bentonite, and the silica content of the Mowry increases upward under each such bed and reaches a maximum directly beneath it. The shale itself contains, beside obviously terrigenous material, montmorillonite, devitrified volcanic ash, cryptocrystalline silica, and organic matter. Silica released in the formation of the bentonite beds has clearly contributed to the siliceous Mowry shale, but Rubey showed that this alone is quantitatively insufficient to account for all the silica in the shale. Moreover, the less siliceous shale above and below also encloses thick bentonite beds. Rubey believed that alteration of finely disseminated volcanic ash, scattered through the shale rather than concentrated in layers, has been the main source of the silica. In any case it seems to have been of volcanic origin.

The Paleozoic sequence in the Ouachita Mountains of Arkansas and Oklahoma (and in the closely related Marathon region of Texas) consists dominantly of sandstone and shale, quartzitic below but approaching graywacke above; it contains a little limestone below but displays an abundance and a wide variety of highly siliceous rocks, such as siliceous shale, chert, and novaculite. This sequence contrasts with the Paleozoic sequence in the nearby Midcontinent area, which includes much limestone and dolostone, and in which chert occurs most commonly only as nodules in the carbonate rocks. Goldstein and Hendricks (1953) have described the petrography of the Ouachita siliceous rocks in detail and have discussed their origin.

The siliceous shale they studied occurs mainly in relatively thin layers in the midst of thick graywackes and shales of the Stanley (Mississippian) and Jackfork (Pennsylvanian) formations; it is generally thinly and wavily laminated, highly carbonaceous, and impregnated with exceedingly fine-grained silica. Radiolarians are abundant, and sponge spicules and plant spores are common in certain beds. The layers appear to represent periods when the normal influx of sand was interrupted and relatively stagnant conditions prevailed. In the Bigfork chert (Ordovician), chert is associated with dark carbonaceous shale of the same type in the upper part of the formation, and with shale and limestone in the lower part. Where chert and shale are associated, the chert is dark and laminated like the shale but even more siliceous. The chert associated with limestone is still purer, mostly lighter, and generally not quite so fine grained (in places it is chalcedonic); it has clearly replaced the limestone, and some of it takes the form of nodules. Finally, the Arkansas novaculite (Devonian and Mississippian), the most siliceous formation of all, contains rocks ranging from similar dark siliceous shale to white massive novaculite. Carbonate is present as scattered grains in some parts of the area, mainly in light-colored novaculite. In this formation, and indeed generally in the rocks studied, radiolarians are abundant in the darker rocks but give way almost entirely to sponge spicules in the lighter rocks, some of which are almost solid spiculite.

Some tuff layers are interbedded in the Stanley formation, and Goldstein and Hendricks conclude that the non-fragmental silica in all these rocks was derived from the submarine alteration of volcanic ash, the novaculite and chert forming where nothing diluted the volcanic silica, the dark siliceous shale where there was some dilution by argillaceous and carbonaceous matter. Radiolarians and sponges throve, they believe, because of the abundant silica in the sea water; redistribution of silica during diagenesis, and especially during deformation or weathering, accounts for that part of the Bigfork chert that replaced limestone. This attractive theory seems based on rather tenuous evidence, however, for, despite their careful petrographic work, they reported no volcanic ash shards in any of the siliceous rocks themselves. Moreover, the Bigfork chert is not the only one of these units associated with limestone; thus, the Arkansas novaculite is contemporaneous with and

presumably grades into limy chert and cherty limestone on the margins of the Ouachita belt (some of these rocks were also studied by Goldstein and Hendricks and they are very similar except for the carbonate content). The solid spiculite reminds one of the diatomite of the Monterey formation and raises further questions. A final choice among the various theories does not yet seem possible.

The Camden chert of Tennessee and the Clear Creek chert of southern Illinois (both basal Middle Devonian) present an allied dilemma. Unlike the otherwise similar and partly contemporaneous Arkansas novaculite, these cherts are richly fossiliferous, the shells now appearing as hollow molds showing surface ornamentation and other features of shell forms in uncommonly faithful detail. Did the chert replace a fossiliferous limestone, completely and precisely avoiding the shells, or was it a primary sediment that hardened around them?

The Rex chert (Permian) of southeastern Idaho, as already mentioned, seems in some respects transitional between bedded chert and nodular chert; it has been described and its origin discussed by Mansfield (1927, p. 78, 367–372) and Keller (1941). Chert of this age is known from Alberta to Utah; in some areas in Idaho, bodies of bedded chert are as much as a hundred feet thick, but in others the chert contains nodules of limestone or grades into massive crinoidal limestone containing much chert in the form of nodules or nodular beds. For the silica in this deposit, Mansfield rejects an organic origin, though sponge spicules are common in certain beds, and also a volcanic origin, on the ground that no volcanic materials accompany the deposit. (Thick bodies of Permian volcanics are present, however, not far to the west in central Idaho.) He follows Tarr generally in believing that the silica came from a peneplaned land mass undergoing chemical weathering and that it was deposited by direct precipitation from sea water over the vast area where the chert is now found. Keller suggests some diagenetic replacement of limestone but like Mansfield holds that the bulk of the chert is a direct precipitate. The chert would thus be essentially an extreme case of the nodular chert associated with carbonate rocks, carbonate being almost absent.

These studies of bedded chert thus indicate diverse origins. Some attribute the silica to chemical weathering on a peneplane, others to emanations accompanying submarine lava flows, still others to submarine alteration of volcanic ash. Some consider the chert itself a primary gelatinous precipitate, others believe that it replaced or at least cemented pre-existing sediments not long after their deposition. All these possibilities must be kept in mind in appraising the origin of other bedded chert formations in the geologic record.

PART IV

SYNTHESIS

Charles Schuchert

Figure 115.   Quarry at Newsom, Tennessee, showing two major paraconformities.   The Laurel, Waldron, and Lego formations are Middle Silurian, the Pegram limestone is lower Middle Devonian, and the Chattanooga shale is Upper Devonian.

15. *The local section*

THE PROBLEMS OF SUBDIVISION

The basic data of stratigraphy are derived from individual sections exposed in local areas. Synthesis becomes possible later as these local sections are correlated one with another, but the first step in working out the geologic history of a region is the objective description of the rocks as they are observed in local outcrops.

Description of anything as complex as the rock sequence, even in a single quadrangle, requires subdivision and the subjective selection of units suitable for description; such units are *formations* and their subdivisions *members, tongues,* and *lenses.*

Figure 116 illustrates the problems of subdivision and nomenclature. It is an idealized cross section of an area more than 100 miles across, having a not uncommon range of facies changes. Of course, these relations would not be known when the geologic study of the region is begun, and they could not be recognized by inspection since only small bits of the whole could be seen at once. A geologist would start with a small area, commonly a quadrangle, and his knowledge would at first be limited to what he could see in that small area.

If he happened to start in quadrangle X, he would find eight fairly distinct and mappable lithologic units, A to H, in normal sequence from oldest to youngest. These he would name and describe as formations, indicating for each its type section, its thickness, its lithologic peculiarities, and, so far as possible, its fossil content. If he worked in quadrangle Z, he would necessarily recognize a totally different sequence of formations, K to P, but his choice of units would likewise be relatively simple and objective.

If, after the local sequences in quadrangles X and Z have been worked out, a geologist should undertake the study of an intermediate quadrangle Y some distance from each of the previously studied areas, he would face several problems of nomenclature. Which of the formations previously named in other areas can be recognized in quadrangle Y? If a unit (e.g., F′) is lithologically similar to a named formation (F) but is either thinner or thicker than the original and presumably represents a different time span, should a new name be given? Should units such as R, S, T, and U be considered tongues of previously named formations? Should units such as V, W, and H′ be considered separate formations, members of one formation, or tongues of previously named formations? Should named formations H and P be considered a single unit embracing also H′ and perhaps V as well? Should unit A′ be identified as formation A and should formation L be suppressed as a synonym of A even though it is almost entirely younger? These are problems now to be faced in almost every areal study, for there are few remaining areas so remote from

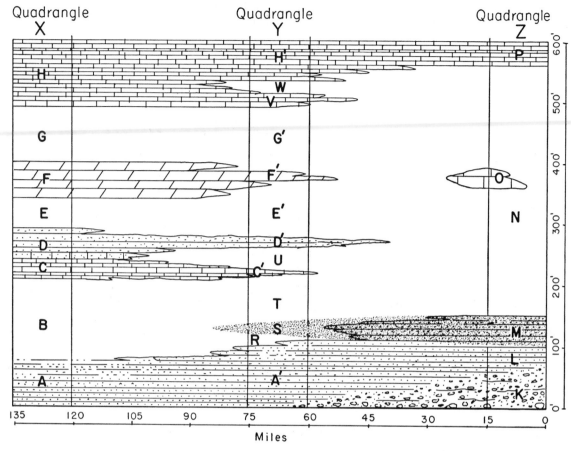

Figure 116. Hypothetical example of facies change to illustrate the range of problems facing a stratigrapher establishing formations in a limited area.

studied sections that at least some named formations cannot be recognized. The answers to questions such as those posed above would be easier if the intervening areas had been worked and the over-all stratigraphic relations as represented in Figure 116 were known. For this reason, reconnaissance excursions across the intervening country to previously mapped areas are commonly useful.

Actually, in many regions the lithologic units are not so simple and obvious as represented in our diagram. In the Appalachian Valley Province, for example, the Upper Cambrian and Lower Ordovician deposits form a monotonous sequence of drab dolostones and limestones some thousands of feet thick, which on casual inspection appears endlessly variable in small details but monotonously alike in the large from top to bottom. For half a century or more these rocks defied satisfactory subdivision, but gradually more subtle characteristics have been found useful in breaking this great mass of strata down into formations.

Ultimately the answers to several of the questions posed above depend on the principles adopted in subdividing and naming the local rock units. Well-defined usages have necessarily grown up as the science of stratigraphy advanced, but usage in North America has tended to diverge in various respects from that in Europe. Only within the last two or three decades have the underlying principles been brought sharply into focus; a noteworthy milestone in the codification of North American usage was the "Stratigraphic Code" of 1933 (Committee on Stratigraphic Nomenclature, 1933; p. 260).

North American stratigraphers have carried their usage wherever they have worked in numbers, notably in northern South America and in Arabia. In Australia, also, a stratigraphic code has been prepared that agrees in most respects with current North American usage (Glaessner and others, 1948; Raggatt, 1950; also, American Commission on Stratigraphic Nomenclature, 1949). In other parts of the world, varieties of European usage are dominant.

UNITS OF SUBDIVISION

Definition of the formation. The fundamental unit in the subdivision of a local section, according to North American usage, is the *formation.* Each sequence of rocks is to be divided exhaustively and without overlap into named formations, virtually the only exception for sedimentary rocks being in first reconnaissance of unexplored areas. The Stratigraphic Code describes the sedimentary formation as "a genetic unit formed under essentially uniform conditions or under an alternation of conditions" (Art. 6), and adds that its limits are to be "drawn at points in the stratigraphic column where lithologic characters change or where there are significant breaks in the continuity of sedimentation" (Art. 5). A more succinct definition in common use is that a formation is "a mappable unit."

There are two main concepts involved in the idea of a formation as thus defined. First, the formation is a unit of *rocks,* distinguished from other units by lithologic characters, which reflect the uniform or uniformly alternating conditions under which it was deposited. "Lithologic" here should be taken as broadly as possible and may include differences in fauna, especially in gross aspect of fauna, though probably not merely specific differences within a single group of animals. But the concept of time as such does not enter; if similar or uniform conditions persisted through the boundary between two time subdivisions, no matter how important, the rocks deposited under those conditions constitute nonetheless a single formation. Nor need the formation be of equal time span throughout. Thus, for example, the unit A–A'–L in Figure 116 is a formation, even though in quadrangle Z it is almost wholly younger than in quadrangle X. Likewise the dolostone, unit F–F', is a single formation, though its time span is far less in quadrangle Y than in X. "Mappable" in the short definition is a corollary of "lithologic," a corollary that is of the utmost practical importance in determining just which of the innumerable possible lithologic distinctions that might be drawn will be the most useful in making subdivisions of the column.

Second, the formation is a *unit* of rocks, specifically a "genetic unit." In other words, gross lithologic similarity or mapping convenience is not sufficient to establish a formation, if in fact the rocks in question do not constitute a unit, if they are not the product of uniform or uniformly alternating conditions. The distinction here is parallel to that drawn in Chapter 6 (p. 134) between a diastem and an unconformity; if over-all conditions have not changed, the rock sequence may logically be placed in one formation, but if they have changed, it should be divided into more than one. It is inevitable that decision on whether the given rocks constitute a "genetic" or "natural" unit cannot be wholly objective; it is inevitable and proper. Subdivision of a stratigraphic sequence into formations is not directly inherent in the rocks themselves, which were not necessarily deposited in such a way as to facilitate their ultimate subdivision by geologists; it is the product of personal judgment, and personal judgment is not wholly objective. But, on the other hand, such subdivision is not wholly arbitrary and subjective either, for it begins, or should begin, from consideration of the objective characters of the rock mass. Thus there will inevitably be strong differences of opinion about the subdivision of given rock sequences, but these differences are not to be lamented; they are signs of healthy growth in our knowledge, provided that no one forgets that there is a tentative subjective element not only in the subdivisions of others but in his own.

Names of formations. According to standard American usage, the name of each formation consists of two parts—for example, Potsdam sandstone, Pierre shale, Monongahela formation. The first part is a locality name, which designates a place at or near which the formation is typically displayed and can be studied; the second term is a lithologic term like sandstone, limestone, redbeds, which indicates the dominant rock type in the formation, or it is simply the word formation if no one rock type is considered dominant. (There is a tendency at present to use "formation" more and more commonly instead of a lithologic term, partly by reaction to cases where a formation was named "quartzite" or "conglomerate" from a few conspicuous beds that make up only a very small part of the unit.) It should be emphasized that both parts of the name are essential to it; generally, indeed, the locality name usurps the function of the full name, but strictly such expressions as "the Potsdam" are no more proper designations than "the sandstone," though either may be used to avoid needless repetition in writing provided the full title has already been given, preferably within the same paragraph.

The prominence of the locality part of formation names probably results from preoccupation with nomenclatural problems revolving around them. It is now generally agreed that no geographic name shall be used for two separate formal stratigraphic units (a few exceptions are permitted by the Code, such as between igneous and sedimentary units if distant, or where the same name has become firmly established in two uses, as Madison for a Cambrian sandstone in Wisconsin and a Mississippian limestone in Montana and Wyoming). Likewise it is generally agreed that in conflicts between names, priority of application shall govern if other considerations are nearly equal, but, on the other hand, stability in nomenclature requires that a well-established name be retained in preference to an older but obscure name. Some writers, indeed, have recommended absolutely strict adherence to the rule of priority, by analogy with biological nomenclature, but they have commonly forgotten that even in biological nomenclature priority has exceptions, as for names before a certain date (1758 for zoology). Unless a similar starting point should be set up for stratigraphic nomenclature, or rather one for each region, attempts to revivify old names, which were commonly based on very incomplete knowledge, will merely perpetuate confusion.

The use of locality names for formations took hold only gradually. They were first widely used in America in the reports of the first geological survey of New York State, especially in the final reports of 1842, but other geologists of that day condemned them as trivial. During the later part of the century, the value of a type locality as a tie point for the concept of a formation became more and more apparent, and by the end of the century locality names were well nigh universal. There was much conflict in usage, however, especially across state lines. In order to avoid this kind of conflict and insure a reasonable uniformity of usage within its own reports, the U. S. Geological Survey early instituted an advisory Committee on Geologic Names, which reviews each report or paper by a Survey geologist, especially each proposal for a new name or a new use of an old one. The result has been a satisfactory (if somewhat conservative) nucleus of uniformity in the reigning chaos.

Realizing the need for more general uniformity, the Association of American State Geologists set up a committee in 1930 to study the matter, and out of this grew a general committee representing that Association, the U. S. Geological Survey, the Geological Society of America, and the American Association of Petroleum Geologists. For this committee, J. B. Reeside, Jr., and W. W. Rubey, under the supervision of H. D. Miser (all of the U. S. Geological Survey), prepared a code of rules to govern stratigraphic nomenclature, and this "Stratigraphic Code" of 1933 (already referred to above, p. 258), as accepted by the committee, has become the standard for sound procedure and is an invaluable reference for American stratigraphers.

As an aid to the work of the Committee on Geologic Names of the U. S. Geological Survey, its longtime secretary, Miss M. Grace Wilmarth, compiled a card catalog of all stratigraphic names given to units in the United States, and later she extended this to all North America. This compilation, as of January, 1936, was published by the U. S. Geological Survey (Wilmarth, 1938), and it is also an invaluable tool for American stratigraphers. The Survey Committee, moreover, has kept the card file up to date, and any geologist who wishes to know if a name has previously been used may write to the Secretary of the Committee for that information.

In 1946, the four organizations responsible for the Code of 1933, together with the Geological Survey of Canada, established the American Commission on Stratigraphic Nomenclature, to review and revise the Code and to act on specific questions of nomenclature arising under it. This Commission has had an active career, publishing (in the *Bulletin of the American Association of Petroleum Geologists,* beginning in 1947) two series: Notes (formal statements of problems presented to the Commission, and informal discussions) and Reports (formal decisions by the Commission), and it is at work on a revision of the Code. The Commission is serving a useful and important function in American stratigraphy, not in deciding questions of stratigraphic fact or interpretation, which it rightly considers no part of its province, but in developing a uniform but usable and flexible system of stratigraphic nomenclature with which to express those facts and interpretations.

Other rock units. The formation is the fundamental rock unit in the American scheme, but flexibility demands other units as well. Several formations that together make a unit of higher order may be classed as a *group,* which, like a formation, is a unit of rocks into the definition of which the concept of time as such does not enter. A group is given a locality name and used as far as the unity it stands for is recognized, even if the named formations within it change entirely from one area to another. The Newark group (Triassic) of eastern North America and the San Rafael group (Jurassic) of the Colorado Plateau are examples. A lithologic term may be used with the group name, if appropriate. The use of groups is not mandatory, and the formations overlying and underlying a group need not belong to any group.

Likewise, units smaller than formations may be recognized. They are called *members* if they are apparently persistent along strike, *tongues* if they disappear (usually by facies change) in one direction, and *lenses* (or lentils) if they disappear in both directions within the mapped area. Members, etc., may receive formal locality names if desirable, and such names have the same standing as formation and group names as regards priority. They do not need to be named so formally, but can be designated as, for example, the upper sandstone member or the white limestone member of the *x* shale (or formation). Moreover, the formation of which they are a part need not be exhaustively divided into members; if, for example, a thick shale formation contains near the middle a thin but distinctive and mappable sandstone unit, that unit could be named the *y* sandstone member of the *x* shale, and the bodies of shale above and below would not need to carry any designation at all, unless the geologist studying the area wished it; indeed, they probably should not be named if they are not lithologically distinct enough to be readily separable should the thin sandstone member be faulted out.

The most common use of tongue is a more special case. In Figure 116 (p. 258), for example, unit W is a tongue of the N shale extending into the H limestone, and unit V is a tongue of the H limestone extending into the N shale. Unit U is another tongue of the N shale. In a case like that shown in Figure 78 (p. 155), where the Mancos shale interfingers in complex fashion with the sandstone facies of the Star Point and Black Hawk formations, it is not necessary that the tongues receive geographic names; the more important tongues may be named if desirable and the minor ones left unnamed.

Deciding whether certain units are to be considered members of a single formation or tongues of two or more distinct formations is commonly a subjective matter. In quadrangle Y of Figure 116, for example, units V, W and H' would appear to persist with little lateral change and to be closely allied genetically, and would probably be considered members of a single formation. In the larger view, on the contrary, V is clearly a lower tongue of unit H and W an upper tongue of unit N, N and H being classed as formations. Neither choice is inherently right or wrong; they merely represent two different ways of looking

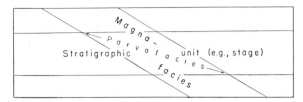

Figure 117. Terminology proposed by Caster (1934) for stratigraphic units within steadily shifting facies.

at the same facts, and either may be preferred according to circumstances. Likewise, in quadrangle Y, unit R is a tongue of the B shale, but unit T might be considered an upper tongue of the B shale, a lower tongue of the N shale, or a separate formation. Units E–E′ and G–G′ might also be considered tongues of the N shale, or they might be regarded as distinct formations, depending commonly on their thickness, uniformity, and persistence. It would be quite acceptable, indeed, to say that *formation* E is a tongue of the N shale.

Stockdale (1931, p. 75–78; 1939, p. 37–40; see also p. 265) has proposed the formal use of the term *facies,* with a geographic name, for a "lateral" subdivision of a formation in the same way that member is used for a "vertical" subdivision, and McKee (1938b, p. 13–14; 1949, p. 47) has suggested the term *phase* for the same thing. Caster (1934, p. 19 ff.) has proposed a more elaborate terminology (Fig. 117) using the term *magnafacies* for a lithologic unit transgressing several "stratigraphic units" (i.e., time-stratigraphic units, *not* formations in the sense of the Code), and the term *parvafacies* for the part of a magnafacies within one "stratigraphic unit." A formal term for such lateral subdivisions of a formation might be very useful, but to date none of these terms has formal status in the Code or by action of the Commission on Stratigraphic Nomenclature.

Further flexibility is added to the scheme of rock units by the provision that, if the conditions warrant, a unit that is considered a group consisting of formations in one area may be considered a formation with members in another. No change in geographic names is necessary, either for the larger unit or its parts; the only restriction is that, where the larger unit is a group, it must be exhaustively divided into formations with geographic names. For example, the Knox group (Upper Cambrian and Lower Ordovician) of part of East Tennessee, composed of five named formations (some of them with members), becomes the Knox dolomite, including certain named members, in other parts of Tennessee and in Georgia. Furthermore, a persistent small unit, of member rank, if traceable through the areas occupied by two different but roughly contemporaneous formations, may rank in each area as a member of the appropriate formation without itself requiring but one geographic name.

Names may also be given to still smaller units below the rank of member, especially to economically important units such as coal beds, bentonite layers, or iron seams, but these names are not considered formal stratigraphic names, and the rules of no duplication and of priority do not apply to them. Thus it is often convenient to use a single geographic name to designate several closely related beds, as, for example, a coal bed, an underclay, and a traceable sandstone layer, or even two or three such sets of beds, such as the Lower, Middle, and Upper Kittanning coal and clay beds and the Kittanning sandstone in the Allegheny formation (Pennsylvanian) of western Pennsylvania and adjacent territory.

European usage. Perhaps the main distinguishing feature that a geologist trained in North American stratigraphic usage finds in European usage is the absence of regularity. Most of the names of rock units consist in Europe as in North America of two parts, a general lithologic term and an identifying (for example, geographic) name, but in Europe there appear to be no general rules applicable to either part. Many, probably a majority, of the European rock units bear locality names, but these are by no means mandatory, and they are mixed in any order and proportion with purely lithologic names, such as *Buntsandstein* or *Grès bigarré* (literally, variegated or motley sandstone); with paleontologic names, such as Lingula flags; or with names based on special features or economic use, such as Millstone grit. The other part of the name is basically lithologic, as with us (though singular and plural forms are mixed without apparent rule—thus, Wenlock shale and Wenlock shales may appear in the same publication), but where we would use the term formation in place of a lithologic term, any term except formation is to be found—in England, for instance, bed or beds, layer, group, stage, or series (the last two apart from their use as time-stratigraphic terms), and on the continent, especially *couches* and *Schichten*. The word formation in England is a general term for any rock unit (thus the term rock group is used as a synonym), but it is never applied to any specific unit. In Germany, on the other hand, the word formation is used only for units of the rank of Cambrian and Triassic, for which we (and the English and generally the French) use the word system (*système*).

Moreover, there appears to be no systematic hierarchy of terms for rock units, like our group, formation, member, bed. A series is generally a large rock unit, and it may be divided into groups or stages or beds, but it may also contain series or it may be applied to units of the lowest rank recognized. Or, rather, the "rank" of a unit may vary from low to high in the same area, depending on the nature of the paper or report, whether generalized or detailed, and terms like series or group applied to the unit give no indication whatever of its relative rank.

Finally, the smaller units with geographic names are not uncommonly more purely local units than in America, where the tendency is always to carry formation names, once established, as far as possible. Thus a single lithologic unit may have several different geographic names in different local areas. In the other direction, however, many of the larger European units, though apparently ranked equally with rock-stratigraphic units and not distinguished from them by their names, are actually time-stratigraphic units and are carried for great distances despite complete changes of facies. Thus a single geographic or other name may signify a variety of lithologic units in different local areas. (Americans must admit, however, that the distinction between rock-stratigraphic and time-stratigraphic units, as set forth in Chapter 17, has only recently become significant in our nomenclature and that similar contradictions could be found in our own litera-

ture.) And, indeed, the fundamental basis of European classification even of local sections, in the fossiliferous rocks at least, appears to be a time-stratigraphic classification rather than the purely rock-stratigraphic classification represented by the American formation (as officially set forth in the Code).

Thus, in general, an American finds European stratigraphic nomenclature a haphazard and unsystematic accumulation of names of many sorts with no apparent guiding principle. To this statement a European might well reply that he finds the American system rigid and unsuited to the infinitely varied data that need to be named and classified, and that his own usage, if confusing and unsystematic at first sight, possesses at least the great virtue of wide flexibility.

DIFFERING CONCEPTS OF THE FORMATION

Examples. Figure 118 (adapted from Baker and Reeside, 1929, Fig. 3) shows a restored cross section of the Permian rocks of part of northern Arizona and adjacent states and illustrates the concept of the formation as a unit characterized by its gross lithology. Each of the named formations includes those rocks in which a particular rock type—cherty limestone, white cross-bedded sandstone, red shale and sandstone—dominates, and because these different rock types intertongue in a complex manner, the formational units into which they are classified intertongue similarly. The units so chosen are, in general, eminently mappable, though some difficulty might be encountered where lateral gradations between the rock types are exposed. On the other hand, it is evident that the time span represented by a formation at one place has no necessary relation to that represented at another, and that two formations can overlap in time to any degree. Thus the Coconino sandstone at the Little Colorado River (near the type area) has almost no beds of the same age as the De Chelly and Cedar Mesa sandstone tongues, yet those tongues are part of the same "genetic unit formed under essentially uniform conditions" as the typical Coconino, conditions whose place of operation shifted with time.

Similar examples could be multiplied. Here it

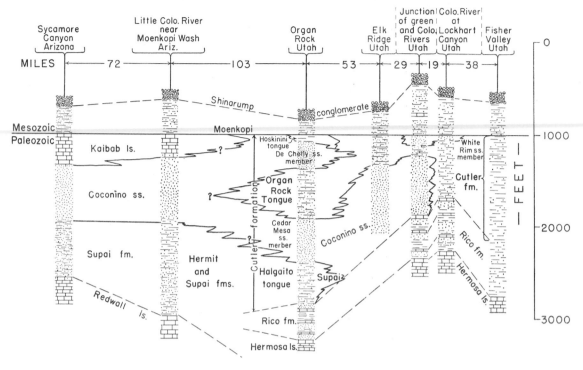

Figure 118. Stratigraphic section of Permian rocks in northeastern Arizona and southeastern Utah. After Baker and Reeside (1929).

will suffice to mention the Monterey formation (Miocene) of California; as described by Bramlette (1946), the Monterey formation is a gross lithologic unit that disregards time, and includes all Miocene (and locally early Pliocene) siliceous rocks—siliceous shale, diatomite, porcelanite, chert, and intermediate types (p. 252)—of the central Coast Ranges of California, but excludes contemporaneously deposited sandstone and non-siliceous shale. Thus the limits of the formation in any area are the limits of the siliceous facies, whatever the time at which deposition of that facies began or ceased in the area.

There are many areas in which the rocks fall naturally in this way into a number of formations, each corresponding to a major rock type, but there are many others where the facts are not nearly so simple. Thus, in the Pennsylvanian rocks of the eastern and central United States gross-lithologic formations are not usable. For example, in Pennsylvania, the Pennsylvanian system is a thick sequence consisting of alternating shale and sandstone, with numerous coal beds in certain parts

of the section and fewer in others, with several thin but persistent limestone layers, and with other special beds here and there. If gross lithology alone is considered, the sequence is virtually a single unit (which continues into the Lower Permian), though a much sandier and even conglomeratic basal part could be separated. But the economic importance of the system is such as to demand its subdivision, and, in fact, subdivision is fairly easy, for most of the coal beds and limestone layers and even some of the sandstone layers are remarkably persistent laterally. By means of such thin but traceable and recognizable units—"key beds"—the whole section can be divided into a sequence of units of convenient size. In the Pennsylvanian of Pennsylvania, out of the many available key beds certain ones have been traditionally chosen as formation boundaries, namely those that divide the sequence roughly into richly coal-bearing and relatively barren formations (in some areas into groups), as shown in Table 14. As a result, these formations do differ to some extent in their over-all lithology,

TABLE 14. MAJOR SUBDIVISIONS OF THE PENNSYL-
VANIAN AND PERMIAN SYSTEMS IN PENNSYLVANIA

Older Names	Modern Geographic Names
Upper Barren shales	Dunkard
Upper Productive Coal Measures	Monongahela
Lower Barren shales	Conemaugh
Lower Productive Coal Measures	Allegheny
Conglomerate or Millstone grit	Pottsville

but the differences are mostly in the proportions of the several rock types, all of which occur to some degree in each of the upper four units, and it would not be possible either to distinguish or to delimit the formations precisely in the field by their gross lithology, but only by using the key beds.

In such a sequence, therefore, the formation limits chosen may well be only a few out of a number of possible limits, and generally they are chosen with two points in mind—the section should be separated, if possible, into at least vaguely differentiated units, as in the case just cited, and the key beds used should be the most persistent available key beds, so that the separation may be carried as far as possible. As a result of the second restriction, formations defined in this way have boundaries that commonly approximate closely to "time-lines"—to contemporaneity. The formations are thus not far from and, indeed, are readily confused with time-stratigraphic units, units of rock *defined* on the basis of the time during which they were deposited (p. 293), but the formations themselves are, nevertheless, truly rock-stratigraphic units, defined on the basis of lithologic characters—in this case key beds. It may even be true that the limits have been chosen deliberately to make the formations as nearly as possible of equal time span throughout, but still the formations are properly rock-stratigraphic units if their actual definition depends on key beds or other lithological characters.

Formations of this sort are probably at least as common in the stratigraphic record as those based on gross lithology. Instructive examples, in addition to those in the Pennsylvanian rocks practically throughout the eastern and central United States, are the subdivisions of the Stanley-Jackfork sequence (Mississippian and Pennsylvanian) in the Ouachita Mountains (Harlton, 1938; Hendricks and others, 1947) and of the lower Lower Cambrian sequence in northeast Tennessee (King and others, 1944).

An apparently similar but not identical concept of a formation is set forth by Stockdale (1931; 1939) in his studies of the Lower Mississippian rocks of Indiana and Kentucky. For him (1939, p. 38, 39), the formation should be "a definite stratigraphic unit with a fixed position in the stratigraphic column and time scale," bounded by "some definite stratigraphic bounding unit or faunal zone, the bounding unit itself being of contemporaneous or nearly contemporaneous age throughout." These formations are then divided into laterally equivalent, contemporaneous, named facies (p. 262) on the basis of lithologic variations within the formations. The formation is, therefore, not strictly a lithologic unit, nor is it defined entirely on the basis of key beds, though certain important key beds and laterally persistent lithologic changes were put to great use by Stockdale in delimiting the formations. The concept of time, in itself, has entered the definition of the formation.

Similar but more explicit in this regard is the usage of G. A. Cooper (1930; 1933) in his papers on the Hamilton group (Middle Devonian) of New York State (p. 138). For Cooper, the Hamilton group is divisible into four formations, the boundaries of which are drawn as nearly as possible along "time-lines" as determined first by faunal differences and second by key beds that mark the limits of the faunal zones. Lithologic units within these formations are separated as members. But each formation corresponds essentially and by definition to a time-stratigraphic unit and may embrace rocks of all the deltaic facies from black shale to redbeds.

Discussion. From the examples given, it is clear that in modern American usage the term formation is used for a wide variety of units, from purely lithologic units with virtually no regard for time to purely time-stratigraphic units with virtually no regard for lithology. In the face of this diversity some authors have indeed recommended abandoning the term altogether. In general, however, two schools of thought are becoming distinct, both of them including able and eminent

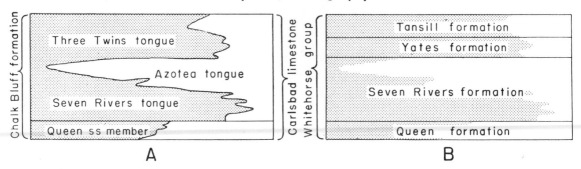

Figure 119.   Alternate classifications of Guadalupian rocks in southeast New Mexico.   From King (in Longwell, Chairman, 1949).

stratigraphers who have thought deeply on the subject. One holds that the formation should be, ideally at least, a unit of constant time span throughout its area of application, and that where the time span changes the name should change. The other holds that time as such has no place in the definition of formations, which should be distinguished fundamentally by their lithologic characters. The latter view is that embodied in the Stratigraphic Code and upheld by the American Commission on Stratigraphic Nomenclature, and we believe it is the opinion also of a majority of North American geologists. Certain qualifications may perhaps be expressed: first, inasmuch as a formation is a lithologic *unit,* lithologic continuity representing uniform conditions of deposition is essential, so that, for example, Devonian limestone resting directly on entirely similar Ordovician limestone may not properly be included in the same formation; and second, "lithologic character" must be interpreted very broadly, including subtle as well as gross distinctions, and key beds as well as over-all lithology. But, given these qualifications, we would strongly recommend to all students of stratigraphy the view that the formation is fundamentally a lithologic unit, as defined in the Code.

King (discussion in Longwell, Chairman, 1949, p. 167–168, Fig. 1) has made some pertinent comments on the differing concepts of the formation. He points out as an example that in the Guadalupian rocks of southeast New Mexico, which lie behind the great Capitan Reef (Fig. 40, p. 93), two quite different formational classifications have been developed (Fig. 119, from King). Reconnaissance surface work divided these rocks

into two complexly intertonguing, gross-lithologic formations, the Carlsbad formation of dolostone and limestone and the Chalk Bluff formation of redbeds, sandstone, and anhydrite. These formations and tongues are readily mapped, and the resulting map indicates the areal distribution of the main rock types. A later subdivision, guided in good part by subsurface data, depends on the detailed tracing of key beds and results in units which approximate a constant time span, though the formations are not defined by time. Such formations are more difficult (though not impossible) to map, but they are more useful for the study of structural features and for the synthesis of geological history, the final aim of stratigraphy. Such a progression, from gross-lithologic time-neglecting formations to key-bed time-approximating formations is perhaps a normal one, to be expected as knowledge of a given area grows. The final step, indeed, would be the delimitation of units deliberately based on and defined by time. But by the time this step is reached, stratigraphic interpretation is advancing beyond the description of the local section, for which rock-stratigraphic units such as the formation are primarily intended, to the correlation and synthesis of regional sequences, and for this purpose quite other units, the time-stratigraphic units, are needed; these units are discussed in Chapter 17. In maintaining, therefore, that the formation should remain fundamentally a lithologic unit, we are not denying the value of units of time-significance, but rather affirming that the two kinds of units, having different functions to perform, should be clearly and consistently distinguished.

CRITERIA FOR SUBDIVISION

The Stratigraphic Code, as quoted above (p. 259), states that the boundaries of formations and similar units are to be "drawn at points in the stratigraphic column where lithologic characters change or where there are significant breaks in the continuity of sedimentation." The two parts of the statement indicate two main types of criteria to be applied in subdividing a sequence of rocks into rock units.

Changes in lithologic character. All changes in lithologic character in a local section reflect changes in the conditions of deposition of the rocks in the section. The lithologic changes may be sharp or gradational, obvious or subtle, readily observed or requiring careful discrimination. Normally, the problem facing the geologist is not the discovery of such changes but the choice, from among a great variety of changes of many kinds, of those most suitable in subdivision. Evidently, from the definition of a formation, he should choose ideally those lithologic changes that express the most fundamental changes in the original environmental conditions, if he can determine which those are. Thus, by the mere statement of the problem, it becomes clear that the selection of formation boundaries is not the elucidation of facts inherent in the rocks themselves, like mineral composition or grain size, but an interpretation made from the rocks by the geologist. As such, it is subject to dispute by other geologists with other interpretations, and this state of affairs is neither to be ignored nor bemoaned. Out of such differences of opinion, where they are the result of careful investigation by men of intelligence and good will, general agreement sooner or later emerges, and the science of stratigraphy makes an advance. Differences of opinion then appear at the next level of detail or interpretation, and so the process continues.

By general agreement, the most "important" changes and the ones most useful in delimiting formations are over-all changes in rock type—from sandstone to shale, from shale to limestone, from limestone to conglomerate. Among other useful changes are changes in color, changes in the thickness of beds or the degree of fissility, changes in weathered appearance or topographic expression. Similarly, changes in readily measured and graphed properties such as resistivity, as recorded by electrical well-logs (p. 274), are eminently useful where the subdivisions must be used principally in subsurface work. In a thick sequence of nearly homogeneous rock, very minor differences in lithology or thin but distinctive layers of some other rock type, which would ordinarily be disregarded, may be used. Again, in thick sequences of heterogeneous rock, built up of relatively thin layers of a few rock types repeated endlessly, with or without order, changes in the proportions of the rock types or thin intercalations of some other rare rock type may make the most satisfactory limits.

But in addition to reflecting the important changes in the conditions of deposition, a classification or subdivision into formations should be convenient for those who must use it, and for the purposes for which they are to use it. Hence it may be desirable to ignore some obvious major changes and select subtle minor ones, if the units that result are more useful. Suppose that a thick sequence of limestone rests on a thin basal sandstone over an important unconformity. For most purposes it would be better to subdivide the limestone into several formations of relatively equal thickness, if differences in grain size, thickness of bedding, or other characters make it possible, leaving the sandstone undifferentiated from the lowest limestone formation or at most recognized as a basal member, rather than simply to divide the sequence on the basis of gross lithology into one thin sandstone and one thick limestone formation. Similarly, as the purposes of investigation differ, the kinds of characters used in subdivision will differ. Thus, changes in resistivity are useless in subdividing a local section being studied for the first time by rapid surface reconnaissance, but they may be the ideal basis for detailed subdivision of the section in an intensively studied oil field.

Where the change selected is sharp, subdivision is relatively easy, but commonly lithologic changes are gradational, either through transitional intermediate rock types or perhaps more typically by interbedding of two separate rock types, the proportions changing steadily through the gradational beds. The problem of selecting a boundary in such a gradational sequence is again largely a matter of convenience. In a gradation between unbroken shale below and unbroken sandstone above, for example, it will ordinarily be more convenient to draw the line at the base of the lowest sandstone layer (or the lowest sandstone layer of more than a certain thickness), for the lowest sandstone layer will ordinarily be much more prominent than the highest shale layer. Under certain circumstances, or for certain purposes, indeed, it may be best to separate the gradational sequence between the unbroken shale and sandstone units as a member or formation in its own right, though one must then draw two difficult boundaries instead of one.

Breaks in the record. As suggested above (p. 259), the unity of a formation should not ordinarily be stretched to cover a break in the record significant enough to rank as an unconformity. To be sure, this "significance" is itself to be evaluated in terms of the purpose of the geologic study being made, so that for reconnaissance mapping a formation might well straddle a disconformity of small hiatus that could not be ignored in more detailed work. Naturally, the criteria required here are precisely those for the recognition and evaluation of unconformities (p. 121).

Changes in fauna. Changes in fauna reflect changes in the biologic conditions accompanying deposition, and thus such changes might also be considered among the criteria for delimiting formations. Indeed, some stratigraphers insist that a formation should never embrace parts of two systems or series, or even of two stages or faunal zones, holding that a change in fauna invariably records a significant break or change in deposition. More than once, certainly, the observation of faunal changes in a sequence has led to the discovery of disconformities or to the recognition of significant changes in lithologic characters, and so to the better delimitation of formations. Because fossils are rarely abundant, however, and because paleontologic distinctions are commonly (and properly) so much a matter for experts, faunal changes *in themselves* (except perhaps for gross ecological changes, as from dominant brachiopods to dominant corals) can-

not supplant changes in lithologic character as the fundamental basis for delimiting formations. We would urge, therefore, a conservative position in this matter, holding with the Stratigraphic Code (Art. 5, Remark c) that "a unit distinguishable from the enclosing rocks only by its fossils shall not, in general, constitute a formation."

On the other hand, fossils are commonly very valuable supplementary aids in recognizing formations, and the geologist may deliberately choose for his formational boundaries those lithologic changes that most nearly coincide (indeed, they may exactly coincide) with faunal changes, even if these are less obvious and readily observed than others he might have chosen. And, of course, in the *correlation* of formations and the delimitation of time-stratigraphic units, fossils, where present, are much the most important criteria.

General remarks. In choosing which lithologic changes shall delimit his formations, the geologist should observe certain general criteria as well. He should strive especially to choose distinctions that are objective and convenient to observe (according to the method of study likely to be employed, such as small-scale mapping, detailed stratigraphic measurement, or study of well samples or electric logs), and he should make his descriptions of them as clear as he may, so that the next observer will have no difficulty in recognizing the same distinctions, however minor and subtle they may be. This, of course, is one of the reasons time span, as such, should not enter into the *definition* of a formation. Generally, moreover, he should try to choose distinctions that are laterally persistent and can be readily traced in the field or from well to well, so that the formations will have as wide an application as possible. Such persistence can best be determined by actual mapping, if the opportunity affords; measured sections may be enough, but characters that appear obvious in well-exposed individual sections are not always the most useful in areal work.

At the present day, to be sure, the geologist rarely finds a completely new and undescribed local section for which he is the first to propose subdivisions. Instead, he finds that his predecessors have already established formations, groups, and members, perhaps brought in from adjacent areas where they were more applicable, perhaps used for different purposes than his. Commonly his first task is to learn to recognize these units and see how far he can make use of them. If, as commonly, he finds them partly but not entirely satisfactory, he must then decide how best to remedy the existing situation. And here he is ordinarily faced with a choice, either to accept the old terminology, patching it up where necessary to suit his needs, or to reject it and propose an entirely new classification. In most cases, there is no easy solution to this dilemma, and much can be said on both sides. Old names are commonly well known and understood, and their modification comes often as a natural evolution of ideas; yet precisely because they are already accepted with one meaning, to alter them may produce considerable confusion. New names are unequivocal (at least if well defined and until the next group of geologists studies the area), but they impose an additional burden on the memory of other stratigraphers, and their relation to the terminology in previous literature is rarely apparent. Perhaps the only advice that can be given is first to determine, without reference to previous terminology, what units appear to fit best the rocks themselves, then to apply old names to these units wherever they correspond in major features to the units as conceived by the previous observers, and finally to observe a proper respect for previous workers even in disagreeing with their results. The geologist who heaps scorn on his predecessors is likely to receive the same treatment from those who follow him.

THE TYPE SECTION

American stratigraphy in the twentieth century has been almost characterized by its concern for type sections. Two extreme points of view have developed, as well as many intermediate ones. One view decries the growing emphasis on the type section and holds that a formation is independent of any one section or locality, though it may be typically displayed by one or by several sections. The other holds that the type section defines the formation, especially as to its time span, and that nothing may be admitted to the formation that cannot be correlated with beds in the type section. (Obviously the latter view goes with a belief that the formation is properly a unit of constant time span.) Probably the great majority of American stratigraphers take an intermediate view.

In developing what we believe to be a sound view of the significance of the type section, and thereby illuminating still further the concept of the formation, we are strongly influenced by the parallel that can be drawn with the view of the significance of the type specimen of a biological species that has been set forth in masterly fashion by George G. Simpson (1940). According to Simpson, the species of the biological taxonomist, though it is an attempt to express a natural grouping of organisms (a "biological species"), is fundamentally a *concept* in the taxonomist's mind, a concept of a group of organisms with certain common characters and also with a certain degree of variability. This concept is based, or should be based, on all the individuals which the taxonomist conceives to belong to the species in question. When proposing a new species, the taxonomist selects one specimen to be a concrete example of his concept and to bear the name of the species, and this becomes the type specimen. The type specimen should illustrate the main common characters of the species, but, of course, it cannot also typify the degree of variability which is as integral a part of the concept of the species as the common characters. Later revisers, with greater knowledge, will commonly find it necessary to revise the species or concept of the original author, changing his list of common characters or the degree of permissible variation. But one thing they must not change; whatever changes they introduce into the concept of the species, the type specimen must still belong to it. The type specimen is, therefore, not a strait jacket restricting the species to specimens identical with itself, but a guide to the concept of the original describer of the species and a stable tie-point, a concrete object to which the name of the species is attached.

So it is with the type section of a formation. The original describer of the formation had in his mind a concept of a unit of rocks, and he selected a given section as a concrete example, typical of the unit as he conceived it. But the type section cannot be expected to display all the features of the formation, especially the degree of variability that the describer was willing to include in it. Later stratigraphers may find it necessary to modify the concept of the particular formation to fit increased knowledge of the rocks, but whatever changes they introduce, the type section should be a tie-point around which the new concepts are built. This does not mean that later workers may not revise the limits of the formation, even in its type locality, if it is necessary to do so in order to make the formation a lithologic unit, but the modifications should preserve to the formation at least the bulk or the most typical part of the original formation in its type section. This rule, like its biological equivalent, should not be broken except on grave provocation, and then only after full publicity and debate. We must, therefore, protest against unilateral alterations of type sections. As an example, Baker, Dane, and Reeside (1947), working in the Jurassic rocks of the Colorado Plateau, found that the type Wingate sandstone at Fort Wingate, New Mexico, is a part, not of the widespread unit long called the Wingate sandstone farther northwest on the Plateau, but of the higher Entrada sandstone of that area. They therefore proposed to abandon the type section of the Wingate, assigning it to the Entrada, and to reserve the name Wingate for the lower sandstone farther northwest. It may well be true that suspension of the usual rule in this case would in the long run be the least disturbing to existing concepts and nomenclature, but we would urge that such a matter not be decided unilaterally but that it be submitted to the American Commission on Stratigraphic Nomenclature, accorded due publicity, and finally decided after all interested parties have had the opportunity to present their views.

In summary, then, we hold that a formation is primarily based on a concept in the mind of its describer, and that the type section is a device for obtaining at least one objective tie-point for that concept. Whoever thereafter uses that formation name implies that he has tried to determine as well as he may what was the original concept of the formation, and that he either accepts that concept or is modifying it within reasonable limits, which should be explicitly stated, and in any case that he still includes within the formation those beds at the type locality that the original describer considered typical.

It follows from this doctrine of the type section that a considerable responsibility rests on the geologist who first describes a formation and selects its type section. In describing the formation he should make as clear as possible the concept he has in mind, and in selecting the type section he should make it as typical as may be, preferably in the area where the formation attains maximum thickness. The section should, if possible, be completely exposed, and, at any rate, it should show the top and base of the formation; the location of the section and of the top and base should be described so that other geologists will have no difficulty in relocating them. Measurements of the type section should be published with the original description, if at all possible. It is very desirable also that the section be fossiliferous, so that collections may be made from it by many observers, and that at least preliminary faunal lists accompany the original description. An excellent discussion of techniques in measuring and describing sections is given in Chapter 3 of Krumbein and Sloss's book, *Stratigraphy and Sedimentation* (1951). It should be emphasized, however, that the geologist who proposes a new formation has responsibilities beyond accurately measuring and describing the type section. The description of the new formation (and, for that matter, of any formation studied stratigraphically) should also provide information on the areal extent of the formation, on the kinds of rock types included, on changes in the proportions of these rock types laterally and vertically within the formation, on its persistent and variable features, and especially on usable key beds it may contain, on other typical localities and sections, on its appearance not only in fresh sections but in weathered outcrops, on the soil that accompanies it, on its topographic expression, and on its total fauna.

16. Correlation

THE MEANING OF CORRELATION

The word correlation has a variety of usages, both vernacular and scientific, but in stratigraphy it has a quite special meaning and should be confined to that meaning. Two units, belonging to different local sections, are said to *be correlative* if they are judged to be time equivalents of each other, and *correlation* is the process by which stratigraphers attempt to determine the mutual time relations of local sections. Thus correlation is concerned with the synthesis of the data of established local sections into a composite time scheme applicable to a whole region.

It should be mentioned here that recently the word correlation, in its stratigraphic usage, has been extended (Krumbein and Sloss, 1951, Chap. 10; Krumbein, 1951, p. 1511) to cover equivalences other than time, specifically equivalences (relations) in terms of lithology (rock units) or fossil content (biostratigraphic units). From this viewpoint, a transgressive sandstone such as the Tapeats sandstone (Cambrian) of the Grand Canyon (Fig. 73, p. 141) would be said to *be correlative* as a rock unit throughout its extent, though it is apparently all Lower Cambrian at one end of the canyon and all Middle Cambrian at the other. Certainly the information that the basal Cambrian sandstone is rising in the section by onlap toward the east has both scientific and economic significance. To the historical geolo-gist it is of cardinal importance in reconstructing the geologic history of the area, while to the petroleum geologist it may suggest a stratigraphic trap. But to say that the two parts of the Tapeats sandstone are correlative obscures both the time and the stratigraphic relations, whereas to state what the time relations really are brings out all the significant facts. We believe, therefore, that it is confusing to extend the stratigraphic term *correlation,* even when qualified as rock-unit cor-relation, to include a relation such as this one of like facies in an onlapping sequence; we would call it physical facies equivalence. Similarly, with respect to the relation between units containing the same fauna (when considered apart from pos-sible time significance), we would call this relation not biostratigraphic correlation but faunal equiv-alence. In what follows, then, correlation refers to time relations and nothing else.

But the determination of the time relations of rock layers from local section to local section cannot be direct; indeed, it is one of thé most difficult tasks facing the stratigrapher. In this task he must call on every possible aid, every possible criterion provided by the rocks, that may enable him to infer their relative or absolute ages; he is shirking his duty if he neglects any of them. There are two principal parts to the task, which are interrelated and mutually helpful; one is to determine the ages relative to each other of the rock units in the various local sections within the region under consideration, the other to determine their ages relative to the standard geological time scale, which serves as a reference for all time designations.

For this task, the stratigrapher has two principal sorts of criteria: the physical or lithologic, and the biological or paleontologic. Now, the same data that serve as lithologic criteria of correlation (time equivalence) may serve also, taken in another light, as criteria of physical facies equivalence, and similarly the biological criteria may serve as criteria of faunal equivalence, but the two uses of the data should be kept distinct. It is precisely for this reason that we deplore the extension of the term correlation to cover other kinds of equivalences than those of time. Moreover, though facies and faunal relations are recorded in the rocks and fossils, and their determination can be reasonably exact and objective, time relations are not so recorded, and their determination remains an ideal, toward which we strive, but which we can only approximate by interpretation and evaluation of the several kinds of factual data provided by the fossils and rocks. It follows that correlation, being, like subdivision of the local section, essentially an interpretation, is the result of personal judgment, and that it can never be wholly objective, a state of affairs that can do no harm if we realize that it holds for our own correlations as well as those of others.

PHYSICAL CRITERIA OF CORRELATION

The basis of most of the physical criteria of correlation is the Law of Superposition, the first fundamental generalization of stratigraphy (p. 110).

Physical continuity. In a single outcrop of bedded rocks, it can be assumed almost without question that any given bed (or bedding plane) is roughly contemporaneous throughout. Exceptions can be imagined, but in general one bed represents a single minor period of deposition, one bedding plane a single minor period of nondeposition or scour, as far as they can be clearly traced as units, though the exact beginning and end of the time span they represent may vary from place to place. Tracing of individual beds and bedding planes is therefore, in theory at least,

an almost unimpeachable method of correlation. In practice, however, it is severely limited, partly because individual beds and bedding planes pinch or die out or merge with others laterally, partly because outcrops are very rarely good enough to permit such tracing, especially if, as is normally the case, the individual bed being traced is but one of a sequence of virtually identical beds. But many other physical methods of correlation are only approximations designed to circumvent the difficulties of this method.

If tracing a single bed is satisfactory correlation, then tracing a unit consisting of beds of like character should be a possible substitute—that is, tracing a member or formation. As formations are in general of mappable dimensions, this is a far more practical procedure, and, indeed, it is the procedure tacitly followed in most geologic mapping of stratified rocks. The map shows the belt of outcrop of each formation or other unit, and unless reasons appear for thinking otherwise, it is generally assumed that the formation is roughly contemporaneous throughout. Within most areas of a size to be covered by a detailed map, especially where outcrops permit continuous tracing, this assumption is probably reasonably valid, but the geologist should always be aware that it is an assumption, that it is almost certainly false in detail, and that it may well be false in its entirety. The Tapeats sandstone (Cambrian) of the Grand Canyon region, mentioned above (p. 271, and Fig. 73, p. 141), furnishes a splendid example. This unit can be traced almost continuously from one end of the Grand Canyon to the other; for long distances it upholds a wide bench, the Tonto Platform, which testifies to its perfect continuity. Yet because of facies shifts the unit is of different ages at the two ends of the canyon, so that physical continuity has failed completely to establish correlation. Presumably, as one traces the unit westward, beds in the upper part extend out into and disappear within the overlying Bright Angel shale, and new beds appear at the base of the unit, until no bed present in the eastern part of the canyon is still represented in the unit in the western part.

Outcrops as continuous as those of the Grand Canyon are, of course, rare, but even with discontinuous outcrops a unit can often be traced satisfactorily by assuming its continuity, an assumption that has proved correct in most cases where it could be tested by wells or mines. Topographic expression is particularly valuable in guiding the interpretation of such discontinuous outcrops. It must never be forgotten, however, that even if continuity is thus suggested or proved, time-equivalence, though perhaps probable, is not assured.

Lithologic similarity. With more and more discontinuous outcrops, and especially where faults or other interruptions prevent tracing of beds or larger units, physical correlation must depend on matching rock types in the hope of recognizing the beds or other units across the discontinuities. Once the matching is accomplished, the problem of whether the units matched are truly correlative is the same as for units followed by physical continuity, except that the distances involved are commonly greater and the chances of facies shifts of the matched units or rock types are therefore increased.

The lithologic characters available for matching units across discontinuities are as diverse as those used in establishing the units themselves (p. 267) —gross lithology, subtle distinctions within one rock type, heavy minerals or microscopic features, data from electric well logs (p. 274), distinctive key beds, even weathering characteristics or topographic expression. Naturally, the greater the number of different and especially of unusual characters that can be matched, the firmer is the matching and through that the correlation. Even unusual characters and unusual combinations of characters in key beds represent, however, special combinations of conditions of deposition that could well be repeated, and, indeed, very commonly the discovery of a distinctive and useful key bed has been followed by the discovery that there are several such beds, perhaps grouped within a narrow stratigraphic interval, perhaps arranged en echelon along strike so that, though most local sections show only one, the bed in one section is not correlative with that in others. Once such facts are known, the several key beds may be almost as useful as if there were only one, or, indeed, more useful if further distinctions can be made between them. For example, the discovery of an altered volcanic ash bed in the

Middle Ordovician Series of the eastern United States offered a magnificent opportunity for close correlation, for by the very nature of an ashfall, at least in shallow seas, it can be considered precisely contemporaneous throughout. But it was shortly found (as might, indeed, have been anticipated) that there were several such beds in that part of the Ordovician section, recording a considerable period of volcanic activity. The first correlations, based on the assumption of a single ash bed, had therefore to be abandoned, but by very careful attention to the details of the several individual ash beds (and of the prominent chert layers that have formed immediately beneath them, layers that in many areas crop out where the weak ash beds are entirely covered), extremely satisfactory correlations over considerable areas can be established.

If it is possible to match not merely one distinctive bed or rock type but a sequence of several, then the strength of the match grows exponentially, *provided* the different components of the sequence are truly independent, as, for instance, several distinctive ash beds. The proviso is necessary because if a given sequence merely reflects an orderly progression of facies, as in marine onlap or offlap, the same sequence, however complicated, appearing elsewhere in the region would prove no more than any one of its members. Spieker (1949) has presented an excellent example of such a facies sequence (a continental replacement) and has discussed the fallacy involved (Fig. 78, p. 155). In the Upper Cretaceous rocks along the Book Cliffs in eastern Utah and adjacent Colorado, it is almost everywhere "possible to start in marine shale of the uppermost Mancos and go upward in order through littoral marine sandstone and coal measures to clastic beds barren of coal." Now, "in any given correlation if two variables agree the force of the conclusion is much more than twice that for agreement as to one variable, and for three or more the certainty of the correlation mounts at an imposing rate. In the present stratigraphic case there are at least five major variables in perfect agreement, and many more minor ones can be aligned. The statistical case would seem to be virtually proved, but the fallacy is that the variables are not independent; on the contrary they are intimately dependent and for purposes of logical analysis they must be treated as one" (Spieker, 1949, p. 68–69). And, as Spieker further points out, it is, in fact, inherently likely that lithologic matching of this one variable —namely, the orderly facies sequence taken as a whole—merely establishes facies equivalence and not true correlation.

Similar caution should be exercised in correlating by means of complicated sequences when the sequences are cyclically repeated, as in the cyclothems of the Pennsylvanian System (p. 109). Evidently each cyclothem in one section will resemble in its main outlines all the cyclothems in another, so that, if direct tracing is not possible, correlation must depend not on the over-all resemblance of the cyclothems but on minor details and especially on irregularities in the individual cyclothems. But if a given cyclothem in one section is lacking one of the usual units, say the shale above the coal, this alone is certainly not enough to permit secure correlation with a cyclothem elsewhere that lacks the same shale, for the absence of a unit normally found is more likely than not to be the result of local irregularities or facies changes. Thus, cyclothems provide no easier and surer method of correlation than is available for non-cyclic beds.

Instrumental well logs. With the growth of the oil industry, the information available to stratigraphers from surface sections has been supplemented by an immense amount of very valuable subsurface information. In the early days of oil well drilling, this information was of roughly the same kind as the surface information, being based on study of the lithology and paleontology of rock samples from the wells, but beginning in the 1920's, methods were developed for obtaining new kinds of data instrumentally from the wells, and these methods have revolutionized the study of subsurface strata. We cannot do justice to these methods in the present chapter but can only mention them and suggest their importance in correlation; the student is referred to the various textbooks of petroleum geology and especially to Chapter 4, "Subsurface Logging Methods," by various authors in the symposium on *Subsurface Geologic Methods* (LeRoy and Crain, Editors, 1949) and Chapter 31, "Subsurface

Techniques" (Busch, 1950), of the book *Applied Sedimentation* (Trask, Editor, 1950).

The first developed and most important of these instrumental methods is the electric log, a set of curves giving continuous measurements of the self-potential of the rocks beside a drill hole, i.e., the electromotive force produced in them by contact of their fluids with the drilling fluid, and of their resistivity, the resistance they offer to an artificially applied electromotive force. The first is measured by lowering a single electrode down the hole, the second by lowering a system of electrodes (and several different sets of measurements may be made with different arrangements of the electrodes; commonly there are three). Figure 120 shows such logs for a number of wells in the West Ranch oil field in Texas (Bauernschmidt, 1944), and it also shows the astonishing amount of detail that these logs record. Infinitely painstaking work on samples from the wells could hardly match this detail, especially if the samples were mixed in coming from the hole, as they commonly are in rotary drilling, and one can understand the dictum that an electric log is to be preferred to a set of rock samples.

Correlation by means of these logs is in principle the same as for any other kind of lithologic similarity; the fidelity with which individual peculiarities recur from well to well (Fig. 120) makes such correlation particularly satisfactory, for one is virtually tracing individual beds. Naturally, such correlations are only good as far as the individual beds or groups of beds continue, but within an area where the beds are persistent, as within an oil field or a basin with a uniform history, electric logs are unsurpassed.

The success of electric logging stimulated the development of several other instrumental logging techniques that provide continuous measurements of some property of the rocks beside a drill hole. Radioactivity is the basis for one of these. Radioactivity logs, like electric logs, consist of two types of curves: one, the gamma-ray curve, measures the natural radioactivity of the rocks, and the other, the neutron curve, measures the radioactivity induced in them by an artificial source of neutrons. Radioactivity logs may show even more detail than electric logs, almost too much,

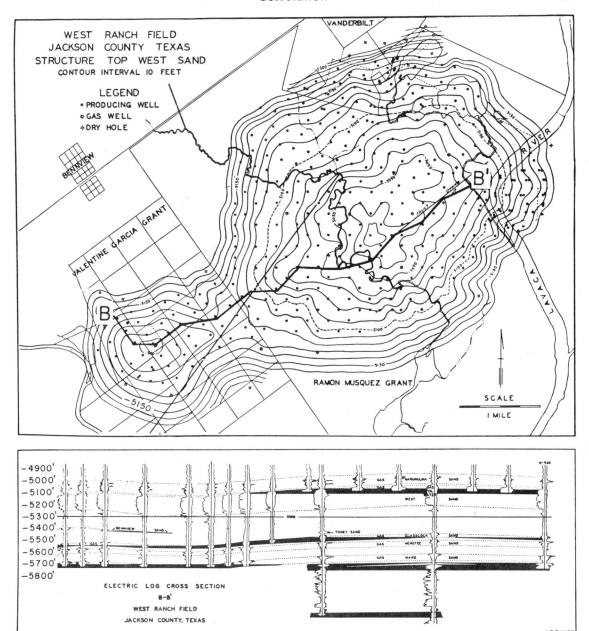

Figure 120. Electric logs. Above, a map of the West Ranch oil field, Jackson County, Texas, contoured on the top of the West sand. Below, a series of electric logs of wells along the line B——B′; the self-potential curve is on the left and the resistivity curve on the right of each log. Solid black shows oil pools. After Bauernschmidt (1944).

indeed, for some purposes; they are used for correlation in much the same way.

Other instrumental methods have been developed to measure continuously the temperature of the fluid in the drill hole and the actual width of the hole itself, which because of caving of weak rock like shale is commonly considerably greater than the width of the cutting tools. These logs can sometimes be used for correlation, but their principal value is in the technology of drilling and production. Drilling-time logs, based on measurements of the progress of the drill, have also been used successfully in correlation.

Stratigraphic position and sequence. If by any means, whether physical or biological, a secure correlation can once be made from a unit or bed in one local section to one in another, it is reasonable enough to suppose that the units next above and those next below the tie-point are likewise correlative, provided there has been no significant break in deposition in the layers concerned in either section. If the rock types involved are not too unlike in the two sections, this reasoning can be applied through considerable thicknesses, correlations being made between beds at roughly the same stratigraphic interval above or below the beds known to be correlative. Even if a minor disconformity intervenes, if it is present at roughly the same position in the two sections, correlation may be suggested. It is evident that such suggestion is far from proof, but often it will serve to draw attention to other features, such as obscure physical or biological changes or inconspicuous key beds, by which the correlation can be more firmly established. Or where no other evidence is available, such correlations may be the best that can be made. An example may be cited from the lower Lower Cambrian detrital rocks of northeast Tennessee (King and others, 1944, p. 27 ff.). A sequence of 4,000 to 7,500 feet of detrital rocks lies beneath the base of the sparsely fossiliferous Shady dolomite (Lower Cambrian) on each of several fault blocks. No fossils but *Scolithus* (vertical tubes in quartzite, probably burrows) are found in the detrital rocks, which consist of alternating and generally lenticular layers of several rock types and cannot be neatly subdivided into units that can be matched from fault block to fault block. But after study it appeared that roughly 1,000 feet, or a little more, below the easily recognized base of the Shady dolomite, there could be found on each fault block a layer or group of layers of white quartzite, commonly with *Scolithus,* and that 2,500 to 3,000 feet below the Shady there was a sharp change from relatively finer-grained rocks above, including some non-silty shale (otherwise rare in the area), to coarser-grained rocks below, commonly conglomeratic.

Because these two changes appeared in relatively consistent stratigraphic positions below a secure datum plane, they were accepted as roughly correlative in the various blocks. (As convenient lithologic changes that could be mapped, they were also used to bound formations, but there is no necessary connection between this use and their use in correlation.)

Naturally, if two firm correlations can be made between two sections, the possibility that the intervening beds are correlative is still more strongly suggested, even if the character of the intervening rocks is quite different in the two sections, again provided that there is no likelihood of an important break in deposition in either of the sections. If, as is common in such cases, it can be shown that the two contrasting rock types lying between the datum planes in the two sections are complementary in the intervening area, the one thickening as the other thins, the case for facies change within contemporaneous, correlative rocks becomes still stronger. Nevertheless, evidence of some other kind should still be sought.

One such kind of evidence would be intertonguing of the two rock types in the intervening area, which proves at least that the periods of deposition of the two rock types overlapped. An intertonguing of different facies may be a useful criterion of correlation in other cases as well; thus, the first clue to the correlation of two lithologically distinct and structurally separated sequences may be the discovery within one sequence of tongues of the rock type characteristic of the other. Under circumstances where the regional geology limits other possibilities, such intertonguing can be a very useful criterion of correlation.

Where other criteria fail, grosser and grosser relations and similarities may need to be used, at least to suggest possible correlations. Such are relations to regional unconformities or to igneous intrusions or the degree of metamorphism. It is obvious that, speaking precisely, the beds next above a regional unconformity are almost certainly *not* of the same age throughout, but where the correlation expected or sought is only to the nearest system, the relation may be useful. For example, in the metamorphic rocks of western New Hampshire (Billings and Cleaves, 1934, and many other reports by Billings and his students), Devonian and Silurian fossils have been found locally in the upper part of the rock sequence. Beneath them is an unconformity, but the rocks below are not markedly more deformed or metamorphosed, except where they are intruded by small igneous bodies that predate the unconformity. Farther west, especially in eastern New York State, where the rocks are hardly or not at all metamorphosed, Silurian rocks rest unconformably on Ordovician rocks. It has seemed reasonable to equate the two unconformities and to suggest that the rocks below are Ordovician in western New Hampshire as well as in New York, but Billings in making this correlation was fully aware of its insecurity, and he has consistently classified the lower rocks as "Ordovician(?)."

Extent of igneous intrusion and degree of metamorphism may likewise provide suggestive evidence for correlation in areas where better evidence is lacking (as in so many areas of Precambrian rock), but the limited extent of intrusive bodies and the abrupt regional changes in metamorphism even in rocks known to be of one age within single igneous and metamorphic regions should never be forgotten, and any conclusions as to correlation based on such evidence should be set forth tentatively and with proper qualifications.

Ages determined by radioactivity. If a radioactive element or isotope is incorporated into a mineral or rock at its formation, *and* if no further introduction or subtraction of material has altered the proportion of radioactive parent and product, then that proportion is a direct measure of the number of years that has elapsed since the formation of the rock or mineral. Several methods of geological dating have been based on this principle, and it is evident that such dating differs from all other criteria of correlation (except such minor methods as varve or growth-ring counts) in giving absolute as well as relative ages. The discovery of methods for determining the absolute age of geologic materials must indeed be ranked as one of the major achievements of twentieth century science (Knopf, 1949a, b).

The most significant method to date depends on the ratio of uranium or thorium, or both, as parents to lead as product. Though thoroughly double-checked determinations by this method are still regrettably few, they have nevertheless enabled us for the first time to estimate with considerable assurance the length of geologic time, its eons and eras, and even to some extent its periods. Other methods are based on the ratio of uranium and thorium to their other end-product, helium, but because helium is a gas that may be lost during the geologic ages, these methods have not been as satisfactory and at present are only of supplementary value. More recently, methods involving the radioactive isotopes of rubidium (product strontium), potassium (products argon and calcium), and, above all, carbon have begun to provide age measurements. The rate of disintegration of the radioactive carbon isotope (C^{14}) is so high that at most it can only be used to date the last few tens of thousands of years, but within that range revolutionary results have already been obtained, which permit for this most recent part of geologic time a relative precision several orders of magnitude higher than any other known method of correlation.

For the methods applicable to earlier geologic time, however, no such precision can be claimed. Each of the methods depends on accurate chemical analysis of the product and parent elements in the rocks, on accurate figures for the present terrestrial proportions of the isotopes of the parent element (except for thorium), and on accurate determination of the rate of disintegration, which must be extrapolated from measurements in the physical laboratory to time spans of millions of years. As a result, even under the best conditions, ages so determined cannot be considered accurate beyond the second significant figure, implying a probable error of several percent. When we consider that 5 percent of 200,-000,000 years (roughly the span of the Mesozoic and Cenozoic together) is 10,000,000 years, we realize that the degree of precision in correlation, that is, in *relative* age determination, that these methods make possible is no more and probably for most cases considerably less than the precision obtainable by fossils and, within local areas, by lithologic criteria. When we also consider that the uranium-thorium-lead method, still the fundamental method, is necessarily largely restricted to minerals from pegmatite deposits, occurring in highly metamorphic areas and commonly dated geologically only by supposed relationships to igneous intrusives, themselves all too seldom accurately dated, we can understand that radioactive age determinations are not likely to displace other methods of correlation, especially paleontologic methods, for the span from the beginning of the Cambrian period to perhaps the middle of the Cenozoic. For the Precambrian or Cryptozoic eon, on the other hand, radioactivity for the first time provides an objective means of correlation, imprecise though it may be, to replace the current subjective schemes, so largely based on the assumption that there have been only two or three "major world-wide orogenies" in the older three-quarters of geologic time.

BIOLOGICAL CRITERIA OF CORRELATION

Fossils and stratigraphy. Just before 1800, William Smith discovered the Law of Faunal Succession, the second fundamental generalization of stratigraphy. He had been collecting fossils as a hobby while working as a surveyor in southern England where the Jurassic strata fall naturally into several distinctive lithologic formations, some of which were extensively quarried. These beds dip gently and can readily be traced across the landscape. Eventually Smith realized that each formation contained a distinctive suite of fossils by which he could identify it without the need of lateral tracing. Thus he conceived the idea of using *guide fossils* as a means of recognizing rocks of equivalent age. Shortly thereafter he visited a friend, the Rev. Mr. Richardson, also a collector of fossils, who was amazed to find that Smith could identify the formation from which each of his collections had come, and who urged him to publish his new discovery.

Smith's idea was quickly adopted by others and proved to be an open-sesame that permitted the synthesis of local details and the construction of a valid geologic column to which sedimentary deposits all over the world could be referred. It is no accident that within the next half century all the geologic systems were established and recognized with assurance across Europe and in North America as well. Almost a century later,

Geikie (1897, p. 241) paid tribute to Smith's work in these words:

While the whole science of geology has made gigantic advances during the nineteenth century, by far the most astonishing progress has sprung from the recognition of the value of fossils. To that source may be traced the prodigious development of stratigraphy over the whole world, the power of working out the geologic history of a country, and of comparing it with the history of other countries, the possibility of tracing the synchronism and the sequence of the geographical changes of the earth's surface since life first appeared upon the planet.

Smith's discovery was purely empirical; he had no idea why distinct faunas succeed one another in the rocks. But the principle of organic evolution, recognized some sixty years later, provided an obvious explanation. Inasmuch as life has evolved continuously throughout its existence on Earth, there has been progressive change from age to age, not only for a limited area but for the Earth as a whole. Trilobites, fusulines, dinosaurs, and nummulites made their separate appearances, each holding the stage for a time and then making a final exit never to reappear. Three-toed horses represent a stage in an irreversible evolutionary sequence. Even on a smaller scale vast experience with the fossil record has confirmed what the principle of evolution would predict—change has been endless and progressive, and the Earth has therefore been peopled by a succession of faunas and floras, each distinct from the rest. Thus the Law of Faunal Succession is now an axiom in geology, which only a few "fundamentalists" would deny.

For precise and detailed correlation, nevertheless, the use of fossils is more difficult and uncertain than William Smith could have guessed, and the problems are more complex, perhaps, than many paleontologists yet realize. Many genera and species were restricted to preferred environments which they followed as the facies wandered, their stratigraphic range in a local section bearing little relation to their total range in time. In biological correlation, therefore, we must never forget the principles of biogeography discussed in Chapter 7.

Guide fossils. Inasmuch as all species and genera of organisms had a beginning in geologic time, and all extinct forms had an ending as well, every fossil is a guide fossil of sorts. But a good guide fossil should have relatively wide geographic distribution and limited stratigraphic range. In general, groups of organisms possessing complicated structures provide better guides than those that are simple, because they have more characters by which evolutionary change can be detected. The ammonites with their complex sutures and the fusulines and orbitoids with their large complicated shells have thus proved to be exceptionally good guide fossils. The value of such shells is enhanced if the group evolved rapidly, since then each detectable variant had a short duration. Groups that are able to swim (e.g., cephalopods) or to float (e.g., graptolites) are especially useful because they ranged widely and were little restricted in distribution by the bottom conditions. On the other hand, some groups of organisms are known to prefer special ecological niches and to have persisted with little change for long periods by following a particular biotope. Such *facies fossils* are of little use in detailed correlation. The "black shale fauna" of the Middle and Upper Devonian of the Appalachian region is a good example.

It must never be forgotten, however, that the stratigraphic range of a fossil cannot be known a priori; it can be determined only by experience. When its range has been determined in a single section or a small area, we proceed with the *tentative* assumption that this is its actual total range and make correlations with adjacent sections accordingly, checking the evidence it provides against all other criteria available. As field work progresses, experience will show that some forms hold a relatively constant stratigraphic position, and they can then be used with increasing confidence. But even after the range of a fossil has been well established in one province, we must be prepared to find that its range is somewhat different in another province. If it appears abruptly in the section, for example, without an obvious immediate ancestor, it is almost certainly an immigrant into the local area, having arrived from some region where it had evolved and where its first appearance is somewhat lower in the section.

In general, of course, a fauna will be more trustworthy than a single species or genus, but here, also, the sudden appearance of a new fauna in one area should raise suspicion that it had been living somewhere else.

Guide fossils have an advantage over almost all other criteria of correlation in that they can be recognized in isolated outcrops or in well cores, permitting immediate correlation across wide gaps, even across water bodies, or in complex structures such as the Alpine folds, where most other criteria fail. Guide fossils are a "first aid," therefore, in all reconnaissance field work. Even if only relatively long-ranging guides can be recognized—those that will place the larger local units in the correct geologic systems—this may be an immense help in organizing the field work for more detailed study.

Not uncommonly, guide fossils will identify deposits whose age would never be suspected on any other basis. To cite but a single illustration, a Lower Devonian formation (the Pillar Bluff limestone) was discovered for the first time in Texas in 1944 (Barnes, Cloud, and Warren, 1946, p. 167). The type section is a small pocket of limestone several inches thick and literally only a few square yards in area, plastered upon the Ellenburger limestone (Lower Ordovician) near Lampasas, in the Llano uplift. This remnant of a formation, almost completely lost by erosion, records an important chapter, otherwise unknown and unsuspected, in the geologic history of Texas.

Stage of evolution. With a broad knowledge of the paleontologic record it is possible to judge the approximate geologic age of a fossiliferous formation—hence its correlation with a standard section—without identifying either genera or species, that is, without recognition of any specific guide fossils. This method is particularly useful in reconnaissance work in remote or little known regions.

If, for example, a formation were found to bear the net-veined leaves of angiosperms, it would be considered not older than Cretaceous, and if these were associated with dinosaur bones, however fragmentary, it could not be younger than Cretaceous. Even this broad generalization would be immensely useful if the age were otherwise unknown. If, in addition, marine tongues were discovered bearing ammonites of distinctive types, the formation might be tied down to a

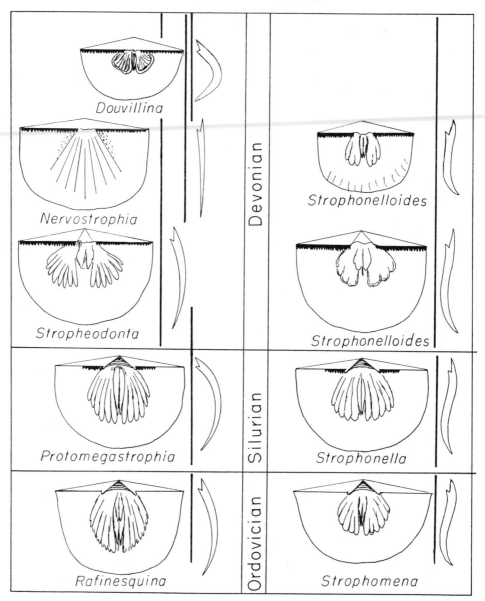

Figure 121. Denticulation of the hinge in the stropheodontid (left) and strophonellid (right) brachiopods. Interior view of a ventral valve and median profile of a complete shell are shown for each of several genera. Denticles in solid black. Range of each genus indicated by a heavy vertical line.

particular part of the Cretaceous System, even though the species were undescribed. Likewise, if a formation bearing net-veined leaves contained abundant mammal bones, even if badly worn and unidentifiable, it could be confidently called post-Cretaceous, and if, among these bones, fragments of three-toed horse skeletons were later found, the age would certainly be within the range from late Eocene to late Miocene. Depending on the size of the skeleton, the relative proportions of lateral and main digits, and the character of the teeth, the age might be pinpointed to a much smaller time-stratigraphic unit.

This principle can be used in many situations, either for broad approximations or for very precise and detailed correlation. For example, during mid-Paleozoic time two prolific tribes of strophomenoid brachiopods, the strophonellids and the stropheodontids, underwent a parallel evolution leading to progressive denticulation of the hinge line (Fig. 121). Both groups were widely distributed over the world and each produced several genera and many species, so that some representatives commonly occur in almost every brachiopod fauna of Ordovician, Silurian, or Devonian age. In the Ordovician rocks all known representatives of either tribe have completely non-denticulate hinge lines, in the Silurian they are all partly denticulate, and in the Devonian the hinges of all are almost completely denticulate, except in the Lower Devonian where there is an overlap of some that are partly denticulate with a majority of completely denticulate forms. With this knowledge, based on much experience in different parts of the world, one may safely refer a fauna containing any of these shells to the proper geologic system by depending on the stage of denticulation of the hinge line.

There are almost endless opportunities to apply this principle as the geologic history of diverse groups of animals and plants becomes known. The zonation of the Lower Carboniferous rocks of England by Carruthers (1910) on the basis of the progressive change in the septa of a simple coral, *Zaphrentis delanouei* Milne-Edwards and Haime, is a classic example. Brinkmann's study (1929) of the evolution of nodes and of the bundling of ribs in the Jurassic ammonite *Zugokosmoceras* (Fig. 69, p. 132)

shows how, under favorable circumstances, the application of biostatistics to such trivial changes may be used to establish the position of a fauna within a few centimeters in a local standard section. Progressive specialization of the septa in diverse tribes of ammonites has made them especially useful in this way, as has progressive evolution of shell structures in the fusulinid foraminifera (Dunbar and Skinner, 1937, p. 581; Dunbar and Henbest, 1942, p. 28–30). Progressive modifications of the glabella and glabellar furrows in some of the trilobites can be used in the same way (Elles, 1924, p. 103–105). Indeed, it is amazing how many groups of organisms, both large and small, provide a basis for zonation and correlation once their evolutionary history is carefully worked out.

Faunal resemblance. In detailed correlation the fossils not uncommonly fail to indicate a clear choice between two or more alternatives. The problem is illustrated by Figure 122 in which Section 1 shows three formations with partially overlapping faunas, some species being restricted to a single formation while others range through two or all three of them. This is the section of reference with which formation D in Section 2 is to be correlated. The latter has some species in common with each of the formations A, B, and C, but its fauna as a whole is not identical with that of any of them. The problem, then, is to decide whether formation D is to be correlated with one of the first three and, if so, with which one.

It is rather common practice to decide on the

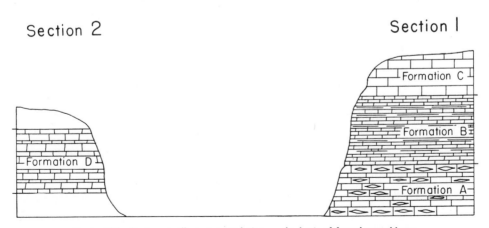

Figure 122. Sections to illustrate correlation on the basis of faunal resemblance.

basis of the number of species or of the percentage of species that the formations to be compared have in common. If, for example, formation D has 20 species in common with formation B but only 10 in common with A and 5 in common with C, it is assumed that it is most nearly equivalent to formation B. Such calculations are likely to be groundless and quite misleading, unless two considerations are taken into account. In the first place, if some of the species involved are known to have a longer range than that represented in the sections under study, their presence or absence there was determined by environmental factors and they have no correlative value for the problem at hand. All such long-ranging species should therefore be eliminated from the calculation. In the second place, since the time range is short, it may be assumed that the local biotope played a major role in determining the composition of each of the faunas. If the lithotope is closely similar in the four formations concerned, we may suppose that the biotopes were also closely alike, but if the lithotopes of formations A, B, and C differ appreciably, the fauna of formation D is likely to resemble that of the formation of a similar lithotope, regardless of precise age. In cases of this kind, some other criterion may be more significant than the statistical analysis of the faunas even if the faunas are large and varied. In any event, where the faunal evidence is somewhat equivocal or even contradictory, correlation based upon it must be considered very tentative. Even a tentative correlation may be useful, however, in guiding further work—provided it is recognized as tentative and does not prejudice the selection of new data.

Proportion of still living species. Lyell's subdivision of the Cenozoic into Eocene, Miocene, and Pliocene Series was based primarily on the percentage of still living species in the several faunas (Lyell, 1830–1833, v. 3, p. 52–60). The marine invertebrate faunas of these rocks in western Europe had already been largely described, and Deshayes, a French paleontologist, had noted that in the deposits of the London and Paris basins less than 4 percent of the fauna (over 1,100 species) consisted of living species, whereas the proportion was about 18 percent in the deposits about Bordeaux in the south of France and

in the basin of Vienna and some other areas, and was between 33 and 50 percent in the formations of Tuscany and the subalpine hills of northern Italy, and in the Crag of England. Lyell, like Deshayes, inferred that these differences indicated a considerable difference in age of the three groups of strata, and he gave them the names Eocene [dawn of the recent], Miocene [less of the recent], and Pliocene [more of the recent]. Lyell added, however: "it must be recollected, that this relation to the recent epoch is only *one* of its [the Pliocene's] zoological characters, and that certain *peculiar species* of testacea also distinguish its deposits from all other strata." Thus, from the first, he used guide fossils as well as the percentage of recent species in recognizing these main subdivisions of the Cenozoic.

As study of the faunas of these and other areas progressed, and the gaps between the Eocene, Miocene, and Pliocene Series were in part filled by adding the Pleistocene, Oligocene, and Paleocene Series to the sequence, the characteristic proportions of living species cited by Lyell were modified from time to time and gradually this basis of classification and correlation lost its significance, yet the names have stuck. One of the most searching criticisms of the method is that of Dickerson (1921), who found that faunal changes and extinctions during the Cenozoic Era have been more rapid in the Temperate Zone than in the Tropics, so that percentages worked out in western Europe are not usable in lower latitudes. The relic faunas preserved about asylums (p. 152) also indicate how the method might fail locally.

Precise local correlation based on long-ranging species. In detailed mapping, where the problem is to match the beds in outcrops a few rods to a few miles apart, fossils can often be used successfully without regard to their total stratigraphic range. A striking example is a bed in the Beil limestone (Middle Pennsylvanian) of the northern Midcontinent region marked by the coral *Campophyllum torquium* Owen. This species is known to range through most of the Pennsylvanian System. In the northern Midcontinent region, however, it normally occurs sporadically and is rarely abundant, except in the Beil limestone where it occurs in such numbers as to attract immediate attention in practically any outcrop along a 200-mile belt. There was no way to know, a priori, that it would be largely limited to a single 4-foot bed over so great an area, but when increasing experience, checked by many other criteria, confirmed this fact, this *Campophyllum* layer became an immensely useful key bed that could be spotted immediately—even in roadside gutters from a moving automobile. It was not sufficient, or necessary, to rely implicitly on this one criterion, for in this region the stratigraphic sequence can generally be checked up and down to other recognizable units, but the value of the *Campophyllum* bed lay in the immediate orientation it gave in the search for other criteria. Obviously, the abundance of *Campophyllum* at this particular time was controlled by favorable environment on a shallow and nearly uniform sea floor. In another province similar conditions would have made it abundant at some different time. Indeed, in the southern Midcontinent region (across central Texas), there are two similar "coral zones" based on *Campophyllum torquium*. Such zones of abundant fossils, like any other aspect of the rock record, reflect the environment of deposition and can be used for correlation only so far as that enviornment persisted simultaneously; wherever the favorable environment shifted geographically with time, the faunal zone will cross time boundaries with the facies.

Examples of similar key beds due solely to environment, and hence subject to the same cautions as the *Campophyllum torquium* bed, could be multiplied ad infinitum.

EVALUATION OF CRITERIA

From what has been written above it must be evident that with a few local exceptions (e.g., volcanic ash falls) there is no single criterion of correlation, either physical or biological, that is precise and infallible or in all cases more dependable than others. The stratigraphic record is vast and complex, reflecting the ever shifting environments and the constantly changing life of the last 500,000,000 years. Synthesis of this record is complicated by its incompleteness. Only parts of the original record are preserved and exposed for study; much of it has been de-

stroyed by erosion, obscured by later deformation, or buried by younger deposits. Only part of the animals and plants that lived are preserved as fossils, and of these we have mostly no more than fragments of the hard parts. Finally, only a small part of the record can be observed from one vantage point or by one individual. As stratigraphers, we grapple with bits and pieces of a jigsaw puzzle that must be fitted together—a jigsaw puzzle in three dimensions, as broad as the land surface of the Earth and miles deep.

In this three-dimensional puzzle we have first to recognize the fragments that belong to a given time unit and piece them together to restore the scene of which they are a part. This is the task of correlation; it is not a simple task. In this puzzle some of the pieces have strongly diagnostic characters and can be placed with some assurance. These are the units with distinctive lithologic peculiarities and/or abundant fossils. Other pieces are rather nondescript and might be mistaken one for another. Such are the common lithotopes that recur in every age, especially those without fossils. Some pieces seem almost to have been designed to deceive—for example, the extreme lithotopes, such as the black shales, that carry specialized faunas and are more alike regardless of age than they are like contemporaneous facies.

In a jigsaw puzzle our criteria are primarily shape and color of the pieces, until a picture begins to emerge and larger relations can be perceived. In our stratigraphic jigsaw puzzle there are many criteria that may be used in fitting the pieces together, but generally only a few of these criteria can be applied in a particular case—and commonly there is some confusion and the criteria do not fully agree, as though the pieces had the right shape but not the right color, or the right color but not the right pattern. It is then wise to remember that there is no single criterion applicable to all cases and none inherently more dependable than all the rest. In various circumstances one or another may be available or may be most useful. And when the different criteria seem contradictory or inconclusive, it may be wise to consider the limitations and the relative advantages of each. Finally, perhaps the best criterion of ultimate success is that, when the pieces are oriented and adjusted, they make a consistent picture.

In any particular stratigraphic problem the merit of a criterion of correlation will depend largely on the purpose in view. In reconnaissance work, or in the study of an area remote from others that have been mapped, the first need is general orientation; it may be sufficient to know that a distinctive rock unit is of Early Devonian or of latest Cretaceous age. For this purpose fossils will give the quickest and the most dependable answer and may, indeed, afford the only criteria available. If, on the contrary, the problem is to map minute details in a well-studied area in order to prove up a possible oil structure, the task may be to match beds to the inch or foot in outcrops scattered over a few square miles or less. Here guide fossils, or even stage of evolution, will be wholly inadequate, and various physical criteria may give the answers, or if fossils are used it will be by recognizing local fossil zones that resulted from local environment of deposition rather from stratigraphic range.

To the student who finds this discussion frustrating and wishes "to have his faith in fossils restored," it may be added that fossils are still as useful as they ever were, and the still-existing chaos in Precambrian correlation as compared with the world-wide synthesis of later geologic history is a measure of their value. For approximate correlation of the larger stratigraphic units they are adequate and dependable. It is only when we strive for greater perfection and finer detail that we find our tools too gross and too blunt. Progress lies, then, in fully recognizing the limitations of our tools and seeking refinements by which they can be made more effective.

To use a different simile, the human eye has lost nothing of its amazing value just because in many fields of science it is no longer adequate to comprehend the details we need to know. The hand lens, the compound microscope, and finally the electron microscope have been developed to give us increasingly great powers of vision. In looking for ever greater detail and perfection in stratigraphic correlation, likewise, we are limited by the powers of resolution of our tools.

CONFLICTING PHILOSOPHIES OF CORRELATION

The development of American stratigraphy in the twentieth century has been strongly influenced by the basic ideas explicitly or implicitly accepted by the majority of stratigraphers as to the kinds of relations, especially correlations, that may be expected among stratigraphic units. During a good part of this period, these ideas have been ranged into two conflicting systems, and stratigraphers have been led to widely divergent interpretations of the same stratigraphic data, according to which of the two systems they have accepted. The effects of this conflict have been widespread and require discussion in any consideration of stratigraphic correlation in America, even though such discussion entails sharply critical judgment of the opinions of outstanding individual stratigraphers.

One of these systems of ideas is inseparably connected with and was largely promulgated by Edward Oscar Ulrich (1857–1944); its principles are clearly set forth in his "Revision of the Paleozoic Systems" (1911), and in a later paper (1916) in which he applied the ideas to a whole series of concrete examples.

Ulrich was one of several eminent stratigraphers who have come out of Cincinnati, bred as it were by the surrounding hills of richly fossiliferous Ordovician rocks. His keen mind, his eye for minutiae, and his extraordinary memory for locations and specimens made him outstanding even among the many able paleontologists of his lifetime. In his earlier years, he was paleontologist for several state surveys in the Midwest, and in 1897 he joined the young U. S. Geological Survey at the time it was carrying on the extensive reconnaissance mapping program that produced 207 geologic folios in 24 years. In these positions, he became one of the leaders in Paleozoic, especially lower Paleozoic, stratigraphy and paleontology from the Appalachians to the Great Plains, and he made imperishable contributions to both fields, above all by his refusal to be content with the current broad subdivisions, either among fossils or formations, and by his insistence on careful discrimination of the lesser units within those subdivisions. He was the pioneer in modern classification of fossil bryozoans, ostracodes, and conodonts, all groups requiring painstaking microscopic study, and likewise in the subdivision of the thick masses of carbonate rocks that characterize much of the Paleozoic, especially the Cambrian and Ordovician, through the eastern and central United States.

The philosophy of correlation that lay behind Ulrich's stratigraphic work is readily understood in the light of his experience. New faunas meant new mapping units to be discriminated within the older broad units, and as each new unit was found it was assigned its place in the steadily growing stratigraphic column. Where faunas were absent, the corresponding rock units were presumed to be absent, and absent because of unconformities resulting from non-deposition; indeed, Ulrich held that virtually all rock units are separated by such unconformities. At no place, therefore, could a complete section be found, the standard column being a composite of units from many different areas, dovetailed into a single sequence. Moreover, Ulrich believed that, at least in the Paleozoic rocks of North America, facies changes are relatively unimportant, being largely confined to a few exceptional areas, and that, on the contrary, each rock unit (of relatively constant lithology throughout) with its own distinctive fauna records one individual advance of a shallow sea over the continental interior, the sea in each advance spreading over only limited areas of the continent and then retreating entirely from it, generally returning on successive advances over quite different areas. Such repeated ingress and regress of the seas in constantly shifting patterns, which Ulrich called "oscillation," was for him the essence of paleogeography.

From these concepts, Ulrich deduced certain principles by which he reinterpreted many of the correlations that had previously been made. Thus he repeatedly reinterpreted what had theretofore been thought to be a broad facies change as a series of separate deposits in separate basins, each deposit being of limited extent and of different age from the others. For the Appalachians, this led to the concept of troughs and barriers, according to which deposits of, for example, sandstone, shale, shaly limestone, and pure limestone, thought by earlier workers to be an orderly succession of facies, were held to have been deposited separately and successively in one or another of four or five parallel troughs, in such manner that no two deposits were contemporaneous.

Illustrations of his method may be taken from his papers of 1916, 1920, and 1924 (Fig. 123). In southern Wisconsin and adjacent parts of Minnesota and Iowa, the following sequence of rock units (all Upper Cambrian except the Oneota dolomite) was recognized by the end of the nineteenth century:

Oneota dolomite (or Lower Magnesian limestone)
Jordan sandstone—Madison sandstone
St. Lawrence dolomite (and shale)—Mendota dolomite
Franconia (or St. Croix) sandstone
Dresbach sandstone

The Madison sandstone and Mendota dolomite were local names given in the vicinity of Madison, Wisconsin, but the units so named were generally agreed to be correlative with the Jordan sandstone and the St. Lawrence dolomite, respectively.

By 1911 (p. 640), Ulrich had come to question at least part of this correlation, and in 1916 he stated that the typical Madison and Mendota, far from being correlative with the Jordan and St. Lawrence, are part of a different system, the Ozarkian, which he had recognized as quite distinct in time span from, and younger than, the Cambrian. He explained that in the vicinity of Madison a shallow and narrow trough had been eroded at the end of Cambrian time through the Jordan sandstone and well into the St. Lawrence dolomite, and that during the Ozarkian this trough was filled with very similar dolomite and sandstone; after the filling of the trough the Oneota dolomite was deposited over the whole region. Ulrich distinguished between the two sets of units on faunal evidence. It happened, however, that another geologist had collected a fauna of 13 species from a dolomite bed near Madison that was admitted by all to be part of the St. Lawrence, and that 10 of these species were also known from the Mendota dolomite. Ulrich nevertheless maintained that he could discriminate the Mendota from the St. Lawrence specimens by minute subspecific differences and that the great

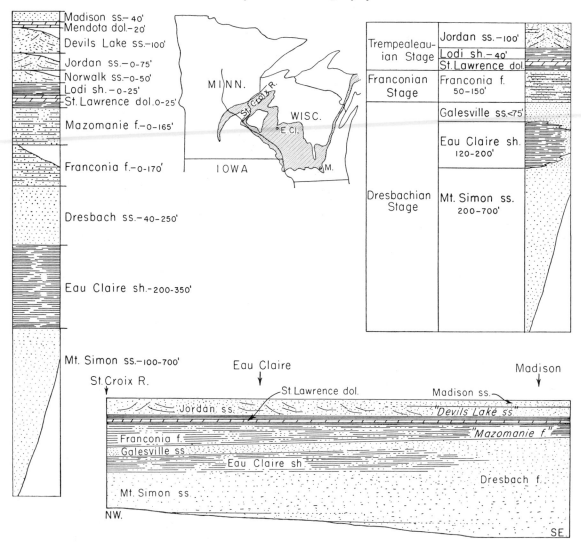

Figure 123. Upper Cambrian correlations in the Upper Mississippi Valley. Left, Ulrich's composite section of 1924; right, composite section as now recognized; center above, outcrop area of the Cambrian formations; below, stratigraphic section across the area, mainly adapted from Twenhofel, Raasch, and Thwaites (1935).

similarity of the two faunas was due to recurrence after the lapse of a considerable part of a period.

Similarly, in 1920 (p. 73–76) Ulrich concluded that the Franconia formation was deposited in a sea that came from the west and that it extended only over the western half of Wisconsin, thinning eastward. He therefore gave a new name, Mazomanie formation, to the deposits about Madison that occupy the stratigraphic position of the Franconia formation and had previously been assigned to it, but which he decided must be younger because they are more calcareous than the type Franconia and overlap the latter. The composite Cambrian section for Wisconsin was finally summarized by Ulrich in 1924 as shown in the left column of Figure 123, with 12 formations and a combined thickness of 1,970 feet.

During the next two decades these rocks were given regional study by geologists representing the three states concerned: Trowbridge and Atwater (1934) for Iowa; Twenhofel, Raasch, and Thwaites (1935) for Wisconsin; and Stauffer, Schwartz, and Thiel (1939) for Minnesota. Although they had some differences over preferred terminology, the three groups agreed closely that the relations are as shown in the section at the bottom of Figure 123, and that the succession of units is as shown in the columnar section above at the right. The Mendota dolomite of Ulrich is a part of the St. Lawrence dolomite; the Norwalk, Devils Lake, and Madison * sandstones are only local facies of the Jordan sandstone; and the Mazomanie is continuous with the Franconia and not lithologically distinct enough to deserve recognition. In short, Ulrich's philosophy led him to recognize 12 formations instead of 6 and to assign them a composite thickness almost 100 percent too great.

The McKenzie shaly limestone (Silurian) of Maryland and Pennsylvania, being the most limy formation in the middle part of the Silurian sequence in the Appalachian belt, had been correlated with the much purer Lockport limestone and dolostone (Middle Silurian) of western New York. The two formations have some fossils in common, but the McKenzie also contains a large fauna of ostracodes not known from the purer limestone. For Ulrich, the difference in the faunas proved that the two units must be different in age and that the McKenzie is Upper Silurian, the Niagaran carbonate rocks being represented in the Appalachians by a disconformity. But Swartz (1934, 1935) later showed that the McKenzie is indeed largely the equivalent of the Lockport limestone.

Beneath the richly fossiliferous Coeymans limestone (basal Devonian) of New York is the Manlius limestone (Upper Silurian), with an impoverished and somewhat dwarfed fauna, probably the result of high salinity (p. 149). In Maryland, however, a limestone unquestionably correlative with the Coeymans is underlain by the Keyser limestone, whose fauna is somewhat richer than that of the Manlius and contains both Manlius and Coeymans elements. Ulrich, accepting the Man-

lius as Silurian, maintained that the Keyser is Devonian but older than the Coeymans, and that it is represented in New York by a disconformity between the Coeymans and Manlius. Yet nowadays the correlation of the Keyser with the Manlius is regarded as firmly established.

In all these cases, difference in fauna and lithology, even if small, was held to be proof of difference in age, the units being mutually exclusive in geographic range and each being represented by disconformities in those areas where the other is present.

The man who in America in the first decades of the century stood for the other system of ideas was Amadeus William Grabau (1870–1946); unfortunately he has left us no adequate short summary of his views of that period, though they are exemplified throughout his *Textbook of Geology* (1920–1921, especially Part II, Historical Geology). Grabau early understood the significance for stratigraphy of the study of the present-day distribution of sediments and faunas, and he was much influenced by the work of Johannes Walther, a European pioneer in the application of that study to historical geology. Grabau's mind, ever eagerly synthetic, saw the whole geologic column in terms of broad facies relationships in the deposits of widespread and semipermanent seas, advancing and retreating over whole continents in long rhythms, which in his later years he called "pulsations" and conceived to be nearly the length of the conventional periods. Unconformities he everywhere minimized, excepting the large ones separating the great pulsations; on the other hand, the mere juxtaposition of two lithotopes such as limestone and black shale in vertical sequence seems often to have suggested to him that they were also lateral equivalents. Thus his *Textbook* contains many diagrams showing facies relationships between formations, for some of which, indeed, evidence was at the time quite lacking, though it later was discovered; in such cases, however, the relations are rarely as simple as he had pictured them. As examples may be cited diagrams showing the relations of the St. Peter sandstone (Middle Ordovician) of the Central States to the rocks above and below, the relations of the Onondaga limestone to the Marcellus shale (Middle Devonian) in New York

State, and the relations within the Trinity group (Lower Cretaceous) of Texas.

Of these two sets of ideas, one stressing disconformities and the other facies, though the latter was more consonant with European thought, the former was dominant in America during the first quarter of the century, largely owing to the immense influence of Ulrich. Moreover, whatever influence Grabau had was lessened when he transferred his life work to China after the First World War. Yet after his departure, the ideas of facies change that he had championed were again brought to the fore, especially by the work of Chadwick, Cooper, and others on the Devonian of New York State (p. 138) and of Stebinger and others on the Cretaceous of the West. On the other hand, in case after case where Ulrich had denied facies and found disconformities, restudy reversed his conclusions, first in the Ozarks with the work of Dake and Bridge, then in the Upper Mississippi Valley, and finally in the Appalachians. Ulrich, indeed, never accepted these new conclusions, but he fought a losing battle against the evidence that continued to accumulate. The importance of facies is now universally acknowledged, though still perhaps not universally put into practice in stratigraphic interpretations, and the concepts of oscillation and of troughs and barriers remain, if at all, only in greatly modified form. For whereas the stratigraphic errors that Grabau made were errors of oversimplification, leading at least in the right direction, the errors that Ulrich made were errors of misinterpretation, and for years his authority stood in the way of further progress. In each of the examples given above (p. 285), and indeed in virtually every one of the illustrations he gave in his 1916 paper, Ulrich was exactly wrong. The faunal differences he recognized are facies differences; thus, the many ostracodes of the McKenzie reflect the muddier environment, and the richer fauna of the Keyser more normal sea water. In the latter case, the long accepted classification of the Manlius as Silurian and the Keyser as Devonian, based on Ulrich's opinions, made it very difficult to re-establish the facts. Even the Ozarkian system, which Ulrich inserted as an entirely new system thousands of feet thick between the Cambrian and the Canadian * or Ordovician, has entirely collapsed, for every unit that Ulrich classified as Ozarkian can now be shown to be correlative with some other unit that Ulrich himself accepted as either Cambrian or Canadian and of which the "Ozarkian" unit is typically a poorly fossiliferous dolostone facies.

To summarize, a brilliantly able paleontologist and stratigrapher allowed his ideas, based on reconnaissance studies, to crystallize into a system of concepts that was widely accepted in North America but that failed to stand up when applied to detailed work. Yet precisely because of his ability and reputation, and because of the tenacity with which he held to his views, a large part of the advance in American stratigraphy in the last thirty years had to be made by direct opposition to his teachings. Even though his major conclusions are now no longer accepted, the debris of his system is widespread in our stratigraphic terminology and even in some of our thinking, hampering the objective discovery and description of the stratigraphic facts.

---

* The Canadian of Ulrich, with minor modifications, is a perfectly satisfactory unit, the chief question with regard to it being whether it should rank as a system, as he thought, or as the basal series of the Ordovician, as most stratigraphers are now inclined to think.

17. *The stratigraphic system*

GROWTH OF THE STRATIGRAPHIC SYSTEM

The lithologic units discussed in Chapter 15 serve well for mapping and for detailed description of the stratified rocks, but they are essentially local. Moreover, their number is legion. The Stratigraphic Lexicon for North America (Wilmarth, 1938) includes more than 13,000 formation names, and when the geology of the other continents has been worked out the valid formations will doubtless exceed 100,000. Each of these will be limited in its extent to a very small part of a single land mass. For synthesis of this local detail, so that the geologic history of a large region, or of the whole Earth, can be worked out, we need units of a different sort, independent of the local lithology. We need a general *time scale* into which events can be fitted in proper chronologic order. But since the time spans are based fundamentally on sequences of stratified rocks, we need also a composite *geologic column* for the Earth as a whole to produce a concrete basis for the subdivisions of the time scale. In both the time scale and the geologic column, moreover, we need a hierarchy of units, both large and small (eons, eras, periods, epochs, and ages of time; systems, series, and stages of rocks). The complex of these units, both the time spans and the rock sections, constitutes the stratigraphic system.

That a sequence of rock layers is equivalent to a time span became evident almost as soon as men discovered the Law of Superposition, that the layers of rock were laid down in sequence one on top of another. The first systematic attempts to formulate this equivalence seem to have taken place just after the middle of the eighteenth century. Johann Gottlob Lehmann (1756), who applied the superposition principle on a wide scale in North Germany, used it to establish the order of age of his three main classes of "mountains," which he distinguished by the rocks that compose them and considered to represent three different periods of deposition, as follows:

3. "Mountains" formed since the Flood by local special events (earthquakes, volcanoes, flooding by rivers and the sea) and consisting of unconsolidated materials (in North Germany chiefly the Drift)—Werner's *Aufgeschwemmtesgebirge* or Drifted (Alluvial) "Mountains."

2. Mountains formed by the general changes at the time of Noah's Flood and consisting of non-crystalline rocks with regular layers; mineral deposits as beds (like coal or the famous copper slate of Mansfeld)—*Flötzgebirge* or Layer Mountains.

1. Mountains formed at the formation of the Earth and consisting of crystalline rocks with steep and unsystematic layering (we would call it foliation); mineral deposits as veins (like the metalliferous veins of Saxony)—*Ganggebirge* or

Vein Mountains, Werner's *Urgebirge* or Primitive Mountains.

Giovanni Arduino (1760) in Italy came to similar conclusions, though we know now he was dealing with somewhat different rocks, and expressed them in the following scheme:

> Volcanic Mountains
> Alluvium of the Plains
> Tertiary Mountains
> Secondary Mountains
> Primitive or Primary Mountains

His lower two classes are roughly the same as Lehmann's, but because of the importance of volcanoes in Italy he further divided the third class; moreover, his Tertiary Mountains include layered but weakly consolidated materials as well as unlayered drift.

But the clearest statement of all of the equivalence of rocks and time is that of Georg Christian Fuchsel (1761). Fuchsel divided the *Flötzgebirge* of Thuringia into 9 rock units which he called series, 6 of which had subordinate basal units called statumina (singular, statumen, support or base). Then, after objectively describing these rock units as such, he proceeded to erect precisely corresponding time units which he called secula (seculum, a life span or generation) and lustra (lustrum, a shorter period of years); he gave each seculum or lustrum the same name as its series or statumen. Already, then, we have a carefully formulated dual classification of time units and rock units.*

During the rest of the eighteenth century, considerable success was achieved in tracing beds by their lithologic characters over large areas in northern Germany, in northern France, and in southern England, and the Law of Superposition was expanded, under the influence of the great

teacher Abraham Gottlob Werner, into the principle that the age of rocks everywhere can be told from their lithologic characters. Applied universally, however, this Wernerian principle soon ran into grave difficulties, and in the first years of the nineteenth century it was discarded in favor of the far more fruitful Law of Faunal Succession, that the age of rocks everywhere can be told from their fossil content. Thereafter the work of constructing a standard chronology for stratigraphy proceeded apace.

No consistent set of units was adopted, however, in which to express this standard, and in the literature of the first half of the nineteenth century we find class, terrain, order, system, formation, series, group, and strata, all applied by different writers to various larger stratigraphic units. The need for greater uniformity became evident and, on the motion of a group of American geologists, the First International Geological Congress was convoked in 1878 in Paris, to study "uniformity in geologic reports with respect to nomenclature and map symbols." International Commissions were appointed to consider these matters, and national committees to work with the Commissions, and these Commissions reported to the Second Congress, held at Bologna in 1881. Their reports were vigorously debated and the proposals in them put to the vote one by one; from these decisions there resulted the dual hierarchy of terms given in Table 15.

The matter was reopened, however, at the Seventh Congress in 1897, and the Eighth Congress at Paris in 1900 adopted a somewhat modified scheme (Table 16), proposed to it by a Commission headed by Eugene Renevier (Commission Internationale de Classification Stratigraphique, 1901). The disappearance of beds

---

* Fuchsel's work is extraordinary in other ways as well. It contains a remarkable geologic map (drawn in perspective) and a cross section that shows that he understood the full implication of dipping layers. Furthermore, whereas for Lehmann only the youngest class was formed by processes like those acting today, Fuchsel laid it down as a principle at the beginning of the explanatory and speculative part of his work (1761, p. 82): "Modus vero quo natura hodierno adhuc tempore agit, et corpora producit, in hac explicatione pro norma assumendus est; alium non novimus." ("Indeed, the manner in which nature at the present time is still acting and

producing things must be assumed as the rule in our explanation; we know no other.") Unfortunately, Werner, in building his celebrated theoretical system of geognosy, seems to have drawn heavily on Lehmann and rather ignored Fuchsel, so that when the principle of uniformitarianism was proclaimed anew by Hutton in Scotland, it took decades to establish it in the teeth of bitter opposition from Werner and all his disciples. Fuchsel wrote his book in Latin, presumably so that it would be accessible to educated men of all nations; as a result it seems to have been read by almost none.

TABLE 15. CLASSIFICATION OF STRATIGRAPHIC UNITS AS ADOPTED BY THE SECOND INTERNATIONAL GEOLOGICAL CONGRESS IN 1881.

Chronologic Terms (time span)	Stratigraphic Terms (rock section)
Era	Group
Period	System
Epoch	Series
Age	Stage
____	Assise (substage, beds)
____	Stratum, bed, etc.

TABLE 17. CLASSIFICATION OF STRATIGRAPHIC UNITS IMPLIED BY THE STRATIGRAPHIC CODE OF 1933.

Divisions of Geologic Time	Divisions or Units of Rocks
Era	____
Period	System
Epoch	Series
Epoch	Group
Epoch (Stage in Pleistocene)	Formation
Epoch (Substage in Pleistocene)	Member, lentil, tongue
____	Bed, stratum, layer

and stratum and the appearance of zone are significant, as is shown in the following paragraphs; Table 16 has no place for local units.

In all these schemes of dual nomenclature, from Fuchsel to Renevier, it is understood that the span of the time units corresponds exactly to the extent of the rock units, and that the same name (for example, Jurassic) shall be used with both; the purpose of the distinction is simply to prevent confusion of the actual time with the rocks deposited during that time. Thus it is correct to say on the one hand that certain dinosaurs lived during the Jurassic Period and on the other that their remains are found in the Jurassic System, but not vice versa. It should be pointed out, however, that the only possible evidence that the dinosaurs lived during the Jurassic Period is precisely that their remains are found in the Jurassic System, so that the first statement actually adds no new information to the second; it merely states the inference instead of the basis for the inference.

The Stratigraphic Code of 1933 (Committee on Stratigraphic Nomenclature, 1933) (p. 258) necessarily considered this matter of time-nomen-

TABLE 16. CLASSIFICATION OF STRATIGRAPHIC UNITS AS ADOPTED BY THE EIGHTH INTERNATIONAL GEOLOGICAL CONGRESS IN 1900.

Chronologic Terms	Stratigraphic Terms
Era	____
Period	System
Epoch	Series
Age	Stage
Phase	Zone

clature. Though no table of units was given in the Code, one can be constructed from its statements (Articles 2 and 24); it is of the same dual type (Table 17). Thus local rock units have been reinstated at the expense of stage and zone.

Schemes of dual nomenclature like these have not been without their critics, however. At the end of the nineteenth century, H. S. Williams (1894 and, in passing, elsewhere) objected to the rigid parallelism of time units and rock units, arguing that the boundaries of rock units need not and ordinarily will not be of the same age throughout, and hence that they cannot correspond to or serve as the basis for time units. He advocated, therefore, a quite different type of dual classification: numerous local rock units based on local sections and having nothing to do with time, relatively few universal time units based on fossils and independent of the lithology of the rocks, and no correspondence between them. Such a sharp distinction was in fact the official practice of the U. S. Geological Survey of which Williams was a member (Powell, 1890, p. 63–64; Walcott, 1903, rule 14, p. 25). A few years later he became a member of the Renevier Commission, and he may have been in part responsible for the deletion of the local units like beds and stratum from that Commission's tabulation of stratigraphic units. Later, however, Williams (1905) receded from some of the conclusions he had drawn, questioning especially whether units based on fossils are really time units, and whether any true time units can be recognized at all.

During the ascendency of Ulrich in American stratigraphy (p. 284), the idea of separating rock units from time units completely, as recommended by Williams, was largely lost sight of; as noted above, the Stratigraphic Code of 1933 im-

TABLE 18. CLASSIFICATION OF STRATIGRAPHIC UNITS PROPOSED BY SCHENCK AND MULLER (1941).

Geologic-Time Units	Time-Stratigraphic Units	Rock-Stratigraphic Units		
Era Period Epoch Age ———	——— System Series Stage Zone	Group	Formation	Member, etc. Bed, etc.

plies an exact parallelism between them, even down to formation and member. The proposals of the Code, however, especially its virtual abandonment of the term stage, led to a vigorous protest (Schenck, Hedberg, and Kleinpell, 1936); discussion was carried on for several years (Schenck and Kleinpell, 1936, p. 215–217; Hedberg, 1937, p. 1975–1976; Kleinpell, 1938, p. 88–99; Tomlinson, 1940; Hedberg, 1941) and finally crystallized in a very important paper by Schenck and Muller (1941), which has been the basis for all further thinking on the subject in America.

Schenck and Muller proposed the scheme of units shown in Table 18 (the headings of the columns have been slightly modified here in accordance with later usage). It is evident that this scheme contains both the dual classifications discussed above. The first two columns (except for the omission of phase) are identical with the classification proposed by the Renevier Commission; like the two columns of that classification they are used with the same names and are only verbally distinct. The third column is contrasted with the first two as Williams had advocated, and Schenck and Muller deliberately placed these terms in the table at right angles to the others so that under no circumstances could they be made to correspond with any of the terms involving time.

The Second World War interrupted discussions of these questions, but as soon as it was over they resumed; the first proposal made to the newly established American Commission on Stratigraphic Nomenclature (p. 261) in 1946 was a proposal by its first chairman, R. C. Moore, to incorporate the scheme of Schenck and Muller explicitly into the Stratigraphic Code (American Commission on Stratigraphic Nomenclature, 1947).* The main business of the Commission since that time has been consideration of these matters in preparation for a revision of the Code, and a number of discussions of these questions have been published in the Notes of the Commission and elsewhere (see especially American Commission on Stratigraphic Nomenclature, 1948, by Flint and Moore; Hedberg, 1948; Teichert, 1950; Woodring, 1953; Rodgers, 1954a; Hedberg, 1954). During this discussion, schemes with as many as five separate categories of units have been proposed, but, in general, opinion has favored the Schenck and Muller scheme with the addition of a category of biostratigraphic units to include zone. The Commission has published first reports on the time-stratigraphic (and geologic-time) units (American Commission on Stratigraphic Nomenclature, 1952, largely taken from Hedberg, 1951), and on the rock-stratigraphic units (American Commission on Stratigraphic Nomenclature, 1956), and it is at work on a similar report on the biostratigraphic units. These reports, when revised in the light of further discussion by stratigraphers generally, will form the basis for a revision of the Stratigraphic Code. The final result of all this debate should be a more useful, precise but flexible, system of stratigraphic units with which to express the description of local sections and the correlation of those sections with each other and with a general standard chronology.

* In this connection it is proper to point out that, while the dual table of classification given in Table 17 can be extracted from the Code, other statements (notably Remark e to Article 2) show that its framers were well aware that terms like system and zone are on a different footing from group, formation, and member. Thus the proposals of Schenck and Muller and of Moore do not necessarily alter the intention of the Code but simply make explicit one way of interpreting it and reject another.

TIME-STRATIGRAPHIC AND GEOLOGIC-TIME UNITS

General. The rock-stratigraphic units of the stratigraphic system are discussed at length in Chapter 15. Our conclusion there is that the formation (and, of course, the other rock-stratigraphic units) should be defined as a lithologic, genetic unit, and that time as such has no place in its definition. These units, which are used in the description of local sections, should always be kept quite distinct from units involving time, which are used in expressing the correlation of local sections with each other and with the standard chronology, itself expressed in time units.

Units involving time are of two kinds: units of rock or time-stratigraphic units, and units of geologic time itself; the two are exactly parallel throughout. Conceptually it would seem that the geologic-time units should be defined first, and the time-stratigraphic units then defined as those rocks laid down within the geologic-time units. But in essence what is known about the Silurian Period, for example, comes exclusively from criteria in the rocks. Historically, also, time units have been created to accommodate rock sections that failed to fit elsewhere; rock sections have not been sought for to fill hitherto known but empty time units. To avoid circular reasoning, therefore, the geologic-time unit (Silurian Period) must be defined as the time span during which the corresponding time-stratigraphic unit (Silurian System) was laid down.

But then how can the Silurian System be defined? In the section in southeastern Wales, it comprises the rocks between such and such limits as chosen by Murchison (and modified by later workers; that the upper limit is still in debate even here does not invalidate the argument), but everywhere else the delimitation, or definition, must depend on criteria of correlation, the criteria discussed in the preceding chapter. Within Wales and western England, physical criteria can be used to some extent, but beyond those bounds only paleontological criteria are valid. Thus certain rocks in America are called the Silurian System only because of fossils contained in them (or if they are unfossiliferous, because of fossils contained in other rocks not too far away with which they can be correlated by physical criteria). Therefore, unless radioactive criteria can achieve a precision that is very much greater than at present (p. 277), the Silurian System is in fact defined by fossils everywhere except in its type region. And this conclusion holds for all the time-stratigraphic units.

That it holds for the smaller ones such as zone and perhaps stage is generally recognized; indeed, it was explicit in the original definitions of both those terms (p. 298–9). But because it is known that fossils are not perfect criteria of time (p. 284), many stratigraphers conclude that zone is therefore not a time-stratigraphic unit at all but a biostratigraphic unit, and a few would transfer stage also. Series and system, however, are considered to have true time significance and hence to be different from zone, to be *defined* by time and not by fossils. But series and system are more satisfactory time-stratigraphic units than stage and zone not because they are in fact defined differently but only because they are larger and grosser, so that the errors of paleontologic correlation are not so apparent—the "limit of resolution" of the criteria is not approached. Historically, series and system, as they have always been used by stratigraphers, are as dependent on fossils as zone, and if zone is a biostratigraphic term, so are they.

Many American stratigraphers, probably a majority, refuse to accept this argument, holding with Hedberg (1951; American Commission on Stratigraphic Nomenclature, 1952, p. 1629) that system, series, and stage must be defined in the first instance by time itself and that their boundaries should be isochronous surfaces. But the only criteria that can be used to detect these isochronous surfaces are precisely the fallible criteria of correlation discussed in Chapter 16, and of these the only ones valid from continent to continent and at the same time precise enough to be useful in constructing a standard stratigraphic chronology are the paleontological criteria. Hence, away from their individual type regions, systems, series, and stages can be delimited (*defined*) only by their fossils.

If, as is probable, the above argument is a minority view, students using this book should not content themselves with our presentation but should read widely the arguments presented by Hedberg and others who have thought carefully on this subject. The final decision will be made neither by our fiat nor by decisions of the Commission but, over the years, by the considered judgment of stratigraphers using these terms and definitions in practical stratigraphic work.

The two geologic eons. If the argument is valid that time-stratigraphic units are fundamentally based on criteria of long-range correlation, which in practice means on fossils, then beds without fossils can be assigned to a time-stratigraphic unit only if other criteria, such as the physical criteria, permit correlation with beds that do contain fossils, and the assignment is only as valid and precise as these other criteria. Such correlation and assignment are, of course, common practice; fortunately it is also common practice to indicate doubtful assignments with question marks.

But the rocks older than those containing the olenellid-archeocyathid fauna of the Lower Cambrian Series contain no fossils that can serve as criteria for correlation; in these rocks correlation can be only by physical criteria. The failure of ordinary physical criteria beyond individual basins of deposition is perhaps nowhere so well demonstrated as by the difficulties encountered in attempting to correlate Precambrian rocks, even within one continuous area like the Canadian Shield. Radioactive criteria are far more hopeful, but the probable errors in the Precambrian are still of the order of 50 or 100 million years and, even so, the dates refer chiefly to pegmatites and the like; the most that has been possible so far has been to date major orogenic belts as Wilson (1952) has done for the Canadian Shield, not to define "series" or "systems."

From the point of view of the practicing stratigrapher interested in determining the age of strata, therefore, geologic time falls into two grand divisions: an older division for which he lacks criteria for long-range correlation, except the imprecise criteria based on radioactivity, and a younger division for which such criteria are provided by the fossil record of organic evolution. These divisions, which are even bigger than eras, may be called *eons,* and the least equivocal and

most significant names for them are those given by Chadwick (1930):

> Phanerozoic (evident life)
> Cryptozoic (hidden life) *

Many conflicting attempts have been made to recognize eras, periods, and even epochs within the Cryptozoic Eon, but their very multiplicity and lack of agreement are the best evidence that as yet no valid basis for this kind of time subdivision of the eon has been found. In contrast, the Phanerozoic Eon divides readily into the full hierarchy of eras, periods, epochs, and ages. And this is natural; stratigraphers developed just this system of units in order to express relative ages within the fossiliferous part of the geologic record. Ages in the Cryptozoic Eon will be determined, when they are determined at all, not relatively by fossils but absolutely by radioactive criteria, and they are likely to require a different form of expression, perhaps something like the numbered years of history, coupled with some statement of probable error.

Our further discussion of geologic-time and time-stratigraphic units applies, then, only to the Phanerozoic Eon.

The eras of the Phanerozoic. The threefold classification of mountains of Lehmann and Arduino underlay later age classifications of rocks as long as rock characters were considered criteria of time. Werner introduced the additional category *Übergangsgebirge* or Transition Moun-

---

* Many other names were proposed at various times to cover the older of these divisions—Protozoic, Hypozoic, Azoic, Eozoic, Archean, Archeozoic, Progonozoic, and probably others—but none of these is satisfactory, either because of its meaning (for example, Azoic) or because common usage now restricts it to only a part of the division (for example, Archean and Archeozoic). The simple term Precambrian is preferable to any of them, but it lacks a satisfactory correlative term for the younger division (post-Precambrian can hardly be considered seriously), and the common tendency nowadays to recognize an Eocambrian or Infracambrian Series (or even System) between the *Olenellus* beds and the "true" Precambrian has rendered it equivocal. We have therefore preferred the pair Cryptozoic-Phanerozoic as convenient, meaningful, and (for the present) unambiguous, the boundary being placed at the beginning of the Cambrian when fossil faunas that can provide criteria of long-range correlation appeared for the first time.

tains below the *Flötzgebirge* and made many subdivisions within the *Urgebirge* and *Flötzgebirge,* in a desperate effort to make his rock classification tally with the observed time-relations. When faunal succession replaced rocks as the basis for time classification, the older classifications were adapted to fit. Finally in 1841 John Phillips [*] (William Smith's nephew), starting from a term of Sedgwick's, proposed a threefold division based on the development of life:

Cainozoic Strata

Mesozoic Strata

Palæozoic Strata

The boundaries which he chose were so reasonable, largely agreeing with the older lithologic classifications, especially Arduino's, yet expressing a natural division of the record of life into "ancient," "medieval," and "modern," that they were quickly accepted and have remained unchanged to the present day. Indeed, in France Phillips' terms are treated as mere synonyms of Arduino's, but Phillips' boundaries are accepted.

These three *eras,* then, are almost universally recognized. They are distinguished not by differences in the rocks but by differences in life. The changes that took place in marine life at the end of the Permian and at the end of the Cretaceous are the most profound that have occurred since the Cambrian; though at each time some kinds of organisms lived through virtually unaffected, others that had been dominant were extinguished or decimated. The end of the Cretaceous also corresponds to a profound change in terrestrial vertebrate life; the great reptiles became extinct and the mammals were released to begin their great expansion.

It is perhaps unfortunate that geologists in North America have commonly associated these two era boundaries with two great orogenies, the Appalachian and Laramide revolutions, and have

[*] Definitively stated in Phillips, 1841, p. 159–161. The growth of Phillips' ideas from the original usage of Palæozoic by Sedgwick, including only the Cambrian and Silurian Systems, may be traced in the articles Phillips wrote for the Penny Encyclopaedia of the Society for the Diffusion of Useful Knowledge (1833–1843), under the headings: Geology (1838), Magnesian Limestone (1839), Organic Remains (1840), Palæozoic Series (1840), and Saliferous System (1841).

thus been led to expect all major time boundaries and faunal changes to be coupled closely with intense diastrophism. In Europe, on the other hand, these boundaries are marked by no angular discordances, at the most by disconformities. In England, where Phillips worked, the Paleozoic-Mesozoic boundary is hidden within the non-marine New Red sandstone; in fact, some British geologists who believe that time boundaries should be prominent rock boundaries have used this fact as an argument against Phillips' whole scheme (Rastall, 1944; Sherlock, 1948). But Phillips had no such idea; his boundaries were intended to reflect not world-wide orogenies but world-wide changes in life, and this they do. Even in North America there is no proof that the Appalachian orogeny came at the end of the Permian Period, and there is excellent evidence that the Laramide orogeny consisted of several pulses, no one of which is known to coincide with the end of the Cretaceous (Spieker, 1946).

Changes have been proposed from time to time in Phillips' scheme, but none of them has received much support. Some geologists have advocated lowering the Paleozoic-Mesozoic boundary by various amounts, even as far as the base of the Pennsylvanian, to make it coincide with a major unconformity; others have proposed splitting the Paleozoic into two eras, either at the end or at the beginning of the Silurian Period. Inability to reach agreement on these changes has doomed them all to failure. A more persistent suggestion has been the separation of the last chapter of geologic time as the Psychozoic Era, on the grounds that the appearance and dominance of man is a change as profound as any that preceded it. Already in the first half of the nineteenth century it was suggested that the Alluvium and Drift should be separated from Arduino's Tertiary and classed as Quaternary, and after the acceptance of the glacial theory for the Drift this became established practice. Application of a -zoic term to the Quaternary was thus a natural development of ideas. But the use of Psychozoic also has been varied, some applying it to the whole Quaternary and some only to the "Recent," the period since the retreat of the ice sheets from Europe and North America, and the period of man's real dominance. The need for such a separation has not been generally felt, however, and the term is now virtually abandoned.

The periods and systems. The geologic *periods* are, as the Stratigraphic Code says (Article 24), "the fundamental units of the standard geologic time scale." Like the eras, the same periods and systems are recognized and understood all over the world, except that there are some differences of opinion as to how many should be recognized, and that major controversies have raged (some still persist) over every one of the boundaries. The usefulness of the systems is attested by their use as chapter headings in practically every textbook of historical geology in the world and also in most compilations of regional stratigraphy.

The list of periods and systems currently accepted is shown in Table 19.

We recommend the usage at the left of the table, but the table also shows other widely accepted usages with which the student must be acquainted if he is to understand stratigraphic literature. These differences are regrettable but can hardly be removed short of international action and agreement; an attempt to compromise the

Carboniferous difficulty by recognizing two subsystems within a Carboniferous System, proposed by the American Commission on Stratigraphic Nomenclature and accepted by the Third Congress of Carboniferous Stratigraphy and Geology at Heerlen in 1951, was rejected by the Nineteenth International Geological Congress in Algiers in 1952, leaving the geologists of each continent to deal with the matter as they see fit.

Restriction of the term Silurian to the post-Ordovician is now standard in all English-speaking countries, but on the continent of Europe the older broader usage is still current, and the Silurian is there divided into two series, or at the most subsystems, called Ordovician and Gothlandian. The Carboniferous is divided into two systems, Mississippian and Pennsylvanian, almost universally in North America and where North American geologists have worked, but nowhere else. A few writers still deny the validity of the Permian System and either make it a part of the Carboniferous (Permo-Carboniferous) or divide it between Carboniferous and Triassic, but no large body of opinion favors such usage. The Germans sometimes call the Permian the Dyassic. Many other periods and systems have been proposed from time to time for parts of the Paleozoic, but they have failed to receive general acceptance even in the countries where proposed.

The three Mesozoic systems are accepted universally; an attempt in North America to divide the Cretaceous into two systems, the Comanche and the Gulf, failed and was abandoned.

Much the commonest division of the Cenozoic Era, both in North America and in Europe, is into two periods, which are still named on Arduino's scheme Tertiary and Quaternary, though Primary and Secondary have been obsolete for about a century except in France, where all four terms are still current and are given era status. Commonly, the French further divide the Tertiary into two periods, the Paleogene (or Nummulitic) and the Neogene (the boundary coming between the Oligocene and Miocene Epochs). A similar subdivision has been advocated sporadically elsewhere (usually with other names, such as Eogene-Neogene or Eocene-Neocene), but not generally accepted.

The separation of the epoch of the late Ceno-

TABLE 19.   CURRENTLY ACCEPTED SEQUENCE OF
PERIODS AND SYSTEMS.

C e n o z o i c Era	Cenozoic	Quaternary	
		Tertiary	Neogene
			Paleogene or Nummulitic
M e s o z o i c Era	Cretaceous		
	Jurassic		
	Triassic		
P a l e o z o i c Era	Permian		
	Pennsylvanian	Carboniferous	
	Mississippian		
	Devonian		
	Silurian	Silurian	Gothlandian
	Ordovician		Ordovician
	Cambrian		

zoic glaciation as a Quaternary Period (or a Quaternary or Psychozoic Era) seems to us to overemphasize its importance. On the one hand, it records a significant and spectacular episode in earth history, concerning which a vast amount of information has been obtained, much of it by methods not available to students of older epochs, methods such as geomorphic studies, correlation by changes in climate or sealevel, varve counts, and the carbon 14 method (p. 277). On the other hand, no marked change in fauna, marine or terrestrial, sets it off (fauna alone is commonly insufficient to distinguish Pleistocene from Pliocene), and the time involved (probably less than a million years) is hardly long enough or its history complex enough to be considered of the same rank as such time spans as the Cretaceous or the Cambrian. We believe, therefore, that the present is still part of the first period of the Cenozoic Era, and that we are still too close to the drastic changes in life brought about by man in the last millennium or two, or to be brought about in the next, to evaluate them in terms of geologic time.

It has often been said that the commonly accepted periods, created in the northern hemisphere, are ill adapted to the southern. Nevertheless, they have been applied without serious difficulty to Australia and South America. But in South and Central Africa there are large bodies of mainly non-marine sediments that are particularly difficult to classify in the standard time scale, notably the Karroo sequence (recognizable also in other parts of the southern hemisphere), reaching from somewhere near the Carboniferous-Permian boundary to somewhere near the Triassic-Jurassic boundary, and the Kalahari sequence, bridging the Mesozoic-Cenozoic boundary. The South Africans have therefore proposed ranking these units as systems, but to do so would defeat the whole purpose of general time-stratigraphic nomenclature. We believe that these units are not time-stratigraphic units at all, but large rock-stratigraphic units, something like the "provincial series" in the Precambrian discussed on p. 298.

Epochs and series. The primary subdivisions of the periods and systems are *epochs* and *series*. Some systems, like the Cambrian and Jurassic, divide neatly into three series that can be recognized almost everywhere (with perhaps some debate about boundaries), and many writers have maintained that such a threefold division is "natural," expressing the transgressive, culminating, and regressive phases of a great marine invasion. But other systems obstinately refuse to subdivide into three, or even to permit the same subdivision in different geologic provinces, and in general such a strait jacket is unwise. The number of series may best be determined independently for each system, and need not be the same in all parts of the world. Thus, the Cretaceous falls naturally into two series in northern Europe and most of North America but into three in the Alps and in Mexico. Although it is convenient for series to be world-wide in acceptance, it is more important at our present state of knowledge for them to correspond with the facts in each major geologic province.

In some systems the individual series have geographic or other distinctive names (e.g., Waucoban, Albertan, and Croixian Series of the Cambrian of North America; Lias, Dogger, and Malm Series of the Jurassic of western Europe). In others, series are designated instead by the adjectives Lower, Middle, and Upper applied to the system name, and the corresponding epochs are designated Early, Middle, and Late; for example:

Late Devonian Epoch—Upper Devonian Series
Middle Devonian Epoch—Middle Devonian Series
Early Devonian Epoch—Lower Devonian Series

(the middle category falls out if only two series are recognizable).

The latter usage is subject to serious ambiguity on two counts. In the first place, a threefold division is not natural for many of the systems. Although the Triassic System, for example, was so named because of its threefold division in Germany, a fourth division was added when the Rhaetic was recognized as Triassic, and in the marine section of the Alpine region six divisions (generally considered stages) are commonly recognized. In the second place, and partly because of the first, the terms—Lower, Middle, and Upper—can mean quite different things to different workers. In Europe, for example, where the Permian is commonly subdivided into two series, Lower Permian includes about half of the system, whereas in America, where four series are recognized, Lower Permian commonly includes only the lowest of these (Wolfcampian). Even more evident is the ambiguity of the term Middle Permian. How shall one divide four series into Lower, Middle, and Upper? Does Middle Permian include only Leonardian, or only Guadalupian, or both? The term Middle Pennsylvanian is equally ambiguous and may mean something very different to a geologist trained in the northern Midcontinent region from what it does to one working in the geosynclinal areas where the lower part of the system is fully developed. Where a series bears a geographic name based on a recognized type or standard section, no such ambiguity is possible. The Desmoinesian Series of the Pennsylvanian System, for example, based on a fossiliferous section of strata in the region of Des Moines, Iowa, can be recognized on a faunal basis over most of the continent, and will be interpreted alike by all competent students. The Guadalupian Series of the Permian, based on certain strata in the Guadalupe Mountain region of Texas, will likewise be recognized wherever its distinctive faunas can be found. We would, therefore, urge the gradual replacement of the designations "Lower," "Middle," and "Upper" by series names based on geographic sections (e.g., Ludlovian or Cayugan Series of the Silurian, Wolfcampian or Sakmarian Series of the Permian).

Within the Cenozoic Era, epochs and series are on a somewhat different footing, and the following list is by now generally recognized as of world-wide extent:

> Pleistocene
> Pliocene
> Miocene
> Oligocene
> Eocene
> Paleocene

Even here, however, there are divergences: the Paleocene is commonly not separated from the Eocene in Great Britain and France, and a final epoch, called Recent, Postglacial, or Holocene, is widely recognized (the Germans prefer Alluvium and Diluvium to Recent and Pleistocene). We believe that marine fauna, terrestrial fauna, and flora all show that the Paleocene is worthy to rank as an epoch with the others; on the other hand, there appears to be no consistent way to separate off the Postglacial, whose length ranges from perhaps 18,000 years at the margins of the last drift sheets to 0 years in Greenland and Antarctica, and which is certainly not marked off by any change in fauna or flora. Because large continental ice sheets still exist and the climate today is not so warm as during the thermal maximum (so-called "postglacial climatic optimum"), let alone the various truly interglacial ages, there is every indication that we are still living in the Glacial or Pleistocene Epoch.

There is another usage of the term series, which we deplore though it was sanctioned by the Stratigraphic Code of 1933. This is the so-called provincial series, which is not a subdivision of a system but a unit including one or several groups. It is thus essentially a rock-stratigraphic rather than a time-stratigraphic unit. In the Phanerozoic there is little need for it and it is little used, but in the Cryptozoic both series and system are common designations for bodies of sediments forming major units in the sections of Precambrian geologic provinces. This usage of the term was recently approved by the American Commission on Stratigraphic Nomenclature (1955). Nevertheless, we believe that no time-stratigraphic units can properly be recognized in the Cryptozoic and that it is unwise to use terms like series and system in two distinct and conflicting ways. We therefore urge that these provincial "supergroups" in the Precambrian (and elsewhere) be given some other frankly rock-stratigraphic designation, such as sequence.

Ages and stages. The concept of the *stage* was created by d'Orbigny (1842, p. 600 ff. [1850]).* Faced by the multiplicity of local lithologic names already in use for Jurassic units in northern Europe, and realizing that facies changes rendered them all suspect if not useless as the basis for a chronologic description of faunas, he proposed instead to divide the Jurassic

---

* D'Orbigny first described stages in 1841 (1840, p. 418 ff.), but the definitive discussion of why he chose to erect them was not published until 1850 (1842, p. 600 ff.). For the dates of publication of the various pages, see Sherborn, 1899.

rocks into ten stages (and the Cretaceous into seven), each characterized by its fauna and by its fauna alone. The usefulness of this kind of subdivision soon became apparent, and, indeed, d'Orbigny's original stages have required remarkably little modification to the present day (Arkell, 1946). To be sure, d'Orbigny accepted the doctrine of the catastrophic creation and extinction of successive fossil faunas and hence he expected to find world-wide faunal units. If uniformitarian ideas have made us realize better than he did how imprecise correlation by fossil faunas may be, they have not lessened the value of these faunas, as opposed to either rocks or individual fossil species, in establishing time-stratigraphic units.

The idea of the stage was quickly applied to the Cenozoic and Triassic deposits of Europe and more slowly to the Paleozoic. In several parts of the section, different sets of stages were set up for different geologic provinces, as for northwestern Europe and the Alps in the Triassic, or for different environments, as for the marine and non-marine Carboniferous of Europe. The tendency recently has been to reduce rather than to increase the number of stages recognized, especially in the Cenozoic where they had proliferated rather wildly, but a world-wide scheme is still far from being worked out. Some of the systems, like the Jurassic and Cretaceous on which d'Orbigny's genius fixed at the start, lend themselves admirably to such a scheme and many of their stages are recognized on every continent, but for others correlations are not yet sufficiently refined. Moreover, stages that are widely recognized can commonly be usefully subdivided in certain provinces into *substages* of more limited application.

D'Orbigny took most of his stage names from localities where good fossiliferous sections can be observed, and this practice has been followed for the most part, though a few non-geographic names have crept in (for example, Tithonian, from classical mythology). Kleinpell (1938, p. 91–92) has argued that the names for stages should never be taken from the same localities as those of contained rock-stratigraphic units, to avoid blurring the distinction between the two categories. There has certainly been too great a tendency to create new stage names simply by adding "-ian" to well-established formation or group names, and thinking has not thereby been clarified. But several of d'Orbigny's stage names were taken directly from rock-stratigraphic units with which they do not necessarily agree in span, and it is unlikely that Kleinpell's counsel of perfection will prevail generally.

In the Stratigraphic Code of 1933, stage is defined as a time term for the individual glacial ages of the Pleistocene; this usage was current in Pleistocene geology in the Midwest for a time, but it has since been repudiated (American Commission on Stratigraphic Nomenclature, 1948) and abandoned, as the time term *age* is available and unequivocal.

The zone. In defining stage, d'Orbigny (1842, p. 604 ff.) also used the term *zone,* stating that such and such a stage was the zone of such and such fossils. Zone was given independent and formal time-stratigraphic status by Oppel (1856–1858), who described it (p. 3) as "a given horizon, that is marked in any one place by a number of species that are constant for it, [and] may be found again even in the most distant region with the same certainty," and (Table, p. 822) as "paläontol. bestimmbare Schichtencomplexe [groups of layers that can be defined paleontologically]." Oppel, like d'Orbigny, was working in the Jurassic rocks of northern Europe, and he subdivided d'Orbigny's 10 stages into 33 zones, two-thirds of them named for individual index species of ammonites; the number has since been raised past 50 (Arkell, 1946). Oppel specifically mentions (p. 812–813), however, the danger that, by the use of the name of one species, "isolated concepts will be substituted for the whole essence of the organized units to be distinguished and used to name them"; he says he used species names rather than locality names (which run a parallel danger) mainly in order to avoid local implications. Thus, he certainly intended that a zone should be defined not by the one species used for the name but, like a stage, by an assemblage of species. The name species need not always be present if the rest of the assemblage is present, and moreover it may occur above or below its zone, but without the assemblage that characterizes the zone.

The difference between zone in this sense and

stage is simply that zone is a finer unit, used to obtain greater precision in correlation where that is possible. By the nature of the criteria of correlation, however, local precision is obtained at the expense of geographic extent, and hence individual zones, even more than stages and substages, tend to be useful mainly within one geologic province. But, as we have argued above, we believe that they are, nevertheless, the same kind of units as stages, series, and systems—namely, units that approximate time equivalence throughout their extent as closely as the available criteria of correlation (chiefly paleontological) permit. And in fact, considering what we know of faunal facies, it is the wide usefulness of zones rather than the limitations on their extent that is surprising.

But the term zone is a very useful general word in the language and can hardly be restricted to this one meaning. It is used in many other ways in geology, as for tectonic zones, metamorphic zones, or zones of certain ore minerals in a mining district, and in stratigraphy, also, it has commonly been used to designate a group of layers characterized by some common property; for example, heavy mineral zones, oil zones, marine zones (Hedberg, 1954, p. 207). (Sometimes it has been used to designate not the layers but the time span of the layers, but this usage is careless, confusing, and unnecessary; the term is not a time term.) In particular, the term has been found very useful to designate the total range in the rocks of a given taxonomic group of fossils, especially a genus or species, whether that range is smaller than a stage or embraces parts of two systems. In the correlation chart of the Pennsylvanian formations in North America, for example (Moore and others, 1944), zones of this sort, based on genera of fusulines, brachiopods, ammonites, crinoids, and plants, served as a framework in terms of which rock-stratigraphic units were correlated. That such large time-stratigraphic units are useful can hardly be doubted. The term *zone of Pseudoschwagerina,* for example, would be understood by competent students all over the world to include the rocks in which this genus may be found, regardless of their preference as to whether these beds should be referred to the Pennsylvanian or Permian system. Such zones are highly flexible, and serve for orientation even though they do not coincide with any formally established time-stratigraphic units.

Whereas none of the other geologic uses of the word zone are likely to be confused with the use in Oppel's sense for a formal time-stratigraphic unit characterized by a faunal assemblage, this last usage could very well be so confused, and it therefore needs to be clearly distinguished. Further, a distinction needs to be made between the total range of a species or genus (or of an assemblage) and its local range in a particular section or region. Accordingly, a rather elaborate terminology has been built up to mark these distinctions and others, as shown in Table 20. How useful all these terms are may be debated. The acme of a form is so largely a matter of ecology that it is of little use in correlation or chronology. The distinction between local range (also often ecologically controlled) and total range is important but commonly very difficult to ascertain, requiring some independent criteria of correlation beside the particular fossil in question. Faunizone is an exact synonym of zone as a formal time-stratigraphic unit, as proposed by Oppel, accepted by the International Geological

TABLE 20. TERMINOLOGY FOR ZONES AND RELATED UNITS. AFTER ARKELL (1933, P. 14–34).

Biological Criteria Distinguishing Unit	Chronologic Terms (Time Span)	Stratigraphic Terms (Rock Section)
Acme (greatest abundance in a local section) of a taxonomic unit	Hemera	Epibole
Local range of a taxonomic unit	Teilchron	Teilzone
Total range of a taxonomic unit	Biochron	Biozone
Range of a faunal assemblage	Moment, Phase, Secule, Chron, or Faunichron	Faunizone, Zone in formal sense (after Oppel)

Congresses, and widely used ever since. In view of the possibilities of confusion, stratigraphers are urged to make their meaning and usage unequivocally clear, whether by using this rather complicated terminology with care or by using the simple word zone, but seeing that each time the word is used it is unambiguous.

As shown in the table, several terms have been proposed as the geologic-time equivalent of the time-stratigraphic term zone (faunizone). Though phase was once adopted by the International Geological Congress, it has had little currency and it is too useful a word in other ways; if a time term is needed at all, we would prefer the word *chron* (and its compounds) as not needed elsewhere, reasonably unambiguous, and mnemonic.

Standard sections of time-stratigraphic units. Like rock-stratigraphic units (p. 269), time-stratigraphic units have type sections (or, for the larger ones, type regions), indicated by the name if it is geographic, where or in terms of which the units were first delimited. But because, in contrast to rock-stratigraphic units, time-stratigraphic units are useful only if they have wide geographic extent, and because adjacent units should, in theory at least, match exactly in time, badly chosen or untypical type sections of these units are much more troublesome, and even well-chosen and typical sections are of little practical use to stratigraphers wishing to recognize the unit on other continents. Type sections are therefore supplemented (and in certain cases, like the Devonian System, are largely supplanted) by *standard sections,* which are rock sections, or, better, groups of sections, chosen after considerable work has been done to serve as standards of reference for a certain part of the geologic column in a certain geologic province. Generally, standard sections are not formally designated, but stratigraphers come to know that such and such a section displays such and such units exceptionally well and that the faunas of those units from that region have been well described; they then refer new sections and new faunas to the older section as a standard.

Take the Devonian System as an example. The system was named for the area where marine beds intermediate in age between Silurian and Carboniferous were first recognized, the county of Devon in southwest England, but an unhappier type region could hardly be imagined; the rocks there are intensely deformed and considerably metamorphosed, and their stratigraphic succession is still not completely understood. Not long after, the well-developed and richly fossiliferous sections of the Ardennes and the Rhineland were discovered, and by common consent (without any formal action) these quickly became the standard sections of the Devonian for Europe and, to a certain degree, for the world. At almost exactly the same time, however, the equally fossiliferous and structurally even simpler Devonian sections of New York State were discovered and described in detail, and these sections have served ever since as a standard for North America. Nevertheless, other standards have been developed in other parts of our continent—for example, the Iowa section for the Midwest and the Nevada section for the Cordillera—and the section along the Mackenzie River will doubtless some day become a standard for the northwest part of the continent. Similarly, one or several standard sections are recognized in South America, South Africa, and Australia.

It is extremely important, of course, that standard sections be intercorrelated as correctly as possible, beginning from the type region or an agreed world standard. Most of the bitter boundary disputes in stratigraphy have arisen because, once a boundary was established in a standard section, stratigraphers using that standard were extremely reluctant to change it, even when it could be shown unequivocally to be incorrect relative to a standard close to the type region or to the type region itself. Commonly they have argued that the boundary they recognized was the most natural, at least for their region, and that if a change must be made it should be made in the other standard or in the type area. In so doing, they have inevitably raised the whole question of the ultimate basis of our time-stratigraphic divisions, a question that has been debated at length since the days of Werner and will doubtless be debated at length for decades to come. Inasmuch as the authors of this book are not in agreement on the matter, the attempt is made in the rest of this chapter not to promulgate the "correct" doctrine but to present all sides of the question as fairly as possible, leaving to the student the task, which is his in any case, of reaching his own decision.

BASIS OF SUBDIVISION OF THE STRATIGRAPHIC RECORD

The faunal changes that distinguish the Phanerozoic Eras have been recognized all over the world wherever fossiliferous rocks are encountered. At the other extreme stand the stages and series, most of which are provincial in extent. In between are the geologic systems, recognized in most parts of the world with boundaries that in some areas are readily defined on faunal and/or structural criteria but in other areas are poorly defined and subject to controversy. The attempt to recognize these boundaries in both kinds of areas has naturally raised the following questions: (1) do the recognized major subdivisions of the stratigraphic column rest on any general physical basis that is both natural and worldwide; (2) is the basis of subdivision natural but imperfect and incomplete; or (3) is it essentially arbitrary and artificial? At present this is a controversial problem and it would certainly be premature to anticipate a final judgment, but as many practical decisions in stratigraphy are influenced by one's philosophical attitude on these questions, it is important to consider the pros and cons.

Theories Based on Orogeny

Growth of ideas. When the geologic systems were established in western Europe early in the nineteenth century, their boundaries were drawn at what appeared to their authors to be natural physical breaks or changes of major importance. In some instances (e.g., the Silurian-Devonian boundary), the break was emphasized by profound unconformity indicating a major hiatus resulting from orogeny; in others (e.g., the Carboniferous-Permian, Permian-Triassic, Triassic-Jurassic, and Jurassic-Cretaceous boundaries), the break was indicated only by lithologic differences suggesting major changes in regimen. In each instance the boundaries of a system

were assumed by its author to be natural, at least in the region under study. Soon after the Cambrian, Silurian, and Devonian Systems were established in England, Murchison traveled widely on the continent and even arranged a visit to Russia in order to see if the new systems could be recognized there also. As geologic study spread over Europe and across North America, the successful recognition of the established systems contributed to a growing confidence that they were natural and world-wide subdivisions of the stratigraphic record. Structural evidence for the major breaks was welcomed, where seen, but commonly was not considered essential. When, for example, the great controversy arose over the Cambrian-Silurian boundary, Sedgwick argued for placing it at a major regional unconformity in the Welsh Border counties, but Murchison vigorously opposed this and wanted to place it much lower. And when, still later, Lapworth proposed the solution that eventually prevailed, separating the Ordovician System from the Silurian, he drew the boundary at the unconformity pointed out by Sedgwick, but his arguments for the new system, and for this particular boundary, were faunal rather than structural.

During the early study of the fine Paleozoic section in New York State, James Hall (1843, p. 17–18) argued that all the strata from the Potsdam to the Chemung sandstone inclusive formed an unbroken sequence and therefore constituted a single unit which he and his colleagues called the New York System. But as it became evident that the systems of Murchison and Sedgwick could be recognized here on a faunal basis, Hall and his colleagues abandoned the New York System and adopted the Cambrian, Silurian, and Devonian Systems instead.

As evidence accumulated that in local regions relatively short episodes of orogeny have alternated with longer periods of diastrophic quiet, the idea of a similar periodicity for the Earth as a whole became dominant. We have already mentioned that in North America the Paleozoic, Mesozoic, and Cenozoic Eras seemed to be neatly separated by the great Appalachian and Laramide revolutions, and similar but lesser and more local orogenies were thought to separate the periods. It remained, however, for T. C. Chamberlin to provide a satisfying philosophical basis for this concept (Chamberlin, 1898a, 1898b, 1909; see summary by Schuchert, 1929). Chamberlin's ideas were accepted in one form or another by practically all the outstanding American geologists of his generation, among them Willis, Barrell, Ulrich, Grabau, and Schuchert. Many Europeans, likewise, have built upon his ideas. From the first, however, there were skeptics disturbed by the regular periodicity attributed to orogeny by theories like those of Chamberlin, and more recently many have flatly denied it. Two of the best statements of this opposed point of view are by Shepard (1923, referring especially to a paper by R. T. Chamberlin, 1914) and Gilluly (1949).

Chamberlin's theory. Although Chamberlin's theory rested upon basic assumptions no longer tenable (his Planetesimal Theory of earth origin), the following of his arguments are common to all theories that have ascribed the subdivisions of the stratigraphic system to natural and world-wide causes:

1. The major relief features of the Earth are the continental masses and the ocean basins, separated by relatively steep continental margins (Fig. 1, p. 2, and Fig. 24, p. 46).

2. The oceans are now a little more than brimful, flooding the continental shelves.

3. Any diastrophic change that increased the capacity of the ocean basins would draw the marine waters off the continents and leave them subject to erosion, producing a break in the sedimentary record on the continents.

4. Any change reducing the capacity of the ocean basins or increasing the volume of ocean water would cause flooding of the lower parts of the continents by marginal or epeiric seas, in which sedimentary deposits would form.

5. Thus, periodic diastrophism causing eustatic changes of sealevel should produce a stratigraphic record with natural units separated by widespread hiatuses.

This and subsequent theories have differed primarily in the basis invoked to account for such periodic diastrophism. Chamberlin believed that the Earth had grown during its cosmic stage by the infall of solid particles (planetesimals), and

that its interior is still shrinking as these particles are compressed under the growing load. He considered the crust to be so strong that it could resist deformation while stresses gradually built up to a critical limit and that then the crust would accommodate itself to the shrunken interior by settling of the sectors under the ocean basins. This would deepen the basins and draw the water off the continents, meanwhile squeezing the margins of the continental sectors to produce fold mountains locally. Following such an episode of crustal readjustment and relief of stresses, another period of stability would ensue until stresses again built up to a critical limit, causing another period of diastrophism. During the stable period, sealevel would gradually rise and flood parts of the continents—first, because the total volume of sea water would be increased by H_2O "sweated out" of the deep interior of the Earth, and, second, because the sediment eroded from the emergent continents would be dumped into the sea, reducing by so much the volume of the ocean basins. According to this view, all the orogenies the world over would fall neatly into one or another of the times of diastrophic readjustments and of continental emergence. Chamberlin argued, furthermore, that organic evolution was accelerated by the physical changes accompanying the continental emergence, so that the lost record was reflected in marked faunal changes.

It is now quite evident that Chamberlin's theory was too ideal and too simple to fit the facts. Not only is the Planetesimal Theory discredited, but there is very serious doubt that the interior of the Earth is shrinking. The philosophical basis for the kind of world-wide diastrophism Chamberlin envisioned has therefore vanished. Furthermore, the crustal stability postulated by Chamberlin between diastrophic revolutions cannot be reconciled with the record. As Shepard (1923) forcefully argued, many local orogenic episodes fall within the recognized periods and not between them. The great revolutions are complex and long enduring; thus, the Laramide revolution includes a chain of disturbances that began in Jurassic time and continued into the Paleocene and Eocene. Moreover, the continents have commonly undergone large-scale deformation during times of submergence (when, according to Chamberlin, they should be stable). The subsidence of a geosyncline and the accumulation of a thick stratigraphic record during a geologic period has normally been accompanied by the rise of adjacent highlands whose erosion supplied the sediment. As Gilluly (1949) has shown, for example, the sediments laid down in the Rocky Mountain geosyncline during Cretaceous time exceed 1,000,000 cubic miles in volume and their source area lay chiefly to the west, between the great interior seaway and the California seaway. To supply this volume of sediment, Gilluly estimates that the average depth of erosion over this source area must have been about 0.5 mile during Early Cretaceous and 4.95 miles during Late Cretaceous time. Making generous allowance for uncertainties, he concludes that the *average* depth of erosion over the source area could not have been less than 3 miles *during* Cretaceous time. This means progressive or repeated uplifts of great magnitude, paralleling the thousands of feet of subsidence in the geosyncline. Spieker's studies in the Wasatch region (Spieker, 1946), among others, have demonstrated that there actually were several sharp orogenic episodes within this source area during Cretaceous time, and that none of these corresponds to the Cretaceous-Cenozoic boundary.

Clearly the continental masses have been far more mobile than Chamberlin believed.

Joly's theory. A quite different philosophical basis for periodic diastrophism was advanced by Joly (1924, 1925) who postulated that heat developed by radioactivity in the quasi-molten subcrust failed to escape as rapidly as it was generated, until gradually the rigid crust was thinned and softened from below. When a certain limit had been reached, the weakened crust yielded to extensive diastrophic adjustments, much of the excess heat escaped through volcanic activity, and some by conduction. As the temperature deep below the surface was thus reduced, the crust again became thicker and stable. Finally, slow build-up of the heat caused another revolution, and so on. Using certain assumptions as to the quantity of radioactive material in the Earth and its distribution below the surface, he estimated that such crustal revolutions should occur at intervals of about 30,000,000 to 50,000,000 years. This he believed to be a basis for separating the periods of geologic time. Joly's hypothesis has never gained support, however—first, because his basic assumptions about the relative mobility of crust and subcrust and the distribution of radioactivity in the subcrust cannot be justified, and second, because radioactive dating of the rocks and other considerations do not support the belief that the periods are subequal in length.

Stille's theory. Without a concrete philosophical basis such as Chamberlin advanced, Stille (1924, 1935, and many other papers) has come to a somewhat similar view from consideration of the geologic evidence. On this view, the Earth has been generally anorogenic during geologic time, though the crust has always been subject to broad warpings, both of uplift and depression (epeirogenic movements); it is at present in an anorogenic phase. From time to time, however, there have been short orogenic epochs during which parts of the crust widely separated over the Earth have been strongly deformed. Thus, relatively long times of quiet have been separated by geologically very short episodes of instability and widespread but local orogeny. Stille believes all local disturbances fit into one or another of these orogenic phases; hence, although breaks and unconformities do not occur everywhere, those that do occur fit into one or another of these short times of revolution. In 1924 he recognized only about 30 such orogenic phases, but as other orogenies were found not to fit into one of these, the number of orogenic phases recognized has increased steadily to more than 50 at present; moreover, he finds no simple periodicity but an unsteady acceleration. Arguments against such episodicity have been effectively marshaled by Gilluly (1949; Stille, Gilluly, and others discussed the matter in the *Geologische Rundschau* in 1950). He concludes that although each orogeny is short-lived at any one place, it is continually and probably irregularly shifting its place of action, both within a given orogenic belt and from belt to belt over the Earth, and orogeny has probably been going on somewhere with more or less intensity all the time.

Theories Based on Epeirogeny

Paleogeographic studies have persuaded many stratigraphers that periods of widespread continental submergence have alternated with others of more or less complete emergence. This idea was set forth at length, with a vast amount of evidence, by Eduard Suess in his great work *Das Antlitz der Erde* (1883–1909), and the lifelong studies of Schuchert leave no doubt that such has been the history of North America. At various times in both the Paleozoic and Mesozoic Eras, epeiric seas have covered 30 to 50 percent of the continent, which at other times, as at present, has stood almost if not quite emergent. This has resulted in subdivisions of the stratigraphic record that, for this continent at least, are natural and useful.

Schuchert and others have attributed the slow ebb and flow of such epicontinental seas to epeirogenic rather than orogenic movements—to broad gentle warping of the crust producing regional uplift or depression with or without local orogeny. A good example would be the late Cenozoic uplift of both the Rocky Mountain region and the Appalachian region, carrying their peneplaned summits to great height. Another may be the slow subsidence of a vast area in the mid-Pacific during Cenozoic time, indicated by the atolls and guyots (Hamilton, 1956).

In so far as such movements have altered the volume of the ocean basins they must have caused eustatic changes in sealevel that would affect all the continents. If the continents had remained stable and such epeirogenic movements had been confined to the ocean basins, uplift in one region might conceivably have been neatly balanced by depression in others so that sealevel would have remained unchanged, but if positive and negative movements did not remain in balance, the rise and fall of sealevel would have caused a world-wide ebb and flow of the seas over the lower parts of the continents. In this case, of course, the breaks would have been synchronous the world over and the stratigraphic system would be natural and complete.

Of course, the matter is not so simple, for the continents as well as the ocean basins were subject to epeirogenic movement. Thus, any continental area that was rising during a time of rising sealevel might remain emergent and, on the contrary, a region that was sinking during a time of falling sealevel might remain flooded during a time of general continental emergence. Evidently, therefore, if eustatic changes of sealevel have occurred on such a scale as to be worldwide in their effects, the stratigraphic system based upon widespread breaks in the record must be imperfect, because warpings of local areas have been out of phase with the rise and fall of sealevel.

If, moreover, these local warpings, acting separately on the different continents, are at all large, they would tend to obscure entirely eustatic changes of less than several hundred feet. But a rise of, say, 200 feet in sealevel all over the Earth requires the displacement of about 5,000,000 cubic miles of water out of the ocean basins (or its addition to the ocean), a volume greater than that of the Arctic Ocean and about $1\frac{1}{2}$ percent of the volume of all the oceans together. If the floor of the entire North Pacific Ocean north of the Hawaiian Islands were to rise 2,000 feet, it would not displace this much water. Quantitatively, therefore, it appears difficult to displace enough water to create eustatic changes large enough to be clearly distinguished from local uplifts and downwarps. Nevertheless, it is generally recognized that at the close of the Paleozoic Era the continents had in some manner become almost completely emergent as they are now, and deep wells on Bikini and Eniwetok Islands (Emery, Tracey, and Ladd, 1954; Ladd, Ingerson, Townsend, Russell, and Stephenson, 1953) indicate that during the Cenozoic Era the ocean floor beneath the far-flung atolls of the mid-Pacific has subsided several thousands of feet.

The problem then remains to decide whether the larger breaks, at least, are in fact so nearly synchronous over a large part of the Earth as to provide a natural and useful basis (however imperfect) for the stratigraphic system, or whether the local and regional movements have predominated to such an extent as to mask the effects of any eustatic changes of sealevel. This problem cannot be decided a priori because we still do not understand the fundamental causes of diastrophism. Paleogeography should provide a method of attack on the problem. If it could be shown, for example, that the major submergences occurred more or less simultaneously in all the continents and the major hiatuses in general are synchronous, a convincing case would be made for a natural basis for subdivision of the stratigraphic record. Unfortunately, the paleogeography of no other continent has yet been worked out in such detail as that of North America (Schuchert, 1955), and there are great regions for which relatively little is known.

There is considerable evidence, however, that essentially world-wide emergence of the continents has occurred at certain times and that very great submergences have occurred on several continents at other times. Toward the close of the Paleozoic Era, for example, the Permian seaways became more and more restricted and the final deposits almost everywhere are non-marine redbeds, no well-established later marine Permian deposits being known. The oldest Triassic marine faunas are likewise restricted to relatively small areas. Certainly the contrast is very great between the marine record of this critical time and that of the Ordovician, the Carboniferous, or the Cretaceous, when seas were widespread over vast areas in several of the continents (e.g., North America, Europe, and Asia).

Likewise it may be significant that, although the geologic systems were established in Europe, they fit well in America where the major submergences fall within the recognized periods and few, if any, straddle a systemic boundary. Controversies over the precise location of the boundaries have been frequent, it is true, but they may be interpreted as imperfections of the system due to local movements out of phase with world-wide conditions. The considerable success that geologists have had in using the established systems in so many other parts of the world likewise suggests that the systems rest on a natural basis, however imperfect.

Theory That the Classification Is Essentially a Convention

The alternative point of view to the theories of a natural diastrophic basis for time-stratigraphic classification is to regard it simply as a convenient and, indeed, necessary human construction, invented in order to divide up the long and complex geologic record. In this view, it is not essential what units are recognized or what boundaries are chosen if only agreement can be reached. Historically, the larger units and their boundaries were created in England and western Europe, and doubtless they are reasonably natural lithologic and diastrophic units in their type areas, but it is not at all necessary that they be natural units of that kind for America and Australia. Their purpose is to provide a common language with which geologists all over the world can express time relations in geologic history; they are only misused if they are distorted to fit the natural diastrophic units of other regions than the type region, for those natural units are properly rock-stratigraphic units.

Advocates of this point of view are those who doubt that there is a natural world-wide basis for classification. They consider the search for such a natural system a search for a will-o'-the-wisp, and the never-ending controversies over natural boundaries a proof that they do not exist. These controversies seem to them to arise mainly because stratigraphers used to boundaries they consider natural in their own region try to impose those boundaries in other regions; all the period boundaries are thus in perpetual debate, and the very purpose of time-stratigraphic classification, to provide a common language, is thereby defeated. They believe we should give up the search for natural divisions because it has proved fruitless and has led only to misunderstandings, and should establish instead a convenient, if arbitrary, scheme by international agreement, modifying the existing scheme as little as possible.

In establishing such a scheme, several factors need to be taken into account, but convenience and usefulness should probably be dominant. First, in order to minimize confusion, the existing scheme should be retained as much as possible, even if a certain lack of logic is thereby perpetuated. Priority has some claims, but where, as for Murchison's base for the Permian System, the original boundary was unsatisfactory and has been abandoned for half a century, an attempt to revive it would be highly inconvenient and undesirable. As noted above (p. 301), the type section of a time-stratigraphic unit is commonly supplemented or even supplanted by standard sections (which may have been unknown to the original describer), and it is in the standard sections that the boundaries ought to be established. Furthermore, original type sections may overlap or they may fail to reach a common boundary, and hence the boundaries of one or the other unit (or of both) have to be shifted to avoid an overlap or a gap. Some approximation to equality in units of the same rank seems desirable; thus American stratigraphers recognize the Mississippian and Pennsylvanian as systems rather than series because they seem to record as long a time and certainly as complex a history (as shown by the number of subdivisions needed to express that history) as the Devonian or Permian. Where possible, major boundaries should be drawn at faunal changes that appear to be significant and relatively world-wide; for example, the base rather than the top of the Tremadoc beds in Wales seems the appropriate base of the Ordovician System because it lies beneath the first of the well-known Ordovician graptolite zones, which are recognized on almost every continent, and also beneath the first of several widespread and well-characterized cephalopod zones.

The scheme, then, would have as its framework accepted standard sections for each of the time-stratigraphic units, established by agreement in (or near) the type regions of those units. These units would then be extended as far as the criteria of correlation would permit; differences of opinion on correlation would, of course, arise, but at least the court of appeal would be an objective standard, not each stratigrapher's idea of what is natural. As the smaller units probably could not be extended throughout the world, stratigraphers in other regions would have the right to set up their own units and standard sections within the larger framework of world-wide units (systems and, where possible, series). The various time-stratigraphic units, therefore, would be distinguished ultimately by the faunas they contain, supplemented by such physical criteria as were useful in extending the boundaries, especially close to the standard sections. Thus, the ultimate basis of time-stratigraphic classification, like that of correlation, would be the sequence of living things produced by organic evolution.

18. Broad patterns in the distribution of sedimentary rocks

STRATIGRAPHY, considered as an attempt to interpret stratified rocks, operates at several levels. We have already discussed the interpretation of specific rock types and of individual sedimentary environments. Over and above these, however, broader patterns are discernible in the distribution of both rocks and environments; thus, both in space and in time, certain rock types are typically associated (for example, graywacke and spilitic lava) and certain environmental patterns are repeated (for example, the pattern expressed by the term geosyncline). Study and interpretation of these broad patterns is an ultimate task of stratigraphy, for which it makes use of and builds upon all its more detailed results, and in pursuing which it finds itself merging more and more with structural geology and petrology, for both of these likewise advance from detailed studies and interpretations to consideration of the same broad spatial and temporal patterns. In this book on stratigraphy, we can only hope to sketch the stratigraphic aspect of these patterns and to suggest what stratigraphy has to offer toward their interpretation, for in the final analysis they must be interpreted not on stratigraphic principles alone, or for that matter on structural or petrologic principles alone, but by a synthesis of all these fields. These patterns appear to reflect fundamental regularities in the processes that affect the Earth's crust, processes that have controlled the unfolding of geologic history.

ROCKS ON THE PLATFORMS

One common association of sedimentary rocks is that found on the *stable platforms* of the continents, such areas as the central United States and the Prairie Provinces of Canada, central European Russia, central Siberia, much of the Sahara, parts of northern and northwestern Australia, and central and southern Brazil. Stability is relative, of course, and some parts of these areas have seen more disturbance than others, but in general none of them has been the site of either great downwarping and thick deposition or great upwarping and accompanying erosion since Precambrian time. Characteristically, the sedimentary sequences of these areas are relatively thin and are made up of thin widespread units, some of them strikingly persistent in rock type over wide areas. Facies changes are not unusual but they are generally gradual; on the other hand, disconformities and especially paraconformities are numerous so that, even leaving diastems out of account, the geologic record in these areas is notably incomplete. Most of the rocks appear to have been deposited in shallow seas, which must therefore have covered vast areas of the various continents at several times; relatively small amounts of sediment were brought into these seas and distributed and redistributed, as on any neritic sea floor, to form sheetlike units. Non-marine sediments are intercalated in some areas, but they, too, are generally in thin units and may show evidence of some similar reworking.

Limestone is perhaps the commonest sedimentary rock in such sequences. In North America, for example, the Ordovician, Silurian, and Devonian formations that once spread widely across the Canadian Shield and still remain in patches are almost exclusively carbonate rocks from Manitoba to Baffinland and from Quebec to Victoria Island. Over the central part of the United States, likewise, they are chiefly limestone or dolostone from Manitoba to Tennessee and from Michigan to Oklahoma. The Mississippian formations are equally calcareous from Illinois westward to the Grand Canyon and northward into Montana and Alberta. Limestone is also common in several other platform sequences, though in a few, for example, the Sahara and Brazil, it is subordinate. Ali kinds of limestone are present in these sequences; organic-fragmental limestone is very abundant, chemical limestone is probably also common, and reefs are prominent though quantitatively minor. Dolostone is also common, probably because so much of the carbonate sediment was deposited in very shallow agitated water; typically, some of the carbonate units are very cherty, others quite free of chert.

Sandstone occurs on the platforms as persistent units, commonly immediately above disconformities and basal to transgressive sequences. Virtually pure quartz sandstone (which may be cemented to quartzite) is common, especially near and at old shorelines; this pure sandstone commonly grades seaward into glauconitic sandstone, limy sandstone, and limestone or dolostone, less commonly into sandy shale. Normally only the most stable minerals are present; besides quartz and cement, the sandstones normally contain zircon, tourmaline, monazite, rutile or some other titanium oxide, and little else.

Shale is present, too, in these sequences, but perhaps is less abundant than either limestone or sandstone; it is generally much more clayey than silty and commonly very limy and fossiliferous, grading laterally and vertically into limestone.

Thus in these rocks the three main sedimentary components—fragments of stable minerals such as quartz, weathering products such as clay, and dissolved matter such as $CaCO_3$ and SiO_2—tend to be largely separated, each accumulating as a distinct rock type. This separation and the characters of the individual rock types all testify to the continued working and reworking that is characteristic of the neritic seas, and the numerous unconformities and the over-all thinness of the sequences show that deposition was generally both slow and interrupted.

Not all parts of the platform are exactly alike, of course, and some may be rather aberrant. Certain *domes* or *axes,* for instance, seem to have been persistently positive; here disconformities multiply, the section is thinned down even more than normal, and evidence of repeated reworking is ubiquitous. Certain other areas seem to have been persistently negative, and some of these form distinct *basins* within the platform. Such basins may have been active only during certain definite time spans; thus, on the North American platform the Michigan basin subsided chiefly in the Silurian and Devonian and the West Texas basin in the Permian. Such basins act as traps for sediment, which is there deposited in thicker units and with less reworking and hence poorer sorting and separation of the components than is normal for the platform; silty shale and sandstone may be prominent here. If the climate is right, their margins may also become the locus of great organic reef barriers, such as the Capitan Reef of West Texas, repeatedly mentioned on preceding pages (Fig. 40, p. 93), and their centers, cut off from open circulation, may be the site of immense deposits of gypsum or anhydrite and rock salt.

ROCKS IN THE GEOSYNCLINES

Geosynclines along the platform margins. James Hall, one of the chief founders of American stratigraphy through his work on the Paleozoic sequence of New York State, early became interested also in the Paleozoic rocks of the Upper Mississippi Valley. As he continued to study these two areas (and many others, especially the Appalachian belt from the Maritime Provinces to Tennessee), he became aware of a marked contrast between them, and in 1857, in a presidential address to the then young American Association for the Advancement of Science,* he pointed out that the Paleozoic section exposed in the folded belt of the Appalachian Mountains and in eastern New York is many times thicker than the contemporaneous flat-lying section in the Upper Mississippi Valley. He also drew at once the conclusion that there is a genetic relation between the linear belt of thick sediments and the linear belt of folding and mountains, and he suggested that such a relation holds for mountain ranges generally throughout the world. This brilliant generalization, that mountain chains everywhere arise along, and by the deformation of, pre-existing belts of abnormally thick sediments, was a major contribution to geology. A few years later, Dana (1873, p. 430) gave the name *geosynclinal* (now universally *geosyncline*) to the broad linear trough in the Earth's crust that permits the accumulation of the thick body of sediments.†

The Paleozoic sequence in the Appalachians differs from that in the Mississippi Valley in more than thickness. Not only are individual contemporaneous units thicker in the Appalachians, but the section is much more nearly complete and part of the greater thickness results from the additional units present. Disconformities are less common (but angular unconformities appear locally along the east margin); on the other hand, facies changes are more abundant and far more abrupt. Thin shale units on the platform turn out to be the feather edges of great detrital wedges, commonly great deltaic masses (pp. 86 and 144), which thicken and coarsen to a maximum near the east edge of the Appalachian Valley and Ridge province. Even in those parts of the section where detrital wedges are absent, the limestone units of the platform thicken enormously as they enter the Appalachians; thus, the

* This address was not published in full for 26 years (Hall, 1883), but various shorter or longer summaries of its ideas were published much earlier (Hall, 1857; Hall and Whitney, 1858, p. 35–44; Hall, 1859, p. 1–96), and they were well known to Hall's contemporaries like Dana.

† Hall and Dana did not agree on what the genetic relation between the thick belt of sediments and the mountains was, but the dispute, which is still going on in other terms today, is not directly the concern of stratigraphy.

Cambrian and Lower Ordovician carbonate sequence is about 1,000 feet thick in southern Minnesota and nearly 2,000 feet thick in eastern Missouri, but 6,500 to 7,000 feet thick in East Tennessee (Fig. 113, p. 239) and 8,000 feet or more thick in central Pennsylvania (about half the beds in the Appalachian sections are older than any in the Mississippi Valley sections), and the proportion of carbonate rock is, if anything, higher in the Appalachian sections.

Much of the Appalachian sequence, despite its greater thickness, consists of the same rock types as the Mississippi Valley sequence—clean quartz sandstone, clayey and limy shale, organic-fragmental limestone, cherty dolostone—and it was evidently deposited in equally shallow water and subject to equal reworking and sorting; deposition must have kept pace, therefore, with the greater subsidence, and at such times an observer lacking subsurface information would probably have been unable to detect a distinction between geosyncline and platform. Other parts of the sequence, however, especially the deltaic detrital wedges within it and the Coal Measures at the top, include much less well-sorted rocks—silty shale, silty sandstone, and sandy conglomerate, all with many of the attributes of graywacke—and evidently at these times material was coming in so fast that reworking was less thorough, the sediments built up above sealevel near the source areas on the east, and sand, silt, and clay were swept across onto the platform, interrupting or replacing the dominant carbonate sedimentation there.

We have stressed the geosyncline in the folded Appalachians because it is the type example of such a geosyncline, but precisely similar relations hold also on the west margin of the central North American platform, where the platform rocks thicken enormously into the Cordilleran geosyncline in northeastern British Columbia, western Alberta and Montana, the Idaho-Wyoming border region, western Utah, and southern Nevada, a belt that has since been strongly folded and faulted but not appreciably metamorphosed. Carbonate rocks make up a large proportion of the thick Paleozoic section in this belt, and clean quartz sandstone is also prominent though less in amount. In the earlier Mesozoic, redbeds and other non-marine deposits on the western part of the platform graded west into thicker marine shale and limestone, whereas, in the Cretaceous, land and sea were reversed and great detrital wedges pushed eastward into a neritic seaway. Similar relations are found going from the Russian platform into the western Urals and from the northwestern Sahara into the Anti-Atlas.

American experience with geosynclines, largely based on the western part of the Appalachians (the Valley and Ridge province) and the eastern part of the Cordillera (west as far as the areas listed above), was codified by Schuchert (1923). Schuchert recognized that some geosynclinal belts are complex and are divided by linear upwarps into several troughs (e.g., the Cordilleran geosyncline during much of the Paleozoic), but for him there was nevertheless a basic pattern, best displayed in the Appalachians: on one side the platform or foreland, with its thin interrupted sequence, in the middle the geosyncline itself, exemplified by the present Valley and Ridge province, and on the other side a complementary *geanticline* (this term is also Dana's) or *borderland,* an upwarp of subcontinental dimensions that lasted as long as the geosyncline and supplied the bulk of its sediments. The type example of such a borderland was Appalachia, but Schuchert found evidence for similar borderlands all around North America: Cascadia west of the Cordilleran geosyncline, Llanoria south of the Ouachitas, and Pearya in the far north, beyond a geosyncline (Franklinian) in the northern part of the Canadian Arctic Archipelago. Furthermore, geosyncline and geanticline alike were integral parts of the continental mass.

Geosynclines along the continental margins. Hall's brilliant generalization, and also the name that Dana attached to it, were soon accepted in Europe and applied to the mountain ranges there, above all to the Alps. A subtle change came over the concept, however, in this transplantation, a change that reflects the great difference between the relatively simple Appalachian folded belt and the enormous complexity of the Alps. Stratigraphic study showed that the Alps and the related mountain ranges, from the Betic Cordillera of southern Spain and the Atlas Mountains of northwest Africa to the Balkans and Anatolia

and, indeed, far beyond through Iran to the Himalayas, have risen on the site of a great trough of deposition, christened by the Europeans Tethys or Mesogea, which lasted from Permian time into the early Cenozoic and had an exceedingly complex history of individual geanticlines and troughs, upwarps and downwarps, with bathyal basins as well as neritic shallow seas. But this great compound trough lay not within a continent but between the two greatest continents, Eurasia and Africa, like the present Mediterranean Sea. For Europeans, therefore, a geosyncline was a complex trough *beside* rather than *on* a continent; indeed, Haug (1900), in the classical presentation of the geosyncline concept in Europe, deliberately contrasted continental areas and geosynclines.

The Alpine geosyncline and the other examples familiar to western Europeans (such as the lower Paleozoic Caledonian geosyncline through northern Great Britain and Norway, and the Hercynian trough containing thick deformed upper Paleozoic sediments and extending from southern Ireland and Brittany across Belgium and central Germany) also differ from the Appalachian Valley and Ridge province in the type of rock they contain. Thick carbonate sequences occur only marginally, as in the Calcareous Alps, or not at all, as in Great Britain, and the bulk of the sediments are quite different. A classic description is that by O. T. Jones (1938) in his presidential address on the evolution of a geosyncline: the Caledonian geosyncline in Wales and nearby parts of England. Clean quartz sandstone, organic-fragmental limestone, fossiliferous limy shale—here all these characterize not the geosyncline but the "shelly" facies of the adjacent platform; in the geosyncline, on the contrary, are found great monotonous sequences of dark shale, sandy shale, silty sandstone, and graywacke, poorly sorted, full of graded bedding, and with only rare fossils and those chiefly graptolites in the least silty shale layers. Also abundant are volcanics, chiefly andesite or basalt and in good part spilitic, lavas and agglomerates and tuffs; half-eroded volcanic islands are still preserved locally, and at times the volcanic activity must have been enormous. None of the common kinds of evidence for the neritic environment are present; there are no signs of reworking or bypassing, no typical sublevation diastems, few disconformities; on the other hand, angular unconformities are not uncommon though not of great regional extent, as though the trough was constantly restless and first one part would be uplifted and eroded, then another. Facies changes are apparently numerous and abrupt, but because of the scarcity of fossils, the general absence of key beds in the monotonous sequences, and the strong deformation the rocks have undergone, they are very difficult to demonstrate. Some parts of the section are very thick, but other parts of apparently equal duration are thin, especially the dark, very fine-grained graptolite shales, and this is interpreted not as the result of winnowing and reworking in the neritic zone but of small supply to basins in the bathyal zone. The contrast with the well-known Appalachian sequence could hardly be more complete.

Where are there such sequences in North America? Americans thought of the Franciscan formation, an immensely thick body of graywacke with spilitic lava and radiolarian chert (p. 253) in the central Coast Ranges of California, or of the Ouachita sequence (p. 253); it is no coincidence that both these sequences contain bedded chert. One of the best descriptions of such a sequence, however, is that of the Archean rocks north of Lake Superior by Pettijohn (1943). Here very thick and poorly sorted sequences of slate, graywacke, and graywacke conglomerate are associated with thick greenstone volcanics; the rocks are intensely deformed and mildly metamorphosed, but many primary features, especially graded bedding and pillow lava, are well preserved. Pettijohn stressed, above all, the contrast between these rocks, obviously "poured in" rapidly into a rapidly subsiding trough in a volcanic region, and the beautifully sorted and separated, thin, endlessly reworked sediments of the central United States, and he expressed the contrast by calling the one sequence geosynclinal and the other platform, as, indeed, Jones had done in Wales and the continental Europeans were apt to do in the Alps and elsewhere.

That the troughs in which such thick sequences were deposited were geosynclines must be admitted, if the term geosyncline is to express the generalizations of Hall and Dana; indeed, Schuchert (1923, p. 197–199) recognized bathyal

troughs along the margins of or between continents as one kind of geosyncline, though he evidently felt they were atypical (just as Haug admitted the existence of intracontinental geosynclines though he, in turn, tended to minimize *their* importance). But that they *alone* are geosynclines, as Jones and Pettijohn seemed to imply, cannot be admitted, not merely because the concept first arose with reference to the quite different sequence in the Appalachian Valley and Ridge province, but because that sequence and the similar sequence in the folded Cordillera are also thick and were also deposited in a major trough in the Earth's crust (Longwell, 1950, p. 416–417). We do not restrict the term laccolith to igneous bodies of exactly the petrographic composition of the Henry Mountains intrusives, for it is clear that Gilbert meant the term to specify form and not content; similarly, we should not restrict the term geosyncline to one or another type of sedimentary sequence, for it, too, describes the form rather than the content of the linear trough and expresses the generalization that mountain ranges have arisen from within such troughs.

At the same time, as studies have been extended over the Appalachians as a whole, we have learned that our previous picture of the Appalachian geosyncline was too simple (Kay, 1937, 1951). While the sequence described above with its high proportion of carbonate rocks and its relatively good sorting was being deposited in what is now the folded belt, other equally thick sequences were apparently being deposited farther east, in what are now the metamorphic belts of New England and the Piedmont, sequences that have much more in common with those described by Jones and Pettijohn. Widespread high-grade metamorphism has obscured evidence of original sedimentary environments and destroyed most of the fossils that might prove the contemporaneity, especially in the Piedmont where most of the rocks are still shown as Precambrian on existing maps; in New England, however, there are a few fossil localities and more than a few belts where it is still clear that the bulk of the stratified rocks were graywacke, sandy shale, and volcanics, with only a little quartzite and limestone, mostly in thin layers. It is possible, therefore, if not probable, that most of the mica and hornblende schist and gneiss so abundant in the eastern Appalachians is similar rock more metamorphosed. A precisely similar view is now prevalent concerning the older rocks of the western Cordillera, beyond the thick folded and faulted carbonate-rich sequence next to the platform (Eardley, 1947).

The traditional picture of low foreland, sinking geosyncline, and high borderland has thus been seriously questioned, and those who question it postulate bathyal Paleozoic troughs set with volcanoes where Appalachia was supposed to have stood. The sediment in the thick graywacke sequences must have come from somewhere, however, and one possibility is a subcontinental Appalachia still farther east, with its roots hidden under the Atlantic Coastal Plain and continental shelf. Another possibility, on the other hand, and one perhaps more consonant with the admittedly little that is known about New England and the Piedmont and also with the considerable that is known about such geosynclines as the Caledonian and the Alpine (Kay, 1951), is that the sediments were derived from islands within the main geosyncline itself, some volcanic and some tectonic but all probably temporary, quickly worn down to be replaced by others. The obvious present-day analogy is the island arcs of eastern Asia, and especially the East Indian Archipelago (p. 62), in which just such dark detrital sediments, mixed with volcanics and with some carbonate (more today because of the importance of the globigerines), are being deposited. Even on this theory, however, the sedimentary troughs must have become fewer and the highlands more continuous as development proceeded until, by late Devonian time in the northern Appalachians and Pennsylvanian time in the southern, most of the area was land shedding debris westward in great quantity into a last vestige of the original geosyncline or across it onto the platform.

As we have so far presented the matter, one might think of the Appalachians or the Cordillera as harboring two geosynclines, one near the platform with generally better sorted sediments and few if any volcanics, the other near the continental margin with poorly sorted graywacke and abundant volcanics, and such an interpretation has been very common, both for these regions and for others, the two geosynclines generally being given separate names (see note below) to emphasize the contrast. But the facts, though meager, are not very favorable to this view; there was no one persistent linear uplift between two separate belts of thick sediments, but rather several temporary uplifts interrupting sedimentation now here, now there (but principally in the outer volcanic part), and the two kinds of sediments tended to interfinger at various times in the complex history of the belt, so that there was no clean separation into two distinct troughs. Now, the term geosyncline has always included composite linear downwarps receiving sediment, as well as simple ones; at the very first, Dana quite specifically mentioned the complex geosyncline in the Cordillera. It would seem most logical, therefore, to consider the entire downwarped belt containing thick deposits, in the Appalachians or the Cordillera or elsewhere, as a single geosyncline, recognizing that the sediments in one part of it may differ consistently from those in another and that in certain areas and at certain stages of development a fairly sharp boundary such as a relatively stable geanticline may have separated different elements. So considered, the geosynclines comprise, to quote Kay (1951, p. 67), "not pairs of troughs extending continuously along the borders of the continents, but linear and arcuate subsiding areas distributed along the borders, with thick volcanic sequences restricted to the outer parts." Not all geosynclines are along the borders of continents, however; the Ural geosyncline, with a non-volcanic belt next to the Russian platform and a volcanic (and metamorphosed) belt farther east, is backed instead by the greatest of the continents.

A note on terminology. The realization that the linear troughs called geosynclines may occur in several different geologic settings and may contain several different kinds of sedimentary sequences has led naturally to attempts to classify them, and, indeed, nearly everyone who wished to present some new theoretical insight into the problem has expressed his ideas by naming some new varieties (except for those who have rejected the name entirely and tried to replace it with another more genetic term, such as geotectocline). The result has been a quite extraordinary proliferation of polysyllabic terminology;

TABLE 21. COMPARISON OF TERMINOLOGIES FOR BROAD GROUPINGS OF SEDIMENTARY ROCKS.

Stille (1936)	Kay (1944, 1947, 1951)	Wells (1949)	Tercier (1939)	Krynine * (1948)	This Chapter
	Hedreocraton (including autogeosynclines)		Epicontinental sedimentation	Orthoquartzite-limestone series	Platform association (including basin associations)
Miomagmatic zone	Miogeosyncline (also deltageosyncline or exogeosyncline)	Ensialic geosyncline	(Not separately recognized)	Mixture of orthoquartzite and low-rank graywacke series	Geosynclinal association, near the platform (including clastic wedges)
Pliomagmatic zone	Eugeosyncline	Ensimatic geosyncline	Geosynclinal sedimentation	Graywacke series, mainly high-rank	Geosynclinal association, far from the platform
	Taphrogeosyncline, zeugeosyncline, or epieugeosyncline		(Continental sedimentation, not discussed)	Arkose series	Association in post-orogenic basins
	Paraliageosyncline		Paralic sedimentation	Graywacke series, mainly low-rank	Association on deltaic coastal plains

* There is unfortunately no readily accessible, reasonably complete, statement of Krynine's ideas in final form, though he has given public lectures on them in many places; see the mimeographed syllabus for his A.A.P.G. lecture tour in 1943, entitled "Diastrophism and the Evolution of Sedimentary Rocks," and a series of seven abstracts in the program of the 1941 meeting of the Geological Society of America (Bull., v. 52, p. 1915–1919). A short summary is provided in his paper of 1948, p. 147–156.

moreover, several different kinds of criteria, both descriptive and genetic, have been used to separate the varieties, which overlap in a confusing manner. Glaessner and Teichert (1947) assembled a glossary of these variety terms a few years ago and found more than thirty; others have been coined since. A few of these terms are being found useful and are making their way into the literature; others were evidently stillborn. Too many of them, though purporting to be names of geosynclines, really refer to the sediments and not the troughs, and in writing this chapter we have chosen to use none of them; instead we have tried to describe the various associations of sedimentary rocks, whether in geosynclines or not, and their characteristic settings. In the present note, however, we attempt to compare the associations we have discussed with certain of the named varieties of geosynclines and with other similar terms.

Schuchert (1923) named several varieties of geosyncline, but he was concerned mainly with their setting—did they lie on the continents or beside or between them (the last he preferred to call mediterraneans rather than geosynclines); were they simple or complex, and did the complex troughs arise by partial deformation and resulting subdivision of simpler ones? Similar considerations prompted other discussions and some simple classifications in the same period (Haug, Cornelius, Cloos, Grabau, and others). But more recently emphasis has shifted to the character of the individual trough as expressed in the sediments it contains; the classifications of Stille, Kay, and Wells are based largely on the contents of the geosynclines and similar ideas underlie the discussions of Tercier and Krynine, though they (like us) prefer to classify sedimentary sequences rather than troughs. These later classifications are compared in Table 21.

Two other terms, flysch and molasse, have been commonly employed in referring to particular associations of sedimentary rocks. Both are formation names (or, better, group names) from the Swiss Alps. The Flysch of Switzerland consists mainly of monotonously repetitive poorly fossiliferous dark shale and siltstone (generally calcareous) in thin layers; much of it also contains layers of graywacke showing graded bedding, some of it contains silty limestone layers, and certain phases contain exotic blocks of all sizes (Wildflysch). It is known to range from Lower Cretaceous to Oligocene, and older representatives of the same lithotope may be masked in the somewhat metamorphic *schistes lustrés* of the Pennine Alps. Even where not metamorphosed the Flysch is strongly deformed, and the scarcity of fossils and key beds has made its stratigraphy difficult to decipher. The Molasse is a younger deposit, Oligocene to Miocene, consisting mainly of light-gray to green calcareous and generally arkosic sandstone and conglomerate. It can be divided into alternating units deposited by fresh water and in shallow seas (in part brackish). Whereas the Flysch is an integral part of the Alpine succession and was deformed with the rest, the Molasse lies mainly under the Swiss Plain north of the Alps, though it, too, was somewhat folded by late orogenic pulses.

As study of the related mountain ranges of Europe progressed, similar and approximately contemporaneous rocks were found elsewhere, and the names, especially flysch, were applied to these, too, as in the Austrian Alps, the Carpathians, the Pyrenees, and the Atlas. Later the names began to be used to designate any deposits of similar character, and in this sense they were imported to North America. Here they have been widely used (Pettijohn, Kay, Krynine) to contrast the graywacke sequence of the volcanic parts of geosynclines with the arkosic sequences of post-orogenic fault troughs, or often merely any pre-orogenic with any post-orogenic detrital sequence. The original Flysch, however, contains no volcanics, and therefore cannot belong to a eugeosyncline as the term is defined by Stille and Kay, and the original Molasse is certainly quite different from the Pennsylvanian and Permian redbeds of the Midcontinent and the Triassic redbeds of eastern North America to which the term has often been applied; indeed, it is more like the Pennsylvanian Coal Measures of the eastern United States. If the names are to be used at all away from the Alpine system, they should be confined to sequences closely comparable to the type sequences and not used indiscriminately merely to signify pre-orogenic and post-orogenic.

OTHER ROCK ASSOCIATIONS

Rocks in post-orogenic basins. Contrasting with the rock associations in geosynclines are those in post-orogenic basins. Krynine, who has emphasized this contrast, has published (1950) a detailed petrographic account of the rocks in part of one such basin, the post-Appalachian Triassic fault trough of New England (p. 213). The sedimentary rocks here are arkose and arkose conglomerate, feldspathic sandstone and siltstone, and silty micaceous shale or mudstone; they are all non-marine and many are red, though some are dark, and related basins farther southwest include minable coal beds. A belt of fanglomerate follows the eastern border fault, which evidently was active throughout deposition, and there is one layer of fresh-water limestone as well as a few layers of calcareous shale. As compared with the rocks on the platforms, the sedimentary components are not sorted out and separated (or only slightly so, into sandier and shalier facies); as compared with the graywacke sequences of the geosynclines, the sediments were derived not from rising islands or land masses resulting from volcanic or tectonic activity and heralding future orogeny but from the worn-down granitic roots of the deformed belt after orogeny was over. Volcanic rocks are present, and also related intrusive sills and dikes, but they are olivine basalt and doler-

ite, unlike the generally somewhat less basic volcanics of the geosyncline (granophyre is known from a few localities in a related fault trough), and they were poured out tranquilly with little pyroclastic or tectonic activity. Yet the sediments accumulated to a minimum thickness of 15,000 feet in Connecticut and 25,000 feet in New Jersey and Pennsylvania.

The Triassic rocks of New England and other parts of eastern North America are not unique; one thinks at once of the Keweenawan redbeds (Precambrian) of Lake Superior, deposited after the deformation of the Huronian rocks, and of the Old Red sandstone (Devonian) of Great Britain, deposited after the Caledonian orogeny. These also are associated with dolerite extrusives and intrusives, and the three are so much alike that they were freely correlated before fossil evidence proved their wide range in age. Likewise the youngest Precambrian rocks in many parts of the great Precambrian shields are closely similar—in the Canadian Shield (beside the Keweenawan) the Athabaska, Et-Then, and Coppermine River groups, and elsewhere the Torridonian of Scotland, the Jotnian of Sweden, the upper Vindhyan of India, and the Waterberg of South Africa. These units have often been correlated, indeed, because of their striking similarity in rock type and in structural setting, and have been taken as evidence of a world-wide period of redbed deposition and dolerite extrusion in late Precambrian time. But the Newark group of eastern North America and the Roraima formation of Venezuela (both Triassic), to mention only two, are no less strikingly similar, and it is now known, furthermore, that the Athabaska sandstone is 1,000 million years older than the Keweenawan, with which it was always correlated. All that the similarity proves is that the last thick sediments in any orogenic area, those in the post-orogenic basins, are apt to be alike, whatever the age of the sediments or the preceding orogeny. Probably similar sediments, though not red, are accumulating today in Owens Valley beside the granitic Sierra Nevada and in other post-orogenic basins in our own Cordillera.

Some post-orogenic sediments, however, are only partly like those described above. The later Devonian and Carboniferous rocks of Gaspé and the Maritime Provinces, deposited in basins after the main pulses of the Acadian or Shickshockian orogeny, generally begin with coarse red arkose and conglomerate, but in the centers of the basins there are thick sections of marine limestone and gypsum in the Mississippian and of non-marine coal-bearing beds in the Pennsylvanian; late pulses of the Acadian orogeny affected the older deposits, and the whole southern part of the area was deformed again in late Pennsylvanian or Permian time. To take another example, Pennsylvanian deformation raised a string of uplifts across Oklahoma and Colorado from the Arbuckles to the Uncompahgres; beside these uplifts thick bodies of red partly arkosic conglomerate and sandstone were deposited, but the redbeds grade laterally off into finer-grained marine sediments and upward into much more widespread Permian redbeds. Here there was no segregated "post-orogenic basin" within an uplifted deformed belt, but only local islands spreading sediment into a wide shallow sea that gradually silted up. Moreover, deformation accompanied as well as preceded deposition, at least in Oklahoma, and in Colorado the whole area was deformed again in the late Cretaceous and early Cenozoic. Still a third variant is the wide irregular basin in which the Permian and Triassic redbeds of northern Europe were deposited after the Hercynian orogeny; arkose and conglomerate are mainly basal, and two major marine invasions deposited the Zechstein and Magnesian limestone (Upper Permian) and the Muschelkalk (Middle Triassic) in the midst of the accumulating redbeds.

Rocks in deltaic coastal plains. Still another common and fairly distinct association of sedimentary rocks is exemplified in the geologic record by the Pennsylvanian rocks of the eastern United States (except New England) and in the modern world by the coastal plain of eastern Sumatra and much of the adjoining shallow Sunda Shelf (Tercier, 1939). The many small rivers of Sumatra bring down sand and mud from the mountain range along its western side and spread them over the flat shelf, which has been alternately low coastal plain and shallow sea floor (van Bemmelen, 1949, v. 1A, p. 298–299, cites evidence of considerable changes in the coast line near Singapore since the tenth century A.D.). On the coastal plain between river channels are large areas of swamp in which richly organic sediments are accumulating; similar accumulations are now lignite in the immediately underlying thick Cenozoic deposits of eastern Sumatra and bituminous coal in the Pennsylvanian of Pennsylvania. The sediments of such a shelf area would be especially affected by minor shifts in sealevel, either the changes caused by the waxing and waning of the Pleistocene and present-day ice sheets, or the ups and downs, whatever caused them, recorded in the Pennsylvanian cyclothems (p. 109). In any case, the resulting sequences consist of endlessly alternating, relatively thin beds of sandstone, shale, coal, and, locally, limestone, some marine, and some non-marine, with or without some cyclical order.

Such deposits, mixed marine and non-marine, are apparently accumulating to great thicknesses elsewhere in the world as well—for example, in the valleys of the lower Ganges and Brahmaputra between the low Indian Peninsula and the high Himalayas and in the Persian Gulf and Mesopotamia between the low Arabian Peninsula and the high Zagros Mountains of Iran. By almost any definition of the term, the linear troughs containing these sediments and those of eastern Sumatra are geosynclines; they even appear to conform to the foreland-geosyncline-borderland pattern, though the borderland has only recently risen, or is still rising, from within a broader complex Cenozoic geosyncline. Similar deposits can be cited from the geologic record—for example, the Upper Cretaceous rocks of the Rocky Mountains, deposited in front of the rising Laramide Mountains (p. 86 and Fig. 78, p. 155), the Coal Measures in the line of major coal basins extending just north of the main Hercynian chain of Europe from southern Wales through Belgium, the Ruhr, and Silesia to the Donetz Basin of Russia, and the Molasse of Switzerland in front of the Alps.

The bodies of sediments mentioned above have all been deposited on one side of a rising land mass, but some similar bodies show no such relation, most notably the Cenozoic deposits of the Gulf Coastal Plain, which were deposited in a great linear trough that extends along the north side of the Gulf of Mexico from Alabama to Texas and northeastern Mexico and has quite properly been called the Gulf Coast geosyncline. Here the sediments were brought in not by many small rivers from a nearby upwarp but by a few large rivers, notably the Mississippi River and the Rio Grande and their ancestors, from uplifts hundreds or thousands of miles away. Yet the type of sediment is the same—rapidly alternating sand and mud, some marine and some non-marine, with layers of lignite in the non-marine portions and rare beds of limestone in the marine. The existence of this enormous mass of detrital sediments deposited far from any source area should be a warning for all who make paleogeographic reconstructions of ancient highlands.

CONCLUDING REMARKS

In order to keep the present chapter within reasonable bounds, we have had to choose for discussion only five kinds of rock associations and to emphasize certain typical examples, thereby seeming to imply that all sequences should fall neatly into one or another of these five kinds and inviting justifiable criticism from those who prefer other lists, longer or shorter and with other members. But we have no such delusions (for this reason, indeed, we have preferred not to formalize the kinds with specially coined names, our own or others'), and we have tried to suggest by added examples the wide ranges in the characters displayed and the numerous transitions. But further stress on the gradations is not amiss.

Thus, on the platforms one finds all gradations from temporarily negative areas through semi-permanent basins to small but sharply-set-off troughs like the Arbuckle-Wichita trough of the lower and middle Paleozoic in Oklahoma, which seems to deserve the name geosyncline because

of its linearity and its subsequent diastrophic history; from here to the major geosynclines is but a step, doubtless bridged by some example. Within the geosynclines, as we have seen, there are two contrasting rock associations and also all possible transitions between them. Again, such post-orogenic basins as the Triassic fault trough of New England contrast strongly with typical geosynclines, yet one could probably find every intermediate step—we have suggested a few. Perhaps what we have called the deltaic coastal plain association is merely a normal, marginal development in the late history of complex major geosynclines—the Pennsylvanian of Pennsylvania is on the edge of the Appalachians, the Cretaceous of the Rockies on the edge of the Cordillera, and the Ganges Valley beside the Himalayas—but once again the Gulf Coast geosyncline is a striking exception. And how is one to classify the Cenozoic troughs of California, such as the San Joaquin Valley and the Ventura basin—as parts of a normal geosyncline (and which parts, for volcanics are sporadic), as post-orogenic basins, or as somehow intermediate?

What stratigraphy has to offer then, to this field where stratigraphy, structural geology, and petrology meet, is a realization of the immense complexity of the geologic record and, so far, only a start toward recognizing significant uniformities in the broad patterns of that record. The idea of the geosyncline as contrasted with the platform expresses one such pattern; the idea that geosynclines are complex and restless and that certain rock types tend to occur on one or the other side of them expresses another; the idea that red arkose and dolerite characterize post-orogenic basins expresses a third. Finally, we must not forget the idea that the patterns themselves are not stereotyped but infinitely varied and transitional, and that the greater part of the work of describing them remains to be done.

Bibliography and author index

Agnew, A. F. See McAllister and Agnew, 1948.

Allee, W. C. See Hesse, Allee, and Schmidt, 1951.

Allen, E. C. See Moberg, Greenberg, Revelle, and Allen, 1934.

Allen, V. T., 1936, Terminology of medium-grained sediments: Natl. Research Council Comm. on Sedimentation Rept. 1935–1936, p. 18–47. **159, 166***

Alling, H. L., 1943, A metric grade scale for sedimentary rocks: Jour. Geology, v. 51, p. 259–269. **164**

American Commission on Stratigraphic Nomenclature, 1947, Note 2—Nature and classes of stratigraphic units: Am. Assoc. Petroleum Geologists Bull., v. 31, p. 519–528. **292**

————1948, Note 5—Definition and adoption of the terms stage and age: Am. Assoc. Petroleum Geologists Bull., v. 32, p. 372–376. **292, 299**

————1949, Note 8—Australian code of stratigraphical nomenclature: Am. Assoc. Petroleum Geologists Bull., v. 33, p. 1273–1276. **259**

————1952, Report 2—Nature, usage, and nomenclature of time-stratigraphic and geologic-time units: Am. Assoc. Petroleum Geologists Bull., v. 36, p. 1627–1638. **292, 293**

————1955, Report 3—Nature, usage, and nomenclature of time-stratigraphic and geologic-time units as applied to the Precambrian: Am. Assoc. Petroleum Geologists Bull., v. 39, p. 1859–1861. **298**

————1956, Report 4—Nature, usage, and nomenclature of rock-stratigraphic units: Am. Assoc. Petroleum Geologists Bull., v. 40, p. 2003–2014. **292**

Andrée, Karl, 1915, Wesen, Ursachen und Arten der Schichtung: Geol. Rundschau, Band 6, p. 351–397. **188**

Androussow, N., 1897, La Mer Noire: 7th Internat. Geol. Cong., Guidebook 29. **60**

Arduino, Giovanni, 1760, Lettera seconda sopra varie sue osservazioni fatti in diversi parti del territorio di Vicenza, ed altrove, appartenenti alla teoria terrestre, ed alla mineralogia: Nuova raccolta d'opuscoli scientifici e filologici [del padre abate Angelo Calogerà], tomo 6: p. cxxxiii–clxxx, Venice. **290**

Arkell, W. J., 1933, The Jurassic System in Great Britain: Oxford, Clarendon. **300**

————1946, Standard of the European Jurassic: Geol. Soc. America Bull., v. 57, p. 1–34. **299**

Arkhangelsky, A. D., 1927, On the Black Sea sediments and their importance for the study of sedimentary rocks: Soc. des Naturalistes de Moscou Bull., Sect. Geol., v. 35, p. 199–289 [not seen]. **60**

Arkle, Thomas, Jr. See Cross, Smith, and Arkle, 1950.

Athy, L. F., 1930, Density, porosity, and compaction of sedimentary rocks: Am. Assoc. Petroleum Geologists Bull., v. 14, p. 1–24. **105**

Atterberg, Albert, 1904, Sandslagens klassifikation och terminologi: Geol. Fören. Förh., Band 25, p. 397–412. **164**

Atwater, G. I. See Trowbridge and Atwater, 1934.

Averitt, Paul See Hendricks, Gardner, Knechtel, and Averitt, 1947.

Bagnold, R. A., 1941, The physics of blown sand and desert dunes: London, Methuen [reprint, 1954]. **17, 18, 20, 21, 65, 190, 191**

Bailey, E. B., and Weir, John, 1933, Submarine faulting in Kimmeridgian times: East Sutherland: Royal Soc. Edinburgh Trans., v. 57, pt. 2, p. 429–467. **177**

Baker, A. A., Dané, C. H., and Reeside, J. B., Jr., 1936, Correlation of the Jurassic formations of parts of Utah, Arizona, New Mexico, and Colorado: U. S. Geol. Survey Prof. Paper 183. **234**

* Boldface numerals at the right of an entry refer to pages in this book on which the reference is cited.

Baker, A. A., Dane, C. H., and Reeside, J. B., Jr., 1947, Revised correlation of Jurassic formations of parts of Utah, Arizona New Mexico, and Colorado: Am. Assoc. Petroleum Geologists Bull., v. 31, p. 1664–1668.   **270**

Baker, A. A., and Reeside, J. B., Jr., 1929, Correlation of the Permian of southern Utah, northern Arizona, northwestern New Mexico, and southwestern Colorado: Am. Assoc. Petroleum Geologists Bull., v. 13, p. 1413–1448.   **263, 264**

Bakewell, Robert, 1815, Introduction to geology (2nd ed.): London.   **116**

Balk, Robert, 1936, Structural and petrologic studies in Dutchess County, New York. Part I: Geologic structure of sedimentary rocks: Geol. Soc. America Bull., v. 47, p. 685–774.   **122**

Bandy, O. L., 1954, Aragonite tests among the Foraminifera: Jour. Sed. Petrology, v. 24, p. 60–61.   **227**

Bär, Otto, 1924, Versuch einer Lösung des Dolomitproblems auf phasentheoretischer Grundlage: Senckenbergiana, Band 6, p. 116–118.   **238, 244**

————1932, Beitrag zum Thema Dolomitentstehung: Centralbl. Mineralogie, 1932, Abt. A, p. 46–62.   **238, 244**

Barnes, V. E., Cloud, P. E., Jr., and Warren, L. E., 1946, The Devonian of central Texas: Univ. Texas Pub. 4301, p. 163–177.   **279**

Barnes, V. E. See also Cloud and Barnes, 1948.

Barrell, Joseph, 1906, Relative geological importance of continental, littoral, and marine sedimentation: Jour. Geology, v. 14, p. 316–356, 430–457, 524–568.   **86**

————1908, Relations between climate and terrestrial deposits: Jour. Geology, v. 16, p. 159–190, 255–295, 363–384.   **211, 213**

————1912, Criteria for the recognition of ancient delta deposits: Geol. Soc. America Bull., v. 23, p. 377–446.   **74**

————1915, Central Connecticut in the geologic past: Connecticut Geol. and Nat. History Survey Bull. 23.   **31, 213**

————1917, Rhythms and the measurements of geologic time: Geol. Soc. America Bull., v. 28, p. 745–904.   **47, 128, 133, 199**

————1925, Marine and terrestrial conglomerates: Geol. Soc. America Bull., v. 36, p. 279–341.   **180**

Barth, T. F. W., Correns, C. W., and Eskola, Pentti, 1939, Die Entstehung der Gesteine: Berlin, Springer.   **227**

Barton, D. C., 1918, Notes on the Mississippian chert of the St. Louis area: Jour. Geology, v. 26, p. 361–374.   **248, 250**

Bartsch, Paul, 1920, Experiments in the breeding of *Cerions:* Carnegie Inst. Wash. Pub. 282.   **146**

Bass, N. W., 1934, Origin of Bartlesville shoestring sands, Greenwood and Butler Counties, Kansas: Am. Assoc. Petroleum Geologists Bull., v. 18, p. 1313–1345.   **70, 73**

Bass, N. W. See also Rubey and Bass, 1925.

Bassler, R. S., 1919, Cambrian and Ordovician: Maryland Geol. Survey.   **180**

Bates, T. F., 1953, Mineralogy of the Chattanooga shale: Geol. Soc. America Bull., v. 64, p. 1529.   **207**

Bauernschmidt, A. J., Jr., 1944, West Ranch oil field, Jackson County, Texas: Am. Assoc. Petroleum Geologists Bull., v. 28, p. 197–216.   **274, 275**

Bavendamm, Werner, 1932, Die mikrobiologische Kalkfällung in der tropischen See: Archiv für Mikrobiologie, Band 3, Heft 2, p. 205–276.   **232**

Bennett, H. S., and Martin-Kaye, P., 1951, The occurrence and derivation of an augite-rich beach sand, Grenada, B.W.I.: Jour. Sed. Petrology, v. 21, p. 200–204.   **183**

Berkey, C. P., 1897–1898, Geology of the St. Croix Dalles: Am. Geologist, v. 20, p. 345–383; v. 21, p. 139–155, 270–294.   **170**

Billings, M. P., and Cleaves, A. B., 1934, Paleontology of the Littleton area, New Hampshire: Am. Jour. Sci., 5th ser., v. 28, p. 412–438.   **276**

Black, Maurice, 1933, The precipitation of calcium carbonate on the Great Bahama Bank: Geol. Mag., v. 70, p. 455–466.   **95, 231, 233, 234**

Black, Maurice. See also Hatch, Rastall, and Black, 1938.

Blackwelder, Eliot, 1909, The valuation of unconformities: Jour. Geology, v. 17, p. 289–299.   **121**

————1918, The climatic history of Alaska from a new viewpoint: Illinois Acad. Sci. Trans., v. 10, p. 275–280.   **196**

————1928, Mudflow as a geologic agent in semiarid mountains: Geol. Soc. America Bull., v. 39, p. 465–483.   **172**

————1931a, The lowering of playas by deflation: Am. Jour. Sci., 5th ser., v. 21, p. 140–144.   **39**

————1931b, Desert plains: Jour. Geology, v. 39, p. 133–140.   **38**

Blanck, Edwin, editor, 1929–1932, Handbuch der Bodenlehre: Berlin, Springer.   **210**

Blissenbach, Erich, 1954, Geology of alluvial fans in semiarid regions: Geol. Soc. America Bull., v. 65, p. 175–189.   **29**

Bøggild, O. B., 1912, The deposits of the sea-bottom: Danish Oceanographical Expeds. 1908–1910 Rept., v. 1, p. 255–269.   **61**

————1930, The shell structure of the mollusks: K. Danske vidensk. Selsk. Skr., naturv. og math. Afd., 9 Raekke, Bind 2, p. 231–326.   **227**

Boltwood, B. B., 1907, On the ultimate disintegration products of the radio-active elements. Part II: The disintegration products of uranium: Am. Jour. Sci., 4th ser., v. 23, p. 77–88.   **127**

Boswell, P. G. H., 1937, The tectonic problems of an area of Salopian rocks in north-western Denbighshire: Geol. Soc. London Quart. Jour., v. 93, p. 284–321.   **105**

————1949, The Middle Silurian rocks of North Wales: London, Edward Arnold.   **105**

Boyd, D. W. See Newell and Boyd, 1955.

Bradley, J. S. See Newell, Rigby, Fischer, Whiteman,

Hickox, and Bradley, 1953; Newell, Rigby, Whiteman, and Bradley, 1951.

Bradley, W. F. See Grim, Dietz, and Bradley, 1949.

Bradley, W. H., 1926, Shore phases of the Green River formation in northern Sweetwater County, Wyoming: U. S. Geol. Survey Prof. Paper 140-D, p. 121–131.   **42**

————1929a, Algae reefs and oolites of the Green River formation: U. S. Geol. Survey Prof. Paper 154-G, p. 203–223.   **234**

————1929b, The varves and climate of the Green River epoch: U. S. Geol. Survey Prof. Paper 158-E, p. 87–110.   **42, 108, 198**

————1931a, Origin and microfossils of the oil shale of the Green River formation of Colorado and Utah: U. S. Geol. Survey Prof. Paper 168.   **42, 197, 227**

————1931b, Non-glacial marine varves: Am. Jour. Sci., 5th ser., v. 22, p. 318–330.   **108**

————1937, Non-glacial varves, with selected bibliography: Natl. Research Council Comm. Geol. Time Rept. 1937, p. 32–43.   **109**

————1940, Geology and biology of North Atlantic deep-sea cores between Newfoundland and Ireland. General introduction: U. S. Geol. Survey Prof. Paper 196, p. xiii–xv [1941].   **49**

————1948, Limnology and the Eocene lakes of the Rocky Mountain region: Geol. Soc. America Bull., v. 59, p. 635–648.   **40, 42**

Bradley, W. H. See also Bramlette and Bradley, 1940.

Bragg, W. L., 1924a, The structure of aragonite: Royal Soc. London Proc., ser. A, v. 105, p. 16–39.   **222**

————1924b, The refractive indices of calcite and aragonite: Royal Soc. London Proc., ser. A, v. 105, p. 370–386.   **220**

————1937, Atomic structure of minerals: Ithaca, Cornell University Press.   **220, 222**

Bramlette, M. N., 1926, Some marine bottom samples from Pago Pago Harbor, Samoa: Carnegie Inst. Washington Pub. 344, p. 1–35.   **232, 235**

————1946, The Monterey formation of California and the origin of its siliceous rocks: U. S. Geol. Survey Prof. Paper 212.   **53, 247, 250, 252, 264**

Bramlette, M. N., and Bradley, W. H., 1940, Geology and biology of North Atlantic deep-sea cores between Newfoundland and Ireland. Part 1: Lithology and geologic interpretations: U. S. Geol. Survey Prof. Paper 196, p. 1–34 [1941].   **48, 56, 57, 60, 174**

Branson, E. B., 1915, Origin of the red beds of western Wyoming: Geol. Soc. America Bull., v. 26, p. 217–230.   **217**

————1927, Triassic-Jurassic "red beds" of the Rocky Mountain region: Jour. Geology, v. 35, p. 607–630.   **217**

Brett, G. W., 1955, Cross-bedding in the Baraboo quartzite of Wisconsin: Jour. Geology, v. 63, p. 143–148.   **189**

Bridge, Josiah, 1930, Geology of the Eminence and Cardareva quadrangles: Missouri Bur. Geology and Mines, 2nd ser., v. 24.   **68**

————1955, Disconformity between Lower and Middle Ordovician series at Douglas Lake, Tennessee: Geol. Soc. America Bull., v. 66, p. 725–730.   **168**

————1956, Stratigraphy of the Mascot-Jefferson City zinc district, Tennessee: U. S. Geol. Survey Prof. Paper 277.   **240**

Bridge, Josiah, and Dake, C. L., 1929, Initial dips peripheral to resurrected hills: Missouri Bur. Geology and Mines Bienn. Rept. [1927–1928], p. 93–99.   **103**

Bridge, Josiah. See also Dake and Bridge, 1932.

Brinkmann, Roland, 1929, Statistisch-biostratigraphische Untersuchungen an Mitteljurassischen Ammoniten über Artbegriff und Stammesentwicklung: Gesell. Wiss. Göttingen, Math.-phys. Kl., Abh., neue Folge, Band 13, no. 3.   **131, 132, 281**

Brokaw, A. L., 1950, Geology and mineralogy of the East Tennessee zinc district: 18th Internat. Geol. Cong. Rept., pt. 7, p. 70–76.   **240**

Brongersma-Sanders, Margaretha, 1948, The importance of upwelling water to vertebrate paleontology and oil geology: K. Nederlandsche Akad. Wetensch. Amsterdam Verh., Afd. Natuurk., Sec. 2, v. 45, no. 4, p. 1–112.   **53, 204**

Brown, F. B. H., 1924, Botanical evidence bearing on submergence of land in the Marquesas Islands: 2nd Pan-Pacific Sci. Cong. Proc., p. 1156–1160.   **58**

Browne, W. R. See David and Browne, 1950.

Bryan, Kirk, 1922, Erosion and sedimentation in the Papago country, Arizona: U. S. Geol. Survey Bull. 730, p. 19–90.   **38**

Buch, Kurt, Harvey, H. W., Wattenberg, Hermann, and Gripenberg, Stina, 1932, Über das Kohlensäuresystem im Meerwasser: Conseil Perm. Internat. pour l'Expl. Mer, Rapp. et Proc.-Verb., v. 79.   **230**

Bucher, W. H., 1918, On oölites and spherulites: Jour. Geology, v. 26, p. 593–609.   **234**

Bucher, W. H. See also Kindle and Bucher, 1926.

Burnside, R. J. See Myers, Stafford, and Burnside, 1956.

Busch, D. A., 1950, Subsurface techniques: Applied Sedimentation, p. 559–578, New York, Wiley.   **274**

Cailleux, André, 1945, Distinction des galets marins et fluviatiles: Soc. Géol. France Bull., 5e sér., tome 15, p. 375–404.   **187**

Cain, S. A., 1944, Foundations of plant geography: New York, Harper.   **145**

Carruthers, R. G., 1910, On the evolution of *Zaphrentis delanouei* in Lower Carboniferous times: Geol. Soc. London Quart. Jour., v. 66, p. 523–538.   **281**

Carsola, A. J., 1954, Recent marine sediments from Alaskan and northwest Canadian Arctic: Am. Assoc. Petroleum Geologists Bull., v. 38, p. 1552–1586.   **24, 52**

Carsola, A. J., and Dietz, R. S., 1952, Submarine geology of two flat-topped northeast Pacific seamounts: Am. Jour. Sci., v. 250, p. 481–497.   **56**

Caster, K. E., 1934, The stratigraphy and paleontology

of northwestern Pennsylvania. Part I: Stratigraphy: Bull. Am. Paleontology, v. 21, no. 71.   **262**

Cayeux, Lucien, 1897, Contribution à l'étude micrographique des terrains sédimentaires: Soc. Géol. Nord Mem., tome 4 [not seen].   **183**

Chadwick, G. H., 1924, The stratigraphy of the Chemung group in western New York: New York State Mus. Bull. 251, p. 149–157.   **138**

————1930, Subdivision of geologic time: Geol. Soc. America Bull., v. 41, p. 47–48.   **294**

————1933, Great Catskill delta: and revision of Late Devonic succession [Upper Devonian revision in New York and Pennsylvania]: Pan-Am. Geologist, v. 60, p. 91–107, 189–204, 275–286, 348–360. [The editor severely mutilated this paper, changing the title and making more than 1,000 other alterations; Chadwick was forced to deny responsibility for the paper and to distribute a list of the most important changes.]   **138**

Chamberlin, R. T., 1914, Diastrophism and the formative processes. VII: Periodicity of Paleozoic orogenic movements: Jour. Geology, v. 22, p. 315–345.   **303**

Chamberlin, T. C., 1898a, The ulterior basis of time divisions and the classification of geologic history: Jour. Geology, v. 6, p. 449–462.   **303**

————1898b, A systematic source of evolution of provincial faunas: Jour. Geology, v. 6, p. 597–608.   **303**

————1909, Diastrophism as the ultimate basis of correlation: Jour. Geology, v. 17, p. 685–693.   **303**

Chaney, R. W., 1948a, The bearing of the living *Metasequoia* on problems of Tertiary paleobotany: Natl. Acad. Sci. Proc., v. 34, p. 503–515.   **153**

————1948b, Redwoods around the Pacific Basin: Pacific Discovery, v. 1, no. 5, p. 4–14, San Francisco, California Acad. Sci.   **153**

Chave, K. E., 1952, A solid solution between calcite and dolomite: Jour. Geology, v. 60, p. 190–192.   **228**

————1954, Aspects of the biogeochemistry of magnesium. 1: Calcareous marine organisms: Jour. Geology, v. 62, p. 266–283.   **228**

Chayes, Felix, 1950, On the bias of grain-size measurements made in thin sections: Jour. Geology, v. 58, p. 156–160.   **225**

Clapp, F. G., 1907, Description of the Rogersville quadrangle [Pa.]: U. S. Geol. Survey Geol. Atlas, Folio 146.   **213**

Clark, P. E. See van Ingen and Clark, 1903.

Clarke, F. W., 1924, The data of geochemistry (5th ed.): U. S. Geol. Survey Bull. 770.   **238, 249**

Clarke, F. W., and Wheeler, W. C., 1922, The inorganic constituents of marine invertebrates (2nd ed., revised and enlarged): U. S. Geol. Survey Prof. Paper 124.   **228**

Clarke, J. M., 1904, Naples fauna in western New York. Part 2: New York State Mus. Mem. 6.   **202**

Cleaves, A. B. See Billings and Cleaves, 1934.

Clements, Thomas, 1952, Wind-blown rocks and trails on Little Bonnie Claire Playa, Nye County, Nevada: Jour. Sed. Petrology, v. 22, p. 182–186.   **173**

Cloud, P. E., Jr., 1942, Notes on stromatolites: Am. Jour. Sci., v. 240, p. 363–379.   **229**

————1955, Physical limits of glauconite formation: Am. Assoc. Petroleum Geologists Bull., v. 39, p. 484–492, 1879.   **184**

Cloud, P. E., Jr., and Barnes, V. E., 1948, The Ellenburger group of central Texas: Univ. Texas Pub. 4621.   **95, 227, 231, 233, 236**

Cloud, P. E., Jr. See also Barnes, Cloud, and Warren, 1946.

Cohee, G. V. See Shepard and Cohee, 1936.

Coleman, A. P., 1926, Ice ages, recent and ancient: New York, Macmillan.   **44**

Collins, C. B., Farquhar, R. M., and Russell, R. D., 1954, Isotopic constitution of radiogenic leads and the measurement of geological time: Geol. Soc. America Bull., v. 65, p. 1–22.   **209**

Commission Internationale de Classification Stratigraphique, 1901, Rapport par E. Renevier: 8th Internat. Geol. Cong., Comptes rendus, fasc. 1, p. 192–203.   **290**

Committee on Stratigraphic Nomenclature, 1933, Classification and nomenclature of rock units: Geol. Soc. America Bull., v. 44, p. 423–459; Am. Assoc. Petroleum Geologists Bull., v. 17, p. 843–868; ibid., v. 23, p. 1068–1099, 1939.   **258–260, 291**

Conant, L. C., 1953, Shallow-water origin of the Chattanooga shale: Geol. Soc. America Bull., v. 64, p. 1529–1530.   **207**

Cooper, B. N., 1944, Geology and mineral resources of the Burkes Garden quadrangle, Virginia: Virginia Geol. Survey Bull. 60.   **233**

Cooper, G. A., 1930, Stratigraphy of the Hamilton group of New York: Am. Jour. Sci., 5th ser., v. 19, p. 116–134, 214–236.   **138, 265**

————1933, Stratigraphy of the Hamilton group of eastern New York: Am. Jour. Sci., 5th ser., v. 26, p. 537–551; v. 27, p. 1–12.   **138, 156, 265**

Cooper, G. A., and Williams, J. S., 1935, Tully formation of New York: Geol. Soc. America Bull., v. 46, p. 781–868.   **156**

Cooper, G. A., and others, 1942, Correlation of the Devonian sedimentary formations of North America: Geol. Soc. America Bull., v. 53, p. 1729–1793.   **112, 138**

Correns, C. W., 1937, Die Sedimente des äquatorialen Atlantischen Ozeans: Deutsche Atlantische Exped. "Meteor" Wiss. Ergeb., Band 3, Teil 3.   **23**

————1950, Zur Geochemie der Diagenese. I. Das Verhalten von $CaCO_3$ und SiO_2: Geochim. Cosmochim. Acta, v. 1, p. 49–54.   **25**

Correns, C. W. See also Barth, Correns, and Eskola, 1939.

Craig, L. C. See King, Ferguson, Craig, and Rodgers, 1944.

Crain, H. M. See LeRoy and Crain, Editors, 1949.

Cressey, G. B., 1928, The Indiana sand dunes and shore lines of the Lake Michigan basin: Geog. Soc. Chicago Bull. 8.   **188**

Crosby, W. O., 1891, On the contrast in color of the soils of high and low latitudes: Am. Geologist, v. 8, p. 72–82.   **211**

Cross, A. T., Smith, W. H., and Arkle, Thomas, Jr., 1950, Field guide for the special field conference on the stratigraphy, sedimentation and nomenclature of the Upper Pennsylvanian and Lower Permian strata (Monongahela, Washington and Greene series) in the northern portion of the Dunkard Basin of Ohio, West Virginia and Pennsylvania: Morgantown, West Virginia Geol. Survey [mimeographed guidebook].   **213, 234**

Crouch, R. W., 1952, Significance of temperature on Foraminifera from deep basins off southern California coast: Am. Assoc. Petroleum Geologists Bull., v. 36, p. 807–843.   **59, 154**

Crowell, J. C., 1955, Violin breccia in Transverse Ranges, California: Geol. Soc. America Bull., v. 66, p. 1546.   **171**

Cumings, E. R., 1932, Reefs or bioherms?: Geol. Soc. America Bull., v. 43, p. 331–352.   **88**

Cumings, E. R., and Shrock, R. R., 1928a, Niagaran coral reefs of Indiana and adjacent States and their stratigraphic relations: Geol. Soc. America Bull., v. 39, p. 579–619.   **103, 145**

————1928b, The geology of the Silurian rocks of northern Indiana: Indiana Div. Geology Pub. 75.
                                                      103, 145, 208

Dake, C. L., 1921, The problem of the St. Peter sandstone: Missouri Univ. School of Mines and Metallurgy Bull., Tech. ser., v. 6, no. 1.   **25, 187**

Dake, C. L., and Bridge, Josiah, 1932, Buried and resurrected hills of central Ozarks: Am. Assoc. Petroleum Geologists Bull., v. 16, p. 629–652.   **103**

Dake, C. L.   See also Bridge and Dake, 1929.

Dall, W. H., 1916, On some anomalies in geographic distribution of Pacific Coast Mollusca: Natl. Acad. Sci. Proc., v. 2, p. 700–703.   **153**

Dall, W. H., and Harris, G. D., 1892, Correlation papers: Neocene: U. S. Geol. Survey Bull. 84.   **148**

Daly, R. A., 1909, First calcareous fossils and the evolution of the limestones: Geol. Soc. America Bull., v. 20, p. 153–170.   **241**

————1936, Origin of submarine "canyons": Am. Jour. Sci., 5th ser., v. 31, p. 401–420.   **13, 14**

Daly, R. A., Miller, W. G., and Rice, G. S., 1912, Report of the Commission appointed to investigate Turtle Mountain, Frank, Alberta: Canada Geol. Survey Mem. 27.   **171**

Dana, J. D., 1873, On some results of the Earth's contraction from cooling, including a discussion of the origin of mountains, and the nature of the Earth's interior: Am. Jour. Sci., 3rd ser., v. 5, p. 423–443, 474–475; v. 6, p. 6–14, 104–115, 161–172, 304, 381–382.   **310**

Dane, C. H.   See Baker, Dane, and Reeside, 1936, 1947.

Dapples, E. C., 1955, General lithofacies relationship of St. Peter sandstone and Simpson group: Am. Assoc. Petroleum Geologists Bull., v. 39, p. 444–467.   **70, 187**

Darwin, Charles, 1859, On the origin of species by means of natural selection: London, Murray.   **116**

David, T. W. E., and Browne, W. R., 1950, The geology of the Commonwealth of Australia: London, Arnold.
                                                       24

Davis, E. F., 1918, The radiolarian cherts of the Franciscan group: California Univ., Dept. Geol. Sci., Bull., v. 11, p. 235–432.   **253**

Davis, W. M., 1898, The Triassic formation of Connecticut: U. S. Geol. Survey 18th Ann. Rept., pt. 2, p. 1–192.   **213**

————1900, The freshwater Tertiary formations of the Rocky Mountain region: Am. Acad. Arts and Sci. Proc., v. 35, p. 345–373.   **37**

Decker, C. E., and Merritt, C. A., 1928, Physical characteristics of the Arbuckle limestone: Oklahoma Geol. Survey Circ. 15.   **223, 224**

DeFord, R. K., 1946, Grain size in carbonate rock: Am. Assoc. Petroleum Geologists Bull., v. 30, p. 1921–1928.   **225**

Deiss, Charles, 1935, Cambrian-Algonkian unconformity in western Montana: Geol. Soc. America Bull., v. 46, p. 95–124.   **125**

De La Beche, H. T., 1851, Geological Observer: London.   **234**

Demarest, D. F.   See Pepper, de Witt, and Demarest, 1954.

de Saussure, N. T., 1792, Analyse de la dolomie: Jour. de physique, tome 40, p. 161–173.   **219**

de Witt, Wallace, Jr.   See Pepper, de Witt, and Demarest, 1954.

Dickerson, R. E., 1921, A fauna of the Vigo group: its bearing on the evolution of marine molluscan faunas: Philippine Jour. Sci., v. 18, p. 1–23.   **282**

Dietz, R. S., and Menard, H. W., 1951, Origin of abrupt change in slope at continental shelf margin: Am. Assoc. Petroleum Geologists Bull., v. 35, p. 1994–2016.   **47, 56, 191**

Dietz, R. S.   See also Carsola and Dietz, 1952; Grim, Dietz, and Bradley, 1949.

Dobbin, C. E.   See Thom and Dobbin, 1924.

Dolomieu, Déodat de, 1791, Sur un genre de pierres calcaires très-peu effervescentes avec les acides, et phosphorescentes par la collision: Jour. de physique, tome 39, p. 3–10.   **219**

d'Orbigny, A. D., 1840, Paléontologie française, Terrains crétacés, tome 1: Paris.   **298**

————1842, Paléontologie française, Terrains oolitiques ou jurassiques, tome 1: Paris.   **298, 299**

Dorsey, G. E., 1926, The origin of the color of red beds: Jour. Geology, v. 34, p. 131–143.   **212**

Drew, G. H., 1913, On the precipitation of calcium carbonate in the sea by marine bacteria, and on the action of denitrifying bacteria in tropical and temperate seas: Marine Biol. Assoc. United Kingdom Jour., new ser., v. 9, p. 479–524; Carnegie Inst. Washington Pub. 182, p. 7–45 [1914].   **232**

Dunbar, C. O., 1940, The type Permian: its classification and correlation: Am. Assoc. Petroleum Geologists Bull., v. 24, p. 237–281.   **141**

———1941, Permian faunas: a study in facies: Geol. Soc. America Bull., v. 52, p. 313–331.   **137**

———1942, Artinskian series: Am. Assoc. Petroleum Geologists Bull., v. 26, p. 402–408.   **141**

———1953, A zone of *Pseudoschwagerina* low in the Leonard Series in the Sierra Diablo, Trans-Pecos Texas: Am. Jour. Sci., v. 251, p. 798–813.   **204**

Dunbar, C. O., and Henbest, L. G., 1942, Pennsylvanian Fusulinidae of Illinois: Illinois Geol. Survey Bull. 67.   **281**

Dunbar, C. O. and Skinner, J. W., 1937, Permian Fusulinidae of Texas: Univ. Texas Bull. 3701, pt. 2, p. 517–825.   **281**

Dunbar, C. O. See also Schuchert and Dunbar, 1934; Weller, Henbest, and Dunbar, 1942.

du Toit, A. L., and Haughton, S. H., 1954, The geology of South Africa [3rd ed.]: Edinburgh, Oliver and Boyd; New York, Hafner.   **44**

Eardley, A. J., 1938, Sediments of Great Salt Lake, Utah: Am. Assoc. Petroleum Geologists Bull., v. 22, p. 1305–1411.   **233, 234**

———1947, Paleozoic Cordilleran geosyncline and related orogeny: Jour. Geology, v. 55, p. 309–342. **313**

Earp, J. R., 1938, The higher Silurian rocks of the Kerry district, Montgomeryshire: Geol. Soc. London Quart. Jour., v. 94, p. 125–160.   **105**

Eaton, J. E., 1929, The by-passing and discontinuous deposition of sedimentary materials: Am. Assoc. Petroleum Geologists Bull., v. 13, p. 713–761. **9, 128**

Ekman, Sven, 1953, Zoogeography of the sea: London, Sidgwick and Jackson.   **145**

Elles, G. L., 1924, Evolutional palæontology in relation to the Lower Palæozoic rocks: British Assoc. Adv. Sci. Rept. Liverpool Mtg., 1923, p. 83–107.   **281**

Emery, K. O., and Rittenberg, S. C., 1952, Early diagenesis of California basin sediments in relation to origin of oil: Am. Assoc. Petroleum Geologists Bull., v. 36, p. 735–806.   **251**

Emery, K. O., Tracey, J. I., Jr., and Ladd, H. S., 1954, Geology of Bikini and nearby atolls. Part I: Geology: U. S. Geol. Survey Prof. Paper 260-A, p. 1–265.   **90, 170, 305**

Emery, K. O., and Tschudy, R. H., 1941, Transportation of rock by kelp: Geol. Soc. America Bull., v. 52, p. 855–862.   **175**

Emery, K. O. See also Ladd, Tracey, Wells, and Emery, 1950; Shepard and Emery, 1941, 1946; Shepard, Emery, and Gould, 1949.

Engel, A. E. J. See Jahns and Engel, 1950.

Ericson, D. B., 1953, Further evidence for turbidity currents from the 1929 Grand Banks earthquake: Geol. Soc. America Bull., v. 64, p. 1560.   **16**

Ericson, D. B., Ewing, Maurice, and Heezen, B. C.,

1951, Deep-sea sands and submarine canyons: Geol. Soc. America Bull., v. 62, p. 961–965.   **59**

———1952, Turbidity currents and sediments in North Atlantic: Am. Assoc. Petroleum Geologists Bull., v. 36, p. 489–511.   **16, 59**

Ericson, D. B., Ewing, Maurice, Heezen, B. C., and Wollin, G., 1955, Sediment deposition in deep Atlantic: Geol. Soc. America Spec. Paper 62, p. 205–219.   **16**

Ericson, D. B. See also Heezen, Ericson, and Ewing, 1954; Heezen, Ewing, and Ericson, 1955.

Eskola, Pentti. See Barth, Correns, and Eskola, 1939.

Ewing, Maurice, Sutton, G. H., and Officer, C. B., Jr., 1954, Seismic refraction measurements in the Atlantic Ocean, Part VI: Typical deep stations, North America Basin: Seismol. Soc. Am. Bull., v. 44, p. 21–38.   **60**

Ewing, Maurice, Vine, Allyn, and Worzel, J. L., 1946, Photography of the ocean bottom: Optical Soc. America Jour., v. 36, p. 307–321.   **46**

Ewing, Maurice. See also Ericson, Ewing, and Heezen, 1951, 1952; Ericson, Ewing, Heezen, and Wollin, 1955; Heezen, Ericson, and Ewing, 1954; Heezen and Ewing, 1952; Heezen, Ewing, and Ericson, 1955.

Fairbridge, R. W., 1950, Recent and Pleistocene coral reefs of Australia: Jour. Geology, v. 58, p. 330–401.   **92, 93, 95**

———1953, The Sahul Shelf, Northern Australia; its structure and geological relationships: Royal Soc. Western Australia Jour., v. 37, p. 1–33.   **95**

Fairbridge, R. W. See also Teichert and Fairbridge, 1948.

Farquhar, R. M. See Collins, Farquhar, and Russell, 1954.

Fearnsides, W. G., 1905, On the geology of Arenig Fawr and Moel Llyfnant: Geol. Soc. London Quart. Jour., v. 61, p. 608–637.   **202**

Ferguson, H. W. See King, Ferguson, Craig, and Rodgers, 1944.

Finley, Robert, Jr. See Fischer and Finley, 1949.

Fischer, A. G., and Finley, Robert, Jr., 1949, Microstructure of some Pennsylvanian nautiloids: Geol. Soc. America Bull., v. 60, p. 1887.   **222**

Fischer, A. G. See also Newell, Rigby, Fischer, Whiteman, Hickox, and Bradley, 1953.

Fischer, Georg, 1934, Die Petrographie der Grauwacken: Preussische geol. Landesanst. Jahrbuch, Band 54, p. 320–343.   **166**

Fisk, H. N., 1944, Geological investigation of the alluvial valley of the lower Mississippi River: Vicksburg, Mississippi River Commission. **31, 34, 37, 75, 77, 86**

———1947, Fine-grained alluvial deposits and their effects on Mississippi River activity: Vicksburg, Mississippi River Commission.   **31, 34**

Fisk, H. N., McFarlan, Edward, Jr., Kolb, C. R., and Wilbert, L. J., Jr., 1954, Sedimentary framework of the modern Mississippi delta: Jour. Sed. Petrology, v. 24, p. 76–99. **9, 64, 75, 78, 79**

Fisk, H. N., and others, 1952, Geological investigation of the Atchafalaya basin and the problem of Mississippi River diversion: Vicksburg, Mississippi River Commission. **31, 77**

Flawn, P. T., 1953, Petrographic classification of argillaceous sedimentary and low-grade metamorphic rocks in subsurface: Am. Assoc. Petroleum Geologists Bull., v. 37, p. 560–565. **166**

Fleming, R. H. See Revelle and Fleming, 1934; Sverdrup, Johnson, and Fleming, 1942.

Flint, R. F., 1957, Glacial and Pleistocene geology: New York, Wiley. **42**

Flint, R. F. See also Longwell, Knopf, and Flint, 1939.

Folk, R. L., and Weaver, C. E., 1952, A study of the texture and composition of chert: Am. Jour. Sci., v. 250, p. 498–510. **246**

Folk, R. L. See also Miller and Folk, 1955.

Ford, W. E., 1917, Studies in the calcite group: Connecticut Acad. Arts and Sci. Trans., v. 22, p. 211–248. **220, 221**

Forel, F. A., 1887, Le ravin sous-lacustre du Rhône dans le lac Léman: Soc. Vaudoise sci. nat. Bull., v. 23, p. 85–107. **13**

Fuchsel, G. C., 1761, Historia terrae et maris, ex historia Thuringiae, per montium descriptionem eruta: Akad. gemeinnütziger Wissenschaften zu Erfurt (Acad. Electoralis Maguntinae scientiarum utilum quae Erfordiae est) Acta, Tomus 2, p. 44–208. **290**

Galliher, E. W., 1935, Geology of glauconite: Am. Assoc. Petroleum Geologists Bull., v. 19, p. 1569–1601; Glauconite genesis: Geol. Soc. America Bull., v. 46, p. 1351–1365. **183, 184**

Gardner, L. S. See Hendricks, Gardner, Knechtel, and Averitt, 1947.

Gautier, E.-F. (translated by D. F. Mayhew), 1935, Sahara: the great desert: New York, Columbia Univ. Press. **39**

Gee, Haldane, 1932, Inorganic marine limestone: Jour. Sed. Petrology, v. 2, p. 162–166. **232**

Gee, Haldane, and others, 1932, Calcium equilibrium in sea water: Scripps Inst. Oceanography Bull., Tech. ser., v. 3, p. 145–190. **231, 232**

Geikie, Archibald, 1897, The founders of geology: London, Macmillan. **278**

———1903, Text-book of geology (4th ed.): London, Macmillan. **122**

Gibson, R. E., Wyckoff, R. W. G., and Merwin, H. E., 1925, Vaterite and μ-calcium carbonate: Am. Jour. Sci., 5th ser., v. 10, p. 325–333. **222**

Gilbert, C. M. See Williams, Turner, and Gilbert, 1954.

Gilbert, G. K., 1890, Lake Bonneville: U. S. Geol. Survey Mon. 1. **40, 74**

———1899, Ripple-marks and cross-bedding: Geol. Soc. America Bull., v. 10, p. 135–140. **188**

———1914, The transportation of débris by running water: U. S. Geol. Survey Prof. Paper 86. **7, 8, 190**

Gilluly, James, 1949, Distribution of mountain building in geologic time: Geol. Soc. America Bull., v. 60, p. 561–590. **303, 304**

Gilluly, James, and Reeside, J. B., Jr., 1928, Sedimentary rocks of the San Rafael swell and some adjacent areas in eastern Utah: U. S. Geol. Survey Prof. Paper 150-D, p. 61–110. **123**

Glaessner, M. F., Raggatt, H. G., Teichert, Curt, and Thomas, D. E., 1948, Stratigraphical nomenclature in Australia: Australian Jour. Sci., v. 11, p. 7–9. **259**

Glaessner, M. F., and Teichert, Curt, 1947, Geosynclines: a fundamental concept in geology: Am. Jour. Sci., v. 245, p. 465–482, 571–591. **314**

Glinka, K. D., 1896, Glauconit: St. Petersburg [not seen]. **183**

Goldman, M. I., 1921, Lithologic subsurface correlation in the "Bend series" of north-central Texas: U. S. Geol. Survey Prof. Paper 129-A, p. 1–22. **184**

———1924, "Black shale" formation in and about Chesapeake Bay: Am. Assoc. Petroleum Geologists Bull., v. 8, p. 195–201. **205**

———1926, Proportions of detrital organic calcareous constituents and their chemical alteration in a reef sand from the Bahamas: Carnegie Inst. Washington Pub. 344, p. 37–66. **235**

Goldman, M. I. See also Vaughan, 1918.

Goldring, Winifred, 1922, The Champlain Sea: New York State Mus. Bull. 239–240, p. 153–194. **149**

Goldstein, August, Jr., 1942, Statistical data on the size distribution of sands and gravels from the Mississippi River and its tributaries: Natl. Research Council Comm. on Sedimentation Rept. 1940–1941, p. 15–25. **187**

Goldstein, August, Jr., and Hendricks, T. A., 1953, Siliceous sediments of Ouachita facies in Oklahoma: Geol. Soc. America Bull., v. 64, p. 421–441. **253**

Gould, H. R., 1951, Some quantitative aspects of Lake Mead turbidity currents: Soc. Econ. Paleontologists and Mineralogists Spec. Pub. 2, p. 34–52. **13**

Gould, H. R., and Stewart, R. H., 1955, Continental terrace sediments in the northeastern Gulf of Mexico: Soc. Econ. Paleontologists and Mineralogists Special Pub. 3, p. 2–19. **51, 235**

Gould, H. R. See also Shepard, Emery, and Gould, 1949.

Grabau, A. W., 1903, Paleozoic coral reefs: Geol. Soc. America Bull., v. 14, p. 337–352. **227, 236**

———1904, On the classification of sedimentary rocks: Am. Geologist, v. 33, p. 228–247. **160, 164, 166**

———1905, Physical characters and history of some New York formations: Science, new ser., v. 22, p. 528–535. **117**

———1906, Types of sedimentary overlap: Geol. Soc. America Bull., v. 17, p. 567–636. **142**

———1907, Types of cross-bedding and their stratigraphic significance: Science, new ser., v. 25, p. 296. **188**

Grabau, A. W., 1913, Principles of stratigraphy: New York, A. G. Seiler. **117, 142, 160, 164, 166, 174, 188**

———1917, Stratigraphic relationships of the Tully limestone and the Genesee shale in eastern North America: Geol. Soc. America Bull., v. 28, p. 945–958. **54, 205**

———1920–1921, A textbook of geology (2 vols.): New York, Heath. **287**

———1931, The Permian of Mongolia: Natural History of Central Asia, v. 4, New York, Am. Mus. Nat. History. **84**

Grabau, A. W., and O'Connell, Marjorie, 1917, Were the graptolite shales, as a rule, deep or shallow water deposits?: Geol. Soc. America Bull., v. 28, p. 959–964. **202**

Greenberg, D. M. See Moberg, Greenberg, Revelle, and Allen, 1934.

Gregory, H. E., 1915, Note on the shape of pebbles: Am. Jour. Sci., 4th ser., v. 39, p. 300–304. **10**

Gressly, Amanz, 1838, Observations géologiques sur le Jura Soleurois [Part I, p. 1–112]: Schweizer. Gesell. gesamten Naturwiss. Neue Denkschr. (Soc. helvétique sci. nat. Nouv. Mem.), Band 2 [part 6]. (Other parts follow in Band 4 [part 4] and Band 5 [part 1].) **135, 136**

Grim, R. E., 1951, The depositional environment of red and green shales: Jour. Sed. Petrology, v. 21, p. 226–232. **184**

———1953, Clay mineralogy: New York, McGraw-Hill. **65, 197, 198**

Grim, R. E., Dietz, R. S., and Bradley, W. F., 1949, Clay mineral composition of some sediments from the Pacific Ocean off the California coast and the Gulf of California: Geol. Soc. America Bull., v. 60, p. 1785–1808. **65, 66**

Gripenberg, Stina, 1939, Sediments of the Baltic Sea: Recent Marine Sediments, p. 298–321, Tulsa, Am. Assoc. Petroleum Geologists. **54, 206**

Gripenberg, Stina. See also Buch, Harvey, Wattenberg, and Gripenberg, 1932.

Hack, J. T., 1941, Dunes of the western Navajo country: Geog. Rev., v. 31, p. 240–263. **21, 65**

Hadding, Assar, 1932, The pre-Quaternary sedimentary rocks of Sweden. IV. Glauconite and glauconitic rocks: Lunds Univ. Årssk., n.f., Avd. 2, Bind 28, no. 2. **184**

Hall, James, 1843, Natural History of New York, Part 4: Geology, Part 4, Survey of the Fourth geological district: Albany, N. Y. **302**

———1857, Direction of the currents of deposition and source of the materials of the older Palæozoic rocks [abstracted from newspaper accounts]: Canadian Naturalist and Geologist, v. 2, p. 284–286; Canadian Jour. Industry Sci. Art, new ser., v. 3, p. 88 (1858). **310**

———1859, Natural History of New York, Part 6, Palæontology, v. 3, containing descriptions and figures of the organic remains of the Lower Helderberg group and the Oriskany sandstone: Albany, N. Y. **310**

———1883, Contributions to the geological history of the American continent: Am. Assoc. Adv. Sci. Proc. 31st Mtg., p. 29–69. **310**

Hall, James, and Whitney, J. D., 1858, Report on the geological survey of the State of Iowa: [Albany, N. Y.]. **310**

Halla, F., 1935, Eine Methode zur Bestimmung der Änderung der freien Energie bei Reaktionen des Typus $A(s) + B(s) = AB(s)$ und ihre Anwendung auf das Dolomitproblem: Zeitschr. physikal. Chemie, Band 175, Abt. A, p. 63–82, 396–399. **238**

———1936, Über die freie Energie bei der Dolomitbildung: Mineralog. Petrog. Mitt., Band 48, p. 275–278. **238**

Hamilton, E. L., 1956, Sunken islands of the Mid-Pacific Mountains: Geol. Soc. America Mem. 64. **305**

Hanna, G. D., 1952, Geology of the continental slope off central California: California Acad. Sci. Proc., v. 27, p. 325–358. **56**

Häntzschel, Walter, 1939, Tidal flat deposits (Wattenschlick): Recent Marine Sediments, p. 195–206, Tulsa, Am. Assoc. Petroleum Geologists. **71, 72**

Hanzawa, Shoshiro, 1940, Micropalæontological studies of drill cores from a deep well in Kita-Daito-Zima (North Borodino Island): Jubilee Pub. in commenoration of Prof. H. Yabe's 60th birthday, v. 2, p. 755–802. **241**

Harlton, B. H., 1938, Stratigraphy of the Bendian of the Oklahoma salient of the Ouachita Mountains: Am. Assoc. Petroleum Geologists Bull., v. 22, p. 852–914. **265**

Harrington, H. J., 1946, Las corrientes de barro ("mudflows") de "El Volcán," quebrada de Humahuaca, Jujuy: Soc. Geol. Argentina Rev., tomo 1, no. 2, p. 149–165. **171, 172**

Harris, G. D. See Dall and Harris, 1892.

Harvey, H. W. See Buch, Harvey, Wattenberg, and Gripenberg, 1932.

Hass, W. H., 1956, Age and correlation of the Chattanooga shale and the Maury formation: U. S. Geol. Survey Prof. Paper 286. **127, 207**

Hatch, F. H., and Rastall, R. H., revised by Black, Maurice, 1938, The petrology of the sedimentary rocks (3rd ed.): London, George Allen and Unwin. **233, 236**

Hatcher, J. B., 1902, Origin of the Oligocene and Miocene deposits of the Great Plains: Am. Philos. Soc. Proc., v. 41, p. 113–131. **37**

Haug, Émile, 1900, Les géosynclinaux et les aires continentales: Soc. Géol. France Bull., 3me ser., v. 28, p. 617–711. **311**

Haughton, S. H. See du Toit and Haughton, 1954.

Hedberg, H. D., 1926, The effect of gravitational compaction on the structure of sedimentary rocks: Am. Assoc. Petroleum Geologists Bull., v. 10, p. 1035–1072. **105**

Hedberg, H. D., 1936, Gravitational compaction of clays and shales: Am. Jour. Sci., 5th ser., v. 31, p. 241–287. **105**

———1937, Stratigraphy of the Rio Querecual section of northeastern Venezuela: Geol. Soc. America Bull., v. 48, p. 1971–2024. **292**

———1941, ' Stratigraphic nomenclature (discussion): Am. Assoc. Petroleum Geologists Bull., v. 25, p. 2202–2206. **292**

———1948, Time-stratigraphic classification of sedimentary rocks: Geol. Soc. America Bull., v. 59, p. 447–462. **292**

———1951, Nature of time-stratigraphic units and geologic-time units: Am. Assoc. Petroleum Geologists Bull., v. 35, p. 1077–1081. **292, 293**

———1954, Procedure and terminology in stratigraphic classification: 19th Internat. Geol. Cong. Comptes rendus, fasc. 13, p. 205–233. **292, 300**

Hedberg, H. D. See also Schenck, Hedberg, and Kleinpell, 1936.

Hedgpeth, J. W., and Ladd, H. S., Editors, 1957, Treatise on marine ecology and paleoecology: Geol. Soc. America Mem. 67. **145, 202**

Heezen, B. C., 1955, Turbidity currents from the Magdalena River, Colombia: Geol. Soc. America Bull., v. 66, p. 1572. **16**

Heezen, B. C., Ericson, D. B., and Ewing, Maurice, 1954, Further evidence for a turbidity current following the 1929 Grand Banks earthquake: Deep-Sea Research, v. 1, p. 193–202. **14, 16**

Heezen, B. C., and Ewing, Maurice, 1952, Turbidity currents and submarine slumps, and the 1929 Grand Banks earthquake: Am. Jour. Sci., v. 250, p. 849–873. **15, 59**

Heezen, B. C., Ewing, Maurice, and Ericson, D. B., 1955, Reconnaissance survey of the abyssal plain south of Newfoundland: Deep-Sea Research, v. 2, p. 122–133. **16**

Heezen, B. C. See also Ericson, Ewing, and Heezen, 1951, 1952; Ericson, Ewing, Heezen, and Wollin, 1955.

Henbest, L. G., 1931, The use of selective stains in paleontology: Jour. Paleontology, v. 5, p. 355–364. **222**

Henbest, L. G. See also Dunbar and Henbest, 1942; Weller, Henbest, and Dunbar, 1942.

Hendricks, S. B., and Ross, C. S., 1941, Chemical composition and genesis of glauconite and celadonite: Am. Mineralogist, v. 26, p. 683–708. **184**

Hendricks, T. A., Gardner, L. S., Knechtel, M. M., and Averitt, Paul, 1947, Geology of the western part of the Ouachita Mountains of Oklahoma: U. S. Geol. Survey Oil and Gas Inv. Prelim. Map no. 66. **265**

Hendricks, T. A. See also Goldstein and Hendricks, 1953; Sears, Hunt, and Hendricks, 1941.

Henson, F. R. S., 1950, Cretaceous and Tertiary reef formations and associated sediments in Middle East: Am. Assoc. Petroleum Geologists Bull., v. 34, p. 215–238. **89, 145**

Hesse, Richard, Allee, W. C., and Schmidt, K. P., 1951, Ecological animal geography (2nd Amer. ed.): New York, Wiley. **145**

Hewett, D. F., 1917, The origin of bentonite and the geologic range of related materials in Bighorn Basin, Wyoming: Washington Acad. Sci. Jour., v. 7, p. 196–198. **167**

———1928, Dolomitization and ore deposition: Econ. Geology, v. 23, p. 821–863. **240**

———1931, Geology and ore deposits of the Goodsprings quadrangle, Nevada: U. S. Geol. Survey Prof. Paper 162. **240**

Hickox, J. E. See Newell, Rigby, Fischer, Whiteman, Hickox, and Bradley, 1953.

Hilmy, M. E., 1951, Beach sands of the Mediterranean coast of Egypt: Jour. Sed. Petrology, v. 21, p. 109–120. **187**

Hind, Wheelton, 1902, On the characters of the Carboniferous rocks of the Pennine system: Yorkshire Geol. Soc. Proc., new ser., v. 14, p. 442–464 [not seen]. **109**

Hjulström, Filip, 1935, Studies of the morphological activity of rivers as illustrated by the River Fyris: Upsala Univ., Geol. Inst. Bull., v. 25, p. 221–527. **6, 7, 8**

———1939, Transportation of detritus by moving water: Recent Marine Sediments, p. 5–31, Tulsa, Am. Assoc. Petroleum Geologists. **7**

Hoffmeister, J. E. See Tracey, Ladd, and Hoffmeister, 1948.

Holmes, Arthur, 1921, Petrographic methods and calculations: London, Murby. **222**

Holtedahl, Olaf, 1921, On the occurrence of structures like Walcott's Algonkian algae in the Permian of England: Am. Jour. Sci., 5th ser., v. 1, p. 195–206. **229**

Hook, J. W. See Oder and Hook, 1950.

Hopkins, C. G., 1899, A plea for a scientific basis for the division of soil particles in mechanical analysis: U. S. Dept. Agriculture Div. Chemistry Bull. 56, p. 64–66. **164**

Hough, J. L., 1956, Sediment distribution in the southern oceans around Antarctica: Jour. Sed. Petrology, v. 26, p. 301–306. **53**

Howell, B. F., and others, 1944, Correlation of the Cambrian formations of North America: Geol. Soc. America Bull., v. 55, p. 993–1003. **287**

Hudson, R. G. S., 1924, On the rhythmic succession of the Yoredale series in Wensleydale: Yorkshire Geol. Soc. Proc., new ser., v. 20, p. 125–135. **109**

Hügi, Th., 1945, Gesteinsbildend wichtige Karbonate und deren Nachweis mittels Färbmethoden: Schweizer. Mineralog. Petrog. Mitt., Band 25, p. 114–140. **222**

Hummel, K., 1922, Die Entstehung eisenreicher Gesteine durch Halmyrolyse (=submarine Gesteinszersetzung): Geol. Rundschau, Band 13, p. 40–81, 97–136. **183**

Hunt, C. B. See Sears, Hunt, and Hendricks, 1941.

Hurd, C. B., 1938, Theories for the mechanism of the setting of silicic acid gels: Chem. Reviews, v. 22, p. 403–422. **245, 249**

Hutton, James, 1795, Theory of the Earth, with proofs and illustrations: v. 1 and 2, Edinburgh, 1795; v. 3, London, 1899.   **116**

Illing, L. V., 1954, Bahaman calcareous sands: Am. Assoc. Petroleum Geologists Bull., v. 38, p. 1–95.
95, 231, 232, 234

Ingerson, Earl. See Ladd, Ingerson, Townsend, Russell, and Stephenson, 1953.

Ingram, R. L., 1953, Fissility of mudrocks: Geol. Soc. America Bull., v. 64, p. 869–878.   **98, 166, 227**

———1954, Terminology for the thickness of stratification and parting units in sedimentary rocks: Geol. Soc. America Bull., v. 65, p. 937–938.   **97, 98, 105**

Ireland, H. A., and others, 1947, Terminology for insoluble residues: Am. Assoc. Petroleum Geologists Bull., v. 31, p. 1479–1490.   **223**

Jahns, R. H., and Engel, A. E. J., 1950, Chaotic breccias in southern California: tectonic or sedimentary?: Geol. Soc. America Bull., v. 61, p. 1474.   **177**

Johnson, D. W., 1939, The origin of submarine canyons: New York, Columbia Univ. Press.   **13**

Johnson, M. W. See Sverdrup, Johnson, and Fleming, 1942.

Johnson, W. D., 1901, The High Plains and their utilization: U. S. Geol. Survey 21st Ann. Rept., pt. 4, p. 601–741.   **37, 174**

Johnston, John, Merwin, H. E., and Williamson, E. D., 1916, The several forms of calcium carbonate: Am. Jour. Sci., 4th ser., v. 41, p. 473–512.   **222**

Joly, John, 1924, Radioactivity and the surface history of the Earth: Oxford, Clarendon.   **304**

———1925, The surface-history of the Earth: Oxford, Clarendon.   **304**

Jones, O. T., 1937, On the sliding or slumping of submarine sediments in Denbighshire, North Wales, during the Ludlow period: Geol. Soc. London Quart. Jour., v. 93, p. 241–283D.   **105**

———1938, On the evolution of a geosyncline: Geol. Soc. London Quart. Jour., v. 94, Proc., p. lx–cx.   **311**

———1940, The geology of the Colwyn Bay district: a study of submarine slumping during the Salopian period: Geol. Soc. London Quart. Jour., v. 95, p. 335–382.   **105**

Kalkowsky, Ernst, 1908, Oolith und Stromatolith im norddeutschen Buntsandstein: Deutsche geol. Gesell. Zeitschr., Band 60, p. 68–125.   **229, 233, 234**

Kay, Marshall, 1937, Stratigraphy of the Trenton group: Geol. Soc. America Bull., v. 48, p. 233–302.   **312**

———1944, Geosynclines in continental development: Science, new ser., v. 99, p. 461–462.   **314**

———1947, Geosynclinal nomenclature and the craton: Am. Assoc. Petroleum Geologists Bull., v. 31, p. 1289–1293.   **314**

———1951, North American geosynclines: Geol. Soc. America Mem. 48.   **312, 313, 314**

Kaye, C. A., and Power, W. R., Jr., 1954, A flow cast of very recent date from northeastern Washington: Am. Jour. Sci., v. 252, p. 309–310.   **194**

Keller, W. D., 1941, Petrography and origin of the Rex chert: Geol. Soc. America Bull., v. 52, p. 1279–1297.   **254**

———1945, Size distribution of sand in some dunes, beaches, and sandstones: Am. Assoc. Petroleum Geologists Bull., v. 29, p. 215–221.   **187**

———1953, Clay minerals in the type section of the Morrison formation: Jour. Sed. Petrology, v. 23, p. 93–105.   **66**

Kendall, P. F., 1929, Upper Carboniferous (B)—The Coal Measures: Handbook of the geology of Great Britain, p. 259–284, London, Murby.   **215**

Keulegan, G. H., and Krumbein, W. C., 1949, Stable configuration of bottom slope in a shallow sea and its bearing on geological processes: Am. Geophys. Union Trans., v. 30, p. 855–861.   **84**

Kindle, E. M., and Bucher, W. H., 1926, Ripple mark and its interpretation: Treatise on Sedimentation [1st ed.], p. 451–483 [2nd ed., p. 632–668], Baltimore, Williams and Wilkins.   **189, 191**

King, P. B., 1942, Permian of West Texas and southeastern New Mexico: Am. Assoc. Petroleum Geologists Bull., v. 26, p. 535–763.   **93, 204**

———1948, Geology of the southern Guadalupe Mountains, Texas: U. S. Geol. Survey Prof. Paper 215.   **62, 93, 233**

King, P. B., Ferguson, H. W., Craig, L. C., and Rodgers, John, 1944, Geology and manganese deposits of northeastern Tennessee: Tennessee Div. Geology Bull. 52.   **265, 276**

Kirk, L. G., 1952, Trails and rocks observed on a playa in Death Valley National Monument, California: Jour. Sed. Petrology, v. 22, p. 173–181.   **173**

Kirwan, Richard, 1794, Elements of mineralogy (2nd ed.), v. 1: London.   **219**

Kleinpell, R. M., 1938, Miocene stratigraphy of California: Tulsa, Am. Assoc. Petroleum Geologists.   **292, 299**

Kleinpell, R. M. See also Schenck, Hedberg, and Kleinpell, 1936; Schenck and Kleinpell, 1936.

Knechtel, M. M. See Hendricks, Gardner, Knechtel, and Averitt, 1947.

Knight, S. H., 1929, The Fountain and the Casper formations of the Laramie Basin: Wyoming Univ. Pubs. Sci. Geology, v. 1.   **188**

———1930, Festoon cross-lamination: Geol. Soc. America Bull., v. 41, p. 86.   **188**

Knight, W. C., 1897, "Mineral soap": Eng. Min. Jour., v. 63, p. 600–601.   **167**

———1898, Bentonite: Eng. Min. Jour., v. 66, p. 491.   **167**

Knopf, Adolph, 1949a, The geologic records of time: Time and its mysteries, ser. 3, p. 31–59, New York, New York Univ. Press.   **277**

————1949b, Time in Earth history: Genetics, paleontology, and evolution, p. 1–9, Princeton, Princeton Univ. Press.   **277**

Knopf, Adolph. See also Longwell, Knopf, and Flint, 1939.

Kolb, C. R. See Fisk, McFarlan, Kolb, and Wilbert, 1954.

Krauskopf, K. B., 1956, Dissolution and precipitation of silica at low temperatures: Geochim. Cosmochim. Acta, v. 10, p. 1–26.   **245**

Kröll, V. S., 1955, The distribution of radium in deep-sea cores: Swedish Deep-Sea Exped. 1947–1948 Repts., v. 10, fasc. 1.   **60**

Krumbein, W. C., 1934, Size frequency distributions of sediments: Jour. Sed. Petrology, v. 4, p. 65–77.   **163**

————1935, Thin-section mechanical analysis of indurated sediments: Jour. Geology, v. 43, p. 482–496.   **225**

————1937, Sediments and exponential curves: Jour. Geology, v. 45, p. 577–601.   **29**

————1939, Tidal lagoon sediments on the Mississippi delta: Recent Marine Sediments, p. 178–194, Tulsa, Am. Assoc. Petroleum Geologists.   **73**

————1941, Measurement and geological significance of shape and roundness of sedimentary particles: Jour. Sed. Petrology, v. 11, p. 64–72.   **185**

————1942a, Criteria for subsurface recognition of unconformities: Am. Assoc. Petroleum Geologists Bull., v. 26, p. 36–62.   **126**

————1942b, Settling-velocity and flume-behavior of non-spherical particles: Am. Geophys. Union Trans. 1942, p. 621–632.   **187**

————1951, Some relations among sedimentation, stratigraphy, and seismic exploration: Am. Assoc. Petroleum Geologists Bull., v. 35, p. 1505–1522.   **271**

Krumbein, W. C., and Pettijohn, F. J., 1938, Manual of sedimentary petrography: New York, Appleton-Century-Crofts.   **162, 197, 225**

Krumbein, W. C., and Sloss, L. L., 1951, Stratigraphy and sedimentation: San Francisco, Freeman.
137, 166, 186, 270, 271

Krumbein, W. C. See also Keulegan and Krumbein, 1949.

Krynine, P. D., 1935a, Arkose deposits in the humid tropics. A study of sedimentation in southern Mexico: Am. Jour. Sci., 5th ser., v. 29, p. 353–363.   **3, 172, 196**

————1935b, Formation and preservation of desiccation features in a humid climate: Am. Jour. Sci., 5th ser., v. 30, p. 96–97.   **200, 213**

————1948, The megascopic study and field classification of sedimentary rocks: Jour. Geology, v. 56, p. 130–165.   **165, 166, 314**

————1950, Petrology, stratigraphy, and origin of the Triassic sedimentary rocks of Connecticut: Connecticut Geol. and Nat. History Survey Bull. 73.
3, 31, 104, 213, 234, 315

Kuenen, P. H., 1937, Experiments in connection with Daly's hypothesis on the formation of submarine canyons: Leidsche Geol. Meded., Deel 8, p. 327–351.
13, 59

————1939a, Sediments of the East Indian Archipelago: Recent Marine Sediments, p. 348–355, Tulsa, Am. Assoc. Petroleum Geologists.   **62**

————1939b, The cause of coarse deposits at the outer edge of the shelf: Geologie en Mijnbouw, Jaarg. 2, p. 36–39.   **48**

————1942, Collecting of the samples and some general aspects: The Snellius-expedition, v. 5, Geological results, pt. 3, Bottom samples, sect. 1, p. 1–46.   **62**

————1950a, Turbidity currents of high density: 18th Internat. Geol. Cong. Rept., pt. 8, p. 44–52.   **13**

————1950b, Marine geology: New York, Wiley.
12, 13, 46, 61, 62

————1952, Estimated size of the Grand Banks turbidity current: Am. Jour. Sci., v. 250, p. 874–884.   **16**

————1956, Experimental abrasion of pebbles: 2. Rolling by currents: Jour. Geology, v. 64, p. 336–368.   **9**

Kuenen, P. H., and Menard, H. W., 1952, Turbidity currents, graded and non-graded deposits: Jour. Sed. Petrology, v. 22, p. 83–96.   **14**

Kuenen, P. H., and Migliorini, C. I., 1950, Turbidity currents as a cause of graded bedding: Jour. Geology, v. 58, p. 91–127.   **14, 59, 108, 109, 192**

Kuenen, P. H. See also Natland and Kuenen, 1951.

Kullenberg, Börje, 1947, The piston core sampler: Svenska Hydrog.-Biol. Skr., 3rd ser., Band 1, Häfte 2, p. 1–46.   **46**

————1955, Deep-sea coring: Swedish Deep-Sea Exped. 1947–1948 Repts., v. 4, Bottom investigations, fasc. 1, p. 35–96.   **46**

Kutscher, Fritz, 1931, Zur Entstehung des Hunsrück-schiefers am Mittelrhein und auf dem Hunsrück: Nassauischer Ver. für Naturkunde Jahrbuch, Band 81, p. 177–232.   **205**

Ladd, H. S., 1950, Recent reefs: Am. Assoc. Petroleum Geologists Bull., v. 34, p. 203–214.   **145**

Ladd, H. S., Ingerson, Earl, Townsend, R. C., Russell, Martin, and Stephenson, H. K., 1953: Drilling on Eniwetok Atoll, Marshall Islands: Am. Assoc. Petroleum Geologists Bull., v. 37, p. 2257–2280.
90, 305

Ladd, H. S., and Tracey, J. I., Jr., 1949, The problem of coral reefs: Sci. Monthly, v. 69, p. 297–305.   **89, 92**

Ladd, H. S., Tracey, J. I., Jr., and Lill, G. G., 1948, Drilling on Bikini Atoll, Marshall Islands: Science, new ser., v. 107, p. 51–55.   **90**

Ladd, H. S., Tracey, J. I., Jr., Wells, J. W., and Emery, K. O., 1950, Organic growth and sedimentation on an atoll: Jour. Geology, v. 58, p. 410–425.   **90, 91, 150**

Ladd, H. S. See also Emery, Tracey, and Ladd, 1954; Hedgpeth and Ladd, 1957; Tracey, Ladd, and Hoffmeister, 1948.

Landes, K. K., 1945, Mackinac breccia: Michigan Geol. and Biol. Survey Pub. 44 (Geol. ser. no. 37), p. 123–153.   **169**

———1946, Porosity through dolomitization: Am. Assoc. Petroleum Geologists Bull., v. 30, p. 305–318.   **240**

Lane, E. W., and others, 1947, Report of the subcommittee on sediment terminology: Am. Geophys. Union Trans., v. 28, p. 936–938.   **161**

Lawson, A. C., 1912, Fanglomerate, a detrital rock at Battle Mountain, Nevada: Geol. Soc. America Bull., v. 23, p. 72.   **174**

———1913, The petrographic designation of alluvial fan formations: California Univ., Dept. Geol. Sci., Bull., v. 7, p. 325–334.   **174**

Lehmann, J. G., 1756, Versuch einer Geschichte von Flötz-Gebürgen: Berlin.   **289**

Leitmeier, Hans, 1916, Zur Kenntnis der Carbonate. II: Neues Jahrb., Beilage Band 40, p. 655–700. **237, 238**

LeRoy, L. W., and Crain, H. M., Editors, 1949, Subsurface geologic methods (a symposium): Golden, Colo., Colorado School of Mines (also in Colorado School of Mines Quart., v. 44, no. 3).   **274**

Lesley, J. P., 1879, Notes on a series of analyses of the dolomitic limestone rocks of Cumberland County, Pa.: Pennsylvania 2nd Geol. Survey Rept. MM, p. 311–362.   **223, 224**

Lill, G. G. See Ladd, Tracey, and Lill, 1948.

Linck, G., 1903, Die Bildung von Oolithe und Rogensteine: Neues Jahrb., Beilage Band 16, p. 495–513.
234

Link, T. A., 1950, Theory of transgressive and regressive reef (bioherm) development and origin of oil: Am. Assoc. Petroleum Geologists Bull., v. 34, p. 263–294.
145

Longwell, C. R., 1922, Notes on the structure of the Triassic rocks in southern Connecticut: Am. Jour. Sci., 5th ser., v. 4, p. 223–236.   **31**

———1928, Geology of the Muddy Mountains, Nevada: U. S. Geol. Survey Bull. 798.   **40**

———1936, Geology of the Boulder Reservoir floor, Arizona–Nevada: Geol. Soc. America Bull., v. 47, p. 1393–1476.   **31, 234**

———1950, Tectonic theory viewed from the Basin Ranges: Geol. Soc. America Bull., v. 61, p. 413–433.
312

———1951, Megabreccia developed downslope from large faults: Am. Jour. Sci., v. 249, p. 343–355.
178, 179

Longwell, C. R., Knopf, Adolph, and Flint, R. F., 1939, Physical geology: Wiley, New York.   **166**

Longwell, C. R., Chairman, 1949, Sedimentary facies in geologic history: Geol. Soc. America Mem. 39.
136, 266

Lovering, T. S., 1923, The leaching of iron protores: solution and precipitation of silica in cold water: Econ. Geology, v. 18, p. 523–540.   **245**

Lowenstam, H. A., 1954, Factors affecting the aragonite: calcite ratios in carbonate-secreting marine organisms: Jour. Geology, v. 62, p. 284–322.   **227, 228**

Lowman, S. W., 1949, Sedimentary facies in Gulf Coast: Am. Assoc. Petroleum Geologists Bull., v. 33, p. 1939–1997.   **51**

Lüders, K., 1939, Sediments of the North Sea: Recent Marine Sediments, p. 322–342, Tulsa, Am. Assoc. Petroleum Geologists.   **53**

Lyell, Charles, 1830–1833, Principles of geology: London, Murray.   **282**

———1838, Elements of geology: London, Murray [Philadelphia and Pittsburgh, Kay, 1839].   **116**

———1845, Travels in North America (2 vols.): London, New York.   **194**

MacCarthy, G. R., 1926, Colors produced by iron in minerals and the sediments: Am. Jour. Sci., 5th ser., v. 12, p. 17–36.   **212**

MacNeil, F. S., 1954, Organic reefs and banks and associated detrital sediments: Am. Jour. Sci., v. 252, p. 385–401.   **88**

Mansfield, G. R., 1927, Geography, geology, and mineral resources of part of southeastern Idaho: U. S. Geol. Survey Prof. Paper 152.   **254**

Marbut, C. F., 1935, Soils of the United States: U. S. Dept. Agriculture, Atlas of American Agriculture, pt. III.   **210**

Marr, J. E., 1925, Conditions of deposition of the Stockdale shales of the Lake District: Geol. Soc. London Quart. Jour., v. 81, p. 113–133.   **197, 202**

Martin-Kaye, P. See Bennett and Martin-Kaye, 1951.

Matson, G. C. See Vaughan, 1910.

Matthews, A. A. L., 1930, Origin and growth of the Great Salt Lake oölites: Jour. Geology, v. 38, p. 633–642.   **234**

Mattox, R. B., 1955, Eolian shape-sorting: Jour. Sed. Petrology, v. 25, p. 111–114.   **187**

McAllister, J. F., and Agnew, A. F., 1948, Playa scrapers and furrows on the Racetrack Playa, Inyo County, California: Geol. Soc. America Bull., v. 59, p. 1377.
173

McFarlan, Edward, Jr. See Fisk, McFarlan, Kolb, and Wilbert, 1954.

McGee, W J, 1897, Sheetflood erosion: Geol. Soc. America Bull., v. 8, p. 87–112.   **38**

McKee, E. D., 1938a, Original structures in Colorado River flood deposits of Grand Canyon: Jour. Sed. Petrology, v. 8, p. 77–83.   **65, 105, 188**

———1938b, The environment and history of the Toroweap and Kaibab formations of northern Arizona and southern Utah: Carnegie Inst. Washington Pub. 492.
262

———1939, Some types of bedding in the Colorado River delta: Jour. Geology, v. 47, p. 64–81.
65, 80, 105, 188

———1943, Some stratigraphic principles illustrated by Paleozoic deposits of northern Arizona: Am. Jour. Sci., v. 241, p. 101–108.   **126**

McKee, E. D., 1945a, Cambrian history of the Grand Canyon region. Part 1. Stratigraphy and ecology of the Grand Canyon Cambrian: Carnegie Inst. Washington Pub. 563, p. 3–168. **126, 140, 141, 143, 145, 155**

———1945b, Small-scale structures in the Coconino sandstone of northern Arizona: Jour. Geology, v. 53, p. 313–325. **65**

———1949, Facies changes in the Colorado Plateau: Geol. Soc. America Mem. 39, p. 35–48. **262**

———1953, Report on studies of stratification in modern sediments and in laboratory experiments: Tucson, Arizona Geological Society. **30, 65, 69, 73, 188**

McKee, E. D., and Weir, G. W., 1953, Terminology for stratification and cross-stratification in sedimentary rocks: Geol. Soc. America Bull., v. 64, p. 381–389. **97, 98, 105, 188**

McQueen, H. S., 1931, Insoluble residues as a guide in stratigraphic studies: Missouri Bur. Geology and Mines 56th Bienn. Rept. [1929–1930], p. 102–131. **223**

Melton, F. A., 1940, A tentative classification of sand dunes—its application to dune history in the southern High Plains: Jour. Geology, v. 48, p. 113–145. **21**

Menard, H. W. See Dietz and Menard, 1951; Kuenen and Menard, 1952.

Merritt, C. A. See Decker and Merritt, 1928.

Merwin, H. E. See Gibson, Wyckoff, and Merwin, 1925; Johnston, Merwin, and Williamson, 1916; Posnjak and Merwin, 1919.

Midgley, H. G., 1951, Chalcedony and flint: Geol. Mag., v. 88, p. 179–184. **246**

Migliorini, C. I. See Kuenen and Migliorini, 1950.

Miller, D. N., Jr., and Folk, R. L., 1955, Occurrence of detrital magnetite and ilmenite in red sediments: new approach to significance of redbeds: Am. Assoc. Petroleum Geologists Bull., v. 39, p. 338–345. **211**

Miller, H. W. See Oder and Miller, 1945.

Miller, W. G. See Daly, Miller, and Rice, 1912.

Millot, Georges, 1949, Relations entre la constitution et la genèse des roches sédimentaires argileuses: Géologie Appl. et Prosp. Min., tome 2, no. 2–4, Nancy. **65, 66**

Miser, H. D., 1934, Carboniferous rocks of Ouachita Mountains: Am. Assoc. Petroleum Geologists Bull., v. 18, p. 971–1009. **177**

Moberg, E. G., Greenberg, D. M., Revelle, Roger, and Allen, E. C., 1934, The buffer mechanism of sea water: Scripps Inst. Oceanography Bull., Tech. ser., v. 3, p. 231–278. **230, 231**

Moore, D. G. See Shepard and Moore, 1954, 1955a, b.

Moore, E. S., 1914, Mud cracks open under water: Am. Jour. Sci., 4th ser., v. 38, p. 101–102. **199**

Moore, R. C., 1934, The origin and age of the boulder-bearing Johns Valley shale in the Ouachita Mountains of Arkansas and Oklahoma: Am. Jour. Sci., 5th ser., v. 27, p. 432–453. **177**

———1936, Stratigraphic classification of the Pennsylvanian rocks of Kansas: Kansas Geol. Survey Bull. 22. **110, 111, 145**

———1948, Stratigraphical paleontology: Geol. Soc. America Bull., v. 59, p. 301–325. **137, 145**

———1949, Meaning of facies: Geol. Soc. America Mem. 39, p. 1–34. **137**

Moore, R. C., and others, 1944, Correlation of Pennsylvanian formations of North America: Geol. Soc. America Bull., v. 55, p. 657–706. **300**

Muller, S. W. See Schenck and Muller, 1941.

Murchison, R. I., 1839, The Silurian System: London, Murray. **166**

Murray, A. N., 1930, Limestone oil reservoirs of the northeastern United States and of Ontario, Canada: Econ. Geology, v. 25, p. 452–469. **240**

Murray, John, and Renard, A. F., 1891, Deep-sea deposits: Challenger Exped. Rept. **56, 184**

Myers, D. A., Stafford, P. T., and Burnside, R. J., 1956, Geology of the late Paleozoic Horseshoe atoll in West Texas: Univ. Texas Pub. 5607. **92**

Natland, M. L., 1933, The temperature- and depth-distribution of some Recent and fossil Foraminifera in the southern California region: Scripps Inst. Oceanography Bull., Tech. ser., v. 3, p. 225–230. **59, 148, 154**

Natland, M. L., and Kuenen, P. H., 1951, Sedimentary history of the Ventura basin, California, and the action of turbidity currents: Soc. Econ. Paleontologists and Mineralogists Spec. Pub. 2, p. 76–107. **59, 194**

Neeb, G. A., 1943, The composition and distribution of the samples: The Snellius-expedition, v. 5, Geological results, pt. 3, Bottom samples, sect. 2, p. 47–268. **4, 62**

Newell, N. D., 1955a, Depositional fabric in Permian reef limestones: Jour. Geology, v. 63, p. 301–309. **89, 229**

———1955b, Bahamian platforms: Geol. Soc. America Spec. Paper 62, p. 303–315. **95, 232**

Newell, N. D., and Boyd, D. W., 1955, Extraordinarily coarse eolian sand of the Ica Desert, Peru: Jour. Sed. Petrology, v. 25, p. 226–228. **17**

Newell, N. D., Rigby, J. K., Fischer, A. G., Whiteman, A. J., Hickox, J. E., and Bradley, J. S., 1953, The Permian reef complex of the Guadalupe Mountains region, Texas and New Mexico: A study in paleoecology: San Francisco, Freeman. **93, 170, 233, 242, 251**

Newell, N. D., Rigby, J. K., Whiteman, A. J., and Bradley, J. S., 1951, Shoal-water geology and environments, eastern Andros Island, Bahamas: Am. Mus. Nat. History Bull., v. 97, p. 1–29. **95**

Newman, M. H., 1933, The Mascot–Jefferson City zinc district of Tennessee: 16th Internat. Geol. Cong. Guidebook 2, p. 152–161. **240**

Niggli, Paul, 1935, Die Charakterisierung der klastischen Sedimente nach der Kornzusammensetzung: Schweizer. Mineralog. Petrog. Mitt., Band 15, p. 31–38. **163**

Noble, L. F., 1941, Structural features of the Virgin Spring area, Death Valley, California: Geol. Soc. America Bull., v. 52, p. 941–999. **177**

Noble, L. F., and Wright, L. A., 1954, Geology of the central and southern Death Valley region, California: California Div. Mines, Bull. 170, Chap. 2, p. 143–160 [1955].   178

Nobles, L. H. See Sharp and Nobles, 1953.

Northrop, John, 1951, Ocean-bottom photographs of the neritic and bathyal environment south of Cape Cod, Massachusetts: Geol. Soc. America Bull., v. 62, p. 1381–1383.   48, 50, 187

————1954, Bathymetry of the Puerto Rico trench: Am. Geophys. Union Trans., v. 35, p. 221–225.   59

Norton, W. H., 1917, A classification of breccias: Jour. Geology, v. 25, p. 160–194.   174, 180

Obruchev, V. A., 1945, Loess types and their origin: Am. Jour. Sci., v. 243, p. 256–262.   23

O'Connell, Marjorie. See Grabau and O'Connell, 1917.

Oder, C. R. L., and Hook, J. W., 1950, Zinc deposits of the Southeastern States: Symposium Min. Resources of Southeastern United States, 1949 Proc., p. 72–87, Knoxville, Tenn., Univ. Tennessee Press.   240

Oder, C. R. L., and Miller, H. W., 1945, Stratigraphy of the Mascot–Jefferson City zinc district: Am. Inst. Min. Metall. Engineers Tech. Pub. 1818; ibid. Trans., v. 178, p. 223–231, 1948.   240, 248

Officer, C. B., Jr. See Ewing, Sutton, and Officer, 1954.

Olson, J. S. See Potter and Olson, 1954.

Oppel, Albert, 1856–1858, Die Juraformation Englands, Frankreichs und des südwestlichen Deutschlands: Stuttgart.   299

Oriel, S. S., 1949, Definitions of arkose: Am. Jour. Sci., v. 247, p. 824–829.   165

Packham, G. H., 1954, Sedimentary structures as an important factor in the classification of sandstones: Am. Jour. Sci., v. 252, p. 466–476.   166

Payne, T. G., 1942, Stratigraphical analysis and environmental reconstruction: Am. Assoc. Petroleum Geologists Bull., v. 26, p. 1697–1770.   225, 236

Pelto, C. R., 1956, A study of chalcedony: Am. Jour. Sci., v. 254, p. 32–50.   246

Pepper, J. F., de Witt, Wallace, Jr., and Demarest, D. F., 1954, Geology of the Bedford shale and Berea sandstone in the Appalachian basin: U. S. Geol. Survey Prof. Paper 259 [1955].
                36, 37, 64, 70, 87, 88, 187, 192, 200

Peterson, J. Q. See Troxell and Peterson, 1937.

Pettijohn, F. J., 1943, Archean sedimentation: Geol. Soc. America Bull., v. 54, p. 925–972.   196, 312

————1948, A preface to the classification of the sedimentary rocks: Jour. Geology, v. 56, p. 112–117.
                236

————1954, Classification of sandstones: Jour. Geology, v. 62, p. 360–365.   166

————1957, Sedimentary rocks (2nd ed.): New York, Harper.   163, 166, 227, 236

Pettijohn, F. J., and Ridge, J. D., 1932, A textural variation series of beach sands from Cedar Point, Ohio: Jour. Sed. Petrology, v. 2, p. 76–88.   162

Pettijohn, F. J. See also Krumbein and Pettijohn, 1938.

Phillips, John, 1841, Figures and descriptions of the Palæozoic fossils of Cornwall, Devon, and west Somerset: London, Longman, Brown, Green, and Longmans.   295

Pia, Julius, 1928, Die Anpassungsformen der Kalkalgen: Paleobiologica, Band 1, p. 211–224, Vienna.
                229, 230

————1932, Die Theorien über die Löslichkeit des kohlensauren Kalkes als Grundlage für das Verständnis der Bildung der Kalksteine. Ein Kapitel aus der physikalischen Chemie, für Geologen und Hydrologen dargestellt: Geol. Gesell. Wien Mitt., Jahrg. 25, p. 1–93.   230

————1933, Die rezenten Kalksteine: Mineralog. Petrog. Mitt., Ergänzungsband.   88, 233

Piggot, C. S., 1937, Core samples of the ocean bottom: Smithsonian Inst. Ann. Rept. 1936, p. 207–216.   46

Pike, W. S., Jr., 1947, Intertonguing marine and nonmarine Upper Cretaceous deposits of New Mexico, Arizona, and southwestern Colorado: Geol. Soc. America Mem. 24.   86

Pirsson, L. V., and Schuchert, Charles, 1915, Text-book of geology: New York, Wiley.   117

Playfair, John, 1802, Illustrations of the Huttonian theory of the earth: Edinburgh.   116

Posnjak, Eugen, and Merwin, H. E., 1919, The hydrated ferric oxides: Am. Jour. Sci., 4th ser., v. 47, p. 311–348.   210

Posnjak, Eugen. See also Tunell and Posnjak, 1931.

Potter, P. E., and Olson, J. S., 1954, Variance components of cross-bedding direction in some basal Pennsylvanian sandstones of the Eastern Interior Basin: geological application: Jour. Geology, v. 62, p. 50–73.
                189

Powell, J. W., 1890, Conference on map publication: U. S. Geol. Survey 10th Ann. Rept., pt. 1, p. 56–79.
                291

Pratje, Otto, 1924, Korallenbänke in teifem und kühlem Wasser: Centralbl. Mineralogie, 1924, p. 410–415.
                148

Price, P. H., 1932, Erratic boulders in Sewell coal of West Virginia: Jour. Geology, v. 40, p. 62–73.   175

Raasch, G. O. See Twenhofel, Raasch, and Thwaites, 1935.

Radczewski, O. E., 1939, Eolian deposits in marine sediments: Recent Marine Sediments, p. 496–502, Tulsa, Am. Assoc. Petroleum Geologists.   23

Raggatt, H. G., 1950, Stratigraphic nomenclature: Australian Jour. Sci., v. 12, p. 170–173.   259

Raggatt, H. G. See also Glaessner, Raggatt, Teichert, and Thomas, 1948.

Rastall, R. H., 1944, Palaeozoic, Mesozoic and Kainozoic: a geological disaster: Geol. Mag., v. 81, p. 159–165. **295**

Rastall, R. H. See also Hatch, Rastall, and Black, 1938.

Raymond, P. E., 1927, The significance of red color in sediments: Am. Jour. Sci., 5th ser., v. 13, p. 234–251. **210, 213**

————1937, Upper Cambrian and Lower Ordovician Trilobita and Ostracoda from Vermont: Geol. Soc. America Bull., v. 48, p. 1079–1145. **180**

————1942, The pigment in black and red sediments: Am. Jour. Sci., v. 240, p. 658–669. **210, 213**

Reeside, J. B., Jr. See Baker, Dane, and Reeside, 1936, 1947; Baker and Reeside, 1929; Gilluly and Reeside, 1928.

Reeves, Frank, 1921, Geology of the Cement oil field, Caddo County, Oklahoma: U. S. Geol. Survey Bull. 726-B, p. 41–85. **104**

Reger, D. B., 1916, Lewis and Gilmer Counties: West Virginia Geol. Survey. **214**

Renard, A. F. See Murray and Renard, 1891.

Renevier, Eugene. See Commission Internationale de Classification Stratigraphique, 1901.

Rettger, R. E., 1935, Experiments on soft-rock deformation: Am. Assoc. Petroleum Geologists Bull., v. 19, p. 271–292. **194**

Reuling, H. T., 1931, Dolomit-Studien im Devon der Eifel: Senckenbergiana, Band 13, p. 271–298. **240**

Revelle, Roger, 1934, Physico-chemical factors affecting the solubility of calcium carbonate in sea water: Jour. Sed. Petrology, v. 4, p. 103–110. **231**

Revelle, Roger, and Fleming, R. H., 1934, The solubility product constant of calcium carbonate in sea water: Fifth Pacific Science Cong. Proc., v. 3, p. 2089–2092. **230, 231**

Revelle, Roger, and Shepard, F. P., 1939, Sediments off the California coast: Recent Marine Sediments, p. 245–282, Tulsa, Am. Assoc. Petroleum Geologists. **52, 62, 206**

Revelle, Roger. See also Moberg, Greenberg, Revelle, and Allen, 1934.

Rice, G. S. See Daly, Miller, and Rice, 1912.

Rich, J. L., 1923, Shoestring sands of eastern Kansas: Am. Assoc. Petroleum Geologists Bull., v. 7, p. 103–113. **70**

————1926, Further observations on shoestring oil pools of eastern Kansas: Am. Assoc. Petroleum Geologists Bull., v. 10, p. 568–580. **70**

————1951, Probable fondo origin of Marcellus-Ohio-New Albany-Chattanooga bituminous shales: Am. Assoc. Petroleum Geologists Bull., v. 35, p. 2017–2040. **207**

Richter, Rudolf, 1927, "Sandkorallen"-Riffe in der Nordsee: Natur und Museum, Band 57, p. 49–62, Frankfurt am Main. **150**

————1931, Tierwelt und Umwelt im Hunsrückschiefer; zur Entstehung eines schwarzen Schlammsteins: Senckenbergiana, Band 13, p. 299–342. **72, 205**

————1935, 1936, 1941, Marken und Spuren im Huns-

rück-Schiefer: Senckenbergiana, Band 17, p. 244–264; Band 18, p. 215–244; Band 23, p. 218–260. **205**

Rigby, J. K. See Newell, Rigby, Fischer, Whiteman, Hickox, and Bradley, 1953; Newell, Rigby, Whiteman, and Bradley, 1951.

Rittenberg, S. C. See Emery and Rittenberg, 1952.

Rivière, André, 1939a, Sur la dolomitisation des sédiments calcaires: Acad. Sci. Paris Comptes rendus, tome 209, p. 597–599. **238, 244**

————1939b, Observations nouvelles sur le mécanisme de dolomitisation des sédiments calcaires: Acad. Sci. Paris Comptes rendus, tome 209, p. 691–692. **238, 244**

————1940, L'eau de mer et les sédiments calcaires: Soc. Géol. France Compte rendu sommaire, 5me sér., tome 10, p. 40–42. **238**

————1941, Sur la réserve alcaline et les carbonates de l'eau de mer: Soc. Géol. France Compte rendu sommaire, 5me sér., tome 11, p. 19–20. **238**

Roberts, R. J., 1951, Geology of the Antler Peak quadrangle, Nevada: U. S. Geol. Survey Geol. Quadrangle Map [10]. **174**

Robinson, G. W., 1932, Soils: London, Murby [3rd ed., 1949]. **210**

Rodgers, John, 1940, Distinction between calcite and dolomite on polished surfaces: Am. Jour. Sci., v. 238, p. 788–798. **222**

————1954a, Nature, usage, and nomenclature of stratigraphic units: a minority report: Am. Assoc. Petroleum Geologists Bull., v. 38, p. 655–659. **292**

————1954b, Terminology of limestone and related rocks: an interim report: Jour. Sed. Petrology, v. 24, p. 225–234. **226**

Rodgers, John. See also King, Ferguson, Craig, and Rodgers, 1944.

Ross, C. S. See Hendricks and Ross, 1941.

Roswall, Gunnar. See Troedsson and Roswall, 1926.

Rothpletz, August, 1892, Über die Bildung der Oolithe: Bot. Centralblatt, v. 51, p. 265–268. English translation by F. W. Cragin: Am. Geologist, v. 10, p. 279–282, 1892. **234**

Roy, C. J., 1945, Silica in natural waters: Am. Jour. Sci., v. 243, p. 393–403. **245, 249**

Rubey, W. W., 1929, Origin of the siliceous Mowry shale of the Black Hills region: U. S. Geol. Survey Prof. Paper 154-D, p. 153–170. **247, 250, 253**

————1931, Lithologic studies of fine-grained Upper Cretaceous sedimentary rocks of the Black Hills region: U. S. Geol. Survey Prof. Paper 165-A, p. 1–54. **4, 108, 197, 198**

————1933, Settling velocities of gravel, sand, and silt particles: Am. Jour. Sci., 5th ser., v. 25, p. 325–338, 512. **4, 5**

————1938, The force required to move particles on a stream bed: U. S. Geol. Survey Prof. Paper 189-E, p. 121–141. **5, 7, 8, 9**

Rubey, W. W., and Bass, N. W., 1925, The geology of Russell County, Kansas: Kansas Geol. Survey Bull. 10, p. 7–86. **37**

Ruedemann, Rudolf, 1925a, The Utica and Lorraine formations of New York. Part 1: Stratigraphy: New York State Mus. Bull. 258.   **140**

———1925b, Some Silurian (Ontarian) faunas of New York: New York State Mus. Bull. 265.   **208**

———1934, Paleozoic plankton of North America: Geol. Soc. America Mem. 2.   **202, 206**

———1935, Ecology of black mud shales of eastern New York: Jour. Paleontology, v. 9, p. 79–91.   **206**

Russell, I. C., 1885, Geological history of Lake Lahontan: U. S. Geol. Survey Mon. 11.   **40, 42**

———1892, Correlation papers: The Newark system: U. S. Geol. Survey Bull. 85.   **213**

———1900, A preliminary paper on the geology of the Cascade Mountains in northern Washington: U. S. Geol. Survey 20th Ann. Rept., pt. 2, p. 83–210.   **170**

Russell, L. S., 1939, Land and sea movements in the late Cretaceous of western Canada: Royal Soc. Canada Trans., 3rd ser., v. 33, sec. 4, p. 81–99.   **86**

Russell, Martin. See Ladd, Ingerson, Townsend, Russell, and Stephenson, 1953.

Russell, R. Dana, 1937, Mineral composition of Mississippi River sands: Geol. Soc. America Bull., v. 48, p. 1307–1348.   **32**

Russell, R. Dana, and Taylor, R. E., 1937, Roundness and shape of Mississippi River sands: Jour. Geology, v. 45, p. 225–267.   **32, 187**

Russell, R. Dana. See also Russell, R. J., and Russell, R. D., 1939.

Russell, R. Doncaster. See Collins, Farquhar, and Russell, 1954.

Russell, R. J., 1936, Physiography of the lower Mississippi River delta: Louisiana Dept. Conserv. Geol. Bull. 8, p. 3–199.   **75, 77**

Russell, R. J., and Russell, R. D., 1939, Mississippi River delta sedimentation: Recent Marine Sediments, p. 153–177, Tulsa, Am. Assoc. Petroleum Geologists.   **75, 79**

Sander, Bruno, 1936, Beiträge zur Kenntnis der Anlagerungsgefüge (Rhythmische Kalke und Dolomite aus der Trias): Mineralog. Petrog. Mitt., Band 48, p. 27–209. English translation by E. B. Knopf: Tulsa, Am. Assoc. Petroleum Geologists, 1951.   **109, 112, 241, 242, 243, 244**

Schenck, H. G., Hedberg, H. D., and Kleinpell, R. M., 1936, Stage as a stratigraphic unit: Geol. Soc. America Proc. 1935, p. 347–348.   **292**

Schenck, H. G., and Kleinpell, R. M., 1936, Refugian stage of Pacific Coast Tertiary: Am. Assoc. Petroleum Geologists Bull., v. 20, p. 215–225.   **292**

Schenck, H. G., and Muller, S. W., 1941, Stratigraphic terminology: Geol. Soc. America Bull., v. 52, p. 1419–1426.   **292**

Schmidt, K. P. See Hesse, Allee, and Schmidt, 1951.

Schott, Wolfgang, 1935, Die Foraminiferen in dem äquatorialen Teil des Atlantischen Ozeans: Deutsche Atlantische Exped. "Meteor" Wiss. Ergeb., Band 3, Teil 3, p. 43–134.   **60**

Schroyer, C. R. See Stauffer and Schroyer, 1920.

Schuchert, Charles, 1923, Sites and nature of the North American geosynclines: Geol. Soc. America Bull., v. 34, p. 151–229.   **311, 312, 314**

———1929, Chamberlin's philosophy of correlation: Jour. Geology, v. 37, p. 328–340.   **303**

———1931, Geochronology, or the age of the Earth on the basis of sediments and life: Natl. Research Council Bull. 80 [Physics of the Earth—IV: The age of the Earth], p. 10–72.   **128**

———1937, Cambrian and Ordovician of northwestern Vermont: Geol. Soc. America Bull., v. 48, p. 1001–1078.   **179**

———1955, Atlas of paleogeographic maps of North America: New York, Wiley.   **306**

Schuchert, Charles, and Dunbar, C. O., 1934, Stratigraphy of western Newfoundland: Geol. Soc. America Mem. 1.   **175, 234**

Schuchert, Charles. See also Pirsson and Schuchert, 1915.

Schwartz, G. M. See Stauffer, Schwartz, and Thiel, 1939.

Schwarzbach, Martin, 1950, Das Klima der Vorzeit: Stuttgart, Ferdinand Enke.   **44**

Sears, J. D., Hunt, C. B., and Hendricks, T. A., 1941, Transgressive and regressive Cretaceous deposits in southern San Juan basin, New Mexico: U. S. Geol. Survey Prof. Paper 193-F, p. 101–121.   **86**

Sharp, R. P., 1940, Ep-Archean and Ep-Algonkian erosion surfaces, Grand Canyon, Arizona: Geol. Soc. America Bull., v. 51, p. 1235–1269.   **68**

Sharp, R. P., and Nobles, L. H., 1953, Mudflow of 1941 at Wrightwood, southern California: Geol. Soc. America Bull., v. 64, p. 547–560.   **172**

Sharpe, C. F. S., 1938, Landslides and related phenomena. A study of mass-movements of soil and rock: New York, Columbia Univ. Press.   **169**

Shelton, J. S., 1953, Can wind move rocks on Racetrack Playa?: Science, new ser., v. 117, p. 438–439.   **173**

Shepard, F. P., 1923, To question the theory of periodic diastrophism: Jour. Geology, v. 31, p. 599–613.   **303**

———1932, Sediments of the continental shelves: Geol. Soc. America Bull., v. 43, p. 1017–1039.   **48**

———1948, Submarine geology: New York, Harper.   **11, 46, 47**

———1953, Sedimentation rates in Texas estuaries and lagoons: Am. Assoc. Petroleum Geologists Bull., v. 37, p. 1919–1934.   **51**

Shepard, F. P., and Cohee, G. V., 1936, Continental shelf sediments off the Mid-Atlantic states: Geol. Soc. America Bull., v. 47, p. 441–457.   **50**

Shepard, F. P., and Emery, K. O., 1941, Submarine topography off the California coast: Canyons and tectonic interpretation: Geol. Soc. America Spec. Paper 31.   **52**

———1946, Submarine photography off the California coast: Jour. Geology, v. 54, p. 306–321.   **46**

Shepard, F. P., Emery, K. O., and Gould, H. R., 1949,

Distribution of sediments on East Asiatic continental shelf: Allan Hancock Found. Pubs., Occasional Paper no. 9, Los Angeles, Univ. Southern California Press. **55**

Shepard, F. P., and Moore, D. G., 1954, Sedimentary environments differentiated by coarse-fraction studies: Am. Assoc. Petroleum Geologists Bull., v. 38, p. 1792–1802. **55, 187, 188**

———1955a, Central Texas coast sedimentation: characteristics of sedimentary environment, Recent history, and diagenesis: Am. Assoc. Petroleum Geologists Bull., v. 39, p. 1463–1593. **51, 55, 73, 187**

———1955b, Sediment zones bordering the barrier islands of central Texas coast: Soc. Econ. Paleontologists and Mineralogists Special Pub. 3, p. 78–96. **51, 55**

Shepard, F. P. See also Revelle and Shepard, 1939; Wanless and Shepard, 1936.

Sherborn, C. D., 1899, On the dates of the "Paléontologie Française" of d'Orbigny: Geol. Mag., decade 4, v. 6, p. 223–225. **298**

Sherlock, R. L., 1948, The Permo-Triassic formations, a world review: London, Hutchinson's Sci. and Tech. Pubs. **295**

Shotton, F. W., 1937, The lower Bunter sandstones of north Worcestershire and east Shropshire: Geol. Mag., v. 74, p. 534–553. **65**

Shrock, R. R., 1948a, Sequence in layered rocks: New York, McGraw-Hill. **105, 106, 112, 194**

———1948b, A classification of sedimentary rocks: Jour. Geology, v. 56, p. 118–129. **164, 166, 219**

Shrock, R. R. See also Cumings and Shrock, 1928a, 1928b.

Simpson, G. G., 1940, Types in modern taxonomy: Am. Jour. Sci., v. 238, p. 413–431. **269**

Skinner, J. W. See Dunbar and Skinner, 1937.

Sloss, L. L., 1947, Environments of limestone deposition: Jour. Sed. Petrology, v. 17, p. 109–113. **236**

Sloss, L. L. See also Krumbein and Sloss, 1951.

Smith, C. L., 1940, The Great Bahama Bank. II: Calcium carbonate precipitation: Sears Found. Jour. Marine Research, v. 3, p. 171–189. **231**

Smith, H. T. U., 1940, Geological studies in southwestern Kansas: Kansas Geol. Survey Bull. 34. **21**

Smith, J. P., 1895, Geologic study of migration of marine invertebrates: Jour. Geology, v. 3, p. 481–495. **153**

Smith, W. H. See Cross, Smith, and Arkle, 1950.

Sollas, W. J., 1883, The estuaries of the Severn and its tributaries: Geol. Soc. London Quart. Jour., v. 39, p. 611–626. **74**

Sorby, H. C., 1879, On the structure and origin of limestone: Geol. Soc. London Quart. Jour., v. 35, Proc., p. 56–95. **233, 234, 236**

———1908, On the application of quantitative methods to the study of the structure and history of rocks: Geol. Soc. London Quart. Jour., v. 64, p. 171–232. **188**

Spieker, E. M., 1946, Late Mesozoic and early Cenozoic history of central Utah: U. S. Geol. Survey Prof. Paper 205-D, p. 117–161. **144, 295, 304**

———1949, Sedimentary facies and associated diastrophism in the Upper Cretaceous of central and eastern Utah: Geol. Soc. America Mem. 39, p. 55–81. **86, 141, 155, 273, 274**

Spurr, J. E., 1894, False bedding in stratified drift deposits: Am. Geologist, v. 13, p. 43–47. **188**

Stafford, P. T., 1955, Zonation of the late Paleozoic Horseshoe Atoll in Scurry and southern Kent Counties, Texas: U. S. Geol. Survey Oil and Gas Inv. Chart 53. **92**

Stafford, P. T. See also Myers, Stafford, and Burnside, 1956.

Stainbrook, M. A., 1935, Stratigraphy of the Devonian system of the Upper Mississippi Valley: Kansas Geol. Soc. 9th Ann. Field Conf., Guidebook, p. 248–260. **180**

———1945, The stratigraphy of the Independence shale of Iowa: Am. Jour. Sci., v. 243, p. 66–83, 138–158. **112**

Stanley, G. M., 1955, Origin of playa stone tracks, Racetrack Playa, Inyo County, California: Geol. Soc. America Bull., v. 66, p. 1329–1350. **173**

Stauffer, C. R., and Schroyer, C. R., 1920, The Dunkard series of Ohio: Ohio Geol. Survey, 4th ser., Bull. 22. **213, 215**

Stauffer, C. R., Schwartz, G. M., and Thiel, G. A., 1939, St. Croixian classification of Minnesota: Geol. Soc. America Bull., v. 50, p. 1227–1243. **287**

Stebinger, Eugene, 1914, The Montana group of northwestern Montana: U. S. Geol. Survey Prof. Paper 90-G, p. 61-68. **86**

Steidtmann, Edward, 1917, Origin of dolomite as disclosed by stains and other methods: Geol. Soc. America Bull., v. 28, p. 431–450. **223, 242**

Stephenson, H. K. See Ladd, Ingerson, Townsend, Russell, and Stephenson, 1953.

Stetson, H. C., 1937, Current-measurements in the Georges Bank canyons: Am. Geophys. Union Trans. 18th Ann. Meeting, p. 216–219. **46**

———1938, The sediments of the continental shelf off the eastern coast of the United States: Massachusetts Inst. Technology and Woods Hole Oceanographic Inst. Papers in Phys. Oceanography and Meteorology, v. 5, no. 4. **48, 187**

———1939, Summary of sedimentary conditions on the continental shelf off the east coast of the United States: Recent Marine Sediments, p. 230–244, Tulsa, Am. Assoc. Petroleum Geologists. **10, 48, 50, 56, 187**

———1949, The sediments and stratigraphy of the East Coast continental margin; Georges Bank to Norfolk Canyon: Massachusetts Inst. Technology and Woods Hole Oceanographic Inst. Papers in Phys. Oceanography and Meteorology, v. 11, no. 2. **47**

———1953, The sediments of the western Gulf of Mexico. Part I—The continental terrace of the western Gulf of Mexico: its sediments, origin and development: Massachusetts Inst. Technology and Woods

Hole Oceanographic Inst. Papers in Phys. Oceanography and Meteorology, v. 12, no. 4, p. 5–45.   **51, 52**

Stetson, H. C., and Upson, J. E., 1937, Bottom deposits of the Ross Sea: Jour. Sed. Petrology, v. 7, p. 55–66.   **24, 53, 174**

Stewart, R. H.   See Gould and Stewart, 1955.

Stille, Hans, 1924, Grundfragen der vergleichenden Tektonik: Berlin, Borntraeger.   **304**

———1935, Der derzeitige tektonische Erdzustand: Preussische Akad. Wiss., phys.-math. Kl., Sitzungsber. 13, p. 179–219. English translation by Hans Ashauer and R. D. Reed: Am. Assoc. Petroleum Geologists Bull., v. 20, p. 849–880, 1936.   **304**

———1936, Die Entwicklung des amerikanischen Kordillerensystems in Zeit und Raum: Preussische Akad. Wiss., phys.-math. Kl., Sitzungsber. 15, p. 134–155.   **314**

Stockdale, P. B., 1931, The Borden (Knobstone) rocks of southern Indiana: Indiana Div. Geology Pub. 98.   **262, 265**

———1939, Lower Mississippian rocks of the east-central interior: Geol. Soc. America Spec. Paper 22.   **262, 265**

Storm, L. W., 1945, Résumé of facts and opinions on sedimentation in Gulf Coast region of Texas and Louisiana: Am. Assoc. Petroleum Geologists Bull., v. 29, p. 1304–1335.   **51**

Stose, G. W., 1909, Description of Mercersburg-Chambersburg district, Pennsylvania: U. S. Geol. Survey Geol. Atlas, Folio 170.   **180**

Straw, S. H., 1937, The higher Ludlovian rocks of the Builth district: Geol. Soc. London Quart. Jour., v. 93, p. 406–456.   **105**

Strøm, K. M., 1939, Land-locked waters and the deposition of black muds: Recent Marine Sediments, p. 356–372, Tulsa, Am. Assoc. Petroleum Geologists.   **61, 203, 204**

Suess, Eduard, 1883–1909, Das Antlitz der Erde: Prague, Leipzig, and Vienna. English translation by H. B. C. Sollas, 1904–1924, The face of the Earth: Oxford, Clarendon Press.   **305**

Sutton, G. H.   See Ewing, Sutton, and Officer, 1954.

Sverdrup, H. U., Johnson, M. W., and Fleming, R. H., 1942, The oceans, their physics, chemistry, and general biology: New York, Prentice-Hall.   **57, 61**

Swan, E. F., 1953, The Strongylocentrotidae (Echinoidea) of the Northeast Pacific: Evolution, v. 7, p. 269–273.   **151**

Swartz, F. M., 1934, Silurian sections near Mount Union, central Pennsylvania: Geol. Soc. America Bull., v. 45, p. 81–133.   **287**

———1935, Relations of the Silurian Rochester and McKenzie formations near Cumberland, Maryland, and Lakemont, Pennsylvania: Geol. Soc. America Bull., v. 46, p. 1165–1194.   **287**

Swartz, J. H., 1929, The age and stratigraphy of the Chattanooga shale in northeastern Tennessee and Virginia: Am. Jour. Sci., 5th ser., v. 17, p. 431–448.   **207**

Sykes, G. G., 1937, The Colorado Delta: Carnegie Inst. Washington Pub. 460.   **80, 81**

Takahashi, J.-I., 1939, Synopsis of glauconitization: Recent Marine Sediments, p. 503–512, Tulsa, Am. Assoc. Petroleum Geologists.   **184**

Taliaferro, N. L., 1935, Some properties of opal: Am. Jour. Sci., 5th ser., v. 30, p. 450–474.   **245**

Tarr, W. A., 1917, Origin of the chert in the Burlington limestone: Am. Jour. Sci., 4th ser., v. 44, p. 409–452.   **245, 248, 250**

———1919, Contribution to the origin of dolomite: Geol. Soc. America Bull., v. 30, p. 114.   **243**

———1926, The origin of chert and flint: Missouri Univ. Studies, v. 1, no. 2.   **250**

———1938, Terminology of the chemical siliceous sediments: Natl. Research Council Comm. on Sedimentation Rept. 1937–1938, p. 8–27.   **159, 247**

Taylor, R. E.   See Russell and Taylor, 1937.

Teichert, Curt, 1950, Zone concept in stratigraphy: Am. Assoc. Petroleum Geologists Bull., v. 34, p. 1585–1588.   **292**

Teichert, Curt, and Fairbridge, R. W., 1948, Some coral reefs of the Sahul Shelf: Geog. Rev., v. 38, p. 222–249.   **92**

Teichert, Curt.   See also Glaessner, Raggatt, Teichert, and Thomas, 1948; Glaessner and Teichert, 1947.

Tercier, Jean, 1939, Dépôts marins actuels et séries géologiques: Éclogae Geol. Helvetiae, v. 32, p. 47–100.   **314, 316**

Thiel, G. A.   See Stauffer, Schwartz, and Thiel, 1939.

Thom, W. T., Jr., and Dobbin, C. E., 1924, Stratigraphy of Cretaceous-Eocene transition beds in eastern Montana and the Dakotas: Geol. Soc. America Bull., v. 35, p. 481–505.   **124**

Thomas, D. E.   See Glaessner, Raggatt, Teichert, and Thomas, 1948.

Thompson, D. G., 1929, The Mohave Desert region: U. S. Geol. Survey Water-Supply Paper 578.   **38**

Thompson, W. O., 1937, Original structures of beaches, bars, and dunes: Geol. Soc. America Bull., v. 48, p. 723–751.   **69, 70**

Thorp, E. M., 1935, Calcareous shallow-water marine deposits of Florida and the Bahamas: Carnegie Inst. Washington Pub. 452, p. 37–119.   **95, 227, 234**

———1939, Florida and Bahama marine calcareous deposits: Recent Marine Sediments, p. 283–297, Tulsa, Am. Assoc. Petroleum Geologists.   **95, 231, 234**

Thwaites, F. T.   See Twenhofel, Raasch, and Thwaites, 1935.

Tieje, A. J., 1923, The red beds of the Front Range in Colorado: a study in sedimentation: Jour. Geology, v. 31, p. 192–207.   **213**

Timmermann, E.   See Wattenberg and Timmermann, 1936.

Tolmachoff, I. P., 1928, Extinction and extermination: Geol. Soc. America Bull., v. 39, p. 1131–1148.   **153**

Tolman, C. F., 1909, Erosion and deposition in the

southern Arizona bolson region: Jour. Geology, v. 17, p. 136–163. **38**

Tomlinson, C. W., 1916, The origin of red beds. A study of the conditions of origin of the Permo-Carboniferous and Triassic red beds of the western United States: Jour. Geology, v. 24, p. 153–179, 238–253. **210, 211**

———1940, Technique of stratigraphic nomenclature: Am. Assoc. Petroleum Geologists Bull., v. 24, p. 2038–2046. **292**

Townsend, R. C. See Ladd, Ingerson, Townsend, Russell, and Stephenson, 1953.

Tracey, J. I., Jr., Ladd, H. S., and Hoffmeister, J. E., 1948, Reefs of Bikini, Marshall Islands: Geol. Soc. America Bull., v. 59, p. 861–878. **90**

Tracey, J. I., Jr. See also Emery, Tracey, and Ladd, 1954; Ladd and Tracey, 1949; Ladd, Tracey, and Lill, 1948; Ladd, Tracey, Wells, and Emery, 1950.

Trask, P. D., 1932, Origin and environment of source sediments of petroleum: Houston, Am. Petroleum Inst. **61, 206**

———1939, Organic content of recent marine sediments: Recent Marine Sediments, p. 428–453, Tulsa, Am. Assoc. Petroleum Geologists. **61, 203**

Trask, P. D., Editor, 1950, Applied sedimentation: New York, Wiley. **274**

Troedsson, G. T., and Roswall, Gunnar, 1926, Nya data angående gränsen emellan Ordovicium och Gotlandium [New data concerning the boundary between the Ordovician and the Gotlandian]: Geol. Fören. Stockholm Förh., Bind 48, p. 441–456. **208**

Trowbridge, A. C., 1911, The terrestrial deposits of Owens Valley, California: Jour. Geology, v. 19, p. 706–747. **28**

———1930, Building of Mississippi delta: Am. Assoc. Petroleum Geologists Bull., v. 14, p. 867–901. **75**

Trowbridge, A. C., and Atwater, G. I., 1934, Stratigraphic problems in the Upper Mississippi Valley: Geol. Soc. America Bull., v. 45, p. 21–79. **286**

Troxell, H. C., and Peterson, J. Q., 1937, Flood in La Cañada Valley, California, January 1, 1934: U. S. Geol. Survey Water-Supply Paper 796-C, p. 53–98. **172**

Tschudy, R. H. See Emery and Tschudy, 1941.

Tunell, George, and Posnjak, Eugen, 1931, The stability relations of goethite and hematite: Econ. Geology, v. 26, p. 337–343, 894–898. **210**

Turner, F. J. See Williams, Turner, and Gilbert, 1954.

Twenhofel, W. H., 1915, Notes on black shale in the making: Am. Jour. Sci., 4th ser., v. 40, p. 272–280. **54, 205**

———1919, The chert of the Wreford and Foraker limestones along the state line of Kansas and Oklahoma: Am. Jour. Sci., 4th ser., v. 47, p. 407–429. **248, 251**

———1923, Development of shrinkage cracks in sediments without exposure to the atmosphere: Geol. Soc. America Bull., v. 34, p. 64. **199**

———1925, Subaqueous formation of mud cracks: Natl. Research Council Comm. on Sedimentation Rept. 1924, p. 75–76. **199**

———1937, Terminology of the fine-grained mechanical sediments: Natl. Research Council Comm. on Sedimentation Rept. 1936–1937, p. 81–104. **159, 166**

———1939, Environments of origin of black shales: Am. Assoc. Petroleum Geologists Bull., v. 23, p. 1178–1198. **207**

———1950, Coral and other organic reefs in geologic column: Am. Assoc. Petroleum Geologists Bull., v. 34, p. 182–202. **95, 229**

Twenhofel, W. H., Raasch, G. O., and Thwaites, F. T., 1935, Cambrian strata of Wisconsin: Geol. Soc. America Bull., v. 46, p. 1687–1743. **286**

Twenhofel, W. H., and others, 1932, Treatise on sedimentation (2nd ed.): Baltimore, Williams and Wilkins. **250**

Udden, J. A., 1898, The mechanical composition of wind deposits: Augustana Libr. Pubs., no. 1. **17, 161**

———1912, Geology and mineral resources of the Peoria quadrangle, Illinois: U. S. Geol. Survey Bull. 506. **109**

———1914, Mechanical composition of clastic sediments: Geol. Soc. America Bull., v. 25, p. 655–744. **17, 161**

———1924, Laminated anhydrite in Texas: Geol. Soc. America Bull., v. 35, p. 347–354. **109**

Ulrich, E. O., 1911, Revision of the Paleozoic systems: Geol. Soc. America Bull., v. 22, p. 281–680. Index: ibid., v. 24, p. 625–668. **126, 206, 284, 285**

———1916, Correlation by displacements of the strandline and the function and proper use of fossils in correlation: Geol. Soc. America Bull., v. 27, p. 451–490. **284, 285, 288**

———1920, Major causes of land and sea oscillations: Washington Acad. Sci. Jour., v. 10, p. 57–78. **285, 286**

———1924, Notes on new names in the table of formations and on physical evidence of breaks between Paleozoic systems in Wisconsin: Wisconsin Acad. Sci. Trans., v. 21, p. 71–107. **285, 286**

———1931, Naylor Ledge, a marine limestone of Canadian age filling caverns in upper Ozarkian formations: Geol. Soc. America Bull., v. 42, p. 348. **111**

United Nations, 1950, Flood damage and flood control activities in Asia and the Far East: United Nations Flood Control Ser., no. 1 [U.N. Pubs., 1951-II F-2]. **83**

Upson, J. E. See Stetson and Upson, 1937.

van Bemmelen, R. W., 1949, The geology of Indonesia: The Hague, Martinus Nijhoff. **316**

Van Burkalow, Anastasia, 1945, Angle of repose and angle of sliding friction: an experimental study: Geol. Soc. America Bull., v. 56, p. 669–707. **104**

Van Houten, F. B., 1948, Origin of red-banded early Cenozoic deposits in Rocky Mountain region: Am. Assoc. Petroleum Geologists Bull., v. 32, p. 2083–2126. **215**

———1953, Clay minerals in sedimentary rocks and derived soils: Am. Jour. Sci., v. 251, p. 61–82. **65**

van Ingen, Gilbert, and Clark, P. E., 1903, Disturbed fossiliferous rocks in the vicinity of Rondout, N. Y.: New York State Mus. Bull. 69, p. 1176–1227. **201**

van Straaten, L. M. J. U., 1953a, Megaripples in the Dutch Wadden Sea and in the Basin of Arcachon (France): Geologie en Mijnbouw, nieuwe ser., Jaarg. 15, p. 1–11. **189**

———1953b, Rhythmic patterns on Dutch North Sea beaches: Geologie en Mijnbouw, nieuwe ser., Jaarg. 15, p. 31–43. **189**

———1954, Sedimentology of Recent tidal flat deposits and the Psammites du Condroz: Geologie en Mijnbouw, nieuwe ser., Jaarg. 16, p. 25–47. **71, 72, 73**

Van Tuyl, F. M., 1916, The origin of dolomite: Iowa Geol. Survey, v. 25, p. 251–421. Summarized in: New points on the origin of dolomite: Am. Jour. Sci., 4th ser., v. 42, p. 249–260, 1916. **237, 242**

———1918, The origin of chert: Am. Jour. Sci., 4th ser., v. 45, p. 449–456. **250**

Vaughan, T. W. (with contribution by G. C. Matson), 1910, A contribution to the geologic history of the Floridian Plateau: Carnegie Inst. Washington Pub. 133, p. 99–185. **234, 235**

Vaughan, T. W. (with contribution by M. I. Goldman), 1918, Some shoal-water bottom samples from Murray Island, Australia, and comparisons of them with samples from Florida and the Bahamas: Carnegie Inst. Washington Pub. 213, p. 239–288. **232, 235**

Verrill, A. E., 1880, Rapid diffusion of *Littorina littorea* on the New England coast: Am. Jour. Sci., 3rd ser., v. 20, p. 251. **147**

Vine, Allyn. See Ewing, Vine, and Worzel, 1946.

Vokes, H. E., 1935, Rate of migration of *Crepidula convexa* Say: Nautilus, v. 49, p. 37–39. **147**

Waagé, K. M., 1950, Refractory clays of the Maryland Coal Measures: Maryland Dept. Geology, Mines and Water Resources Bull. 9. **110**

Wadell, Hakon, 1932, Volume, shape, and roundness of rock particles: Jour. Geology, v. 40, p. 443–451. **184, 185, 186**

———1933, Sphericity and roundness of rock particles: Jour. Geology, v. 41, p. 310–331. **184, 185, 186**

———1935, Volume, shape, and roundness of quartz particles: Jour. Geology, v. 43, p. 250–280. **185, 186**

Walcott, C. D., 1903, Nomenclature and classification for the Geologic Atlas of the United States: U. S. Geol. Survey 24th Ann. Rept., p. 21–27. **291**

Walther, Johannes, 1893–1894, Einleitung in die Geologie als historische Wissenschaft: Jena, Fischer. **24**

———1910, Die Sedimente der Taubenbank im Golfe von Neapel: K. Preussische Akad. Wiss. Abh., phys.-math. Kl., Jahrg. 1910, Anhang, Abh. 3. **151**

———1919–1927, Allgemeine Paläontologie: Berlin, Borntraeger. **151**

Wanless, H. R., 1922, Lithology of the White River sediments: Am. Philos. Soc. Proc., v. 61, p. 184–203. **37, 234**

———1923, The stratigraphy of the White River beds of South Dakota: Am. Philos. Soc. Proc., v. 62, p. 190–269. **37**

Wanless, H. R., and Shepard, F. P., 1936, Sea level and climatic changes related to late Paleozoic cycles: Geol. Soc. America Bull., v. 47, p. 1177–1206 (see also p. 2008–2014). **110**

Wanless, H. R., and Weller, J. M., 1932, Correlation and extent of Pennsylvanian cyclothems: Geol. Soc. America Bull., v. 43, p. 1003–1016. **109**

Wanner, Johannes, 1916, 1924, Die Permischen Echinodermen von Timor: Paläontologie von Timor, Lief. 6, Band 11; Lief. 14, Band 23. **153**

Warren, L. E. See Barnes, Cloud, and Warren, 1946.

Wattenberg, Hermann, 1933, Kalziumkarbonat- und Kohlensäuregehalt des Meerwassers: Deutsche Atlantische Expedition "Meteor" Wiss. Ergeb., Band 8, p. 122–333. **230, 231**

———1936, Kohlensäure und Kalziumkarbonate im Meere: Fortschr. Mineralogie, Band 20, p. 168–195. **231**

Wattenberg, Hermann, and Timmermann, E., 1936, Über die Sättigung des Seewassers an CaCO₃ und die anorganogene Bildung von Kalksedimenten: Annalen der Hydrographie und maritimen Meteorologie, Band 64, p. 23–31. **231**

Wattenberg, Hermann. See also Buch, Harvey, Wattenberg, and Gripenberg, 1932.

Weaver, C. E. See Folk and Weaver, 1952.

Weidman, Samuel, 1904, The Baraboo iron-bearing district of Wisconsin: Wisconsin Geol. and Nat. History Survey Bull. 13. **68, 170**

Weir, G. W. See McKee and Weir, 1953.

Weir, John. See Bailey and Weir, 1933.

Weller, J. M., 1930, Cyclical sedimentation in the Pennsylvanian period and its significance: Jour. Geology, v. 38, p. 97–135. **109, 110**

Weller, J. M., Henbest, L. G., and Dunbar, C. O., 1942, Stratigraphy of the fusuline-bearing beds of Illinois: Illinois Geol. Survey Bull. 67, p. 9–34. **109**

Weller, J. M. See also Wanless and Weller, 1932.

Wells, F. G., 1949, Ensimatic and ensialic geosynclines: Geol. Soc. America Bull., v. 60, p. 1927. **314**

Wells, J. W., 1947, Provisional paleoecological analysis of the Devonian rocks of the Columbus region: Ohio Jour. Sci., v. 47, p. 119–126. **137**

Wells, J. W. See also Ladd, Tracey, Wells, and Emery, 1950.

Wentworth, C. K., 1922, A scale of grade and class terms for clastic sediments: Jour. Geology, v. 30, p. 377–392. **161**

Wentworth, C. K., 1928, Striated cobbles in southern States: Geol. Soc. America Bull., v. 39, p. 941–953.   **24, 175**

——1931, The mechanical composition of sediments in graphic form: Iowa Univ. Studies in Nat. History, v. 14, no. 3.   **17**

——1933, Fundamental limits to the sizes of clastic grains: Science, new ser., v. 77, p. 633–634.   **161**

——1935, The terminology of coarse sediments: Natl. Research Council Comm. on Sedimentation Rept. 1932–1934, p. 225–246.   **159**

Wentworth, C. K., and Williams, Howel, 1932, The classification and terminology of the pyroclastic rocks: Natl. Research Council Comm. on Sedimentation Rept. 1930–1932, p. 19–53.   **159**

Wethered, Edward, 1890, On the occurrence of the genus *Girvanella* in oölitic rocks, and remarks on oölitic structure: Geol. Soc. London Quart. Jour., v. 46, p. 270–283 (also v. 51, p. 196–209, 1895).   **234**

Wheeler, W. C. See Clarke and Wheeler, 1922.

White, I. C., 1903, The Appalachian coal field: West Virginia Geol. Survey, v. 2, p. 81–716.   **214**

Whiteman, A. J. See Newell, Rigby, Fischer, Whiteman, Hickox, and Bradley, 1953; Newell, Rigby, Whiteman, and Bradley, 1951.

Whitney, J. D. See Hall and Whitney, 1858.

Wilbert, L. J., Jr. See Fisk, McFarlan, Kolb, and Wilbert, 1954.

Williams, H. S., 1894, Dual nomenclature in geological classification: Jour. Geology, v. 2, p. 145–160.   **291**

——1905, Bearing of some new paleontologic facts on nomenclature and classification of sedimentary formations: Geol. Soc. America Bull., v. 16, p. 137–150.   **291**

——1913, Recurrent *Tropidoleptus* zones of the Upper Devonian in New York: U. S. Geol. Survey Prof. Paper 79.   **153**

Williams, Howel, 1933, Geology of Tahiti, Moorea, and Maiao: B. P. Bishop Mus. Bull. 105.   **232**

Williams, Howel, Turner, F. J., and Gilbert, C. M., 1954, Petrography: San Francisco, Freeman.   **166**

Williams, Howel. See also Wentworth and Williams, 1932.

Williams, J. Stewart. See Cooper and Williams, 1935.

Williamson, E. D. See Johnston, Merwin, and Williamson, 1916.

Wilmarth, M. G., 1938, Lexicon of geologic names of the United States (including Alaska): U. S. Geol. Survey Bull. 896.   **260, 289**

Wilson, J. T., 1952, Some considerations regarding geochronology with special reference to Precambrian time: Am. Geophys. Union Trans., v. 33, p. 195–203.   **294**

Wilson, W. B., 1950, Reef definition: Am. Assoc. Petroleum Geologists Bull., v. 34, p. 181.   **88**

Wolansky, Dora, 1933, Untersuchungen über die Sedimentationsverhältnisse des Schwarzen Meeres und ihre Anwendung auf das nordkaukasische Erdölgebiet: Geol. Rundschau, Band 24, p. 397–410.   **60**

Wollin, G. See also Ericson, Ewing, Heezen, and Wollin, 1955.

Woodford, A. O., 1925, The San Onofre breccia: California Univ., Dept. Geol. Sci., Bull., v. 15, p. 159–280.   **31**

Woodring, W. P., 1931, Age of the orbitoid-bearing Eocene limestone and *Turritella variata* zone of the western Santa Ynez Range, California: San Diego Soc. Nat. History Trans., v. 6, p. 371–387.   **153**

——1953, Stratigraphic classification and nomenclature: Am. Assoc. Petroleum Geologists Bull., v. 37, p. 1081–1083.   **292**

Worzel, J. L. See Ewing, Vine, and Worzel, 1946.

Wright, L. A. See Noble and Wright, 1954.

Wyckoff, R. W. G. See Gibson, Wyckoff, and Merwin, 1925.

Yonge, C. M., 1930, A year on the Great Barrier Reef: London, Putnam.   **208**

Zingg, Theodor, 1935, Beitrag zur Schotteranalyse: Schweizer. Mineralog. Petrog. Mitt., Band 15, p. 39–140.   **186**

Subject index

* Asterisks refer to illustrations.